The United States has used military forc[e] [as an] instrument of diplomacy on many occa[sions in many] areas of the world in the years since the [war.] This book describes and analyzes the circumstances accompanying 215 shows of force and examines how effective these actions were in helping to attain U.S. foreign policy objectives.

Which type of force (air, ground, naval) was most often used? What did the forces do and how effective were they? Of what significance was Soviet involvement when U.S. military power was called upon to influence events? Was the threat presented by the alerting or deployment of strategic nuclear forces or by very large conventional forces especially telling? How clear is it that a desired effect was in fact caused by the demonstration of force?

Barry Blechman and Stephen Kaplan explore these and other questions, examining also such elements as a President's domestic popularity and personal diplomacy preceding or during crises that led to U.S. military demonstrations. Complementing their analysis are five sets of case studies describing ten instances of the use of American military power to influence events in Central and Eastern Europe, the Middle East, South and Southeast Asia, and the Caribbean. The case studies—by David K. Hall, William B. Quandt, Jerome N. Slater, Robert M. Slusser, and Philip Windsor—focus on the reasons for U.S. action and the methods adopted, on the behavior of other parties, and on the relation between the use of force and the resolution of the crisis.

The book's main conclusion is that the demonstrative use of U.S. armed forces has often stabilized a deteriorating situation enough to avoid further deterioration, relieved domestic and international pressure for more drastic and possibly self-defeating action, and gained time for diplomacy to achieve a more lasting remedy.

Barry M. Blechman, head of the Brookings defense analysis staff at the time this study was prepared, became an assistant director of the U.S. Arms Control and Disarmament Agency in 1977. Stephen S. Kaplan, a research associate in the Brookings Foreign Policy Studies program, is also a coauthor (with Philip J. Farley and William H. Lewis) of *Arms across the Sea* (Brookings, 1978).

FORCE
without
WAR

FORCE
without
WAR

U.S. Armed Forces as a Political Instrument

BARRY M. BLECHMAN

STEPHEN S. KAPLAN

with

DAVID K. HALL

WILLIAM B. QUANDT

JEROME N. SLATER

ROBERT M. SLUSSER

PHILIP WINDSOR

THE BROOKINGS INSTITUTION
Washington, D.C.

Copyright © 1978 by

THE BROOKINGS INSTITUTION

1775 Massachusetts Avenue, N.W., Washington, D.C. 20036

Library of Congress Cataloging in Publication Data:

Blechman, Barry M
   Force without war.

   Bibliography: p.
   Includes index.
   1. United States—Foreign relations—1945–
2. United States—Military policy. I. Kaplan,
Stephen S., joint author. II. Title.
E744.B585   327.73   78-12416
ISBN 0-8157-0986-2
ISBN 0-8157-0985-4 pbk.

9 8 7 6 5 4 3 2 1

TO LINDA AND SUE

THE BROOKINGS INSTITUTION is an independent organization devoted to nonpartisan research, education, and publication in economics, government, foreign policy, and the social sciences generally. Its principal purposes are to aid in the development of sound public policies and to promote public understanding of issues of national importance.

The Institution was founded on December 8, 1927, to merge the activities of the Institute for Government Research, founded in 1916, the Institute of Economics, founded in 1922, and the Robert Brookings Graduate School of Economics and Government, founded in 1924.

The Board of Trustees is responsible for the general administration of the Institution, while the immediate direction of the policies, program, and staff is vested in the President, assisted by an advisory committee of the officers and staff. The by-laws of the Institution state: "It is the function of the Trustees to make possible the conduct of scientific research, and publication, under the most favorable conditions, and to safeguard the independence of the research staff in the pursuit of their studies and in the publication of the results of such studies. It is not a part of their function to determine, control, or influence the conduct of particular investigations or the conclusions reached."

The President bears final responsibility for the decision to publish a manuscript as a Brookings book. In reaching his judgment on the competence, accuracy, and objectivity of each study, the President is advised by the director of the appropriate research program and weighs the views of a panel of expert outside readers who report to him in confidence on the quality of the work. Publication of a work signifies that it is deemed a competent treatment worthy of public consideration but does not imply endorsement of conclusions or recommendations.

The Institution maintains its position of neutrality on issues of public policy in order to safeguard the intellectual freedom of the staff. Hence interpretations or conclusions in Brookings publications should be understood to be solely those of the authors and should not be attributed to the Institution, to its trustees, officers, or other staff members, or to the organizations that support its research.

Foreword

SINCE the Second World War the United States has continually devoted substantial resources to the development and deployment of strategic weapons and conventional armed forces. It has done so not only to be prepared for war, but also to deter hostile foreign behavior, to reassure allies and other friends, and to deal with potentially dangerous contingencies. Faced with untoward developments, U.S. policymakers have often turned to the military to reinforce diplomacy and other means of achieving foreign policy objectives.

The Korean and Vietnam wars, the Berlin blockade, the Cuban missile crisis, the 1973 Middle East war, and a number of other major crises in which U.S. armed forces were involved are well known. Not so well recognized is that since the Second World War U.S. authorities have alerted or deployed military units on more than two hundred occasions to achieve specific objectives, large or small, that seemed important enough to warrant some show of American military power. This study presents a historical record of military operations in support of American diplomacy in the postwar era and examines their effectiveness.

After introducing their book, Blechman and Kaplan devote chapter 2 to an interpretation of the historical record focused on the political context of incidents and on the types, size, movements, and activities of the military units involved. In chapters 3-5, they subject thirty-three incidents to rigorous comparative analysis so as to obtain an aggregate sense of the effectiveness of military force as a political instrument and to determine the significance of variations in force strength, tactics, other diplomatic stratagems, and the contextual characteristics of incidents. Chapters 6-10 present case studies carried out with systematic reference to a common set of questions. The five authors of the case studies examine ten postwar crises and—without denying the uniqueness of political events—support a number of general inferences. In the final chapter, Blechman and Kaplan conclude that although U.S. political-military operations have not served well as permanent remedies for difficult international problems, they have been generally successful in stabilizing situations so as to gain time for other forms of diplomacy to achieve lasting solutions.

Barry M. Blechman, the former head of the Brookings defense analysis staff, is assistant director of the U.S. Arms Control and Disarmament Agency. Stephen S. Kaplan is a research associate in the Brookings Foreign Policy Studies program and a coauthor of *Arms across the Sea* (Brookings, 1978). The case studies were carried out by academic specialists, working as members of the Brookings associated staff: David K. Hall is assistant professor of political science at Brown University; William B. Quandt, formerly of the University of Pennsylvania, is director of the Middle East office of the National Security Council staff; Jerome N. Slater is professor of political science at the State University of New York at Buffalo; Robert M. Slusser is professor of history at Michigan State University; and Philip Windsor is a reader in international relations at the London School of Economics and Political Science.

The research upon which this book is based was supported by the Advanced Research Projects Agency of the Department of Defense and was reviewed by the Office of Naval Research under Contract N00014-75-C-0140. A further contract allowed the data collected at Brookings in the course of the study to be prepared for use by other researchers through the Cybernetics Technology Office of the Advanced Research Projects Agency and the Inter-University Consortium for Political and Social Research. Brookings and the authors are grateful for this assistance and the personal support of Robert A. Young and Stephen J. Andriole, former and current directors, respectively, of the Cybernetics Technology Office of the Advanced Research Projects Agency.

The cooperation of various members of the staffs of governmental historical offices listed in appendix A simplified the collection of data. The authors are grateful for the assistance of the following members of their staffs: Gloria Atkinson, Bernard F. Cavalcante, Lloyd Cornett, Captain Mary F. Edmonds (USMC), Philip A. Farris, Barbara A. Gilmore, Alfred Goldberg, Mary Haynes, Virginia R. Hildebrand, Arthur G. Kogan,

William G. Lewis, E. E. Lowry, Jr., Walter L. McMahon, Gabrielle M. Neufeld, Earl G. Peck, Gene C. Sands, David Schoem, Brigadier General Edwin H. Simmons (USMC, Retired), John Slonaker, Nina F. Statum, Russell B. Tiffany, John B. Wilson, and Hannah M. Ziedlik.

Valuable assistance was also provided by Herbert Block, Leonard G. Campbell, Henry H. Demsko, Brigadier General Bertram K. Gorwitz (USA, Retired), Captain F. Brayton Harris (USN), Steven Mitnick, Alfred B. Stille, Rodney G. Tomlinson, and Harry Zubkoff.

The members of the Brookings advisory committee for the study—Graham T. Allison, Robert R. Bowie, General Andrew J. Goodpaster (USA), Rear Admiral M. Staser Holcomb (USN), Ernest R. May, and Charles W. Yost—made helpful comments and suggestions. Joseph I. Coffey, Peter Karsten, and Robert B. Mahoney, Jr., also contributed useful criticism. The authors and the institution also thank Alexander L. George, George H. Quester, and Helmut Sonnenfeldt for evaluating the manuscript as outside readers.

At Brookings, advice and assistance were received from Robert P. Berman, Michael R. Leavitt, Henry Owen, and Robert G. Weinland. The principal research assistants during the study were Christine K. Lipsey and Faith Thompson Campbell; they were aided by Marjorie A. Toohy, John J. MacWilliams III, and Dennis Olson. Ruth Kaufman and Deborah M. Styles edited the manuscript. Its factual content was verified by Penelope S. Harpold. Georgina S. Hernandez, Jeanane Patterson, and Pamela S. Trussell provided secretarial assistance. The index was prepared by Diana Regenthal.

The views expressed in this book are the authors' alone and should not be interpreted as representing the official policies, either expressed or implied, of the Advanced Research Projects Agency, the Department of the Navy, or the U.S. government; nor should they be ascribed to the officers, trustees, or other staff members of the Brookings Institution.

BRUCE K. MACLAURY
President

October 1978
Washington, D.C.

Contents

Appendixes

Index   565

Tables

Appendix Table

Figures

And Aaron cast down his rod before Pharaoh and before his servants, and it became a serpent.

Exod. 7:10

CHAPTER ONE

Introduction

ON NOVEMBER 11, 1944, the Turkish ambassador to the United States, Mehmet Munir Ertegün, died in Washington; not a very important event at a time when Allied forces were sweeping across France and Eastern Europe toward Germany, and Berlin and Tokyo were approaching *Götterdämmerung.* Sixteen months later, however, the ambassador's remains were the focus of world attention as the curtain went up on a classic act in the use of armed forces as a political instrument. On March 6, 1946, the U.S. Department of State announced that the late Ambassador Ertegün's remains would be sent home to Turkey aboard the U.S.S. *Missouri,* visibly the most powerful warship in the U.S. Navy and the ship on board which General Douglas MacArthur had recently accepted Japan's surrender.

Between the ambassador's death and this announcement, not only had World War II ended, the cold war—as yet untitled—had begun. In addition to conflicts between the United States and the Soviet Union over Poland, Germany, Iran, and other areas, the Soviet Union had demanded the concession of two Turkish provinces in the east and, in the west, a base in the area of the Dardanelles.

On March 22 the *Missouri* began a slow journey from New York harbor to Turkey. At Gibraltar the British governor had a wreath placed on board. Accompanied by the destroyer *Power,* the great battleship was met on April 3 in the eastern Mediterranean by the light cruiser *Providence.* Finally, on the morning of April 5, the *Missouri* and her escorts anchored in the harbor at Istanbul.[1]

1. Log of the U.S.S. *Missouri.*

1

The meaning of this event was missed by no one; Washington had not so subtly reminded the Soviet Union and others that the United States was a great military power and that it could project this power abroad, even to shores far distant. Whether the visit of the *Missouri,* or it together with other U.S. actions that followed, deterred the Soviet Union from implementing any further planned or potential hostile acts toward Turkey will probably never be known. What is clear is that no forceful Soviet actions followed the visit. Moreover, as a symbol of American support for Turkey vis-à-vis the Soviet Union, the visit of the *Missouri* was well received and deeply appreciated by the government of Turkey, the Turkish press, and presumably by the Turkish citizenry at large. The American ambassador stated that to the Turks the visit indicated that "the United States has now decided that its own interest in this area require it to oppose any effort by [the] USSR to destroy Turk[ey's] independence and integrity."[2]

Three decades later, on August 18, 1976, two American officers supervising the pruning of a tree in the Korean demilitarized zone were attacked by North Korean soldiers and killed. The U.S. response was prompt. The UN military commander in Korea, General Richard G. Stilwell, accused North Korea of "deliberate murder" and demanded an apology and punishment of the North Koreans involved. Secretary of State Henry A. Kissinger termed the attack "premeditated murder," demanded "amends," and warned that such attacks would not be tolerated.

At the same time certain military preparations were taken: U.S. forces in Korea were placed on increased alert, U.S. tactical aircraft squadrons flew to Korea from bases in the United States and Okinawa, and the aircraft carrier *Midway* and accompanying vessels sailed from Yokosuka, Japan, for Korean waters. Finally, a few days after the initial incident, a large force of American and South Korean soldiers entered the demilitarized zone and cut down the offending tree while armed helicopters circled overhead and B-52 bombers flew near the border.

North Korea never did apologize for the incident, nor did it announce (publicly at least) any punishment for the North Korean soldiers involved in the incident. A North Korean representative at the Military

2. U.S. Department of State, *Foreign Relations of the United States, 1946,* vol. 7: *The Near East and Africa* (Government Printing Office, 1969), p. 822. Also see Stephen G. Xydis, "The Genesis of the Sixth Fleet," *U.S. Naval Institute Proceedings,* vol. 84 (August 1958), pp. 41–50.

Armistice Commission did, however, describe the incident as "regretful" —a marked departure from previous behavior. And at a subsequent meeting North Korea submitted several businesslike proposals for avoiding such incidents in the future.[3]

Earlier in the summer of 1976 the United States was involved, albeit less directly, in another international incident. Following the July raid by Israeli commandos on Entebbe airport in Uganda to free passengers of a hijacked aircraft held hostage by a Palestinian group, longstanding tensions between Uganda and Kenya intensified markedly. The two states had not gotten along for some time, but when the Israeli raiders landed at the Nairobi airport on their way back to Israel with the freed hostages, Uganda's President Idi Amin threatened military retaliation.

As the war of words between Ugandan and Kenyan leaders continued, a U.S. P-3C maritime patrol aircraft landed at the Nairobi airport, apparently the first sign of what was to become a routine operation. A day later the U.S. frigate *Beary* entered the Kenyan port of Mombasa for what was termed a "courtesy port call." And at the same time the U.S. aircraft carrier *Ranger* entered the Indian Ocean from the Pacific for a "routine periodic deployment." Although U.S. officials refused to publicly link any of these military operations to the Uganda-Kenya tension, U.S. reporters were told privately that they were meant as a show of support for Kenya.[4]

In each of these three incidents, as in hundreds of others since 1945, U.S. military forces were used without significant violence to underscore verbal and diplomatic expressions of American foreign policy. Historically, of course, the United States has not been the only nation to use its armed forces for political objectives; all the great powers have engaged in such activity, and in the last three decades the Soviet Union has been a frequent practitioner of the political use of the armed forces.

This book has two broad objectives:

First, to describe the historical record; that is, to identify the incidents in which the United States has used its armed forces for political objectives since the Second World War, and to determine the broad trends in such uses of the armed forces in terms of the context in which the military units were employed, and variations in the size, type, and activities of the military units themselves.

3. Based on reports in the *New York Times*, August 19–27, 1976.
4. *New York Times*, July 13, 1976, and *Baltimore Sun*, July 30, 1976.

Second, to evaluate the effectiveness of the armed forces as a political instrument, in the short term and over a longer period, by analyzing the consequences of such factors as: the size, type, and activity of military units involved in the incident; the nature of the situation at which they were directed; the character of U.S. objectives; the international and domestic context in which the incident occurred; and the extent and type of diplomatic activity that accompanied the use of the armed forces.

The Armed Forces as a Political Instrument

A state has many means at its disposal to obtain objectives abroad. These may include personal diplomacy, alliances, trade, aid, cultural and scientific exchanges, emigration and immigration policies and other domestic policies, covert activities, and the use of the military. These instruments, together, are an orchestra, to be used in accordance with the differing requirements of individual scores.

Clausewitz taught that although a state might use military force to obtain an objective through violent actions, the goal is never violence per se but rather the achievement of an objective otherwise unobtainable. He saw war as "a continuation of political intercourse with an admixture of other means."[5] So, too, the armed forces—by their very existence as well as by their general character, deployment, and day-to-day activities—can be used as an instrument of policy in time of peace. In peace, as in war, a prudent statesman will turn to the military not as a replacement or substitute for other tools of policy but as an integral part of an "admixture . . . of means."

The United States has utilized its armed forces often and in a wide variety of ways since the Second World War. Most of these uses have had a political dimension; that is, they were liable to influence the perceptions and behavior of political leaders in foreign countries to some degree. This study is concerned with only some of these uses of the armed forces: those in which the armed forces were used in a discrete way for specific political objectives in a particular situation. To establish a framework for evaluating these discrete activities, however, we first discuss the full range of uses of the armed forces which may have political consequences, some

5. Karl von Clausewitz, *On War*, trans. O. J. Matthijs Jolles (*Infantry Press Journal*, 1950), p. 596.

of which are liable to be of greater continuing significance than the episodic uses discussed in the balance of the book.

Size and Character of Standing Armed Forces

The recruitment of military personnel and the procurement of weapons signal not only that a state has a capability for warfare, but also that it has the will to allocate a portion of its resources to this end, demonstrating a resolve to defend what it defines as its interests in the international arena. The greater the resources allocated to the armed forces, the more clearly this resolve is likely to be perceived. Foreign audiences are attentive to changes in the size and composition of military forces; while some may only take note of changes, others may be influenced to act differently than they would have otherwise. Still others may be especially gratified or, on the other hand, may become particularly anxious. Consider, for example, the rearmament of the Federal Republic of Germany in the 1950s. German rearmament was strongly supported by the United States, while the Soviet Union, on the other hand, became extremely anxious and hostile. And even Bonn's erstwhile allies in Western Europe were discomforted to varying degrees. Yet those perceptions, and probably the actions taken by each of the observing nations as a result of those perceptions, stemmed only from the coming into existence of German armed forces—the new German army did not have to undertake any specific activities to have such political effects.

Aside from the size of the force, the relative sophistication of weaponry and the reputation of military personnel are likely to have different political impacts. In the immediate postwar period, for example, the United States' monopoly of nuclear weapons was of great importance to the common perception that it was the most powerful nation. Similarly, once the Soviet Union also obtained a nuclear capability, that was of great value to the success of Soviet diplomacy. Given these precedents, it should not have been surprising that several nations—France, China, and perhaps others—sought to enhance their influence in world affairs through the development of nuclear weapons.

The possession of advanced conventional weapons can confer political influence as well, because of the image of power which those weapons project and because they are perceived as a symbol of a nation's modernity and technological prowess, and hence of its standing in the world.

Aircraft carriers, nuclear submarines, supersonic aircraft, and advanced tanks not only improve a nation's ability to fight wars, they also influence the attitudes and behavior of other states toward their possessor. No nation has benefited as much in this regard as has the United States. The B-29 bomber, the *Missouri*-class battleship, the *Midway*-class aircraft carrier were potent symbols of American power in the immediate post-war period. Successive generations of bombers, fighter aircraft, warships, and ground combat equipment have helped to maintain the image of the United States as a nation in the forefront of military technology, an image that conditions the reactions of friends and foes alike to expressions of U.S. desires. The Soviet Union too has obtained political advantage by the development and display of advanced weapon systems. The effective use of these systems by other nations, as in the October 1973 war, has amplified this Soviet image.

The political significance of new types of weaponry derives not only from the technical capabilities they represent but from the test of the battlefield. The specters of Hiroshima and Nagasaki certainly contributed to the success of American and, later, Soviet diplomacy. If nuclear weapons had never been used, their destructive capability and decisiveness might have been doubted, or they might have been classed with chemical and bacteriological weapons: weapons whose use would be so abhorrent that they could be more or less discounted in the calculations of foreign policymakers.

Similarly, a military service which has a reputation for competence—hard training, close attention to weapons maintenance, professionalism, toughness—generally receives more respect and imparts greater political influence than one lacking such a reputation. An armed force seen as unfit and unpracticed will have the opposite impact. During the 1950s and even the 1960s, for example, the Spanish armed forces were regarded as not only ill equipped but composed of a moonlighting officer corps and poorly trained conscripts. Consequently, while those favoring Spain's entry into NATO always cited the size of the Spanish army, critics railed about its quality. By contrast, the Yugoslav and Turkish armed forces, while grossly inferior in numbers and equipment to those of the Soviet Union, are reputedly so able to provide a good accounting of themselves in conflict that Moscow may be deterred from engaging in aggression against these countries.

Performance in war, of course, is of primary significance to the reputation of armed forces and to the consequent assumptions and decisions of policymakers. A third of a century and more than a generation later, reputations forged or lost in World War II continue to have considerable significance for the political influence of various armed forces. Both the forces that gave a good accounting of themselves (such as the Soviet Army) and those that did not (such as the Italian Army) are remembered. Performance, more than victory or defeat, is the key. In the aftermath of the 1948, 1956, and 1967 Arab-Israeli wars, both Israel's image and the political clout of its military forces were enhanced, while Egypt's and Syria's images were tarnished; yet Jordan, also on the losing side, found its image and influence greater than might have been expected. So, too, after the 1973 Middle East war, both Egypt and Syria gained in reputation despite their military defeat.

Deployment and Operations

By emplacing ground or air forces in a foreign nation, or by regularly operating naval forces in a certain region, a state may become better prepared for, and able to react more quickly to, conflict in that region. Moreover, it will be more difficult for the state making the overseas deployment to ignore untoward events. At the extreme, forces deployed abroad will become automatically involved in outbreaks of conflict, as when they are located at the edge of a demilitarized zone across a traditional invasion route. In less extreme and more frequent cases, the fact that military personnel (and often their dependents) are located in an area of potential conflict means that the state making the deployment can ill afford to shut its eyes to potential threats in that region. Hence the location of forces abroad can sometimes support a nation's policies more directly and effectively than can a force of equal capability which is kept at home, even when provisions are made to move the latter force quickly and effectively when needed. The key is that when the force is not located in the region of concern, the deploying nation has greater flexibility in identifying those events requiring force, and thus its commitments are perceived as somewhat less certain.

When forces are deployed abroad the deploying nation's promises and commitments become more credible, as do its threats and warnings. The emplacement of forces abroad also may increase a state's general influence in the region, both as an expression of interest and as a demonstration of the viability of its instruments of power. For these reasons the United States has maintained army and air force units in Europe, Japan, Korea, and elsewhere for more than twenty-five years. And it is largely for these reasons too that the United States, and now the Soviet Union, maintain standing naval deployments in several parts of the globe.

There are various political effects following from the activities undertaken by armed forces—excluding still those activities specifically directed at particular situations. For one, the cohesion of alliances may be strengthened by regular military exercises, both unilateral and bilateral. The annual REFORGER exercise, in which U.S. ground troops are airlifted to central Europe and engage in maneuvers with other NATO forces, supports the credibility of the United States' preparedness to quickly reinforce the Seventh Army—the permanent U.S. ground force presence on the continent. Exercises of this nature, if not of the same scope, also are conducted in support of U.S. allies in southern Europe and in the Far East. Similarly, the annual UNITAS exercise in which U.S. ships circle South America and engage in antisubmarine warfare and other exercises with the navies of various Latin American states helps to maintain favorable relations between U.S. and Latin American armed forces. In each of the above instances the exercise supports and reinforces the perceptions established by U.S. diplomacy: the United States is concerned with the target states' security and interests, and the United States is willing and able to aid them militarily in the event of various contingencies.

Visits of military ships and planes to foreign locations on the occasion of inaugurations, holiday celebrations, air shows, regattas, and other special events can also have political consequences. Visits whose main purpose is to provide rest and recreation to their crews, to replenish consumables, or to make minor repairs may have a similar, if less pointed, political dimension. The friendly presence of a nation's military personnel in a foreign city, if well received, can serve to affirm the visiting state's interest in good relations and, often enough, support for the host state. By sending a symbol of its sovereignty—a warship or military aircraft unit—to a place where, in all likelihood, the safety of the military personnel and the ships or aircraft themselves are dependent upon the goodwill of the host nation, the visiting nation expresses trust in the host as well as confidence in its strength and good intentions. Visits also allow a nation to show off fighting capabilities and military technology. The visual impression made by a modern warship or military aircraft may not be measured easily, but neither can it be argued that such sights do not leave some impression.

Frequently, visits become so routine that they pass almost unnoticed. A sudden change in a previously established pattern of visits would be noticed, however. In 1976, for example, a U.S. warship visited Haifa, Israel—for the first time in more than ten years. The event was trumpeted in the Israeli media and noted in major U.S. and European newspapers, whereas similar visits to Italian ports—a long-standing practice—pass unnoticed. The cancellation of a previously planned visit also draws attention. It is a common way to express displeasure with a decision, policy, or stance of the host country. For example, during the tenure of the Allende regime in Chile, a planned visit by the U.S. aircraft carrier *Enterprise* was canceled.

Armed forces, being well-organized, highly disciplined, well-equipped, mobile, and *existing* national resources, can be quite useful to another state in various contingencies not involving conflict, particularly disaster relief or prevention. Ground troops have been used to fight fires, remove snow, clean up after tidal waves, and search for survivors after floods, earthquakes, storms, and other natural calamities. Aircraft can rapidly transport skilled military and civilian personnel, field hospitals, medicine, shelters, and even food. Ships, though they usually cannot respond as quickly as can aircraft, are able to deliver larger amounts of supplies more efficiently over a longer period of time. On occasion, moreover, ships close to a disaster have provided immediate aid of great significance.

No nation has been as active as the United States in providing disaster assistance and similar supportive activities. Britain and France have engaged in these practices for an even longer period than has the United States, mainly in their former colonies. In more recent years the Soviet Union has followed this lead. The usual objective of these actions, to the extent that they do not spring solely from humanitarian motives, is to create a good impression or reservoir of goodwill which can be drawn upon at some future time. Rarely is a specific political objective sought through these efforts. Interestingly, states prone to natural disasters (because of their geographic location and world weather patterns) have come to expect support from particular nations, especially from the United States. The absence of participation in disaster relief and rescue efforts, therefore, may be very noticeable and have impact.

Military Assistance

Armed forces also are used to implement arms transfers and to train foreign military personnel. Whether or not arms transfers provide a vehicle for influence with regard to particular issues is a contentious point; there seems little doubt, however, that they often tie countries more closely together in a broad sense. Where an arms transfer program is successful in this political dimension, there will tend to be less suspicion, better communications, and a greater openness between the military personnel (and sometimes the political leaders) of the donor and recipient nations. This has been the case, for example, with respect to the United States and Western European nations. On occasion, moreover, the initiation, continuance, or curtailment of particular arms transfers may result in the attainment of specific policy objectives.

Sizable arms transfers necessarily involve the use of military personnel from the donor country to instruct recipient country personnel in the usage and maintenance of weapon systems and corresponding military tactics. These military advisers can make contacts with, and may obtain the trust and confidence of, the officers with whom they deal. There often is a professional camaraderie among military officers, as in any profession, which can overshadow national distinctions. In consequence, the advisers may be useful conduits for communicating policy and for creating a favorable impression in the donor country. And individual officers may sometimes be able to influence their professional counterparts on particular issues. These consequences, which can be turned into political gain, may be made more important insofar as a sizable number of nations are ruled by serving or ex-professional military officers.

Other points of contact between U.S. and foreign military men are military schools such as West Point and the Command and General Staff College at Fort Leavenworth. Of course, familiarity need not always lead to respect; it sometimes breeds contempt. All nations that maintain large arms transfer programs have occasionally had to cope with tensions between advisers and students or incidents involving visitors and citizens of the host country.

Of a perhaps less tenuous character are the physical dependencies created by arms transfers. The fact that a nation's armed forces are dependent upon military equipment fabricated in another state may predispose the recipient to wish to please the donor. Again, this relationship obviously is not absolute: some recipient countries have been willing to alienate their donors; the recent experience of the Soviet Union in Egypt is an obvious and pointed example. Still, there is a price to pay for such disruptions—if nothing else, a degradation in military capabilities while new equipment is sought. This wish to keep the supplier country content is likely to be stronger if financial gains are included in the transfer (for example, if it is a grant rather than a sale), if stocks of spare parts and consumables are kept low, and if the recipient country is in immediate danger of military confrontation. Yet even in certain cases where all factors pointed to great dependency on the part of an arms recipient, the political influence that usually is assumed to flow from arms transfers has proven to be illusory.

Discrete Political Operations

All these ways in which the armed forces serve political functions—by their existence and character alone, by their location abroad, by the carrying-out of routine exercises and visits, and by their provision of military assistance and various forms of support in situations not featuring conflict—are virtually ignored in this study. The focus here is a single aspect of the armed forces as a political instrument—the use of discrete military moves to influence a particular situation.

In taking this focus the study's approach may be somewhat misleading, a caveat which readers should bear in mind. In one sense, the fact that a discrete use of the armed forces has taken place in itself indicates a failure of policy. When U.S. policy is unambiguous, when that policy is in accord with the reality of limits on the U.S. ability to influence world affairs, when U.S. military forces are sized commensurately with the tasks set for them, when they are deployed, equipped, and trained so as to make their ability to carry out those tasks (and the nation's will to use them in those roles) unquestionable, then situations requiring a discrete use of force are less likely to arise. In effect, a discrete political use of the armed forces is a belated attempt to make clear a policy intent or military capability which for one reason or another—domestic dissension, uncertain or inept leadership, inadequate military preparation, situational factors, or the unreality of the policy objective itself—has come into question.

Thus, in many cases the discrete use of armed forces indicates that the previously mentioned, more fundamental political roles of the armed forces have fallen into disrepair. Or put another way, it is when a discrete use of the armed forces is not required that the political functions of the armed forces are being best fulfilled. For example, it may be argued that during those periods when the Soviet Union did not put pressure on the Western position in Central Europe (as in Berlin), and thus no special military steps were needed, U.S. troops deployed in Europe were achieving their principal political goal—persuading Soviet decisionmakers to accommodate themselves to the status quo in Europe.

In this study, however, we count as incidents only those instances when, to continue the example, the Soviet Union did put pressure on Berlin and the United States did react with discrete military activity. We did not record, nor obviously could we record, those times when Soviet decisionmakers debated, or individually considered, applying pressure to Berlin and then thought better of it, although in terms of reducing the risk of war and stabilizing international politics it is these latter effects of the U.S. military presence that were most beneficial. This bias in the study should be kept in mind.

The Basic Concept

In some cases it is obvious that a particular use of the armed forces constitutes a discrete political-military operation and thus falls into the area of interest of this study. In many others, however, it is not. Thus, one of the first tasks was to define rigorously the concept under investigation. The definition that was employed for this purpose follows:

A political use of the armed forces occurs when physical actions are taken by one or more components of the uniformed military services as part of a deliberate attempt by the national authorities to influence, or to be prepared to influence, specific behavior of individuals in another nation without engaging in a continuing contest of violence.

Thus, a political use of the armed forces was inferred to have taken place if five elements were present in a situation.

1. A physical change in the disposition (location, activity, and/or readiness) of at least a part of the armed forces had to occur. Mere references by policymakers to the military (verbal threats) were not considered to constitute a use of the armed forces. Military activities were

taken to include: the use of firepower; the establishment or disestablishment of a permanent or temporary presence abroad; a blockade; an interposition; an exercise or demonstration; the escort or transport of another actor's armed forces or matériel; a visit by a military unit to a foreign location; an evacuation; the operation of reconnaissance, patrol, or surveillance units in a non-exercise context; or a change in readiness status. Readiness measures included changes in alert status, the mobilization or demobilization of reserve forces, and the movement of units toward or away from specific locations.

2. Behind this activity there had to have been a certain consciousness of purpose. Only in those cases when a specific political impact could be considered a significant objective of the national command authority— that is, a member of the National Security Council—in initiating action, did the incident qualify for inclusion in the study.

3. Decisionmakers must have sought to attain their objectives by gaining influence in the target states, not by physically imposing the U.S. will. Generally speaking, armed forces may be used either as a political or as a martial instrument. When used as a martial instrument a military unit acts to seize an objective (occupy territory) or to destroy an objective (defeat an invading army). In both of these examples, attainment of the immediate objective itself satisfies the purpose for which the force was used. When used as a political instrument, the objective is to influence the behavior of another actor—that is, to cause an actor to do something that he would not otherwise do, or not to do something that he would do otherwise. Thus, the activity of the military units themselves does not attain the objective; goals are achieved through the effect of the force on the perceptions of the actor. Only instances of force used in this latter fashion were of interest here.

4. Decisionmakers must have sought to avoid a significant contest of violence. Although a war may result from a use of the armed forces which otherwise meets the terms of the definition, the initiation of war must not have been the *intent* of the action. Although even the most intense and protracted war may constitute a political use of the armed forces—if the objective is to cause the opponent to capitulate without necessarily totally destroying his capacity to fight—such large-scale uses of violence were not of interest in this study.

5. Some specific behavior had to have been desired of the target actors. A use of the armed forces had to have been directed at influencing

specific behavior in a particular situation; or, at least, to have occurred because of concern with specific behavior.

The delimitation of the political uses of the armed forces examined in this study may be further clarified by listing the sorts of military activity which were excluded.

1. The Korean War and the U.S. involvement in the war in Indochina between March 1965 and March 1972 were excluded. U.S. armed forces were used in these conflicts primarily as a martial instrument—that is, to wage war. Objectives were gained or lost as a direct result of the outcome of violent interactions between opposing forces. The symbolic value of the military force, the effect of its use on the perceptions and expectations of decisionmakers, was relatively unimportant.[6]

2. Uses of U.S. armed forces deployed abroad to defend directly U.S. property, citizens, or military positions were not considered political incidents for our purposes. In these incidents, components of the armed forces were used in response to immediate threats. Examples would include actions by troops patrolling the Korean demilitarized zone, the use of Army troops in the Panama Canal Zone to control demonstrations, and incidents at Guantanamo between Marine sentries and suspected infiltrators. This military activity was not designed to cause foreign policymakers to terminate the undesirable activity, but to terminate it in a direct fashion (for example, by shooting an infiltrator). However, in those cases when the United States reinforced a military deployment overseas in response to infiltration or some other hostile activity, it was assumed that the symbolic political value of the reinforcement was at least as important as any immediate improvement in military capabilities. Thus, incidents of the latter type were considered political uses of the armed forces.

3. The psychological reinforcement of previously established behavior through the continuous presence or operation of military forces abroad also was excluded. While the stationing of U.S. armed forces

---

6. The U.S. air war against North Vietnam was initially aimed at a political objective—to compel the DRVN to halt its support for the war in the South. Increasingly, however, this political aim was subsumed by the military objective of stopping the traffic to the South directly. The political objective gained prominence again only during the 1972 "Linebacker" operations. Insofar as it was impossible to define the break-points precisely, we arbitrarily excluded from this analysis the air strikes against the North once the United States stopped identifying a specific incident leading to each strike in March 1965.

abroad certainly is a political act, and is perhaps the most important political function served by them, such activity helps to maintain previously established behavior rather than to establish new behavioral patterns. Only the initial establishment of an overseas presence, the disestablishment of such a presence, or a significant change in the size of the overseas deployment was included in the list of incidents. The continuing effects of maintaining forces overseas are examined only as an independent variable influencing the effectiveness of discrete political uses of force.

4. Routine activity primarily directed at maintaining or improving combat readiness was excluded. This category includes most training exercises and maneuvers and most visits to foreign ports by U.S. warships. Although there are often political side effects of these interactions between U.S. military forces and individuals in foreign nations, most routine military activity is simply not deliberate in its political consequences.

5. Miscellaneous forms of support provided routinely to foreign governments in non-conflict situations were not considered. Examples include disaster relief, search and rescue operations, and the movement of refugees. Usually these operations have had a political objective, but a diffuse and long-term one: to enhance U.S. influence in the recipient nation. Consequently, they did not meet the definitional requirement of specificity.

6. The provision of military assistance was not considered. Again, this activity encompasses an important political dimension, but the factors determining the success or failure of military assistance—which is usually given over a protracted period of time—are likely to be quite different from those affecting the outcome of discrete political uses of the armed forces.

7. Incidents in which noncombatant forces were used to evacuate American citizens from areas of impending conflict were not included. Actually, such incidents are rare, insofar as most instances of evacuation have coincided with the use of combatant forces. And in these latter incidents the primary purpose usually was not to rescue Americans directly but to cause foreign leaders to stabilize a threatening situation. Cases in which combatant forces were employed were included in the list of incidents.

8. The use within the United States of active or reserve military forces to control civil disturbances, to aid in relief efforts following national

disasters, and to achieve other objectives was not examined. Uses of the armed forces abroad sometimes serve primarily domestic political objectives, however, and these were included in the study.

Incidents and Sources

The sources examined for the development of a list of incidents fall broadly into three categories: official records of military organizations, such as fleet histories; chronologies of international events, such as that which appears in the *Middle East Journal;* and compilations of U.S. military activity prepared by government agencies and other researchers for various purposes. A full list of sources consulted, together with methodological notes, is presented in appendix A.

Using our restrictive definition, 215 incidents were identified in which the United States utilized its armed forces for political objectives between January 1, 1946, and December 31, 1975—an arbitrary cutoff date. A list of these incidents appears in appendix B. The character of the incidents and the character of the U.S. military involvement in them are described and analyzed in chapter 2.

We are confident that the list of incidents is an adequate representation of all those instances in which U.S. armed forces were used in a way that would fit the terms of the definition. Analysts undertaking a similar study on a classified basis have indicated that there is a correlation of 0.89 between the incident list in appendix B and a list of incidents which, under the terms of the definition employed in this study, their data would indicate have taken place. Moreover, the set of incidents utilized in this study are distributed roughly congruently over time with the set of incidents that would be derived from the classified data.[7]

We are less confident, however, about descriptions of the military units which took part in the incidents. Reporting on this sort of data in the unclassified literature—even in official documents—tends to be incomplete, nonsystematic, and sometimes contradictory. The activities of military units which are easy to keep track of—like aircraft carriers—tend

7. Robert B. Mahoney, Jr., "A Comparison of the Brookings and CNA International Incidents Projects," Center for Naval Analyses, Professional Paper 174 (February 1977; processed).

to be reported more often and more completely than the activities of other types of units—for example, submarines, to cite an extreme case. Furthermore, because the reporting of military activity on an unclassified basis has varied over time, findings concerning the type, number, or activity of military units involved in the incidents should be considered tentative.

The Question of Utility

When do discrete uses of the armed forces help to satisfy U.S. foreign policy objectives with regard to particular situations abroad? Do the size, type, or activities of the forces involved matter? Can utility be enhanced by diplomatic or other levers of policy in conjunction with the military operation? What role does the balance of U.S. and Soviet strategic forces play, and how does Soviet involvement affect outcomes? Are particular types of objectives more likely to be satisfied than others?

Answers to these and a number of related questions are important, for the usage of military power as a means of diplomacy can risk the security and well being of the United States and importantly affect U.S. and other international relationships both immediately and for a long time afterward. Although on some occasions the risks of intervention may be small, in many instances it is difficult to determine all possible dangers and the likelihood of their being realized. Military action in still other situations may clearly entail great risk—particularly if the USSR is an actor and committed to a different result, or if another opponent is prepared to use violence as a last resort. The political use of military power in a discrete instance may also lead to unwanted dependency on the United States and the hostility, not only of antagonists, but of other nations in the affected region. Relations with the USSR, China, and uninvolved U.S. allies may be made more difficult. In light of the Vietnam War experience, the effect of U.S. military activities abroad on the political culture of the United States and the fabric of American politics should also be considered. Before reaching a judgment that military intervention is necessary for the preservation of highly important U.S. interests and accepting the immediate and long-term risks that may be apparent, policymakers would be wise to also consider the utility of political-military operations that have gone before. Two means of approach were taken in evaluating this past effectiveness.

These two approaches, aggregate analysis and case study, respectively present macro- and micro-views of the same phenomena. The value of the first is that it permits broad generalizations which might be applicable in the future when the armed forces were used for political objectives. Individual case studies can confirm or disprove these generalizations, allow the inference of propositions related to the peculiarities and complexities of specific situations, and provide a sense of the psychological climate and individual concerns that condition the choices of policymakers. In short, the two approaches are complementary; each has advantages and disadvantages, but together they afford greater understanding than either can provide separately. The findings from these two approaches are integrated in the concluding chapter of the study.

For the aggregate analysis, a 15 percent sample of thirty-three incidents was selected, as described in appendix C, for systematic and rigorous analysis of outcomes. For each of the incidents in the sample, the available literature, documents, and newspaper accounts were investigated so as to determine the following: (1) U.S. objectives vis-à-vis each participant, and whether or not those objectives were satisfied within six months and retained over three years following the use of U.S. armed forces; (2) the size, type, and activity of U.S. armed forces involved in the incident; (3) the character of the targets in relation to U.S. objectives; (4) other activities (for example, diplomatic) undertaken in support of U.S. objectives along with the use of the armed forces; and (5) certain U.S. domestic conditions. In the analysis, the degree of satisfaction of U.S. objectives is related to each of these other factors with the aim of highlighting the crucial variables determining whether a political use of the armed forces is likely to be successful or not. This analysis is presented in chapters 3 through 5. A bibliography for the thirty-three sample incidents is presented in appendix D.

Although the methodology utilized in this analysis is quantitative, only simple descriptive statistics are employed. No attempt was made to construct causal models of the behavior being investigated. In part this stems from a concern that the analysis be understandable to readers lacking a technical background. Of greater importance, though, is the crude nominal and ordinal nature of most of the data, which simply do not lend themselves to highly sophisticated statistical techniques. To ignore this debility and utilize more elaborate methods would risk overinterpreting the data and perhaps misleading the reader.

More detailed assessments were made of the specific mechanisms through which military operations affected the perceptions and decisions of foreign policymakers in ten case studies. Five specialists were asked to address a lengthy set of questions concerning the United States' use of armed forces in each of two incidents. The questions required that each analyst describe in some detail: (1) U.S. objectives, (2) the instruments of policy directed at those objectives, (3) the character of the situation (and particularly the concerns of foreign decisionmakers), and (4) most important, the outcomes of the situation.

Cases were selected to highlight variations in the particular circumstances in which the United States has used its armed forces for political objectives since 1945. For example, the investigator dealing with intra-Arab conflicts was asked to examine both the 1958 Lebanese civil war and the 1970 Jordanian civil war, to shed light on how changes between 1958 and 1970 in the global and Mediterranean balance of military power between the United States and the Soviet Union may have affected the utility of U.S. armed forces in these situations. Time was not the only factor used to distinguish among cases, however. There were two Berlin crises in a period of only three years, for example, the main difference between them being the style and content of the U.S. response. The five sets of case studies are presented in chapters 6 through 10.

Finally, it is very important to draw a distinction between the *utility* of the political use of the armed forces and the *wisdom* of carrying out such operations. The former is addressed in this study, the latter is not. In evaluating the utility of political uses of the armed forces, the methodology employed accepts the objectives of U.S. decisionmakers as given, and assesses only whether or not those objectives were achieved. The question of the wisdom of establishing those objectives is beyond the scope of this study. Nor do we try to judge the long-term security consequences of the political use of armed forces. One or a series of military actions may protect U.S. interests in a specific instance, increase the credibility of U.S. commitments generally, and alert foreign leaders to carefully consider their actions which might affect U.S. interests. On the other hand, the use of American military forces may be perceived as unnecessary or wrongful saber-rattling and lead to an undesired escalation of tensions or new incidents. Moreover, local beneficiaries of American support may be stigmatized as dependent clients, lacking internal bases of support and acting solely upon U.S. command. The creation of perceptions like these does not enhance the image of America around the world and may, over the long term, cause serious problems for the protection of American interests. Possible effects such as these fall beyond the scope of this study.

PART ONE

Aggregate Analyses

CHAPTER TWO

The Historical Record

THE 215 incidents in which the United States employed its armed forces for political purposes between 1946 and 1975 do not constitute a homogeneous set. As might be expected, the incidents varied widely in the size and composition of the American military forces which became involved, ranging from a visit to a foreign port by a single warship to the deployment of major ground, air, and naval units against a backdrop including the mobilization of reserves and the placing on alert of strategic nuclear forces. More important, they also varied in their fundamental political context. The situations in which the United States used its armed forces for political objectives were sometimes tense international confrontations; sometimes minor disturbances in international relations; and at still other times there was no conflict—the forces were used to strengthen ties between the United States and other nations.

We first examine five contextual features: time, region, type of political situation at which the U.S. military action was directed, the level of involvement by the Soviet Union and China, and the participation of other actors. In order to put these factors in perspective we begin with a substantive, multidimensional characterization of the incidents. Our purpose is not to present a history of the political use of the military, but rather to examine a number of the historical dimensions of these actions which may be particularly relevant to understanding current and future usages of the armed forces as a policy instrument.[1]

1. It is also worth noting that, notwithstanding the inclusion of appendixes A and B, and documentation appearing in footnotes, many of the actual data and "coding" judgments on which the analysis is based are not presented. The inclusion of this material simply was not practical. Additional data are available, however. A computer tape and accompanying codebook have been prepared for use by inter-

The Political Environment

A few types of situations in each region of the world accounted for a
very large proportion of the incidents in which the United States used its
armed forces for political objectives.

Only three U.S. actions took place in South Asia, all related to wars
between India and its neighbors—in 1962 with China, and in 1965 and
1971 with Pakistan. Eight of the ten incidents that took place in sub-
Saharan Africa involved internal strife in Zaire or Tanzania, principally
in the early and mid-1960s. In the third area of relatively low activity,
South America, virtually all of the incidents concerned relatively minor
U.S. demonstrations of friendship to various states.

In the Central American/Caribbean area, where a much greater number of incidents took place, nearly one-half involved the rise to power of
Fidel Castro, attempts to oust him from power, Castro-supported insurgencies, or the security of the U.S. base at Guantanamo. All of these
incidents took place between 1958 and 1965. Several other incidents also
involved Cuba—the most important concerning attempts by the Soviet
Union to enhance its military position in the area (the 1962 missile crisis
and the construction of submarine facilities in 1970). Almost another
one-third of the incidents in the Caribbean concerned domestic conflicts
in either Haiti or the Dominican Republic, or disputes between those two
states.

Of twenty incidents in the Far East more than half concerned conflict
between China and Taiwan, the last such incident taking place in 1963.
Most of the remaining incidents concerned North Korea's conflict with
South Korea and attacks on U.S. military units on or near the Korean
peninsula. The last such incident before our 1975 cutoff point was in
1971.[2]

In Southeast Asia one-half of the incidents were related to North Vietnam's support of, or participation in, conflicts within the former SEATO

---

ested scholars. Further information in this regard may be obtained by contacting
U.S. Department of Defense, Advanced Research Projects Agency, Cybernetics
Technology Office.

2. Of course the U.S. military deployments which followed the tree-cutting
incident in August 1976 would have met the terms of the definition of a political use
of military force. The necessity to impose a cutoff on the data collection did not allow its inclusion, however.

protocol states of South Vietnam, Laos, and Cambodia. These incidents occurred either between the initiation of conflict in the area in the late 1950s and full U.S. entry into the war in 1965, or between the mining of Haiphong harbor in 1972 and the collapse of governments friendly to the United States in 1975. Another 10 percent of the incidents in Southeast Asia stemmed from the colonial war in Indochina between France and the Viet Minh. A third type of situation provided another 15 percent of the incidents: domestic strife in Indonesia and the "confrontation" with Malaysia, beginning in 1956 and lasting until President Sukarno was ousted from office in 1966.

In the Middle East, one-third of the incidents were accounted for by either internal strife in Jordan and Lebanon, or those two nations' bilateral relations with the United States. Only three of these types of incidents occurred in the last ten years of the study period (1966–75), however.[3] One-fourth of the Middle East incidents were directly related to the Arab-Israeli conflict, most frequently stemming from violence between Egypt and Israel. Of perhaps greater significance, three-fifths of the Arab-Israeli incidents occurred in the last ten years. Most of the remaining incidents that took place in the Middle East involved U.S. demonstrations of friendship to various states, the Yemeni civil war, or Arab oil policy.

Perhaps the most significant feature of the incidents in Europe is the fact that the Soviet Union participated in three-fourths of them. Of this subgroup, almost two-fifths concerned U.S. actions to reassure individual states coming under Soviet pressure, particularly Greece, Turkey, and Yugoslavia in the early postwar years. Another one-fourth of the European incidents in which the Soviet Union participated pertained to Berlin, the last such incident taking place in 1965; a further one-fourth concerned either U.S. responses to other hostile Soviet acts or U.S. initiatives to reduce tension in Europe. Of those European incidents in which the Soviet Union was not involved, more than one-half were related to Cyprus.

During the last five years covered in the study (1971–75), U.S. actions related to the war in Southeast Asia accounted for the majority of the incidents. The last of these were the evacuations from Vietnam and Cambodia and the *Mayaguez* incident, all three symbolic of the termina-

3. Again, additional incidents have taken place—e.g., in Lebanon—after the December 1975 cutoff imposed on the data collection.

tion of U.S. commitments and military involvement in this area. Also of particular prominence in the 1970s were actions taken with regard to the Arab-Israeli conflict and Arab oil policy.

From another perspective, it is interesting that a large number of incidents during the last ten years involved either the termination of involvements abroad (for example, the 1973 mineclearing of Haiphong harbor) or actions aimed at improving relations between states (for example, visits to ports in the Soviet Union in 1971 and 1975).

Distribution of Incidents over Time

The thirty years covered seem to fall somewhat naturally into four periods: 1946–48, 1949–55, 1956–65, and 1966–75. For the three years immediately following the Second World War the annual average number of incidents (8.0) ran slightly above the average for the entire thirty-year period (7.2 incidents per year). After 1948, however, the United States began to use its armed forces less frequently for political purposes; the annual average for the period 1949–55 was only 3.4. Beginning in 1956 the use of armed forces for political objectives became more common, and the number of incidents per year increased gradually, peaking at twenty incidents in 1964. On the average, 12.0 incidents occurred each year during the period 1956–65, which stands quite apart as a time of great American activism. This activist period ended abruptly in 1966, when there were only three incidents. And the frequency of incidents has remained relatively low ever since.

What accounts for these changes in the number of incidents each year? To answer this question we examined the relationship between variation in the annual number of incidents and a number of indices reflecting either changes in the international environment in which U.S. policy functioned, or domestic changes in the United States. Statistics summarizing the most interesting relationships are presented in table 2-1.

Of the international indices the factor most closely related to changes in the frequency of incidents was whether or not the United States was or recently had been involved in a limited war. During and following both the Korean and Vietnam Wars, policymakers employed U.S. armed forces in discrete political operations far less often than they did at other times. This stands to reason: fewer unengaged forces were available, and military officials would have been reluctant to become involved in situa-

Table 2-1. *Simple Correlations between Annual Number of Incidents and Various Measures of Change in the International and Domestic Environment*

Measure of change	All incidents	Incidents involving U.S. use of one or more major components of force[a]
U.S. not engaged in Korean and Vietnam wars[b]	0.39	0.35
U.S. not engaged in Korean and Vietnam wars in past three years[c]	0.58	0.31
Opportunities[d]	0.44	0.29
Relative U.S. and USSR nuclear strength[e]	−0.37	−0.27
President's popularity[f]	0.50	0.50
National confidence[g]	0.58	0.45

a. A major force component is defined as: (a) ground combat forces larger than one battalion; or (b) naval forces at least as large as two carrier (or battleship) task groups; or (c) land-based combat air units at least as large as one air wing. For a discussion of the concept of a "major force component," see pp. 49–50.

b. The periods 1946–49, 1954–64, and 1973–75.

c. The periods 1946–49 and 1957–64.

d. The annual number of "intra-nation and inter-nation hostilities (i.e., revolts, crises, coups, unrest, dyadic, and multidyadic wars)," as defined and determined by Edward E. Azar, *Probe for Peace: Small State Hostilities* (Burgess, 1973); and updated by Edward Azar in "An Inventory of Intra-Nation and Inter-Nation Hostilities" (University of North Carolina–Chapel Hill, Conflict and Peace Data Bank, 1976; processed).

e. End-of-year ratio of force loadings: number of nuclear weapons deployed on U.S. and Soviet inter-continental ballistic missiles, submarine-launched ballistic missiles, and long-range bombers; on U.S. intermediate-range ballistic missiles and bombers when they were deployed in Europe; on U.S. forward deployed aircraft carriers when they were included in plans for strategic strikes. "Annual Defense Department Report, FY 1977" (1976; processed), and previous reports; "Statement of Secretary of Defense Melvin R. Laird Before a Joint Session of the Senate Armed Services Committee and the Senate Sub-committee on Department of Defense Appropriations, on the Fiscal Year 1971 Defense Program and Budget" (February 20, 1970; processed), pp. 56–59; "The Development of Strategic Air Command, 1946–1973" (SAC, 1974; processed); Stockholm International Peace Research Institute, *World Armaments and Disarmament: SIPRI Yearbook 1974* (MIT Press, 1974), pp. 105–10; International Institute for Strategic Studies, *The Military Balance, 1971–1972* (London: IISS, 1971), p. 56; Norman Polmar, *Aircraft Carriers* (Doubleday, 1969), pp. 503–08, 596–600.

f. Annual average approval of the President's performance, as surveyed by the Gallup poll. George H. Gallup, ed., *The Gallup Poll*, vols. 1–3 (Random House, 1972); *The Gallup Opinion Index*, Report No. 56 (February 1970), pp. 8–16, and succeeding supplements.

g. Annual average Standard and Poor's composite stock price index discounted for both inflation and real economic growth. *Standard and Poor's Trade and Securities Statistics*, 1976 Edition (Standard and Poor's Corp., 1976), p. 4; *Economic Report of the President, January 1976*, p. 171. The index of national confidence was constructed by dividing the 1946 U.S. gross national product by the current year gross national product and multiplying by the Standard and Poor's index figure for the current year.

tions which might have resulted in new demands on U.S. military resources. Also, once the Korean and Vietnam conflicts became unpopular in the United States, political leaders were likely to have been loath to risk further alienation of their constituents. This latter explanation is highlighted by the relatively sharp increase in the correlation when three years (an arbitrary choice) were added to the actual period of fighting. Apparently, the psychological consequences of a direct military involvement persist beyond the war itself, and have an important effect on policy decisions.

A second international factor which is relatively highly correlated with the frequency of U.S. use of the armed forces for political purposes is the number of opportunities presented by the international system. This too is an obvious relationship. When fewer situations develop in which the armed forces can play a role, there are likely to be fewer uses of force.[4]

A third factor which is relatively closely related to the frequency of U.S. political uses of the armed forces is the overall U.S.-Soviet balance of strategic nuclear weapons. The strategic balance may be measured in a number of ways. The ratio of U.S.-Soviet force loadings, or numbers of nuclear weapons on delivery vehicles able to reach the other super-power's territory, was used as the pertinent index in this analysis.[5] The correlation here is an inverse one. As the Soviet Union gained in nuclear strength relative to the United States, especially after the mid-1960s, the United States employed its armed forces less frequently for political objectives. This relationship was not notably strengthened by lagging the nuclear balance one year behind the incident frequency—testing the hypothesis that it takes time for actual military strength to affect behavior. Nor was it notably strengthened by having the nuclear balance index lead incident frequency by one year—testing the hypothesis that projections of future strength are the pertinent influence on national behavior.

As to the relationships between the frequency of political uses of the armed forces and indices of domestic changes in the United States, two interesting results were obtained: (a) a strong correlation exists between increases in the number of incidents and the President's popularity; and (b) an even stronger correlation exists between the number of incidents and the nation's sense of confidence. Presidential popularity was measured by the annual average percentage of respondents who approved the President's performance in the Gallup poll. National confidence was

4. Data on international and intranational conflicts compiled by Edward Azar at the University of North Carolina were used to index opportunities. See table 2-1, note d.

5. See table 2-1, note e.

measured by making use of the Standard and Poor's average annual composite stock price index.[6]

Of course, a stock price index may reflect a number of things besides "outlook" or "sense of confidence"—it may also reflect inflation and real economic growth. The effects of these two factors were therefore separated out, that is, discounted.[7] The residual index reflects, in one sense, investors' outlook. A rise may indicate buoyancy in the national spirit and a more optimistic view of the future; a decline, a more gloomy attitude. The strong positive correlation suggests that at times when the nation was more confident the armed forces were used more frequently for political purposes.

For all of these relationships, measures of covariance were recomputed using the annual frequency of only those incidents in which the United States employed major components of its armed forces.[8] This step almost always reduced the strength of the correlation. A further examination of the incidents in which one or more major force components were employed revealed that they tended to occur with greater regularity than did incidents in which lesser forces were used. This regularity is largely explained by the durability of many of the political situations U.S. policymakers chose to face with large military units. In short, a sizable proportion of these incidents were strongly related to one another. By contrast, many smaller U.S. military demonstrations occurred in response to situations of a transient character, bearing little relation to one another; hence their greater variability in frequency.

Of course, the variables mentioned need not be independent determinants of the United States' proclivity to use the armed forces for political objectives. Many of these factors are likely to vary, to some degree, in similar directions at the same time. Regression analysis was used to measure the degree to which each of these variables, singly and in combina-

6. *Standard and Poor's Trade and Securities Statistics,* 1976 edition (Standard and Poor's Corp., 1976), pp. 2, 4. This index is based on a mathematical formula applied currently to a series of 500 stocks considered in four main groups and 88 subgroups. Aside from other stock market indices, we might have used the index of consumer sentiment developed at the Survey Research Center at the University of Michigan. One problem, however, is that it covers only the years since 1953.

7. Changes in the gross national product were used to signify real and inflationary growth. Gross national product figures were taken from *Economic Report of the President, January 1976,* p. 171.

8. See table 2-1, note a.

Table 2-2. *Annual Number of Incidents as a Function of Selected Variables*

Annual number of incidents, Y, as a function of	Regression equation	R^2	F-statistic	Standard error
X_1 (U.S. not engaged in Korean and Vietnam Wars in past three years) + X_2 (opportunities)	$Y = -1.59$ $+5.7\ X_1$ $+0.30\ X_2$	0.57	18.18 (d.f. = 2/27)	3.13
X_1 (U.S. not engaged in Korean and Vietnam Wars in past three years) + X_2 (national confidence)	$Y = -3.71$ $+4.62\ X_1$ $+0.47\ X_2$	0.57	18.10 (d.f. = 2/27)	3.14
X_1 (U.S. not engaged in Korean and Vietnam Wars in past three years) + X_2 (national confidence) + X_3 (opportunities)	$Y = -3.51$ $+5.14\ X_1$ $+0.26\ X_2$ $+0.17\ X_3$	0.60	13.00 (d.f. = 3/26)	3.09

tion, could be used to account for variations in the frequency with which the United States used its military forces for political purposes.

We found that three of the factors examined were most important in determining when the United States turned to the armed forces to attain political objectives. Past or present involvement in either the Korean or the Vietnam War would appear to be the most important factor. When either the number of opportunities presented by the international system or the previously mentioned index of the nation's confidence was added to that involvement, 57 percent of the variation in the annual number of incidents could be accounted for. The use of all three independent variables raised the strength of the regression equation only slightly. Adding presidential popularity did not raise the equation's strength at all; substituting the latter for "national confidence" made little difference. The most significant regression statistics are summarized in table 2-2.[9]

9. Robert B. Mahoney, Jr., used the list of incidents presented in appendix B as a dependent variable—i.e., the number of times each year in which the U.S. armed forces were used as a political instrument in an incident—and the following as independent variables: the state of the strategic balance, Soviet conflictual behavior toward the United States, the amount of conflict throughout the world, and American

Figure 2-1. *Comparison of Actual and Estimated Number of Incidents,*
1946–75

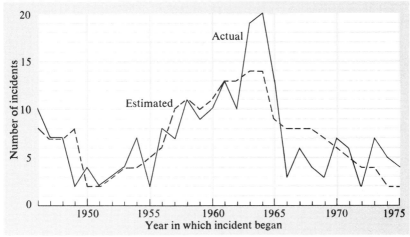

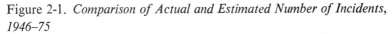

Figure 2-1 presents the annual number of incidents that would be
estimated on the basis of the following independent variables: non-
Korean and Vietnam War years (also excluding the three-year periods
after each of those conflicts), "national confidence," and "opportunities."
Figure 2-1 also provides, for each year, a graphic comparison between
the number of incidents that would be estimated on the basis of this equation and the number of incidents that actually did occur. The reader
should note not only the closeness of the "fit" between these numbers,
but also the degree of similarity in directional changes.

A reasonable inference that may be drawn from this analysis is that
as memories of the Vietnam conflict recede from the American consciousness, the nation may once again more frequently employ its armed forces
for political objectives, especially if an increasing number of "opportunities" are presented by the international environment, *or* if the nation's
sense of confidence returns to previously high levels. If the executive can
restore confidence in its ability to correctly gauge national interest in its
conduct of foreign affairs, if Congress eases off from stricter scrutiny and

involvement in limited wars. Among the results of a multiple regression analysis reported are the following figures: $R = 0.84$ and $R^2 = 0.70$. See Robert B. Mahoney,
Jr., "American Political-Military Operations and the Structure of the International
System," paper presented at the annual meeting of the International Studies Association, Section on Military Studies, Ohio State University, Columbus, October 1976.

the restrictions it has imposed on presidents since the early 1970s, and if the American people again become sanguine about the United States' ability to play a forceful role in world affairs, the domestic conditions would exist for the executive to carry out foreign political-military operations in discrete situations more frequently once again. As to opportunities, in addition to persisting domestic instabilities in scores of new nations, there is the continued hostility between Israel and its Arab neighbors as well as among various Arab nations; the potential for crisis in Yugoslavia after the Tito era; the possibility of new eruptions between Greece and Turkey and on the Korean peninsula; turmoil on the African Horn and in sub-Saharan Africa; and so forth. If the past is a guide, however, we would not expect very many or major U.S. interventions in sub-Saharan Africa, the Indian Ocean area, or South America; nor are U.S. policymakers likely to engage again easily in Southeast Asia.

Regional Focus of Incidents

The regional focus of U.S. political uses of the armed forces has varied widely over time, as shown by the data in table 2-3. Over the full period the incidents were distributed relatively evenly, except for the Southern Hemisphere, in which relatively few incidents took place. Europe, the Middle East, Southeast and East Asia, and the Central American/ Caribbean area each accounted for approximately one-fifth to one-fourth of the total number of incidents.

The Western Hemisphere accounted for more than one-fourth of the incidents. These have been highly specialized, however, with regard to both time and location. Virtually all of these incidents occurred on islands in, or in nations on, the littoral of the Caribbean. And about three-fourths of the Western Hemisphere incidents took place during the most active period, 1956–65. Another one-fourth of the incidents took place in Southeast and East Asia and were more evenly distributed over time. Interestingly, the United States used its armed forces for political objectives in Southeast and East Asia relatively less from 1956 to 1965 than it did both before and after that period. During the period leading up to the Vietnam War, Fidel Castro was more often the target of U.S. military activities than was Ho Chi Minh. Europe accounted for one-fifth of the incidents, as did the Middle East, but during the last ten years of the

Table 2-3. *Distribution of Incidents by Time Period and Region*
Percentage of total for time period

Time period	Western Hemisphere	Europe	Middle East and North Africa	South Asia and sub-Saharan Africa	Southeast and East Asia
1946–48	21	63	13	0	4
1949–55	13	29	8	4	46
1956–65	37	12	15	9	27
1966–75	13	15	32	4	36
1946–75	28	20	18	6	28

study period these two regions combined saw about one-half of the incidents.

What is remarkable is how little attention South Asia and sub-Saharan Africa have received. Indeed, the Southern Hemisphere generally has been the target of very few political uses of U.S. armed forces. When South America, exclusive of Venezuela (a Caribbean littoral state), is split off from the Western Hemisphere figures and added to the South Asian and sub-Saharan African total, it raises the latter's share of the overall number of incidents to only 13 percent. Either the United States had little interest in what occurred in these distant regions, or it did not expect that the armed forces would be an effective instrument of policy in the Southern Hemisphere. Certainly there were numerous "opportunities" for the use of U.S. armed forces of the type that elsewhere may well have elicited a response.

Finally, it should be emphasized that, regardless of these thirty-year trends, the last half decade of the study time frame was dominated by incidents in Southeast Asia and the Middle East. The end of the war in Vietnam and changing perceptions of U.S. interests in Southeast Asia would seem to make new actions in that area unlikely. The Middle East, by contrast, promises no such change in attention or involvement. The Arab-Israeli conflict continues, regimes in the area remain fragile, intra-Arab conflicts abound, and the oil issue looms large in calculations of U.S. decisionmakers. At the same time, both the Soviet Union and the United States are deeply involved, and the executive, the Congress, and the American public are in general accord on policy in this area. Also in the eastern Mediterranean, hostility between Greece and Turkey exists over Cyprus as well as over other issues, and there remains the possibility of an international crisis developing over Yugoslavia following the death of President Tito.

Political Situation

Of the numerous ways to characterize the political situation, two deserve mention here. First, the 215 incidents were divided into two categories: those that were essentially intranational in nature and those that were essentially international. The latter were further compartmented, depending upon whether or not the United States was judged to be a primary actor in the pertinent events or relationships leading up to the introduction of U.S. armed forces. In table 2-4, the percentages of incidents in each category are displayed by time period.

Of note is the sharp increase in the share of incidents attributable to intranational events during the period of greatest U.S. activism, 1956–65. During this period intranational situations accounted for slightly more than one-half of the incidents, as compared to the one-third share typifying the remainder of the thirty years. In fact, the increase in U.S. involvements in intranational situations accounts for about one-half of the rise in total U.S. activity during 1956–65. Much of this rise is attributable to U.S. efforts to help various nations in the Caribbean defeat Cuban-sponsored insurgencies. Other types of situations which contributed to the increase in intranational involvements included domestic conflicts in Laos and South Vietnam and difficulties in the Congo.

Intranational situations were further subdivided into five categories. Three of these—insurgency, civil war, domestic turmoil—involved violence to varying degrees and accounted for about three-fourths of the total U.S. uses of the armed forces directed at intranational situations (or one-third of all incidents). The other two subcategories were coups and constitutional changes of government. Clearly, the United States became involved in intranational situations mainly when violence was threatened or actually occurred. The activist period (1956–65) featured a greater incidence of involvements in insurgencies and coups: overall, 63 percent of the intranational situations occurred during the activist period, but 81 percent of the insurgencies and 75 percent of the coups took place during those ten years.

Table 2-4. *Distribution of Incidents by Time Period and Political Situation*

Percentage of total for time period

		International	
Time period	Intranational	Initially involving U.S.	Not initially involving U.S.
1946–48	33	38	29
1949–55	38	20	42
1956–65	52	25	23
1966–75	34	26	40
1946–75	44	26	30

Use of the armed forces for political objectives directed at *international situations,* on the other hand, shows no clear pattern over time. International uses too were subdivided, to characterize either the specific relationship that the U.S. armed forces were attempting to influence or the specific event to which the United States was reacting.

International situations not involving the United States initially were divided into: (a) wars between two or more states, (b) sporadic armed conflicts between two or more states, (c) unfriendly but nonviolent relations between states, and (d) friendly relations between states. Most (67 percent) of the U.S. actions directed at international situations also involved violence—both full-blown wars and sporadic conflicts. As in the intranational situations, the United States seemed to act mainly when conflict was threatened or manifest.

International situations in which the United States was a primary actor from the onset included those in which the United States responded to specific hostile acts directed at itself, its military forces stationed in a foreign country, American citizens abroad, or property owned abroad by American citizens. These hostile acts were either political initiatives or physical attacks organized by foreign governments or by nongovernmental groups. There were a total of thirty-six such incidents (17 percent of the total). Most of those which involved real or potential physical actions against U.S. property or military forces took place in the Caribbean area, usually involving Cuba; most of those which involved hostile political initiatives—usually by the Soviet Union—occurred in Europe.

Identity of Participants

One of two criteria had to be satisfied for an actor to be considered a participant in an incident: (a) it had to have been a specific target of U.S. decisionmakers in using the armed forces, in that the United States must have desired that the actor perform, or not perform, a specific act or, more subtly, be impressed in a particular fashion; or (b) the actor had to play a special role in determining the outcome of the incident. Mere interest in an incident or essentially inconsequential behavior on the part of an actor was not considered enough to warrant inclusion. The application of these rules is of course as reliant on judgments as on apparent facts. It was our judgment, for example, that by the terms of our definition Israel was not an actor in the 1957 Syrian crisis, South Vietnam was not an actor in the 1959 Laotian crisis, and Japan was not an actor in the 1968 *Pueblo* crisis. Others might reach different judgments on these questions.

In this sense, the Soviet Union or China participated in 41 percent of the 215 incidents. The proportional participation of each one dropped off sharply after 1955. Soviet participation rose slightly during the last ten years, but Chinese participation continued to decline (see table 2-5).

Both Soviet and Chinese participation were closely related to the location of the incident. The Soviet Union was involved in 75 percent of the incidents in Europe, 60 percent of those in sub-Saharan Africa, 39 percent of those in the Middle East, and only 7 percent of those in the Western Hemisphere. The Chinese were not involved in any of the incidents in these four regions. China or the Soviet Union was involved in 85 percent of the incidents in East Asia but only one-third of those in Southeast Asia. Thus the overall decline in both Soviet and Chinese partici-

Table 2-5. *Percentage of Incidents in Which the Soviet Union and China Participated, 1946–75*

Time period	Soviet Union	China
1946–48	63	4
1949–55	42	21
1956–65	28	14
1966–75	30	11
1946–75	34	14

Table 2-6. *Number of Incidents Involving Each Principal Participant*

Country or organization	Number of incidents
USSR	73
United Kingdom	35
China	30
Cuba	25
North Vietnam	21
France	17
Egypt	16
United Nations	16
South Vietnam	14
Israel	13
National Liberation Front (South Vietnam)	13
Taiwan	12
Turkey	12
Organization of American States	11
Dominican Republic	10
Greece	10
Jordan	10
Yugoslavia	10

pation reflects mainly the reduction in the number of incidents in the regions of their greatest interest—Europe and East Asia, respectively.

In the incidents in which either did participate the Soviet Union or China threatened to use, or actually employed, its own armed forces roughly one-half of the time. In another 20 percent of the incidents they *may* have used or threatened to use force, but the data are insufficient to be certain. Only one hostile act directed at the United States by China resulted in a U.S. use of armed force. It is arguable, though, whether Peking was simply not as hostile toward the United States as is generally imagined, or was merely cautious and selective in manifesting its hostility.

On the average, two other participants were involved with the United States in each incident. As might be expected, a relatively small number of actors accounted for a very large proportion of the total participation (table 2-6). The Soviet Union was by far the most active state. Besides the Soviet Union, only two other nations—Britain and France—participated in incidents outside their own immediate region. Eighteen actors accounted for more than one-half of the total; the leading five actors alone accounted for almost one-third.

Almost one-half of the total extraregional involvements took place in the Middle East, reinforcing its characterization as the crossroads of the world.

Trends in the Size, Type, and Activity of Participating Military Forces

The incidents described above were not ephemeral events. On the average, the United States employed units of its armed forces in these incidents for ninety days; the maximum level of force employed in the incidents was exerted, again on the average, for fifty-six days. Still, most of the 215 incidents in which the United States utilized its armed forces for political objectives were relatively minor; neither the stakes involved (at least for the United States), the amount of force employed, nor the activity of U.S. forces ever attained significant proportions. In other incidents, however, significant U.S. political objectives were at stake and commensurate levels of force were employed. And in a few incidents the very survival of the nation seemed to be threatened, indirectly if not directly, and the full panoply of the nation's armed forces was employed to avert the disaster which seemed otherwise inevitable.

Are certain "modal" components of force utilized when events seem to necessitate a demonstrative use of force? Do these modalities vary in different regions or political contexts? These and similar questions are addressed in the following pages with a view toward discerning the consistencies as well as the variations in the historical pattern.

Naval Forces

Throughout the postwar period the United States has turned most often to its Navy when it desired to employ components of the armed forces in support of political objectives. Naval units participated in 177 of the 215 incidents, or more than four out of every five. Land-based forces were used in many fewer incidents, and rarely without the simultaneous participation of naval units. Land-based air units participated in 103 incidents, or roughly one-half of the total number. Ground combat units took part in only 45 incidents, or about one-fifth of the total.[10] Moreover, whereas naval forces alone were employed in 100 incidents, landbased air units alone took part in only 22 incidents. Ground combat forces alone were used in only 3 incidents. The combination of landbased air and ground combat units without naval participation also was rare; there were only 12 such cases. These frequencies are summarized in figure 2-2.

This reliance on naval forces has been the case in all parts of the world throughout the postwar period. It has been sensitive neither to Soviet or Chinese participation in the incidents nor to the political context which led to the U.S. use of force. Navy participation ranged from a "low" of 77 percent of the incidents in sub-Saharan Africa and South Asia to a "high" of 85 percent of the incidents in East Asia. Navy participation in the other regions fell within this relatively narrow range. Although Navy participation sometimes varied sharply from one year to the next, it has been consistently high over time. Indeed, in only five years (1949, 1953, 1955, 1960, and 1966) did the Navy participate in less than 70 percent of all incidents. For nine of the years the Navy was involved in every political use of the armed forces. Since 1955 the Navy has been involved, on the average, in more than nine out of every ten incidents.

Navy participation also has not varied significantly with political context. Naval forces were employed in 76 percent of the incidents stemming from international situations in which the United States was involved from the beginning, 83 percent of the intranational situations, and 86 percent of those situations characterized as international but not involving the United States initially. Soviet or Chinese participation did not seem to make much difference; nor did it matter whether or not the USSR or China threatened, or actually employed, force in the incidents when they did participate. Navy involvement ranged narrowly between 78 and 84 percent as a function of the level of Soviet or Chinese involvement.

In short, the Navy clearly has been the foremost instrument for the United States' political uses of the armed forces: at all times, in all places, and regardless of the specifics of the situation. The reasons for this dominance are not difficult to discern. First, ships are easier to move about than are Army or land-based aircraft units, and can be moved at less incremental cost and more rapidly than can any land-based unit of comparable

10. Excludes Marine units when deployed by ship.

Figure 2-2. *Number of Incidents in Which Naval, Ground Combat, and Land-Based Air Units Participated*[a]

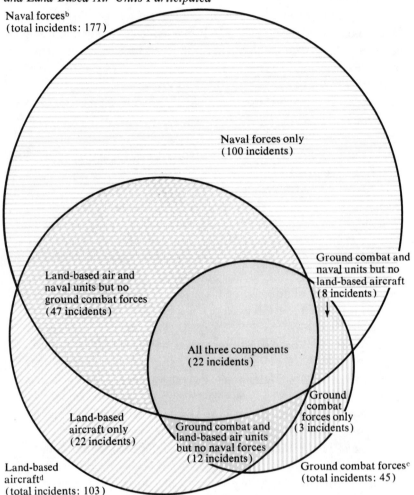

Naval forces[b]
(total incidents: 177)

Naval forces only
(100 incidents)

Land-based air and
naval units but no
ground combat forces
(47 incidents)

Ground combat and
naval units but no
land-based aircraft
(8 incidents)

All three components
(22 incidents)

Land-based
aircraft only
(22 incidents)

Ground combat and
land-based air units
but no naval forces
(12 incidents)

Ground
combat
forces only
(3 incidents)

Land-based
aircraft[d]
(total incidents: 103)

Ground combat forces[c]
(total incidents: 45)

a. Information was unavailable on the type(s) of forces used in one incident.
b. Includes Marine Corps units when deployed on amphibious vessels.
c. Army units, and Marines when not deployed on amphibious vessels.
d. Includes Navy land-based maritime patrol aircraft and Army helicopter transportation units.

size. Because a larger portion of the Navy's support is organic to the combat unit (that is, a ship as compared to a battalion or a squadron), the establishment of communications and logistics flows can be accomplished with less difficulty.

Second, warships on the scene of a disturbance are less disruptive psychologically than are land-based forces and thus are likely to be less offensive diplomatically; if desirable, naval forces can remain nearby but out of sight. Fewer inhabitants of the target state are likely to be aware of their presence than would be the case for land-based units, and contacts between sailors and local citizens can be more tightly controlled than is the case with land forces. Naval forces can be used more subtly to support foreign policy incentives—to underscore threats, or warnings, or promises, or commitments—than can land-based units, and they can do so without necessarily tying the President's hand. Of course, if the President wished to make a hand-tying gesture—for example, to demonstrate resolve—he would be better advised to turn to land-based forces for the political demonstration. Such voluntary cessions of flexibility are rare in international politics, however.

Third, the frequent recourse to the Navy is partly the result of tradition or habit. For most of U.S. history the Navy was the only military instrument which could be used for these purposes—there were no or few forces abroad, and the rapid movement of land-based forces was impossible. As a consequence the Navy, far more than the other two military services, has come to think of its employment for political objectives as one of its principal missions ("show-the-flag," "presence," "crisis diplomacy"), and has incorporated certain measures in the design of its forces which enable it to perform better in such operations—for example, the construction of underway support ships which permit operations in regions remote from bases.

AIRCRAFT CARRIERS. Not surprisingly, the U.S. Navy in the thirty years under study most often utilized sea-based airpower. Aircraft carriers took part in 106 incidents in all; about 60 percent of those involving naval forces and slightly less than one-half of all the incidents.[11] Carriers were used proportionally more during the 1949–55 period, which was a time generally of lesser naval participation (see table 2-7).

Aircraft carriers were used more often in regions where the United States maintained a continuous carrier presence than elsewhere. In the Seventh Fleet's operating area, carriers took part in 75 percent of those incidents in East Asia in which any naval forces were involved, and 63 percent of those in Southeast Asia. In the Sixth Fleet's area, carriers

---

11. It is possible that carriers were used in eight additional incidents, but the data are too fragmentary to be certain.

Table 2-7. *Use of Naval Forces and Aircraft Carriers, by Time Period*

| Period | Naval participation as a percentage of all incidents | Carrier participation as a percentage of | |
		All naval involvements	All incidents
1946–48	88	52	46
1949–55	71	82	58
1956–65	83	59	49
1966–75	83	56	47

participated in 55 percent of the total naval involvements in both the Middle East/North Africa and Europe. The latter were primarily incidents in the Balkans and Cyprus. Elsewhere the use of carriers was not nearly so common; they were used in less than one-third of the Navy's involvements in Africa, South Asia, and the Western Hemisphere.

Of course, the decision to use or not to use a carrier in a particular incident may be as much a function of the nature of the situation as it is of the immediate availability of carrier decks. For example, incidents in the Western Hemisphere typically did not involve the USSR or any other actor with sizable military forces, and hence could be handled by lesser U.S. forces. Apparently the carriers are deployed on a continuous basis in those areas in which they are likely to be needed, rather than being used in certain areas simply because they are available. This hypothesis is supported by two observations.

First, carriers were more often used in political contexts characterized by international violence than in other types of situations. Carriers participated in 70 percent of the former but in only 49 percent of all other types of political contexts. Presumably, faced with the prospect of intervening in a shooting war, the United States turned to its more powerful warships.

Second, there is a clear relationship between Soviet or Chinese involvement and the use of carriers. Aircraft carriers were involved in 65 percent of those incidents in which U.S. naval forces were used and Russian or Chinese military forces also participated, and in 67 percent of those U.S. naval involvements in which the Soviet Union or China threatened to but did not actually employ armed forces. On the other hand, carriers were involved in only 26 percent of those incidents in which the U.S. Navy and the Soviet Union or China participated, but in which the USSR and China neither employed nor threatened to employ force. And carriers took part in only 46 percent of those U.S. naval involvements in situations in which there was no Soviet or Chinese participation.

It should be noted that Soviet and Chinese threats of or resort to military activity occurred usually in East Asia, the Middle East, and Europe— the areas where carriers were most readily available. Thus there is again the question of whether the carrier deployments in these regions stem from anticipation of Soviet/Chinese military activity. Other possibilities are that such forward-deployed U.S. forces have provoked greater levels of Soviet or Chinese involvement and military activity, and that both these U.S. and Soviet/Chinese actions have been related to still other factors (for example, the degree of local conflict).

In fifty-one incidents only one carrier task-group took part; two carrier task groups were utilized on twenty-five occasions, and three on eleven occasions. More than three carrier task groups took part in eleven incidents, the largest carrier deployments taking place during the Offshore Islands crisis (1958), the Cuban missile crisis (1962), the crisis which followed North Korea's shooting down of an EC-121 aircraft (1969), and in response to the North Vietnamese Easter offensive in 1972.

AMPHIBIOUS FORCES. In seventy-one incidents (40 percent of the Navy involvements and 33 percent of all the incidents) amphibious forces were used.[12] Participation by amphibious units tended to be proportionally even regardless of region, with the exceptions of Southeast Asia, where amphibious units participated in a larger share of the incidents (54 percent), and East Asia, where amphibious participation was lower (10 percent). In Southeast Asia amphibious operations were attempts to bolster the former SEATO protocol states, or preparations for various contemplated but never executed operations related to incidents involving Indonesia.

There were no significant variations over time in the use of amphibious forces, although during the last three years of the study period (1973–75), amphibious forces were involved in 43, 60, and 75 percent of the naval incidents, respectively (for a total of nine incidents out of sixteen). The length of this trend is too short to impute any great significance to it, however, and an explanation is offered below.

As would be expected, there was considerable overlap between the use of amphibious forces and aircraft carriers. U.S. decisionmakers have

12. There were ten additional incidents in which amphibious forces might have been employed, but the data are incomplete.

been reluctant to commit ground forces without also dispatching air cover. Amphibious forces alone participated only in fifteen incidents. Both amphibious forces and aircraft carriers were involved in fifty-six incidents, one-fourth of the total number of incidents. This is an extraordinarily high percentage and demonstrates the central role played by the "Navy/Marine team" in political-military operations.

Ground Combat Forces

The Army has been used least often as a discrete instrument for political objectives. This is not to gainsay the Army's importance, for the maintenance of a continuous U.S. ground force presence in Europe and Korea may well be the most important way in which U.S. armed forces have served political objectives, by conditioning the expectations of foreign leaders to such an extent that discrete uses of forces have been needed less often. U.S. decisionmakers have turned to the Army only infrequently, however, when desirous of a discrete, demonstrative, politically oriented use of force as defined in this study.

All told, Army ground combat forces took part in thirty-nine incidents, 18 percent of the total.[13] When the Army did become involved, it typically did so in force. In over one-fourth of the incidents in which Army ground combat forces were employed more than one full division was used. Four of these eleven major incidents occurred between 1968 and 1973; four others occurred between 1958 and 1962. More than one-half of the Army's multiple division involvements (six incidents) took place in Europe, generally stemming from controversies over Berlin.

The next most frequent level of Army ground force operation was of multiple battalion through full brigade size.[14] There were nine of these incidents but the last one occurred in 1964. This probably reflects constraints on Army resources due to the deployment of considerable forces to Vietnam while maintaining large forward deployments in Europe and Korea. Indeed, Army manpower was so tight that troop levels in Europe had to be drawn down during the Vietnam buildup. Given the strain these demands placed on Army manpower, Army ground combat forces seem to have been utilized elsewhere during the period of the Vietnam War only for the most serious contingencies, those in which larger than

---

13. Army ground forces were possibly used in two additional incidents.
14. Usually there are three or four battalions in an Army brigade.

brigade-size forces were required. A similar gap in battalion-level operations occurred during the Korean War. While there was one multiple-battalion operation in 1946, in 1947, and in 1948, and then one again in both 1954 and 1955, there were none from 1949 through 1953. Most of these multiple-battalion-level operations took place in Europe (five of nine incidents). Three others occurred in Southeast Asia.

Marine Corps

Often when U.S. decisionmakers wished to inject ground forces quickly into a situation, or at least to threaten such an action, they turned to the Marine Corps. Marine ground combat forces took part in seventy-seven incidents, twice the Army total.[15] In all but six of these incidents the Marines were moved to the region of the incident, or had already been deployed in that region, on amphibious ships.

This dependence on the Marines is not hard to understand. Indeed, the sort of limited politically oriented operation which makes up most of the incidents may well constitute the essence—that is, the central self-perception or purpose—of the corps. Marine units have been used in such operations as far back as the Napoleonic Wars, and the corps' official history lists a sizable number of incidents which took place before the Second World War that would meet the terms of our definition of a political use of the armed forces.[16]

Moreover, the Marines are equipped, trained, and organized for quick reaction, limited operations, and flexible utilization. Most important, Marine Corps units have been maintained afloat in the Mediterranean, the Western Pacific, and often in the Caribbean, throughout the postwar period. Most of the incidents in which Marine ground combat forces took part involved solely these forward-deployed units. For these reasons the Marine units employed in these incidents most frequently ranged in size from several companies up to a full battalion—the size of the units maintained afloat. Forty-four of the seventy-seven incidents involving Marine ground combat forces included units of roughly battalion size.

15. Marine Corps ground combat units possibly were involved in fourteen additional incidents.

16. Capt. William D. Parker, USMCR, *A Concise History of the United States Marine Corps, 1775–1969* (Historical Division, Headquarters, United States Marine Corps, 1970).

Land-based Air Forces

Three types of land-based air units were employed during the study time period, for a total of 103 incidents. Land-based air units provided the only U.S. military presence in only twenty-two of these incidents, however. Most frequent was the use of *transport aircraft*—either to move U.S. equipment or, less often, to move U.S. troops to a target state or to transport a target nation's equipment or troops within the region of concern. Fixed-wing aircraft were used in these roles on fifty-two occasions; helicopters on fourteen occasions.[17] The size of the units involved ranged from less than one squadron (or one helicopter company) in about one-fourth of the cases, to one or more wings in another one-fourth of the incidents.

Land-based combat aircraft were utilized more sparingly: Air Force units took part in thirty-four incidents, Marine Corps units in twelve incidents;[18] in five of these incidents aircraft from both services were involved. Full wings or even larger units took part in 60 percent of these cases. One factor which may have affected the decision as to the size of the unit required was Soviet participation; the Russians took part in more than one-half of the cases in which land-based combat aircraft were used, far more than their rate of participation in all cases. A concentration of land-based combat air operations during the 1958–62 period reflected mainly tensions in Central Europe: one-third of the uses of land-based combat aircraft occurred during these five years, but only one-fourth of all the incidents.

Finally, in twenty-seven incidents the United States used *land-based patrol or reconnaissance aircraft* for political objectives.[19] Most frequently these were Navy maritime patrol craft, looking for suspected Cuban-supported guerrillas in the Caribbean. Sixteen of the twenty-seven incidents took place during the 1956–65 period, the time the United States was most active in seeking to help governments in the Third World to defend themselves against domestic movements supported by foreign nations. Two-thirds of these incidents took place in the Caribbean.

17. Fixed-wing aircraft may have been used in five additional incidents; helicopters may have been used in four additional incidents.

18. Air Force and Marine air combat units may each have been involved in one additional incident.

19. Land-based patrol or reconnaissance aircraft may also have been involved in two additional incidents.

Strategic Nuclear Weapons

A special note should be made of the implicit, and sometimes explicit, threat to use nuclear weapons. Of course, nuclear weapons are deployed abroad for use in tactical warfare. The Seventh Army in Germany and the Eighth Army in South Korea have included units equipped with short-range surface-to-surface missiles; Air Force tactical squadrons deployed in Europe and Asia have maintained stocks of nuclear ordnance. Warships often have nuclear warheads on board for surface-to-air missiles and antisubmarine weapons; aircraft carriers may carry nuclear air-to-ground ordnance. Consequently, any movement or other involvement of these forces in an incident may imply, in one sense, a nuclear signal. But because these forces are primarily for conventional warfare their involvement does not necessarily imply that U.S. decisionmakers intended a nuclear threat. There are other forces, however, which play a primary role in plans for strategic nuclear war against the Soviet Union, and the involvement of one of these units would be open to interpretation as a nuclear threat. For this reason we have noted whenever a force, which at the time had a designated role in U.S. plans for strategic nuclear war, took part in one of the political incidents in such context that a nuclear signal of some type could be inferred. There were nineteen such incidents (table 2-8), including five distinct subtypes:

1. An overt and explicit threat was directed at the USSR through global actions of U.S. strategic forces in four incidents—the Suez, Lebanon, and Cuban missile crises and the October 1973 war in the Middle East. The small number of these incidents demonstrates the relative caution with which U.S. decisionmakers have approached the risk of nuclear war.

2. In ten incidents Air Force strategic bombers were moved either closer to the Soviet Union or China, placed on increased alert, or their withdrawal from a region abroad was delayed, in the context of U.S.-Soviet or U.S.-Chinese tension. Six of these incidents occurred in Europe, the first in 1946 when, after a U.S. aircraft was downed over Yugoslavia, six B-29s were deployed to Germany and rather ostentatiously flew along the border. Such a display was repeated on three other occasions in 1948, related to Berlin incidents. The fifth occurred in 1950 when, in the aftermath of the outbreak of the Korean War, U.S. strategic bombers were

Table 2-8. *Incidents in Which Strategic Nuclear Forces Were Involved*

Incident	Date
U.S. aircraft shot down by Yugoslavia	November 1946
Inauguration of president in Uruguay	February 1947
Security of Berlin	January 1948
Security of Berlin	April 1948
Security of Berlin	June 1948
Korean War: Security of Europe	July 1950
Security of Japan/South Korea	August 1953
Guatemala accepts Soviet bloc support	May 1954
China-Taiwan conflict: Tachen Islands	August 1954
Suez crisis	October 1956
Political crisis in Lebanon	July 1958
Political crisis in Jordan	July 1958
China-Taiwan conflict: Quemoy and Matsu	July 1958
Security of Berlin	May 1959
Security of Berlin	June 1961
Soviet emplacement of missiles in Cuba	October 1962
Withdrawal of U.S. missiles from Turkey	April 1963
Pueblo seized by North Korea	January 1968
Arab-Israeli War	October 1973

stationed in Europe. The last of them occurred during the Berlin crisis of 1961, when the planned withdrawal of B-47s from Europe was delayed.

Deployment of U.S. strategic aircraft to the Western Pacific occurred four times—once to reassure South Korea and Japan in connection with the end of the Korean War, twice during China-Taiwan offshore islands crises, and finally during the *Pueblo* crisis.

3. In two incidents—Jordan in 1958 and the 1958–59 Berlin crisis—Sixth Fleet aircraft carriers, then playing a key role in U.S. strategic strike plans, were used to help attain political objectives.

4. In two peculiar incidents, U.S. long-range bombers assigned to the Strategic Air Command were flown to nations in the Western Hemisphere (Uruguay in 1947 and Nicaragua in 1954), apparently to reassure U.S. allies. The Nicaragua case makes some sense perhaps, insofar as it occurred in connection with maneuvers to overthrow the Soviet-supported Arbenz government in Guatemala.

5. Finally, in one case a U.S. strategic submarine, the *Sam Houston,* was used to reassure a U.S. ally. In 1963, following the withdrawal of U.S. intermediate-range ballistic missiles from Turkey, the *Sam Houston* visited Izmir. That port visit, the only such visit to a foreign port by a

U.S. strategic submarine that we know of, clearly was meant to demonstrate to Turkey that the United States retained a strategic presence in the region.

In short, the United States has used nuclear threats sparingly; moreover, their use was more common in earlier years—when the U.S. strategic position vis-à-vis the Soviet Union was dominant—than more recently. One-half of the nuclear incidents occurred during the first ten years (one-third) of the study period. Three-fourths occurred during the first fifteen years (one-half) of the study period. During the last ten years, there were only two incidents involving strategic nuclear threats.

Again, remember that the references above relate solely to discrete political uses of nuclear weapons. Like Army ground troops deployed overseas, strategic nuclear forces serve vital political objectives on a continuous basis, perhaps thus obviating the need for discrete and explicit utilization.

Levels of Force Used in Incidents

Variations in the types and size of military units which have been involved in the incidents, and the infrequent inclusion of strategic nuclear forces, make it difficult to discuss in the aggregate the significance of the involvement in terms of the level of force mustered by the United States. To alleviate this difficulty a scale was constructed which, based on the historical data, roughly ranked "military level of effort." For example, when combatant naval forces were involved in an incident they typically included one carrier task group. A carrier task group was therefore considered to constitute the "standard" naval force component. The use of two or more carriers in an incident constituted a "major" component of force. When the naval forces did not include an aircraft carrier, the incident was considered to have been less significant in that it required only a "minor" component of force. Similar assessments were made for ground forces[20] and land-based air forces,[21] with the results shown in table 2-9. Granted, the units listed for each rank are quite different in terms of manpower or any other measure of size. However, that is not the point. What the classification does is to provide a rough ranking of "military level of effort" based on aggregate past experience.

20. Army and Marine Corps units.
21. That is, Air Force and Marine Corps aircraft.

Table 2-9. *Level of Force Uses by Type of Force*

Level of force	Type of force		
	Naval	*Ground*	*Land-based air*
Major	Two or more aircraft carrier task groups	More than one battalion	One or more combat wings
Standard	One aircraft carrier task group	No more than one battalion, but larger than one company	One or more combat squadrons, but less than one wing
Minor	No aircraft carriers included	No more than one company	Less than one combat squadron

Next, these levels of conventional force were combined with the strategic nuclear factor in an intuitive fashion, resulting in the scale shown below.

Level of force scale, in descending order of magnitude

1. Use of strategic nuclear unit plus at least one "major" force component (naval, ground, or air)
2. Two or three "major" force components used, but not strategic nuclear units
3. Either one "major" force component *or* strategic nuclear unit used
4. At least one "standard" component of force used, but no "major" components and no strategic nuclear units
5. "Minor" components of force used only, and no strategic nuclear units

Considering the types of incidents which have occurred, it was our judgment that the use of any strategic nuclear force unit implied a greater threat or show of support than did the use of standard or minor conventional force components. Two or three major conventional force components, however, seemed to imply a greater threat or support than did the use of only a strategic force unit—for example, the U.S. forces used in 1965 in the Dominican Republic and in response to North Korea's shooting down a U.S. Navy EC-121 aircraft in 1969, as compared with the use of individual strategic force units for various visits and overflights which have been previously described. The greatest levels of force used were a combination of strategic nuclear units and two or three major conventional units, as for example in the Cuban missile, Offshore Islands, and several Berlin crises, and in the 1973 Middle East war. Nuclear force "use," as previously noted, refers to the involvement of

Table 2-10. *Level of Effort in Descending Order of Magnitude*

Level of effort	Number of incidents	Percentage distribution of incidents
1	15	7.0
2	18	8.4
3	46	21.4
4	64	29.8
5	72	33.5

weapon platforms which had a role at the time in strategic nuclear strike plans, leading to a reasonable inference that a nuclear signal of some sort was intended. As might be expected, in terms of military level of effort most of the incidents were of less significance, as shown in table 2-10. The most significant incidents, the thirty-three which scored a one or two on the level-of-effort scale, were distributed relatively evenly among Europe, the Middle East, East Asia, and Southeast Asia. Five of the eight incidents in Europe concerned Berlin, but the last of these occurred in 1961. In fact there have not been any significant incidents in Europe since 1968. By contrast, significant incidents in the Middle East have occurred more recently, the last in 1973. Surprisingly, only two of the eight significant incidents in the Middle East stemmed from the Arab-Israeli conflict; the other six had to do with intra-Arab conflicts.

There were seven significant incidents in East Asia, three stemming from the civil war in China, and four from conflict on the Korean peninsula. Like Europe, East Asia was not the scene of any significant incidents in 1970–75. The six significant incidents in Southeast Asia all had to do with the Indochina war, and highlight the United States' entry into and exit from that conflict.

Finally, there were four significant incidents in the Caribbean, two of which were related to the Dominican Republic. It is fascinating that the 1954 decision by the Arbenz government in Guatemala to accept military aid from the Soviet bloc was sufficient to occasion a major response from the United States, which included the temporary deployment of strategic bombers to Nicaragua—meant, it would appear, as a signal of American commitment—and the movement of an aircraft carrier task group, a reinforced Marine amphibious battalion and air-wing, land-based patrol aircraft squadrons, and several related actions.

Table 2-11. *U.S. Level of Military Effort, by Region and Time Period*

Number of incidents

Region or time period	Military level of effort					Total incidents
	1	*2*	*3*	*4*	*5*	
Western Hemisphere	2	2	6	18	32	60
Europe	5	3	12	19	4	43
Middle East	4	4	7	7	16	38
Sub-Saharan Africa and South Asia	0	0	0	6	7	13
Southeast Asia	0	6	17	8	10	41
East Asia	4	3	4	6	3	20
Total incidents	15	18	46	64	72	215
Time period						
1946–48	2	1	6	11	4	24
1949–55	4	1	7	7	5	24
1956–65	7	10	27	33	43	120
1966–75	2	6	6	13	20	47
Total incidents	15	18	46	64	72	215

Table 2-12. *U.S. Level of Military Effort as a Function of Soviet-Chinese Participation*

U.S. level of effort	Percentage of instances in which USSR/China			
	Used force	Threatened to use force	Participated, but did not use force	Did not participate
1. Nuclear weapons plus major component	53	27	0	20
2. Two or three major components	39	6	11	44
3. Nuclear weapons or one major component	15	4	22	59
4. Standard components only	16	9	13	63
5. Minor components only	11	7	15	67
All levels	19	8	14	59

The distribution of incidents by U.S. level of military effort, region, and time period is shown in table 2-11.

There is a strong relationship between U.S. military level of effort and Soviet or Chinese participation. As shown in table 2-12, the United States used major force components proportionally more often when either the USSR or Chinese military forces actually were, or threatened to become, involved in incidents.

Activities and Readiness

Typically, U.S. armed forces employed for political objectives did very little in an operational sense. In sixty-eight incidents (about one-third of the total) the military activity could only be characterized as, at most, providing a presence. That is, forces were moved from one place to another, or their alert status was raised, but they did not undertake any specific operation.[22] Presumably, the movement or change in alert status was meant to prepare for some activity which might have become necessary, and to remind participants of U.S. military power so that they would be reassured or intimidated, as the case may have been.

Most often the forces that were used for these "presence" missions, as well as most other activities, came from standing U.S. deployments nearby. In 167 incidents, three-fourths of the total, U.S. forces already operating within the theater which was the scene of the situation of concern were either moved or placed on an increased alert status without movement. In only ninety-two incidents, less than one-half of the total, were U.S. forces operating outside the theater of concern redeployed or placed on a greater alert status. Reserve forces were mobilized in only three incidents.

The data in table 2-13 summarize the activities of U.S. armed forces in the 215 incidents. In view of the Navy's dominant position in past experience, the table separates those incidents in which naval forces were involved from those in which they were not. As noted, simply providing a presence was by far the most frequent activity; the Caribbean, the

---

22. This conceptualization of the mission of "presence" is of course more limited than that of many policymakers and military planners, who include in their conceptualization routine deployments, visits, and exercises in an area. But the focus of this study is on the discrete use of armed forces for particular policy objectives in specific situations.

Table 2-13. *Activities of Naval and Other U.S. Armed Forces for Political Objectives, 1946–75*

	Number of incidents	
Type of activity	Naval forces	Other forces alone
Providing a U.S. presence	68	1
Visit	44	0
Patrol/reconnaissance/surveillance	35	9
Exercise/demonstration	29	1
Movement of military equipment or forces to a target	22	8
Movement of a target's military forces or equipment	13	8
Evacuation	18	1
Use of firepower	14	4
Emplacing ground forces or occupying territory	10	8
Interposition	6	1
Escort of a target's forces	5	2
Demonstrating transit rights	4	3
Blockade	3	0
Other	4	0

Middle East, and Southeast Asia were each the scene of one-fourth of these actions.

Visits to foreign ports and the conduct of patrols or other reconnaissance and surveillance missions tied as the second most frequent activity. Europe accounted for one-half of the port visits, the vast majority of these visits being paid by Sixth Fleet ships to allies along the northern Mediterranean littoral.[23] About one-half of the reconnaissance activities took place in the Western Hemisphere, mainly during the 1956–65 period, when the United States was most actively concerned about Communist infiltration into the hemisphere.

Most of the thirty exercises or demonstrations were in Europe. In the thirty instances of transporting military equipment to a target state, the Middle East was the most frequent destination. Other types of activity, generally of a manifestly more "military" nature, were undertaken in no more than one-tenth of the incidents and included the following:

1. Firepower or other physical force was used in only eighteen incidents, nine of them in Southeast Asia (exclusive of the period March

23. Only port visits which clearly served specific political purposes were included in the list of incidents.

1965 to March 1972). Such "violence" was used on only four occasions before 1964, in four incidents in each of 1964 and 1965, and six times over the period of 1971–75.

2. Most frequent non-naval activities included reconnaissance, the movement of a target state's military forces or equipment, and the movement of equipment to a target state.

3. When U.S. ground forces actually were emplaced on foreign soil, as contrasted to the movement or alert of Marines on amphibious ships without disembarkation, they were moved by air almost as often as by sea.

4. Traditional naval activities—interposition, escort, demonstration of transit rights, and blockade—took place relatively infrequently.

5. Fully 40 percent of the armed evacuations mentioned in the incident list took place in the Caribbean.

In summary, although U.S. armed forces have been used frequently for political objectives over the past thirty years, only relatively infrequently have they had to do anything in a specific operational sense. Typically, the armed forces—and particularly naval forces—have provided a U.S. presence on (or near) the scene of the incident, and presumably have prepared to take action, but the situations precipitating the military activity have generally run their courses before the armed forces were required to take more specific action. When specific operations were carried out, they most often were of a passive character (for example, visits, patrols). Manifestly military actions—for example, the use of firepower, the establishment of a blockade—were called for very infrequently.

Patterns of Involvement and Action

Considering that naval forces were used in fully four-fifths of the incidents, it is not surprising that the distribution of naval actions by level of armed forces parallels the distribution of incidents generally. To be otherwise, a greatly disproportionate usage of naval forces would have had to occur in conjunction with one or several levels of armed forces. Naval participation ranged narrowly, however—between 75 and 91 percent—in relation to the five levels of armed forces considered (table 2-14).

Land-based air and ground forces, it will be recalled, were used much

Table 2-14. *Level of Armed Forces by Intensity of Incidents as*
Measured by Type of Force and Activity

	Type of force			Activity	
Level of armed forces	Naval	Land-based air	Ground	Mani-fest[a]	Latent[b]
Distribution of force type and activity by level of armed forces					
1. One or more major components and nuclear force unit	6.8	14.6	20.0	20.5	3.5
2. Two or three major components; no nuclear force units	9.0	15.5	22.2	18.2	5.8
3. One major component or nuclear force unit	20.9	20.4	33.3	31.8	18.7
4. Standard component	32.8	17.5	11.1	15.9	33.3
5. Minor component	30.5	32.0	13.3	13.6	38.6
Force type and activity as a percentage of incidents in which each level of armed forces was used					
1. One or more major components and nuclear force unit	80.0	100.0	60.0	60.0	40.0
2. Two or three major components; no nuclear force units	88.9	88.9	55.6	44.4	55.6
3. One major component or nuclear force unit	80.4	45.7	32.6	30.4	69.6
4. Standard component	90.6	28.1	7.8	10.9	89.1
5. Minor component	75.0	45.8	8.3	8.3	91.7

a. Use of firepower or other physical force, blockade, interposition, emplacement of ground forces, exercise of right of transit.
b. Activities other than those included in note a.

less frequently than naval forces—in approximately one-half and one-fifth of the incidents, respectively. As compared with the use of naval forces the use of land-based air and especially ground forces occurred proportionally more often in incidents involving larger forces: while 16 percent of the incidents in which naval forces participated involved the use of the two highest force levels on the scale, such incidents constituted 30 percent of those in which land-based air elements participated and 42 percent of those in which ground forces were used. Viewed another way, while almost two-thirds of the naval involvements included only standard or minor force components, only one-half of the land-based air and one-fourth of the ground force actions were associated with these two lowest levels of forces. Not surprisingly, land-based air elements participated less frequently than naval forces in incidents involving lower force levels, and ground forces participated less frequently still. Indeed, while ground forces were used in three-fifths of the incidents in which the two highest levels of force were used, they were turned to in less than one-tenth of the incidents employing only the two lowest force levels.

Land-based air units participated in every incident when the highest of the five force levels was used and in nine-tenths of those actions when there was resort to the second highest force level, as contrasted with those relatively lower frequencies of participation noted with regard to ground forces. When policymakers have considered it necessary to use the highest force levels they have turned first to land-based air, second to naval, and third to ground forces. Quite clearly, ground forces have been used only with the greatest reluctance.

In brief then, naval units have been used with relatively equal and high frequency, whatever the force level policymakers felt it necessary to apply. As compared with naval forces, land-based air units were used more often in association with higher levels of force, and have been called upon first in conjunction with the highest force level (in terms of our scale). Finally, ground forces, although used least frequently whatever the level of force, were used much more often in major than in lesser actions.

The activities of U.S. armed forces can be divided into two broad categories: actions of a relatively more manifest character, and a residual category of more latent types of military activity. The first grouping included the use of firepower (for example, bombing) and other actions involving physical force, the imposition of a blockade, interposition, the emplacement of ground forces, and the exercise of a right of transit. The residual grouping included such activities as presence, visits, surveillance, exercises, and demonstrations.

Almost three-quarters of the incidents in which the more manifest activities were performed involved the use of a major conventional force component or nuclear-capable force units. By contrast, almost three-fourths of those incidents in which U.S. forces engaged in less manifest activities involved only standard or minor conventional force components. Thus, as compared with the use of standard and minor components, which were called upon almost always for purposes of *show,* more serious business was assigned more frequently to larger forces.

CHAPTER THREE

The Question of Utility:
Theory and Practice

To WHAT EFFECT have decisionmakers turned to the armed forces as an instrument with which to support policy? During the three decades after World War II ended, on the average, U.S. armed forces were used as a political instrument once every other month. Both policymakers and the public at large have an interest in knowing whether or not these actions were of value in supporting American foreign policy and, in addition, what difference it made, if any, when the armed forces were used in particular ways, when certain sizes or types of forces were used, or when special situational factors were present.

We examine in these next three chapters the relationship between the use of armed forces and the behavior desired of each of the other actors in thirty-three incidents, which together comprise a 15 percent sample of the full 215-incident file. We cannot assess whether or not a particular behavior was the result of a particular use of force. Establishing causality is too heavy a burden to place on our data, and we therefore leave that task to the case studies. Rather, in these chapters we measure a less complicated phenomenon: the extent to which the use of armed forces was associated, in aggregate, with positive and negative outcomes related to the behavior desired of the other actors in the sample incidents.

A sample was used for the analysis insofar as it was impossible to investigate the utility of using armed forces in all 215 incidents. The choice of a thirty-three-incident (15 percent) sample constituted a compromise between two conflicting concerns: considering an adequate number of

58

cases and the necessity to consider each case adequately. The sample was structured to proportionally represent the full set of incidents in terms of: the size of the U.S. military involvement; the degree of Soviet involvement; the nature of the East-West relationship at the time; and the situational context in which incidents occurred.

The sample also closely reflects many other profile characteristics of the full file. To the extent that the selection procedure did skew the sample in terms of time and place, it gave proportionally more emphasis to the Middle East and the past decade, and proportionally less emphasis to Europe and the first postwar decades, than the full file would have given. Details of the sample selection process and of the degree of similarity between the sample and the 215-incident file are presented in appendix C. Table 3-1 describes some characteristics of the selected incidents and will familiarize readers with the sample; additional details are presented in chapters 4 and 5.

Objectives, Not Motives

The focus of this analysis is on the performance, by other actors in an incident, of behavior desired by U.S. policymakers, *not* on whether the motives of U.S. policymakers were satisfied. Motivation is extremely difficult, if not impossible, to determine in any situation, let alone in thirty-three international incidents. Motives, among other things, may be singular or multiple in number, subliminally or consciously held, and future- or present-oriented. Further, a President's motives may be of a personal nature, they may relate to domestic political matters, or they may concern the "national interest" of the United States.

For example, what were President Kennedy's motives when he confronted the Soviet Union in the Cuban missile crisis? Was it a concern for the physical defense of the United States, Soviet aggressiveness in the world at large, American leadership in the West, the forthcoming congressional election, his own influence and relations with the Congress, his leadership of the Democratic party? Was it one, some, or all of the above? What were President Eisenhower's motives in sending troops to Lebanon in 1958, President Truman's in sending ground troops to Europe following the onset of the Korean War, or President Ford's in responding to Cambodia's seizure of the *Mayaguez* and its crew?

Table 3-1. *Description of Incidents in the Sample*

Date U.S. use of force was initiated	Situation	Region	Context	Principal actors
1. Apr. 1946	Communist threat in *Greece* preceding outbreak of civil war	Europe	Intrastate, non-violent	Greece, Greek Communist party, United Kingdom, Soviet Union, Yugoslavia
2. Nov. 1947	Communist threat in *Italy* preceding 1948 elections	Europe	Intrastate, non-violent	Italy, Italian Communist party
3. Aug. 1953	Security of *Japan*/*South Korea* after Korean War	East Asia	Interstate, non-violent	China, Japan, North Korea, South Korea, Soviet Union
4. Apr. 1956	British influence in *Jordan* threatened	Middle East	Interstate, non-violent	Jordan, United Kingdom
5. July 1956	Egypt nationalizes *Suez* Canal	Middle East	Interstate, non-violent	Egypt, France, United Kingdom, Soviet Union
6. Oct. 1956	Security of U.S. military bases/personnel in *Morocco*	Middle East	Violent threat to U.S. armed forces	France, Morocco
7. Aug. 1957	Political developments in *Syria*; security of U.S. allies	Middle East	Interstate, non-violent	Iraq, Jordan, Lebanon, Saudi Arabia, Syria, Syrian armed forces group, Egypt, Turkey, Soviet Union
8. May 1958	Security of Vice President Nixon in *Venezuela*	Central America/Caribbean	Violent threat to U.S. vice president	Venezuela
9. Apr. 1959	Cuba supports insurgents in *Panama*	Central America/Caribbean	Intrastate, violent	Cuba, Panama, Panama insurgents, Organization of American States

	Event	Region	Type	Actors
10. Aug. 1959	Civil war in *Laos*	Southeast Asia	Intrastate, violent	China, Laos, North Vietnam, Pathet Lao, Soviet Union
11. Feb. 1960	Exiles overfly *Cuba*; security of Guantanamo	Central America/ Caribbean	Intrastate, violent	Cuba, Cuban exile group
12. July 1960	Breakdown of order in *Congo*	Sub-Saharan Africa	Intrastate, violent	Belgium, Congo, Katanga, United Nations, Soviet Union
13. June 1961	Trujillo assassinated in *Dominican Republic*	Central America/ Caribbean	Intrastate, violent	Dominican Republic, Dominican armed forces–civilian group
14. July 1961	Iraq threatens to invade *Kuwait*	Middle East	Interstate, non-violent	Arab League, Iraq, Kuwait, United Kingdom
15. Feb. 1962	Communist gains in *South Vietnam*	Southeast Asia	Interstate, violent	North Vietnam, South Vietnam, Viet Cong
16. May 1962	Civil War in *Laos*	Southeast Asia	Intrastate, violent	China, Laos, Laos neutralists, North Vietnam, Pathet Lao, Thailand, Soviet Union
17. Feb. 1963	Inauguration of President Juan Bosch in *Dominican Republic*	Central America/ Caribbean	Intrastate, non-violent	Dominican Republic, Dominican armed forces
18. Jan. 1964	Coup and war in *South Vietnam*	Southeast Asia	Intrastate, violent	North Vietnam, South Vietnam, South Vietnam armed forces, Viet Cong
19. July 1964	Cuba supports insurgents in *Dominican Republic*	Central America/ Caribbean	Intrastate, violent	Cuba, Dominican Republic, Dominican insurgents
20. Jan. 1965	*Tanzania* accuses U.S. of planning a coup	Sub-Saharan Africa	Hostile but non-violent political act directed at U.S.	Tanzania

Table 3-1 (*continued*)

Date U.S. use of force was initiated	Situation	Region	Context	Principal actors
21. Feb. 1965	War in *South Vietnam* (Qui Nhon barracks attacked)	Southeast Asia	Violent attack on U.S. armed forces	North Vietnam, South Vietnam, Viet Cong
22. May 1965	Cuba supports insurgents in *Venezuela*	Central America/Caribbean	Intrastate, violent	Cuba, Venezuela, Venezuelan insurgents
23. Aug. 1967	*Cyprus* crisis	Europe	Intrastate, violent	Cyprus (government; Greek populace), Cyprus (Turkish populace), Greece, Turkey, United Kingdom, United Nations
24. Jan. 1968	North Korea seizes U.S.S. *Pueblo*	East Asia	Violent attack on U.S. armed forces	North Korea, South Korea, Soviet Union
25. Dec. 1968	Israel attacks *Lebanon* (Beirut airport)	Middle East	Interstate, violent	Israel, Lebanon, Palestinians, United Nations
26. Apr. 1969	*North Korea* shoots down U.S. EC-121	East Asia	Violent attack on U.S. armed forces	North Korea, South Korea, Soviet Union
27. Aug. 1970	*Rogers Plan* cease-fire accepted by Egypt, Israel, and Jordan	Middle East	Interstate, violent	Egypt, Israel, Jordan, Soviet Union
28. Oct. 1970	USSR establishing base at *Cienfuegos* (Cuba)	Central America/Caribbean	Hostile but non-violent political act directed at U.S.	Cuba, Soviet Union
29. May 1972	North Vietnam offensive in *South Vietnam*	Southeast Asia	Interstate, violent	China, North Vietnam, South Vietnam, Soviet Union

30. Dec. 1972	*Vietnam* peace negotiations stalled	Southeast Asia	Interstate, violent	North Vietnam
31. Feb. 1973	Civil war in *Laos*	Southeast Asia	Intrastate, violent	Laos, Meo Tribe, North Vietnam, Pathet Lao
32. May 1973	Conflict between *Lebanon* and Palestinians	Middle East	Intrastate, violent	Israel, Lebanon, Palestinians, Syria
33. Nov. 1974	Availability and price of oil from *Persian Gulf* area; Arab-Israeli conflict	Middle East	Unfriendly but non-violent relations with U.S.	Egypt, Organization of Arab Petroleum Exporting Countries, Saudi Arabia

After any international incident there is always considerable dispute as to "why" U.S. policymakers behaved as they did. Post-facto explanations by the decisionmakers themselves (as in memoirs) do little to ease such speculation; for there is then a question as to the motives behind the explanation. There is much less argument, however, about the behavior that was sought of the other parties to the incidents. In that regard there is usually firmer evidence: statements, written communications, and so on. Thus, while there is considerable dispute about why President Kennedy acted as he did in the Cuban missile crisis, there is little argument about his principal operational objective vis-à-vis the Soviet Union: the withdrawal of Soviet offensive missiles and bombers from Cuba. Similarly, President Eisenhower sought to ensure that a leftist or Arab nationalist government allied with Egypt was not installed in Lebanon in 1958, President Truman sought to deter Soviet aggression and to reassure European allies, and President Ford sought to obtain the release of the *Mayaguez* and its crew.

In each incident the desired outcomes may have been only instrumental to other objectives policymakers had in mind, and seldom able to satisfy all their underlying motives. However, the immediate outcomes were the focus of their attention and the usually necessary first steps. And it was to obtain these operational objectives that policymakers expended their energies and the nation's resources, including the use of the armed forces. Perhaps President Ford's fundamental strategic objective was to avoid giving further evidence of U.S. weakness after the defeat in Vietnam. But to accomplish that, he had to first obtain the release of the *Mayaguez*. President Ford's underlying personal motives are, at best, uncertain. His strategic objectives are debatable. But his operational objective is clear.

This is not to argue that operational objectives are always easily and surely identified. Indeed, there are many situations in which it is difficult to do this, if only because they are essentially minor incidents which have passed relatively unnoticed and for which there is little information available. In other cases the policymakers themselves were unclear about the facts of the situation and, at times, about what it was they wanted to happen (or not to happen). It is no easy task, for example, to determine what exactly U.S. officials had in mind regarding Spanish behavior when they allowed a naval visit to Spain in 1952. Nor is it easy to accept without question the official explanation that what President Nixon hoped to obtain by deploying the *Enterprise* to the Indian Ocean during the

1971 Bangladesh war was the deterrence of an Indian attack on West Pakistan.[1]

Nevertheless, we concluded that to focus on operational objectives—the behavior desired of the individual foreign actors in the incident by U.S. policymakers—would allow the consideration of more objectively determined and empirically verifiable phenomena without risking the validity of the study's results. Policymakers must deal more directly with operational objectives than with underlying strategic objectives or personal motives. Consequently, operational objectives tend to be expressed in relatively tangible and specific terms and their satisfaction or non-satisfaction can be judged much more easily. There is much greater agreement among public documents, memoirs, and scholarly studies of incidents as to what the decisionmakers' operational objectives were than as to either fundamental strategic objectives or personal motives.

Furthermore, it is the operational objectives which, in one sense, most strongly affect the success or failure of a foreign policy and the interests of the United States. Foreign decisionmakers do not often react to strategic objectives or personal motives; they are more likely to respond to the manifestations or non-manifestations of those underlying goals which are expressed in specific operational objectives, the decisions taken to obtain those objectives, and the resulting U.S. activity—military, diplomatic, or other.

Still, it is important to be aware that the choice of operational objectives entails a degree of analytic sacrifice. Operational objectives in an incident may be only ostensible, or no more than incidental to broader goals that policymakers have in mind—for example, in sending troops to Lebanon in 1958, President Eisenhower was certainly as much concerned to strengthen the credibility of U.S. commitments and respect for American interests in the Middle East generally, as he was to influence developments in Lebanon. Although it is not clear how this more fundamental strategic objective could have been attained without satisfaction of operational objectives pertaining to the situation in Lebanon, these more basic objectives of policymakers remain important in their own

1. Theodore J. Lowi, "Bases in Spain," in Harold Stein, ed., *American Civil-Military Decisions* (University of Alabama Press, 1963), pp. 667–705; Elmo R. Zumwalt, Jr. (Admiral, USN Ret.), *On Watch: A Memoir* (Quadrangle, 1976), pp. 363–69; James M. McConnell and Anne M. Kelley, "Superpower Naval Diplomacy in the Indo-Pakistani Crisis," Center for Naval Analyses, Professional Paper 108 (February 1973; processed).

right. Fundamental objectives enjoy greater durability than operational objectives and in the longer term are of greater significance. The case studies illustrate these differences between strategic and operational objectives.

In many instances policymakers will have conflicting objectives in mind as regards a single actor. After President Nasser nationalized the Suez Canal, President Eisenhower sought to persuade Britain and France not to intervene militarily; but he was also concerned not to alienate London and Paris and thereby weaken the Atlantic alliance. In the immediate aftermath of the assassination of Rafael Trujillo in the Dominican Republic in 1961, President Kennedy wanted Trujillo's political heirs to give up power. At the same time he was concerned to prevent the latter from acting violently toward American citizens, insofar as the United States was implicated in the plot.

When multiple objectives concerning a single actor's behavior do exist, one particular concern will typically command more attention than the others and dominate U.S. decisions. In fact, the two cases just cited are unusual, in that they were the two in the sample that were least clear in this regard. There was much less difficulty in determining, for example, that President Truman's principal objectives in using the armed forces to influence political developments in Italy in 1947–48 were to maintain the de Gasperi government in power (by winning the April 1948 elections) and to caution the Italian Communist party against engaging in large-scale violence. Notwithstanding President Nixon's motives for ordering the "Christmas" bombing of Hanoi in December 1972, it seems obvious that his principal operational objective was that North Vietnam should sign an acceptable peace agreement.

This is not to suggest that the objective singled out is the most important from the perspective of the "national interest" or even the interest of the President. The chosen objective may instead reflect only a determination about what is feasible under the circumstances and what will obtain consensus support. It may also reflect an appreciation of the greater risks that might be necessary in order to obtain more ambitious goals. In any case, our study of the political use of the armed forces indicates that, for whatever reason, one operational objective dominates decisions vis-à-vis each actor. Our identification of what these dominant operational objectives may have been is of course subject to review and debate.

Neither Success nor Failure, but Outcomes

It would be best if the utility of using armed forces as a political instrument could be discussed point-blank in terms of success or failure in achieving specific objectives; or, alternatively, in terms of the circumstances in which armed forces were used with success or failure. However, "success" and "failure" imply causation, which cannot be determined absolutely. Moreover, insofar as political phenomena are concerned, it is impossible to determine the linkages that are necessary to provide an empirical chain of evidence similar to that provided by physical scientists. In order to even approach the reliability of the latters' type of work, a much larger number of incidents would have to be examined, verifiable interviews would have to be held with individual participants, who would have to be reasonably precise in stating what their perceptions and calculations were during incidents. It goes without saying that these individuals would have to be honest, self-conscious, and able to recollect their thoughts at the time. Obviously, none of this is feasible.

Short of this ideal approach, the scientific method might have been brought to bear in this analysis if the sample of incidents selected could have been compared with a group of incidents in which armed forces might have been used as a political instrument, but, for one reason or another, were not. Following a comparative analysis of this nature it would be possible to infer that the use of armed forces was a necessary condition for "success," if outcomes were consistently positive when armed forces were used and consistently negative when they were not used. If outcomes were either unfavorable or favorable in both types of incidents, it might have been inferred that the use of armed forces was unnecessary.

This approach also would require that a much larger number of incidents be examined and that the two sets of incidents be comparative— that is, share a large number of similar characteristics including that the objectives of policymakers and use of force by other actors be comparable. Such experimentalism is a regular mode of analysis where the subjects of inquiry are protons, laboratory-bred rats, and even controlled groups of human beings. But this approach does not lend itself very well to analyses in which the subjects are individuals and groups in diverse societies with different values, levels of information, and so forth. The less the similarity between incidents, the greater the number of incidents that have to be examined. The simple pairing of incidents that differ in single major characteristics, such as occurring at different times or involving different actors, would be especially questionable.

This study does strive for scientific verifiability to the degree that "before and after" comparisons were possible with reference to individual incidents. If an incident comprised a number of rounds, rather than running smoothly from a starting point to a finishing point, a comparison could be made between two or more of those rounds; for example, between the period before armed forces were used by U.S. policymakers and the period after they were used. Of course, other developments might have occurred independently or in response to U.S. actions, and thus lessened the validity of even comparisons like these.

Still, the data problems are such that we had to adopt even more modest goals and methods of inquiry. Our focus is on the *outcomes* related to the principal behavior desired by U.S. policymakers of each other actor in the thirty-three incidents. Favorable or unfavorable outcomes were determined both for the six-month period following the use of armed forces and for a longer period thereafter (the following two and a half years). The consideration of only short-term outcomes would be misleading insofar as some are likely to be ephemeral. The longer term perspective allows a consideration of "durability."

In focusing on shorter and longer term outcomes related to the operational objectives of U.S. policymakers, the study refrains from attempting to assess the enduring implications and widespread ramifications—that is, the greater "wisdom"—of U.S. actions with respect to more general national interests. Not that this is unimportant. One can readily imagine instances in which desired outcomes were obtained in the immediate sense, and perhaps even retained over a longer term, but at the same time consequences of a more important and adverse nature were set in motion.

For example, actors earlier coerced into performing some specific behavior may later increase the size of their armed forces or develop new weapon systems having important implications for U.S. national security —consider, for example, the proposition that the Cuban missile crisis led the Soviet Union to further increase the size of its strategic weapons program, or that General de Gaulle was confirmed in his belief that France should develop an independent nuclear capability as a result of U.S. actions during the Suez crisis.

Moreover, other actors, not party to the incident at all, may sometimes draw undesired conclusions or take actions adversely affecting U.S. security and other interests. Perhaps Peking felt freer to initiate the 1958 Offshore Islands crisis because of its perception that the United States was too involved in Lebanon to support Taiwan firmly. Was Khrushchev's behavior in the 1961 Berlin crisis influenced by President Kennedy's minimal support of the Cuban exiles during the Bay of Pigs disaster? We may never know the answers, but questions such as these are important. For this study, however, simply determining the utility of using armed forces for particular outcomes was an extremely laborious task, and it was impossible to also consider the long-term consequences of those actions for the nation's interests in a wider context.

It should also be borne in mind that outcomes may not be related even indirectly to the use of armed forces. The political use of the military is often accompanied by policy statements, diplomatic communications, the manipulation of economic assistance and arms transfers, and covert activities. These other instruments may be more or less important for achieving objectives than the use of the armed forces. Such behavior may also clarify or reinforce the meaning of the use of the military, or, alternatively, confuse and undermine its meaning.

Of further significance to the choices made by foreign decisionmakers whom U.S. policymakers are attempting to influence are their own domestic and foreign pressures and constraints. As intervening variables, the perceptions, sources of motivation, and strength of commitment of a target are surely of great significance. Although the United States might clearly signal a threat of the use of force, a foreign leader may perceive only a weak U.S. commitment; domestic considerations may make a target act against its own better judgment; and nothing at all may avail when an actor identifies an objective with its own sense of destiny. As discussed elsewhere, the "confident use of a strategy of coercive diplomacy" will include a consideration of all of these factors.[2]

The sum—clearly a complex one—of the variables influencing a target's decisions is a screen through which the armed forces used as a political instrument, and other U.S. policy instruments, must usually penetrate in order to achieve a desired outcome. Different screens will present differing degrees of difficulty. Insofar as the analysis here considers only the direct and simple association between the use of armed forces and outcomes, and does not discuss the use of other U.S. policy

---

2. Alexander L. George, David K. Hall, and William E. Simons, *The Limits of Coercive Diplomacy: Laos, Cuba, Vietnam* (Little, Brown, 1971), p. 216.

instruments or the calculi of foreign decisionmakers, the findings of our analysis can only be suggestive. To regard these findings as conclusive would be to ignore the possibility of their including spurious relationships. The discussion in chapter 5 of the significance of other types of U.S. behavior and important situational characteristics, in fact, should temper the findings in this chapter and chapter 4.

The method of analysis utilized here breaks reality down into parts which cannot be cumulated simply. Understanding lies rather in a complex calculus, including factors not considered in these chapters; it being our judgment that only some, and not all, of the relevant variables could be investigated successfully at the present time. The validity of the findings resulting from the partial analysis in these chapters may be tested in the case studies, which take a holistic approach and consider the perceptions and motivations of foreign decisionmakers at length.

Finally, and notwithstanding the focus of this analysis being on the association between the use of armed forces and outcomes, it is often difficult not to make at least implicit inferences of success or failure. The full implications of such inferences therefore deserve elaboration.

"Success" in using armed forces in order, for example, to reinforce the performance of a desired behavior would imply a determination that the actor was otherwise unresolved as to whether to continue to perform the desired action, *and* that the use of armed forces by the United States was perceived and did indeed persuade the actor not to change the behavior in question. If the desired behavior was going to be performed in any case, the use of force would be of no consequence, even if the actor did perceive and consider it. "Failure" would imply that the actor did not perceive the use of force or did perceive it but was not influenced by it. Thus, failure can be determined with greater confidence: all that is necessary is to observe the nonperformance of a desired behavior.

Alternatively, success could imply that a use of the armed forces influenced the views and confidence of others around an individual actor, and thereby caused the actor to perform the desired behavior in a more circuitous fashion. Insofar as only a very few political leaders rule with absolute authority, the influence exerted upon factions and individuals, as well as upon formal or informal policy debates in general, may be the most frequently effective avenue to a satisfactory outcome.

The conclusion that armed forces were used successfully where the objective was to modify the actor's behavior, or to cause an actor to do something different, would imply a similar finding—that the actor performed a desired behavior to at least some degree in consequence of a U.S. use of the military, and that in the absence of this action the desired behavior would not have been performed.

Modes and Styles

When the essential character of relations between two actors is hostile, armed forces typically are used as an instrument of coercive diplomacy. Military units are used in one of two modes in order to present a threat to a target: (1) to *deter* the target from an undesired action or from stopping a desired action; or (2) to *compel* the target to do or to stop doing something. Thus, for example, the Soviet Union presumably was deterred from carrying out various threats in the 1961 Berlin crisis and compelled in the 1962 missile crisis to stop activating and eventually to withdraw the missiles and bombers it had emplaced in Cuba. By contrast, North Korea was not deterred by the U.S. military response to the seizure of the *Pueblo,* insofar as North Korean forces shot down a U.S. Navy EC-121 aircraft over international waters a little more than one year later. Nor was North Vietnam compelled to terminate its support for the war in South Vietnam by several discrete political uses of armed forces by the United States in the early 1960s.

Even as armed forces are used to coerce an antagonist, they may at the same time be used in one of two other modes to support a non-antagonist: (1) to *assure* a second target so that it will continue to do or not to do something; or (2) to *induce* a second target to do or to stop doing something. The literature of coercive diplomacy has devoted much less attention to assurance and inducement than it has to deterrence and compulsion.[3] When using armed forces, however, policymakers often

3. Of this literature, see, for example, James F. Cable, *Gunboat Diplomacy* (Praeger for the International Institute for Strategic Studies, 1971); George and others, *Limits of Coercive Diplomacy;* Alexander L. George and Richard Smoke, *Deterrence in American Foreign Policy: Theory and Practice* (Columbia University Press, 1974); Paul G. Lauren, "Ultimata and Coercive Diplomacy," *International Studies Quarterly,* vol. 16 (June 1972), pp. 131–65; Edward N. Luttwak, *The Political Uses of Seapower* (Johns Hopkins University Press, 1974); Bruce M. Russett, "The Calculus of Deterrence," *Journal of Conflict Resolution,* vol. 7 (June 1963), pp. 97–109; Thomas C. Schelling, *Arms and Influence* (Yale University Press, 1966); J. David Singer, "Inter-Nation Influence: A Formal Model," *American Political Science Review,* vol. 57 (June 1963), pp. 420–30; Oran R. Young, *The Politics of Force: Bargaining During International Crises* (Princeton University Press, 1968).

consider the assurance or inducement of non-antagonists to be as important as the deterrence or compulsion of antagonists. In the aftermath of North Korea's seizure of the *Pueblo,* for example, President Johnson sought to deter any further hostile action by Pyongyang and to compel the release of the *Pueblo* and its crew. But in ordering a large naval demonstration and the reinforcement of the U.S. air forces in the Far East he also sought to assure South Korea so that it would not remove the ground forces it then had deployed in Vietnam. Similarly, the permanent emplacement of ground forces in Japan and South Korea at the end of the Korean War was as much to assure those states and thus solidify their ties with the United States as it was to deter new aggression by North Korea and China.

In this study, all four modes of use of the armed forces—deter, compel, assure, and induce—are examined. By comparing uses of the armed forces to support—that is, assure or induce behavior—with uses to coerce —that is, deter or compel behavior, the utility of using the armed forces as a "reward" may be contrasted with the utility of their use as "punishment." The comparison of uses of the armed forces to insure the continued performance of existing behavior—that is, to assure or deter— with uses to obtain changed behavior—that is, to induce or compel— permits examination of the relative value of using armed forces for the purposes of behavior reinforcement and modification.

Regardless of mode, armed forces may be used either directly or indirectly; this is what we term "style of use." A *direct* use of the armed forces occurs when the activities of the military units involved clearly are aimed at a particular target without intermediaries. In sending U.S. Marines to Thailand during the 1962 Laotian crisis, for example, President Kennedy used the armed forces *directly* to assure Bangkok that the United States remained committed to Thailand's security and to deter both the Pathet Lao and North Vietnam from certain actions in Laos. The Marines also served *indirectly,* however, to compel the Soviet Union and China to take steps to control the Laotian crisis. Neither China nor the Soviet Union were threatened themselves with violence by the Marine deployments; only their allies were threatened *directly.* Moscow and Peking were coerced indirectly to the degree that they were concerned with their clients' well-being and found the U.S. threat credible.

Occasionally, alerted or deployed armed forces are used in none of the four modes mentioned above vis-à-vis a particular actor (or actors)—

and thus are used neither directly nor indirectly—but rather as a latent instrument. In such instances policymakers desire that an actor should do or not do something specific, and the direct or indirect use of armed forces is contemplated to this end. Changes in the disposition of military units may even be made. However, while these actions may demonstrate U.S. concern to all parties, no specific attempt is made to communicate the relationship between the military activity and the desired behavior. Indeed, the target state may neither anticipate, observe, nor otherwise become aware of the military activity.

For example, when the situation on Cyprus began to simmer in 1967, elements of the Sixth Fleet were deployed closer to the area. In taking this action there was no clearly formulated or signaled intent on the part of U.S. policymakers to coerce or support the various actors involved; rather the Johnson administration sought to be prepared to take coercive or supportive actions if the crisis developed further. At the same time it was assumed that fleet movements would be observed by the participants in the crisis and evaluated in light of previous U.S. behavior and current policy statements. In short, when used as a latent instrument, military activity will often serve to remind the actor that the United States can and might act. This is akin to what James Cable has termed the "catalytic" use of force. "A situation arises," Cable relates, "pregnant with a formless menace or offering obscure opportunities. Something, it is felt, is going to happen, which might somehow be prevented if force were available at the critical point. Advantages, their nature and the manner of their achievement still undetermined, might be reaped by those able to put immediate and appropriate power behind their sickle."[4]

Uncertainty of the observer as to what is expected is an important element in latent uses of the armed forces. In 1956, after King Hussein dismissed General John Glubb as commander of Jordan's Arab Legion, elements of the Sixth Fleet were placed on alert and other ships were moved eastward in the Mediterranean in an atmosphere marked by confusion on the part of U.S. decisionmakers as to whether Glubb's dismissal was an isolated action or indicative of a broad erosion in Jordan's relations with Great Britain. The connection between this naval activity and behavior desired of either Amman or London was never made clear. Nonetheless, the military preparation may have become known to or

4. Cable, *Gunboat Diplomacy,* p. 49.

been expected by Amman, and thus have predisposed Hussein to consider the U.S. reaction to his next steps. Similarly, the British government was certainly aware of, and probably reassured by, the naval activity.

In each of the sample incidents examined in this study armed forces were used as an instrument of coercive rather than cooperative diplomacy—that is, in each incident the overriding relationship was hostility between two foreign actors or between a foreign actor and the United States, and U.S. policymakers used or contemplated the use of armed forces to coerce one or more targets. As an instrument of cooperative diplomacy the armed forces are not used to coerce an actor or to intervene in a situation in any martial way—they are not meant to present a threat. Nor are they intended as a show of support to one actor vis-à-vis another. Rather, the armed forces are used to symbolize a desire or willingness to obtain, strengthen, or solidify a particular relationship and, by doing this, to assure the continuance or induce the initiation of some behavior desired of the target.

Two examples in the 1970s are the use of the helicopter carrier *Iwo Jima* and later the *Inchon* to sweep mines from the Suez Canal, thus helping to improve relations with Egypt in 1974, and the exchange of port visits by U.S. and Soviet warships in May 1975, intended to strengthen the atmosphere of détente. The previous background to these two incidents most certainly did include hostility between the United States, on the one hand, and Egypt and the Soviet Union, respectively, on the other. However, the specific uses of the armed forces under question clearly were meant to express a willingness to cooperate.

Cooperative uses of armed forces have occurred far less frequently than have coercive uses. This is probably because, while armed forces are clearly a superior instrument of coercion (or of showing support for actors in conflict situations), many other instruments of policy—for example, economic aid and cultural tours—are available for and are better suited to expressing friendship.

Characteristics of the Sample

Table 3-2 presents in categorical terms, for each actor in the incidents of the sample, the principal action desired by U.S. policymakers and the mode and style in which armed forces were used in order to obtain that behavior. It also lists the outcomes relative to each objective six months and three years following the U.S. use of force. Relationships between outcomes and objectives, and the significance to outcomes of different modes and styles of using armed forces, are analyzed in chapter 4. The observations in table 3-2 do not represent "data," but rather judgments made jointly by the authors, based on an examination of the bibliography presented in appendix D. Although in most cases outcomes were patently obvious, in others they are somewhat ambiguous. In these cases, the reasonableness of our judgments is critical to the validity of the analysis.

For only one of the 116 participants in the thirty-three incidents examined was it not possible to determine the U.S. operational objective.[5] In eight other instances an objective was determined vis-à-vis a specific actor, but the use of the armed forces in the crisis was clearly not pertinent to that objective. For example, in sending Marines to Morocco in 1956 in the midst of disturbances resulting from France's actions during the Suez crisis and in Algeria, the Eisenhower administration sought to insure that Rabat would protect American citizens and military installations. France was an actor in the situation and the objective of U.S. policy at the time was to persuade France to withdraw gracefully from North Africa. But the use of the Marines was in no way related to that objective, only to the objective vis-à-vis Morocco.

Nor was the reinforcement of Guantanamo in 1960, following an overflight of Cuba and dropping of leaflets and perhaps a bomb by Florida based anti-Castroites, aimed at the anti-Castro group in any way. The concern, it would appear, was to deter a Cuban reprisal against Guantanamo. While it was an actor, the exile group was not a target of U.S. military activity. Similarly, Jordan was an important actor in the Middle East cease-fire agreement in August 1970, but the U.S. use of reconnaissance aircraft to observe the cease-fire in the Suez Canal area was not directed at Jordan.

In several instances we could not determine outcomes. For example, it was not evident whether, following U.S. military actions, Cuba cur-

5. That is, Katanga Province (led by Moise Tshombe) in the 1960 Congo crisis. This incident encompasses only the first stage of that crisis: the period between the outbreak of the mutiny by the *Force Publique* in July 1960 and the coup d'état staged by Joseph Mobutu in mid-September 1960. The objective of ending Katanga's secession appears to have been embraced by U.S. policymakers only after the Kennedy administration took office. During the earlier months Katanga was certainly an issue, but no clear policy objective appears to have been formulated. Perhaps the best examination of administration attitudes toward Katanga, but one that we do not find conclusive, is the analysis by Stephen R. Weissman, *American Foreign Policy in the Congo, 1960–64* (Cornell University Press, 1974), pp. 74–77.

Table 3-2. *Actors, Principal Actions Desired of Them, Modes and Styles of Force Used, and Outcomes*

Incident and actors	Substantive action desired of actor	Mode and style in which armed forces were used[a]	Outcome[b] 6 months	3 years
1. Greece, 1946				
Greek Communist Party	Do not use force against government of Greece	D	N	N
Greece	Maintain regime authority	A	P	P
United Kingdom	Continue relationship with Greece	(L)	P	N
Soviet Union	Do not begin to support or spur undesired behavior by Greek Communists	D	P	P
Yugoslavia	Do not begin to support or spur undesired behavior by Greek Communists	D	N	N
2. Italy, 1947				
Italian Communist Party	Do not use force against government of Italy	D	P	P
Italy	Maintain regime authority	A	P	P
3. Japan/South Korea, 1953				
China	Do not use force again against South Korea	D	P	P
Japan	Maintain security (sovereignty)	A	P	P
North Korea	Do not use force again against South Korea	D	P	P
South Korea	Maintain security (sovereignty)	A	P	P
Soviet Union	Do not use force (overflights) again against Japan	D	P	P
4. Jordan, 1956				
Jordan	Continue relationship with United Kingdom	(L)	P	N
United Kingdom	Continue relationship with Jordan	(L)	P	N

Crisis / Actor	Objective			
5. Suez, 1956				
Egypt	Restore relationship with United Kingdom	(L)	N	N
France	Do not use force against Egypt	(L)	N	n.a.
United Kingdom	Do not use force against Egypt	(L)	N	n.a.
Soviet Union	Do not begin to support or spur undesired behavior by Egypt	(L)	N	N
6. Morocco, 1956				
Morocco	Protect U.S. military installations in Morocco	C	P	P
France	None relevant	..	..	..
7. Syria, 1957				
Egypt	Do not begin to support or spur undesired behavior by Syria	(L)	N	N
Iraq	Provide support to Turkey	I	N	N
Jordan	Provide support to Turkey	I	N	N
Lebanon	Provide support to Turkey	I	N	N
Saudi Arabia	Provide support to Turkey	(L)	N	N
Syria	Give up regime authority	C	N	N
Turkey	Initiate use of force against Syria	A	P	n.a.
Soviet Union	Do not begin to support or spur undesired behavior by Syria	(D)	N	N
Syrian armed forces group	Seize regime authority	I	N	N
8. Venezuela, 1958				
Venezuela	Protect Vice President Nixon and party	C	P	n.a.
9. Panama, 1959				
Cuba	Curtail support of insurgents in Panama	C	P	P
Panama insurgents	Terminate use of force against government of Panama	C	P	N
OAS	Provide support to Panama	(A)	P	P
Panama	Maintain regime authority	A	P	P

Footnotes to table on page 82.

Table 3-2 (continued)

Incident and actors	Substantive action desired of actor	Mode and style in which armed forces were used[b]	Outcome[b] 6 months	Outcome[b] 3 years
10. *Laos, 1959*				
China	Curtail support of Pathet Lao	(C)	N	N
Laos	Maintain regime authority	A	P	N
North Vietnam	Terminate use of force against government of Laos	C	P	N
Pathet Lao	Terminate use of force against government of Laos	C	P	N
Soviet Union	Curtail support of Pathet Lao and North Vietnam	(C)	N	N
11. *Cuba, 1960*				
Cuba	Do not take action against U.S. base at Guantanamo	D	P	P
Cuban exile group	None relevant	...	...	...
12. *Congo, 1960*				
Belgium	Maintain alliance with U.S.	(L)	P	P
Congo	Do not allow USSR influence in Congo	(L)	N	P
Katanga	Don't know, but none apparently relevant	...	...	...
United Nations	Restore order in Congo	A	P	P
Soviet Union	Do not begin to support or spur undesired behavior by Congo (Lumumba government)	(L)	N	N
13. *Dominican Republic, 1961*				
Dominican Republic	Give up regime authority	C	P	P
Dominican armed forces– civilian group	Seize regime authority	A	P	P

14. Kuwait, 1961				
Arab League	None relevant	:	:	:
Iraq	Do not use force against Kuwait	(L)	P	P
Kuwait	Maintain security (sovereignty)	(L)	P	P
United Kingdom	Continue relationship with Kuwait	A	P	P
15. Vietnam, 1962				
North Vietnam	Curtail support of Viet Cong	(C)	N	N
South Vietnam	Continue (increase) use of force against Viet Cong	I	P	N
Viet Cong	Terminate use of force against government of South Vietnam	C	P	N
16. Laos, 1962				
China	Curtail support of Pathet Lao	(C)	P	N
Laos	Give up regime authority	(L)	P	P
Laotian neutralists	Seize regime authority	(L)	P	P
North Vietnam	Curtail support of Pathet Lao	C	P	N
Pathet Lao	Terminate use of force against government of Laos	C	P	N
Thailand	Maintain alliance with U.S.	A	P	P
Soviet Union	Curtail support of Pathet Lao	(C)	P	N
17. Dominican Republic, 1963				
Dominican Republic	Maintain regime authority	A	P	N
Dominican armed forces	Do not use force against government of Dominican Republic	D	P	N
18. Vietnam, 1964				
North Vietnam	Curtail support of Viet Cong	C	N	N
South Vietnam	Continue (increase) use of force against Viet Cong	I	N	N
South Vietnam armed forces	None relevant	:	:	:
Viet Cong	Terminate use of force against government of South Vietnam	C	N	N

Table 3-2 (continued)

Incident and actors	Substantive action desired of actor	Mode and style in which armed forces were used[a]	Outcome[b] 6 months	3 years
19. Dominican Republic, 1964				
Cuba	Do not begin to support or spur undesired behavior by Dominican insurgents	D	P	P
Dominican Republic	Maintain regime authority	A	P	N
Dominican Republic insurgents	Do not use force against government of Dominican Republic	D	P	N
20. Tanzania, 1965				
Tanzania	Do not take action against U.S. citizens or assets	(L)	P	n.a.
21. Vietnam, 1965				
North Vietnam	Terminate use of force against South Vietnam	C	N	N
South Vietnam	Continue (increase) use of force against Viet Cong	I	N	N
Viet Cong	Terminate use of force against government of South Vietnam	(C)	N	N
22. Venezuela, 1965				
Cuba	Curtail support of insurgents in Venezuela	C	DK	N
Venezuelan insurgents	Terminate use of force against government of Venezuela	(C)	N	N
Venezuela	Maintain regime authority	A	P	P
23. Cyprus, 1967				
Cyprus	Maintain regime authority	(L)	P	P
Turkish Cypriots	Do not use force against government of Cyprus	(L)	P	P
Greece	Maintain alliance with U.S.	(L)	P	P
Turkey	Do not use force against Cyprus	(L)	P	P
United Kingdom	Continue relationship with Cyprus	(L)	P	P
United Nations	Provide support to Cyprus	(L)	P	P

24. *Pueblo*, 1968				
North Korea	Do not use force again against U.S. armed forces	D	P	N
South Korea	Continue to use force in South Vietnam	I	P	P
Soviet Union	Do not begin to support or spur undesired behavior by North Korea	(D)	P	P
25. *Lebanon*, 1968				
Israel	None relevant	:	:	:
Lebanon	Maintain regime authority	(L)	P	P
Palestinians	Do not use force again against Israel	(L)	N	N
United Nations	None relevant	:	:	:
26. *EC-121*, 1969				
North Korea	Do not use force again against U.S. armed forces	D	P	P
South Korea	Maintain alliance with U.S.	A	N	N
Soviet Union	Do not begin to support or spur undesired behavior by North Korea	(D)	P	P
27. *Rogers Plan*, 1970				
Egypt	Do not use force again against Israel	D	P	P
Israel	Do not use force again against Egypt	I	P	P
Jordan	None relevant	:	:	:
Soviet Union	Do not begin to support or spur undesired behavior by Egypt	(D)	P	P
28. *Cienfuegos*, 1970				
Cuba	Do not allow Soviet submarine base in Cuba	C	P	P
Soviet Union	Terminate construction of submarine base in Cuba	C	P	P
29. *Vietnam*, 1972a				
China	Curtail support of North Vietnam	(C)	DK	N
North Vietnam	Terminate use of force against South Vietnam	C	P	N
South Vietnam	Continue (increase) use of force against Viet Cong and North Vietnam	A	P	N
Soviet Union	Curtail support of North Vietnam	(C)	DK	N

Table 3-2 (continued)

Incident and actors	Substantive action desired of actor	Mode and style in which armed forces were used[a]	Outcome[b] 6 months	Outcome[b] 3 years
30. *Vietnam, 1972b*				
North Vietnam	Terminate use of force against South Vietnam	C	P	n.a.
31. *Laos, 1973*				
Laos	Maintain regime authority	A	P	N
Meo Tribe	Continue use of force against Pathet Lao	A	P	N
North Vietnam	Terminate use of force against Laos	C	P	N
Pathet Lao	Terminate use of force against government of Laos	C	P	N
32. *Lebanon, 1973*				
Israel	None relevant	..	..	..
Lebanon	Continue (increase) use of force against Palestinians	(L)	P	N
Palestinians	Terminate use of force against government of Lebanon	(L)	P	N
Syria	Do not use force against Lebanon	(L)	P	N
33. *Persian Gulf, 1974*				
Egypt	Negotiate with Israel	(C)	P	n.a.
OAPEC	Maintain oil flow to West	D	P	..
Saudi Arabia	Maintain oil flow to West	D	P	..

a. Mode in which armed forces were used: A (assure); C (compel); D (deter); I (induce). Where the mode is not in parentheses, armed forces were aimed at an actor directly; where the mode is in parentheses, armed forces were used indirectly. Latent uses of armed forces, in which instances armed forces were not used in any one of the four modes vis-à-vis an actor, are also presented in parentheses, as (L).

b. Outcome: N (operational objective not satisfied); P (operational objective satisfied); DK (don't know); n.a. (not applicable).

tailed its support of the insurgents in Venezuela in 1965, or the Soviet Union and China exerted pressure on Hanoi to halt the 1972 spring offensive. Longer term outcomes of the 1974 use of naval forces in the Persian Gulf area could not be determined because of our research cutoff date. In a number of instances the objective was irrelevant from the longer term perspective.

In table 3-3, all operational objectives of U.S. policymakers in the thirty-three incidents are categorized and tallied according to the modes and styles in which the armed forces were used for political purposes. Insofar as the sample is representative of the full 215 incidents these data

Table 3-3. *Objectives, Modes, and Styles of Using Armed Forces*
Number of instances in each category

Operational objectives of U.S. policymakers	Modes of use				Style of use			Total
	Assure	Deter	Induce	Compel	Total direct uses	Total indirect uses	Latent uses	
Use of force	3	10	5	13	29	2	9	40
Continue use	2		4		6	0	1	7
Do not use		4			4	0	6	10
Initiate use	1				1	0	0	1
Do not use again		6	1		7	0	1	8
Terminate use				13	11	2	1	14
Regime authority	9	0	1	2	12	0	4	16
Give up				2	2	0	1	3
Maintain	8				8	0	2	10
Seize	1		1		2	0	1	3
Nonviolent support given by one actor to another	1	7	3	11	10	12	5	27
Curtail				11	4	7	0	11
Do not initiate		7			3	4	3	10
Provide	1		3		3	1	2	6
Relationship of U.S. ally with another actor	1	0	0	0	1	0	5	6
Continue	1				1	0	4	5
Restore					0	0	1	1
Other objectives	5	3	0	5	12	1	5	18
All objectives	19	20	9	31	64	15	28	107

can inform us as to why and how the armed forces are used for discrete political operations.

When U.S. armed forces were used as a political instrument, the operational objectives of American policymakers usually included one or more of four types of behavior: the use of force by one actor against another; nonviolent support given by one actor to another; the authority of a certain regime; and the relationship of a U.S. ally with another nation. For example, during the 1962 Laotian crisis, the operational objectives of the Kennedy administration were that the Pathet Lao should terminate its use of force against the Laotian government; that the Soviet Union, China, and North Vietnam should curtail their support of the Pathet Lao; that the Laotian government of Boun Oum and Phoumi Nosavan should give up power; and that the Laotian neutralists led by Prince Souvanna Phouma should obtain power. The fourth type of objective—an ally relationship—did not figure in this incident. Objectives related to these four basic concerns accounted for 37 percent, 25 percent, 15 percent, and 6 percent, respectively, of the total 107 operational objectives sought in the thirty-three incidents.[6]

When the operational objective concerned the use of force by an actor, in most cases the specific objective was that the target should not use force—"do not use force," "do not use force again," "terminate the use of force." In only a few instances was the objective that an actor should use force and in only one instance—the 1957 Syrian crisis—did Washington seem to seek the initial use of force by target; in the others the operational objective was that an actor should continue to use force.[7]

When the operational objective concerned nonviolent support given by one party to another, again the United States usually sought an end of support—"curtail support," "do not begin to support or spur undesired behavior." In all but two such instances, the U.S. target—that is, the actor lending support to another—was a Communist state, generally the Soviet Union or China, and at times North Vietnam, Cuba, or Yugoslavia. Most of the few instances when the U.S. operational objective was to encourage third party support were related to the 1957 Syrian crisis.

6. Percentages presented in tables are to the nearest tenth of a percentage point; those presented in the text are to the nearest percentage point.

7. Patrick Seale, *The Struggle for Syria: A Study of Post-War Arab Politics, 1945–1958* (Oxford University Press, 1965), pp. 293–96; Miles Copeland, *The Game of Nations: The Amorality of Power Politics* (Simon and Schuster, 1969), pp. 187–88.

Regime authority refers to the political will and courage to hold on to or seize political authority—that is, control the state. As noted, in the 1959 Laotian crisis one principal operational objective of U.S. policymakers was to embolden the Laotian government so that it would not allow its authority to disintegrate. U.S. armed forces were used in a similar fashion to support the governments of Greece and Italy in the immediate postwar years. Most frequently the U.S. objective was a positive one, that an actor should maintain its control of a state. However, on two occasions (Syria, 1957; Dominican Republic, 1961) the U.S. operational objective was that an existing government should be changed.

The fourth type of operational objective—the relationship of a U.S. ally to another actor—stands out especially with reference to latent uses of the armed forces. In all of these instances the U.S. objective was that Britain should retain a degree of influence with a third party. For example, after General Glubb was dismissed in 1956 by King Hussein, Washington desired that London reconfirm its special relationship (and influence) with Jordan.

The operational objectives in the miscellaneous category included the protection of U.S. citizens and military installations, the maintenance of the security of states in threatening but nonviolent situations, the maintenance of U.S. alliances, Soviet access to military facilities in third nations, and others.

U.S. armed forces were used to assure, compel, deter, or induce specific behavior as regards roughly three-fourths of the targets. As concerns the remaining one-fourth, armed forces were used only as a latent instrument. Armed forces were most frequently used to compel, least frequently to induce, behavior. To assure and to deter fell between these two extremes in frequency of occurrence. If the four modes are grouped together, the instances are evenly divided between actions to reinforce (assure or deter) behavior and actions to modify (induce or compel) behavior. On the other hand, the operational objective was much more frequently to coerce (compel or deter) behavior than it was to support (assure or induce) behavior.

Armed forces were used directly—that is, to support militarily or to coerce a particular actor—60 percent of the time. Armed forces were used indirectly—that is, to support or coerce one actor by militarily supporting or coercing another actor—14 percent of the time. They were used solely as a latent instrument in 26 percent of the instances.

CHAPTER FOUR

Findings

How frequently have positive outcomes occurred when the armed forces have been used as a political instrument, in the short term and over the longer term? Have positive outcomes occurred more often when certain types of operational objectives were sought? Can different frequencies of positive outcomes be associated with different modes or styles of using the armed forces? Can differing levels, types, and activities of forces employed in these incidents be associated with different frequencies of positive outcomes? The three basic questions confronted are: (1) What is the relationship between outcomes and the use of armed forces generally? (2) What is the apparent importance to this relationship of different operational objectives? (3) What is the significance of using armed forces in different ways?

Overall Outcomes of Incidents

Overall—looking at all of the operational objectives of policymakers in an incident—were the short and longer term outcomes of the incidents favorable or unfavorable? In some incidents, of course, all outcomes were positive (for example, Cienfuegos, 1970); in others, outcomes were uniformly negative (for example, Vietnam, 1965); in still others, results were mixed. One approach to determining the overall result is to establish a particular percentage of positive outcomes as a criterion.

When a criterion is used that if two-thirds of U.S. operational objectives in the incident are fulfilled then the overall outcome is considered favorable, it may be said that in the short term the outcomes of twenty-four incidents (three-fourths) were favorable and of nine were not (see table 4-1). Obviously, not every incident is as important as the next, nor is every operational objective in an incident as important as every other objective. No weighting schemes were considered, however.

Over the longer term, this overall favorable outcome rate dropped to less than one-half; only thirteen outcomes were favorable and sixteen were unfavorable. If the sizable proportion of favorable short-term outcomes was at least in part related to the use of the armed forces, we might infer that the efficacy of those actions declined considerably over just a few years; of course, in the interim policymakers may have failed to take other actions, including the further use of force, necessary to insure the sustenance of favorable outcomes over the longer term. Or changes in circumstances may have rendered those earlier outcomes untenable. Whichever is the case, it is certain that the use of the armed forces was not alone able to sustain a large proportion of favorable outcomes over the longer term.

Table 4-1. *Overall Outcomes of Sample Incidents*[a]

Incident	6 months	3 years	Incident	6 months	3 years
1. Greece, 1946	U	U	17. Dominican Republic, 1963	F	U
2. Italy, 1947	F	F	18. Vietnam, 1964	U	U
3. Japan/South Korea 1953	F	F	19. Dominican Republic, 1964	F	U
4. Jordan, 1956	F	U	20. Tanzania, 1965	F	n.a.
5. Suez, 1956	U	U	21. Vietnam, 1965	U	U
6. Morocco, 1956	F	F	22. Venezuela, 1965	U	U
7. Syria, 1957	U	U	23. Cyprus, 1967	F	F
8. Venezuela, 1958	F	n.a.	24. *Pueblo*, 1968	F	F
9. Panama, 1959	F	F	25. Lebanon, 1968	U	U
10. Laos, 1959	U	U	26. EC-121, 1969	F	F
11. Cuba, 1960	F	F	27. Rogers Plan, 1970	F	F
12. Congo, 1960	U	F	28. Cienfuegos, 1970	F	F
13. Dominican Republic, 1961	F	F	29. Vietnam, 1972a	F	U
14. Kuwait, 1961	F	F	30. Vietnam, 1972b	F	n.a.
15. Vietnam, 1962	F	U	31. Laos, 1973	F	U
16. Laos, 1962	F	U	32. Lebanon, 1973	F	U
			33. Persian Gulf, 1974	F	n.a.

a. F, favorable; U, unfavorable; n.a., not applicable.

Individual Outcomes and the Political Use of Armed Forces

In table 4-2 data are presented showing the share of all outcomes which were positive from the U.S. perspective, broken down by the objectives of U.S. policymakers and the modes and styles in which armed forces were used in order to achieve those objectives.

In the short term, favorable outcomes occurred with respect to a large proportion (73 percent) of the objectives for which U.S. armed forces were used as a political instrument. However, this proportion declined substantially when objectives were evaluated over the longer term. Indeed, outcomes pertaining to more than one-half of the principal objectives were not positive after three years. To take an extreme case, all of the outcomes following the use of B-52 bombers over Laos in early 1973 were positive in the short term. The Laotian government of Prince Souvanna Phouma continued to act with some confidence; the Meo tribe continued to fight in support of that government; and North Vietnam and the Pathet Lao did terminate their direct and immediate use of force. Over the longer term, however, none of these outcomes was sustained; new fighting began and eventually Laos was taken over by the Pathet Lao.

The decline in the frequency of favorable outcomes between the short and longer term periods occurred for every type of objective but the miscellaneous category "other," and with respect to every mode and style of using armed forces. These distinctions are discussed below.

Substantive Objectives

Of the three principal categories of objectives, positive outcomes occurred most often in the short term when the U.S. operational objective concerned regime authority, less often when the operational objective concerned the use of force by another actor, and least often in regard to third party support. Over the longer term, positive outcomes also were most frequent when the operational objective concerned regime authority, although the decline in the frequency of positive outcomes was substantial. No real distinction can be made between the frequencies of positive outcomes with respect to the other two principal categories of operational objectives, both of which were very low.

Table 4-2. *Percentage of Outcomes Which Were Positive from the U.S. Perspective, by Type of Objective and Mode and Style of Use of Force*

Item	After 6 months		After 3 years	
	Percentage of positive outcomes	Size of denominator	Percentage of positive outcomes	Size of denominator
Objectives				
Use of force	75.0	40	30.6	36[a]
Continue use	71.4	7	14.3	7
Do not use	70.0	10	50.0	8[b]
Initiate use	100.0	1	...	0[c]
Do not use again	87.5	8	75.0	8
Terminate use	71.4	14	0.0	13[e]
Regime authority	87.5	16	62.5	16
Give up	66.7	3	66.7	3
Maintain	100.0	10	60.0	10
Seize	66.7	3	66.7	3
Third party support	45.8	24	29.6	27
Curtail support	50.0	8[d]	9.1	11
Do not initiate	50.0	10	50.0	10
Provide	33.3	6	33.3	6
Ally relationship	83.3	6	33.3	6
Continue	100.0	5	40.0	5
Restore	0.0	1	0.0	1
Other	88.9	18	92.3	13[e]
Mode of use of force				
Assure	94.7	19	61.1	18[a]
Compel	67.9	28[d]	17.9	28[d]
Deter	85.0	20	66.7	18[b]
Induce	33.3	9	22.2	9
Style of use of force				
Direct	79.4	63[c]	44.1	59[e]
Indirect	53.8	13[b]	28.6	14[e]
Latent	67.9	28	52.0	25[d]
Total	73.1	104[d]	43.9	98[f]

a. No outcome could be determined in four instances.
b. No outcome could be determined in two instances.
c. No outcome could be determined in one instance.
d. No outcome could be determined in three instances.
e. No outcome could be determined in five instances.
f. No outcome could be determined in nine instances.

Outcomes were positive in almost nine out of every ten instances in the short term and in almost two out of every three in the longer term when regime authority was of concern. Outcomes were most often positive in the short term when the objective was to embolden or give confidence to an actor to maintain its authority—for example, the use of force in 1959 to insure that the government of Panama would deal firmly and effectively with a Cuban-supported insurgency. In the June 1961 incident in the Dominican Republic, the objectives—that the Trujillo family should give up power and that another group should seize power— were realized in November 1961 (just before the six-month cutoff point), but only after a second use of the armed forces by the Kennedy administration.

When another actor's use of force constituted the principal operational objective of U.S. policymakers, outcomes were favorable in three out of every four instances in the short term and in three out of every ten instances over the longer term. Excluding the single instance when the objective was that an actor should "initiate" the use of force, differences in the frequencies of positive outcomes were small in the short term, although outcomes were somewhat more frequently positive when the objective was that force should not be used again. In the longer term, outcomes were much more frequently positive when the objective was that force should not be used again or should not be initiated than when U.S. policymakers sought to persuade an actor to continue or terminate the use of force. Regarding the last, positive outcomes never endured for three years.

One reason why outcomes were relatively more frequently positive in the short term and much more frequently so over the longer term when the objective was that an actor should not use force *again* (after having just used force) was probably that the relevant actors, in at least a number of those instances, had no intention of using force again. Two of these outcomes pertained to Israel's and Egypt's non-use of force during the three-year period between the August 1970 ceasefire and the October 1973 war. In two other instances, China and North Korea may have had no intention of using force in the three years immediately following the Korean War, whether or not the United States permanently emplaced troops in the Far East. The one instance of an unfavorable outcome of an incident in this category was North Korea's shooting down of the U.S. Navy EC-121 a little over a year after the *Pueblo* was seized.

Outcomes were least frequently positive when objectives concerned support given by one actor to another actor—for example, North Vietnam's continued support of the Viet Cong and the Pathet Lao in the early 1960s. These outcomes were positive in less than one out of every two instances in the short term and in less than one out of every three in the longer term. Favorable outcomes were particularly infrequent in the longer term when the objective was that an actor should curtail its support of another actor.

All four of the instances in which outcomes were negative and the objective was that support should be given by one actor to another were related to the 1957 Syrian crisis when the Eisenhower administration desired that several Arab states support Turkey vis-à-vis Syria.

As to the fourth category of objectives—concerning a U.S. ally's relationship with another actor—outcomes were positive in the short term in all five instances when the objective was that an ally should continue a relationship—and maintain its influence—with another actor. Over the longer term, however, only two of these five outcomes remained positive. Both the short and longer term outcomes were negative in the one instance when the objective was that an actor should restore a relationship with an ally—Egypt in the crisis following President Nasser's nationalization of the Suez Canal in 1956.

Modes of Use—Reinforcement or Modification

In the language of coercive diplomacy, the proportions of short-term positive outcomes were exceptionally high when armed forces were used to reinforce behavior. Despite a considerable decline, positive outcomes also predominated over the longer term in these instances. When the objective was to assure that an action would be performed (for example, that the United Nations would act to restore order in the Congo in 1960), positive outcomes occurred with regard to 95 percent of the objectives after six months, and 61 percent of the objectives after three years. When the objective was to deter behavior (for example, that Cuba should not take action against the U.S. base at Guantanamo in 1960), positive outcomes occurred 85 percent of the time after six months and 67 percent of the time after three years.

Favorable outcomes occurred less often when the operational objective was to modify behavior, particularly over the longer term. After three years, positive outcomes occurred with regard to only 18 percent of the objectives when armed forces were used to compel an action (for example, to influence China and the Soviet Union to curtail their support of the Pathet Lao in 1959); and with regard to 22 percent of the objectives when policymakers sought to induce an action (for example, to persuade South Vietnam to take more effective military action against the Viet Cong). The greater short-term proportion of positive outcomes occurred when the objective was to compel an action; unfortunately, the decline over time was most pronounced in these cases as well (from 68 percent to 18 percent). The decline was smaller when the concern was to induce behavior, but this reflects the extremely low proportion of favorable outcomes even after six months.

If outcomes related to the use of armed forces to assure and deter (reinforce) behavior are combined, 90 percent were positive in the short term and 64 percent were favorable over the longer term. If those outcomes related to the use of armed forces to compel and induce (modify) behavior are taken together, 59 percent were favorable in the short term and 19 percent were favorable in the longer term. Why were outcomes more frequently positive when policymakers sought to reinforce rather than to modify behavior? Two explanations may be offered.

In many instances in which U.S. policymakers wanted to reinforce behavior the actor may have intended to continue the desired behavior in any case. Hence the objective sought by the United States was not in question, and the use of armed forces was irrelevant in those instances. It may also be true that it is simply easier to reinforce than to modify behavior. The behavioral psychology literature suggests that this is the case for individual behavior. Moreover, aside from the decisionmaker's anxiety about the unknown, and his greater comfort in repeating familiar behavioral patterns, it may be especially difficult to induce or compel new behavior because of political constraints on the target actor. He naturally wants to avoid losing face and, consequently, power and influence, domestically and internationally.

We cannot discount entirely the possibility that behavior apparently compelled or induced would also have occurred in some cases irrespective of whether the armed forces were used or any other action was taken. To suggest otherwise is to assume that the use of the armed forces by itself indicates that a change in behavior sought by U.S. policymakers is otherwise unacceptable to a target. Such instances of "apparent" success in modifying behavior would seem less likely than "apparent" success in the reinforcement of behavior; they are possible, however.

It might also be mentioned that, insofar as policymakers may understand intuitively that it is easier to reinforce than to modify behavior, they may be more willing to attempt the former than the latter. In some instances, actions supposedly designed to reinforce foreign behavior may simply be a form of posturing—that is, "deterring" an actor that is not contemplating undesired behavior and "assuring" a supposed victim that is not in any danger.

When armed forces were used to assure that an action would be performed, it made virtually no difference what the objective was, short-term outcomes being almost uniformly positive. When armed forces were used coercively—to compel or deter, or supportively to induce behavior—outcomes were more frequently positive when the operational objective was the use of force by another actor. Thus, following the shooting down by North Korea of a U.S. Navy EC-121 aircraft in 1969, Pyongyang did not provoke the United States further, being deterred perhaps by the large U.S. naval forces which were deployed in the Sea of Japan and the aircraft deployed from South Vietnam to South Korea. By contrast, the visit of the battleship *Missouri* to Athens in April 1946 did not deter Yugoslavia from lending support to the Communist-led insurgency in Greece which began not too long after the *Missouri*'s visit.

Style of Use—Direct, Indirect, or Latent

Outcomes were positive much more frequently both in the short and longer terms when armed forces were used directly rather than indirectly. However, short-term outcomes were almost as frequently positive when armed forces were used as a latent instrument as when they were used directly; in the longer term, outcomes were most often positive when the armed forces were used only latently. Whether or not the initial conditions in these incidents were more conducive to favorable outcomes, prudence would appear to have had its virtues.

When armed forces were used directly, outcomes were very frequently positive in the short term except when the operational objective concerned support given by one actor to another. The same was true as concerns latent uses. When third party support was of concern, outcomes were most frequently positive when armed forces were used indirectly. In the longer term the difference with regard to the last was minimal, however.

Finally, it is worthwhile to note declines in the percentages of positive outcomes when armed forces were used directly and the objectives concerned either regime authority or the use of force by another actor. In no instance did a positive outcome endure when it was desired that the use of force by an actor should be terminated. By contrast, positive outcomes endured in more than four out of five instances when the objective was that an actor should not use force again (after having just used force).

Outcomes and the Level, Type, Movement, and Activities of Armed Forces

In April 1969 North Korean aircraft attacked and shot down an unarmed U.S. Navy EC-121 reconnaissance plane flying on a routine mission. All of the crew members were killed. Only months earlier the crew of the *Pueblo* had been released. In response to this new provocation President Nixon ordered a show of force of major proportions: six aircraft carriers, the battleship *New Jersey,* three cruisers, and sixteen destroyers were directed to the Sea of Japan, the Yellow Sea, and other waters proximate to the area; land-based combat aircraft were redeployed from South Vietnam to South Korea; and various units in the United States were readied for deployment to the Far East.

In radically different circumstances and at quite the other end of the spectrum of forces that might be used as a political instrument, a single destroyer was dispatched in response to the sudden worsening of relations between the United States and Tanzania in January 1965. Similarly, when the Soviet Union appeared to be in the process of establishing a submarine base in Cuba in 1970, only a destroyer and reconnaissance aircraft were utilized. And concern with developments in Morocco during the Suez crisis led to the deployment of only a company of Marines.

Do positive outcomes occur more often when greater amounts of force or particular types of forces are used, or when those forces do certain things? These and similar questions are explored in this section. Table 4-3 describes the level, type, and activities of U.S. armed forces in the sample incidents.

The data in table 4-3 indicate that units associated with strategic nuclear forces were used together with at least one major conventional component of the armed forces in two of the incidents (Japan/South Korea, 1953; *Pueblo,* 1968). In four incidents, two or more major conventional components, but no strategic nuclear units were used (Syria, 1957; Dominican Republic, 1961; EC-121, 1969; Vietnam, 1972a); and in nine other incidents a single major conventional component was utilized. Nuclear forces were not used alone in any of the sample incidents. No more than standard or minor components of conventional armed forces and no nuclear force units were used in the remaining 18 incidents.

Table 4-4 compares the force levels used in the thirty-three sample incidents with those force levels used in the other 182 incidents in the full 215-incident file. The data in this table indicate that the sample underrepresents incidents when lower levels of armed forces were used and overrepresents incidents in which major force components were used apart from strategic nuclear-associated units. This is because one of the four variables that was used to derive the sample pertained to the level of force used; the sample was structured to include a significant number of incidents when policymakers made use of major force components.

Short and longer term outcomes are tallied with reference to the levels and types of armed forces used in the incidents, and their specific activities, in table 4-5.

Level of Armed Forces

The data show that definitely in the short term and generally speaking in the longer term too, *outcomes were less often positive when greater levels of force were used, unless nuclear-capable forces were used together with one or more major conventional components.* The use of greater levels of armed forces was probably associated with situations or objectives presenting implicitly a greater degree of difficulty or implying a greater level of risk. For example, it may have been a more difficult task to oust governments in power in Syria (1957) and the Dominican Republic (1961) than it was to successfully counter Cuban-supported insurgencies in the Caribbean (Panama, 1959; Dominican Republic, 1964; Venezuela, 1965). Similarly, it may have been more difficult to show North Korea that an attack on an American ship would not be tolerated (*Pueblo,* 1968), or to control the situation in Southeast Asia (Vietnam, 1964 and 1965), than it was to insure the safety of American citizens and

Table 4-3. Level, Type, and Activity of Armed Forces[a]

Incident	Overall level of armed forces used	Army (AR) or Marine (MC) ground forces	Air Force (AF) or Marine (MC) combat aircraft	Battleship (BB), aircraft carrier (CV), or helicopter carrier (LPH)	Other	Activity
1. Greece, 1946	4			1 BB		Visit
2. Italy, 1947	4			1 CV		Visit
3. Japan/South Korea, 1953	1	DIV MC	U AF, ? MC			Emplacement, visit
4. Jordan, 1956	3	BAT MC (A)		2 CV		Presence
5. Suez, 1956	3	COM MC		2 CV		Exercise
6. Morocco, 1956	5	BRG MC (A)			U TA	Emplacement
7. Syria, 1957	2	BAT AR		3 CV	S TA	Exercise, transport, visit
8. Venezuela, 1958	4	BAT MC (A)		1 CV	U TA	Presence
9. Panama, 1959	5				U PA, 2 SC	Surveillance
10. Laos, 1959	3	BRG MC (A)	S MC	3 CV	L TA	Presence, surveillance, transport
11. Cuba, 1960	4					Emplacement
12. Congo, 1960	4	COM MC (A), U AR		1 CV	L TA	Evacuation, transport
13. Dominican Republic, 1961	2	U MC (A), BRG AR	U AF, U MC	3 CV, ? LPH		Exercise
14. Kuwait, 1961	3	BAT MC (A)				Presence
15. Vietnam, 1962	5	COM AR		2 CV	S TH	Emplacement, tactical support, transport
16. Laos, 1962	3	BRG AR, BAT MC (A)		1 CV, 1 LPH	1 SS, U TA, ? TH	Emplacement, surveillance, presence, visit, (?) transport
17. Dominican Republic, 1963	4	BAT MC (A), BRG AR		1 LPH		Visit
18. Vietnam, 1964	3	BRG AR		U CV, ? LPH	W TA	Presence
19. Dominican Republic, 1964	5	U MC			U PA, U SH	Surveillance

#	Event	Level	Ground	Air	Carrier/BB	Other	Purpose
20.	Tanzania, 1965	5		S AF	3 CV	1 SC	Presence
21.	Vietnam, 1965	3				U SH	Bombing
22.	Venezuela, 1965	5			1 CV		Presence
23.	Cyprus, 1967	4			3 CV		Presence
24.	*Pueblo*, 1968	1		W AF			Presence
25.	Lebanon, 1968	5	U AR		1 BB	U SH	Presence
26.	EC-121, 1969	2	U MC (?A)	W AF	6 CV	U PA	Presence, surveillance
27.	Rogers Plan, 1970	5				U TA	Surveillance
28.	Cienfuegos, 1970	5				U PA / 1 SC	Escort, surveillance
29.	Vietnam, 1972a	2		W AF	6 CV		Blockade, bombing
30.	Vietnam, 1972b	3		W AF	U CV		Bombing
31.	Laos, 1973	3		W AF			Bombing
32.	Lebanon, 1973	5				U SH	Presence
33.	Persian Gulf, 1974	4			1 CV		Exercise

a. U, size unknown; ?, possibly.

Level of armed forces used (i.e., *alerted and/or deployed*) (see table 2-9, above, for definitions of components):
1. One or more major components and strategic nuclear force unit
2. Two or more major components; no strategic nuclear force unit
3. One major component; or strategic nuclear force unit
4. Standard component
5. Minor component

Army/Marine ground forces:
A   Afloat
COM   Less than or equal in size to a company
BAT   More than a company but less than or equal in size to a battalion
BRG   More than a battalion but less than or equal in size to a brigade
DIV   More than a brigade but less than or equal in size to a division

Air Force/Marine combat aircraft:
L   Less than a squadron of aircraft
S   More than or equal in size to a squadron but less than a wing
W   More than or equal in size to a wing

Other
SC   Naval surface combatant
SS   Submarine
PA   Fixed wing maritime reconnaissance/patrol aircraft
TH   Transport helicopter
TA   Transport aircraft; see combat aircraft re unit size
SH   Ship; type unknown but probably not a battleship, aircraft carrier, or helicopter carrier

Table 4-4. *Level of Armed Forces Used in Sample and Non-Sample*
Incidents

	Sample incidents		Non-sample incidents	
Level of armed forces used	*Number*	*Percent of total*	*Number*	*Percent of total*
1. One or more major components and nuclear force unit	2	6.1	13	7.1
2. Two or more major components; no nuclear force unit	4	12.1	14	7.7
3. One major component or nuclear force unit	9	27.3	37	20.3
4. Standard component	8	24.2	56	30.8
5. Minor component	10	30.3	62	34.1
Total	33	100.0	182	100.0

military installations abroad (Morocco, 1956; Venezuela, 1958; Cuba, 1960; Tanzania, 1965).

Even if larger forces were more likely to have been used in order to achieve more difficult objectives, the fact remains that those objectives were less frequently realized than were the easier objectives for which smaller units of the armed forces were used. The implication is that policymakers ought to be wary of using armed forces for political objectives when they believe that objectives, though difficult to attain, will require only sizable components of conventional force. A large risk of failure would appear to be taken when policymakers believe important interests are at stake but are unwilling to brandish nuclear-capable forces. Whether or not the nation should walk on such thin ice, or, alternatively, turn to its nuclear forces, will depend on a calculus of costs and benefits peculiar to the policymakers faced with such decisions. Some elaboration is in order.

OUTCOMES AND THE USE OF STRATEGIC NUCLEAR FORCES. As mentioned earlier, units associated with strategic nuclear forces were used together with major conventional force components in only two sample incidents (Japan/South Korea, 1953; *Pueblo,* 1968). However, in the complete file of 215 incidents, nuclear and major conventional force components were used together on fifteen occasions (see table 4-6),

Table 4-5. *Percentages of Positive Outcomes, by Level, Type, and Activities of Forces Used*

	6 months		3 years	
Level, type, and activities of forces	*Percentage of positive outcomes*	*Number of instances*	*Percentage of positive outcomes*	*Number of instances*
Level of armed forces				
One or more major components and nuclear force unit	100.0	8	87.5	8
Two or more major components; no nuclear force unit	47.6	21	18.2	22
One major component or nuclear force unit	63.0	27	25.0	24
Standard component	83.3	24	70.0	20
Minor component	87.5	24	50.0	24
Type of armed forces				
Ground force	59.6	52	39.6	48
CV/BB/LPH	64.3	70	39.1	64
Land-based combat aircraft	83.3	24	48.0	25
Other	66.1	56	37.0	54
Activities				
Bombing, blockade, emplacement, or tactical support	85.2	27	35.7	28
Other	68.8	77	47.1	70

ranging from the deployment of a few Strategic Air Command bombers to the global alert and deployment of U.S. strategic forces (as occurred during the Cuban missile crisis). Considering the importance of the potential role of nuclear weapons, we departed from the sample to look more closely at these fifteen incidents.

The Soviet Union was an actor in twelve of the incidents, nine of which may be termed crises—that is, the superpowers confronted each other in a situation in which American policymakers perceived a danger of an imminent conflict between the United States and the Soviet Union. In the three other incidents in which Soviet involvement was a factor, policymakers used nuclear-capable forces as a warning to a third actor, or as a warning to the Soviet Union in a situation in which policymakers probably did not perceive a serious danger of imminent superpower conflict.

Again, using a criterion of two-thirds, the *overall* outcomes of the cases involving nuclear forces appear to have been favorable in nearly every

Table 4-6. *Incidents in Which Nuclear and Major Components
of Conventional Armed Forces Were Used Together, 1946–75*

Incident	Degree of Soviet involvement and nature of situation[a]
1. Security of Berlin, April 1948	A
2. Security of Berlin, June 1948	A
3. Korean War: security of Europe, July 1950	A
4. Security of Japan/South Korea, August 1953	B
5. China-Taiwan conflict: Tachen Islands, August 1954	C
6. Guatemala accepts Soviet bloc support, May 1954	B
7. Suez crisis, October 1956	A
8. Political crisis in Lebanon, July 1958	C
9. Political crisis in Jordan, July 1958	C
10. China-Taiwan crisis: Quemoy and Matsu, July 1958	A
11. Security of Berlin, May 1959	A
12. Security of Berlin, June 1961	A
13. Soviet emplacement of missiles in Cuba, October 1962	A
14. *Pueblo* seized by North Korea, January 1968	B
15. Arab-Israeli War, October 1973	A

a. A: Soviet Union an actor; danger of imminent superpower conflict perceived by U.S. policymakers. B: Soviet Union an actor; no serious danger of imminent superpower conflict perceived by U.S. policymakers. C: Soviet Union not an actor.

one of these fifteen incidents in the short term, and in three-fourths of them over the longer term. Virtually the same may be said about individual outcomes: approximately nine-tenths were positive in the short term; three-quarters were positive over the longer term.

Both in the short term and over the longer term, positive outcomes were especially frequent when the U.S. operational objective was to assure behavior, and much less frequent—approximately six out of ten—when U.S. policymakers sought to compel behavior. When the objective was to deter behavior, outcomes were invariably positive in the short term, although the frequency of positive outcomes declined somewhat over the longer term: after three years, approximately seven of ten outcomes were positive. U.S. policymakers almost never sought to induce behavior by an actor in these incidents. Thus, the pattern which emerges over the longer term is that when nuclear forces were used together with a major conventional force component, positive outcomes were least frequent when policymakers sought to *compel* an actor to do something, more frequent when the objective was to *deter* an action, and most frequent when policymakers sought to *assure* behavior.

Of the twelve occasions when the operational objective was to coerce—that is, compel or deter—Soviet behavior, outcomes appear to have been positive in ten instances in the short term and in nine over the longer term; in short, frequencies of positive outcomes were very much the same as those in the fifteen "nuclear" incidents generally. All the instances in which coercive objectives were not attained were related to the security of, and Western access to, Berlin, an issue that appears now to have been defused. These three incidents in which the Russians were not successfully coerced over the longer term constitute one-third of those incidents in which a serious superpower confrontation occurred.

Type of Armed Forces Used

It was observed in chapter 2 that some types of military units were employed more frequently than others as a political instrument. For example, naval forces were turned to more frequently than land-based units, including the use of aircraft carriers as compared with Air Force and Marine aircraft, and Marine units on board amphibious ships as compared with shore-based Army and Marine units. An important question is whether different types of forces are associated with different frequencies of favorable outcomes. If so, policymakers may want to consider not only how much force but what kind of force they should employ. We have already discussed the utility of strategic nuclear units which, in addition to representing a level of force, also constitute a very particular type of force. We turn now to the utility of different types of conventional force units.

The use of land-based combat aircraft stands out as being proportionally most often associated with positive outcomes. Moreover, in eight of nine incidents the use of land-based combat aircraft was associated with the use of at least one major conventional force component—that is, one of the three "highest" force levels. Even discounting the two incidents in this subset in which both nuclear and major conventional forces were used together, it would appear that positive outcomes occurred more frequently when land-based combat aircraft were used than when major ground force or naval force components were introduced. It is worth noting that, like nuclear-associated units, land-based combat aircraft were never used as a latent instrument. It is likely that target actors view the distinctive capabilities of these two types of forces with greater alarm,

Table 4-7. *Outcomes and Type of Ground Forces*

	Percentage of positive outcomes	
Ground forces used	6 months	3 years
Amphibious only	39.1	15.0
Land-based only	66.7	53.3
Land and amphibious together	85.7	61.5

and that they also perceive their use as signaling greater determination on the part of U.S. policymakers.

A similar finding concerns the relationship between positive outcomes and land-based ground forces as compared to troops based on ships. The data in table 4-7 suggest that both in the short term and over the longer term, positive outcomes were much more frequent when land-based rather than amphibious ground forces were used (leaving aside the use of other types of forces in these incidents). Positive outcomes were even more frequent, however, when land-based and amphibious ground units were used together. Thus, amphibious ship-based ground forces would appear to have been a useful complement to land-based ground forces.

The distinction made between land-based and amphibious forces is not strictly a distinction between the Army and the Marines. While the amphibious ground units that were employed were always Marines, land-based ground forces included Marine and Army units.

Activities

Notwithstanding the lesser frequency of positive outcomes when larger conventional forces were used, positive outcomes, at least in the short term, occurred more frequently when the armed forces components involved engaged in activities of a more manifest nature (for example, bombing); the frequencies of positive outcomes when manifest and less-manifest activities were engaged in being 85 percent and 69 percent, respectively. On the other hand, more manifest actions were not associated more frequently with favorable outcomes over the longer term. In fact, the less manifest activities of smaller conventional forces were more often associated with positive outcomes over the longer term.

Positive outcomes did occur more often when manifest activities were

Table 4-8. *Percentage of Positive Outcomes, by Activities and Style of Use of Force*

	Direct		Indirect		Latent	
Activities	6 months	3 years	6 months	3 years	6 months	3 years
Bombing, blockade, emplacement, or tactical support	90.5	40.0	50.0	0.0	100.0	100.0
Other	73.8	46.2	55.6	50.0	65.4	47.8

aimed directly rather than indirectly at an actor (see table 4-8). If armed forces were used directly and engaged in more intense activities when policymakers faced more difficult situations, then it might be argued that, considering the minimal difference between the frequencies of positive outcomes when intense and less-intense activities were undertaken, the frequency of positive outcomes when intense activities were undertaken was higher than would have been expected otherwise. As concerns indirect uses of force, the denominators are small, but the outcomes were wholly negative over the longer term, which suggests that more manifest but indirectly aimed activities were futile.

PRESENCE. Of particular interest is the activity termed presence, or mere appearance on the scene. In ten incidents this was the only activity performed by U.S. forces which, typically, included naval combatants either alone or in the company of Marine amphibious units—for example, in immediate response to the mob violence that was directed at Vice President Nixon and his party in Caracas in May 1958, a presence was established near the Venezuela coast by an aircraft carrier task force and a battalion-sized Marine amphibious force.

In these incidents the proportion of positive outcomes was 81 percent in the short term and 52 percent over the longer term. While both of these figures are relatively high, two or more major force components (apart from nuclear force units) were not used in any of these actions; thus one might have expected more frequent favorable outcomes than usually was the case. In the three incidents when one major force component alone established a presence, the frequency of positive outcomes was an average 63 percent in the short term and a relatively higher than average 38 percent over the longer term. The higher figures for the ten "presence" incidents together thus reflect the outcomes of six incidents in

Table 4-9. Levels, Types, and Activities of Armed Forces, and Combination of Modes

| | Percentage of positive outcomes in each cell | | | | | | | |
| | Reinforce (assure and deter) | | Modify (compel and induce) | | Support (assure and induce) | | Coerce (compel and deter) | |
Variable	6 months	3 years	6 months	3 years	6 months	3 years	6 months	3 years
Level of armed forces								
1. One or more major components and nuclear force unit	100.0	85.7	100.0[a]	100.0[a]	100.0[a]	100.0[a]	100.0	80.0
2. Two or more major components; no nuclear force unit	75.0	42.9	37.0	7.7	44.5	12.5	60.0	25.0
3. One major component or nuclear force unit	100.0[a]	50.0[a]	53.8	0.0	66.7	33.3	63.6	0.0
4. Standard component	83.3	60.0	100.0[a]	...	100.0[a]	75.0[a]	80.0	50.0
5. Minor component	100.0	75.0	80.0	45.5	100.0	66.7	83.3	53.8
Type of armed forces								
Ground forces	89.0	68.8	50.0	9.5	63.0	40.0	70.0	31.8
CV/BB/LPH	83.0	55.0	48.0	8.3	62.0	41.2	66.7	22.2
Land-based combat aircraft	94.0	66.7	66.7	20.0	78.0	44.4	87.0	50.0
Other	87.5	66.7	55.6	18.5	62.5	40.0	70.4	33.3
Activities								
Bombing, blockade, emplacement, tactical support	100.0	70.0	73.3	6.3	87.5	37.5	82.4	27.8
Other	86.2	61.5	50.0	28.6	70.0	52.6	71.0	42.9

a. Denominator was less than five.

which major force components were not used and one incident in which a major component was used together with nuclear force units. In "presence" cases the style of use of armed forces was usually latent. In short, outcomes were very frequently positive when relatively small forces were deployed in a low-keyed fashion, while policymakers sought to wait upon rather than press developments.

In four other incidents the only activity performed was surveillance, or surveillance and presence together—for example, the use of a destroyer, a minesweeper, and P2V aircraft to patrol the Caribbean in response to a Cuban-supported landing of insurgents in Panama in April 1959. In these incidents the frequency of positive outcomes was 93 percent in the short term and 69 percent over the longer term. While minor force components were used in three of these four cases, in every instance those forces were used directly or indirectly to obtain U.S. objectives. Thus, the selective use of a small force to patrol an area or perform a reconnaissance mission would appear to have been adequate.

The Association between Outcomes, the Use of Armed Forces, and Modes

When used in a particular mode, are some levels, types, or activities of armed forces more often associated with positive outcomes? Are forces of a particular nature, used in a particular way, better utilized in one mode than in another? Do particular uses of force matter when the operational objective is to reinforce rather than modify an actor's behavior, or to support rather than coerce a target? Table 4-9 presents data pertinent to these questions.

Level of Armed Forces

It was previously noted that outcomes were less often positive when larger conventional forces were used apart from nuclear force units. This appears to have been true generally when the objective was either to *deter* or to *compel* an actor. However, when the U.S. objective was to *assure* that an actor would do something, positive outcomes almost always occurred irrespective of the level of force used; and when the objective was to *induce* behavior, positive outcomes occurred only when a very low level of force was used. Thus, a "continuum of ease" as concerns the four modal uses of force runs as follows: assure, deter, compel, induce.

Even when greater levels of force were used, positive outcomes occurred more often when the objective was to compel an antagonist than when the objective was to induce a friend. Further, outcomes were positive only moderately often in the short term when the largest conventional forces and no nuclear forces were utilized to compel an actor. Over the longer term, virtually no differences in positive outcome frequency occurred whether compulsion or inducement was the objective.

While the reinforcement of behavior (assurance and deterrence) was more often associated with positive outcomes than the modification of behavior (compulsion and inducement) when large conventional forces were used, this was much less likely when lesser levels of force were used. Minor actions to modify a particular behavior—which perhaps were aimed at easier objectives—were often associated with positive outcomes.

Type of Armed Forces

Whether the objective was to reinforce or modify behavior, or to support or coerce an actor, the use of land-based combat aircraft was associated with higher percentages of positive outcomes than were ground forces or major naval forces. The only mode in which this was not the case was the assurance of behavior, when outcomes were frequently positive irrespective of the type of force used. Curious, though, is the decline in positive outcomes in the longer term when land-based combat aircraft were used and the aim was to assure behavior; perhaps more important, when combat aircraft were used to deter an actor, the percentage of positive outcomes did not decline over the longer term.

Activities

Of special value for modifying behavior, at least in the short term, was the engagement of the forces in more manifest military activities, especially when the objective was to compel an actor to do something. Again though, over the longer term, these actions too were futile. More manifest activities appear to have been of great value for reinforcing behavior, especially when deterrence was the aim. Those highly positive short-term figures concerning actions to both support and coerce actors reflect outcomes when the objective was to assure and deter behavior, respectively.

Summary

In the short term, a large proportion (73 percent) of the outcomes related to U.S. objectives in the thirty-three incidents were favorable. Of the three principal categories of objectives, positive outcomes were most frequent when armed forces were aimed at objectives related to regime authority, less frequent when they were aimed at the use of force by another actor, and least frequent when they were aimed at an actor supporting a third party. Over the longer term, the frequency of favorable outcomes declined substantially with regard to all three of these major categories of objectives.

Favorable outcomes occurred far more frequently when the objective was to reinforce (assure or deter) behavior than when it was to modify (compel or induce) behavior, both in the short term and in the longer term. In frequency of positive outcomes the four modes might be arranged from easiest to most difficult, as follows: assure, deter, compel, induce. When armed forces were used in one of these four modes rather than as a latent instrument, outcomes were most frequently positive when they were used directly (reflecting outcomes related to the use of force by another actor and regime authority) rather than indirectly (reflecting, in turn, outcomes related to third party support).

In both the short and longer terms, outcomes were less frequently positive when greater levels of force were used, except when strategic nuclear force units were used together with one or more major conventional force components. The use of larger conventional forces alone did not compensate for the greater difficulty of the situations in which the larger forces might have been employed. Such compensation, it might be inferred, may be obtained by the use of strategic nuclear forces.

The type of force proportionally most often associated with positive outcomes was land-based combat aircraft. Especially significant was the fact that such aircraft were used most typically in incidents in which at least one major force component was used. Positive outcomes were less frequent when ground and naval forces were used. However, the greater frequency of positive outcomes when land-based combat aircraft were used as compared with naval or ground forces was more apparent in the short term than in the longer term.

It was also observed that positive outcomes were much more frequent when only land-based ground forces were used as compared with the use of only ship-based ground forces—leaving aside the use of other types of forces. This and the suggestion above about the efficacy of land-based combat aircraft suggest the generally greater utility of land-based forces as compared with sea-based forces.

Positive outcomes in the short term were often associated with the engagement of armed forces in manifest activities—even when the concern was to modify behavior. Over the longer term, though, manifest activities were not associated with noteworthy frequencies of favorable outcomes. Indeed, in those instances in which manifest activities had been the order of the day, the decline in favorable outcomes was dramatic.

CHAPTER FIVE

Situational Factors

THE political context of the various incidents in the sample also influenced outcomes. Before some incidents U.S. armed forces had been deployed, and sometimes used, in the region of interest; treaties implying U.S. commitments had been signed; the size of the U.S. military deployment in the area had been altered; and presidential or other official statements had been made pertinent to the incident. Other incidents were preceded by no such history. Moreover, during the incidents, the amount, quality, and character of verbal statements and other U.S. diplomatic behavior varied, as did presidential popularity. Of further interest is the association between outcomes and Soviet participation in an incident as well as the character of overall U.S.-Soviet relations.

Previous Uses of U.S. Armed Forces in the Region

Some incidents took place in regions where the United States had been recently, or was currently, engaged in a war. Indeed, in these cases the incidents generally were outgrowths of those conflicts. For example, the Truman administration's concern with Communist movements in Greece and Italy in the immediate post–World War II period was a consequence of the political vacuum that followed the war. U.S. efforts to reassure Japan and South Korea in 1953 were directly related to the way in which the Korean War ended. Incidents during 1972 and 1973 in Southeast Asia were related to the Vietnam War.

With regard to other incidents, the United States had used armed forces as a political instrument in the region on numerous occasions within past years. For example, in the five years before the 1964 action to deter a Cuban-supported landing of insurgents in the Dominican Republic, there had been no less than twenty-six U.S. political uses of force in the Caribbean area. In a similar period before the Qui Nhon incident in South Vietnam in 1965, U.S. armed forces had been used in fifteen incidents in Southeast Asia.

By contrast, in other areas U.S. armed forces had been used rarely, if at all, before an incident. No U.S. military actions had taken place in sub-Saharan Africa in the five years preceding the 1960 Congo crisis; only one had occurred in East Asia in the same number of years before North Korea's seizure of the *Pueblo*.

In the longer term, positive outcomes were not associated with previous U.S. military involvements in a region (see table 5-1). However, in the short term a pattern does emerge: positive outcomes occurred more frequently when U.S. armed forces previously had been used in the region. Positive outcomes were especially frequent for incidents that took place in Europe right after World War II, East Asia after the Korean War, and Southeast Asia after the U.S. withdrawal of ground troops from Vietnam; favorable outcomes occurred much less often in regions where U.S. armed forces had been used only infrequently—less than once a year, on the average, during the previous five years.

We may speculate, therefore, that demonstrated U.S. willingness to engage in major conflict in a region before an incident caused actors in the region to become more sensitive to signals of U.S. resolve to become involved militarily if necessary. In other words, when used against a backdrop that includes a demonstrated willingness to act, armed forces

Table 5-1. *Relationship of Outcomes to Recent U.S. Military Involvement in a Region*

Number of incidents, or war occurring in region during past 5 years	Percentage of positive outcomes	
	6 months	*3 years*
0–4 incidents[a]	62.5	42.9
5–10 incidents[a]	73.0	37.5
11 or more incidents[a]	70.8	52.0
War	89.5	45.0

a. These cutoff points were used so that there might be a relatively equal number of sample incidents in each grouping.

may be especially effective. Conversely, in regions where U.S. armed forces were used infrequently in past years, actors may have been more prone not to take a threatened U.S. use of armed forces seriously.

This stands to reason. The theoretical literature has long emphasized the importance of credibility for bargaining in conflict situations.[1] And anyone who has played poker seriously can attest to the importance of a player's reputation when it comes to having threats taken seriously. In those areas where such a U.S. reputation was absent, foreign leaders may have been more confident in testing the degree of U.S. commitment and more willing to risk action in opposition to American interests. The existence of a reputation for action in a region, on the other hand, may have led foreign leaders to be more cautious and better prepared to retreat.

Where U.S. troops previously had fought in wars, or where a large number of incidents had occurred, outcomes were positive proportionally more often when either nuclear forces were used *with* a major force component, or two or three major components of the armed forces were used *apart* from nuclear forces. A possible explanation is that, against such a backdrop, foreign decisionmakers may believe the United States is really serious only when larger forces are used. In the short term, every outcome was positive when those levels of force were used subsequent to high U.S. past involvement. When two or three major conventional force components were used alone and without such a backdrop of prior U.S. military involvement, only one-third of the outcomes were positive. In the longer term one-third of the outcomes were positive when there was a significant prior U.S. military involvement; in its absence only one-eighth were positive.

Prior Change in the Size of U.S. Forces Deployed in the Region

During the past three decades major U.S. naval, air, and ground forces have been permanently stationed in Europe, the Mediterranean, the Far

---

1. See Fred C. Iklé, *How Nations Negotiate* (Harper and Row, 1964), pp. 74–86; Oran R. Young, *The Politics of Force: Bargaining During International Crises* (Princeton University Press, 1968), pp. 35–36; Robert Jervis, *The Logic of Images in International Relations* (Princeton University Press, 1970), pp. 78–102.

East, and the Western Pacific. Smaller combat forces have also been stationed in the Panama Canal Zone, the Caribbean, and the Persian Gulf. No combat units have been permanently stationed in the Southern Hemisphere.

There has been much speculation that changes in U.S. troop levels abroad tend to destabilize a region; most often this speculation stresses that reductions in U.S. troop levels will encourage foreign decisionmakers hostile to the United States or its allies to become more aggressive. Others have argued that increases in U.S. troop levels tend to be provocative, forcing antagonists to demonstrate that they will not be cowed; thus, it is argued, stability in U.S. troop levels overseas is a necessary if not a sufficient condition for world peace. This theory is not supported by our evidence.

The measure used was the percentage change in the number of U.S. military personnel in the region in the two-year period before the incident. In the short term, outcomes were more frequently positive when there had been either a previous increase or decrease in the size of forces deployed than when there had been no change, or when no prior deployment had been maintained (see table 5-2). Outcomes were most frequently positive where there had been a previous decrease in the size of U.S. forces. The decreases were not sufficient to constrain U.S. flexibility in these incidents; if necessary, the United States was able to move other forces into the area rapidly, but there was no need to use major force components. Whereas major force components were used in one-half of the incidents preceded by an *increase* of 10 percent or greater in

Table 5-2. *Outcomes and Previous Change in U.S. Regional Deployment*

	Percentage of positive outcomes	
Change in regional deployment in past two years	*6 months*	*3 years*
Increase of 10 percent or greater	73.3	41.9
Increase or decrease less than 10 percent	60.5	28.1
Decrease of 10 percent or greater	95.2	52.4
No prior deployment	60.0	75.0

Sources: *Fiscal Year 1976 and July–September 1976 Transition Period for Military Procurement, Research and Development, and Active Duty, Selected Reserve and Civilian Personnel Strengths,* Hearings before the Senate Armed Services Committee, 94:2 (GPO, 1975), p. 118; *Fiscal Year 197S Authorization for Military Procurement, Research and Development, and Active Duty, Selected Reserve and Civilian Personnel Strengths, Part 4: Manpower,* Hearings before the Senate Armed Services Committee, 93:2 (GPO, 1974), pp. 1072–78; Office of the Assistant Secretary of Defense/Comptroller, Directorate for Information Operations.

the size of the regional U.S. deployment, and in almost three-fifths of those incidents preceded by increases *or* decreases of less than 10 percent, major force components were used in fewer than two-fifths of those incidents preceded by a *decrease* of 10 percent or greater. Presumably, the force reductions that were made before incidents were not sufficient to bring the credibility of U.S. threats or promises into serious question.

Most significant increases in the size of U.S. forces took place in climates of increased tension—for example, in Europe right after World War II, and in the Caribbean and Southeast Asia in the early 1960s. These increases seem to have had a positive effect on the outcome of subsequent incidents.

Commitments

Before sending Marines and combat aircraft to Japan at the end of the Korean War, the United States and Japan had signed, in September 1951, a security treaty, one portion of which allowed the stationing of U.S. forces in Japan to protect "against armed attack from without." Two weeks before the radar picket ship *Kretchmer* arrived off the Cuban coast at Cienfuegos, Henry Kissinger, briefing newspaper editors in Chicago, drew an analogy between the United States stationing Polaris submarines in the Black Sea and the Soviet Union establishing a base in Cuba for strategic submarines. Ten days later Dr. Kissinger warned Moscow that the establishment of an SSBN base would be viewed as a "hostile act."[2] By contrast, no treaty, administration statement, or any other relevant action preceded the U.S. response to, for example, the Congo crisis in 1960 or North Korea's seizure of the *Pueblo* in 1968.

In examining prior U.S. diplomatic actions which might have influenced foreign decisionmakers either apart from or in conjunction with the use of armed forces, we considered whether or not one of the following three conditions had existed: (1) a treaty between the United States and one of the actors that might be reasonably interpreted as a U.S. commitment to, or expression of support for, the objectives of U.S. policymakers in the incident; (2) when such a treaty did not exist, a statement with similar intent by the President, the Secretary of State, the Assistant to the President for National Security Affairs, or the Secretary

2. Marvin Kalb and Bernard Kalb, *Kissinger* (Little, Brown, 1974), pp. 210–11.

Table 5-3. *Outcomes and Prior U.S. Commitment*

Treaty statement or action interpretable as a commitment to or supportive of desired outcomes	*Percentage of positive outcomes*	
	6 months	*3 years*
Treaty	76.2	29.5
Statement by President, Secretary of State, Assistant for National Security Affairs, or Secretary of Defense[a]	100.0	100.0
Other statement or action[a]	62.1	39.3
None of the above	72.0	66.7

a. During the six months preceding the use of armed forces.

of Defense; or (3) in the absence of either (1) or (2), a statement by another U.S. government official or the use of nonmilitary foreign policy instruments (for example, an increase in economic aid) which highlighted the ties between the United States and another actor in the incident.

Intuitively it would seem that a treaty and, to a lesser extent, a statement by the President or one of his top foreign policy advisers would be given greater weight by a foreign decisionmaker than would either a statement by a lesser U.S. official or a nonverbal executive action. On the other hand, it might be that treaties become relevant and statements are made by senior officials in precisely those situations which present the greatest degree of difficulty—that is, when positive outcomes are hardest to obtain. In any case, positive outcomes did occur proportionally more frequently in the short term when a treaty existed, or a previous statement had been made by the President or one of his three most senior advisers, than when a lesser official had made a statement or some other action had been taken (see table 5-3). Indeed, the fact that only a lesser official evinced concern with the situation may have been taken as an expression of a weak U.S. position. Note that positive outcomes were more frequent when no U.S. statements or diplomatic actions were taken prior to the incident than when only minor actions were taken.

This last finding, however, must be tempered by the fact that incidents which were not preceded by any of the above-mentioned actions were those in which the armed forces were used as a latent instrument or which presented a relatively unexpected threat to American citizens, property, or armed forces abroad. Our earlier warnings against attributing causality to these findings are still appropriate.

Positive outcomes were associated most frequently with statements by senior administration officials (where a treaty did not exist), rather than with the existence of a treaty. Negative outcomes often occurred in the presence of a treaty, both in the short and longer terms; these were frequently associated with incidents in Southeast Asia—and the SEATO protocol—before the U.S. engagement in the ground war in South Vietnam.

The limited number of cases and other methodological difficulties previously discussed make it difficult to draw conclusions concerning the effects of these prior actions in incidents involving different levels of force. Still, one result stands out: in instances where a treaty existed and two or more major conventional force components were used, more than 70 percent of the outcomes were positive in the short term. By contrast, when only lower level officials took action and two major force components were used, only 36 percent of the outcomes were positive. We may speculate that the existence of a U.S. treaty commitment served in these incidents as an early caution to foreign decisionmakers not to discount the possibility of strong U.S. action. As a result, their expectations of success may have been lower and a wider path left open for retreat. Without a treaty legitimating the U.S. interest the use of large forces may have been too unexpected by the targets to have established a credible commitment in short order. Reinforcing statements by lesser officials may have gone unnoticed, been interpreted as a signal of a less than full commitment, or been made too late to affect foreign behavior. Still, even the existence of a treaty was to no effect in the longer term, all of the relevant outcomes being negative.

Administration Attention and Use of Coercive Rhetoric

Sometimes the use of armed forces was accompanied by a strong administration statement relating the reasons for the action and making both its supportive and coercive objectives explicit. Such was the case, for example, in May 1972, when President Nixon related in a television address to the nation why he had ordered the mining of Haiphong harbor and the renewed bombing of North Vietnam. Perhaps the most dramatic instance of such communication in the postwar era was President Kennedy's television speech announcing the "quarantine" of Cuba at the onset of the 1962 missile crisis.

Table 5-4. *Relationship of Outcomes to Statements by U.S. Officials*

	Percentage of positive outcomes			
	Any related statement		Coercive statement	
Statement on situation by	6 months	3 years	6 months	3 years
President	66.7	34.1	53.8	16.7
Secretary of State, Assistant for National Security Affairs, Secretary of Defense	55.0	50.0	57.1	36.8
Other U.S. official	86.7	50.0	80.0	42.9
None of the above	95.2	54.5	81.8	52.8

Alternatively, the President and other administration officials have sometimes coupled the use of force only implicitly with a statement expressing concern, interest, or a description of U.S. objectives; at times, the use of force was not mentioned at all. For example, after U.S. naval vessels began to "show the flag" in Italian ports and adjoining waters prior to the April 1948 elections, President Truman issued a statement expressing hope for "a free and independent Italy" and his intention, if that objective was threatened, "to consider what means would be appropriate for the maintenance of security and peace" in Italy.[3] Similarly, in regard to the issue of a Soviet submarine base in Cuba in 1970, Secretary of State William Rogers related during the incident that the United States had evidence "beyond a doubt" of Soviet base construction and was watching the situation "very closely." A week later, lower level U.S. officials stated that the continuing presence of two Soviet barges in Cienfuegos was causing concern.[4] Still other uses of force were wholly unaccompanied by any public statement concerning either the fact that armed forces were being used or even what the incident was.

Table 5-4 presents data which may shed light on the association between favorable outcomes and the level and type of public attention given to the incident by administration officials. The statements that were considered include *only* those made publicly at the time armed forces were used, and exclude those made before the use of force.

Positive outcomes did not occur proportionally more often when state-

3. *New York Times,* December 14, 1947. This statement was issued on the eve of the withdrawal of the last U.S. Army troops from Italy.
4. *New York Times,* October 10, 1970, and October 16, 1970.

ments were made by the President or other high administration officials than when statements were made by lesser officials or no statements were made at all. A finding not shown in the table, however, is that when major conventional force components were used, positive outcomes did occur more frequently when the President himself took note of the incident. In the short term, 59 percent of the outcomes were positive when a presidential statement was made; only 43 percent were positive when statements were made by one of the other three senior officials.

On the other hand, coercive statements by the President or his three senior advisers were not associated frequently with positive outcomes when made in conjunction with the use of major conventional force components apart from nuclear-capable forces. Positive outcomes were more frequently associated with both coercive statements by lesser administration officials and no coercive statements at all than with coercive statements by the President and his three principal advisers. If only those incidents are examined in which more than one major force component was used apart from nuclear-capable forces, and in which a coercive statement was made by either the President or one of the other three senior officials, positive outcomes resulted 27 percent of the time in the short term and never over the longer term. When coercive statements were not made by one of these individuals the figures were 70 percent and 40 percent, respectively. The same pattern also appears for incidents in which only one major force component was used.

Of further interest is the significance of coercive statements by the President and his three senior advisers for the reinforcement and modification of behavior. The data in table 5-5 indicate that coercive statements by the President and other high officials, while perhaps of some value when the objective was to assure and deter behavior, were asso-

Table 5-5. *Outcomes, Coercive Statements, and Behavior Reinforcement and Modification*

Coercive statement made by President or one of three senior advisers	Percentage of positive outcomes			
	6 months		3 years	
	Reinforce	Modify	Reinforce	Modify
Yes	92.9	33.3	72.7	5.6
No	88.5	84.2	61.5	31.6

ciated with a low frequency of positive outcomes when the aim was to compel or induce behavior. In considering only those incidents in which major force components, apart from nuclear force units, were used, outcomes in the short term were almost entirely unfavorable (8 percent) when coercive statements aimed at modifying behavior were made; nor did such statements make a difference when the concern in these incidents was to reinforce behavior.

Personal Diplomacy

In almost one-third of the incidents a senior administration official went abroad to engage in what is often termed personal diplomacy. These missions took many forms. For example, following President Nasser's nationalization of the Suez Canal, Deputy Under Secretary of State Robert Murphy and then Secretary of State Dulles went to London. The Murphy mission, President Eisenhower stated, "was to urge calm consideration of the affair and to discourage impulsive armed action."[5] Secretary Dulles had a similar objective on his first trip to London during the crisis. In a second visit in mid-August he took part in the London Conference, which ultimately drew up a proposed compromise agreement between the British and French position on the one hand and the Egyptian position on the other. In turn, this agreement was taken to President Nasser by Prime Minister Robert Menzies of Australia, accompanied by, among others, Deputy Under Secretary of State Loy Henderson. A year later, it may be added, Henderson was in Turkey and a number of Arab capitals coordinating policy in regard to the Syrian crisis. In a more recent example, after the *Pueblo* was seized then Deputy Secretary of Defense Cyrus Vance was dispatched to Seoul.

Table 5-6 presents data associating positive outcomes with instances in which senior officials or other envoys did or did not go abroad on special diplomatic missions. On the whole, both in the short and longer terms, outcomes were less frequently positive when personal diplomacy was engaged in. This was particularly the case in those incidents when large force components were used. When a special visit was combined with the use of one or more major conventional force components *apart*

5. Dwight D. Eisenhower, *The White House Years: Waging Peace, 1956–1961* (Doubleday, 1965), p. 37.

Table 5-6. *Outcomes and Personal Diplomacy*

Type of incident	Visit to an actor state by administration official or special envoy	Percentage of positive outcomes	
		6 months	3 years
All incidents	Yes	54.3	29.4
	No	82.6	51.6
Major force component used	Yes	34.8	18.2
	No	81.8	40.6
Standard or minor force component used	Yes	91.7	50.0
	No	83.3	62.5

from nuclear weapons, only 25 percent of the outcomes were positive in the short term; in the longer term, only 11 percent of the outcomes were positive. When such forces were used and no special diplomatic mission went abroad, 79 percent of the outcomes were positive in the short term, and 30 percent were positive in the longer term. It made little difference whether or not a special envoy was sent abroad when lesser armed forces were used.

How does one explain the figures when larger conventional force components were used? Did the envoys bungle their missions and thereby make positive outcomes less likely than if they had not gone at all? Or were special missions made only in the most difficult situations, those least likely to end positively in any case? While instances of the former may be found, the latter is a more reasonable proposition. Either way, however, our findings would not support the hypothesis that these missions make positive outcomes likely.

Presidential Popularity

It often has been suggested that a President's foreign policy is more likely to be effective if the President is popular at home, if his policy has the support of the broad body politic. Presumably, foreign actors believe that a President who is more rather than less popular is better able to carry through on threats or promises and to do so over a sustained period. The evidence in this study provides mixed support for this hypothesis.

Table 5-7. *Outcomes and Presidential Popularity Preceding the Use of Armed Forces*

Percent who "approve" the President's performance (Gallup poll)	Percentage of positive outcomes	
	6 months	3 years
0–59	94.7	47.1
60–66	56.7	28.6
67–72	61.9	52.6
73–100	80.0	30.0

Sources: George H. Gallup, ed., *The Gallup Poll*, vols. 1–3 (Random House, 1972); *The Gallup Opinion Index*, Report 56 (February 1970), pp 8–16, and succeeding supplements.

For each incident in the sample, data were collected as to the percent of people interviewed in the last Gallup poll before the U.S. use of force who "approved" the performance of the President. These figures were divided into ranked quartiles (see table 5-7), ranging from 43 percent (Lebanon, 1968) to 80 percent (Vietnam, 1964).[6]

In the short term, outcomes were proportionally most frequently positive when the President's popularity was lowest, and next most frequently positive when it was highest. Thus it would be difficult to argue that foreign decisionmakers were more often swayed by a popular—that is, "stronger"—President. If anything, a more powerful argument is that outcomes were more often positive when the President was least popular and, perhaps, perceived to be most desperate. To the extent the data in table 5-7 explain anything, they suggest a curvilinear relationship—that is, both of the above-mentioned theses are correct and outcomes are more often positive when the President's popularity is at an extreme, either high or low.

It is also of interest to consider the change in the President's popularity during the period in which armed forces were used. These changes ranged from only one or two percentage points, during such incidents as the Nixon visit to Venezuela in 1958 and General Kassem's threat to Kuwait in 1961, to an increase of six percentage points during the period

6. Because data were not collected if the last poll preceded the incident by more than two months, the following four incidents were not included in the analysis: Greece (1946), Italy (1947), Morocco (1956), and Cyprus (1967). Data were obtained from George H. Gallup, ed., *The Gallup Poll*, vols. 1–3 (Random House, 1972); *The Gallup Opinion Index*, Report 56 (February 1970), pp. 8–16, and succeeding supplements.

in which President Nixon ordered the mining of Haiphong harbor and renewed the air war against North Vietnam in 1972, and a decrease of twenty percentage points when U.S. forces were used in Laos in 1973.

Of course these increases and decreases in the President's popularity may have been totally unrelated to the foreign incidents and the accompanying use of U.S. armed forces. Probably the changes in popularity during dramatic incidents, such as the 1968 *Pueblo* crisis, were related at least in part to those incidents and the U.S. actions, but it is doubtful that changes in presidential popularity coincident with minor events, such as the use of U.S. armed forces to deter a Cuban-supported insurgency in the Dominican Republic in 1964, were at all related to those incidents. This notwithstanding, the association of a change in presidential popularity with the use of armed forces may affect the perceptions of foreign actors and hence the effectiveness of the use of force.

As a measure of the change in the President's popularity during the period when armed forces were used, we took the difference in the percent of people who "approved" the President's performance in the last Gallup poll taken before, and first poll taken after, the use of the U.S. armed forces. Polls taken more than two months before or after the use of armed forces were not considered, however; hence data were available only for twenty of the thirty-three incidents. Of those, the percent of people who "approved" the President's performance increased in seven incidents and decreased in thirteen.

In the short term, 85 percent of the outcomes were positive in incidents in which presidential popularity increased; 74 percent were positive in incidents in which the President's popularity declined. The difference is too small to make very much of; it provides only limited support for the argument that outcomes are more often positive when presidential popularity increases rather than decreases. Moreover, in five of the seven incidents in which there was an increase in presidential popularity, that increase was of three percentage points or less; while in seven of the thirteen incidents in which there was a decline in presidential popularity, the decline was of at least five points. Apparently a decline in presidential popularity is not very likely to affect the outcome of an incident.

If only those incidents are examined in which major force components apart from nuclear forces were used (levels 2 and 3 in table 5-8), in the short term 82 percent of the outcomes were positive when presidential popularity increased and only 59 percent were positive in those instances

Table 5-8. *Level of Armed Forces Used and Change in Presidential Popularity*

Level of armed forces used	Percentage of short-term positive outcomes	
	Popularity increased[a]	Popularity decreased[a]
1. One or more major components and nuclear force unit	...	100.0[b]
2. Two or more major components; no nuclear force unit	71.4	27.3
3. One major component or nuclear force unit[c]	100.0[b]	81.2
4. Standard components	...	100.0
5. Minor components	88.9	100.0

a. The percentage of those who "approve" the President's performance during the period in which armed forces were used increased (decreased).
b. Denominator was less than five.
c. Nuclear force units were not actually used alone in any of the sample incidents.

when the President's popularity declined. When two or three major conventional components were used apart from nuclear forces (level 2 above), these figures were 71 percent and 27 percent respectively (see table 5-8). While it might be argued that, when larger conventional forces were used, outcomes were more often positive if the President's popularity increased rather than decreased while force was being used, another view might be that presidential popularity was a function of whether outcomes were positive or negative. Either way, it is interesting to observe the existence of a "positive" relationship between outcomes in these types of incidents and presidential popularity.

Incidents in which major conventional force components were used generally received greater public attention than did incidents in which lesser forces were used. For each incident, the average number of pertinent *New York Times Index* lines per day was calculated. The incidents were then divided into two groups on the basis of whether they received more or less than the median number of lines per day. Most of the incidents in which at least one major force component was used fell into the group receiving more than the median number of lines per day. By contrast, most of those incidents in which lesser forces were used fell into the group receiving less than that number.

If only those incidents are considered in which at least one major conventional force component was used and the average number of *New*

York Times Index lines per day was above the median, then in the short term 75 percent of the outcomes were positive when the President's popularity increased, but only 21 percent were positive when presidential popularity declined. Thus it might be suggested that if presidential popularity increased rather than decreased in a climate of relatively high public attention to the incident, then outcomes in incidents in which major force components were used were more often positive.

The Role of the Soviet Union

The Soviet Union was a participant in twelve of the sample incidents; it used or threatened to use its armed forces in six of these incidents (see table 5-9). In the twelve incidents in which the U.S.S.R. was an actor, U.S. armed forces were used twice as a latent instrument, in six instances to deter, and in four instances to compel, Soviet behavior. Considering only operational objectives related to Soviet behavior, positive outcomes occurred 64 percent of the time in the short term and 50 percent over the longer term. As compared with the average short and longer term figures for operational objectives pertaining to other actors, this indicates a greater degree of intractability in the short term but a slightly more moderate Soviet stance in the longer term.

The frequency of positive outcomes for incidents in which the U.S.S.R. was an actor was 63 percent in the short term and 43 percent in the longer term, but for incidents in which Moscow was not an actor these figures were 83 and 45 percent, respectively. In short, there is a sugges-

Table 5-9. *Outcomes and Degree of Soviet Involvement*

| | Percentage of positive outcomes | |
Degree of Soviet involvement	6 months	3 years
Soviet Union a participant and used or threatened to use force[a]	52.2	37.5
Soviet Union a participant but did not use or threaten to use force[b]	72.4	48.1
Soviet Union not a participant	82.7	44.7

a. Incidents include Syria, 1957; Congo, 1960; *Pueblo*, 1968; EC-121, 1969; Cienfuegos, 1970; Vietnam, 1972a.

b. Incidents include Greece, 1946; Japan, 1953; Suez, 1956; Laos, 1959; Laos, 1962; Rogers Peace Plan, 1970.

tion that Soviet participation was of little consequence in the longer term, but of significance in the short term. Furthermore, the data in table 5-9 indicate that, in the short term, positive outcomes were less frequent the greater the degree of Soviet involvement. Over the longer term, although positive outcomes occurred with similar frequencies whether or not the U.S.S.R. participated in an incident, Soviet willingness to use or to threaten to use force was associated with proportionally fewer positive outcomes.

It was suggested in chapter 4 that outcomes were less frequently positive the greater the level of armed forces used, except when nuclear forces were used in addition to major conventional forces. This association becomes especially apparent when only incidents in which the Soviet Union was an actor are considered.

For analytic purposes, we also divided the sample incidents into the following groups: (1) incidents in which both American and Soviet allies were participants and the Soviet Union also was a participant; (2) incidents in which both American and Soviet allies participated but the Soviet Union did not; (3) incidents in which an American ally participated but neither the Soviet Union nor any Soviet ally did; and (4) all others. Table 5-10 presents data concerning frequencies of positive outcomes for these groups of incidents, further subdivided by the degree of Soviet involvement. To summarize:

—Outcomes were positive in all instances in the short term, and very frequently in the longer term, when policymakers were able to deal with

Table 5-10. *Combinations of Types of Actors in Incidents*

	Percentage of positive outcomes	
Types of actors	*6 months*	*3 years*
American ally and Soviet ally; Soviet Union used or threatened to use force	47.1	22.2
American ally and Soviet ally; Soviet Union a participant but did not use or threaten to use force	72.4	48.1
American ally and Soviet ally; Soviet Union did not participate	71.0	34.4
American ally but not USSR or Soviet ally	100.0	71.4
Other	81.8	83.3
All incidents	73.1	43.9

U.S. allies without the presence (even in strictly a political sense) of the Soviet Union or Soviet allies.

—Outcomes were much less frequently positive when an American ally faced a Soviet ally, irrespective of whether or not the Soviet Union participated.

—Outcomes were positive least frequently when an American ally faced a Soviet ally which had the support of the Soviet Union, and when Moscow used or threatened to use its armed forces.

It may be hypothesized that whether Soviet allies were participants, and whether the Soviet Union used or threatened to use its armed forces, were important factors in determining the outcomes of incidents. When Moscow was a participant, but did not use or threaten to use force, Soviet participation did not seem to matter. If anything, it may be argued that in the longer term Soviet influence had a moderating effect on its allies.

Conflict and Cooperation between the Superpowers

Edward Azar has developed a data bank that attempts to quantify conflictive and cooperative behavior among thirty-one nations for each year since 1948.[7] The data are summarized in the form of aggregate statistics with reference to overall cooperative and conflictive relationships between each of the thirty-one nations and every other nation for each year. Under this system, individual cooperative acts directed by one actor toward another are coded one through seven, and conflictive acts are coded nine through fifteen. The score of one is awarded to the most extreme cooperative act and the score of fifteen is awarded to the most extreme conflictive act. A score of eight is awarded to a "neutral" act.

For each incident we determined the mean level of cooperative and conflictive behavior directed by each of the superpowers toward the other during that year, and then grouped incidents by their scores. The groups were established so as to obtain a relatively equal number of incidents in each group. Tables 5-11 and 5-12 present data showing associations between outcomes and these scores.

At least in the short term, outcomes of incidents were more frequently

7. See Edward E. Azar and Thomas J. Sloan, *Dimensions of Interaction: A Source Book for the Study of Behavior of 31 Nations from 1948 through 1973* (University of Pittsburgh, International Studies Association, Occasional Paper 8, 1975).

Table 5-11. *Outcomes and the Degree of Cooperative Behavior between the United States and the Soviet Union*[a]

| Azar scale: | Percentage of positive outcomes | |
mean score	6 months	3 years
Cooperative behavior by Soviet Union directed at United States		
1. 5.9–6.3	87.5	33.3
2. 6.4–6.5	72.0	70.8
3. 6.6–6.9	62.5	32.4
Cooperative behavior by United States directed at Soviet Union		
1. 5.9–6.4	80.8	20.8
2. 6.5–6.6	71.4	43.8
3. 6.7–6.9	69.4	57.1

Source: Edward E. Azar and Thomas J. Sloan, *Dimensions of Interaction: A Source Book for the Study of the Behavior of 31 Nations From 1948 Through 1973*, and updated by authors (International Studies Association, 1975), pp. 5–8, 145–48.

a. Data were unavailable for two incidents (Greece, 1946; Italy, 1947).

positive when, in their broader relations, the United States and the Soviet Union acted more cooperatively toward each other (table 5-11). Looking at the percentage differences in positive outcomes between each of the three levels on the two scales, the degree of Soviet cooperative behavior appears a more discriminatory and therefore significant factor than the degree of U.S. cooperative behavior. The observed pattern is more pronounced if only incidents in which the Soviet Union participated are examined; and the pattern is most pronounced when only incidents in which Moscow used or threatened to use force are considered.

Thus, the dominant factor, and a significant one, would appear to have been Soviet cooperative behavior directed at the United States, as compared with American cooperative behavior directed at the Soviet Union. This is not illogical; the frequency of positive outcomes, especially in incidents in which the Soviet Union was an actor and the superpowers were protagonists, might be expected to reflect the Soviet side rather than the American side of the relationship.

The association between positive outcomes and Soviet *conflictive* behavior directed at the United States is less clear. Still, outcomes were most frequently positive when Soviet behavior was least conflictive, both in the short term and in the longer term. Moreover, the relatively high short-term figure when Soviet conflictive behavior was greatest is largely

Table 5-12. *Outcomes and the Degree of Conflictive Behavior between the United States and the Soviet Union*[a]

Azar scale: mean score	Percentage of positive outcomes	
	6 months	*3 years*
Conflictive behavior by Soviet Union directed at United States		
1. 9.4–9.7	93.1	50.0
2. 9.8–9.9	56.3	35.5
3. 10.0–10.5	72.2	44.1
Conflictive behavior by United States directed at Soviet Union[b]		
1. 9.6–9.7	92.3	61.5
2. 9.8	53.3	12.5
3. 9.9	68.3	38.5
4. 10.0–10.1	73.3	60.0

Source: Same as table 5-11.
a. Data were unavailable for two incidents (Greece, 1946; Italy, 1947).
b. Four groups rather than three were used because of the distribution of incidents.

accounted for by outcomes to incidents in which the Soviet Union was not an actor.

Two important points emerge out of this examination of Soviet and American conflictive and cooperative behavior. First, positive outcomes occurred more frequently (a) the greater the general cooperative behavior between the superpowers, and (b) when the superpowers acted least conflictively toward each other. Second, this was especially so for incidents in which the Soviet Union was a participant. The clearest indicator of positive outcomes in the short term was cooperative behavior directed by the Soviet Union toward the United States.

By themselves, these findings argue for the pursuit of détente. However, insofar as Soviet cooperative behavior directed toward the United States appears more significant than U.S. cooperative behavior directed at the USSR, it might be inferred that the critical element is overriding Soviet interest in good relations with the United States.

The Strategic Weapons "Balance"

A major issue in recent years has been the significance of the strategic weapons balance between the United States and the Soviet Union for the successful pursuit of American interests abroad. Some have argued that the *decline* in the U.S. strategic weapons position vis-à-vis the Soviet Union has already had, or will soon have, an adverse impact on the success of American foreign policy generally. Others have taken the view that the present balance is adequate from the U.S. perspective and that the relative decrease in U.S. capability which has occurred has not adversely affected the successful pursuit of American interests abroad.

Two indicators of the strategic weapons balance are the relative number of strategic nuclear warheads deployed by each superpower (or force loadings), and the number of delivery vehicles each of the superpowers maintains in its inventory which are capable of reaching the territory of the other.[8]

In 1953, when the Eisenhower administration threatened to use and several times brandished nuclear weapons in the Far East, the United States had approximately 800 aircraft capable of carrying nuclear weapons and more than 1,600 nuclear bombs. The Soviet Union, meanwhile, had no nuclear weapons deployed operationally. However, by the time of the 1968 *Pueblo* crisis—the other incident in the sample in which the United States used a nuclear-capable strategic unit—the U.S. advantage in delivery vehicles had been reduced to approximately 2 to 1, and the advantage in force loadings to 4 to 1. By the 1972 "Christmas" bombing of North Vietnam, these figures were approximately 1 to 1 and 2.6 to 1, respectively—the United States retained an advantage in numbers of warheads, but had "lost" the advantage in delivery vehicles. Table 5-13 presents data showing the association between positive outcomes and the ratios of U.S. and Soviet launchers and warheads.

In general, the data do not support propositions as to the importance of the strategic balance. It was not true that positive outcomes were proportionally less frequent, the less the U.S. advantage vis-à-vis the Soviet Union in the number of either nuclear warheads or delivery vehicles.

The *same* pattern emerges, moreover, if only incidents in which the Soviet Union participated are examined: for example, using force loadings as a proxy for the strategic balance, short-term outcomes were posi-

8. Calculations of the number of delivery vehicles include: U.S. intermediate range missiles that were emplaced in Europe between 1959 and 1963; number of U.S. aircraft on forward deployed aircraft carriers between 1951 and 1961 when these aircraft were included in strategic planning; and forward-based intermediate-range nuclear bombers such as the B-47 and B-58. The calculations exclude, however, Soviet intermediate-range bombers and missiles.

Table 5-13. *Outcomes and the Strategic Weapons Balance*

Ratio between United States and Soviet Union	*Percentage of positive outcomes*	
	6 months	*3 years*
Number of warheads (force loadings)		
100 or greater:1	57.9	38.2
10–99.9:1	70.6	41.2
9.9 or less:1	93.8	53.3
Number of delivery vehicles		
100 or greater:1	83.3	75.0
10–99.9:1	46.2	18.2
5–9.9:1	78.6	46.4
4.9 or less:1	84.2	47.2

Sources: "Annual Defense Department Report, FY 1977" (1976; processed), and previous reports; "Statement of Secretary of Defense Melvin R. Laird Before a Joint Session of the Senate Armed Services Committee and the Senate Subcommittee on Department of Defense Appropriations, on the Fiscal Year 1971 Defense Program and Budget" (February 20, 1970; processed), pp. 56–59; "The Development of Strategic Air Command, 1946–1973" (SAC, 1974; processed); Stockholm International Peace Research Institute, *World Armaments and Disarmament: SIPRI Yearbook 1974* (MIT Press, 1974), pp. 105–10; International Institute for Strategic Studies, *The Military Balance, 1971–1972* (London: IISS, 1971), p. 56; Norman Polmar, *Aircraft Carriers* (Doubleday, 1969), pp. 503–08, 596–600.

tive 43 percent of the time when the U.S. strategic advantage was 100 to 1 or greater, 82 percent when the U.S. strategic advantage ranged between 10 and 99 to one, and 92 percent when the U.S. advantage was less than 10 to 1. If we look at a still smaller set—those incidents in which the Soviet Union used or threatened to use force, these figures were 11, 50, and 90 percent, respectively. Thus, although outcomes were less frequently positive when Moscow was most deeply involved, our data would not support a hypothesis that the strategic weapons balance influences the outcome of incidents in which both the United States and USSR are involved.

Structure of the Situation

Finally, a critical factor in determining outcomes may be whether the initial situation or context in which armed forces were used was one of conflict within a state or conflict between states. Issues essentially internal to a state simply may or may not be more controllable than issues between states.

It might be hypothesized that insofar as the United States often used armed forces to support existing governments, outcomes were more often favorable when those governments had to deal principally with an internal rather than external antagonist. Governments usually have at their disposal a greater amount, if not a monopoly, of force and a larger information or propaganda apparatus than any other actor within a state. Conversely, though, it might be suggested that when U.S. armed forces were used to support a government, it was because these advantages had been eroded (consider the weakness of the Diem government in South Vietnam in the early 1960s), or were not relevant to the situation (for example, the position of the Bosch government vis-à-vis the military in the Dominican Republic in 1963).

Incidents of an interstate nature have been subcategorized into those in which the United States was involved initially and those in which it was not. Table 5-14 lists the frequency of positive outcomes for each of these two groups of interstate incidents, and for intrastate incidents.

The data indicate that positive outcomes were least frequent, both in the short term and over the longer term, when the situation was of an interstate nature *not* initially involving the United States directly. Outcomes were most frequently positive in the short term when the situation was of an intrastate nature. In interstate incidents not initially involving the United States, the U.S. objective was somewhat more frequently to modify behavior than it was to reinforce it; in intrastate incidents the reverse was the case. Since it is generally easier to reinforce than to modify behavior, positive outcomes might well have been related to the nature of the task, or the mode in which armed forces were used, rather than to the nature of the situation.

A further indicator that intrastate incidents presented less difficulty than interstate incidents not initially involving the United States is that lesser levels of force were used in intrastate incidents. Major force components were used with respect to 70 percent of interstate incidents, but in only one-third of the intrastate incidents.

Table 5-14. *Outcomes and the Structure of the Situation*

| | Percentage of positive outcomes | |
| | 6 months | 3 years |
Type of situation		
Interstate: U.S. not involved directly	58.8	37.5
Interstate: U.S. involved directly	76.5	58.3
Intrastate	81.1	44.4

In interstate incidents in which the United States was involved directly, the operational objective also was more often to modify than to reinforce behavior; yet positive outcomes occurred in three out of every four instances in the short term, and in three out of every five over the longer term. Hence, if the mode in which armed forces were used is an indicator of degree of difficulty, then it may be argued that positive outcomes occurred most frequently—and *notwithstanding* that difficulty—in incidents in which the United States was involved directly. Presumably it was in this type of incident that foreign actors were most likely to perceive the United States as seriously committed.

Summary

In the short term, positive outcomes were more frequent in those incidents which were preceded by U.S. military actions in the region, especially where the backdrop of a prior U.S. engagement in a war existed. Things also worked out well more frequently when, preceding incidents, U.S. deployments in the region had been increased or decreased, as compared to when no changes had been made in prior deployments or when no prior deployments had existed. The data do not support the hypothesis that decreases in force size are generally harmful; they do support a hypothesis that increases may be helpful.

Positive outcomes also occurred proportionally often when pertinent treaties or statements by the President and senior administration officials had been made before the incident. However, such outcomes were not more frequent when the President or one of his most senior foreign policy advisers took public notice of the incident after the use of armed forces had been initiated; nor were favorable outcomes more frequent when coercive statements were made or when special envoys went abroad and engaged in personal diplomacy during the incident.

Positive outcomes were especially frequent when the President's popularity was either very low or very high, as measured before the use of armed forces, being most frequent when the President was least popular and presumably lowest in standing with the American people. In these instances, foreign decisionmakers might have perceived the President as being especially committed, if not desperate, to obtain his objectives. Conversely, the high proportion of positive outcomes when the President was relatively popular may have been the result of foreign decisionmakers believing that the President would be able to stand firm insofar as he had public support generally. Generally speaking, the proportion of positive outcomes was the same regardless of what had happened to the President's popularity during the period in which armed forces were used.

As compared to outcomes in incidents in which the USSR was not a participant, positive outcomes were less frequent when the Soviet Union was a participant, and least frequent when Moscow used or threatened to use force. Moreover, the association suggested in chapter 4 between the frequency of positive outcomes and the level of armed forces used by policymakers was found to be particularly strong for incidents in which the USSR was an actor. In pursuing its own objectives and supporting allies and clients, the Soviet Union was a powerful adversary. Recognizing this, U.S. policymakers used larger contingents of the armed forces in incidents in which Moscow was a participant; but these forces could not wholly compensate. And when Moscow was heavily committed, as indicated by the use of or threat to use force, American objectives were not likely to be obtained even in the short term.

The frequency of positive outcomes also varied with the level of cooperative behavior directed by the Soviet Union at the United States. The greater the level of Soviet cooperative behavior directed at the United States, the more frequently outcomes were positive; this relationship being stronger with reference to incidents in which the Soviet Union was an actor, and strongest in relation to incidents in which Moscow used or threatened to use force.

Especially noteworthy is the fact that our data do not support a hypothesis that the strategic weapons balance between the United States and the USSR influences outcomes. No support was found for the thesis that positive outcomes would occur more often when the United States had the advantage over the Soviet Union in ratios of delivery vehicles and numbers of warheads.

Finally, outcomes were more often positive when the United States was involved directly in a situation. Perhaps other actors perceived that the United States was especially committed in these incidents. Outcomes were much less frequently positive when the situation was of an interstate nature and the United States was not involved directly. Outcomes were most often positive when policymakers dealt with intrastate situations; however, these incidents probably presented a lesser degree of difficulty.

PART TWO

Case Studies

CHAPTER SIX

The Laotian War of 1962 and the Indo-Pakistani War of 1971

DAVID K. HALL

THE Laotian war in 1962 and the war between India and Pakistan in 1971 are two Asian crises in which both superpowers, and China, were intimately involved. In each of these crises, U.S. policymakers deployed military forces in order to influence local actors, and perhaps Moscow and Peking as well. Still, U.S. armed forces were deployed with different degrees of skill in international climates and local political situations wholly different from each other. Not surprisingly, the outcomes were dissimilar. Why was this so? Insofar as the different outcomes may have been related to the distinctive situational characteristics and to the different ways in which instruments of American foreign policy were orchestrated, policymakers faced with similar decisions in the future might use these experiences to better understand the circumstances in which a use of force may be helpful and how to use force and other policy instruments effectively.

THE LAOTIAN WAR OF 1962

GEOGRAPHY determined that Laos would be a battlefield of the cold war. At the close of the 1954 Geneva Conference, Laos was a sparsely populated land of mountains and jungle, a weak and vulnerable nation separating the Communist and non-Communist nations of Asia. On the north, it bordered the newly Communist states of China and North Vietnam; on the south it bordered Thailand, South Vietnam, and Cambodia. The 1954 Geneva accords required the Viet Minh to withdraw to North Vietnam, and the Pathet Lao, the Laotian Communist movement, to move back to the northern provinces of the country pending its integration into a coalition government. All nations except France were proscribed from establishing military bases in Laos. External economic and military aid, such as the U.S. programs begun in 1950, were permitted to continue. An International Control Commission (ICC) in Laos was created to police the agreements and report any violations to the permanent cochairmen of the Geneva Conference, the United Kingdom and the USSR.[1]

When French colonial rule in Southeast Asia collapsed, defense against further Communist expansion in Asia fell to the United States. The U.S. administration of Dwight Eisenhower believed that establishment of pro-Western governments in both Laos and South Vietnam was vital not only to the political security of Thailand, Cambodia, Malaya, and Indonesia, but to the entire island chain of Japan, Formosa, and the Philippines. In September 1954, the Southeast Asia Treaty Organization (SEATO) was created to deter further Communist expansion. Initial signatories included the United States, the United Kingdom, France, Thailand, Australia, New Zealand, the Philippines, and Pakistan. A protocol attached to the mutual security pact unilaterally extended its defensive provisions to Laos, South Vietnam, and Cambodia. During the following years, the Eisenhower administration poured $300 million into Laos in the form of military and economic assistance. State Department, CIA, and military officers in Laos covertly supported Lao politicians who favored close ties with the United States and neighboring Thailand, and opposed a coalition government that included Pathet Lao representation. When, in 1958, Laotian Prime Minister Souvanna Phouma integrated the Pathet Lao into his cabinet and

1. This survey of the Laotian historical context, 1962, draws heavily on a similar introduction found in an earlier case study by this author, "The Laos Crisis, 1960–61," published in Alexander L. George, David K. Hall, and William E. Simons, *The Limits of Coercive Diplomacy: Laos, Cuba, Vietnam* (Little, Brown, 1971), pp. 36–85. Among the standard works on post-World War II Laotian history and U.S. foreign policy toward Laos are: Arthur J. Dommen, *Conflict in Laos: The Politics of Neutralization* (Praeger, 1964; rev. ed., 1971); Hugh Toye, *Laos* (Oxford University Press, 1968); Charles A. Stevenson, *The End of Nowhere* (Beacon Press, 1972); Martin E. Goldstein, *American Policy Toward Laos* (Associated University Presses, 1973); Marek Thee, *Notes of a Witness* (Random House, 1973).

the parliament, to comply with the Geneva agreements, U.S. operatives orchestrated Souvanna's removal from power by staging a parliamentary crisis.[2]

After Souvanna Phouma was replaced by a pro-American regime and the Pathet Lao was forced out of the government, Laos drifted steadily toward civil war. The United States threw its support behind the Royal Lao Army and its young commander, General Phoumi Nosavan, a cousin of Thai Premier Sarit Thanarat. The Pathet Lao retreated to the Laotian provinces bordering North Vietnam and China, where they began systematically to organize the mountain tribes. The civil war was precipitated by a neutralist coup against the pro-American regime, which led to the reappointment of neutralist Souvanna Phouma as prime minister in August 1960. Thailand imposed a crippling blockade of all food and fuel going to Laos through Thailand. When the United States refused assistance against the blockade, Souvanna established diplomatic relations with the USSR and opened negotiations with the Pathet Lao. In November 1960, when General Phoumi Nosavan's troops in southern Laos massed for attack on the capital, Souvanna turned to the USSR for an emergency airlift of food, oil, and arms. The assistance came too late. Souvanna Phouma and his neutralist military forces were driven into northern Laos, where they quickly established a new seat of government. The USSR and other Communist states granted diplomatic recognition and military support. In Vientiane, a second government headed by Prime Minister Boun Oum and Deputy Prime Minister Phoumi Nosavan received diplomatic recognition and military assistance from the United States.[3]

Despite its temporary victory, the new regime headed by Boun Oum and Phoumi quickly demonstrated its military ineffectiveness in the escalating war. By the end of April 1961, the united forces of neutralist Kong-Le and the Pathet Lao, with the assistance of North Vietnam and the USSR, had mounted a counteroffensive that threatened Vientiane and the royal capital of Luang Prabang. The new U.S. administration of John Kennedy was reluctant to intervene militarily to stem the tide. There was heavy pressure from SEATO members Thailand and the Philippines to do so, but the United Kingdom and France favored negotiation. Events in Cuba and Berlin seemed more important; U.S. conventional forces were unprepared; and the Royal Lao Army seemed irresponsible. All of the

2. Hall, "The Laos Crisis," pp. 37–39.
3. Ibid., pp. 39–40.

Joint Chiefs of Staff insisted on prior presidential assurances of rapid
military escalation, including permission to use nuclear weapons, should
North Vietnam or China respond to U.S. force.[4]

During March and April 1961, President Kennedy readied U.S.
Marines in Japan, Thailand, and the Gulf of Siam for possible introduction into Laos should a cease-fire not be reached. At the same time, the
United States decided to seek the political neutrality of Laos and to participate in a new, enlarged Geneva Conference to consider the problem.

In May 1961, resolution of the war entered a phase of protracted and
complex international negotiation. The Geneva Conference on Laos convened and a shaky cease-fire was arranged. At Geneva on June 4, Soviet
Premier Nikita Khrushchev and President Kennedy agreed on the importance of establishing an effective cease-fire in Laos and on the need for
international agreements to ensure Laotian neutrality. In October, at the
Laotian village of Ban Hin Heup, Souvanna Phouma, Boun Oum, and
Souphanouvong (leader of the Pathet Lao) agreed to create a coalition
government with Souvanna Phouma as prime minister. In December,
envoys from the fourteen nations represented at Geneva drafted an agreement guaranteeing the international neutrality of Laos.[5]

Final resolution of the war awaited formation of a universally recognized Laotian government that could initial the Geneva accords. Such a
government seemed impossible, because the exact assignment of ministries
within any coalition produced unresolvable differences of opinion among
the neutralists, rightists, and Communists. General Phoumi Nosavan
stubbornly insisted that the rightists be assigned the cabinet portfolios of
defense, which controlled the army, and interior, which controlled the
police and courts. Despite U.S. pressure on Phoumi to concede the defense and interior ministries to the neutralists, the deadlock persisted.
Laotian Communist forces attempted to break the stalemate by attacking
5,000 of Phoumi's troops at the provincial capital of Nam Tha, in the
northwestern corner of Laos, in early May. Phoumi's troops abandoned
Nam Tha after a brief battle on May 6, and fled across the border into
Thailand, some eighty miles to the south. Fearing a permanent breakdown in the year-long cease-fire and a loss of diplomatic bargaining
power with the Communist forces, Kennedy ordered the U.S. Seventh

4. Ibid., pp. 48–63.
5. Ibid., pp. 58–74; Thee, *Notes of a Witness,* pp. 175–84; Goldstein, *American
Policy Toward Laos,* pp. 252–53.

Fleet into the Gulf of Siam and landed 5,000 U.S. combat troops in neighboring Thailand.[6]

The rout of Phoumi's troops and the landing of American armed forces in Thailand urged events in Laos quickly toward a political solution. On June 11, the neutralists, Communists, and rightists agreed to an internationally neutral coalition government in which the prime minister, defense minister, and interior minister were neutralist officials and the Communists and rightists held an equal number of ministries. On July 23, 1962, the foreign ministers of the fourteen nations at the Geneva Conference initialed the "Declaration on the Neutrality of Laos." Between July and November the 5,000 U.S. combat forces sent to Thailand were gradually withdrawn to their original stations in the Philippines, Okinawa, Guam, and Hawaii. In Laos, complying with the Geneva accords, the United States withdrew its 666 military advisers to the Royal Lao Army and the USSR removed its 500 military advisers to the Communist forces. Kennedy had achieved his minimal objectives of disengagement of American and Soviet soldiers in Laos, a face-saving political settlement that did not threaten his international or domestic standing, and temporary removal of any direct military threat to the bordering state of Thailand.[7]

U.S. Behavior

The Nam Tha incident in May 1962 affected directly the paramount U.S. interest in Laos: the strategic relationship between Laos and its neighbor, Thailand.[8] U.S. officials had long felt Laos had little intrinsic value, but harmonious relations with Thailand—which was far more important because of size and because it was the headquarters for SEATO—depended on U.S. willingness to prevent the growth of Communist influence in Laos. After the Indochina war, Thailand's overriding security concern was Communist expansion into the Mekong River valley of Laos and the organization of subversive activities among the Thai-Lao and Vietnamese living in the northeastern region of Thailand facing Laos. By

6. Thee, *Notes of a Witness,* pp. 225–53.
7. Ibid., pp. 270–75, 292–96, 308–35.
8. For one American policymaker's perception of this relationship, see Roger Hilsman, *To Move a Nation: The Politics of Foreign Policy in the Administration of John F. Kennedy* (Doubleday, 1967), pp. 91–94.

May 1962 the Kennedy administration itself had become worried about the insurgency linkage between Laos and Thailand. On May 5, one day before the fall of Nam Tha, Max Frankel of the *New York Times* reported:

The administration fears that developing subversive activity in Thailand may soon lead to open Communist guerilla warfare there and further extend the trouble zones of Southeast Asia.

Communists from North Vietnam and Laos are said to be helping insurgents in the backward regions of northeastern Thailand along the Laotian frontier. Officials are especially worried about the area's fate if the precarious cease-fire in Laos is broken.

State and Defense Department officials conveyed their concern to members of Congress at a special briefing two weeks ago. . . .

The secret briefing of about fifteen members of Congress was conducted . . . by W. Averell Harriman, Assistant Secretary of State for Far Eastern Affairs, and William P. Bundy, Deputy Assistant Secretary of Defense for International Security.[9]

On May 1, a week after the secret Harriman-Bundy congressional briefing, Deputy Assistant Secretary for International Security Haydn Williams sent a letter to Representative Edwin Dooley, warning that the situation in Thailand could become especially serious if efforts to establish a neutral government in Laos failed "and if Laos goes Communist." "There would then be on the Thai borders in this most crucial northeast area a government which would very possibly give support to the infiltration of guerillas."[10]

Close relations between the United States and Thailand dated from 1950, when both nations became alarmed at Communist power in China and Vietnam.[11] In the summer of 1950, Thailand quickly dispatched troops and food to South Korea, and the United States responded with military, economic, and technical assistance for Thailand. Government cooperation grew particularly close after the anti-Communist strongman Sarit Thanarat staged a military coup in 1957. During the late 1950s, while the Eisenhower administration was openly striving for a pro-American government in Laos, Sarit began "secretly to funnel soldiers, arms, equipment, and money into Laos to prop up the rightist [pro-

9. *New York Times,* May 6, 1962.
10. Ibid.
11. For a thorough history of the growth of American-Thai cooperation, see Donald E. Neuchterlein, *Thailand and the Struggle for Southeast Asia* (Cornell University Press, 1965), pp. 93–257.

American] regime of his Laotian kinsman, General Phoumi Nosavan."[12] By the time the Laotian civil war broke out in August 1960, the Thai government felt fully confident that its U.S. ally, acting either unilaterally or collectively through SEATO, would prevent any leftward drift in Laos, Thailand's buffer with China and North Vietnam.[13] However, the Thai government was profoundly shaken when, in the spring of 1961, SEATO deadlocked on collective action against the successful Pathet Lao–neutralist counteroffensive and the Kennedy administration refused to intervene militarily. Thai suspicions deepened during 1961–62, when the United States accepted Souvanna Phouma as the next head of government, and then tried to coerce Phoumi to drop his demand for control of the defense and interior ministries in a coalition government. Bangkok opened talks with the USSR on trade and cultural exchanges, and the diplomatic world speculated that Thailand might move toward neutralism and withdraw from SEATO.

The Kennedy administration hurried to reverse the erosion in relations with Thailand by initiating a series of high-level visits by Vice President Lyndon Johnson, General Maxwell Taylor, and Attorney General Robert Kennedy. Their efforts brought Thai Foreign Minister Thanat Khoman to Washington for a round of consultations in March 1962. The joint communiqué issued by Thanat and Secretary of State Dean Rusk formally pledged the United States, without prior consent of other SEATO members, to meet militarily any Communist attack on Thailand. Two weeks later, Assistant Secretary of State W. Averell Harriman flew to Bangkok to reassure Sarit that the United States, in exchange for Thai support for Souvanna Phouma's coalition government, would prevent the Communists from seizing control of Laos. By April 1962 the U.S. diplomatic offensive had reversed much of the damage done in 1961. Then, suddenly, the credibility of these promises seemed at stake when the cease-fire at Nam Tha unexpectedly collapsed in May 1962.

The Kennedy administration recognized the high cost of failing to respond to the breakdown of the Laotian cease-fire. On the other hand, by May 1962 there was a common recognition by the President, his top civilian advisers, and the Joint Chiefs of Staff that Laos was a decidedly undesirable location for direct military intervention. The mountainous

12. T. D. Allman, "Big Brother Is Watching," *Far Eastern Economic Review* (October 9, 1969), p. 124.
13. Ibid., pp. 224–36.

jungle terrain, the tropical climate, and the almost complete absence of communication and supply lines made Laos a military nightmare for U.S. conventional forces.[14] The risk of provoking a Korean-type counterintervention by either the Chinese or the North Vietnamese army was considered substantial.[15] The Kennedy administration had been unable to obtain firm pledges of military support in Laos from either the United Kingdom or France, the other major powers in SEATO,[16] and the complete lack of fighting spirit in the 50,000-man Royal Lao Army made it a certainty that any war would be completely shouldered by the United States and its Asian allies.[17]

The possibility that Thailand might take unilateral military action in Laos added to U.S. concern. By spring 1962, U.S. intelligence had confirmed the presence of 10,000 North Vietnamese soldiers and a sizable contingent of Chinese military advisers in northern Laos. Any Thai military movement across the border risked confrontation with North Vietnam or China and the end to U.S. hopes for a peaceful retreat from Laos. The Kennedy administration had ample evidence that Thailand might take unilateral action if the Communists sought to exploit their military position. In April 1961, when the Pathet Lao pushed to within ten miles of Thakhek on the Laotian side of the Mekong River, Sarit publicly announced that Thai troops would go into action if the town were attacked. On February 13, 1962, when the May 1961 cease-fire momentarily broke down around Nam Tha, Sarit ordered Thai armed forces to move up to the northern border for the first time since a 1941 demilitarization agreement between France and Thailand. Sarit's order was given without prior consultation with the United States or SEATO.[18]

Mingled with Kennedy's international concerns was a natural presidential wariness of the domestic political implications of the Laos problem. Congressional leaders of both parties had made known their opposition to direct U.S. combat involvement as early as April 1961, but a number of

14. *New York Times,* January 6, 1961; *Life,* March 21, 1961, pp. 22–23.

15. Arthur M. Schlesinger, Jr., *A Thousand Days: John F. Kennedy in the White House* (Houghton Mifflin, 1965), pp. 310, 315–16; Hilsman, *To Move a Nation,* pp. 147–49.

16. *New York Times,* January 4, 1961; Harold Macmillan, *At The End of the Day, 1961–1963* (Macmillan, 1973), pp. 237–41.

17. Hugh Sidey, *John F. Kennedy, President* (Atheneum, 1963), pp. 76–77; Theodore C. Sorensen, *Kennedy* (Harper and Row, 1965), p. 642.

18. Neuchterlein, *Thailand and the Struggle for Southeast Asia,* pp. 170, 200, 227; *New York Times,* February 14, 1962.

conservative congressmen were opposed to a negotiated settlement with the Pathet Lao. When Phoumi and Boun Oum refused to agree to a coalition government, except on terms unacceptable to the neutralists and Communists, the Kennedy administration suspended in February 1962 the $3 million monthly assistance check that met the Lao Army's payroll. In response, the official organ of the Republican National Committee criticized Kennedy for "forcing the legitimate government of Laos into a perilous coalition with the Reds."[19] When Nam Tha fell on May 6, several conservative Republicans took the floor in the Senate and House of Representatives to attack the administration for failing to support the rightists and resorting to economic coercion against the United States' own clients. On May 10, while the National Security Council was weighing the American response, former President Eisenhower publicly expressed his doubts about the planned coalition government, observing that this was "the way we lost China."[20] Kennedy and his advisers were abundantly aware by May that a total victory by the Pathet Lao would bring Republican charges that another Democratic administration had materially contributed to the loss of an Asian ally to communism.

In addition to Kennedy's concerns, the bureaucratic perspective of the State Department represented by Assistant Secretaries Averell Harriman and Roger Hilsman was particularly influential on U.S. decisionmaking. Since the Laotian cease-fire of May 3, 1961, much of the day-to-day responsibility for managing the problem had fallen to these two senior officials. A major question raised by the fall of Nam Tha was whether it constituted an isolated incident or whether it was the first step in a general Communist offensive. Three days before the battle, the Pathet Lao and their Vietnamese supporters had also captured the last airfield in northern Laos, and some intelligence reports suggested Communist troop movements south toward the Thai border. Whether a large-scale campaign was beginning was difficult to determine, but Harriman and Hilsman argued that it made little difference. The complete rout of Phoumi's 5,000-man garrison would tempt the Communists to go farther now, whether or not that was their original intent. The U.S. strategy of deterrence in Laos had depended on the quite modest but still important strength of the Lao Army, even though this dependence had considerably complicated simultaneous attempts to pressure Phoumi into a coalition government. This

19. *New York Times,* February 15, 1962.
20. *New York Times,* May 11, 1962.

presumed strength had now been thoroughly discredited, and deterrence depended completely on external military forces.

Harriman and Hilsman warned Kennedy that the Pathet Lao and their allies had little incentive to resume political negotiations unless they genuinely feared American intervention. A *credible* signal of U.S. determination to resist further Communist military nibbling would now require moving American troops into Thailand, not just repeating the naval shows of force in the Gulf of Siam ordered by Eisenhower in January 1961 and by Kennedy again in May 1961.[21] Enough action had to be taken to make the threat convincing, but under no circumstances—even in the face of additional cease-fire violations—should U.S. military action call into question continued U.S. willingness to press for a negotiated neutralization of Laos.[22]

The breakdown in the Laotian cease-fire found the U.S. government generally unified behind Kennedy's operational objectives of reestablishing the May 1961 cease-fire and moving the three Laotian political factions back to the negotiating table.[23] After Phoumi's forces were routed at Nam Tha, even the Joint Chiefs were willing to concede the wisdom of a negotiated settlement rather than an attempt to retake lost territory with the discredited Lao Army.[24] The fall of Nam Tha reactivated the articulation of these frequently enunciated U.S. objectives in several channels. Communication was particularly intense with the USSR, the Communist nation perceived as most sympathetic to U.S. objectives in Laos and the nation most capable of exerting leverage over the Pathet Lao and North Vietnamese because of its role as the principal supplier of material to both the Communist and the neutralist forces. U.S. Ambassador to the USSR Llewellyn Thompson met with Soviet Foreign Minister Andrei Gromyko on May 8 and with Soviet Premier Khrushchev on May 13 to convey U.S. concern at the breakdown of the cease-fire and a desire that the USSR dissuade the Communist forces from further military action.[25]

21. The most thorough account of the Eisenhower administration's response in late 1960 to the deteriorating Laotian civil war is Stevenson, *End of Nowhere*, pp. 121–28. On Kennedy's use of force in March 1961, see Hall, "The Laos Crisis," pp. 58–67.

22. Hilsman, *To Move a Nation*, pp. 142–51.

23. Acquiescence in these administration objectives had been painfully achieved within the security bureaucracy during the preceding months. For details, see Stevenson, *End of Nowhere*, pp. 129–70.

24. Hilsman, *To Move a Nation*, pp. 143–44.

25. *New York Times*, May 9 and 14, 1962.

Similar American views were pressed in Washington on May 9 and May 15 in direct talks between Harriman, Secretary of State Rusk, and Soviet Ambassador Anatoly Dobrynin.[26] At a presidential press conference on May 9, Kennedy stated that the United States and the USSR were hopeful that they could "bring about a restoration of the cease-fire [sic]."[27]

On May 12, with heavy pressure from Harriman and Hilsman and with the concurrence of Defense Secretary Robert McNamara and Joint Chiefs of Staff Chairman Lyman Lemnitzer, who had just returned from an inspection tour of Southeast Asia, Kennedy privately authorized the movement of 4,000 U.S. servicemen to Thailand from their normal stations in the Philippines, Okinawa, Guam, and Hawaii. Included in the President's authorization were 1,800 Marines of the Third Marine Division in Okinawa; 1,200 infantry soldiers from the First Battle Group, Twenty-seventh Infantry based in Hawaii, and 1,000 airmen from tactical fighter groups based in the Philippines, Guam, and Okinawa.[28] On the same day, the State Department announced that a U.S. aircraft carrier task force and a Marine battle group of 1,800 men would be moving in the direction of Indochina. On May 14, without public announcement, a U.S. Army battle group of 1,000 infantrymen, already in Thailand on temporary duty for a SEATO airborne exercise ("Air Cobra," staged in early May), was moved into northeastern Thailand, some thirty miles from the Laotian border.[29]

On the afternoon of May 15 a presidential message announced that 4,000 American Marines, infantrymen, and airmen would be landing in Thailand in the coming days, and would "remain there until further orders."[30] At the Pentagon, McNamara revealed the creation of a new U.S. Military Assistance Command, Thailand, to be headed by General Paul D. Harkins, already chief of U.S. Military Assistance Command, South Vietnam.[31] On Okinawa an additional 5,000 American troops were alerted for possible embarkation for Thailand.[32] U.S. fighters,

26. *New York Times,* May 10 and 16, 1962.
27. "The President's News Conference of May 9, 1962," *Public Papers of the Presidents of the United States: John F. Kennedy, 1962* (GPO, 1963), p. 378.
28. *New York Times,* July 1, August 9, and May 13, 1962.
29. *New York Times,* May 15, 1962.
30. "Statement by the President Announcing the Dispatch of Additional U.S. Forces to Thailand, May 15, 1962," *Public Papers of the Presidents: John F. Kennedy, 1962,* p. 396.
31. *New York Times,* May 16, 1962.
32. Goldstein, *American Policy Toward Laos,* pp. 261–62.

tankers, and cargo planes were transferred from Hawaii to the Philippines where they would be in a better position to support U.S. troops destined for Thailand.[33]

During the week following Kennedy's May 15 declaration, U.S. combat troops arrived in Thailand and were deployed along a defensive perimeter in northeastern Thailand facing the Mekong River border with Laos. Eighteen hundred Marines from the Third Marine Expeditionary Brigade, including their helicopters and jet fighters, were stationed at Udon, only forty miles south of the Laotian administrative capital of Vientiane. Upon arrival, U.S. troops began combined military exercises with Thai forces to acclimate American personnel to the terrain and weather of Thailand.[34] By the first week of July, when U.S. combat strength peaked, some 5,000 American reinforcements had arrived in Thailand—a thousand more than originally contemplated by Kennedy.[35] Combined with the 1,000-man U.S. Army battle group, 700 U.S. Army Engineers, and 300 members of the U.S. Military Assistance Advisory Group already in Thailand at the time of the fall of Nam Tha, total U.S. military strength in Thailand crested at 7,000 during the first days of July.[36]

U.S. military actions in May 1962 were designed to deter further warfare, or advocacy of warfare, by parties involved in the Laotian confrontation. Above all, this show of U.S. armed strength was intended to deter military advances by Pathet Lao and North Vietnamese troops and to discourage Chinese advocacy of such advances. But the Kennedy administration also saw U.S. troop landings in Thailand as a means of strengthening the hand of Moscow, which had been quietly working with

33. *New York Times*, May 22, 1962.

34. *New York Times*, May 18, 21, and 23, 1962.

35. The arrival of 5,000 U.S. servicemen, rather than the 4,000 originally authorized by Kennedy, resulted from deployment in Thailand of 2,800 Marines rather than the 1,800 initially projected. Whether Kennedy was apprised of this disparity cannot be determined. For published references to the presence of 2,800 Marines in Thailand, see *New York Times*, July 28, 1962, August 19, 1962.

36. For a description of the work of the U.S. Army Engineers in Thailand in 1962, see Ernest L. Hardin, Jr., "Road-Building in Thailand," *Army Information Digest* (November 1962), pp. 28–31. Seven years later, in the context of congressional debate over the extent of the U.S. defense commitment to Thailand, the past and current American ambassadors to Thailand erroneously stated that the Kennedy administration had deployed 10,000 ground and air force personnel to Thailand in spring 1962. See *United States Security Agreements and Commitments Abroad: Kingdom of Thailand*, pt. 3, Hearings before the Senate Foreign Relations Committee, 91:1 (GPO, 1970), pp. 614–15, 646, 874.

Washington since April 1961 to find a peaceful resolution to the East-West confrontation. Collapse of the cease-fire at Nam Tha was taken by the Kennedy administration as a dangerous sign that Moscow's influence over the more aggressive Pathet Lao, Vietnamese, and Chinese had declined. To a lesser degree, U.S. troop movements were intended to pre-empt any untoward and complicating military initiative by Thailand's Marshal Sarit.[37]

Public statements by U.S. officials, however, only hinted at the possible use of U.S. armed forces in Laos. Administration fears of provoking Communist escalation, of inadvertently deepening the limited U.S. commitment to Laos, or of giving the recalcitrant Laotian rightists renewed hope of support all militated against explicit warnings. One of the sternest U.S. statements of the crisis, the State Department announcement on May 12 that U.S. troops would be moving toward Indochina, had described the action as not just another "show of force," but as an effort to position troops for direct military action if Communist advances continued in Laos.[38] But Kennedy's presidential message justifying the landing of U.S. forces in Thailand described the action as a "defensive act," designed "to help insure the territorial integrity" of Thailand. No mention was made of Laos. Only Kennedy's remark that forces "would remain there until further orders" hinted at their possible use in Laos.[39]

The restricted nature of the U.S. mission was underscored in Saigon on May 17 when General Harkins, commander of the new United States Military Assistance Command, Thailand, told the press that U.S. troops entering Thailand were under strict orders not to enter Laos, and could not react militarily unless Thailand were invaded. The next day in Bangkok, Harkins went further, noting that "the troops do not have the right to fire on suspected infiltrators [into Thailand] as of now."[40] Such caution proved a minor embarrassment to Kennedy, when he was asked in a presidential press conference on May 23 to comment on reports that U.S. troops in Thailand were not carrying ammunition. The following day, the U.S. military command in Bangkok announced that live ammunition had been issued to U.S. troops.[41]

37. *New York Times,* May 14 and 15, 1962; Stevenson, *End of Nowhere,* p. 175.
38. Hilsman, *To Move a Nation,* p. 146; *New York Times,* May 13, 1962.
39. "Statement Announcing the Dispatch of Additional U.S. Forces to Thailand, May 15, 1962," *Public Papers: Kennedy, 1962,* p. 396.
40. *New York Times,* May 18 and 19, 1962.
41. *New York Times,* May 24 and 25, 1962.

The post–Nam Tha military lull was broken in late May by minor fighting in northern and southern Laos. Secretary of State Rusk warned of "very serious problems," and the American press reported intensive administration discussion of military contingency plans for Laos, including the occupation of southern Laos by U.S. forces in Thailand. Such rumors ceased only when a successful Laotian government was formed in June.

While the introduction of U.S. troops in Thailand was designed to force a new cease-fire, the Kennedy administration simultaneously increased its political and economic pressure on its balking Laotian clients. Throughout the spring the U.S. government had been pressing the rightists to drop their demand for control of the defense and interior ministries in a coalition government. Washington had suspended its monthly $3 million payroll assistance, and had also hinted that it might terminate deliveries of military equipment to Laos.[42] On March 24, at a personal meeting in Thailand with General Phoumi, Assistant Secretary Harriman was brutally frank. American troops would not come to Laos and die for him, Harriman told Phoumi. The only alternative to a neutral Laos was a Communist one. Phoumi would be responsible for the destruction of his country. Talking to reporters afterward, Harriman implied that military aid would soon be stopped if there were no agreement on a coalition government.[43]

When the Nam Tha garrison collapsed on May 6, the Kennedy administration was furious with Phoumi. The recalcitrance of the Boun Oum-Phoumi regime had led the Communists to break the cease-fire and endangered Washington's neutralization plans; and furthermore, American military experts had been urging Phoumi for weeks to withdraw his 5,000 troops from the highly vulnerable Nam Tha garrison deep in northern Laos. Some U.S. officials suspected that Phoumi had intentionally provoked the Communists in order to coerce the Kennedy administration to resume its support for his regime.

On May 12, after the fall of Nam Tha, the *New York Times* reported that Phoumi and Boun Oum "were being told that their careers were in peril unless they agreed to meet the neutralist terms for a coalition."[44] In

42. *New York Times,* May 30 and June 1, 1962.

43. Stevenson, *End of Nowhere,* p. 173; see also Joseph Alsop, "Mad Hatter's Tea Party," *New York Herald Tribune,* April 23, 1962.

44. *New York Times,* May 13, 1962.

a confidential message to the Vientiane government from its Laotian embassy in Washington, Harriman was reported as saying,

the Nam Tha events have completely destroyed the U.S. government's confidence in the personality of General Phoumi. The United States cannot extend to him its aid, neither militarily nor financially, or otherwise. The United States cannot support a government in which General Phoumi is the most important personality. General Phoumi ought better to attend to his army, rendering in this way better service to his country than as a political leader.[45]

The U.S. government rejected requests by the rightists for replacement of the more than $1 million in American arms, ammunition, and equipment lost or destroyed during the Nam Tha battle.[46] In a series of state visits to Thailand, South Vietnam, South Korea, Japan, Taiwan, Malaya, and the Philippines immediately before and after the military defeat, Washington actively discouraged other Asian allies from extending the political or economic support sought by Phoumi and Boun Oum.[47] By landing American troops in Thailand, the Kennedy administration signaled that Vientiane should not see the action as a direct show of U.S. support. On May 18 Harriman told the Laotian ambassador in Washington that the United States did not foresee a need to dispatch U.S. troops to Laos, "as Chinese troops would never be so foolish as to invade Laos. General Phoumi cannot cause the outbreak of a world war. By his irresponsible deeds he will only destroy his own country. It is not he who dictates the policy of the United States."[48] The U.S. ambassador in Vientiane stressed to the Laotian government that U.S. troops had arrived only to defend Thailand, and had no intention of intervening in Laos.[49]

Target Behavior

The behavior of the USSR was crucial to the Kennedy administration's hopes for reestablishing the cease-fire line and completing the Laotian coalition. By May 1962 the United States and the USSR had a well established history of cooperation on Laos. In April 1961, following military threats by the United States, the USSR had actively assisted in bringing

45. Thee, *Notes of a Witness,* pp. 266–67n.
46. *New York Times,* May 26, 1962.
47. *New York Times,* May 28, 1962.
48. Thee, *Notes of a Witness,* p. 239.
49. Ibid., p. 251.

about the cease-fire demanded by Kennedy as a prerequisite to U.S. participation in a reconvened Geneva Conference on Laos. At the Vienna summit talks between Khrushchev and Kennedy in June 1961, the two leaders had agreed that Laos was not worth a direct superpower confrontation. In the words of their joint communiqué on June 4, they pledged "their support of a neutral and independent Laos under a government chosen by the Laotians themselves, and of international agreements for insuring that neutrality and independence, and in this connection they have recognized the importance of an effective cease-fire."[50] By September 1961 the United States, the USSR, and the United Kingdom had privately reached the confidential "Pushkin Agreement"—named after Georgi Pushkin, Soviet deputy foreign minister and chief Soviet delegate to the Geneva Conference—which called for the USSR and the United Kingdom, as cochairmen of the Geneva Conference, to ensure the compliance of members of their political blocs with any negotiated agreements on Laos.[51]

The USSR's cooperation with the United States reflected its own limited interests in Laos. Soviet intervention in the civil war, in December 1960, had been motivated by its growing competition with China for the favor of North Vietnam. The Soviet campaign for influence in North Vietnam had begun in August 1960, with the extension of large credits for industrial expansion. In the winter of 1960 the USSR could not remain aloof from the Laotian civil war for fear of strengthening the pro-Chinese faction in Hanoi.[52] But the Kennedy administration's offer of neutralization was satisfactory for Soviet interests. While willing to assist an inexpensive war of national liberation in Southeast Asia, Khrushchev had no desire to remain militarily involved in a civil war that threatened to escalate into a Korean-style local war and that had little relevance to basic Soviet interests. Soviet assistance in the neutralization of Laos gave evidence of Soviet support for North Vietnam's interests, and allowed the USSR to argue privately in both Hanoi and Peking that, with patience, Laos would, in Khrushchev's graphic phrase, "fall into our laps like a ripe apple."[53]

When negotiations to complete the Laotian coalition government stale-

---

50. *Department of State Bulletin,* vol. 44 (June 26, 1961), p. 999.
51. Stevenson, *End of Nowhere,* pp. 165–66.
52. Hall, "Crisis in Laos," p. 44.
53. Hilsman, *To Move a Nation,* pp. 130–31.

mated in early 1962, however, the USSR attempted to wash its hands of the thorny problem. In letters to the Communist parties of North Vietnam and China in mid-March, Moscow stated that the USSR was satisfied with the de facto division of power within Laos, but felt that the Vietnamese, Chinese, and Laotian Communists were in a better position to judge what practical steps should be taken next. When the Soviet ambassador in Laos became aware of the Communist forces' plans for a military attack on Nam Tha, he adopted the view that a military loss by Phoumi might drive the Laotian rightists back to the bargaining table.[54] The May breakdown in the cease-fire found the USSR still in agreement with the United States on the objectives of preventing military escalation and completing the coalition government, but the question now existed whether the USSR had leverage on the course of events.

In high level talks in Washington and Moscow on May 8 and 9, the U.S. government reiterated to the USSR its determination to reestablish the cease-fire and complete the coalition government.[55] On May 12 the State Department announced major U.S. troop movements toward Indochina, and by May 13 the American press was speculating that some troops would be landed in Thailand.[56] A clear-cut Soviet response to American communications came on May 15. In a private meeting with Secretary of State Rusk requested by the USSR, Soviet Ambassador Dobrynin relayed to Rusk Premier Khrushchev's continued desire to create a coalition government in Laos in the spirit of the Khrushchev-Kennedy Vienna communiqué. Because of Phoumi's part in causing the breach, however, the USSR felt that the United States had particular responsibility for reinforcing the cease-fire.[57] After his meeting with Rusk, Dobrynin told the American press that it was necessary to put into effect the agreement that was reached at Vienna in June 1961 between Khrushchev and Kennedy.[58]

Official Soviet reaction to the actual American landings in Thailand was moderate and belated. On May 17, Foreign Minister Andrei Gromyko called the military action "very bad," and claimed that it "just complicated the situation."[59] The next day, while on a goodwill tour of

54. Thee, *Notes of a Witness,* pp. 240–43, 248.
55. Ibid., p. 251.
56. *New York Times,* May 14, 1962.
57. Thee, *Notes of a Witness,* p. 239.
58. *Christian Science Monitor,* May 16, 1962.
59. *New York Times,* May 18, 1962.

Bulgaria, Khrushchev seemed determined to dramatize the potential dangers of the situation for his Chinese, Vietnamese, and Laotian comrades. He firmly predicted that U.S. forces would become involved in a shooting war: "They arrived with their weapons. They did not come to play golf. They will shoot, and those they shoot will shoot back." He made no suggestion, however, that U.S. military moves posed a threat to successful completion of negotiations on Laos. He consoled his fellow Communists with the additional prediction that "the Americans may fight fifteen years if they want to, but it will not help." The masses in Southeast Asia, he assured, were certain to win over the capitalists in the end.[60]

Khrushchev's signal to his Communist allies was reiterated by *Pravda* on May 20. Implying that U.S. actions were not the purely "defensive act" painted by American officials, this official newspaper of the Communist party of the USSR condemned the United States for "preparing for intervention in Laos," which "would certainly widen the military conflict and enhance the danger of war not only on the borders of Laos but also in the whole of Southeast Asia. . . . In that case the military intervention of the United States in Laos also would turn into a collective intervention and would inevitably provoke a counteraction by the other side."[61] *Pravda* concluded that failure to resolve the Laos problem was the worst possible outcome for all parties. During a national radio and television speech from Moscow on May 25, in what was to be the last major Soviet comment on Laos before the incident was resolved, Khrushchev stated that while the landing of U.S. troops in Thailand "seriously hinders a settlement of the Laotian problem," "the Soviet Government has been doing everything in its power to put an end to the war in Laos. . . . The Soviet Government firmly adheres to the position that it is essential to promote the formation in Laos of a coalition government headed by Souvanna Phouma."[62] Despite Khrushchev's criticism of Kennedy's action, U.S. officials were convinced that the USSR privately was not displeased by the support this lent Soviet warnings to Hanoi and Peking.[63] The moderation of Khrushchev's statements and the generally optimistic tone of the Soviet press on Laos seem to support the accuracy of Washington's analysis.

The USSR's response to U.S. pressure was reasonable. The costs to it

60. *New York Times*, May 19, 1962.
61. *New York Times*, May 21, 1962.
62. *New York Times*, May 26, 1962.
63. *New York Times*, May 16, 1962.

of temporarily restraining pro-Communist advances and working toward a coalition government, as the United States insisted, were quite negligible when compared to the potential costs and risks associated with a continued military campaign by the Communist forces. Laotian neutralization would, in fact, constitute a significant victory for Soviet foreign policy—the elimination of a former U.S.-client regime, its replacement by the Soviet-sponsored Souvanna Phouma regime, and, in general, a vivid demonstration of Khrushchev's claim that peaceful coexistence could achieve socialist victories while avoiding major wars with the United States. An apparent international victory at small cost would be welcome compensation for recent failure at Berlin. While the Vietnamese and Chinese might question the failure to exploit fully the military balance of power within Laos, the chance for political success was clearly high if American influence was withdrawn. In contrast, the risks associated with continued fighting were considerable. The possibility that Kennedy was not bluffing could not be ignored, and it was uncertain that the United States could constrain the Thai government. Any escalation would be difficult for the USSR to avoid, with its 500 advisers in the country lending airlift, logistics, and advisory service to the Pathet Lao.[64]

The United States held both local and strategic superiority vis-à-vis the USSR. Involvement in a war in Southeast Asia would divert resources from more important issues. The Pathet Lao might be even less amenable to Soviet influence and more susceptible to Chinese influence than a neutralist coalition under Souvanna. In general, from the Soviet perspective, the risk of major costs to physical and economic well-being resulting from renewed fighting in Laos outweighed the minimally greater security and influence associated with complete Communist victory, as opposed to a neutralist coalition government.

A more hostile but weaker target of U.S. military signaling was the People's Republic of China (PRC). Unlike the Soviet Union, which chose to aid the Communist forces in Laos largely out of deference to Hanoi's desires, the PRC had a direct and major security interest in the removal of pro-Western influence from its border and the establishment there of a neutral, or preferably pro-Chinese, buffer state. To this end, since 1958 China had supported both the Laotian government of Souvanna Phouma

64. *United States Security Agreements and Commitments Abroad: Kingdom of Laos,* pt. 2, Hearings before the Senate Foreign Relations Committee, 91:1 (GPO, 1970), p. 419.

and, in a minor fashion, the military activities of the Pathet Lao.[65] But
in 1962 China had neither the economic, political, nor military power to
impose its will in Laos. Economically, China faced severe national problems resulting from the aftereffects of the unsuccessful "great leap forward" program, the withdrawal of Soviet economic and technical assistance, and a recent series of poor grain harvests.[66]

China's political relations with the USSR were strained. The USSR had
far greater leverage in North Vietnam and Laos because of its role as
principal source of supplies. Militarily, the United States appeared increasingly potent and dangerous because of Kennedy's emphasis on conventional and guerrilla warfare. And China remained completely dependent on the strategic protection of the USSR, even as the reliability of
that protection was increasingly in doubt.

Laos was not the PRC's dominant security concern at the time.
Throughout the spring, the Chinese nationalists threatened to take military advantage of the economic dislocation evident on the mainland; the
PRC responded by intermittent shelling of Quemoy and Matsu and massing troops opposite the offshore islands in mid-June. An equally serious
problem was the increasing number of troop and plane incidents in April
and May on the India-China border and the series of formal protests ex-
changed between the two countries.[67] These conditions and concerns
made China willing in the spring of 1962 to give political and advisory
support to a Pathet Lao–North Vietnamese tactical blow against Phoumi's
troops at Nam Tha, but unwilling to be directly involved or to lend support to larger military plans. China's immediate interests were adequately
served by the basic objectives of neutralizing Laos in international affairs
and pressing Phoumi into a neutralist-led coalition government.[68]

Although not as intimately involved as the USSR in the international
diplomacy over Laos, the PRC had still abundant opportunity by May
1962 to become thoroughly familiar with the Kennedy administration's
attitudes, both as a member of the fourteen-nation Geneva Conference
and through the more private United States-PRC ambassadorial talks in
Warsaw. At Geneva, American and Chinese differences on the implemen-

65. Chae-Jin Lee, *Communist China's Policy Toward Laos: A Case Study, 1954–
1967* (Center for East Asian Studies, University of Kansas, 1970), pp. 42–71.
66. Thee, *Notes of a Witness*, pp. 249–50; *New York Times*, May 5 and 27,
1962.
67. *Peking Review*, February 23, May 4 and 18, June 8 and 15, 1962.
68. Thee, *Notes of a Witness*, pp. 244–45.

tation of Laotian neutrality had been meticulously mediated and compromised by May 1962, through the efforts of the British and Soviet representatives. At Warsaw, the United States and the PRC had signaled, as early as June 1961, their mutual desire to settle the Laotian issue through international guarantees of Laotian neutrality.[69] Because of this prior communication, Chinese reaction to the landing of U.S. combat troops in Thailand was surprisingly temperate by the day's standards. No formal protest or statement on the matter was made by the Chinese Foreign Ministry.[70] Government reaction was spelled out in greatest detail in a front page editorial in the official *Peking Daily* on May 19. Acknowledging Kennedy's objectives of "an effective cease-fire and prompt negotiations for a government of national union," the editorial correctly noted that the possibility of U.S. intervention in Laos turned on the future of the Laotian rightists: having entered Thailand "to shore up the Phoumi-Boun Oum group by deploying military forces in the Mekong area" and "failing to do so, it would carry out direct armed intervention and extend the Laotian war." (The Chinese interpreted another motive for U.S. landings as being in line with their view of U.S. capitalist imperialism— "armed occupation of Thailand.") But the editorial clearly signaled Peking's willingness to permit internal resolution of the Laotian civil war and reluctance to become involved militarily except as a response to U.S. military intervention in Laos.

We have always maintained that Laotian affairs must be settled by the Laotians themselves, that the affairs of the Southeast Asian countries must be settled by the people of these countries themselves, and that no foreign country should interfere. The Chinese people firmly oppose U.S. imperialist armed intervention in Laos, and absolutely cannot tolerate the establishment by U.S. imperialism in areas close to China of any new military bridgeheads directed against this country.[71]

Meanwhile, in Geneva, China demanded immediate and complete withdrawal of U.S. forces from the Thai-Lao border, but made no threats to boycott the sessions or refuse to sign any agreements reached at them.[72]

Acquiescing to U.S. operational objectives was, in fact, far easier for China than it was for the USSR. China's potential gains from the acces-

69. Lee, *Communist China's Policy Toward Laos*, pp. 72–96; Kenneth T. Young, *Negotiating with the Chinese Communists* (McGraw-Hill, 1968), pp. 248–49.

70. *New York Times*, May 19, 1962.

71. *Peking Review*, May 25, 1962.

72. Lee, *Communist China's Policy Toward Laos*, p. 88.

sion of a neutral Laotian government were considerable, while the likely costs of military escalation were ominous. Guarantees of neutrality would include the withdrawal of foreign military personnel and the termination of all external military relationships; this promised to remove Laos from the protective orbit of SEATO and thus weaken this long-resented anti-Chinese alliance. Further, a neutral government in Laos would probably mean an increase in the influence of the PRC vis-à-vis the USSR. Soviet military personnel, one of the major sources of Soviet influence over the Pathet Lao and the neutralists, would have to be withdrawn. Because of Laos' proximity to China, the PRC had the advantage in any peaceful competition to develop influence through economic and cultural ties. In a joint statement signed with Chinese Premier Chou En-lai, in April 1961, Souvanna had agreed to establish diplomatic, economic, and cultural relations with Peking. In January 1962 China had established a legal basis for ongoing involvement in Laos by agreeing with Souvanna on Chinese construction of a major road running from Mengala, China, to Phong Saly in northern Laos.[73]

The costs of major fighting in Laos, on the other hand, were potentially heavy for the PRC. China would find it extremely difficult to stand aloof from any major war on its southern border, and yet the Soviet move toward disengagement from Laos indicated that the USSR would be quite reluctant to lend major assistance there. In March 1962, when Chinese officials in Laos asked the Soviet ambassador for increased supplies for the Pathet Lao, the Soviet response was evasive.[74] Nor would China find it easy to conduct military operations in Laos. Only 25,000 Chinese troops were customarily stationed near Laos, and intervention in force would create formidable logistical problems because of the rugged terrain of both China's bordering Yunnan Province and northwestern Laos.[75] These factors had all contributed to China's careful avoidance of direct military involvement in Laos, even when Souvanna Phouma had personally requested the assistance of Chinese pilots in 1962.[76]

Thus, in terms of Chinese physical and economic well-being, as well as China's long-term influence over events in Laos, support for a neutral

73. *New York Times,* January 14, 1962.
74. Thee, *Notes of a Witness,* pp. 249–50.
75. *New York Times,* May 19, 1962.
76. Thee, *Notes of a Witness,* p. 245n.

government was preferable to all other avenues open to the PRC in May 1962.

The third target of U.S. military actions in May 1962 was the Democratic Republic of Vietnam (DRV). While American officials estimated that DRV soldiers constituted only 9,000 to 10,000 of the combined Communist and neutralist force of 35,000, these North Vietnamese soldiers were considered to be by far the best enemy troops. Washington felt it highly unlikely that any major fighting could continue in Laos without the active encouragement and support of Hanoi. North Vietnam had, in fact, founded the Pathet Lao organization, trained, armed, and developed it, and provided troops to assist its military operations. Souphanouvong, leader of the Pathet Lao, was married to a Vietnamese Communist party official, and had spent much of his life in Vietnam.[77] Field reports from Laos suggested that the attacks at and around Nam Tha in May 1962 had been led by North Vietnamese soldiers.[78]

The DRV's overriding interests in Laos were maintenance of a nonbelligerent government on its western border and continued, unhindered ability to utilize the Ho Chi Minh infiltration trails into South Vietnam, which ran through the jungles of eastern Laos and constituted the principal supply route to the Communist insurgents in the South. The eruption of the Laotian civil war in December 1960 had allowed North Vietnam to make major advances toward both of these goals. During the December 1960–May 1961 fighting before the cease-fire, the North Vietnamese and the Pathet Lao had been able to gain complete military control of eastern Laos, with its key points of access to South Vietnam.

By September 1961, all parties to the Laotian problem had agreed that a neutralist coalition government under Souvanna would succeed the former pro-American regime of Phoumi and Boun Oum. The Geneva negotiations during the last half of 1961 had resulted in technical compromises between the Communist and non-Communist delegates, which did not pose any serious challenge to these gains. The conference representatives had agreed that all foreign military personnel were to be with-

77. P. J. Honey, *Communism in North Vietnam: Its Role in the Sino-Soviet Dispute* (MIT Press, 1963), p. 93.
78. Hilsman, *To Move a Nation,* pp. 140–41. Later interviews by Paul Langer and Joseph Zasloff confirmed this. See their *North Vietnam and the Pathet Lao: Partners in the Struggle for Laos* (Harvard University Press, 1970), p. 78.

drawn from Laos, and that Laotian territory was not to be used as a corridor for aggression against other states (such as South Vietnam), but the authority and resources given to the International Control Commission to supervise and enforce these agreements were completely inadequate to prevent any discreet use of eastern Laos by North Vietnam.[79]

In late 1961 and early 1962, however, Phoumi showed signs of revitalizing the Royal Lao Army and reneging on his October 1961 pledge at Ban Hin Heup to join in a neutralist-dominated coalition government. His refusal to relinquish to Souvanna control of the police forces and of the Royal Lao Army, his massing of troops at Nam Tha, his military probes beyond the Nam Tha garrison, and his resistance to U.S. economic and political pressure all signaled challenges to the desirable status quo in Laos that the DRV had established in 1961 by force of arms. Furthermore, the Communists could not wholly discount the possibility that U.S. policy was shifting back to the offensive. In late March 1962, the Communists made the decision to apply new military pressure on Phoumi at Nam Tha, but to avoid a serious escalation of the war. As the Vietnamese and Pathet Lao explained privately, their strategy was "to aim at a vital and politically sensitive section of the front," "to destroy as much of enemy forces and material as possible," and "to retain a local character." The action was timed for the last days of the May dry season to preclude counterattack. The main objective was to force the rightists back to the coalition negotiations on terms favorable to the Pathet Lao.[80]

The attack on Nam Tha had succeeded beyond the expectations of the Vietnamese and Pathet Lao, and had aroused some discussion among the Communists as to whether or not their forces should push to the Mekong River, but American intervention in Thailand on behalf of a cease-fire and resumed tripartite talks provided whatever additional incentive was needed to induce the Communists to settle for their initial objective of obtaining a coalition government including Communist representation.[81] Cooperation promised to enhance North Vietnam's goals of influence both in Laos and South Vietnam. During the 1961–62 cease-fire, the DRV actively pursued a series of bilateral agreements with Souvanna

79. Ibid., pp. 79–80, 239; Lee, *Communist China's Policy Toward Laos,* pp. 80–86.
80. Thee, *Notes of a Witness,* p. 245.
81. Dommen, *Conflict in Laos,* p. 219.

Phouma's government in northern Laos that legitimated its increased involvement in the country: agreements on broadcasting (June 7), foreign training grants (July 13), commercial relations (July 13), exchange of payments (July 13), economic assistance (December 15), construction of roads (March 10), and Lao students in North Vietnam (March 10).[82] The North Vietnamese as well as the Pathet Lao were convinced that a neutral coalition government merely represented the first step toward eventual Communist control, but achieved through less provocative political means.[83] With the preliminary Geneva agreements as background, compliance with U.S. operational objectives promised to obtain removal of American and other SEATO personnel from Laos, while allowing the DRV to proceed with quiet use of the Ho Chi Minh trails. Negotiated neutrality would establish an important precedent in Southeast Asia, and Hanoi hoped to extend that precedent to future talks on the status of South Vietnam.[84] On the other hand, the DRV had much to lose by provoking U.S. intervention. Recognition of this prospect was reflected in the carefully controlled strategy designed for the Nam Tha assault. Escalation in Laos would strain relations with the USSR and the PRC, and would divert energy from the more immediate and important goal of communizing South Vietnam. At its most extreme, U.S. intervention might threaten the physical safety of North Vietnam itself.

The Laotian neutralists and Communists were not primary targets of the administration's military signaling after the capture of Nam Tha, because the Kennedy administration had concluded that any sustained Pathet Lao–neutralist offensive against the numerically superior Royal Lao Army was unlikely without active military leadership and material support from the USSR, North Vietnam, and China. The perception that the military strategy of the indigenous Laotian forces was determined by decisions reached in Moscow, Peking, and Hanoi had been strongly reinforced by Kennedy's 1961 success in arranging a Laotian cease-fire through direct diplomatic and military pressure on the USSR and by Khrushchev's subsequent confidential promise to guarantee Communist compliance with any neutralization agreements signed at Geneva.[85]

82. Ibid., pp. 212, 230.
83. Goldstein, *American Policy Toward Laos,* p. 270.
84. Thee, *Notes of a Witness,* pp. 249, 283–87.
85. Hall, "Crisis in Laos," pp. 51–78; Stevenson, *End of Nowhere,* pp. 164–66.

The fourth major target of American military signaling was the Thai government of Field Marshal Sarit Thanarat. As previously noted, Thailand's paramount security concern since the Communist victory in China had been the possible expansion of communism into the Mekong River valley of Laos and externally encouraged subversion among the Thai-Lao and Vietnamese living in northeastern Thailand near the Laotian border. Thailand's military alliance with the United States within SEATO had been the keystone of its strategy for combating these threats since 1954. While the Thai government was dismayed in 1961 by Kennedy's refusal to intervene militarily on behalf of the Phoumi-Boun Oum regime in Laos, it was strongly reassured in the spring of 1962 by the Rusk-Thanat communiqué promising U.S. defense of Thailand without regard for action taken by other SEATO members.

The U.S. increase of military forces in Thailand was designed to re-assure Sarit of the reliability of recent American security pledges, but there is no evidence to indicate that the Thai government sought such a dramatic gesture. Kennedy's decision on May 12 to deploy servicemen to Thailand was strictly a unilateral initiative of the U.S. government, which necessitated a last-minute, pro forma agreement by Marshal Sarit to a "Thai request" for such an American landing.[86] With 1,000 U.S. infantry-men already in Thailand as a result of SEATO's recent "Air Cobra" ex-ercises, and with another 1,000 U.S. military personnel present in Thailand with the Army Corps of Engineers and Military Assistance Advisory Group, Sarit apparently felt little need for further reassurance as to the American commitment to his nation's defense. While Thai officials were alarmed at the possibility of increased subversion in the northeast as a result of recent Communist gains in Laos, they did not consider the sta-tioning of U.S. combat troops in Thailand directly germane to this problem.

Bangkok's increased confidence in the reliability of the American de-fense commitment to Thailand had been indicated during the days before the fall of Nam Tha. In late April, at the urging of Harriman, Sarit had taken the important step of publicly throwing his influence behind a coalition government for Laos. Abandoning his prior position that a coalition under Souvanna Phouma would mean eventual Communist con-

86. Goldstein, *American Policy Toward Laos,* pp. 260, 270.

trol of Laos, Sarit officially announced on April 25—only hours before Laotian Premier Boun Oum's arrival in Bangkok—that a coalition should now be acceptable to all Lao parties:

> The United States has confirmed that it is the best solution. . . . The United States must have considered all reasons and circumstances before reaching such a decision. . . . If bad results follow this later . . . the United States will not deny its responsibility and might step in to solve the situation in time.[87]

After the loss of Nam Tha, which further convinced the Thai government that the Lao Army could not resist the Communists in serious fighting, Sarit brought pressure on his cousin Phoumi to drop his objections to participation in the proposed neutralist coalition.[88]

Despite Thailand's generally favorable reaction to the U.S. show of force, the Kennedy administration's desire to encourage multilateral participation proved to be an element of friction between Washington and Bangkok. The United States had long preferred the broadest possible military and political front in response to Asian security problems, but Thailand—after SEATO's failure to intervene in Laos in the spring of 1961—wished to dissociate American action from SEATO for fear that SEATO's chronic disunity might hinder U.S. response to some future threat to Thailand, or even provide a pretext for Washington's refusal to honor its pledges. It was with considerable reluctance, therefore, and only after five days of public and private pressure from American officials, that Sarit formally requested on May 21 the token military forces offered by Great Britain, Australia, and New Zealand.[89]

Third Party Behavior

Phoumi Nosavan had hoped that the defeat of his forces at Nam Tha and exaggerated claims of Communist advances would result in direct intervention by the United States, but the military debacle had the opposite effect, eliminating any remaining U.S. desire to support its ineffectual client.[90] Under the combined pressure of military defeat, continued eco-

87. *Christian Science Monitor*, April 25, 1962.
88. Thee, *Notes of a Witness*, p. 262.
89. *New York Times*, May 18 and 19, 1962; *Wall Street Journal*, May 17, 1962; *Christian Science Monitor*, May 21, 1962.
90. Thee, *Notes of a Witness*, p. 248.

nomic and political pressure from the Kennedy administration, and a clear signal that U.S. troops in Thailand would not assist the Lao Army, Phoumi capitulated to U.S. demands that he join the proposed Laotian coalition government on terms dictated by Souvanna Phouma.

Signs of Phoumi's new flexibility had emerged, in fact, before the defeat at Nam Tha. On May 3, three days before the battle, Souvanna Phouma was informed in Paris by American Ambassador to France James Gavin that Phoumi was now ready to resume coalition negotiations without insisting on keeping the defense and interior portfolios.[91] After their military defeat and the new ultimatums from Washington, Phoumi and Boun Oum cabled Souvanna in Paris on May 14 to indicate their willingness, "under certain conditions," to accept a coalition in which the key interior and defense ministries would be given to neutralists. While in Taiwan on May 15, Phoumi and Boun Oum publicly stated that they were willing to turn government control over to Souvanna, if he could "prove he is not working for the Communists." The support this shift in attitude gave to U.S. objectives was evident the next day, when Souphanouvong notified the International Control Commission that he was willing to reopen negotiations with the rightists and Souvanna Phouma.[92] On May 17, in response to a cable from Souvanna in Paris stating his willingness to return to Laos but "without conditions" alluded to by Phoumi and Boun Oum, the rightists reiterated their request for Souvanna's return and dropped all mention of prior "conditions" for participation in a coalition government.[93] On June 8, at the first full exchange of views among the three factions, Phoumi agreed to cede the portfolios of defense and interior as well as foreign affairs to Souvanna. The last major obstacle was cleared for formal signing of a coalition agreement on June 12.[94]

The United Kingdom, as a long-suffering advocate of a neutral Laos and as cochairman of the permanent Geneva Conference, functioned as a supportive and sympathetic American ally after Kennedy's shift to the need for U.S. disengagement from the political and military quagmire of Laos. The May 1961 cease-fire and reconvening of the Geneva Conference had originated from a *joint* U.K.-U.S. proposal presented to the

91. Ibid., p. 259.
92. *New York Times,* May 16 and 17, 1962.
93. *New York Times,* May 18, 1962.
94. Thee, *Notes of a Witness,* pp. 270–75.

USSR.[95] The confidential Pushkin Agreement of September 1961 had called for *British* responsibility for ensuring Western compliance with any international provisions negotiated at Geneva.[96] The United Kingdom had long been more resistant than the United States to being drawn into a Laotian war—even if this required turning a blind eye to North Vietnamese use of the Laotian corridor—but the potential new threat to Thailand posed by the fighting in May 1962 cast a new perspective on the problem for the United Kingdom, just as it did for the United States. As later recounted by then Prime Minister Harold Macmillan,

These threats to Thailand introduced a new complication and one in which the British Government was much more closely involved.

The defeat of the Laotian Government's forces at Nam Tha caused great alarm in Thailand. The way seemed to be open to an invasion by the Pathet Lao and their Communist supporters. Thailand, as a loyal member of the SEATO alliance, was entitled to support in case of need.[97]

In response to the U.S. request on May 16 for allied solidarity, Macmillan not only offered Thailand a token force of British jet fighters, but also recruited participation by other SEATO members as well.

I immediately informed both [Australian Prime Minister] Menzies and [New Zealand Prime Minister] Holyoake that if we received a formal request for help we would send a squadron of Hunters. Menzies replied very properly that Australia would be ready to send jets to Thailand if the Thais made a request, but he was most anxious that any action should be taken in the name of SEATO and the obligations under that treaty, even if some SEATO powers made no contribution. Holyoake made a similar reply. He was willing to send a small force of "jungle troops, transport freighters and perhaps a frigate." He added, with his usual good sense: "We appreciate that the objective is to show as many flags as possible in Thailand."[98]

When Sarit finally requested SEATO forces on May 21, these British, Australian, and New Zealand symbols of collective defense were dispatched to Thailand.

With the breakdown of the Laotian cease-fire and the apparent threat to Thailand, Macmillan rediscovered the urgency of a successful diplomatic resolution to the protracted war. "I felt much more anxious to press

95. Hall, "Crisis in Laos," p. 60.
96. Stevenson, *End of Nowhere,* pp. 164–65.
97. Macmillan, *At the End of the Day,* p. 241.
98. Ibid.

on with the Geneva Conference," he later recalled.[99] On May 9, only three days after the fall of Nam Tha, London's chief Geneva negotiator and High Commissioner for Southeast Asia, Malcolm MacDonald, arrived in Laos. Meeting with top officials of the Pathet Lao and the neutralists, he underscored the necessity of reestablishing the cease-fire, but at the same time relayed the message that Phoumi Nosavan now seemed ready to return to the negotiating table without insisting on the defense and interior portfolios. MacDonald also informed the leftists and neutralists that the United States promised to increase its pressure on Laos and Thailand to settle the war peacefully. The Pathet Lao informed MacDonald that there could be no return of the territory taken in recent fighting, but that coalition talks could resume if Phoumi demonstrated a sincere desire to negotiate. This information was relayed to the United States, and within a few days Washington decided to drop its initial demand for return to the status quo ante in Laos.[100]

Simultaneously, at the major power level, the United Kingdom reinforced U.S. efforts to enlist Soviet support for moving the participants back to the bargaining table. On May 8, in the first Western communication to the USSR regarding Nam Tha, the British and American ambassadors in Moscow met jointly with Foreign Minister Gromyko to stress their governments' concern for restabilizing the cease-fire.[101] The landing of U.S. troops in Thailand on May 15 was viewed by the Macmillan government as a logical complement to its own continuing search for a diplomatic solution. In prepared statements to Parliament that same day, the British foreign secretary and lord privy seal stressed the British hope that the USSR would use its influence privately to restore the cease-fire in Laos, and the British Foreign Office emphasized the government's support for the U.S. troop landings.[102] With the signing of the three-faction coalition agreement in Laos on June 12, Khrushchev cabled Macmillan: "I wish to express my satisfaction that the collaboration of the Governments of the USSR and Great Britain as the co-Chairmen of the Geneva Conference has played its own useful role in clearing the paths towards a peaceful solution of the Laos question."[103]

99. Ibid., p. 242.
100. Thee, *Notes of a Witness,* p. 261.
101. *New York Times,* May 9, 1962.
102. *New York Times,* May 16, 1962.
103. Macmillan, *At the End of the Day,* p. 243.

Outcomes

The Kennedy administration's immediate operational objectives were achieved after the defeat of the Laotian Army at Nam Tha. A cease-fire was reestablished, the long-sought three-faction coalition government was created and a fourteen-nation agreement on the permanent neutrality of Laos was formally ratified at Geneva on July 23, 1962. With respect to the specific targets of U.S. military signaling during this period, we have already noted the close conformity between actual Soviet behavior and that desired by the Kennedy administration. The USSR both publicly and privately reaffirmed its year-long support for a neutral coalition regime in Laos. Khrushchev publicly—and we can surmise privately—warned his fellow Communists against the dangers of provoking the United States to direct military intervention in Laos. In a note to Kennedy published on June 12, Khrushchev announced his complete satisfaction with the Laotian coalition agreement of that same day and his intended support during the coming months for the implementation of Laotian neutrality:

> The formation of a coalition Government of national unity of Laos opens the way toward completing in the near future the work done at the Geneva conference toward a peaceful settlement of the Laotian problem and giving life to the agreements worked out at that conference, which constitute a good basis for the development of Laos as a neutral and independent state. . . .
>
> I will avail myself of the occasion to express satisfaction over the fact that the mutual understanding we achieved [when] meeting in Vienna last June on the support of neutral and independent Laos begins to be translated into life.[104]

On July 23, the USSR initialed at Geneva the Declaration on the Neutrality of Laos, which pledged each of its fourteen signatories to:

1. Do nothing to impair the sovereignty, independence, neutrality, unity, or territorial integrity of Laos.

2. Refrain from direct or indirect interference in Laotian internal affairs.

3. Refrain from bringing Laos into a military alliance.

4. Respect Laotian wishes not to recognize the protection of any military alliance, including SEATO.

104. *New York Times,* June 13, 1962.

5. Refrain from introducing into Laos any military personnel.

6. Refrain from establishing in Laos any foreign military bases or strongpoints.

7. Refrain from using Laotian territory for interference in the internal affairs of other countries.

The behavior of the People's Republic of China after the fall of Nam Tha was also compatible with Kennedy's operational objectives. Reversing their behavior during the spring of 1961, when the Chinese openly encouraged the Pathet Lao and North Vietnamese to pursue their military superiority, Chinese leaders eschewed any such offensive rhetoric and instead confined themselves to warning the United States of the hazards of intervening in Laos. In an official Chinese statement issued the day after formation of the Laotian coalition government, Peking argued:

The development of the situation in Laos in the past year and more is convincing demonstration that the domestic aspect of the Laotian question can be settled reasonably only through peaceful consultations among the three political forces in Laos, and that no outside interference or attempts to impose one's will on others can succeed.[105]

On June 14, the *Peking Daily* printed an editorial stating that the new coalition government "will pave the way for completion of the work of the enlarged Geneva Conference and the realization of peace, independence and neutrality for Laos."[106] On July 23 China initialed the Declaration on the Neutrality of Laos at Geneva.

In the days immediately after the fall of Nam Tha, North Vietnam's behavior also supported Kennedy's short-term operational objectives. No major military battles occurred within Laos after May 6, although a few minor skirmishes took place on May 27 in northwest and southern Laos. In a private conversation with Souvanna Phouma in Hanoi on June 16, DRV Prime Minister Pham Van Dong stated that his government was "interested in easing Souvanna Phouma's tasks and would comply with any demands by the Laotian government." The only exception would be, he implied, use of the infiltration routes through Laos into South Vietnam, which he candidly admitted the DRV employed for moving "contacts and movement of cadres, not military units." Even this matter could be resolved, Pham Van Dong argued, with resolution of the Vietnam

105. *Peking Review,* June 15, 1962.
106. *Peking Daily* editorial, reprinted in *Peking Review,* June 15, 1962.

problem in the manner envisioned by the original 1954 Geneva accords.[107] On July 23 Hanoi joined the thirteen other Geneva participants in ratifying the Declaration on the Neutrality of Laos.

The responses of the principal parties involved in Laos in the final days before the Geneva accords have historical significance beyond peaceful resolution of a minor military incident. U.S. actions represented in microcosm the general Kennedy administration response to the Communist threat in Southeast Asia: continued disengagement, with minimized costs, from the weak and relatively defenseless country of Laos, with simultaneous establishment of new and harder battlelines in the stronger nations of Thailand and South Vietnam. In May 1961, after reluctantly forgoing a military intervention in Laos to rescue the inept, pro-American regime of Phoumi and Boun Oum, Kennedy countered with a broad new commitment against further Communist gains in South Vietnam. In what the Pentagon Papers described as post-Laotian crisis reassurance of U.S. allies, on May 11, 1961, the White House secretly ordered 500 American military advisers to South Vietnam, a campaign of clandestine warfare against the North by CIA-trained South Vietnamese agents, and a doubling of U.S. military assistance to Vietnam.[108] While continuing with Laotian disengagement in the spring of 1962 through attempts to coerce the Laotian rightists into a coalition government, the administration mollified the troubled Thai government with the Rusk-Thanat communiqué. With U.S. perception of threats to both the face-saving Laotian disengagement and the new security pledges to Thailand resulting from Nam Tha's capture, the temporary dispatch of 5,000 U.S. servicemen to Thailand became another episode in a series of similar retrenchments.

The events of May and June were particularly fateful for American–North Vietnamese relations. The apparent Soviet assistance in urging the North Vietnamese to halt military operations reinforced in the minds of American decisionmakers the conviction that the USSR could be induced and had the power to influence Hanoi to call off military operations elsewhere, including South Vietnam. This conviction had first emerged in the American perception of Southeast Asia in May 1961, when the USSR

107. Ibid.
108. Neil Sheehan and others, *The Pentagon Papers* (Bantam Books, 1971), pp. 87–93.

had helped by urging North Vietnam to accept the initial Laotian cease-fire. In drawing this conclusion, the Kennedy administration—as well as two succeeding American administrations—would badly underestimate North Vietnam's freedom of maneuver. Then, too, this misguided conviction failed to give adequate weight to the great psychological importance of South Vietnam to Hanoi or the conclusions the North Vietnamese themselves would draw from their relations with the USSR. "This Soviet pressure, which was later viewed as a source of shame by the proud Vietnamese, made Hanoi *less* rather than *more* likely to let its actions be influenced by the Russians again."[109]

In fact, North Vietnam's conclusions on the utility of military operations in pursuit of political objectives, as drawn from the Laotian experience, most closely approximated those of China. From Peking's point of view, the last months before the Geneva accords constituted additional evidence that nothing was ever achieved at the conference table without struggle on the battlefield. Only when the U.S. "imperialists" and their Laotian "reactionaries" had suffered military defeat were they forced to accept the Geneva agreements.[110] China's conclusions did not, however, foreshadow any increased desire to become directly involved in the military events in Southeast Asia or any decreased wariness about military confrontation with the United States. In succeeding years, as in 1962, China remained satisfied with its indirect influence through Hanoi.

The events of May and June 1962 had more peaceful implications for future relations with the USSR. For Khrushchev, resolution of the Laos dilemma represented both the fruits of negotiations with the United States dating from spring 1961, and a major victory for his strategy of peaceful coexistence in a world of nuclear weapons. Hope for similar peaceful outcomes was voiced in his June 13 note to Kennedy:

> The example of Laos indicates that provided there is desire to resolve difficult international problems on the basis of cooperation with mutual account of the interests of all sides, such cooperation bears its fruit.
>
> At the same time, the results achieved in the settlement of the Laotian problem strengthen the conviction that success in solving other international problems which now divide states and create tension in the world can be achieved on the same road as well.

109. Arthur J. Dommen, "Laos: The Contest of Wills," *Current History*, vol. 61 (December 1971), p. 352.

110. Lee, *Communist China's Policy Toward Laos*, pp. 92–93.

As to the Soviet Government, it has always adhered, as it does now, to this line, which in present conditions is the only correct policy in international affairs according with the interests of peace.[111]

In spite of the October missile crisis—set in motion by Soviet decisions made in March—the events in Laos were symbolic of both improving relations between the USSR and the United States and the growing ideological rift between Soviet peaceful revolution and Chinese armed struggle. In compliance with the Geneva accords, the USSR withdrew from Laos the 500 military technicians it had had there since early 1961. During the following years, and despite renewed Laotian warfare that led to the covert reintroduction of U.S. forces, the USSR scrupulously adhered to the Geneva agreements and maintained proper diplomatic relations with the U.S.-supported government of Souvanna Phouma.[112]

The impact of the U.S. troop landings was perhaps greatest on American-Thai relations. As an action justified in terms of the March 1962 Rusk-Thanat communiqué, the response both reinforced the credibility of U.S. pledges and, more significant, provided a major boost to the creeping U.S. commitment to Thailand. Despite the gradual withdrawal of U.S. combat troops from Thailand between July and November, the military relationship between the two nations had been altered. As American Ambassador Young later described the situation, "the United States, in agreement with the Government of Thailand, made arrangements to leave all the necessary combat and logistic equipment ready in Thailand for another deployment."[113] When fighting broke out in Laos in May 1963, and again in May 1964, the United States moved its Seventh Fleet into the South China Sea and seriously considered combat deployments to Thailand.[114] By 1965 the American commitment had progressed to include a confidential U.S.-Thai Contingency Plan for U.S. defense of Thailand against military invasion, despite the absence of any congressionally ratified bilateral defense treaty between the two nations.[115]

111. *New York Times,* June 13, 1962
112. Stevenson, *End of Nowhere,* pp. 190–93; *United States Security Agreements and Commitments Abroad: Kingdom of Laos,* pt. 2, Hearings, pp. 403–19.
113. Kenneth T. Young, Jr., *The Southeast Asia Crisis* (Oceana Publications, 1966), p. 54.
114. Stevenson, *End of Nowhere,* pp. 182, 192–93, 201.
115. *United States Security Agreements and Commitments Abroad: Kingdom of Thailand,* pt. 3, Hearings, pp. 653–56, 666, 680–81, 747.

The increasing U.S. commitment to the defense of Thailand and the escalating Vietnam War eventually led the Johnson administration to abandon Kennedy's distinction between the military defense of Thailand and direct U.S. defense of non-Communist Laos. By June 1964 the Johnson administration had embraced Thailand's preference for a policy of full participation in the Laotian fighting. The United States began a secret air war over Laos conducted from Thai airfields, and reintroduced U.S. and Thai army personnel into the Royal Lao Army. By 1969 the cost to the United States of participation in the secret war in Laos had reached an annual $500 million, and Thailand had 5,000 "volunteers" on Laotian soil.[116]

The dispatch of U.S. combat troops to Thailand in May 1962 constituted an interesting benchmark in the accumulation of presidential war powers in Southeast Asia. In April 1961, when faced with the decision of whether or not to commit U.S. troops into Laos as a means of deterring further fighting, Kennedy had consulted congressional leaders from both political parties at some length.[117] In May 1962, however, when faced with a comparable choice of whether or not to send combat troops to Thailand, with the possibility of their becoming involved in fighting, Kennedy reached his decision without congressional consultation.[118] On the day the troops landed in Thailand the President briefed congressional leaders on the decision he had taken three days earlier. It is equally noteworthy that this unilateral exercise of war power did not prompt a single negative statement by a member of Congress on presidential usurpation of authority, to judge from the *Congressional Record* or principal metropolitan newspapers.

The landing of U.S. troops in Thailand had a marginal but positive influence on both public and congressional attitudes toward Kennedy. In a random survey of 200 Americans, the *Wall Street Journal* found Kennedy's action had "overwhelming support." At the same time, the newspaper found that

many feel the stand in Thailand against the Communists must not be extended into neighboring Laos, which is considered less defensible. And even people in

116. *Far Eastern Economic Review,* October 9, 1969, pp. 124–25; Victor Marchetti and John D. Marks, *The CIA and the Cult of Intelligence* (Knopf, 1974), p. 62.
117. See Joseph Alsop, "Beginning of an Ending," *Washington Post,* February 19, 1962.
118. *Time,* May 25, 1962, p. 22.

favor of some action in Laos generally concede there is no point in trying to recover the areas currently controlled by the Reds.

About 20 percent of the more than 200 people interviewed were vague about the issues involved in the crisis.[119]

Support for Kennedy's attempt to avoid direct U.S. intervention in Laos held firm within Congress after the fall of Nam Tha. Floor criticism was confined to the more conservative members of the Republican party, and their complaints faded quickly after U.S. troops moved into Thailand. But the movement of U.S. combat troops in and out of Thailand had little lasting political influence. Its impact on the congressional elections of 1962 was soon swamped by the more emotional and important issue of U.S. policy toward Cuba.

In retrospect, it now seems clear that a Kennedy decision *not* to move U.S. troops to Thailand would have had little effect on the outcome of the military incident in Laos or the signing of the Geneva accords. North Vietnam, China, and the USSR—each for its own reasons—at least temporarily supported a political settlement of this international problem. Thailand would not have been noticeably dismayed by U.S. failure to dispatch combat forces. The Sarit regime had not sought such military action; recent diplomatic reassurances combined with the 2,000 American soldiers already in Thailand constituted ample evidence of the U.S. defensive commitment. Nor did Thailand perceive the direct relevance of U.S. combat to its most pressing concern of Communist insurgency. It now seems evident that the absence of a bold military response would not have posed a domestic political threat to the Kennedy administration either. The partisan impact of Laos turned on Kennedy's ability to prevent a total and highly visible military conquest by the Pathet Lao–Vietnamese forces. Because of the Communist nations' commitment to a neutral coalition government, the partisan threat was in fact a chimera. Kennedy had paid his political price in 1961 when he openly redirected U.S. policy toward Laotian neutrality. By May 1962, as the *Wall Street Journal* survey indicated, the American public had become highly sophisticated in discerning the advisability of defending Thailand rather than Laos.

In retrospect, it does not seem likely that introduction of U.S. combat forces into the Mekong River valley of Laos—the maximum military response seriously contemplated by Kennedy—would have materially

119. *Wall Street Journal*, May 18, 1962.

altered the eventual outcome of the incident. As the State Department had calculated in May 1962, Communist forces in Laos and reserves in North Vietnam and China would have attacked U.S. forces only in response to a clear attempt to *recapture* territory already lost.[120] Introduction of U.S. troops might have complicated quick formation of a Laotian coalition regime—because of heightened suspicions of the United States by the Communist nations and/or renewed stubbornness on the part of the Laotian rightists—but the prevailing international unanimity as to the wisdom of temporary neutralization made probable an eventual political settlement short of war. Had the introduction of U.S. troops into Laos permanently prevented completion of the Geneva accords, the likely effect would have been to accelerate the movement toward the de facto partition of the country that emerged in 1963 when the coalition government collapsed. U.S. military action in Laos short of combat with Communist soldiers would not have had an appreciable effect on American-Thai relations or on Kennedy's partisan fortunes beyond that which occurred as a result of the actual introduction of U.S. combat forces in Thailand.

Evaluation

Despite the apparent success of the movement of U.S. troops into Thailand in May 1962—the reestablishment of the cease-fire, the formation of a neutralist-led coalition government, and the eventual ratification of the Geneva accords on Laos—a careful analysis of the events indicates that the use of American armed forces had little influence on the outcome of the incident. Before the attack by Communist forces on General Phoumi Nosavan's troops at Nam Tha, Vietnamese, Chinese, and Pathet Lao officials had agreed to a highly limited military strategy designed to reactivate the long-stalled coalition negotiations. The limited nature of the Communists' objective is manifest in their failure to pursue further military action after the fall of Nam Tha and *before* the landing of U.S. troops in Thailand—that is, between May 6 and May 15. This unexpected opportunity did prove enticing for the Pathet Lao leaders, who had most to gain from toppling the Boun Oum-Phoumi regime. "In Vientiane six

120. Hilsman, *To Move a Nation,* p. 143.

months later, Souphanouvong revealed that a difference of opinion had existed within the NLHS Central Committee as to whether the Pathet Lao should press all the way to the Mekong after the collapse of Phoumist resistance."[121] But it is also clear that any such decision in favor of a larger military campaign would have stimulated significant counter-pressure from the USSR and possibly China and North Vietnam, all of which were both publicly and privately committed—at least tempo-rarily—to the establishment of a neutral government.

Phoumi's new flexibility on the terms of coalition government was not the result of American military action. By early May 1962 U.S. political and economic pressures against Vientiane were on the verge of success. As previously noted, three days *before* the fall of Nam Tha, the United States informed Souvanna Phouma that Phoumi was ready to drop his insistence on control of the defense and interior ministries. Whatever political intransigence Phoumi still retained on May 3 was quickly swept away three days later by the ignominious defeat of his soldiers at Nam Tha. Communist armed forces—not American combat troops—provided the final leverage needed to crush the rightists. In fact, a principal con-cern during U.S. troop landings in Thailand was the possibility that Phoumi might find in this action grounds for *reasserting* his independence from U.S. policy. U.S. military action was in this respect a *threat to,* rather than a support for, the complex political formula required to accomplish Kennedy's operational objectives.

In sum, Kennedy's ability to nudge the Laotian war toward a tempo-rary solution acceptable to the United States can be ascribed to political, military, and economic action taken *before* May 15, and not to the actual landing of American combat troops in neighboring Thailand. Available evidence does not suggest that this U.S. military action endangered the successful conclusion of the Geneva accords in July 1962, but the possi-bility remained that U.S. officials had found proof of the utility of a particular military action where, in fact, none existed.

In the light of the concerns and interests motivating Kennedy during the May 1962 episode, the policymaking process by which the President reached his decision appears to have been oddly incomplete. During the days preceding the decision of May 12 no serious consultations were held with the Thai government to determine *if* Sarit desired such a show of

---

121. Dommen, *Conflict in Laos*, p. 219.

force or *if* he considered it germane to the credibility of recent U.S. defense pledges. The available *hard* military intelligence did not imply the need for such action. As Hilsman himself notes, U.S. intelligence from Laos showed "no further troop movement" in the days after Nam Tha, despite Vientiane's exaggerated claims to the contrary.[122] Whatever Kennedy's personal concern about domestic political sentiment, he chose to consult only with Eisenhower—who privately recommended a strong military signal—rather than to conduct a more comprehensive canvass of prevailing political opinion.[123] In the end, the decision to land U.S. troops hinged heavily on the strongly advocated Harriman-Hilsman calculation—which now appears to have been in error—that "unless the United States responded promptly and effectively, the Communist side would be encouraged to step up their military effort."[124]

If the utility of U.S. military action in May 1962 can be strongly questioned, the broader intent of this armed response deserves higher praise. Kennedy was cognizant—probably more so than any of his principal advisers—of the limited utility of any show of force and the possible concessions that he might be forced to make to achieve his operational objectives. Even if Communist forces had continued to advance in the weeks after Nam Tha, it is unlikely that Kennedy would have ordered U.S. intervention until the capital of Vientiane was directly threatened. In March 1961 Kennedy had confided this fact to Arthur Schlesinger and Walter Lippmann.[125] Kennedy's extreme care on May 15 to commit the United States only to the defense of Thailand reflected his determination to avoid inflexible obligations to the defense of Laos. Military action was to be employed—as it had been by the Communists—only to reactivate stalled negotiations, even if this required additional military losses.

Kennedy's overriding objective in Laos remained, as it had been since May 1961, the establishment of a negotiated neutralist coalition—whatever its uncertain affiliation and effectiveness—which would permit the United States an honorable retreat from a strategically weak position. In 1961 some optimistic administration officials had thought of the accession of a neutral government as an effective means of denying North Vietnam use of the Ho Chi Minh trails into the South. By May 1962

122. Hilsman, *To Move a Nation,* p. 141.
123. Ibid., pp. 144–45.
124. Ibid., p. 141.
125. Schlesinger, *A Thousand Days,* pp. 331–32.

Kennedy and his principal advisers were much more realistic. Shortly before the October 7, 1962, deadline for foreign withdrawal of troops from Laos, when the International Control Commission had counted only forty departing North Vietnamese, Harriman told Kennedy that matters were going "just about as unsatisfactorily as we expected."[126] By 1962 Kennedy retained few illusions about the likely costs of political compromise over Laos. When the tripartite coalition government disintegrated in 1963, leaving Souvanna Phouma's neutralists as well as Phoumi Nosavan's rightists allied with the United States, the outcome represented an unexpected victory for Kennedy's strategy, which helped to stabilize the military balance in Laos until 1969.[127]

THE INDO-PAKISTANI WAR OF 1971

IN 1947 the Asian subcontinent, which now consists of India, Pakistan, and Bangladesh, was partitioned into the two sovereign states of India and Pakistan. Pakistan comprised the territory of West Pakistan, on the northwestern border of India, and the separate territory of East Pakistan, located 1,000 miles to the east and encircled by eastern India. The division into states had been made on the basis of divergent religious and cultural nationalities, with both East and West Pakistan ruled by Muslims, and India by Hindus.

Since 1947 the two nations have waged three major wars against each other. In 1947 and again in 1965, fighting occurred over control of the state of Kashmir, which lies between northwestern India and West Pakistan. When Kashmir's Hindu maharaja ceded authority over his predominantly Muslim nation to India in 1947, Pakistan and India went to war. The fighting ended with Kashmir temporarily partitioned along a cease-fire line supervised by UN forces. In 1965 a second inconclusive war for Kashmir occurred.[128]

The Indo-Pakistani war of 1971 concerned principally the territory of East Pakistan—now independent Bangladesh. Political tension had existed between East and West Pakistan since 1947. West Pakistan had

126. Stevenson, *End of Nowhere*, p. 179.
127. Ibid., pp. 180–221.
128. William Barnds, *India, Pakistan, and the Great Powers* (Praeger, 1972), pp. 38–43.

a history of firm control by a traditional Muslim plutocracy. Political and social events in East Pakistan were increasingly influenced by the Bengali-speaking Muslim middle class of professionals and merchants. The Bengalis of East Pakistan increasingly saw themselves as the victims of economic exploitation by the West, the traditional seat of political authority. Trade between the two was one-sided, the East typically supplying raw and semiprocessed materials to the West, while repurchasing finished products. Legal restrictions on the foreign purchase of competitive finished products and an overvalued national currency contributed to the East's large trade deficit with the West. What foreign exchange was earned from Eastern exports was centrally managed in the Western capital of Islamabad and used largely to finance foreign imports to West Pakistan. These factors, coupled with the West's superior geography, climate, and educational system, led to a widening economic gap between the two regions.[129] In 1960, the per capita income of West Pakistan was 32 percent higher than that of the East; by 1970, the West's per capita income stood 61 percent higher. By 1970, the fragile political and religious ties between the Bengali-dominated East and Punjabi-dominated West were rapidly disintegrating.

The national elections held in December 1970 caused the decisive break between the two regions. In March 1969, after months of domestic agitation against the decade-old military dictatorship of General Ayub Khan, a military coup brought to power General Yahya Khan, who promised eventual civilian rule and a more equitable social order. In the December 1970 National Assembly elections the Awami League party, headed by Bengali nationalist leader Sheikh Mujib Rahman, unexpectedly won all but two of the East's allotted seats. The Awami League's platform included political autonomy for the East within a highly decentralized Pakistani federal structure. The election results thus constituted a political disaster for both Yahya Kahn and Ali Bhutto, leader of the West's majority Pakistan People's party. Bhutto persuaded Yahya to postpone temporarily the National Assembly, which was scheduled to convene in March. Mujib responded with a general strike and a campaign of civil disobedience in the East. Amidst political wrangling over the date and location for convening the National Assembly, West Pakistani troops

129. Pran Chopra, *India's Second Liberation* (MIT Press, 1974), pp. 64–65; William J. Barnds, "Pakistan's Disintegration," *The World Today*, vol. 27 (August 1971), pp. 319–29.

were secretly airlifted to the East. By March 25, when Yahya announced that the opening of the assembly had been indefinitely postponed, some 40,000 pro-government armed forces were in the East.

On the evening of March 25, after a day of bloody military battles between Bengali nationalists and West Pakistani units, Sheikh Mujib was arrested for treason. While Bengali liberation radios proclaimed the new independent state of Bangladesh, Yahya Khan ordered the forcible reimposition of political order in the East. Despite international protests by India, the USSR, and other nations about widespread West Pakistani atrocities against the Bengalis, by mid-April formal military resistance within East Pakistan had been temporarily suppressed. The nucleus of a large Bengali guerrilla army, however, had safely crossed into neighboring India. In Calcutta, capital of the Indian state of West Bengal, the escaped deputy leader of the Awami League established a provisional government-in-exile for Bangladesh.[130]

From March to December 1971 the Pakistani civil war was marked by the deaths of some one million East Pakistani civilians and increasing Bengali guerrilla warfare against the occupying troops from the West. As the death toll mounted, some 10 million Bengalis fled for safety to the Indian states bordering East Pakistan. This massive influx of refugees placed a severe financial burden on India—despite international relief assistance—and increased India's stakes in the outcome of the civil war. New Delhi provided increasing economic and military assistance to the Mukti Bahini, the Bangladesh freedom fighters, operating from Indian soil. In October, Pakistani armed forces moved up to the India–East Pakistan border in an effort to control infiltration by the Mukti Bahini. In response, India concentrated regular military forces in strength in the frontier zones along the East Pakistan–India border. By November, border confrontations—mortaring and shelling, tank engagements, and jet aircraft duels—between Pakistani and Indian troops along the eastern border had become frequent.

In the months before the war both India and Pakistan attempted to consolidate their international support. On August 9 India officially concluded a twenty-year Treaty of Peace, Friendship, and Cooperation with the USSR. Late in October, Prime Minister Indira Gandhi began a six-nation tour of Europe and the United States designed to communicate

130. Robert Jackson, *South Asian Crisis: India, Pakistan, and Bangladesh* (Praeger, 1975), pp. 21–38.

the gravity and urgency of the refugee problem and to demonstrate that the new Indo-Soviet treaty had not altered India's professed international neutrality. Simultaneously, Ali Bhutto led a senior delegation of Pakistani leaders to Peking to obtain an increased commitment from the People's Republic of China (PRC) to Pakistan in the event of war with India. At the United Nations Pakistan pressed for the establishment of an international peacekeeping force along the India–East Pakistan border as a means of protecting East Pakistan, but the USSR blocked such efforts within the Security Council.[131]

On December 3, in an apparent attempt to defend the beleaguered East through offsetting territorial gains in the West or by inducing the great powers to impose peace along the Bangladesh border to obviate a full-scale international war, Pakistan launched a major air and ground offensive on Indian military forces stationed along the West Pakistan–India border. In response, India quickly settled for a defensive military strategy in the West but a decisive, liberating military offensive against Pakistani units in the East. On December 5 the United States began attempts to obtain a cease-fire resolution in the UN Security Council; the USSR twice vetoed such proposals. India extended diplomatic recognition to the new, independent state of Bangladesh on December 6; Pakistan immediately terminated diplomatic relations with India. On December 8 the UN General Assembly approved a resolution calling for an immediate cease-fire and withdrawal of armed forces to their own sides of the border, but Yahya Khan's hopes that the great powers would collectively intervene to stop the war did not materialize. Late on December 10, in a move designed to signal U.S. resistance to any Indian military offensive against West Pakistan, the United States dispatched a ten-ship naval task force from the Seventh Fleet off South Vietnam toward the Bay of Bengal. This late military action by U.S. armed forces proved counterproductive. By December 15, when the task force reached the Bay of Bengal, India had already eliminated Pakistani military resistance in the East, established an air and sea blockade isolating East Pakistan, and unilaterally chosen to confine its attention in the West to the long-disputed territory of Kashmir. The effects of U.S. military action were to prompt precautionary military countermeasures by India, intensify Indian animosity toward the United States, increase Indian-Russian diplomatic

131. Ibid., pp. 55–105.

and military cooperation, and encourage Pakistani leaders to delay the transfer of power in the East to Bengali nationalists.

After thirteen days of fighting in Bangladesh the Pakistani army surrendered on December 16. On December 17, Indian Prime Minister Indira Gandhi declared a unilateral cease-fire along the stalemated West Pakistan front. Gandhi's order was reciprocated that same day by Pakistani President Yahya Khan.[132]

In January 1972 the United States withdrew its naval task force from the Indian Ocean. The United States recognized the new state of Bangladesh on April 4, 1972, but American diplomatic, economic, and military pressure on India during the December 1971 war left U.S. relations with India tense and difficult during the years that followed.

U.S. Behavior

The behavior of the U.S. government during the 1971 Indo-Pakistani war was dictated by both the very personal concerns of President Richard M. Nixon and the broader strategic threat to the United States posed by the possible disintegration of the nation of Pakistan. U.S. favoritism toward Pakistan before and during the December war was to some extent an extension of Nixon's own affective relationships with the warring nations. His antipathy toward India dated from the Eisenhower administration's negative appraisal of India's international neutrality in the cold war and from Nixon's indifferent receptions in that country while vice president.[133] During the 1960 presidential campaign the Indian press had endorsed the candidacy of John Kennedy. On a private trip to India soon after his narrow loss to Kennedy, Nixon felt insulted by the meager attention given him by the Indian government. His relations with Prime Minister Gandhi had always been cool. When Nixon met briefly with Gandhi on his 1967 global tour, the Indian prime minister could "scarcely conceal her boredom with her visitor."[134] Visiting New York in October 1970 for the United Nations' twenty-fifth anniversary celebration, Gandhi declined Nixon's invitation to dinner at the White House with scant

132. Ibid., pp. 106–45.
133. Eisenhower, *Waging Peace*, pp. 110–14.
134. Krishan Bhatia, *Indira: A Biography of Prime Minister Gandhi* (Praeger, 1974), p. 250.

explanation. During her state visit to Washington in November 1971, a month before the war, Gandhi contributed to an already tense atmosphere by refusing Nixon's request to pull back Indian troops from the East Pakistan border. She then criticized administration policy on the Bengali refugees at a White House reception to which Nixon had invited several of his vocal congressional opponents.[135]

Nixon's coolness toward India was in marked contrast to his warm feelings for Pakistan. He, more than any other senior member of the Eisenhower administration, had advocated U.S. arms assistance to Pakistan in 1954. On his private visits to Pakistan after his 1960 election defeat and again in 1967, he was accorded lavish and friendly welcomes. Meeting Pakistani President Yahya Khan in August 1969, Nixon asked Yahya to serve as a "courier" between Washington and Peking, to explore the Chinese leaders' reactions to Nixon's tentative moves to improve Sino-American relations. Yahya's successful service as the White House's secret channel to Peking between August 1969 and July 1971, when Henry Kissinger stopped in Pakistan on his way to China, steadily increased Nixon's appreciation of and debt to him. In Washington on October 25, 1970, Nixon observed to Yahya that "nobody has occupied the White House who is friendlier to Pakistan than me."[136]

China's diplomatic alignment with Pakistan and against India—dating from the 1962 Chinese-Indian border war—provided Nixon additional personal incentive for favoring Pakistan during the Indo-Pakistani war. The President's opening toward China was crucial both to his vision of a new, more complex international balance of power orchestrated from Washington and to his domestic political claim to superiority as an international statesman. During the months after Nixon's July 15 announcement that he would make his historic first visit to Peking, the administration devoted extraordinary efforts to avoiding any possible barriers to successful completion of the trip. Provocative U.S. intelligence operations were suspended. Kissinger returned to Peking during the week of October 20–26 to resolve remaining technical details. On October 25, with Kissinger still in Peking, the U.S. government stood aloof while the United

135. Ibid., pp. 250–54; Henry Brandon, *The Retreat of American Power* (Doubleday, 1973), pp. 259–61.
136. Quoted by G. W. Choudhury, "Reflections on Sino-Pakistan Relations," *Pacific Community,* vol. 7 (January 1976), p. 266. The most detailed accounts of Yahya Khan's role as Nixon's China courier are Choudhury's article, and Marvin Kalb and Bernard Kalb, *Kissinger* (Little, Brown, 1974), pp. 223–44.

Nations evicted Taiwan from its seat in the UN General Assembly. Only five days before the full-scale outbreak of the Indo-Pakistani war, the New China News Agency officially announced agreement to February 21 as the date for Nixon's arrival in China. When the war broke out on the subcontinent on December 3, it logically followed that the administration would be heavily influenced by its desire to avoid any last-minute strain in relations with China—suggesting a U.S. policy favoring China's ally Pakistan.[137]

The personal attitudes aroused by the combatants and the war's sensitive relationship to the coming China visit made Nixon take extra care to be sure that his subordinates were clear as to the general direction he wished U.S. policy to take. As assistant to the President for national security affairs, Henry Kissinger informed the National Security Council's Washington Special Action Group (WSAG) on December 3, the day war began,

I am getting hell every half hour from the President that we are not being tough enough on India. He has just called me again. He does not believe we are carrying out his wishes. He wants to tilt in favor of Pakistan.[138]

The Indo-Pakistani war, however, engaged fundamental strategic interests of the U.S. government transcending Nixon's attitudes toward the combatants or his rapprochement with the PRC, and these fundamental concerns became increasingly important to all senior officials—Nixon and Kissinger included—when India seemed assured a quick victory in the East. By December the White House had already conceded India's and the Mukti Bahini's success in Bangladesh; as Kissinger noted at the WSAG meeting on December 4, "Everyone knows how all this will come out and everyone knows that India will ultimately occupy East Pakistan."[139] But at the next WSAG meeting on December 6 the Nixon-Kissinger fear of an even more profound shift in the world balance of power was evident. If it achieved a military victory in the East, the White House wondered, would India shift its forces from East to West, assume the offensive, and seize large portions of West Pakistan from its traditional rival? According to Marvin and Bernard Kalb, Kissinger

believed that if Pakistan were to disintegrate under Indian economic and military pressure, then India would completely dominate the subcontinent, Soviet

137. Kalb and Kalb, *Kissinger,* pp. 252–55.
138. Jackson, *South Asian Crisis,* p. 213.
139. Ibid., p. 217.

influence would skyrocket, the strategic balance would be disrupted, China would become alarmed, and a major war, involving the big powers, could erupt.[140]

At the WSAG meeting on December 6 Kissinger alerted the departmental officers to the fact that "it is quite obvious that the President is not inclined to let the Paks be defeated."[141] At the next meeting of WSAG, on December 8, Kissinger articulated the White House strategic perception:

If the Indians smash the Pak air force and the armored forces [in the West] we would have a deliberate Indian attempt to force the disintegration of Pakistan. The elimination of the Pak armored and air forces would make the Paks defenseless. It would turn West Pakistan into a client state.[142]

In the light of the White House's affective, political, and strategic stakes in the viability of an autonomous Pakistan, the administration quickly adopted as its principal objective a policy of deterring India from taking offensive military action against West Pakistan. This approach encountered minor opposition from other senior U.S. officials. Assistant Secretary of State for Near Eastern and East Asian Affairs Joseph Sisco was frank in questioning the necessity for U.S. deterrence. At the important WSAG session on December 8, Sisco tactfully parried Kissinger's contention that India might be attempting "to force the disintegration of Pakistan." According to minutes of the session,

Mr. Sisco stated that if the situation were to evolve as Dr. Kissinger had indicated then, of course, there was a serious risk to the viability of West Pakistan. Mr. Sisco doubted, however, that the Indians had this as their objective. He indicated that [Indian] Foreign Minister Singh told [American] Ambassador Keating that India had no intention of taking any Pak territory. Mr. Sisco said it must also be kept in mind that Kashmir is really disputed territory.[143]

But Sisco found little overt support for his doubts among other senior officials. Only Deputy Defense Secretary David Packard reinforced Sisco, and then on the basis of the likely effectiveness of the Nixon-Kissinger deterrence policy, rather than on the more fundamental issue of India's true intentions.

Mr. Packard stated that the overriding consideration is the practical problem of either doing something effective or doing nothing. If you don't win, don't

140. Kalb and Kalb, *Kissinger,* p. 258.
141. Jackson, *South Asian Crisis,* p. 223.
142. Ibid., p. 226.
143. Ibid.

get involved. If we were to attempt something it would have to be with a certainty that it would affect the outcome. Let's not get in if we know we are going to lose. Find some way to stay out.[144]

Outside of Washington the major critic of U.S. involvement on the side of Pakistan was, to no one's surprise, American Ambassador to India Kenneth B. Keating. Throughout the war, in a stream of cables to Washington, Keating urged a policy of "genuine neutrality" and reported that U.S. covert favoritism was "having no appreciable effect on Yahya and was confusing the Indians."[145] But Keating's efforts were partially offset by comparably impassioned pro-Pakistani appraisals forwarded to Washington by U.S. Ambassador to Pakistan Joseph Farland.

In general, however, the principal actions of the U.S. government during the war were dictated by Nixon and Kissinger. During the months preceding November, most senior State Department officials had been preoccupied by the seemingly more important issues east and west of the subcontinent. Sisco and his bureau personnel had themselves been largely absorbed with Secretary of State William P. Rogers' attempt to carve out a role as a constructive mediator in the explosive Middle East. Planning within the National Security Council (NSC) system had been dominated by the negotiated withdrawal of U.S. forces from Vietnam and the diplomatic breakthrough with China. When the December war broke out, decisionmaking was quickly centralized at the top of the NSC system, where Nixon and Kissinger were able to dominate discussion and options. The continuous series of WSAG meetings "served as a mechanism both to legitimize the 'tilt' policy formulated by Nixon and Kissinger and to ensure White House policy was understood by those officials responsible for implementing various manifestations of the tilt."[146]

Before, and to a lesser extent during, the fourteen-day December war, congressional and public opinion narrowed the magnitude of executive discretion—particularly with respect to U.S. policy as formally declared. Since 1967, because of the constant tension between India and Pakistan, an official American embargo had been imposed on the shipment of all "lethal" military equipment to Pakistan. Although the Nixon administra-

---

144. Ibid., p. 227.

145. W. Norman Brown, *The United States and India, Pakistan, Bangladesh* (Harvard University Press, 1972), p. 414; *Time,* August 23, 1971, p. 15.

146. Joan Hochman, "The Suspension of Economic Assistance to India," *Appendices: Commission on the Organization of the Government for the Conduct of Foreign Policy,* vol. 3 (GPO, 1975), p. 113.

tion announced termination of the limited U.S. military assistance program to Pakistan in April 1971, $35 million of "nonlethal" military assistance already contracted for, and the cash sale of such "nonlethal" items as trucks, transport aircraft, communications equipment, and *ammunition* to Pakistan continued until congressional pressure in early November forced the administration to revoke these export licenses. Congress registered similar disapproval of Pakistan's bloody civil war in July, when the House Foreign Affairs Committee voted against the 1972 appropriations for development aid to Pakistan.[147]

Domestic political pressure on the Nixon administration may have slowed down open diplomatic support for Pakistan against India until the December war, but it did not deter covert administration favoritism toward Islamabad. According to Joan Hochman, Nixon himself privately announced his "tilt" policy to the Washington Special Action Group at a meeting in mid-September.[148] Once full-scale conventional warfare began on December 3, the administration abandoned its pretense of neutrality and the pro-India sentiment of Congress and the public had little impact on the private manifestations of the Nixon-Kissinger "tilt."

From December 3 onward the Nixon administration explicitly communicated its general conclusion that India was principally responsible for the war, and that the United States intended to deter any Indian military action against West Pakistan. On December 4, as Marvin and Bernard Kalb recount,

State Department spokesman Robert McCloskey summoned the Saturday morning contingent of reporters into his second-floor office. Sisco, looking uncomfortable, stalked into the room, carrying his White House instructions from Kissinger. "India bears the major responsibility," he charged, "for the broader hostilities which have ensued."[149]

At the United Nations on December 5 and 6, U.S. Ambassador George Bush sponsored cease-fire resolutions calling for the withdrawal of all troops to their own side of the border. These resolutions effectively favored the retreating Pakistanis. Bush let it be known to reporters that

147. Melvin Gurtov, *The United States Against the Third World* (Praeger, 1974), pp. 171–75; Jackson, *South Asian Crisis,* pp. 84, 93.

148. Hochman, "Suspension of Economic Assistance to India," p. 110. Jack Anderson, however, dates Nixon's personal statement to the WSAG members sometime in August. See Jack Anderson with George Clifford, *The Anderson Papers* (Random House, 1973), p. 212.

149. Kalb and Kalb, *Kissinger,* p. 259.

the U.S. government considered India clearly "the major aggressor."[150] In response to public criticism of the Nixon administration's anti-India statements, Kissinger convened a press background briefing on December 7 to elaborate on White House policy. Kissinger disclaimed any anti-India bias, but at the same time made it clear that the administration considered India's military attack on East Pakistan unnecessary, asserting "we believe that what started as a tragedy in East Bengal is now becoming an attempt to dismember a sovereign state and a member of the United Nations."[151]

Nixon's and Kissinger's fears of India's military intentions in West Pakistan were given fuel on December 8 with the report by CIA Director Richard Helms:

Mrs. Gandhi has indicated that before heeding a UN call for cease-fire, she intends to straighten out the southern border of Azad [Pakistani-controlled] Kashmir. It is reported that, prior to terminating present hostilities, Mrs. Gandhi intends to attempt to eliminate Pakistan's armor and air force capabilities.[152]

The next day, according to Marvin and Bernard Kalb, Kissinger called Indian Ambassador L. K. Jha to the White House, confronted him with the CIA intelligence report on Gandhi's intentions, and demanded that India reconsider this action.[153] Meanwhile, Under Secretary of State John Irwin cabled the American Embassy in India: "In view of intelligence reports spelling out Indian military objectives in West Pakistan, we do not want in any way to ease Indian Government concerns re help Pakistan might receive from outside sources."[154] At the United Nations on December 12, U.S. Ambassador Bush presented a letter to the president of the Security Council that argued: "With East Pakistan virtually occupied by Indian troops, a continuation of the war would take on increasingly the character of armed attack on the very existence of a member-State of the United Nations." During Security Council debate Bush called for "a clear and unequivocal assurance" that India did not intend to annex Pakistan territory and "change the status quo in Kashmir."[155]

150. *New York Times*, December 6, 1971.
151. Jackson, *South Asian Crisis*, p. 209.
152. Ibid., p. 225.
153. Kalb and Kalb, *Kissinger*, p. 260.
154. Jackson, *South Asian Crisis*, p. 232.
155. Ibid., pp. 128–29.

That same day, December 12, Nixon and Kissinger chose to broaden their deterrence communications to include the USSR. As they flew to the Azores for a summit meeting with French President Georges Pompidou, they instructed Jacob Beam, U.S. ambassador to Moscow, to inform the Soviet Foreign Ministry that Nixon would have to reconsider his scheduled visit to Moscow if the USSR allowed India to carve up West Pakistan. On the return flight from the Azores on December 14, with the war still raging and no word from the Soviet Foreign Ministry, Kissinger confidentially informed the traveling pool of White House reporters that if the USSR did not restrain India within a few days, "the entire U.S.-Soviet relationship might well be reexamined." The importance of the statement led the *Washington Post* to ignore Kissinger's usual anonymity and to name him directly as the source of the ultimatum.[156]

Paralleling the administration's increasingly specific and threatening verbal communications during the war was a carefully tailored escalation of U.S. economic and military sanctions designed to give both credibility and potency to the punishment implied in the oral communications. On December 1, in the light of the increasing number of military incidents along the East Pakistani borders, the Nixon administration announced cancellation of export licenses for $2 million in arms bound for India and a freeze on all future licenses for arms to India.[157] When full-scale war broke out on December 3 the United States escalated its economic sanctions. That day Nixon ordered suspension of all pending development loans for India and suspension of $72 million in Public Law 480 credit assistance.[158] Three days later Charles Bray, a State Department official, announced the suspension of $87.6 million in development loans to India, stating that the United States "was not going to make a short-term contribution to the Indian economy to make it easier for the Indian government to sustain its military efforts."[159] At the December 8 WSAG session Kissinger inquired "what the next turn of the screw might be" in the light of India's potential military threat to the West. Maurice Williams, deputy administrator of the Agency for International Development (AID), and Deputy Defense Secretary David Packard explained the dif-

---

156. David Wise, *The Politics of Lying* (Random House, 1973), pp. 300–01.
157. *New York Times,* December 2, 1971.
158. Jackson, *South Asian Crisis,* p. 212.
159. Hochman, "Suspension of Economic Assistance to India," p. 105.

ficulties associated with canceling foreign assistance already committed through irrevocable letters of credit to U.S. suppliers. Kissinger instead ordered AID to exclude from the coming fiscal year budget any requests for assistance from India.[160]

These decisions involved significant sums, but the total impact on the $64 billion Indian economy was predictably small. One is forced to conclude that Nixon and Kissinger were attempting to signal the possibility of more severe economic and military sanctions if India continued its military offensive, rather than trying actually to cripple the Indian economic base. *Not* suspended during the war were $30 million in U.S. project aid loans to India for specific purposes and $105 million in commodity import assistance. Moreover, at the international financial institutions during December and January, American representatives did not interfere with the normal extension of new loans and credit to India.[161]

Following the administration's policy of progressive escalation of threats, Kissinger inquired at the WSAG meetings on December 6 and 8 into the legality of authorizing Jordan or Saudi Arabia to transfer previously supplied American weapons to Pakistan. The congressional ban on direct transfer of lethal weapons precluded any deliveries of replacement arms from the United States. Although State Department spokesman U. Alexis Johnson referred to such action as a "token" gesture unlikely to narrow substantially the Pakistani defense gap, it is clear that Kissinger had in mind the demonstrative impact of such outside involvements. Acting under Kissinger's orders, Under Secretary of State John Irwin sent cables to the American embassies in India, Saudi Arabia, Jordan, Iran, and Pakistan instructing that "we do not want in any way to ease Government of India's concerns regarding help Pakistan might receive from outside sources. Consequently, embassy should henceforth give GOI no repeat no assurances regarding third country transfers."[162] When, in response to Yahya Khan's pleas, Jordan's King Hussein privately asked the administration to agree to the transfer of eight Jordanian F-104 jets to Pakistan, Nixon ignored the consensus of the WSAG members and secretly authorized Jordan's transfer of *ten* American-supplied planes to Pakistan.[163] Libya chose to send American-supplied F-5 jets

---

160. Jackson, *South Asian Crisis,* pp. 225–26.
161. Hochman, "Suspension of Economic Assistance to India," p. 105.
162. Anderson, *Anderson Papers,* p. 228.
163. Ibid., pp. 249–52.

to Pakistan as a show of Islamic solidarity without requesting U.S. approval.[164]

From thoughts about American arms assistance—to the extent that it was politically viable—Nixon and Kissinger soon progressed to thoughts about a direct demonstration of American arms. During the last days of November, as fighting escalated in East Pakistan, the U.S. Defense Department had expanded the operational zone of the Seventh Fleet to include the Bay of Bengal. When word arrived in Washington on December 8 that the Indian cabinet was discussing a possible military offensive against West Pakistan, "Urgent huddles in the White House led to a decision on 10 December to assemble in Malacca Strait a United States task force, spearheaded by the aircraft carrier *Enterprise,* the Navy's most powerful ship."[165]

The four Soviet ships already in the Bay of Bengal were overshadowed by U.S. Task Force 74 of the Seventh Fleet, assembled off Singapore. It consisted of the *Enterprise,* the world's largest attack carrier, with seventy-five nuclear-armed fighter-bombers on board; the amphibious assault carrier *Tripoli,* carrying a Marine battalion-landing team of 2,000 troops and twenty-five assault helicopters; three guided-missile escorts, the *King, Decatur,* and *Parsons;* four gun destroyers, the *Bausell, Orleck, McKean,* and *Anderson;* and a nuclear attack submarine.[166] Countries along the intended route of the task force were informed in advance of the ships' movements, so word of the implied American threat reached New Delhi as early as December 11.[167] During the night of December 13–14, Task Force 74 went through the Strait of Malacca. On December 15 the U.S. combat ships entered the Bay of Bengal. Washington announced that day that the task force might help evacuate Pakistani forces from the East after a cease-fire. Despite the official end of the Indo-Pakistani war on December 17, Task Force 74 remained in the Indian Ocean until January 1972, when its ships retired to their original stations off Vietnam and at Subic Bay in the Philippines.[168]

164. *New York Times,* March 29, 1972.
165. Jackson, *South Asian Crisis,* p. 230.
166. Anderson, *Anderson Papers,* p. 264; James M. McConnell and Anne M. Kelley, "Super-Power Naval Diplomacy: Lessons of the Indo-Pakistani Crisis 1971," *Survival* (November–December 1973), p. 289.
167. Chopra, *India's Second Liberation,* pp. 197–99.
168. McConnell and Kelley, "Super-Power Naval Diplomacy," pp. 289–90.

Target Behavior

U.S. behavior during the December war was directed toward the three targets of India, the USSR, and China, with India the principal target of U.S. action. While the war against Pakistan found India firmly united behind the leadership of Prime Minister Indira Gandhi and her Congress party—as indicated by the party's sweep of the national elections in March 1971—Gandhi was under considerable domestic pressure to give direct economic and military assistance to the Bangladesh independence movement. The international dispute over East Pakistan had engaged a number of major Indian interests. Pakistan's weakened condition presented India with the opportunity to establish itself as the sole power on the Asian subcontinent and the chance to recoup national prestige lost at the hands of the Chinese in 1962. The fighting also posed major threats. Pakistan's diplomatic alignment with China meant that any war risked renewed fighting with China. During the year, India's relations with the United States had deteriorated as word leaked of continuing U.S. shipments of nonlethal military equipment to Pakistan, and as the Nixon administration steadily improved relations with India's adversary, China. Faced with the possibility of a war with Pakistan that would put India against the combined opposition of the United States and China, New Delhi felt compelled to seek countersupport from the USSR. The rapid consummation of the Indo-Soviet Treaty of Peace, Friendship, and Cooperation, only three weeks after Nixon's July 15 announcement of his forthcoming trip to China, was a major step in this direction. But this counterbalancing strategy also threatened India with the possible loss of international neutrality and flexibility by hardening its alliance with the USSR.[169]

The most pressing problem of the war was that of the East Pakistani refugees, and the solution of this matter governed India's behavior before and during the December war. Between late March and early December an estimated 9.5 million Bengali refugees crossed into India to escape the genocidal fighting. By late 1971 the financial burden on India of provid-

169. Jackson, *South Asian Crisis,* pp. 61–71.

ing refugee assistance had reached $3 million a day. Only part of that cost was offset by international relief contributions.[170]

Even more worrisome to the government in New Delhi, however, was the mounting potential for violence in India. The Indian state of West Bengal, to which most of the refugees had fled, was a Muslim-dominated state, politically and economically unstable in the best of times. During 1971 West Bengali Muslims grew increasingly resentful that the East Pakistani refugees, many of them Hindus, received better food, shelter, clothing, and medical care than did the native Indians themselves. Gandhi was aware of the growing potential for violence, and assured the West Bengalis that she had "no intention of allowing them [the refugees] to settle here; neither have we any intention of asking them to go back merely to be butchered."[171] To avoid either of these undesirable alternatives, however, required a resolution of the East Pakistani civil war on terms favorable to the Bengali nationalists. By the time the government in Islamabad ordered the military attack in the West, the Indian government was strongly motivated, as well as militarily prepared, to impose a quick solution to the Bangladesh problem that would permit refugee resettlement. War with Pakistan provided the necessary opportunity.

The Nixon administration's vigorous campaign at the United Nations to arrange a cease-fire and mutual withdrawal of opposing forces during the war's first days alerted the Indian government to the U.S. objective of preventing "forceful dismemberment" of a longtime ally. India registered its perception of this objective in several fashions. On December 6, Indian Foreign Secretary T. N. Kaul summoned American Ambassador Keating to inform him of India's "shock and surprise" at the stand the United States was taking in the United Nations.[172] Two days later a senior Indian official rejected Kissinger's claim that India's military action had undercut promising opportunities for a political resolution of the East Pakistani problem, and described U.S. proposals for a political settlement as "neither new nor realistic."[173] The fact that U.S. policy was widely known was indicated by a demonstration on December 7 outside the American

170. *New York Times,* December 12, 1971.
171. "Picking Up the Pieces," *New Republic,* vol. 166 (January 1 and 8, 1972), p. 8.
172. *New York Times,* December 7, 1971.
173. *New York Times,* December 9, 1971.

embassy by thirty members of the Indian Parliament protesting U.S. attempts to arrange a cease-fire through the UN Security Council.[174] When the Nixon administration shifted its attention toward the more feasible objective of deterring major Indian military action against West Pakistan, the Indian government quickly sought to signal that it had no desire to destroy the sovereignty of West Pakistan. At a Washington news conference on December 3 the Indian ambassador to the United States told reporters that India wanted "neither Pakistani territory or people."[175] In response to Kissinger's assertion at the WSAG session on December 8 that an Indian attack on Pakistani forces in Azad Kashmir (the Pakistani state of Kashmir) would be equivalent to "a deliberate Indian attempt to force the disintegration of Pakistan," Assistant Secretary Sisco reminded Kissinger that "Foreign Minister Singh told Ambassador Keating that India had no intention of taking any Pak territory."[176]

The Nixon administration continued to push for unequivocal assurances of West Pakistani sovereignty, and the Indian government sought to provide these. At a massive public rally on December 12, Prime Minister Gandhi said in words meant for Washington:

We are not facing this grave danger . . . because we want to occupy somebody's territory or we want to destroy some nation. We have never wanted this. We have never wanted any nation, including our neighbor, to be destroyed. . . . We are not fighting to occupy any country's territory or to destroy it. I repeat this because propaganda of this kind is being spread in the world to discredit us.[177]

At the United Nations that same day, in response to Ambassador Bush's demand for "a clear and unequivocal assurance that India does not intend to annex Pakistan territory and change the status quo in Kashmir," Indian Ambassador Swaran Singh replied that "India has no territorial ambitions in Bangladesh or in West Pakistan."[178] Other major states, such as the United Kingdom and France, were persuaded by the veracity of

---

174. *New York Times,* December 8, 1971.

175. *New York Times,* December 4, 1971.

176. Jackson, *South Asian Crisis,* p. 226.

177. *U.S. Foreign Broadcast Information Service Daily Report,* no. 239 (December 13, 1971), p. O 1. Hereafter *FBIS.*

178. Jackson, *South Asian Crisis,* p. 129. Singh's silence on Kashmir apparently reflected his uncertainty over the actual status of fighting in the area as well as India's traditional refusal to recognize the legitimacy of any Pakistani claims to the region.

Indian assurances despite their knowledge of U.S. intelligence. India's last attempt to mitigate the White House's suspicion of its intentions came on December 15. In a personal letter to Nixon sent on December 15 and released to the public the next day, Gandhi wrote: "We do not want any territory of what was East Pakistan and now constitutes Bangladesh. We do not want territory of West Pakistan."[179] On December 15, the day Gandhi's letter arrived in Washington, State Department spokesman Robert McCloskey told the press that India still had not replied to a U.S. request for assurances that it would not move on West Pakistan after defeating the Pakistanis in the East.[180]

On December 11 the Indian government learned of the White House's decision the previous day to organize a naval task force for possible use in the Bay of Bengal. The extension of the Seventh Fleet's operational zone to the Indian Ocean the previous week had alerted New Delhi to possible initiatives by U.S. naval forces. News of the organization and tentative destination of Task Force 74 appears to have reached India via other governments in the region that Washington had informed of the pending U.S. force movement.[181] New Delhi obtained confirmation of U.S. naval activities on December 12 through intercepted Pakistani communications as well as from news reports arriving from Southeast Asia. In a story dated December 12 the *New York Times* reported from Saigon that the *Enterprise* and several escort ships had left Vietnamese waters on December 10 for the Strait of Malacca to await final instructions there before proceeding up the Bay of Bengal.[182]

The Indian government may have learned quickly of the organization and destination of Task Force 74, but found it extremely difficult to interpret the purpose of the naval force, or credibly to link its mission to Nixon's objective of deterring military action against West Pakistan. For some four days Indian defense officials pondered the likely purpose of the U.S. task force; apparently they never reached a definitive conclusion. Instead the Indian government chose to take precautionary military measures against those probable American actions it considered most threatening. It quickly discarded the Defense Department's formal explanation, made both in Saigon and by Defense Secretary Melvin Laird in Washing-

179. *New York Times,* December 17, 1971.
180. *New York Times,* December 16, 1971.
181. Chopra, *India's Second Liberation,* p. 197.
182. *New York Times,* December 13, 1971.

ton, that Task Force 74 was part of contingency planning for the evacuation of some 47 Americans who voluntarily remained in Dacca after the British Air Force evacuated 114 U.S. nationals on December 12.[183] The Indian government considered it improbable that the United States would not consult India before sending into the war zone a powerful armada including a nuclear-powered and -armed aircraft carrier, for the sole purpose of evacuating fewer than fifty Americans.[184] The idea that the naval task force intended forcibly to break the Indian blockade of East Pakistan—either to link U.S. Marines with Pakistani troops or to escort Pakistani reinforcements to the East—was also quickly rejected on the grounds that this would risk war with the Soviet ships in or near the Bay of Bengal. It seemed to Indian government officials that Nixon did not have enough political support in the United States for a presidential war against India. They felt that the task force might be intended merely to divert Indian naval and air attention away from the Pakistanis, but they thought the best response to this contingency was to disregard the American ships and to increase military efforts toward a quick conclusion of the war.[185]

The most plausible military mission for the U.S. task force, in the official Indian view, was to evacuate Pakistani troops to the West before the fall of Bangladesh. The presence of the American amphibious assault carrier *Tripoli,* with its helicopters and Marine battalion, seemed to imply such a mission. Indian intelligence in Washington and Dacca reported discussions and preparations for evacuation. On December 15 the Pentagon officially stated that the U.S. task force might help to evacuate Pakistani troops after a cease-fire. Indian military planners expected the evacuation to be carried out either by a U.S. helicopter airlift of the Pakistani officer corps to the American flotilla or by a more massive troop evacuation on numerous small vessels from East Pakistani harbors under the protective umbrella of Task Force 74. Either possibility was cause for grave concern, for it would place India in the position of having to initiate military action against nonbelligerent American forces. To prevent any such peaceful evacuation the Indian Air Force was quickly ordered to destroy all ships in East Pakistani harbors, to keep all East Pakistani airports under constant attack to deter possible helicopter landings, and to

183. Jackson, *South Asian Crisis,* pp. 139–41.
184. Chopra, *India's Second Liberation,* p. 198.
185. Ibid., pp. 201, 204.

make preparations to sink any Pakistani troop ships attempting to link up with the U.S. task force. By December 15 New Delhi was convinced that these operations would make it impossible for the U.S. troops to link up with Pakistani troops unless American forces first initiated military action against the Indian Air Force and Navy—an action they felt the United States was unlikely to take because of the political and military risks involved. When Bangladesh fell on December 16, a large number of Indian leaders and citizens were convinced that the American task force would in fact have attempted an evacuation of Pakistani troops to the West if India had not taken preventive military countermeasures and if East Pakistani resistance had not collapsed so quickly.[186]

Few Indian officials seem to have given serious thought during the war to the possibility of a link between the movement of U.S. naval forces and the principal Nixon-Kissinger objective of impressing New Delhi with the dangers of any major military action against West Pakistan. While gunboat diplomacy was temporarily considered as a possible motive for U.S. naval action, the target of this threat was seen not as Indian action in the *West,* but as ongoing Indian advances in the *East.* And in the light of India's existing commitment in the East and its imminent military victory, this misapprehension of U.S. intent merely stimulated increased defiance on the part of Indian officials.[187] In fact, East Pakistan's hopeless military position convinced New Delhi that evacuation, and not gunboat diplomacy, was the true motive behind U.S. naval action. The Indian government's confusion was wholly understandable. Washington's official explanations of the task force emphasized evacuation operations in the East rather than deterrence in the West. The Indian government thought it had made it clear to the Nixon administration in numerous authoritative communications that it did not entertain major ambitions in the West. In this respect the Indian government drew the important distinction between offensive military action designed to consolidate control over the long-disputed territory of Kashmir versus offensive action designed to undermine the sovereignty of West Pakistan. The Indian government assumed that the Nixon administration perceived and appreciated this distinction. Finally, the initial movements of Task Force 74 seemed potentially relevant to events in East Pakistan but geographi-

186. Ibid., p. 203.
187. Ibid., pp. 198–201.

cally remote to events in the West. In the Bay of Bengal, U.S. naval air power was a full 1,300 miles from the Western battle front.[188]

In the end, Gandhi and her advisers chose to stop short of her contemplated goal of retaking some or all of Azad Kashmir. While this action conformed to the objective of the Nixon administration, the available evidence suggests that India's motives in not attacking Azad Kashmir were unrelated to the activities of the U.S. naval task force. According to Chopra's detailed analysis of the Indo-Pakistani war,

The political advantages of an immediate and unilateral cease-fire, partly conceived in terms of prestige, were weighed against the military advantages of inflicting further attrition on the enemy and capturing some crucial territorial point. Within a few hours Mrs. Gandhi consulted senior cabinet colleagues, the three Chiefs of Staff, and leaders of the main Opposition parties in Parliament. [Foreign Secretary] Swaran Singh, who was still in New York, was consulted over the telephone. In varying degrees nearly all of them preferred the political advantage, Swaran Singh most of all because, he said, such a gesture would put India's critics in the wrong and the effect of the adverse vote in the UN would be greatly diluted. The Soviet Union had the same preference. . . . Its preference was for an immediate cease-fire because of the isolation in which it was placed at the UN by the vote in the General Assembly.[189]

Furthermore, India was not interested in pressing its luck with the People's Republic of China, which had begun troop movements along India's northern border and had issued two sharp warnings to New Delhi on the morning of December 16. But Gandhi's call for a cease-fire in the West was unrelated to the military threat the United States attempted to convey through its naval operations in the Bay of Bengal. Military

188. Ibid., pp. 205–08. The *Enterprise* had moved south and west, to a point southwest of Ceylon, by the 16th, however. All in all, the seeming inappropriateness of U.S. military action to the administration's primary diplomatic interest appears in part to have been the result of the limited military options served up to the White House by Navy planners. Classified documents held by Jack Anderson indicate that the U.S. Navy was primarily interested in demonstrating its capability to counter the growing Soviet naval presence in the Indian Ocean since Britain's announced withdrawal "east of Suez," and was only marginally attuned to the administration's objective of deterring a land and air offensive by India against West Pakistan. Thus, the Navy's "Outline Plan for Show of Force Operations in the Pakistan-India Area" called for shadowing Soviet and Indian ships in the Bay of Bengal, but forecast no projection of naval power into the Arabian Sea off West Pakistan, because of the absence of Soviet operations in the area. Nixon approved the Navy's operational plan for Task Force 74 with only minor alterations. For details, see Anderson, *Anderson Papers,* pp. 259–66.

189. Chopra, *India's Second Liberation,* pp. 212–13.

counteraction by both India and the USSR soon offset some of the coercive impact of Task Force 74, and most concerned parties felt the threat of U.S. intervention on the subcontinent lacked credibility. What effective deterrence the United States was able to exercise against the Indian government was grounded not in military threats but in the international political isolation that attached to India and the USSR as a result of U.S. diplomatic efforts in the UN Security Council and General Assembly.

A secondary target of U.S. deterrence strategy during the fourteen-day war was the USSR, India's principal ally during the last months of 1971. Because of the Sino-Soviet rift and the strategic location of India and Pakistan on China's southern border, the USSR had pursued closer ties with both subcontinent powers simultaneously since the mid-1960s. In 1966 Moscow played an important role as mediator between the two countries, sponsoring the meetings at Tashkent that concluded the 1965 Indo-Pakistani war over Kashmir. At the World Congress of Communist parties in September 1969, Communist Party First Secretary Leonid Brezhnev had proposed an "Asian collective security system," which most leaders took to be a Soviet attempt to line up India, Pakistan, and other Asian nations against China.[190]

The beginning of the Pakistani civil war in March 1971 found the USSR still pursuing its good neighbor policy with both Pakistan and India, and during the next months Moscow tried to avoid taking sides in the dispute over East Pakistan. From April through July, Moscow made several amicable signals toward Pakistan: a Soviet agreement to double imports of Pakistani leather, a Soviet commitment to construct a Pakistani steel mill, continued Soviet economic aid, and private Soviet communications implying that Moscow saw the civil war as an "internal affair."[191] At the same time, in deference to India's sentiments, the USSR strongly urged Pakistan to find a quick political solution to the civil war "in the interest of preserving peace in the area"—possibly through direct negotiations with Sheikh Mujib and the Awami League, as demanded by India.[192] Although the USSR discontinued its shipments of arms to Pakistan in 1970, it maintained substantial deliveries of arms to India throughout 1971.

190. Marcus F. Franda, "India and the Soviets: 1975," *American Universities Field Staff Reports*, vol. 19 (June 1975), p. 10.
191. Jackson, *South Asian Crisis*, pp. 39–40, 48, 69–70.
192. Ibid., pp. 36–37, 172.

The USSR was nudged from neutrality in the dispute during the summer of 1971 by Pakistan's active cultivation of Chinese support against India and by Nixon's dramatic breakthrough in relations with China. Pakistan's efforts to gain a public commitment of Chinese military action against India in the event of an Indian attack on East Pakistan and China's willingness to lend both political and material support to Pakistan steadily eroded the Soviet incentive to remain neutral. In addition, Nixon's July 15 announcement of his China trip opened the door for possible collaboration between China and the United States in support of the two nations' mutually preferred client, Pakistan. When alarmed Indian officials approached the USSR for offsetting support, Moscow saw advantages in strengthening its political relationship with New Delhi. On August 9 a twenty-year Indo-Soviet Treaty of Peace, Friendship, and Cooperation was signed in both capitals. Article IX of the treaty stipulated:

Each High Contracting Party undertakes to abstain from providing any assistance to any third country that engages in armed conflict with the other Party. In the event of either being subjected to an attack or a threat thereof, the High Contracting Parties shall immediately enter into mutual consultations in order to remove such threat and to take appropriate effective measures to ensure peace and security of their countries.[193]

The treaty did not, however, mean complete Soviet commitment to India's position on East Pakistan. In private conversations with Indian officials, Soviet officials tirelessly advocated military nonintervention in the civil war.[194] Soviet support for Indian military action was impossible because of Moscow's simultaneous courtship of the Islamic states of the Middle East. The "Islamic Republic of Pakistan," with the world's largest Muslim population, was fully supported in its dispute with India by the Arab (Muslim) states of the Middle East. Nor was the USSR eager to harm its improving relations with the United States, in the light of their mutual interests in strategic arms control, a Berlin treaty, and expanded economic relations. On October 12, with the USSR anxious to counter improving relations between China and the United States, Nixon announced that he had accepted an invitation to visit Moscow in the latter part of May 1972. Given this array of international interests, the most that Moscow was able to concede to the Indian government in re-

193. Ibid., p. 190.
194. Ibid., pp. 85–87; Chopra, *India's Second Liberation,* pp. 90–91.

gard to the Pakistani civil war was India's right to adopt unilaterally whatever means it deemed necessary to relieve the political and financial pressure placed on it by fighting. Meanwhile, from August 9 on, the USSR would provide through its UN Security Council membership an effective shield against imposition by the United Nations of a political settlement to the civil war that was unsatisfactory to India.[195]

The USSR did not become a major target of U.S. signaling until the last days of the Indo-Pakistani war, when Nixon and Kissinger concluded that India intended to attack West Pakistan and that direct American leverage against Gandhi's government was insufficient to prevent this. Before December 13 Moscow had received at least two noteworthy indications of the Nixon administration's desire to induce the USSR to "restrain" India from military action. In November Nixon had sent a personal letter to Soviet Premier Aleksei Kosygin urging superpower restraint in the escalating crisis. Then, on December 7 in a background press briefing, Kissinger said in response to questions about the diplomatic impact of Soviet support for India:

> We believe that the basis of a peaceful evolution with the Soviet Union requires that both countries exercise great restraint in the many crisis areas around the world and that they both subordinate short-term advantages to the long-term interests of peace. . . .
>
> The attempt to achieve unilateral advantage sooner or later will lead to an escalation of tensions, which must jeopardize the prospects of relaxation. We hope that the Soviet Union will use its undoubted influence to approach problems in the subcontinent in the same spirit and not to jeopardize the very hopeful evolution that has started by a short-term approach. But we are still waiting to see. We have no judgment yet.[196]

Not until December 13, when U.S. Ambassador Jacob Beam carried to the Soviet Foreign Ministry the Nixon-Kissinger message that the President's trip to Moscow might be jeopardized by India's "dismemberment" of West Pakistan, did the U.S. government make clear the overriding objective of U.S. diplomatic and military pressure. (Beam's mission was preceded on December 12 by Ambassador Bush's demand at the United Nations that India publicly declare that it had no territorial ambitions in West Pakistan and Kashmir.) After December 13 Moscow received several reiterations of U.S. objectives. With the collapse of East Pakistan at hand, Kissinger privately informed the White House press

195. Jackson, *South Asian Crisis,* p. 103.
196. *New York Times,* December 14, 1971.

pool on December 14—with an eye to signaling Moscow—that "the U.S. is definitely looking to the Soviets to become a restraining influence in the next few days. But if the Russians continue to deliberately encourage military actions, a new look might have to be taken at the President's summitry plans."[197]

Although White House press secretary Ronald Ziegler that same evening officially denied speculation that the United States was considering cancellation of the Moscow summit, he did confirm that this might occur under a "highly hypothetical situation": "If the Soviets continued to support Indian military action and the Indians should move into West Pakistan, this could very well affect future relations with the Soviet Union. But we have no reason to suspect this will occur. We have every expectation the fighting will stop in South Asia."[198]

By December 13 the Soviet leaders were generally aware of the Nixon administration's primary objective. On the day Beam carried the Nixon-Kissinger message to the Soviet Foreign Ministry, Soviet Ambassador to India Nikolai Pegov reportedly informed the Indian government that, in the USSR's estimation, "the movement of the Seventh Fleet is an effort by the U.S. to bully India, to discourage it from striking against West Pakistan, and at the same time boost the morale of the Pakistani forces."[199] Although Moscow's evaluation of U.S. objectives was less ominous than New Delhi's less accurate surmise that Task Force 74 was assembled to evacuate Pakistani troops, Pegov made it clear that the USSR was interested in preventing escalation in the West. According to the U.S. Central Intelligence Agency (CIA), the Soviet ambassador advised New Delhi on December 13 that

India should try to occupy Bangladesh in the quickest possible time and that it should then accept a cease-fire. . . . India has achieved a marvelous military victory, Pakistan is no longer a military force, and it is therefore unnecessary for India to launch an offensive into West Pakistan to crush a military machine that no longer exists.[200]

According to Marvin and Bernard Kalb, after the war Kissinger took this and other U.S. intelligence as proof

that the warning from the plane [by Nixon and Kissinger on December 12] had compelled the Russians to lean on India, and that the cease-fire was a

197. Kalb and Kalb, *Kissinger,* p. 262.
198. *New York Times,* December 15, 1971.
199. Jackson, *South Asian Crisis,* p. 231.
200. Anderson, *Anderson Papers,* p. 233.

result of this pressure. By claiming that he had "saved" West Pakistan, Kissinger could assert that he had rescued an ally of the United States and a friend of China, and that his new "leverage" magic had worked to advance American interests on the subcontinent; the balance, however tenuous, had been preserved, and Moscow had been taught still one more lesson about global responsibility.[201]

Kissinger's analysis assumes that the Indian cease-fire was motivated by Soviet pressure rather than by the other Indian diplomatic and military interests indicated above. The available data suggest that Kissinger was mistaken. Several days before the end of the war the U.S. military attaché in Nepal reported that conversations with Indian officials convinced him that, after victory in the East, Indian forces would withdraw to their prewar positions in the West provided Pakistan did the same.[202] Even while warning on December 8 of a possible Indian offensive in the West, the CIA reported that the "Indian Government hopes that all major fighting will be over by the end of December 1971," which would certainly have been impossible if India had entertained any major military objectives in the West.[203] Indian scholar Pran Chopra argues, based on extensive interviews with senior Indian officials, that by the time the USSR made known its preference for a cease-fire in West Pakistan Gandhi and her advisers had already reached a similar position largely independent of Soviet opinion.[204]

Whether or not the USSR brought effective pressure on New Delhi to forgo an offensive in the West, it is important to emphasize that Soviet and Indian support for a cease-fire was *not* the result of U.S. military pressure generated by Task Force 74. When they first received word of Task Force 74 on December 11, Moscow and New Delhi decided to exchange high-level diplomatic missions as a sign of mutual support under the terms of Article IX of the Indo-Soviet Treaty. On December 11, D. P. Dhar, chairman of India's foreign policy planning committee, left for Moscow, while Soviet First Deputy Foreign Minister Vasily V. Kuznetsov left with a five-member delegation for Delhi.[205] CIA intelligence reports from New Delhi indicate that U.S. military pressure on

201. Kalb and Kalb, *Kissinger,* pp. 262–63. See also Chopra, *India's Second Liberation,* p. 205.
202. Anderson, *Anderson Papers,* pp. 233–34.
203. Ibid., p. 287.
204. Chopra, *India's Second Liberation,* pp. 212–13.
205. Ibid., pp. 198–99.

Moscow was ineffective. According to the CIA, Soviet Ambassador Pegov informed Indian officials on December 13:

Pakistan is trying to draw both the United States and China into the present conflict. The Soviet Union, however, does not believe that either country will intervene. . . .
Pegov noted that a Soviet fleet is now in the Indian Ocean and that the Soviet Union will not allow the Seventh Fleet to intervene.[206]

Pegov's claim was backed by action. When the war broke out the USSR had a minesweeper and a destroyer in the Indian Ocean nearing the end of their routine six-month tour, as well as a conventional attack submarine and a tank landing ship. When an additional Soviet destroyer and minesweeper arrived in the Indian Ocean on December 5 for routine relief of duty, Moscow decided to maintain all six ships in the war zone. On December 7 two additional Soviet combat ships were dispatched from Vladivostok to the Indian Ocean: a cruiser armed with surface-to-surface cruise missiles (SSM) and a submarine armed with anti-ship missiles.[207] Formation of U.S. Task Force 74 on December 10 did little to deter the USSR from further military action; U.S. behavior, in fact, seems to have had the effect of escalating Soviet actions. On December 13, as Pegov was informing the Indian government of the USSR's pledge to prevent intervention by the Seventh Fleet, a second Soviet anti-carrier task force—a cruiser armed with SSMs, a destroyer, a submarine armed with SSMs, and an attack submarine—was organized at Vladivostok and dispatched toward the Bay of Bengal.[208]

Whatever Soviet pressure was applied to India appears to have been motivated by considerations other than fear of U.S. military action. As Chopra indicates, the USSR's preference for Indian acceptance of a cease-fire in West Pakistan was heavily influenced by the political "isolation in which it was placed at the UN by the vote in the General Assembly."[209] Two vetoes cast by the USSR on December 5 were required to prevent Security Council passage of a binding resolution calling for a cease-fire and withdrawal of all troops to their own side of the border. On December 7, with frustration running high at the inability of the United Nations to act, the UN General Assembly—acting under the

206. Jackson, *South Asian Crisis,* p. 231.
207. McConnell and Kelley, "Super-Power Naval Diplomacy," p. 289.
208. Ibid., pp. 290–91.
209. Chopra, *India's Second Liberation,* p. 213.

"Uniting for Peace" procedures for the sixth time in its institutional history—overwhelmingly approved (104 to 11) an Argentine resolution calling for a cease-fire and troop pull-back. On December 13, with India still advancing, the United States reintroduced a cease-fire resolution in the Security Council, forcing the USSR to cast its third blocking veto.

This solitary defense of India against the tide of international sentiment proved particularly embarrassing to Soviet diplomacy in the Middle East. The Arab states brought heavy diplomatic pressure on Moscow to modify its UN position, not only because of Pakistan's Islamic culture, but also because Soviet opposition to the UN-mandated withdrawal of Indian troops seemed to weaken a similar 1967 UN resolution calling for Israeli withdrawal from occupied Arab lands.[210] The USSR hoped to avoid the prolonged rupture in political relations with Pakistan that was likely to follow from its acquiescence to an Indian attack on West Pakistan. Moscow still hoped for close relations with both subcontinent powers at the expense of China; its month-long delay in recognizing the independent state of Bangladesh underscored its eagerness to avoid a full diplomatic break with Pakistan. The military threats that might have influenced the USSR to counsel Indian restraint did not originate from the United States but from the People's Republic of China. Although Moscow did not expect China to intervene because of events in Bangladesh, an attack on West Pakistan—the only nation friendly with the PRC on its vulnerable western border—would have posed a serious risk of Chinese intervention.

The PRC was apparently also a target of U.S. behavior during the December 1971 war, although concrete evidence of this is admittedly limited. Kissinger's trips to China in July and October, and the announcement on November 29 of Nixon's arrival in Peking on February 21, make it difficult to imagine that latent concern over last-minute complications did not give the White House added incentive for signaling its full support for the two nations' common client, Pakistan. Henry Brandon, a well-informed White House correspondent, has gone so far as to argue that "perhaps more than anything it was the new relationship with China that influenced the President and Dr. Kissinger. It gave them a vested interest in maintaining the integrity of Pakistan, allied with a desire to show Peking that cooperation with the United States can have its advan-

210. *New York Times,* December 6, 1971.

tages."[211] The WSAG documents make no reference to administration concern over relations with China, but sensitivity to China's position can be detected in Kissinger's December 14 background briefing of White House reporters: "Asked what the Soviet motive is in its behavior on the India-Pak war, Kissinger said it is apparently to humiliate China—to show the world that China cannot prevent what is happening in Pakistan."[212] Kissinger indicated that Nixon shared this evaluation.[213]

The primary Chinese interests engaged by the Indo-Pakistani war were the desire to deny any major expansion of Soviet power in southern Asia and the need to preserve Pakistan as a viable buffer and a partial counterbalance to India's growing power. The official conclusion of the Indo-Soviet Treaty on August 9 increased China's concern over encirclement from the north and south by the USSR and India. Peking saw the erosion of Pakistani strength on the subcontinent as a further tightening of the circle.

During 1971 China provided Pakistan with extensive diplomatic, economic, and military assistance in its growing dispute with India but, like the USSR, China remained wary of making any firm military commitment to its subcontinent client over the war issue. In a letter of April 13 that governed PRC policy throughout 1971, Chinese Prime Minister Chou En-lai wrote President Yahya Khan: "Should the Indian expansionists dare to launch aggression against Pakistan, the Chinese Government and people will, as always, firmly support the Pakistan Government and people in their just struggle to safeguard state sovereignty and national independence."[214] Chou's commitment failed to refer to Chinese defense of Pakistan's "unity"—a term that came to be viewed as synonymous with East Pakistan—nor did it mention direct armed support. Despite Pakistani pressure the PRC refused to increase its public commitment during succeeding months. In India, Chinese behavior was interpreted to mean continued material support from the PRC for Pakistan's efforts in the East, but direct Chinese military support only if Pakistan's very existence was threatened in the West.[215]

No direct evidence emerged during the war of China's appraisal of

211. Brandon, *Retreat of American Power,* p. 252.
212. Kalb and Kalb, *Kissinger,* p. 261.
213. *New York Times,* December 15, 1971.
214. Jackson, *South Asian Crisis,* p. 173.
215. Ibid., pp. 42–43, 94–96.

U.S. operational objectives or use of military forces. During this period the official Chinese media were filled with belligerent attacks on Soviet and Indian "social imperialism" in Pakistan and on the two nations' refusal to accept the UN General Assembly resolution for a cease-fire and troop withdrawal. It may be possible to infer, from the absence of official Chinese comment on U.S. policy in the subcontinent during these two weeks, a generally favorable reaction in China to the U.S. position supporting Pakistan. In fact, from December 3 through December 17, the only official Chinese reference to U.S. action was a statement that the UN Security Council session on December 13 had been convened at the request of the American representative Bush, to consider a U.S. cease-fire proposal.[216] An additional indication of a generally favorable Chinese response to U.S. policy might be Peking's announcement on December 13 of the release of CIA spy Richard Fecteau and U.S. citizen Mary Harbert and the reduction of the life sentence of CIA spy John Downey.[217]

Although the meager evidence available suggests that Peking viewed Washington's pro-Pakistan policy favorably, there is also some later indication that China did not fully endorse the U.S. military signaling in the Bay of Bengal, particularly when subsequent events suggested that the U.S. naval presence would not be temporary. On December 29, in an article entitled "Soviets Step Up Expansion, Aggression in the Indian Ocean," the New China News Agency also took the opportunity to criticize the presence of U.S. naval power in the Indian Ocean:

When the Indian aggressor troops, armed with Soviet weapons, were pressing toward Dacca, U.S. imperialism in contention with social-imperialism for hegemony over the South Asian subcontinent and the Indian Ocean, made a show of force to the Soviet Union and India by dispatching an aircraft carrier and some other warships of its Seventh Fleet to the Bay of Bengal. . . . Soviet revisionism recently accused U.S. imperialism of pursuing a "gunboat policy," declaring that "the Indian Ocean is not an American lake." But at the same time it regards the Indian Ocean as a "Soviet lake" and frantically pursues a social-imperialist "gunboat policy" by dispatching its own task force there to contend with U.S. imperialism for domination over the Indian Ocean. The aggression and expansion in the Indian Ocean by Soviet revisionism and U.S. imperialism have long aroused the strong discontent and opposition of the medium-sized and small countries in Asia and Africa.[218]

216. *FBIS*, no. 241 (December 15, 1971), p. A 3.
217. *FBIS*, no. 239 (December 13, 1971), p. A 1.
218. *FBIS*, no. 250 (December 29, 1971), p. A 5.

Chinese criticism intensified when the Defense Department announced on January 6 that Task Force 74 would temporarily remain in the Indian Ocean to counter the Soviet naval presence and that U.S. naval operations would be expanded in the region. In a January 14 article, "U.S.-Soviet Scramble for Hegemony in South Asian Subcontinent and Indian Ocean," *Peking Review* warned:

As our great leader Chairman Mao teaches us, "The imperialist wolves must remember that gone forever are the days when they could rule the fate of mankind at will and could do whatever they liked with the Asian and African countries." The affairs of the South Asian subcontinent can only be handled by the peoples of the area. No domination or carving up of the area by U.S. imperialism and Soviet revisionism will be tolerated.[219]

Peking was thus not as enthusiastic about the arrival of U.S. troops as the White House might have anticipated.

During the second week of the Indo-Pakistani war, with China's concern over Indian-Soviet intentions in West Pakistan increasing, Peking chose to make its own veiled show of force—apparently without intentional coordination with U.S. military moves to the south. Evidence of Chinese military preparations was first reported in Washington on December 10. Interpreting Chinese radio transmissions gathered by U.S. reconnaissance satellites, the CIA stated:

On 8 and 9 December, an air net terminal for Tibet and West China was noted passing hourly aviation surface reports to Peking for 11 Chinese civil weather stations along routes and areas adjacent to the border of India. . . . The continued passing of weather data for these locations is considered unusual and may indicate some form of alert posture.[220]

The CIA also noted that "war preparation" efforts had been observed in Tibet during the past months, and that the 157th Infantry Regiment of Yatung, Tibet, had just recalled its personnel to carry out an "urgent mission."[221] Later that night the U.S. military attaché in Nepal cabled from Katmandu that "the Indian high command had some sort of information that military action was increasing in Tibet" and that "both the USSR and India embassies have a growing concern that PRC might intervene."[222] During the next two days both Indian and American in-

219. *Peking Review,* January 14, 1972.
220. Anderson, *Anderson Papers,* p. 262.
221. Ibid.
222. Ibid., pp. 316–17.

telligence intercepted high-level Pakistani communications informing Eastern military commanders not to accept a cease-fire in the light of imminent military assistance "from the north and the south." In New Delhi on December 13 official Indian spokesmen informed the press that Chinese troop movements of unknown size had begun at two points along the mountainous northern border.[223] On December 16 China increased the military tension both by formally protesting to the Indian government an alleged crossing of the China-Sikkim boundary by Indian soldiers and by issuing a major government statement calling "absolutely impermissible" India's desire "not only to swallow up East Pakistan, but also to destroy Pakistan as a whole."[224] Later that day, before diplomatic and military escalation could proceed, Gandhi announced a unilateral cease-fire in the East and a cease-fire in the West for the following morning.

Third Party Behavior

Pakistani President Yahya Khan did have a major role in the outcome of the Indo-Pakistani war, but he was not an intentional target of U.S. military signaling during the fourteen days of fighting. Yahya became president of Pakistan in March 1969, when he led a military coup against long-time dictator Ayub Khan. He centralized civilian and military authority under his leadership to an unprecedented degree, proclaiming himself not only president but also commander-in-chief, chief martial law administrator, minister of defense, and minister of foreign affairs.[225] After the disastrous national assembly elections in December 1970, Yahya further centralized authority by dissolving his cabinet. According to the former Pakistani communications minister, by this action Yahya became

completely dependent upon bureaucrats and generals who provided only those reports and assessments that were pleasing to the ears of their boss. Yahya, like Ayub before him, demonstrated the military dictator's paucity of sources for honest, independent, and accurate advice. This lack of good advice was

223. *New York Times,* December 14, 1971.
224. *Peking Review,* December 17, 1971.
225. Jackson, *South Asian Crisis,* pp. 21–24.

largely responsible for Yahya's incredible errors during the crisis, and for the immense suffering that resulted.[226]

Yahya was representative of the interlocking commercial-military-bureaucratic elite that had dominated Pakistani political affairs since 1947. The members of that elite were the principal beneficiaries of the inequities between West and East Pakistan and had an overwhelming incentive for maintaining the Pakistani status quo.[227] Like most Westerners, Yahya and his military backers underrated the determination of the traditionally less martial Bengalis. He also underestimated the legitimacy of Sheikh Mujibur Rahman as spokesman for Bengali aspirations. With regard to India, Yahya allowed himself to see the crisis as a personal test of strength with New Delhi's female prime minister and as a holy war against Hindus. "If that woman thinks she can cow me down," he told a visiting Chinese delegation, "I refuse to take it. If she wants a war, I'll fight her!"[228] After Yahya's poorly organized air strike against Indian forces in the West on December 4, the *Pakistan Times* proclaimed: "Plainly Islam is the issue between India and Pakistan. Only those qualify to fight the battle of Pakistan who are prepared to fight the battle of Islam. . . . For us there is no choice but to fight, if need be, to the last man."[229]

American-Pakistani relations reached a low ebb in late 1965 when the Johnson administration suspended military and economic assistance to Pakistan and India during the Kashmir war. Relations gradually improved as the United States resumed its economic assistance and modified the arms embargo to permit sale of spare parts and nonlethal supplies. During Nixon's presidency ties continued to improve, largely because of changing U.S. policy toward China. On his summer tour of Asia in 1969 Nixon stopped briefly in Pakistan. He privately told Yahya of his determination to open a diplomatic dialogue with China, and asked him to be his conduit to Peking. When the two presidents met again in October 1970, Nixon asked Yahya Khan to inform the Chinese leaders of Wash-

226. G. W. Choudhury, *India, Pakistan, Bangladesh, and the Major Powers* (Free Press, 1975), p. 212.
227. Louis Dupree, "The Military Is Dead! Long Live the Military!" American Universities Field Staff Reports, vol. 13 (April 1969).
228. John G. Stoessinger, *Why Nations Go to War* (St. Martin's Press, 1974), p. 165.
229. Ibid., p. 167.

ington's desire to open direct American-Chinese talks "at a high level." From December 1970 until July 1971, Yahya served as middleman in a secret exchange of presidential notes between Washington and Peking that culminated in Kissinger's secret visit to China during a three-day "visit" to Pakistan.[230] Yahya Khan remained convinced throughout 1971 that his role as liaison between them ensured that Peking and Washington would bail him out of any international problem into which he stumbled. When Pakistan's former communications minister asked Yahya in September 1971 about the growing crisis with India, he was assured that "both Chinese and Americans will help us, how could they forget our services in the last two years." This happy delusion persisted when war began.[231]

Yahya's diplomatic strategy rested on the assumption that the great powers and the United Nations would intervene to prevent or halt a dangerous subcontinent war from spiraling out of control. This might be accomplished by setting up a UN Observer Group similar to the one that had supervised the Kashmir truce line since 1949. Yahya's assumption gained support early in the war, when the United States and China sponsored UN resolutions calling for an immediate cease-fire and withdrawal of all armed personnel to their own sides of the border. But the UN role quickly fell afoul of a series of Soviet vetoes in the Security Council. At that point, the Pakistani government made a direct appeal for unilateral intervention by its allies. On December 9, a "ranking Foreign Ministry official" in Islamabad "called on the world at large, particularly the big powers, to take appropriate action against what he charged was 'naked and barbarous aggression' by India," according to the *New York Times* correspondent in Pakistan.[232]

Yahya saw as the first signs of an affirmative response to his call for help the creation of Task Force 74 on December 10 and rumors of Chinese troop movements along India's northern border. Yahya's optimistic interpretation of U.S. intentions may have been the result not only of his services for the White House but also of misleading information

230. Kalb and Kalb, *Kissinger*, pp. 223, 233–34, 237, 243–44; Choudhury, "Reflections on Sino-Pakistan Relations," pp. 262–66.
231. Choudhury, "Reflections on Sino-Pakistan Relations," p. 266.
232. *New York Times*, December 10, 1971.

from his close friend, U.S. Ambassador Joseph Farland.[233] Whatever the primary explanation, American and Chinese military maneuvers gave Yahya the reinforcement he needed to cling to his great power strategy. On December 10, Pakistani military commanders in the East requested authorization from Islamabad for a transfer of power to the clearly victorious Bengalis. But the next day, acting on its conviction about American and Chinese intentions, Islamabad radioed its Eastern commanders that there would be no cease-fire. That evening a government spokesman explained to newsmen that "Pakistan has evoked understandings and agreements with other countries to meet the situation created by India's naked aggression."[234]

Unrealistic expectations of a savings intervention lingered for several more days. According to Pakistani Prime Minister Nurual Amin, "even a day before admitting the loss of East Pakistan, Yahya Khan assured me that our forces were in control and were expecting a Chinese intervention and the American Seventh Fleet any moment."[235] Presidential reassurances such as these affected the expectations of other West Pakistanis. On December 13, Pakistani news services misleadingly reported that "President Nixon yesterday sent to the Indian Prime Minister, Mrs. Indira Gandhi, a categorical warning raising the possibility of direct American intervention in the Indo-Pakistan conflict."[236] On the morning of December 17, twelve hours after official surrender in the East, Rawalpindi's leading newspaper plaintively asked if there was still a chance of military help from the United States Seventh Fleet and from China.[237] These false hopes postponed by several days—possibly as many as five—the official surrender of Pakistani forces in the East.

A second unexpected effect of Task Force 74 on Pakistani attitudes after the war was resentment of the misleading U.S. military signals. The

233. According to Anderson's analysis, which is based in part on interviews with Farland, "Yahya Khan had an extraordinary relationship with American Ambassador Joseph Farland; they met almost daily and sometimes shared a bottle of Scotch. . . . Other ambassadors stationed in Islamabad complained that Yahya saw no foreign envoy other than Farland during November and December 1971." See Anderson, *Anderson Papers*, p. 220.
234. *FBIS*, no. 239 (December 13, 1971), p. Q 1.
235. Chopra, *India's Second Liberation*, p. 209.
236. *FBIS*, no. 239 (December 13, 1971), p. Q 1.
237. *New York Times*, December 18, 1971.

depth and duration of such resentment are impossible to judge, but it is clear that the U.S. military action only diminished the gratitude the United States had won among Pakistanis during the first week of the crisis by its vigorous attacks on India in the United Nations.[238] Informed Pakistani opinion, like that in India, found it difficult to decipher the White House's objectives for Task Force 74. Writing in *Pakistan Horizon* immediately after the war, a senior professor at Karachi University could only conclude: "The purpose of the diversion of the naval vessels was not too clear. Was it to pressurise [sic] India into agreeing to a cease-fire in West Pakistan, or was it to impress upon the Soviet Union that its presence in the Indian Ocean would not be allowed by the United States to go unchallenged."[239]

During the December war, neither India nor the USSR accepted U.S. attempts to impose a cease-fire and troop withdrawal in East Pakistan. The gravity and urgency of the Bengali refugee problem and the domestic commitment to liberation ruled out compliance by India, and the USSR was unwilling to risk its political capital with India for the sake of marginally improved relations with the White House. The subsequent and more realistic U.S. objective of deterring a major Indian military offensive against West Pakistan met with greater success. Despite India's early inclination to step up operations in West Pakistan after victory in the East—if only to strengthen its hold on Kashmir—it undertook no major operations in the West after the cease-fire in the East on December 16. (Even then, India occupied more than 2,500 square miles of West Pakistani territory before December 17; this land was returned under the Simla agreements of July 1972.) This second administration objective was aided by the USSR, which made known to the Indian government its strong preference for a cease-fire in West Pakistan after Indian liberation of the East. To the extent that U.S. behavior was guided by the objective of protecting its fledgling relationship with China, one must conclude that Chinese behavior conformed to that desired by Nixon. Nixon's trip to China proceeded without incident and officially inaugurated a new era of diplomatic cooperation between the two nations.

The permanent effects of the Indo-Pakistani war on U.S. external relations are clearly visible only in the instance of the relationship with India.

238. Ibid.
239. Khurshid Hyder, "United States and the Indo-Pakistan War of 1971," *Pakistan Horizon* (First Quarter, 1972), p. 70.

The formation of the impoverished and unstable state of Bangladesh proved to be of little significance to the security of the United States. No major U.S. alliance system was materially altered by the war. Pakistan had effectively withdrawn from the Southeast Asia Treaty Organization (SEATO) in 1965, when the Johnson administration refused to deliver aid during the Kashmir war; its official withdrawal from SEATO in November 1972 merely formalized the status quo. As the WSAG concluded during the December war, the United States had no legal obligation to protect East Pakistan from India under the charter of the Central Treaty Organization (CENTO). In the light of recent political pressures from the USSR, however, Pakistan has demonstrated some renewed interest in closer relations with Iran, Turkey, and the United States within the CENTO alliance structure.[240]

The Indo-Pakistani war did not have a lasting effect on U.S. bilateral relations with the USSR or China. Compared with strategic arms, economic relations, Vietnam, the Middle East, or Taiwan, policy toward the Asian subcontinent was of marginal importance to U.S. relations with Moscow and Peking. This might not have been the case if the USSR had been able to exploit militarily the events of December 1971 after the war. But in the end, India proved unwilling to abandon its military non-alignment to repay Soviet military and diplomatic help. The USSR has been unable to transform its Indo-Soviet Peace, Friendship, and Cooperation Treaty into the first link in the formal Asian collective security system—the Russian SEATO—long championed by Brezhnev.[241] Despite Moscow's urging, New Delhi has refused to grant rights for naval bases for Soviet ships. And India has continued to join with other littoral states of Asia in pressing for creation of an Indian Ocean "zone of peace," which would exclude American and Soviet naval power.[242] The USSR has also been unable to obtain a military toehold in Bangladesh. Moscow has, in fact, lost influence recently as a result of the military coup removing Sheikh Mujibur Rahman and the increasing political and military tension between Bangladesh and India.[243]

240. Choudhury, *India, Pakistan, Bangladesh, and the Major Powers*, pp. 233–34.
241. Franda, "India and the Soviets," p. 10; Choudhury, *India, Pakistan, Bangladesh, and the Major Powers*, pp. 220–26.
242. Franda, "India and the Soviets," p. 10.
243. Marcus F. Franda, "India's Northern Border: In the Wake of Bangladesh," *American Universities Field Staff Reports*, vol. 19 (June 1975).

Although U.S. relations with the USSR and China were not significantly influenced by the Indo-Pakistani war, U.S. relations with India were. While the Nixon administration's "tilt" was not the beginning of deteriorating relations with India, its behavior during the 1971 war greatly accelerated the downward spiral.

The vigorous and open White House support for Pakistan came as a profound shock to New Delhi, and triggered anti-U.S. sentiment throughout India. Indian hostility has since been directed not only at the U.S. government—its foreign policy, diplomats, AID, CIA, and Peace Corps— but also at American scholars, businessmen, journalists, students, and tourists.[244] Strong official criticism of Washington's decision in February 1975 to lift its ten-year embargo on the sale of lethal arms to the subcontinent can be traced in part to New Delhi's continuing sensitivity to the events of 1971. India's opposition to U.S. plans for expanded naval facilities on the Indian Ocean atoll of Diego Garcia is reinforced by memories of American gunboat diplomacy during the December war.

The relevance of the 1971 war to American relations with Pakistan lies in the basic continuity of U.S. policy since that time. Salvaging what it could from defeat, the Nixon administration chose to demonstrate its continued concern for the security and well-being of Pakistan by selling nonlethal military supplies and extending economic assistance. Simultaneously it attempted to mitigate the adverse impact of this assistance on U.S. relations with India. The decision in February 1975 to resume the cash sale of lethal arms to Pakistan, over India's protests, indicated a similar willingness by the Ford administration to aid Pakistan militarily, at some cost to relations with India. With Islamabad still unwilling to accept the status quo in Kashmir, and with the USSR and China siding with India and Pakistan respectively on the issue, the potential remains for another awkward U.S. choice among subcontinent combatants.

While the foreign impact of the administration's behavior was mixed, the domestic effects were uniformly negative. A Louis Harris survey found the American public disapproved of Nixon's handling of the crisis by a two-to-one margin.[245] It seems evident that this negative evaluation was caused by behavior contrary to the public's self-image—that is, by

---

244. Marcus F. Franda, "Indo-American Relations: A Year of Deterioration," *American Universities Field Staff Reports*, vol. 17 (January 1973).

245. William J. Barnds, "India, Pakistan and American Realpolitik," *Christianity and Crisis* (June 12, 1972), p. 143.

official support of a brutal military regime against the world's most populous democracy. The administration's conduct did not, however, have a major impact on Nixon's position within the Republican party, his chances for reelection in 1972, or the success of other political candidates. Despite widespread public opposition to the White House's policy on the subcontinent, by the time of the election the subject was unimportant in comparison with Nixon's most popular stands on Vietnam, China, the USSR, and arms control.

The most profound domestic effect of the administration's behavior was on its relations with the Washington political community. Both Nixon's and Kissinger's credibility with Congress and the news media were adversely affected by the contradictions between the White House's professed neutrality in the war and the anti-Indian tenor of its public actions and confidential deliberations. The inconsistencies reinforced earlier suspicions caused by White House claims of a total embargo on arms for Pakistan and later discoveries of continuing pipeline deliveries. The numerous leaks from press conferences and secret documents during and immediately after the crisis also indicated the adverse impact on legitimate confidentiality that accompanied Nixon's attempts to exclude Congress and the bureaucracy from effective participation in policy-making. The longer term impact of the White House exclusiveness practiced during the Indo-Pakistani war and on other occasions would be felt in the War Powers Act and the congressional attempt to impeach Nixon.

A decision by the Nixon administration not to deploy Task Force 74 into the Bay of Bengal would have favorably affected U.S. international interests, but it would not have altered the domestic political consequences of administration policy. Much of the anti-U.S. backlash in India during and after the war resulted from the White House's heavy-handed attempt to intimidate the Indian government by displaying naval force. The absence of U.S. military power would have done much to reduce the visibility of U.S. opposition to Indian policy, and would have complicated the Soviet attempt to portray itself as New Delhi's indispensable protector. There is no strong evidence to suggest that India would have made major acquisitions in West Pakistan in the absence of U.S. forces. The crucial deterrents appear to have been international political pressure and the possibility of Chinese military involvement. An additional factor may have been the obvious problems associated with assimilating millions of embittered Pakistani Muslims. Future U.S. relations with China or Pakistan would not have been much affected by the absence of Task Force 74; both nations considered the flexing of U.S. naval power in the Indian Ocean to have been a mixed blessing at best. The adverse domestic consequences of the White House policy had little to do with the deployment of naval power, however. The hostile reactions of the general public, Congress, and the news media grew out of disagreement with the administration's pro-Pakistan foreign policy and the deceptive packaging of that policy to minimize public opposition. Strong disagreement with the administration's policy was evident long before the creation of Task Force 74.

Only the most massive military intervention by the United States could have significantly altered the tide of events in the Indo-Pakistani war. The outcome in East Pakistan owed as much to local political dynamics and the military efforts of the Mukti Bahini as it did to the external power of the Indian government given so much credit by the Nixon administration. Once full-scale war was launched on December 3, the U.S. capacity for military deterrence was eliminated. An attempt by Prime Minister Gandhi to reverse the war decision would have threatened her regime's existence. With military resistance in the East eliminated in ten days of fighting, the United States was confronted with a fait accompli reversible only through military strength beyond the capacity of U.S. forces in Asia. U.S. intervention would have required military action against Soviet naval forces; it would have abruptly ended superpower cooperation on numerous issues more vital than the disposition of the subcontinent. The dependence of the new American-Chinese relationship on Peking's assumption of a diminishing U.S. military presence in Asia meant that U.S. intervention on the subcontinent—even in support of China as an ally— might well have ended the Washington-Peking dialogue. Most important, both India and the USSR had correctly calculated that the post-Vietnam redefinition of U.S. interests and ability to influence foreign events, combined with the general war weariness of the American public, precluded any sustained U.S. military action on the Asian subcontinent.

Evaluation

Although both India and the USSR decided against a major Indian offensive aimed at West Pakistan, there is little evidence to suggest that this conformity with the U.S. objective was a result of the deployment of U.S. naval forces. The Indian government failed to perceive a link between U.S. naval operations in the Bay of Bengal and the President's determination to deter military action in the West; instead, New Delhi chose to interpret the American action as an attempt to evacuate Pakistani forces from East Pakistan. India's decision not to launch a major offensive in the West was dictated by its political isolation at the United Nations, its fear of Chinese intervention, and, apparently, diplomatic pressure from the USSR. A similar conclusion must be drawn with respect to Soviet behavior. Although it is clear that the USSR advised Gandhi against an attack on West Pakistan, this advice was not motivated by the arrival of U.S. naval forces in the Bay of Bengal. Moscow's principal concern was the impact such a war might have on its other interests—with the Arab states, with the United States, with the international community generally. The USSR dismissed the possibility of U.S. military intervention on the subcontinent. Finally, U.S. relations with the People's Republic of China continued to improve after the Indo-Pakistani war, but there is no evidence that the U.S. naval presence contributed to this trend. The vociferous U.S. condemnation of India at the United Nations, in tacit coordination with the PRC, was more than sufficient to demonstrate U.S. support for the line China favored. With even Peking hesitant to back Islamabad's genocidal war against the Bengalis, there is no reason to believe that China took the deployment of U.S. forces as a test of good faith. In fact, the U.S. task force appears to have interjected a minor note of discord into U.S.-Chinese relations because of Peking's backing for the Third World movement to create an Indian Ocean zone of peace barring superpower naval forces.

The deployment of U.S. forces did stimulate hostile political and military responses by India and the USSR antithetical to Washington's desire for a cease-fire and withdrawal of forces in the East. Learning of the formation of Task Force 74, the Indian government quickly invoked the defensive provisions of the new Indo-Soviet Treaty through the exchange of high-level diplomatic missions. Gandhi's public speeches adopted the new message that India would not be intimidated by outside powers. The Indian Air Force began destroying the East Pakistani ships and airfields that would be needed to evacuate personnel to the approaching U.S. task force. The net effect of Task Force 74 was to drive India closer to the USSR, arouse anti-American passions, and prompt effective military countermeasures, without securing for Washington any additional leverage over the direction of events in East Pakistan.

The appearance of U.S. naval forces did nothing to induce greater Soviet cooperation on the war in the East, but it did present Moscow with a low-risk opportunity for a psychological victory over Washington. Calculating that there was a negligible chance of actual U.S. intervention, the USSR responded to word of Task Force 74 with assurances of protection to New Delhi and with a large-scale naval deployment, which put twenty-six Soviet ships into the Indian Ocean by December 31. The final collapse of Pakistani resistance in the East, with both Soviet and American naval forces looking on from the Bay of Bengal, conveyed the illusion of Soviet deterrence of American intervention, and also suggested a lack of resolve on the part of the more powerful American task force. This imagery was given strength by the U.S. failure to communicate intelligibly to India and other parties the relationship it intended between Task Force 74 and events in the West.

The unintended impact of U.S. military action on Pakistan has been noted; the creation of Task Force 74, in combination with similar military preparations by China, gave the desperate Yahya Khan the misleading impression of imminent allied intercession. The effect was to postpone by several days Islamabad's acceptance of a cease-fire in the East. Moreover, the false hopes engendered by American and Chinese preparations heightened many Pakistanis' disappointment in the United States and China when the external help promised by Yahya Khan failed to materialize at the conclusion of the war.

Even within the context of the Nixon-Kissinger value system little merit can be found in the deployment of U.S. naval forces during the Indo-Pakistani war. The attempt at coercion through the threat of military punishment was doomed to failure, because the conditions requisite to such a strategy were absent. First, while Task Force 74 contained substantial gross military capability, the exact nature and positioning of this capability made it of little relevance to the war. By December 14, when Task Force 74 was ordered through the Straits and into the Bay of Bengal, the fighting in the East was effectively over. Only a massive introduction of American ground troops could have reversed the outcome. Yet as Chopra informs us, the Indian "navy estimated that the [American] force had a limited capacity for sustained action on land."[246] The threat was appropriately downgraded. While the rough stalemate in the

246. Chopra, *India's Second Liberation*, p. 202.

West made the introduction of naval air power from Task Force 74 potentially germane, its location in the Bay of Bengal, some 1,300 miles from the Western battle front, made the actual use of this power impossible. In general, the United States did not have effective and usable military options on the subcontinent because of the nature and positioning of its forces. Second, if the effectiveness of the U.S. threat was in doubt, its credibility was even more dubious. The imbalance between the very limited U.S. interests on the subcontinent and the very high cost of U.S. intervention was simply too great to support a credible threat of force. This widespread perception was fully reinforced by the absence of a public or private statement from Nixon, Kissinger, or Rogers threatening the introduction of U.S. military power. Third, the war weariness and pro-Indian sentiment of the American public made domestic political support inadequate for a credible threat of intervention against India. Chopra indicates that the Indian cabinet drew the appropriate conclusion: "The Prime Minister and her seniormost advisers ruled out the . . . possibility on the basis that a lame duck President would not dare risk a mainland war with India on an issue on which he carried an even smaller proportion of visible domestic support than he did on Viet Nam."[247]

In general, the contextual pattern of the crisis was unsuited for inducing in the minds of Indian and Soviet officials a fear of unacceptable military escalation by the United States. In the absence of the required conditions, the Nixon administration's military choice was not so much the one identified by Packard as "either doing something effective or doing nothing," as it was of doing something *ineffective* or doing nothing. Apparently this lack of leverage was recognized to a degree by the White House. "We realized full well," states Nixon's 1972 Foreign Policy Report, "that there were objective limits to what the United States could do. South Asia was a region in which we had no preeminent position of influence."[248] Despite this, and somewhat mysteriously, the White House made the militarily ineffectual choice.

The lack of wisdom manifest in the U.S. force movement is compounded by the recognition that the White House's own objectives were fully achievable without the resort to counterproductive military threats. Nixon's desire to maintain good working relations with Pakistan and

247. Ibid., p. 204.
248. *U.S. Foreign Policy for the 1970s: The Emerging Structure of Peace,* A Report to the Congress by Richard Nixon (February 9, 1972), pp. 142–43.

China was amply serviced and provided for during the first week of the war through highly visible diplomatic and economic sanctions taken by the U.S. government against India. Although early U.S. intelligence, suggesting Gandhi's consideration of a major offensive in the West, might have suggested precautionary formation of Task Force 74, the administration's decision on December 14 to send the task force through the straits required systematic denial of the numerous Indian assurances of December 12 and 13 that it no longer planned significant military action in the West, whatever its previous inclination.

Of values Nixon and Kissinger chose to discount in their use of military power, none was more obvious than the negligible importance they assigned to U.S.-Indian relations. Instead they gave paramount importance to strategic relationships with China and the USSR, in line with the new five-power world balance of power—United States, USSR, China, Japan, and Western Europe—they envisioned. By assuming this perspective the White House both downgraded the local causes of the Indo-Pakistani conflict and overestimated the role outside powers could play in the regional dispute.

The Nixon-Kissinger procrustean attempt to impose a five-power world on subcontinent events may go far toward explaining some of the administration's miscalculations: its overestimation of its power to induce Yahya Khan into a peaceful solution of the civil war and, therefore, its indignation at Gandhi's invasion; its exaggeration of the USSR's leverage over India in the midst of war; its miscalculation of its own ability to intimidate India through a show of force. In the end, the administration's great-power hubris proved to be self-defeating, forcing it into a costly and belated recognition of the strength and independence of India. As Gandhi observed after the war, "A great power must take into account the existence not only of countries with comparable power, but of the multitude of others who are no longer willing to be pawns on a global chessboard."[249]

COMPARISON OF THE TWO WARS

A COMPARISON of the Laotian and Indo-Pakistani wars reveals some caveats and lessons regarding the deployment of American armed forces

249. Indira Gandhi, "India and the World," *Foreign Affairs,* vol. 51 (October 1972), p. 75.

to obtain diplomatic bargaining power. During both wars the latent belief of U.S. officials in a great power political order led them to overestimate Moscow's control over the military actions of its allies. The eventual breakdown of the Laotian cease-fire at Nam Tha resulted from limited Soviet control over its clients' military strategy; those military restrictions Moscow was able to impose during 1961–62 were purchased at the price of diminished control over subsequent strategy in Vietnam. That Khrushchev also overrated Soviet control over the fighting is implied by his apparently sincere but never fulfilled promise to ensure Communist compliance with the neutralization accords. In 1971 the Nixon administration overestimated Soviet control over Indian military strategy. This judgment resulted in shock at New Delhi's offensive (despite numerous intelligence warnings) and a presumption that continued fighting meant Moscow was encouraging the war rather than using what Kissinger described as its "undoubted influence" to stop it. In fact, Moscow's acquiescence in New Delhi's planning—in a fashion similar to its behavior with regard to Laos—reflected a more realistic appraisal of its limited leverage on such a vital Indian problem.

Washington's inclination to overestimate the leverage other great powers have over local warfare is ironic in the light of numerous examples, including the Laotian and Indo-Pakistani wars, of uncontrolled military action by American clients. Both Phoumi Nosavan's massing of troops at Nam Tha and Yahya Khan's air strike against India on December 3 were contrary to U.S. policy. The uncontrollable behavior of allies seriously compounds the problem of tailoring a suitable U.S. response to a military attack against a client regime. The deployment of U.S. forces may be inaccurately seen by a client as nonverbal approval of its political and military strategy, prompting false hopes, which seriously hinder a compromise settlement to the fighting. The Nixon administration appears to have been unaware of this possibility in December 1971, and made little effort to communicate to Pakistan the limited nature of the mission of Task Force 74. Because of its stormy relations with the Laotian rightists and the Thai government, the Kennedy administration was more alert to possible miscommunication in May 1962, but its ability to restrain the rightists after Nam Tha may have resulted from their loss of independent military capability and the previous months of U.S. economic sanctions, which conditioned them to expect little help from Washington. Similar conditions did not exist when Pakistan learned of Task Force 74, and are unlikely to exist often between the United States and an ally. The possibility of inappropriate client response is a chronic problem in the deployment of American armed forces.

While Kennedy's dispatch of troops to Thailand proved unnecessary to his neutralization objective, this military action did not have the adverse impact on U.S. credibility and prestige, nor did it cause the hazardous military escalation by the opposing side, that occurred as a result of Nixon's show of naval force. A comparison of the two cases highlights some of the general factors that dictated this difference in outcomes. First, although Kennedy's modest neutralization objective was clear to all parties to the Laotian war, because of both the protracted international negotiations and Kennedy's own public statements in May 1962, the Nixon administration's shifting objectives during the Indo-Pakistani war gave credence to claims that the White House had failed in its attempts to prevent an Indian victory in the East or to evacuate Pakistani troops before the fall of Bangladesh. Second, while Kennedy's troop deployment to Thailand seemed compatible with his professed objective of achieving a neutralization of Laos that preserved Thailand's essential security interests, the Nixon administration's deployment of naval forces into the Bay of Bengal seemed at variance with its public and private emphasis on deterring an Indian offensive in the West. This apparent contradiction between means and ends further reinforced the belief that the United States had suffered a military defeat in the East. Third, while U.S. combat forces in Thailand constituted a potent and usable instrument vis-à-vis 35,000 modestly trained and equipped neutralist and Communist forces in Laos, Task Force 74 appeared unsuited for resisting the massive Indian and Bengali armies in the East, except through resort to its unusable nuclear weapons. Finally, the credibility of *any* American use of force was markedly different in the two instances. In 1962, the U.S. commitments to Laos and Thailand were visibly cemented by American military advisers, military aid, and formal treaty pledges. The general public supported military resistance to a Communist victory in Southeast Asia. In 1971, neither active military cooperation nor relevant treaties committed the United States to Pakistan's defense. A war-weary Congress and public sided with India on the Bangladesh issue.

While a comparison of the two cases suggests real differences in the skill with which Kennedy and Nixon deployed forces for deterrence purposes, it is important to emphasize that the differences in outcome were equally influenced by background factors over which Kennedy and Nixon had little control. The Nixon administration's attempt, through domestic deception, to compensate for the absence of conditions favoring successful use of force only compounded the political losses that it predictably suffered. Only through a sober contextual analysis of the relevant domestic and international forces can policymakers expect to distinguish successfully those instances in which armed forces have bargaining utility from those more numerous situations in which the deployment of military power is counterproductive.

Finally, our two cases suggest that the impact of military signaling on the successful resolution of international conflict is typically less decisive than the impact of undramatic political and economic forces. The prevailing constellation of Soviet, Chinese, Vietnamese, and Laotian interests, all blended and mirrored in the pre-crisis draft of the Geneva accords, left little chance for major escalation in Laos after Nam Tha, except through military overreaction by the Kennedy administration or the Thai government. In 1971, the absence of internal political and economic pressures on New Delhi compelling military action in the West, diplomatic pressures against such an offensive, and the obvious political and economic problems of assimilating Pakistani territory were more important than military threats in deterring an Indian offensive in the West.

It is understandable that a tendency exists, among senior U.S. officials, toward post-crisis emphasis on the contribution to peace made by military action. Few political executives can be expected to have both the intellectual detachment and the political courage to state publicly that the risks of escalation associated with U.S. military deployment were assumed unnecessarily. A critical appraisal of the self-serving accounts is an important function of the professional analyst.

CHAPTER SEVEN

Lebanon, 1958, and Jordan, 1970

WILLIAM B. QUANDT

ON SEVERAL occasions since the Second World War the United States has been involved in acute crises in the Middle East. As a global super-power with particularly strong interests in that region, the United States has rarely been indifferent to the dangers of conflict between the Arabs and Israelis and among the Arab states themselves. Twice the United States has reacted to regional conflicts with particularly strong displays of military force, in Lebanon in 1958 and in Jordan in 1970.

In the studies that follow, particular attention will be paid to the rela-tionship between force and diplomacy. Several important themes emerge from a careful comparison of these two crises. It is worth noting them before examining the cases in more detail:

—In both the Lebanese and Jordanian crises U.S. decisionmakers were more concerned by the global dimensions of the conflicts than by their regional implications. In particular, the President was attentive to the role the USSR perceived for itself in the region. In Lebanon, however, once U.S. military force was introduced, a diplomatic effort was launched that was closely attuned to the local situation. In Jordan, where U.S. forces played a less direct role, and where few diplomatic contacts were made with the local adversary forces, the U.S.-Soviet aspect of the conflict remained paramount.

—Despite the emphasis on the global nature of the crises, U.S. policies were most successful in terms of the limited regional objectives that were sought. Order was restored to Lebanon, King Hussein remained in power, American lives were protected. The more grandiose goals, such as checking the spread of Soviet influence in the Middle East, remained elusive.

—U.S. actions in both crises were aimed at influencing both adversaries and friends. Ironically, it appears in both cases that the friends were more influenced by U.S. policies than the adversaries.

—In Lebanon, the use of force preceded the resort to diplomacy. In Jordan, diplomacy and the threat to use force went hand in hand; and force had a much greater role in signaling intentions than in Lebanon.

—The Lebanese civil war was not dealt with primarily as an extension of the Arab-Israeli conflict. By contrast, the Jordanian crisis was intimately related to the Palestinian-Israeli problem, and thus, in the view of President Nixon, to the danger of superpower confrontation. In both cases, however, the fear of general war was present.

—In both crises, the initial U.S. objectives were remarkably similar: to protect American lives and to help friendly governments remain in power. The turning point in each case came as a result of unanticipated external events: the coup in Iraq on July 14, 1958, and the Syrian intervention in Jordan on September 18–19, 1970.

—In both cases, U.S. restraint and control over the use of force were essential to the successful outcomes. A greater reliance on force would almost certainly have been counterproductive.

—The lessons learned by U.S. policymakers from the two cases were dramatically different. In the case of Lebanon, U.S. intervention was followed by a scrapping of the Eisenhower Doctrine and an opening toward Egypt. Following the Jordanian crisis, by contrast, Nixon seemed more convinced than ever that a U.S.-Israeli strategic alliance against the USSR and its clients was the key to maintaining regional stability.

An analysis of these two dramatic crises raises questions about the role of U.S. military forces in the Middle East. In pursuit of its interests the United States has long maintained a significant capability for armed intervention in this region. The Sixth Fleet, normally with two aircraft carriers at its disposal, has been the visible mainstay of the U.S. military presence in the eastern Mediterranean. In addition, the 82nd Airborne Division and units in Europe have been available for intervention. Only in Lebanon in 1958, however, have U.S. forces been ordered to intervene in the Middle East.

The United States has generally chosen to remain militarily uninvolved in purely inter-Arab disputes. Only when the Soviet or Arab-Israeli dimensions of inter-Arab rivalries become involved has the U.S. response been particularly strong, as in 1958 and 1970. On the whole, this has probably been a wise policy, since the United States has little ability to influence inter-Arab politics directly. In the Lebanese civil war of 1975–76, the United States sensibly refrained from military intervention. It is hard to see how U.S. military power could have been usefully employed in such a conflict, other than for the limited purpose of evacuating U.S. citizens.

The Sixth Fleet, as well as other U.S. military capabilities, is not easily related to U.S. policy objectives in the Middle East. Part of its value is symbolic, a tangible sign of U.S. power. But if that were all, it would hardly justify the considerable expense of maintaining two aircraft carriers and numerous other ships in the Mediterranean. The strategic purposes of these forces may justify their presence, quite apart from regional objectives, although this seems unlikely.

The ostensible reason for their existence is their regional peacekeeping function. Of the regional tasks assigned to the Sixth Fleet, two have stood out in recent years: to deter Soviet military intervention in the Middle East, and to protect Israel. There is some reason to doubt whether the fleet has accomplished either of these objectives particularly well. Soviet military involvement in Egypt grew from 1967 to 1972, despite the presence of the Sixth Fleet. In 1967 and 1973 Arab countries were not deterred from making threats against Israel. Nonetheless, the Sixth Fleet has been useful in such crisis situations as Lebanon in 1958 and Jordan in 1970, primarily as a signal of U.S. intentions. As a fighting force the Sixth Fleet is basically an unknown quantity, and it is difficult to justify its specific composition on military grounds alone. The presence of one or two carrier task forces in the Mediterranean does not seem to make much difference in normal times. In a crisis, additional force is needed to make military action credible in any case.

One is tempted to conclude that the military forces that the United States has maintained in the eastern Mediterranean have played only a limited role in the pursuit of U.S. policy objectives in the Middle East. The USSR has taken them seriously, but probably more as a tripwire that could activate NATO than in their own right. The local parties have certainly taken note of them, but not to the point of sacrificing their own objectives or moderating their own behavior. Israel has not viewed them as a substitute for its own strength.

The Jordanian crisis, and to a lesser degree the Lebanese landings of 1958, raise other troubling questions. What would have happened if the United States had become involved in actual hostilities? Would U.S. forces have done well against determined opponents? Can airpower alone, or even in combination with a small number of ground troops, deal with likely regional military contingencies of the future? Middle East armies of the 1970s are, after all, large, well-equipped, and experienced.

If the prospects for effective U.S. military intervention in the Middle East seem dim, the likelihood is much greater that regional U.S. forces, linked to a strong global military posture, will effectively deter large-scale Soviet military interventions in the Arab-Israeli area. In both crises examined here the USSR behaved circumspectly. It recognized that the United States had serious commitments at stake and was determined to act if necessary. The presence of the Soviet squadron in the Mediterranean in 1970 did little to change this reality.

Given the nuclear stalemate and the continuing superpower rivalry in the Middle East, there are likely to be occasions in the future when force and diplomacy will again be involved on behalf of U.S. interests. Force may be a useful adjunct to diplomacy but it cannot substitute for it. Nor can a regional show of force dramatically alter the U.S.-USSR strategic balance. If there is a lesson to be learned from these cases it is that Middle East crises must be dealt with in regional, not just global, terms. Successful diplomacy, even more than successful military operations, requires a knowledge of the local terrain. This was eventually recognized in Lebanon in 1958, but was ignored in Jordan in 1970. As a result, U.S. policy after September 1970 remained stuck in an inflexible mold, whereas after 1958 it was responsive to new regional trends.

U.S. INTERVENTION IN LEBANON, 1958

ON JULY 15, 1958, U.S. Marines waded ashore on the beaches of Lebanon in what has proved to be a unique example of direct military intervention by the United States in the Middle East. Within weeks, 14,000 U.S.

troops were deployed in Lebanon, and other military units elsewhere in the world had been mobilized for action in the Middle East. By October, however, the crisis was over and all U.S. forces were withdrawn. There had been few hostilities and virtually no casualties. In retrospect, many observers wondered about the wisdom of the U.S. use of force in Lebanon. What were the motives that lay behind President Dwight Eisenhower's decision? Who were the targets of the action? And in the light of subsequent developments was the action justifiable?

Historical Background

The decision to land U.S. troops in Lebanon was the result of a particular view of the world, and especially of the Middle East, that existed in Washington circles in mid-1958, combined with a crisis produced by a coup d'état against the pro-Western regime in Iraq on July 14. A few years earlier or a few years later the United States might have reacted quite differently, but in 1958 Egypt's President Gamal Abdel Nasser seemed a menacing force in the Middle East, a force that, consciously or unconsciously, was serving Soviet objectives at the expense of the West.

The emergence of Nasserism in the Arab world can be traced to 1955 and 1956, especially to the abortive British-French-Israeli military campaign against Egypt. Nasser's prestige among Arabs soared after the Suez crisis, while pro-British and pro-Western regimes came under mounting nationalist and radical pressures. Having helped ensure the failure of the Suez venture, the United States stepped into the perceived vacuum by announcing early in 1957 that it would provide aid, including the use of military force, to any Middle Eastern state threatened by international communism. The Eisenhower Doctrine, as this policy came to be known, reflected the widespread U.S. concern with instability and growing Soviet influence in the Middle East, a concern that had been dramatically intensified by the Soviet-Egyptian arms deal of 1955.

Of all the states in the Arab world, only Lebanon enthusiastically endorsed the Eisenhower Doctrine. At least its president, Camille Chamoun, and his conservative Christian supporters did. Other Lebanese, especially the Muslims, resented such close alignment with the West, preferring that Lebanon align itself with the forces of Arab nationalism as represented by Nasser. Lebanon's complex communal structure, with a population composed of numerous Christian and Muslim sects, served to translate the debate over Lebanon's foreign policy orientation into a serious domestic political crisis.

Since independence, Lebanese domestic political life has revolved around delicate sectarian balances, which have provided established political families with a share of power and access to considerable wealth. The National Pact of 1943 enshrined the principle that the president of Lebanon would always be a Maronite Christian, the prime minister a Sunni Muslim, the speaker of the Chamber of Deputies a Shii Muslim; and other important posts were also to be distributed on a sectarian basis. In the Chamber of Deputies the ratio of Christians to Muslims was to be maintained at six to five, thus ensuring Christian predominance within the system, despite demographic changes that eventually produced a Muslim majority.[1]

By 1958 Lebanese political life was factionalized along several lines. President Chamoun was widely believed by rival establishment politicians, both Muslim and Christian, to have been responsible for trying to destroy their power bases in the 1957 elections and through administrative reforms promulgated in March 1958. Saeb Salam, Rashid Karami, and Kamal Jumblatt were particularly outspoken in their opposition, and all became active in leading the insurgents after the May 8 incident that sparked serious fighting throughout much of Lebanon. The Maronite Patriarch and Christian leaders such as Hamid Frangiah also opposed Chamoun. On ideological grounds Arab nationalists and Baathists rejected Chamoun's pro-Western inclinations; on socioeconomic grounds many poor, rural Lebanese resented the liberal, urban-oriented policies of the regime. On the whole, the insurgents found their strongest backing among the rural poor, the alienated intelligentsia, and rival traditional leaders.

Chamoun's support came from some conservative Arabs in Christian areas of Mount Lebanon, some figures in the business and banking community, and some middle class, secular intellectuals. While lacking a strong mass base, Chamoun was able to count on the support of the two best organized political parties in Lebanon, the Parti Populaire Syrien (PPS) and the Kataeb of Pierre Gemayel. Most of Chamoun's support

1. Michael Hudson, *The Precarious Republic: Political Modernization in Lebanon* (Random House, 1968), pp. 44, 52.

thus came from comparatively well-off Christian groups and businessmen in urban areas.[2]

Elsewhere in the Middle East in 1957 tensions were also rising. In Jordan the traditionally pro-British monarchy was under pressure from Arab nationalist sentiment, particularly strong among the Palestinians, to align Jordan more closely with Nasser's Egypt. The king, fearing for his throne, decided to move against the nationalists in the spring and successfully restored his authority. The United States had played a part by maneuvering the Sixth Fleet in the eastern Mediterranean as a visible symbol of U.S. support for the king. The situation in Jordan remained under control, but plots and counterplots kept tensions high.

It was Syria, however, more than Jordan, where radical nationalism and perhaps even communism seemed to some observers to be on the verge of political success in 1957. Syria had never been the model of a stable moderate polity, but in 1957 the trend toward radicalism and violence appeared particularly pronounced. The United States, in collaboration with Iraq, Turkey, and perhaps others, was actively trying to forestall a radical or Communist takeover in Syria, but these plans were unmasked by the Syrians in the late summer, serving to heighten the sense of crisis in the region.[3]

Meanwhile, in Lebanon, parliamentary elections were held in 1957, yielding results that were highly unfavorable to the left and the Arab nationalists generally. Accusations of electoral fraud were widespread, and the already serious communal and political strains in Lebanon were further exacerbated.

In the light of these developments the United States and the United Kingdom began, in November 1957, to develop contingency plans for military intervention in Lebanon and Jordan in the event of an actual or imminent coup d'état in either country. The United States could rely primarily on the Sixth Fleet, and the British could draw on forces stationed on Cyprus. U.S.-British military planning proceeded and by mid-1958 both parties were prepared to act in the Middle East if the decision were made to do so.

2. Ibid., pp. 110–16.
3. Patrick Seale, *The Struggle for Syria: A Study of Post-War Arab Politics, 1945–1958* (Oxford University Press, 1965), pp. 291–96, gives some evidence of a U.S. plot in August 1957.

Events Leading to Crisis

On February 1, 1958, Egypt and Syria announced the creation of the United Arab Republic (UAR), with Nasser as president of the new entity. The initiative for the merger of the two states had come from Syria, but the effect in the United States and the United Kingdom was to cause anxiety about Nasserism sweeping the Middle East. And behind Nasser, it was suspected, stood the USSR.

Within Lebanon, the creation of the UAR added to the conflict that had been developing for several months. Compounding the problem, President Chamoun let it be known that he might seek a constitutional amendment allowing him to serve a second six-year term when his mandate expired in September.

On May 8 violence erupted in the wake of the assassination of an anti-Chamoun journalist. Three days later Chamoun informed U.S. Ambassador Robert McClintock that he might ask for outside help. On May 13, as the Lebanese president accused the UAR of interfering in Lebanese internal affairs by supplying weapons to the insurgents, in Washington Eisenhower met with Secretary of State John Foster Dulles and other advisers to decide upon a response to Chamoun's query as to "what our actions would be if he were to request our assistance."[4]

The next day McClintock was authorized to tell Chamoun that the United States was prepared, upon request from the Lebanese president and government, to send forces to assist Lebanon in its military efforts to defend its independence. Before sending troops, however, the United States would expect Lebanon to file a complaint in the United Nations against external interference and to marshal the support of some other Arab country. Finally, the United States made it clear that troops would not be sent to keep Chamoun in office after his constitutionally sanctioned term expired in the fall.[5]

Verbal support for Lebanon was also forthcoming from Washington. On May 17, an unidentified Air Force spokesman stated that U.S. troops might be sent to Lebanon if they were requested. A few days later, on

4. Dwight D. Eisenhower, *The White House Years: Waging Peace, 1956–1961* (Doubleday, 1965), p. 266; Robert McClintock, "The American Landing in Lebanon," *U.S. Naval Institute Proceedings* (October 1962), pp. 65–69.
5. McClintock, "American Landing in Lebanon," pp. 65–69.

May 20, Dulles asserted that the Eisenhower Doctrine was applicable to the situation in Lebanon even if communism was not behind the troubles. Two days later U.S. and British military teams met in Cyprus to discuss contingency plans.[6]

As violence in Lebanon continued to spread, transport aircraft were sent from the United States to Germany for the possible evacuation of U.S. citizens from Beirut. Army units in Europe were also placed in a higher state of readiness. In early July units of the Sixth Fleet moved closer to the Lebanese coast, and Dulles announced that the United States reserved the right to intervene in Lebanon under Article 51 of the UN Charter.

While the crisis in Lebanon alone had brought the United States to the brink of intervention, it was the news that reached Washington early on July 14, that the monarchy had been overthrown in Iraq, that tipped the scales in favor of the use of force. That morning President Eisenhower, with virtually no dissent from his advisers, decided to respond to President Chamoun's urgent request for aid by ordering U.S. troops into Lebanon.

U.S. Behavior in the Crisis

President Eisenhower, by all accounts, had few doubts that his decision to send troops was a wise one. In his memoirs he acknowledged the risks of alienating the Arab world and of "general war with the Soviet Union," but concluded that to do nothing would be worse.[7] Eisenhower and Dulles were clearly concerned with Nasser's growing influence and with communism. The events in Lebanon, and more dramatically in Iraq, evoked the fear that Western influence would be eliminated from a strategically vital area of the world.

Domestic politics must also have been on the President's mind. The Suez crisis of October–November 1956 and subsequent developments in the Middle East had alienated some sectors of American opinion. Congressional elections were looming in the fall. Eisenhower may well have felt that decisive action in the new crisis developing in Lebanon would help restore his own prestige and also help his party in the congressional

---

6. Alexander L. George and Richard Smoke, *Deterrence in American Foreign Policy: Theory and Practice* (Columbia University Press, 1974), p. 344.

7. Eisenhower, *Waging Peace*, p. 274.

elections. While domestic politics have rarely been mentioned by participants in these events, it would be surprising if they were absent from the President's considerations.

At a meeting at the State Department early on July 14, before the President's decision to intervene, John Foster Dulles, Joint Chiefs of Staff Chairman General Nathan D. Twining, and CIA Director Allen Dulles, along with a number of other senior advisers, agreed that if the United States did nothing: (1) Nasser would take over the whole area; (2) the United States would lose influence not only in the Arab states of the Middle East but in the area generally, and our bases throughout the area would be in jeopardy; (3) the dependability of the United States' commitments for assistance in the event of need would be brought into question throughout the world.[8]

These general concerns led to a predisposition to "do something" to be in a position to influence events in the area after the Iraqi coup.[9] The President had apparently felt frustrated by earlier instances when the United States had not been able to act effectively to counter what he believed to be Communist provocations. Perhaps the experience in Syria in 1957, when covert U.S. intervention had failed, was on his mind. Eisenhower described his feelings as early as May 1958, when President Chamoun had tentatively asked for help:

Against similar provocations in the past the United States had for one reason or another often been unable to lend a hand. But here was one case where it appeared, if the Lebanese government should call upon us for help, we might move firmly and in full accord with the local government and the principles of the United Nations.[10]

Oil and the Arab-Israeli conflict were no doubt on the minds of some Washington policymakers as they planned the response to Chamoun's call for help, but there is little evidence that these interests were much discussed. The British were more preoccupied with oil and urged this concern upon Eisenhower, but the U.S. posture was guarded. The idea of promoting a counterrevolution in Iraq, while appealing to some U.S. policymakers such as General Twining, never seems to have been taken very seriously by Eisenhower, although plans were advanced to protect

8. U.S. State Department, Memorandum for the Record, "Meeting re Iraq" (July 14, 1958; processed).
9. Malcolm Kerr, "The Lebanese Civil War," in Evan Luard, ed., *The International Regulation of Civil Wars* (Thames and Hudson, 1972), p. 78.
10. Eisenhower, *Waging Peace*, p. 266.

Kuwait from Iraqi aggression. Nor is there evidence that the United States acted in Lebanon primarily to forestall a trend that might have culminated in full-scale Arab-Israeli war.[11] In fact, Eisenhower on several occasions in the first days of the crisis reportedly considered the merits of "unleashing" Israel against Nasser, and General Twining seriously proposed that Israel should seize the West Bank of Jordan as part of an area-wide counteroffensive that would include British intervention in Iraq and Turkish intervention in Syria.[12] Needless to say, such thoughts were not translated into policy, but the fact that they were considered suggests that prevention of an Arab-Israeli war was not seen as the priority concern for the Eisenhower administration.

Operational Objectives

If the broad concerns behind U.S. policy in the Lebanon crisis can be comparatively easily discerned, what of the more concrete operational objectives? What did the United States hope to accomplish through its military deployments and its diplomacy?

Eisenhower's decision to use force in the Lebanon crisis was meant to influence both adversaries and friends. Principal among the adversaries was the USSR. U.S. action was designed, among other things, to deter the USSR from exploiting for its advantage a volatile situation growing out of the events in Iraq and Lebanon. Eisenhower and Dulles judged that the USSR would not react militarily, although others such as Twining and some State Department officials were considerably less sanguine. Even the pessimists, however, felt that "we should face the risk now [of general war] as well as any time."[13]

Apart from the hope that U.S. military action would prevent the USSR from gaining ground in the Middle East, an objective that was formulated in particularly vague terms, the more concrete goals involved Lebanon, Jordan, and Iraq. In Lebanon the United States hoped to ensure that the shock waves of the Iraqi revolution would not exacerbate the tensions that had engulfed the country in civil war during the preceding months.

The objective sought by Eisenhower in Lebanon, then, was a rela-

11. Kerr, "Lebanese Civil War," pp. 79–80, provides the most cogent argument that intervention in Lebanon was intended to prevent a chain reaction that could have ended in Arab-Israeli war.
12. Interviews with ranking U.S. officials involved in the Lebanon decision.
13. Loy Henderson, in "Meeting re Iraq."

tively limited one—to prevent dissident forces, backed by the UAR, from overthrowing the legal government and endangering American lives. Most U.S. officials seem to have endorsed this policy, although the U.S. ambassador in Beirut was opposed to the landing of the troops, and subsequently went to considerable lengths to ensure that they did not inadvertently clash with the Lebanese Army under the command of General Fuad Chehab.[14]

It has been argued by some observers that the real objective of the U.S. forces in Lebanon was to stage a counterrevolution in Iraq.[15] The coup in Iraq was indeed the critical event leading to U.S. intervention, and there were some in the U.S. government who contemplated a major operation throughout the Middle East that would simultaneously deal with the anti-Western regimes in the UAR and Iraq, relying on some mixture of U.S., British, Israeli, and even Turkish forces to do the job. The British were also proponents of broad action to protect the Western position in the area, but were unwilling to act alone.[16] Prime Minister Harold Macmillan had been in Washington during June to discuss the situation in the Middle East, and when the Iraqi revolution occurred he immediately sought Washington's views. To his obvious dismay, Washington was prepared only to send troops into Lebanon, and he was urged to hold his own forces in reserve.[17] It was only a few days later that the United States promised support for British forces to intervene in Jordan at King Hussein's request. By then, the hope of restoring a friendly regime in Baghdad had faded, but the British continued to show concern with Iraqi designs on Kuwait, a fear that came to be taken seriously in Washington as well.

While it is impossible to be certain that Eisenhower did not envisage the use of force to overthrow the new Iraqi regime, it seems more likely that, in the wake of the July 14 revolution, he wanted to have some forces in the area in case events took an unexpected turn. After all, the new regime was an enigma. Was it Nasserist, or possibly even Communist?

14. See the account in Charles W. Thayer, *Diplomat* (Harper, 1959), chaps. 1–3.

15. Peter Lyon, *Eisenhower: Portrait of the Hero* (Little, Brown, 1974), p. 775, argues that counterrevolution in Iraq was seriously considered. He bases this conclusion on the size of the U.S. force in Lebanon, which he gives as 114,000, relying on the misprint in Eisenhower's memoirs, *Waging Peace*, p. 286, where the figure of 114,357 is given. The correct figure is 14,357.

16. Harold Macmillan, *Riding the Storm, 1956–1959* (Macmillan, 1971), pp. 506–25.

17. Ibid., p. 512.

Could it hold onto power, or would some other faction of the army try to seize control? If a group of pro-Western officers were to call for help how should the United States respond? What if the new Iraqi regime were to try to annex Kuwait? It seems fair to assume that Eisenhower wanted to be in a position to deal with such contingencies if they should arise. Thus, a minimum U.S. force in Lebanon and a British force in Jordan, plus other U.S. deployments elsewhere in the world, would provide the capability that might be needed if the situation in the area were to take an unexpected dangerous turn. In the event, of course, nothing of the sort outlined here happened, and Robert Murphy, the deputy under secretary of state, was even sent to Baghdad to reassure the new rulers there that the United States was not plotting against them.[18]

In brief, the use of force by the United States in the Lebanon crisis was related to a set of general objectives involving Lebanon and British policy in Jordan:

1. Prevent the spread of instability (Nasserism, communism) to the remaining pro-Western Arab regimes of Lebanon, Jordan, Kuwait, and Saudi Arabia.

2. Deter Soviet adventurism in the area.

3. Develop the capability to act in or against Iraq should circumstances require.

4. Enhance U.S. credibility as an ally and as a superpower.

And to some specific objectives:

1. Stabilize the situation in and around Beirut, by the use of force if necessary (control airport, protect presidency).

2. Evacuate and protect U.S. citizens if necessary.

3. Coordinate a response with the British and limit the scope of their action to Jordan.

Patterns of Communication

To convey these operational objectives to the intended targets of U.S. actions during the crisis a variety of means were employed. Before the crisis, the goals of preventing the spread of communism and of supporting pro-Western regimes had been enshrined in the Eisenhower Doctrine and had been periodically repeated by Dulles. Once the crisis entered its new phase on July 14, however, a restatement of purposes was neces-

18. Eisenhower, *Waging Peace,* p. 281.

sary. Eisenhower concentrated first on the British allies to ensure that their response would be consistent with U.S. plans to act unilaterally in Lebanon. Eisenhower reportedly talked to Macmillan by telephone in the morning of July 14, although the content of that communication is unknown.[19] Later that afternoon, after giving the order to land troops the next day in Lebanon, Eisenhower again called Macmillan to inform him of his decision. Macmillan stressed that the issue was not Lebanon alone, but rather that it involved broader developments in the area and that some action in Jordan was also essential.[20] Eisenhower suggested that the United Kingdom hold its forces in Cyprus in reserve for the time being. According to Eisenhower, Macmillan wanted his assurance that "we were in this together, all the way. This I gave him with the understanding that I could take action only one phase at a time."[21] Two days later, Macmillan sent Foreign Secretary Selwyn Lloyd to Washington, where he found the U.S. attitude improving.[22] In talks with Lloyd, Eisenhower and Dulles promised "moral and logistical support" for the British operation in Jordan and agreed to work to get Israeli permission for overflights.[23]

Eisenhower was aware of the need to defend his policy before U.S. and international opinion. On July 14 he met with congressional leaders, among whom several were critical of the decision and questioned the assumption that Nasser was a tool of the Communists. As troops were disembarking in Lebanon on July 15, Eisenhower released a statement at the White House which stressed that the purpose of the military operation was to defend Lebanon's independence and integrity.[24] A similar message was sent to Congress, and Ambassador Henry Cabot Lodge made the same point at the United Nations, where a meeting of the Security Council had been called for July 15. Finally, Eisenhower gave a public address to the nation that same evening.

In his speech, Eisenhower referred to such precedents as the civil war in Greece in 1947, the Communist takeover in Czechoslovakia in 1948, the fall of China to the Communists in 1949, and Communist threats in

---

19. Robert Cutler, *No Time for Rest* (Little, Brown, 1965), p. 363.
20. Macmillan, *Riding the Storm*, p. 512.
21. Eisenhower, *Waging Peace*, p. 273.
22. Macmillan, *Riding the Storm*, p. 515.
23. Eisenhower, *Waging Peace*, p. 279. Eisenhower refused to commit U.S. forces to Jordan but promised to help ensure the success of the British operations if they got into trouble.
24. Ibid., pp. 271–74.

Korea and Indochina beginning in 1950. The implication was that communism lay behind the events in Lebanon as well. Nonetheless, Eisenhower did indicate the limited scope of U.S. action, emphasizing that he
hoped rapid UN action to protect Lebanon's independence would "permit the early withdrawal of United States forces." Nothing was said of
broad concerns with Iraq, oil, or the Arab-Israeli conflict. For public
purposes this was a Lebanese crisis, behind which communism's malign
influence could be detected. In brief, public statements did little to clarify
specific U.S. objectives, serving rather to justify the operation in terms of
the Eisenhower Doctrine.

Perhaps the most important means of clarifying U.S. objectives to the
key actors in the crisis was through Robert Murphy's diplomatic mission
to the area. At Dulles's suggestion, Eisenhower agreed to send Murphy
to Lebanon, where he arrived on July 19. Murphy quickly concluded
that communism had nothing to do with the crisis in Lebanon, and in
talks with various Lebanese leaders helped to work out the elements of
the political compromise that resulted in General Chehab's election to
the presidency on July 31.[25] Shortly thereafter, U.S. troop strength in
Lebanon was reduced.

In addition to his diplomatic efforts in Lebanon, Murphy also traveled
to Baghdad and Cairo to reassure Iraq's new ruler, Abd al-Karim Qasim,
that U.S. troops in Lebanon were not aimed at Iraq and to reestablish
contact with Nasser, whose intentions in the area were of continuing
concern to Washington. The net effect of the Murphy mission was to
scale down the scope of U.S. objectives to the restoration of order and
political stability in Lebanon. The more grandiose anti-Communist, anti-
Nasser, and anti-Iraq goals faded into the background as the worst fears
of policymakers proved to be unfounded. The landings of U.S. troops
may have had a calming effect on the area, and, having served that purpose at the outset, they became less relevant to subsequent events than
Murphy's diplomatic efforts. From the initial pursuit of vague, global
objectives, the United States increasingly limited its goals to ensuring an
orderly transition to a new regime acceptable to Nasser and to the majority of Lebanese. Unlike Eisenhower's public statements, which tended
to obscure the goals of U.S. action in Lebanon, Murphy's talks in Lebanon, Iraq, and Egypt appear to have helped clarify and set limits on the
military operations.

25. Robert Murphy, *Diplomat Among Warriors* (Doubleday, 1964), p. 450.

Military Operations

In mid-May, shortly after President Chamoun had accused the UAR of intervention in Lebanon's internal affairs and had queried the United States on its attitude in the event that a request for military assistance were forthcoming, Eisenhower authorized a number of steps that prepared the way for later military action. First, the Marine contingent of the Sixth Fleet was doubled in strength to over 3,500 men. Second, arms were sent to Lebanon by air and sea. Third, transport aircraft were sent to Germany in the event that U.S. citizens had to be evacuated from the Middle East. Twenty-two Army units in Europe were also placed on alert. All of these actions in May had no visible impact on the crisis, and it was not until July 14 that a second series of moves was ordered, this time including the landing of troops in Lebanon.

As soon as the news of the Iraqi coup reached Washington, Eisenhower met with his diplomatic and military advisers and ordered a worldwide military alert of U.S. forces. Strategic Air Command planes were prepared for takeoff if necessary. The Sixth Fleet, including the aircraft carriers *Essex, Saratoga,* and *Wasp,* was ordered to move toward the eastern Mediterranean. Joint Chiefs Chairman Twining was ordered to implement the plan for landing U.S. troops in Lebanon the next day.[26]

On the afternoon of July 15 the 2nd Battalion of the 2nd Marine Regiment, consisting of 1,700 men, landed on the beaches of Lebanon. U.S. Ambassador Robert McClintock, who disapproved of the landing, was worried that the Lebanese Army might oppose the Marines by force. There were, in fact, elements in the Lebanese armed forces that apparently favored resisting the U.S. landing. General Chehab had tried to keep the army out of the civil war, and now was confronted with an external threat as well. Ambassador McClintock recognized the danger and rushed to the point of debarkation, where he managed to convince Chehab to restrain his forces. The Lebanese Army then escorted the Marines to designated areas. U.S. forces were thereafter deployed with utmost care to avoid unintended clashes.[27]

26. Cutler, *No Time for Rest,* p. 364.
27. Kerr, "Lebanese Civil War," pp. 79–80, argues that the key to the success of the intervention was the avoidance of violence. The troops by their mere presence had a calming effect, and the subsequent deployment of troops away from rebel-held areas helped to avoid hostile encounters. See McClintock, "American Landing in Lebanon," and Colonel H. A. Hadd, "Orders Firm but Flexible," *U.S. Naval Institute Proceedings* (October 1962), for details on operational problems of the landing and disputes over the chain of command.

The next day, July 16, the 3rd Battalion of the 6th Marine Regiment landed, with the 1st Battalion of the 8th Marine Regiment arriving on the 18th. Two Army battle groups in Germany, the 187th Airborne and 503rd Airborne, were on call and could arrive in the area within twelve hours. In addition, tactical aircraft were flown to Turkey and the Sixth Fleet was reinforced.

General Twining also recommended the deployment of Air Force tankers into forward positions, as well as an increased level of readiness for the Strategic Air Command. According to Eisenhower, Twining advised him that these moves would be visible and might cause some misinterpretation of U.S. intentions, to which the President responded by ordering the moves precisely to underscore U.S. "readiness and determination without implying any threat of aggression."[28]

Other military preparations were considered as well, such as the movement overseas of two full divisions. But "shipping was short," and Eisenhower decided not to charter additional vessels. Instead he merely ordered Twining "to keep a roster of available shipping." "Part of the 82nd Airborne Division [however] was held ready for quick airlift to Europe."[29]

Finally, and presumably in response to British urgings, Eisenhower approved a recommendation from the Joint Chiefs for a seaborne movement of a Marine Corps regimental combat team then stationed on Okinawa to the Persian Gulf. There, in Eisenhower's view, it could help deter an Iraqi move into Kuwait or help protect other friendly governments. Twining was ordered to "be prepared to employ, subject to [Eisenhower's] approval, *whatever* means might become necessary to prevent any unfriendly forces from moving into Kuwait."[30] It seems clear that Eisenhower was referring to the possible use of nuclear weapons, an issue that was discussed several times during the crisis.

Despite pressure from Macmillan, Eisenhower decided against send-

28. Eisenhower, *Waging Peace,* p. 276. In his memoirs, *Neither Liberty Nor Safety: A Hard Look at U.S. Military Policy and Strategy* (Holt, Rinehart and Winston, 1966), pp. 64–65, General Nathan Twining takes a very hawkish view of the Lebanon crisis, arguing that the State Department "backpedaled" by ordering U.S. troops not to go into Lebanon with nuclear-tipped rockets. On page 148 he claims that "the Soviet bluff to take over Lebanon was called" by U.S. military action in the crisis.

29. Eisenhower, *Waging Peace,* p. 276.

30. Ibid., p. 278; emphasis in original.

ing U.S. troops into Jordan. He did, however, agree to help the United Kingdom with logistics and supply problems. This involved airlifting some equipment and supplies from Lebanon to Jordan, and Eisenhower even contemplated resupplying British forces from the U.S. air bases at Dhahran in Saudi Arabia. The Saudis, however, withheld permission for such an operation, although this apparently would not have deterred Eisenhower from using them in an emergency.[31]

At peak strength, the U.S. military presence in Lebanon consisted of more than 14,000 troops, about 8,000 Army and 6,000 Marines. The Sixth Fleet, with nearly 70 ships and 40,000 men, played a key role in support of the landing. Marines and Army paratroopers were airlifted from the United States and West Germany, and support aircraft were flown from bases in the United States.[32]

As the crisis eased, U.S. troops began their withdrawal in mid-August, the last contingent leaving Lebanon on October 28. No combat had occurred involving the Lebanese Army, and only one U.S. fatality was registered, the result of a sniper bullet.

The Relationship of Force to Objectives

The use of force was primarily intended to stabilize the volatile situation in Lebanon, and to a large degree it was successful in doing so. U.S. troops were available to help the legitimate government maintain order if necessary, but their mere presence had a calming effect, and virtually no hostile encounters occurred. The U.S. ambassador in Beirut worked closely with Lebanese Army Commander Chehab to avoid unintended confrontations, and after the first few days the danger of hostilities was on the wane. Thus one of the President's immediate objectives was accomplished rapidly, although the smooth transition from the Chamoun regime to that of Chehab required the diplomatic skills of Robert Murphy as much as the presence of 14,000 U.S. soldiers. Table 7-1 summarizes the interlocked political and military moves in Lebanon.

A second objective was to ensure stability in Jordan, but without the use of U.S. troops. To achieve this goal Eisenhower was obliged to coordinate carefully with Macmillan, restraining the British from envision-

31. Ibid., p. 280.
32. Lt. Col. M. M. Bodron, U.S. Army, "U.S. Intervention in Lebanon—1958," *Military Review* (February 1976).

Table 7-1. *Political and Military Developments in the Lebanon Crisis*

Date	Military moves	Diplomatic moves	Events in Lebanon	International reaction
May 8			Anti-Chamoun journalist assassinated. Violence erupts in Tripoli.	
May 11			Chamoun informs Ambassador McClintock he might ask for help from U.S.	
May 12			Disorders spread to Beirut. Anti-U.S. demonstrations.	
May 13		Eisenhower meets with Dulles and other advisers to decide on response to possible appeal from Chamoun.	More disturbances. Lebanon accuses UAR of "massive intervention." Sends protest note.	
May 14	U.S. Navy announces that size of amphibious force in Mediterranean is being doubled.	Ambassador McClintock informs Chamoun that U.S. would be prepared in some circumstances to send troops to Lebanon. Explicit conditions spelled out. Troops would not be sent to keep Chamoun in office.		
	U.S. supplies anti-riot equipment to Lebanon.			
	U.S. and UK start "routine" maneuvers in central Mediterranean.			

Date			
May 17	18 Globemaster planes flown from Donaldson Air Base, South Carolina, to West Germany for possible evacuation of U.S. citizens. Another 22 on alert.	State Dept. announces that consideration would be given to Chamoun call for troops.	Tass statement that U.S. or other intervention could have serious consequences for peace in the Middle East.
May 19	NATO naval exercise switched to eastern Mediterranean so U.S. and British ships can be available for possible evacuation operation.		
May 20		Nasser confers with U.S. Ambassador Hare on Lebanese crisis. Dulles says Eisenhower Doctrine is applicable to Lebanon.	
May 22	U.S.-British military teams in Cyprus to discuss contingency plans.	Lebanon asks for urgent meeting of UN Security Council; charges UAR interference.	
June 6			UN Security Council begins debate on Lebanon.
June 14–16			Heavy fighting in Beirut.
June 19–20			Hammarskjöld in Beirut.
June 26–27			Heavy fighting in Tripoli.

Table 7-1 (continued)

Date	Military moves	Diplomatic moves	Events in Lebanon	International reaction
July 3	6th Fleet moves closer to Lebanese coast (early July).		Hammarskjöld says there is no evidence to warrant charge of UAR intervention.	
July 14	Eisenhower receives Lebanese request for troops, orders military alert. SAC planes prepared for takeoff, 6th Fleet ordered to move toward eastern Mediterranean.	Eisenhower calls for emergency meeting of UN Security Council.		Coup in Iraq; pro-Western monarchy overthrown.
		NSC meeting; Eisenhower decides to send troops.		
	Twining ordered to implement plan for landing troops.	Eisenhower talks to Macmillan twice by telephone; suggests U.K. hold forces in reserve.		
	Macmillan orders 6,000 British troops to prepare for movements to Middle East.			
July 15	2nd Battalion of 2nd Marine Regiment disembarks, Lebanon.	Ambassador Lodge presents U.S. resolution in UN to end infiltration of illegal arms and personnel.		Meeting of UN Security Council.
	U.S. naval, air, and army units ordered to "improved readiness positions" to support Marines.	McClintock negotiates with General Chehab.		

July 16	3rd Battalion of 6th Marine Regiment lands.	U.S. informs NATO allies of move as Marines land.	Nasser flies to Moscow.
	187th and 503rd Airborne on call in Germany.	Eisenhower addresses nation.	
	82nd Airborne held ready for airlift to Europe.	Murphy leaves for Lebanon.	
	Eisenhower approves recommendation for seaborne movement of Marines from Okinawa.	Lloyd flies to Washington at invitation of Dulles, who promises "moral and logistic support" for British operation in Jordan.	
July 17	British paratroopers land in Jordan.	Lloyd and Dulles confer.	Nasser in Moscow discusses U.S. intervention. Khrushchev decides to stage maneuvers on Turkish border.
	U.S. jets from 6th Fleet cover British landings.		
	U.S. paratroopers airlifted from W. Germany to Adana, Turkey.		

Table 7-1 (*continued*)

Date	Military moves	Diplomatic moves	Events in Lebanon	International reaction
July 18	1st Battalion of 8th Marine Regiment lands.	Ambassador Hare calls on Ali Sabri to ensure that UAR fully understands why U.S. acted as it did. U.S. warns UAR any attack on its military units could have "grave consequences."		Nasser arrives in Damascus. Attacks occupation of Lebanon. Large scale anti-U.S. and anti-British demonstrations in Moscow.
July 19	More Marines, 1,700 paratroopers land in Lebanon.			Khrushchev proposes summit meeting to Eisenhower, Macmillan, de Gaulle, and Nehru.
July 20		Lloyd returns to London.		
July 21	Copies of leaflets explaining U.S. landing signed by Eisenhower dropped over Lebanon by U.S. planes. 1st Marine Division alerted for move to Middle East.			NATO council meeting. Israeli Prime Minister David Ben Gurion says recent events in Middle East increase "danger of Israel's encirclement by President Nasser."
July 22		Eisenhower replies to Khrushchev's letter, suggests heads-of-government meeting best held through UN.		Macmillan proposes that summit conference be held in New York at special meeting of UN Security Council.

Date			
July 23	U.S. aircraft demonstrate over Lebanon in "salute to people."		Khrushchev sends letters to Eisenhower, Macmillan, de Gaulle, accepts proposals for summit conference within Security Council framework, says it should begin July 28.
July 24			
July 25		Eisenhower tells Khrushchev U.S. will not limit conference to discussion of U.S.-British military actions. Says July 28 is too early for start of conference.	
July 26	More U.S. forces reported heading toward area.		
July 27			
July 28			
July 29			
July 30		Murphy in Amman.	Khrushchev accuses Eisenhower of delaying tactics on conference.

Table 7-1 (*continued*)

Date	Military moves	Diplomatic moves	Events in Lebanon	International reaction
July 31		Eisenhower and Macmillan propose summit meeting to be held August 12 (letters to Khrushchev).	Chehab elected president.	UN Observer Force makes 2nd report; finds no evidence of infiltration from UAR.
Aug. 1				
Aug. 2	1,800 more troops and tank battalion land, 3,000 more on way.			
Aug. 3	U.S. lands 2,200 more troops. Total now 13,300.			
Aug. 4	Anglo-American airlift over Israel ceases.			
Aug. 5				Khrushchev withdraws support for summit conference after visit to Peking.

ing a major combined operation in the Middle East, while facilitating the more limited task of moving British forces into Jordan and keeping them adequately supplied. As part of this package the United States apparently agreed to help look after British oil interests, especially in Kuwait. To fulfill the conditions of this agreement the United States transferred to the Middle East some forces from Okinawa. It seems unlikely that the new regime in Iraq was contemplating an attack on Kuwait at that time, but the movement of forces to the Persian Gulf was as much intended to reassure the British as to deter Qasim. The net effect of these U.S. military moves was to guarantee that the British acted in Jordan on the same pattern as the Americans in Lebanon. While Macmillan was less than overjoyed with the scope of the operations, he was unable to move independently and thus British policy fell into line with that chosen by Eisenhower. Once again Eisenhower succeeded in achieving one of his specific objectives.

The more sweeping goals of preventing the spread of Nasserism and communism were beyond the reach of U.S. and British policy. How the use of force could achieve such goals, short of mounting coups d'état in Damascus, Baghdad, and Cairo, was a bit of a mystery. While the regimes in Beirut and Amman were able to achieve a degree of stability and strength thanks to U.S. and British support, the forces of radical nationalism remained strong in the Arab world and were essentially unaffected by the Lebanon crisis and the U.S. reaction to it. Measured by the maximum objective of thwarting Nasserism, Eisenhower's decisions were not a success, and shortly after the withdrawal of U.S. forces from Lebanon in October the Eisenhower Doctrine was effectively put on ice and a new policy of attempted rapprochement with Nasser was initiated.

Reflecting on the crisis, Eisenhower certainly felt that the use of force had been justified in terms of the limited objectives sought. In his memoirs, Eisenhower termed the operation "highly satisfactory," crediting it with the achievement of a peaceful resolution of the Lebanese internal conflict:[33]

One additional benefit to the West, intangible and unpublicized but nevertheless important, came out of the affair. This was a definite change in Nasser's attitude toward the United States. . . . In our action and the Kremlin's cautious reaction he found much food for thought, it would appear. Presumably he concluded that he could not depend completely on Russia to help him in any

33. Eisenhower, *Waging Peace*, pp. 288–89.

Middle East struggle, and he certainly had his complacency as to America's helplessness completely shattered.[34]

From Eisenhower's perspective, it seems clear, a major achievement of the Lebanon operation was the demonstration that the United States was capable of acting decisively, a lesson that he apparently thought was particularly important to convey to the USSR and to the nonaligned countries in mid-1958.

The Impact on Domestic Lebanese Politics

The U.S. intervention in Lebanon stimulated a search for a political solution to the crisis. A successor to Chamoun had to be found who was acceptable to the Arab nationalists as well as the Christian community. General Fuad Chehab, head of the army, quickly emerged as a man capable of attracting broad support. He had the advantage of being relatively nonpartisan, not tied to the traditional establishment, and sufficiently neutralist in his ideology to be tolerated by the Nasserists. He was easily chosen as president on July 31 and subsequently named one of the prominent leaders of the insurgents, Rashid Karami, as prime minister.

Under Chehab's presidency Lebanon recovered quickly from its civil war; a strong executive emerged and Lebanon once again began to develop rapidly. But underlying social and economic problems were not resolved; the rigidities of the sectarian-based political system were not eliminated; and under the weak leadership of the 1960s strains began to appear.

After the 1967 Arab-Israeli war, external pressures on Lebanon mounted, leading to a severe crisis in 1969 over the issue of the Palestinian presence in Lebanon. In subsequent years tensions remained acute, and Lebanese political life began to polarize along a complex sectarian and class-based line. By 1975 civil war had once again engulfed Lebanon, resulting in the Syrian military intervention of early 1976. Unlike the 1958 civil war, however, neither major power showed an interest in intervening militarily. The 1958 crisis had done little to help solve Lebanon's internal problems, and perhaps that realization served as a note of caution for outside powers when the much more bloody and prolonged civil war began in 1975.

34. Ibid., p. 290.

Egyptian Reactions

Egypt's President Nasser was clearly one of the primary targets of the U.S. policy adopted in January 1957 and implemented in Lebanon in July 1958. It is thus worth investigating how he reacted to the landing of U.S. forces.

At the time of the Lebanon crisis, Nasser was at the peak of his career as an Arab nationalist leader. After the Suez crisis in 1956 his status in Egypt and elsewhere in the Arab world had grown. Radical nationalists in numerous Arab countries looked to him for inspiration and support. The Syrian Baath party went so far as to plead for political union with Egypt, which was realized with the creation of the UAR early in 1958.

Nasser had ambivalent feelings toward the United States. From 1952 to 1954 he was on close terms with U.S. officials and was viewed in Washington as a promising moderate Arab leader. The conclusion of an arms deal with the USSR in 1955, however, had cooled the relationship between Cairo and Washington considerably, and the Dulles-Eisenhower decision to withdraw the offer to finance the Aswan High Dam in mid-1956 was a further blow to the chances of maintaining friendly ties. Eisenhower's stand against the British, French, and Israeli attack on Egypt in October 1956 created a momentary sense of gratitude on the part of Nasser, but the subsequent development of the Eisenhower Doctrine, so clearly aimed at "containing" Nasserism, undermined what little goodwill existed toward the United States in Cairo. By 1958 Nasser was deeply suspicious of U.S. intentions in the area. A conspirator by background and distrustful by nature, Nasser saw the United States actively working against him throughout the Arab world.

Although Nasser was an advocate of Arab unity he had entered the union with Syria only reluctantly. There was no indication that he hoped to add Lebanon to the UAR, although he clearly did oppose the strongly pro-American policies of President Chamoun. When incipient civil war broke out in Lebanon in May, Nasser no doubt helped to provide arms and money to his supporters.

Nonetheless, Nasser did not seem to want a full-scale test of strength in Lebanon. In June, Nasser surprised Eisenhower by not objecting to the dispatch of UN observer teams to Lebanon. This was followed by a direct bid from Nasser to the United States offering to use his influence to end the crisis in Lebanon. The conditions that he posed were that

Chamoun finish his term in office; that he be succeeded by General Chehab; and that the rebels be offered amnesty. Eisenhower notes that these were "not wholly unreasonable" conditions.[35] In fact, they later became the basis for the U.S.-sponsored settlement of the crisis.

Nasser learned of the coup in Iraq and of the U.S. decision to send troops to Lebanon while on a visit to Yugoslavia. After some hesitation he decided to fly to Moscow for consultations with the Soviet leadership. He seemed particularly fearful that the United States might use Turkey to invade Syria, now the northern region of the UAR. In 1957, when a similar danger had existed, the USSR had staged troop maneuvers on the Turkish border and warned Turkey not to intervene in Syria. At a minimum Nasser must have hoped for a repeat of this performance. By the time Nasser left Moscow, Soviet Premier Nikita Khrushchev had promised to maneuver twenty-four divisions on the Turkish frontier, although he reportedly warned Nasser, "It is only a maneuver."[36]

In addition to securing a minimal degree of Soviet support against the U.S. intervention, Nasser also directed that Egyptian arms be sent to the new regime in Iraq. Preventing a counterrevolution in Baghdad was clearly high on his agenda.

While Nasser was apparently concerned when he first learned of the U.S. use of force that his interests and influence in the Arab world were the target of the operation, he soon realized that the U.S. objective was essentially limited to Lebanon and was not incompatible with his own goals there. He was able to confirm this through his talks with Robert Murphy, and by fall of 1958 he saw that U.S. troops were not planning to remain in Lebanon indefinitely. Subsequently, even in moments of great anger at the United States, Nasser did not list the Lebanon landings as one of the U.S. crimes against the Arab world. By 1959, in fact, he was talking to Washington again about aid while publicly quarreling with Khrushchev and Qasim.

Perhaps Eisenhower was correct: Nasser was impressed both by the U.S. ability to act and by the restraint that characterized the operation and the subsequent diplomacy. In this sense Nasser may have been influenced by the U.S. resort to force, although it would be hard to point to any specific action that Nasser did or did not take as a direct result of

35. Ibid., p. 268.
36. Mohamed Heikal, *The Cairo Documents* (Doubleday, 1973), p. 135.

the U.S. military action in Lebanon. Certainly Nasser was not deterred from seizing control of Lebanon, since that was not high on his list of priorities, although some of his followers in Lebanon moderated their behavior once U.S. forces intervened.

The Soviet Reaction

The USSR, in a general way, was the second principal target of the U.S. intervention in Lebanon. Eisenhower and Secretary of State Dulles were both confident that the USSR would not react militarily to the U.S. action in Lebanon, "particularly if other parts of the Middle East were not involved in the operations," as Eisenhower was later to write.[37]

Since early 1955 the Soviet leaders—Nikita Khrushchev in particular—had embarked upon a policy of weakening Western influence in the Middle East by offering arms to "anti-imperialist" regimes. Egypt was the key to this strategy. The most important Soviet objective was to undermine the military posture of the United States in the Middle East, and for this the USSR was prepared to cooperate with regimes that were decidedly non-Communist in their internal makeup. Nasserism, with its anti-Western overtones and its goal of removing foreign bases from Arab soil, suited the Soviet objective nicely. The USSR did not have to do much but supply military and economic aid.

The overthrow of the pro-British regime in Baghdad—the only Arab regime that had agreed to join a pro-Western defense pact—was precisely the kind of development that the USSR welcomed. When Nasser arrived in Moscow on July 17, he found Khrushchev "terribly excited," according to Mohamed Heikal, who was present at the meeting. But he also gave the impression that "he was finding it difficult to formulate a policy because events were moving so quickly and so dangerously."[38]

For several hours Nasser and Khrushchev discussed U.S. intentions. According to Egyptian sources, Khrushchev thought that the Americans had lost their senses. Nasser pressed for Soviet assurances in the event that the United States staged a major counteroffensive in the Arab world, leading Khrushchev to reply, according to Heikal, "Frankly, we are not ready for confrontation. We are not ready for World War III." Khru-

---

37. Eisenhower, *Waging Peace*, p. 266.
38. Heikal, *Cairo Documents*, p. 132.

shchev even refused to issue an ultimatum, settling instead for a policy of staging maneuvers on the Turkish border.[39]

On the diplomatic front the USSR strongly opposed the U.S. and British actions in the United Nations but failed to achieve any results. On July 20 Khrushchev suggested to Eisenhower a summit meeting, a proposal that was refused. This led to a long, and largely ritualistic, exchange of letters between Eisenhower and Khrushchev over the next several weeks.[40] All of this was superseded by a UN General Assembly debate in August, which ended with a call for UN measures that would lead to the withdrawal of foreign troops from Lebanon and Jordan.

From the little that is known about Soviet behavior in the Lebanon crisis, it appears that Eisenhower was generally correct in his assessment of the probable Soviet reaction to a show of force by the United States. If part of the objective of the exercise was to demonstrate that the United States had both the will and the capability to act in pursuit of its interests, the point seems to have gotten through to Khrushchev. As such, it was one among many of the tests of strength between the superpowers in secondary regions that characterized the cold war. In this instance the United States seemed to have the upper hand.

The British Role

As is typically the case when the United States resorts to the threat or actual use of force, part of the exercise is intended to influence friends. In this case the United Kingdom was very much on Eisenhower's mind during the first few days of the crisis. For at least eight months British and U.S. military teams had been working on plans for intervention in Lebanon and Jordan. A joint operation had clearly been envisioned. Yet, when the moment of truth came, British and U.S. objectives were not entirely congruent. Part of the U.S. effort thus became to persuade the British to act within a relatively limited framework, rather than to stand aside entirely or to aim for a major restoration of Western influence in the Arab world.

Macmillan had traveled to Washington in early June to talk about the Middle East situation. He was particularly anxious that U.S. and British policies be closely coordinated. The lessons of Suez weighed heavily on

39. Ibid., pp. 133–34.
40. Eisenhower, *Waging Peace*, pp. 283–85, 287–88.

him. Thus it was with some embarrassment that he learned from Eisenhower on July 14 that the decision had been made in Washington to respond favorably to Chamoun's request for intervention, but that it preferred to act alone. Macmillan chided Eisenhower, perhaps not so gently, with the suggestion that he was "doing a Suez on me."[41]

Subsequent contacts revealed that Dulles was hesitant about British intervention in Jordan. Macmillan did not want to go in only to be abandoned by the United States. To avoid misunderstandings, Macmillan sent Foreign Secretary Lloyd to Washington on July 16, where he extracted a promise of support for British intervention in Jordan in response to King Hussein's request. He must also have received assurances that the United States would not be indifferent to an Iraqi move against Kuwait. Thus, while refusing to help the British restore their position in Iraq, Eisenhower was prepared to limit the damage to British interests elsewhere and to assist in the British deployments to Jordan. The British were less than enthusiastic at the degree of cooperation they received from their superpower ally, but had no alternative but to play by Eisenhower's rules. As often seems to be the case, it is easier to influence friends than adversaries. More than Nasser or the Soviet leaders, the British were directly affected by the decisions made in Washington. They were told in no uncertain terms that the U.S. objectives were limited, a message that soon reached the ostensible targets of the action as well—namely, Nasser and Khrushchev.

Outcomes of the Crisis

A balanced assessment of U.S. behavior in the Lebanon crisis is made difficult by the suspicion that the outcome might have been much the same if the United States had done nothing. Even Eisenhower expressed some doubts on this score.[42]

It is impossible to pinpoint specific actions taken by Nasser, the Soviet leaders, or the Iraqis that related directly to the U.S. intervention and that decisively affected the outcome of the crisis. Yet it would be wrong to dismiss the intervention as inconsequential. Within Lebanon a volatile situation was brought under control after the arrival of U.S. forces. Robert Murphy was able to help negotiate a successful resolution

41. Macmillan, *Riding the Storm,* p. 512.
42. Eisenhower, *Waging Peace,* p. 289.

of the crisis, not only because of his personal skills but also because he could use the presence of U.S. forces as a lever against both Chamoun and the rebels. Thus, at least within Lebanon, the U.S. action had the intended effects. By restoring stability in Lebanon at a very tense moment in the Arab world, the United States may have helped forestall a chain reaction leading to the downfall of the monarchy in Jordan, seizure of the West Bank of Jordan by Israel, and even a general Arab-Israeli conflict. While it is only speculation that any of this would have happened if order had not been restored in Lebanon, the above sequence of events is not implausible and would have engaged important U.S. interests.

In the five years following the Lebanon crisis the Middle East remained an area of instability, but U.S. interests and those of U.S. friends and allies were not seriously affected. Inter-Arab tensions increased but the Arab-Israeli dispute remained under control. The UAR was dissolved when Syria seceded from it in September 1961, and Qasim was overthrown in a coup in February 1963. Chehab brought a period of order to Lebanon but fundamental issues that had sparked the 1958 crisis remained unsolved and led to later outbursts of violence.

In terms of global politics the Lebanon crisis did not have long-lasting consequences. It was not a turning point in the cold war. Soviet leaders did not change their behavior in any significant way because of U.S. behavior in Lebanon, although they may well have concluded that a naval capability in the Mediterranean would be a useful asset. The USSR began to acquire such a capability in the mid-1960s.

In its relations with Nasser, the United States seems to have learned something from the Lebanon crisis. From 1959 on, U.S. policymakers no longer saw Nasser as an appendage of Moscow nor were they quite so fearful of Nasser taking over the Middle East. A PL-480 aid program for Egypt was instituted, and for several years relations seemed to be improving.

Evaluation

The commitment of U.S. troops to Lebanon, combined with the diplomatic efforts of Robert Murphy, had precisely the effects within Lebanon that Eisenhower and Dulles hoped. But the key to success lay in the restraint with which the operation was conducted. Had hostilities occurred between U.S. and Lebanese forces, the U.S. mediating role would have been seriously jeopardized. It was at least in part luck that prevented any clashes from occurring in the first few days.

While it is impossible to know what might have happened in Lebanon if the U.S. troops had not arrived, there is every reason to believe that the authority of the Chamoun regime would have been eroded further and a peaceful transfer of power would have been complicated. Continuing turmoil in Lebanon could have contributed to instability elsewhere, such as in Jordan.

If the United States had not acted as it did in Lebanon, the United Kingdom would have been unwilling and probably unable to intervene in Jordan. The British presence there no doubt helped to strengthen the somewhat shaky regime of King Hussein. Had Hussein been overthrown or assassinated, a distinct possibility given the atmosphere in the region following the Iraqi coup, Israel would probably have seized the West Bank of Jordan. A full-scale Arab-Israeli conflict could not then have been far off. Given this danger, the U.S. reluctance to join Britain in the Jordan operation is somewhat surprising. In any event, the key to British action lay in Washington, and a major consequence of the U.S. decision to intervene in Lebanon was that the United Kingdom agreed to mount a parallel operation in Jordan. At the same time, the U.S. commitment to limited goals served also to constrain the scope of British intervention and to rule out the possibility of counterrevolution in Iraq.

From Eisenhower's perspective, considering the domestic and international pressures he faced, the policy of intervention in Lebanon was a wise one. He was able to appear decisive yet not reckless. He combined the use of force with effective diplomacy. The outcome was generally successful, the costs were modest, and the consequences on the whole were favorable to U.S. interests.

Yet there is something unsettling about a decision to commit U.S. forces that is based on such shaky premises as those that underlay the Lebanon landings. The driving force behind the decision was a desire to stop the spread of communism and Nasserism, but the U.S. action was incapable of achieving such nebulous purposes. It was able to help restore order in Lebanon; U.S. diplomacy was able to help mediate the Lebanese internal conflict; the United States was able to assist the United Kingdom in providing aid to King Hussein. These were reasonable, legitimate objectives. Viewed dispassionately, they also contributed to the stability of the Arab-Israeli balance. And yet these were not the terms in which the issue of intervention was discussed. A much more ambitious set of goals was initially articulated, and only after the decision had been made to commit U.S. forces were the objectives of the operation consciously scaled down, in part to counter British pressures to expand the scope of intervention.

On the whole the Lebanon decision is most admirable in its contribution to upholding U.S. national interests when examined in terms of its results; when the premises that lay behind the decision are examined closely, one can only feel that there was a large element of chance that contributed to the positive outcome. For example, during the first few days after the decision there were several occasions when top decision-makers discussed the merits of "unleashing" Turkey and Israel as part of an area-wide counteroffensive. Similarly, the use of nuclear weapons was considered, particularly with reference to any Iraqi moves against Kuwait. Nuclear-capable howitzers were even landed in Lebanon, although this does not necessarily imply that their use was ever contemplated. Nonetheless, it is not difficult to imagine, given the perceptions that prevailed at the time in Washington, that the initial U.S. commitment to the use of force could have escalated rapidly had any of a number of developments occurred. If the Lebanese Army had resisted the Americans with force, if a pro-Western faction in the Iraqi military had requested aid, if rebellion had broken out in Jordan, if the regimes in Saudi Arabia and Kuwait had been threatened, then the likelihood of deeper U.S. military involvement would have been very great, precisely because the limited nature of U.S. goals was not well articulated in the first few days of the crisis. With time, Eisenhower, and perhaps even Dulles, did come to appreciate that neither Nasserism nor communism was the issue that they were confronting, and the Murphy mission was a sensible outcome of the recognition that diplomacy offered the hope of a solution, whereas force would merely help to stabilize the Lebanese situation without resolving the conflict.

While the use of force in Lebanon in 1958 can be justified in terms of U.S. national interests, the caveat must be borne in mind that the premises of action as publicly and privately stated by Eisenhower and Dulles at the time were not consistent with a restrained use of force. The intervention proved to be a success in terms of the limited goals sought in Lebanon, but there was considerable danger that the more nebulous purposes that lay behind the action could have led to an expanded commitment that probably would have been counterproductive in terms of U.S. interests. The lesson seems to be that the use of force unaccompanied by a clear understanding of objectives runs the danger of unintended escalation. Fortunately, in the case of the Lebanese crisis, events did not develop in such a way that an open-ended commitment to the use of force was ever made. One is left with the strong feeling, however, that it was circumstances more than self-restraint that helped ensure that the use of force in Lebanon during the first few crucial days remained limited in scope and objectives. Thus it was possible to establish at an early date a balance between force and diplomacy, and between the abstract goals that had led to the commitment to use force and the concrete realities of the Lebanese situation.

U.S. POLICY IN THE JORDAN CRISIS, 1970

DURING Richard M. Nixon's first term as President of the United States, the Middle East was a region of continuing preoccupation for policy-makers. The President referred to the area as a "powder keg," and likened it to the Balkans before 1914. At issue was not only the persistent conflict between Israel and its Arab neighbors but also the U.S.-Soviet relationship, since both sides were increasingly involved on opposite sides of the major regional disputes. Nixon's fear was that a crisis in the Middle East could lead to superpower confrontation; his hope, until early 1970, had been that Moscow would cooperate in working for a compromise peace settlement. In September 1970, with the outbreak of civil war in Jordan, the fear became a virtual reality and the hope faded into the background.

Regional and International Developments

The outcome of the Arab-Israeli war in June 1967 set the stage for the Jordanian crisis of September 1970. Israel had scored a brilliant military victory but had been unable to turn battlefield success into political settlement with the Arabs. The Arabs insisted on an Israeli commitment to withdraw from the newly occupied territories—Sinai, the Golan Heights, Jerusalem, and the West Bank—as a precondition for any form of peace agreement. The result was a standoff which left Israel in control of the territories and the Arabs unreconciled to the new status quo.

Two new factors, however, ensured that the de facto situation would not remain quiet for long. First was the emergence of a militant and increasingly popular Palestinian guerrilla movement committed to the goal of freeing Palestine from Zionist control by means of armed struggle. The *fedayeen,* as they were called in Arabic, had become such a major political force in the Arab world by mid-1968 that Egypt's President Nasser was obliged to offer them firm support or risk undermining even further his sagging prestige. Despite its popularity, however, the fedayeen movement remained faction-ridden and relatively unsuccessful on the battlefield.[43]

By 1969 the Israelis were able to prevent most fedayeen efforts to cross the cease-fire lines from Jordan and Lebanon, and within the West Bank and Gaza the fedayeen found it extremely difficult to maintain a political infrastructure, let alone to carry out military operations. As a result, the fedayeen increasingly concentrated in Jordan, and to a lesser degree in Lebanon, where the regimes were reluctant or unable to move against them. By mid-1970 the Palestine Liberation Organization (PLO), the umbrella organization linking most of the fedayeen factions, constituted something of a state within a state in Jordan.

The second major development after 1967 was the growth of Soviet involvement in Egypt and Syria. Initially the USSR had concentrated on rebuilding the shattered defenses of its two key clients in the Middle East, a task that was essentially completed by the end of 1968. In March 1969 President Nasser began a "war of attrition" along the Suez Canal, which gradually escalated in intensity and scope as the Israelis responded with "deep penetration bombing," using newly supplied Phantom jets, toward the end of the year. Egypt was coming under substantial military pressure, and finally in January 1970 Nasser made a secret trip to Moscow to ask for an acceleration of Soviet aid, particularly in the form of air defense equipment and Soviet combat personnel. The USSR responded positively, and shortly thereafter began deliveries of a sophisticated air defense system. In April Soviet fighter pilots were noted for the first time helping defend Egyptian airspace. This represented a quantum jump over previous levels of Soviet involvement in the conflict, and greatly raised the risk of superpower confrontation.

43. On the Palestinian movement, see William B. Quandt and others, *The Politics of Palestinian Nationalism* (University of California Press, 1973).

In response to the deteriorating political situation in the Middle East, the Nixon administration had initiated early in 1969 a series of talks, the most important of which were with the USSR, designed to produce a joint proposal for settling the Arab-Israeli conflict. Nixon and Kissinger at the time were interested in the possibility of establishing "linkages" among various issues that were being negotiated with the USSR—strategic arms limitations and Vietnam in particular—and they hoped that the USSR would prove cooperative in the Middle East. By fall of 1969 the USSR had managed to extract some concessions from Nasser on the nature of a peace agreement with Israel; now Soviet leaders were asking Nixon to commit the United States to the principle of full withdrawal from the territories occupied by Israel in the 1967 war. After considerable debate in Washington, a draft of a joint U.S.-Soviet proposal for an Egyptian-Israeli agreement was handed to the USSR in late October 1969. It contained the principles of Israeli withdrawal from Sinai and Egyptian commitment to peace. On December 9 Secretary of State William Rogers publicly revealed the essence of the proposal, henceforth dubbed the "Rogers Plan," but two weeks later the USSR officially rejected it, primarily because of Nasser's unwillingness to acquiesce in its terms. The Israelis had also rejected the plan, so U.S. diplomacy came to a sudden halt. Nixon and Kissinger, who had harbored some misgivings all along about the State Department's handling of the talks with the USSR, were particularly angry at Moscow for its uncooperative stance. A harder line, directed from the White House, began to appear, while the State Department tried to find some way to pick up the pieces of its failed diplomatic effort.

Toward Confrontation in Jordan

It was the next Rogers initiative that precipitated the Jordan crisis. During May, June, and July, tension rose rapidly in the Middle East, with the USSR engaging in combat operations over Egypt and the fedayeen threatening the stability of the regime in Jordan. In response to the continuing deterioration of the regional situation, Rogers proposed in mid-June a simple formula for a cease-fire and the beginning of talks on a settlement. After more than a month of delays the parties to the conflict agreed to the proposal. Finally, on August 7, the fighting stopped as a standstill cease-fire went into effect. The State Department was elated.

Within hours of the cease-fire, however, new problems arose. First, the Israelis were angry at the United States for the way in which the cease-fire was announced. Then they charged that the Egyptians were violating the standstill provisions, a point that the United States was initially unable to confirm. Second, the Palestinians violently attacked the cease-fire, seeing it as a prelude to their own extinction as a fighting force in Jordan. Nasser ordered the closing of the Palestinians' broadcasting facilities in Cairo, and King Hussein began to make clear his intentions to restore law and order in his shaky kingdom.

By late August the United States had confirmed that Egypt had technically violated the terms of the cease-fire by completing construction of surface-to-air missile sites within the Suez Canal Zone, and by rotating some missiles from active to inactive sites. Nixon and Kissinger felt the USSR was partly responsible for the violations, and this very much colored their subsequent perceptions of regional developments.

Meanwhile, the fedayeen, badly divided and very much on the defensive, met in Amman to decide on a course of action. The militant groups called for a new regime in Jordan, while others were reluctant to make a final break with Nasser and to risk confrontation with the well-armed Jordanian military. The debate was settled in early September when the Popular Front for the Liberation of Palestine (PFLP), a small, radical fedayeen group led by George Habash, hijacked four international airliners.[44] One was flown to Cairo, where it was destroyed on the ground after its passengers had been evacuated. Three others were flown to a desert airstrip in Jordan where the passengers were held hostage by the PFLP. Among the passengers were many Europeans and Americans. An international crisis had begun.

Civil War

The simmering crisis in Jordan exploded on September 15, when King Hussein appointed a new government with responsibility to restore order. Two days later the Jordanian Army went into action, concentrating initially on driving the fedayeen from Amman. The PFLP had by now released all but fifty-four hostages and had destroyed the three aircraft,

44. An unsuccessful attempt to hijack one other airliner was led by Leila Khaled of the PFLP.

but the efforts to exchange the hostages for fedayeen held by European governments were meeting with little success. Henceforth the PFLP took a back seat as the larger fedayeen groups assumed the burden of staving off the onslaught of the Jordanian Army. Within days the fedayeen were being driven north by the army. On the night of September 18–19 the first indications were received that tanks from Syria, painted with the colors of the Palestine Liberation Army, had entered the fighting in the north. The following evening the Syrians launched a full-scale armored intervention with elements of two divisions.

The aid from Syria reversed the course of the battle, and on September 21 the important town of Irbid fell to the Palestinians and Syrians. King Hussein appealed for outside help, and the United States and Israel quickly worked out a plan for intervention if the situation in Jordan were to deteriorate further. The next day the Jordanian Air Force went into action without encountering any opposition from the Syrian Air Force, and Syrian tanks were withdrawn by September 23. On September 25 a cease-fire went into effect, in part because of the efforts of President Nasser. The Egyptian president, however, was not in good health. On September 28, having convened a gathering of Arab heads of state to resolve the Jordanian civil war, he suffered a heart attack and died, bringing to an end an era in Middle East history.

The Jordanian conflict was particularly dangerous because of the threat of outside intervention. The Iraqis had forces in Jordan but they never entered the fray. The Israelis nearly did, but the success of Hussein's own army on September 22 made the Israeli involvement unnecessary. The United States went to the brink of encouraging Israeli intervention, but held back once the Syrians began to withdraw. On balance, the crisis ended well for the United States, Jordan, and Israel. But the role played by the intricate maneuvers of U.S. and Israeli forces in obtaining this outcome is still obscure.

The Actors and Their Objectives

The key actors in the drama that unfolded in September 1970 were the fedayeen, the Jordanian government, Israel, Egypt, Syria, Iraq, the United States, and the USSR. Each had a different stake in the crisis and each saw it in terms of distinctive goals.

The Fedayeen

For the fedayeen, the minimal objective was survival as a viable political force. This meant retaining a foothold in Jordan, the country with the largest concentration of Palestinians. Different factions within the PLO had other goals as well. The PFLP, which had instigated the crisis, was thoroughly opposed to the idea of a political settlement with Israel and was seeking to sabotage the recent Rogers initiative. In addition, PFLP fortunes had been on the wane since the previous June, and the group was anxious to demonstrate the bankruptcy of PLO Chairman Yasir Arafat's more conciliatory policies. Arafat himself was struggling to maintain his position of leadership at the head of a badly fractionated movement. He could not afford to let the PFLP appear as the sole defender of the Palestinian cause, and yet he doubtless feared that his cadres in Fatah, the largest of the fedayeen groups, would pay the highest price in the event of a showdown with the Jordanian Army. If it came to a show of force Fatah would not stand aside, but some outside help would be needed.

Jordan

King Hussein had tolerated the Palestinian fedayeen presence in Jordan longer than some of his advisers—especially Wasfi Tal, Zaid Rifai, and Zaid Ben Shakir—had thought wise. The August cease-fire provided Hussein the chance to reestablish his authority without alienating his key Arab ally, President Nasser. Both Jordan and Egypt, for different reasons, favored the pursuit of a political settlement. Syria, Iraq, and the Palestinians were adamantly opposed to such a course. To avoid total isolation, then, Hussein needed Nasser. Even more, however, he needed the loyalty of his armed forces, largely of Bedouin origins in the upper ranks and intensely anti-fedayeen. There were rumors of dissatisfaction in the army with the king's unwillingness to defend his regime against the threats of the guerrillas. But Hussein, mindful of the need for Nasser's support, could not risk initiating hostilities against the fedayeen. The PFLP hijacking altered the situation, however, and provided Hussein with the opportunity to reestablish his authority without breaking with Nasser. After all, the PFLP action had been just as much aimed at Nasser as at Hussein. By bringing the Palestinians under control, Hussein would be serving both his own narrow regime interests and those of the Arab "moderates" who were favorable to a political settlement with Israel.

Syria

Syrian objectives during the crisis reflected an underlying division within the regime. In power in Damascus since February 1966, the left wing of the Baath party was split into civilian and military factions. The civilians were self-professed Marxists, or at least leftists, and tended to follow a militant policy toward Israel. President Nureddin al-Atasi and Salah Jadid, head of the Baath party, represented this group. They did not hold Nasser in high regard; they were barely on speaking terms with the rival Baath leaders in Baghdad; and they took pride in their sponsorship of the fedayeen. One significant fedayeen group, Saiqa, was directly under their control. The military wing of the party, by contrast, was less ideological, more skeptical of the effectiveness of guerrilla warfare against Israel, and determined not to be drawn into a disastrous military operation because of the extreme policies of the civilians. Air Force Commander Hafiz al-Asad and Army General Mustafa Tlas were key actors in this group.

Both Syrian factions probably hoped that, whatever else happened, the Palestinian guerrillas in Jordan would not all be driven into Syria, which would have placed strains on the regime and would inevitably have drawn it into unwanted conflicts with Israel. Although Syria was already host to nearly 200,000 Palestinians, fedayeen within the country were kept under strict control, and military operations from Syrian territory against Israel were proscribed. An influx of armed fedayeen fleeing Jordan could only add to the regime's problems. Apart from this area of agreement, however, the two groups could not be expected to work closely together. In fact, each was doubtless watching for mistakes or weaknesses on the part of its rival. The Jordanian crisis provided opportunities to score points at one another's expense. The rather confusing and tentative nature of Syrian involvement in the crisis can only be understood against this background of internal political division.

Iraq

The Iraqi government was less intimately involved in the crisis, although it stridently opposed the cease-fire and was militantly anti-Nasser.

The Iraqi press and radio attacked the regimes in Damascus and Amman, as well as Cairo, but the major preoccupation of the Hassan al-Bakr regime in Iraq was the consolidation of its recently acquired power and the festering Kurdish insurrection, aided by Iran, in the north. Approximately 20,000 Iraqi troops, however, were stationed in Jordan, and the regime announced in August that one of its missions was to defend the Palestinians against all plots.[45] But when confronted with a full division of the Jordanian Army, the Iraqi forces refrained from any direct involvement in the fighting.

Israel

The Israeli government was very clear in its objectives during the crisis. First, it was determined to prevent the fedayeen from seizing power in Amman. Second, the crisis provided an opportunity to heal a year-long breach with the United States by demonstrating the compatibility of the aims of the two countries. Israel had long been anxious to show that it could be a strategic asset to the United States, not just a charity case. Third, the Israelis were determined not to allow Syrian or Iraqi troops to overthrow King Hussein. The Israeli leadership by far preferred Hussein among the Arab leaders, and they were committed to helping him remain in place. A shift in the balance of power in the Arab world at that particular moment could have serious consequences.

Egypt

President Nasser was more uneasy about his country's objectives in the crisis. Egypt's acceptance of the Rogers proposal for a cease-fire had helped set the stage for the showdown in Jordan, and Nasser was now being denounced by his long-time protégés, the Palestinians, for encouraging and supporting his former antagonist, King Hussein. Nasser now needed Hussein, and thus was not prepared to offer full backing for the militant Palestinians. At the same time he was not willing to stand idly by if Hussein went too far. At another time, if the option of a political

45. For example, on August 17, 1970, after a meeting between Arafat and the Iraqi leadership, Baghdad Radio announced that "Iraq has placed her forces on the eastern front at the disposal of the resistance movement." In early September the theme was repeated several times, as Iraqi military leaders paid visits to their troops in Jordan.

settlement were to fail, he might once again find the fedayeen useful to his strategy. The preferred outcome from his standpoint would be a restoration of Hussein's authority without a complete defeat for the fedayeen.

The United States

In Washington, Nixon and Kissinger saw the crisis on several levels. The most serious aspect was the threat of indirect Soviet intervention to disrupt the prospects of reaching a political settlement in the area. Ever since the Soviet rejection of the Rogers Plan in December 1969, the President had been suspicious that the Soviet leaders were trying to create tensions in the area as a way of undermining U.S. influence. The record was not one to inspire confidence: massive arms shipments to Nasser early in the year; the provision of combat pilots; and apparent complicity in Egyptian violations of the August cease-fire. While the Soviet leaders had obviously not precipitated the Jordan crisis, at the White House it was feared that they might try to profit from it. Compounding these suspicions was the fact that early in September U.S. intelligence sources had discovered that the USSR was constructing a submarine base in Cuba.[46]

Washington officials were also concerned by the regional aspects of the crisis. Nixon was strongly anti-fedayeen, seeing them as a disruptive, terrorist force that played into the hands of the USSR, and was anxious to see their trouble-making potential ended. More to the point, the administration wanted to keep in power King Hussein, a good friend of the United States. Nixon and his adviser for national security affairs, Henry Kissinger, felt that it was important for the United States to support its friends in need, especially those who had the capacity and willingness to stand up and fight. This, after all, was what the Nixon Doctrine was all

---

46. The Soviet dimension of the crisis stands out in Nixon's retrospective analysis of the situation he faced in September 1970:

"If Syria had attacked Jordan successfully, Israel would have pounced. Then the Russians would have moved, and we would have had a confrontation.

"We had to give assurances that the Israelis would not move; and assurances to King Hussein to stand firm. That gave the Russians pause. Then the Syrians pulled back."

Quoted from Frank van der Linden, *Nixon's Quest for Peace* (Robert B. Luce, 1972), p. 85.

about. Nixon liked Hussein. He saw him as tough, courageous, and moderate on the Arab-Israeli issue. If there was ever to be a peace settlement, Hussein was expected to play a major part in helping to resolve the ticklish Palestinian problem. Finally, the administration was haunted by the scenario of another full-scale Middle East war if Hussein were to fall. In that contingency, Syria, Iraq, Saudi Arabia, and Israel might all move to seize parts of Jordan. Egypt could be drawn in, with Soviet involvement not far behind. The United States would then face the prospect of intervention to protect Israel and its interests in the Arabian Peninsula on very unfavorable terms.

The third level of concern for the United States was the fate of the U.S. citizens who were held hostage by the PFLP. This was a serious issue, and contingencies for going to their rescue were considered throughout the crisis. Some scenarios envisaged a limited use of force to rescue the hostages and to evacuate Americans from Jordan, with the added benefit of providing some tangible aid to Hussein in the process. The danger, of course, was that the hostages might be killed by their captors if force were used to rescue them. Nor was it known exactly where they were being held after September 12.

The USSR

The Soviet objectives are most difficult to discern. The Soviet leaders certainly hoped to maintain their credibility as good friends of the Arabs, especially of Syria and Egypt. As such, they were not particularly worried by King Hussein's difficulties. At the same time they did not want a full-scale confrontation with the United States. The crisis presented them with serious dangers and relatively few opportunities. How they would choose among their various goals would be determined by events on the ground and by the response of the United States. Moscow was not strongly committed to any particular outcome, provided its primary interests in Cairo and Damascus were not affected.

U.S. Behavior in the Crisis

U.S. policy during the Jordan crisis was very much the product of the perceptions of President Nixon and Henry Kissinger. In their view, the time had come to demonstrate U.S. resolve and determination to the leadership in Moscow. To some degree this was related to recent Soviet behavior in the Middle East, but Soviet behavior elsewhere was also of concern. Jordan provided an opportunity to make the point with the USSR that détente and negotiations did not provide a license to fish in troubled waters. Nor was the United States incapable of defending its interests elsewhere because of the continuing crisis in Vietnam. (It should be recalled that the situation in Southeast Asia had been a major preoccupation during the early part of the year, with the overthrow of Prince Sihanouk and the subsequent U.S. military intervention in Cambodia.) The message that the United States was able and willing to stand up to the USSR was no doubt also meant to impress the Chinese leadership in Peking, with whom indirect contacts were under way to develop a relationship founded on the mounting anti-Soviet sentiments of Chairman Mao Tse-tung and his colleagues.

In addition, the President had several bureaucratic-domestic concerns in mind as he dealt with the crisis. In 1970 congressional elections would be held, and no administration wants to face elections while engaged in a public quarrel with the Israelis. Until mid-1970 the State Department had guided the conduct of Middle East policy, culminating in the August cease-fire and the subsequent crisis in U.S.-Israeli relations. Nixon and Kissinger were angry at the bureauracy's handling of the Israeli relationship, and by September they were asserting close White House control over policy toward the Middle East. It was clear that Nixon, sensitive to his domestic political base, would not gratuitously offend the Israelis. In fact, the crisis might provide an opportunity for cementing the U.S.-Israeli relationship, with both strategic and political dividends.

Operational Objectives

The operational objectives of the President shifted once the Syrian military intervention began. Up until that time the objectives were primarily to obtain the release of the hostages held by the PFLP, then to ensure that King Hussein would remain in power once fighting had broken out. In addition, the President was hoping to deter military intervention by Iraqi and Syrian forces by hinting that the United States might itself intervene in such circumstances. Finally, the United States was most anxious to deter direct Soviet intervention in the conflict.

Once the Syrians had intervened, on September 18–19, the operational objectives shifted. The first priority was to enlist Soviet support to persuade the Syrians to withdraw. The second goal, to develop a credible military option in the event that King Hussein's regime was threatened, required close consultations with the Jordanians and the Israelis.

Within the administration there was virtual unanimity over these objectives. Earlier there had been a few voices that had referred to the king as a "wasting asset," but this was no longer a prevailing view. The new U.S. ambassador to Jordan, L. Dean Brown, for example, actively supported the goal of aiding the king. The State Department, while only marginally involved in the formulation of policy in the crisis, saw the need to preserve the possibility of a peace settlement.[47] The military was skeptical that the United States could project adequate power, especially ground forces, into the area in the event of a full-scale crisis but did not oppose the thrust of the President's policy. The negotiations with the Israelis, which might have proved divisive, were handled almost entirely by Kissinger and thus the rest of the bureaucracy was not in a position to object. On balance, then, the administration appeared united, purposeful, and clear-headed about its goals. The USSR and Syria had no reason to hope for divided counsels in Washington or the constraining influence of public or congressional opinion.

Communication Patterns

Nixon and Kissinger went to considerable lengths to ensure that the USSR, and to a lesser degree Syria, Iraq, and the Palestinians, understood U.S. objectives and what the consequences of their actions would be. The most explicit threat of U.S. military intervention in the event of Syrian or Iraqi involvement in the Jordanian conflict came on September 17. President Nixon was visiting the Midwest at the time. He had spoken in Kansas City the previous day and had denounced the fedayeen. While

47. Secretary Rogers was much less prone than Nixon and Kissinger to see the USSR as deeply involved in the Jordanian crisis. He reportedly recommended a joint U.S.-Soviet initiative to end the fighting. Marvin Kalb and Bernard Kalb, *Kissinger* (Little, Brown, 1974), pp. 201–02.

passing through Chicago he gave an "off-the-record" interview to editors of the *Chicago Sun-Times,* the gist of which appeared later that day in print.[48] In essence, Nixon was quoted as saying that he would be inclined to order U.S. troops into Jordan if either Syria or Iraq intervened in the fighting that was just breaking out. In addition, he reportedly said that it would not be such a bad thing for the USSR to believe that the United States was capable of "irrational action."

After Syrian tanks entered the fray, Kissinger, Rogers, and Assistant Secretary of State Joseph Sisco were all used as channels of communication to the USSR. Their tone was tough and the message was simple: Call off your friends, or the consequences will be nasty. On September 20 Rogers warned the Syrians to end their "invasion" of Jordan.[49] Nixon sent one official message through the State Department to Soviet Premier Aleksei Kosygin, then relied on less direct means to drive home the point.[50] Sisco stressed the danger of Israeli intervention to the Soviet chargé in Washington.[51] The President explicitly decided against calling a UN Security Council meeting. U.S. military moves were designed to reinforce the basic message. Finally, on September 22 Kissinger attended a reception at the Egyptian Interests Section, where he deliberately sought out the ranking Soviet diplomat, Yuli Vorontsov, to tell him cryptically that the United States expected the Soviet leaders to persuade

48. *Chicago Sun-Times,* September 17, 1970; *New York Times,* September 19, 1970. The President was also worried about the hostages, according to Press Secretary Ronald Ziegler: "The President asked me to point out to you and to have it clearly understood that the holding of United States citizens is deplorable and that those who hold them will be held directly and completely responsible for their safety." *New York Times,* September 18, 1970.

49. The essence of the Rogers statement (*New York Times,* September 21, 1970) was as follows: "We have been informed that tank forces have invaded Jordan from Syria during the night and have moved toward Ramtha. We have also been informed that Jordanian armor is resisting this invasion. We have condemn this irresponsible and imprudent intervention from Syria into Jordan. This action carries with it the danger of a broadened conflict. We call upon the Syrian Government to end immediately this intervention in Jordan and we urge all other concerned governments to impress upon the Government of Syria the necessity of withdrawing the forces which have invaded Jordan."

50. On September 20 Nixon told Rogers to send Moscow the "sternest note" ever on the Syrian intervention. Sisco delivered this message to the Soviet chargé d'affaires, Yuli Vorontsov, that morning, and Rogers met with the Soviet diplomat that evening to emphasize the urgency of the situation.

51. Kalb and Kalb, *Kissinger,* p. 201.

their friends to withdraw quickly. "You and your client started it, and you have to end it."[52]

At no time during the crisis did the United States try to communicate directly with the Syrians, Iraqis, or Palestinians. The state of political relations did not hold out much promise of success in any event but, more important, the administration was treating the crisis primarily on the U.S.-Soviet plane. With the Jordanians, however, communications were frequent, usually passing through the newly arrived Ambassador Brown and King Hussein and his closest advisers, especially Zaid Rifai. This was primarily used for information about how the battle was going and how the Jordanians assessed their needs. There was little attempt to influence Jordanian behavior, except by way of telling the king what the United States and Israel were planning.

Detailed and complex negotiations did take place between Israel and the United States. The U.S. goal was to ensure that Israel would not act on its own in ways that would complicate the situation, while nonetheless preparing for a controlled use of force if a contingency should arise in which Israeli action was needed to save King Hussein. This required fine tuning, since Hussein obviously did not want Israel to appear as his rescuer if any other alternative could be found. Nor did he want Israeli ground troops pouring into northern Jordan. Thus the United States had to reassure the Israelis that U.S. aid would be forthcoming if Israel did act, while at the same time ensuring that any Israeli move would be carefully coordinated with King Hussein.

These negotiations with Israel took place through several channels. In the early phase of the crisis, on September 18, Israeli Prime Minister Golda Meir happened to be in Washington to see Nixon about aid. Joint intervention in Jordan was reportedly not discussed at that point, since the Syrians had not yet entered the fighting in force. A few days later, however, at the peak of the crisis on September 20, Prime Minister Meir and Ambassador Itzhak Rabin were in New York. Kissinger reached them by phone for preliminary discussions of joint planning, then spent much of the day of September 21 with Rabin to work out details. Rabin provided the main channel of communication thereafter to the Israeli leadership, and Kissinger monopolized the talks on the U.S. side. The

52. The Vorontsov encounter is described by Kalb and Kalb in *Kissinger,* p. 207, and by Henry Brandon, *The Retreat of American Power* (Doubleday, 1973), p. 137.

meetings were private and their contents have never been fully revealed.[53] It appears, however, that agreement was reached late on September 21 that Israel would be prepared to intervene in Jordan by air and ground if Hussein's position were to deteriorate further. The United States promised to deter Soviet intervention against Israel and to provide assistance if Egypt attacked. These contingency arrangements were subject to review and to King Hussein's approval. Jordan had made clear its objection to Israeli ground forces entering northern Jordan, although Israeli air strikes and a diversionary armored thrust into Syria would have been acceptable. As it turned out, however, the following day the Jordanian Air Force went into action and did quite well. By September 23, Syrian tanks were being withdrawn and the United States was telling the Israelis not to move.

The crisis came to a close without direct intervention by Israel or the United States, but it was a near thing. Had the communications between the two, and with King Hussein, been less well managed, it is not difficult to imagine the Israelis acting in ways that would have complicated Hussein's position and greatly expanded the conflict. The U.S. role was indispensable, both as coordinator of Israeli and Jordanian moves and as guarantor that Israeli security would not be jeopardized if military action were undertaken against the Syrians. Private and very restricted means of communication were used in fulfillment of these roles, in contrast to the obvious public messages intended for the USSR and its friends.

The subtlety and nuances of the objectives sought from Israel and Jordan required utmost secrecy in communications; the effort to deter Syria and the USSR, and to persuade Moscow to pressure the Syrians, required a blunter, more public message, backed up by the movement of forces and a few private communications. On balance, however, Nixon did not go to great lengths to communicate with the Soviet leaders, and certainly not with the Syrians or Palestinians. The hot line was not used during the crisis.

Military Moves

Throughout the Jordanian crisis President Nixon paid careful attention to the preparation and movement of U.S. military forces. Because

53. Kalb and Kalb, *Kissinger*, pp. 201–03; *New York Times*, October 8, 1970.

military force was viewed as an important adjunct to diplomacy, most military moves were publicized, either through Defense Department announcements or leaks to the press.

In addition to the "signaling" aspect of military moves, U.S. forces were being prepared for several possible contingencies. At the lowest end of the spectrum of force, evacuation of U.S. citizens might require a limited intervention. Paratroopers would try to secure Amman airport, then transport aircraft would land to evacuate U.S. citizens. An effort might also be made to rescue the hostages if they could be located. A variant of this option included a small show of force to bolster King Hussein.

Once Syrian armed forces entered the battle, other contingencies were considered. Air strikes from the carriers of the Sixth Fleet against Syrian tanks were a possibility. The option of land-based airstrikes, using British bases in Cyprus, was also discussed but was discarded as less effective than carrier-based air strikes. Finally, some consideration was given to the introduction of ground forces into Jordan although this option was not viewed with much enthusiasm by the Pentagon.

The difficulty of organizing a substantial U.S. strike force against the Syrians led to consideration of the Israeli alternative. Israel could assemble ground and air forces to move into Jordan or Syria on short notice. The Israelis wanted assurances from the United States, however, that if Egypt or the USSR were to respond to an Israeli military move the United States would intervene if necessary. Thus the United States had to be prepared to counter any Soviet military moves—which did not seem very likely—and to protect Israel against any Egyptian attack. It is not known if specific plans were ever drawn up for these contingencies.

The sequence of military moves by the United States reflected the evolution of the crisis in Jordan. From an initial concern with freeing the hostages held by the PFLP and evacuating Americans, the emphasis shifted after September 18 to countering the Syrian intervention and then to providing a deterrent against Soviet or Egyptian military involvement.

In the first phase the President ordered six C-130 transport aircraft to Incirlik, Turkey, on September 10. These might be used for evacuation from Jordan. The 82nd Airborne Division in North Carolina was also placed on semi-alert status. The following day, twenty-five F-4 Phantom jets were flown to Incirlik from Europe along with four more C-130s.

The F-4s would be available to escort the C-130s into Jordan. Also on September 11 some ships of the Sixth Fleet were reported en route to an undisclosed location. These moves were all noted in the press over the next several days, prompting the fedayeen to warn that the United States was planning to intervene militarily in Jordan. The official statements from the White House, however, stressed the routine, precautionary nature of these steps, linking them to possible evacuation.[54]

The next phase of the crisis began on September 15, when King Hussein informed the United States and the United Kingdom that he intended to move against the fedayeen the following day. The Washington Special Action Group (WSAG) met that evening to consider evacuation and the "question of outside intervention to support the King."[55] The decision was made during the WSAG meeting to order the aircraft carrier *Saratoga* to proceed from the western to the eastern Mediterranean, where it would join the carrier *Independence* east of Cyprus. An airborne battalion in West Germany was also placed on semi-alert, and additional C-130s were ordered to Turkey. These steps became known publicly on September 17 when the Defense Department announced them, along with the early departure from Norfolk of a helicopter carrier, the *Guam,* with a Marine battalion landing team on board, and several other amphibious ships to join the Sixth Fleet in the eastern Mediterranean. Secretary of Defense Melvin Laird placed these moves in the context of possible evacuation; the State Department, when queried, would not rule out armed intervention if necessary to save American lives.

That evening the WSAG recommended that a third carrier, the *John F. Kennedy,* proceed from the Atlantic to the eastern Mediterranean. Earlier that day in Chicago the President had stated off the record that he would be inclined to intervene in Jordan if Syria or Iraq sent in troops. On September 18 the Defense Department made further announcements of fleet movements and the dispatch of C-130s to Europe and Turkey.

When news reached Washington late on September 19 that a large armed force from Syria had entered Jordan, the President immediately raised the alert status of the 82nd Airborne Division and the airborne battalion of the 8th Infantry Division in West Germany. The Sixth Fleet was ordered to move farther east. The following day, the *Independence*

54. Ronald Ziegler, statement to press, September 11, 1970.
55. *New York Times,* September 17, 1970.

Table 7-2. *Political and Military Developments of the Jordan Crisis*

Date	U.S. military moves	U.S. diplomatic/political moves	Regional developments	Soviet reaction
Sept. 10	82nd Airborne Division on semi-alert status. 6 C-130s ordered to Incirlik, Turkey.			
Sept. 11	25 F-4 fighters ordered to Incirlik, along with 4 more C-130s. Ships of 6th Fleet reported leaving port.	White House terms 6th Fleet moves "routine precautions in such a situation for evacuation purposes."	Palestinian fedayeen warn of U.S. plans to intervene in Jordan.	
Sept. 12		Rogers announces resumption of economic aid to Israel and increase in military aid.	Fedayeen blow up hijacked airliner in Jordan, release some hostages. Of remaining 54, 38 are American.	
Sept. 13		Rogers meets with Nixon to discuss U.S. hostages in Jordan.		
Sept. 14				
Sept. 15	Carrier *Saratoga* ordered to eastern Mediterranean. Airborne units in West Germany on semi-alert. More C-130s to Turkey.	Nixon plans to visit Europe and 6th Fleet on Sept. 27. WSAG meets for two hours to discuss evacuation and "question of outside intervention to support the King."	Hussein informs U.K. and U.S. that he will form military government and move against fedayeen.	

Sept. 16		Nixon speech at Kansas State University on "law and order"—denounces "Palestinian guerrillas."	Hussein names military government. Sporadic fighting begins between army and fedayeen. Martial law declared in Jordan. Prime Minister Meir leaves Israel for Washington on "private visit."
Sept. 17	Defense Department briefs on naval movements. Carrier *JFK* ordered from Atlantic to eastern Mediterranean.	Kissinger informs Nixon at 2 A.M. that Jordan has gone on offensive. Defense Secretary Laird says U.S. is ready to evacuate Americans from Jordan "if necessary." State Department will not rule out intervention. WSAG meets in evening. Nixon briefs Chicago editors on Jordan crisis: favors intervention to protect Hussein if Syria or Iraq intervenes. Reported in *Sun-Times* in late edition. Press Secretary Ziegler holds fedayeen responsible for safety of American hostages.	Heavy fighting begins in Amman at 5 A.M.

Table 7-2 (*continued*)

Date	U.S. military moves	U.S. diplomatic/political moves	Regional developments	Soviet reaction
Sept. 18	Defense Department announces further naval moves and additional C-130s to Europe and Turkey.	Prime Minister Meir meets President Nixon on aid and Jordan crisis.	PFLP warns of U.S. intervention.	USSR warns against outside intervention in Jordan. Joins President Nasser in calling for cease-fire. Tass refers to British and U.S. military moves.
	Plans to evacuate up to 450 are revealed.	Ziegler denies that U.S. has decided one way or another on intervention.	First reports of Syrian tanks crossing into Jordan.	
		Kissinger informs Nixon at Camp David of Vorontsov message on Soviet restraint. Nixon skeptical.		Chargé Vorontsov tells Sisco that USSR is trying to restrain Syrians; denies Soviet involvement.
Sept. 19	Nixon raises alert status of 82nd Airborne and units in West Germany.	Laird sees no need for U.S. intervention unless situation deteriorates.	Full-scale Syrian intervention during night of Sept. 19–20. Nasser calls for cease-fire.	Tass statement viewed as warning to Syria and Iraq. (Gwertzman, *New York Times*.)
	6th Fleet ordered farther east.			
Sept. 20		Rogers calls on Syria to halt "invasion" of Jordan.	King Hussein calls for help from any quarter.	
		Nixon orders State Department to send "sternest note" ever to USSR. Delivered by Sisco to Vorontsov in morning. Sisco warns that Israel may move against Syria.	Irbid falls to Syrian-Palestinian forces.	
		Kissinger contacts Rabin and Meir in New York on Hussein appeal for help.		

Sept. 21	Plane from 6th Fleet flies to Tel Aviv to coordinate target information. Press reports on U.S. military moves of previous days.	Daylong WSAG meeting. Nixon meets Rogers, Laird, Kissinger, Moorer for 2½ hours in morning. Kissinger and Rabin work out joint U.S.-Israeli plan of action. Approved by Nixon in evening.	Meir returns to Israel, arriving in afternoon. Arab leaders meet in Cairo on Jordan crisis. Kuwait ends subsidy to Jordan. Jordanian forces falling back toward Amman.	Vorontsov calls Sisco to say USSR has warned against all outside intervention. Delivers moderate Soviet note in evening. Asks U.S. to restrain Israel.
Sept. 22		State Department says USSR claims to be restraining Syria. Kissinger tells Vorontsov to call off the Syrians in meeting at Egyptian reception in evening.	Jordanian Air Force goes into action. Syrian intervention is slowed.	
Sept. 23		White House welcomes Syrian withdrawal. Sisco tells Israel not to move against Jordan.	Jordanian troops advance toward Syrian border. All Syrian tanks withdraw by noon.	
Sept. 24		Nixon, Rogers, Mitchell, and Meany go golfing at Burning Tree Country Club. Crisis is considered over.		
Sept. 25			Cease-fire announced in Jordan.	Podgorny speech in evening and Tass statement imply USSR restrained Syria and Iraq.

was reported off the Lebanon-Israel coast; the *Saratoga* was still en route to join the *Independence*. Reports on the status of the *Guam* and the airborne units in Germany were also made public.

As the crisis reached its peak on September 21, news of the movement of the carrier *JFK* was released, and a plane from the Sixth Fleet flew to Tel Aviv, reportedly to discuss target coordination. No effort was made to disguise these moves.[56] By this time, Nixon wanted to make sure that the USSR recognized the danger of the situation caused by the Syrian intervention. Within forty-eight hours the crisis was virtually over, as the Syrian armed forces withdrew. No other military maneuvers were made, although President Nixon did carry out a prearranged visit to the carrier *Saratoga* on September 27, as part of an effort to symbolize U.S. power and interests in the Mediterranean.

In brief, military and diplomatic moves were closely coordinated in Washington, and were designed to meet different aspects of the unfolding crisis. Table 7-2 highlights the relationship between political and military decisions and regional developments.

Ironically, during all of the maneuvers and hints that the United States might intervene in the crisis, the key policymakers in Washington were acutely aware of the limited military capability at their disposal. In particular, substantial ground forces needed to enter Jordan and to rescue the hostages were not available on short notice. Air power from the Sixth Fleet could be called upon, but even that capability was not overwhelming and was no match for what Israel could produce. When it became clear that Israel was prepared to lend its weight to the U.S. effort to shore up Hussein's throne the offer was welcomed. Since Israel desired a guarantee against Soviet intervention, the Sixth Fleet could be used as a visible symbol of such a guarantee.

While U.S. force was judged to be important as the crisis unfolded, senior U.S. decisionmakers were uneasy about the actual use of force. U.S. military maneuvers were designed primarily to convey signals to the USSR. There was little desire, particularly on the part of the military, to intervene directly in the fighting. The more serious the crisis became, the more valuable the option of Israeli intervention seemed. If the Syrian Air Force had intervened, Israel, not the United States, would have reacted militarily. Nixon and Kissinger felt that it was the combination

56. The plane's mission was deliberately leaked to the press. Van der Linden, *Nixon's Quest for Peace*, p. 83.

of U.S. and Israeli military power that played a major part in resolving the crisis. Unilateral U.S. action appeared increasingly undesirable as its consequences were examined, but the Israeli option helped protect the United States from having its bluff exposed as a rather empty one.[57] Ultimately, both the United States and Israel were relieved when King Hussein with his own forces was able to handle the Syrian threat and restore order within Jordan.

The Soviet Response

The primary thrust of U.S. policy during the crisis was directed at the USSR. Syria and Iraq may have been seen at the outset as important targets of Washington's coercive diplomacy, but Moscow was the channel through which pressure was to be brought to bear on the Soviet-supported regimes in Damascus and Baghdad.

Although the USSR has not revealed much about its role in the Jordanian crisis, it did not seem to feel that any major Soviet interests were at stake. Washington's view that the USSR was intimately involved in the Syrian intervention is certainly an exaggeration. Soviet relations with the Palestinians at the time were not particularly close. Egypt's President Nasser was still the primary Soviet client in the Arab world, and Nasser was moving slowly toward a political settlement, in conformity with professed Soviet desires. The Jordan crisis was an embarrassment to Nasser and, it would appear, to the USSR as well. Clearly the Soviet leaders would not wring their hands over King Hussein's overthrow by the Palestinians, but this was not a Soviet priority and the risks of such a move must have been obvious.

A primary Soviet objective as the crisis deepened appeared to be the prevention of U.S. or Israeli military intervention. The method chosen was not saber rattling but rather an effort to convey an image of moderation to Washington.

The USSR clearly took the threat of U.S. intervention seriously. Presumably it was Nixon's veiled threat, coupled with strong diplomatic messages, that underscored the seriousness of the U.S. stance. Moscow's

57. Given enough time the United States could have sent a sizable fighting force to Jordan. But the pace of events on the ground required rapid action, measured in hours, not days. While U.S. air power could react quickly, it would have taken much longer for ground troops to reach the area. It was here that Israel had a great advantage.

first official reaction to the crisis came on September 19, when Tass warned against "foreign armed intervention" in the crisis.[58] The next day, at the peak of the conflict, Radio Moscow warned against U.S. military intervention.[59] In its private diplomacy with Washington, however, the USSR denied any responsibility for the Syrian intervention and claimed to be working for an end to the fighting.

As early as September 18 the USSR had reportedly sent Nixon a moderate message that it would not intervene and that it would restrain Syria.[60] This theme was repeated on September 21 in a message to Nixon, along with efforts by Vorontsov to ensure that the United States would not unleash Israel. Some evidence was beginning to accumulate by then in Washington that the USSR was trying to persuade the Syrians to back down. It was known that the Soviet ambassador in Damascus had talked to Syrian leaders. On September 22 a State Department spokesman said, "We were told that the Soviet Government is in touch with the Syrian Government." The next evening Soviet President Nikolai Podgorny confirmed this in a speech.[61]

58. The Tass statement included the following: "It is believed in the Soviet Union that foreign armed intervention in the events in Jordan would aggravate the conflict, hamper the Arab liberation struggle for liquidating the consequences of Israeli aggression, for a lasting peace with justice in the Middle East, for restoration of their violated rights and national interests." After warning of the moves of the U.S. Sixth Fleet the statement went on to say: "Other reports indicate that plans for military intervention in the conflict in Jordan are being hatched by definite circles in certain countries. Such a development would aggravate the situation in the Middle East and would not only endanger the independence of Jordan and other Arab countries, but would essentially complicate the international situation as well." The *New York Times,* September 20, 1970, carried an article by its Moscow correspondent interpreting this as a warning to Syria and Iraq.

59. See Abraham Becker and others, *The Economics and Politics of the Middle East* (American Elsevier, 1975), p. 94.

60. Brandon, *Retreat of American Power,* p. 135.

61. "In its appeals made recently to a number of states—both those belonging and those not belonging to the area—the Soviet Union stressed the inadmissibility of external interference in Jordan, under whatever pretext whatsoever." Tass later elaborated on this statement with a foreign ministry statement to the effect that contacts had been made in Damascus, Baghdad, Amman, and Cairo, expressing "the firm conviction that everything should be done to end as soon as possible the fratricidal fighting in Jordan." *New York Times,* September 24, 1970. The author, in an interview with a high-ranking Jordanian official, was told that the Jordanians learned after the crisis that the USSR did try to restrain the Syrians and urged them to withdraw their forces. Mohamed Heikal, *The Road to Ramadan* (Quadrangle, 1975), pp. 98–100, states that the USSR passed on to Nasser the contents of the U.S. message of September 20 and urged "utmost restraint" on the Egyptians because of the dangerous international situation.

The USSR did send several ships into the Mediterranean to reinforce the Soviet squadron, but the Soviet squadron did not interfere with the Sixth Fleet's movements, limiting itself instead to a monitoring role. On the propaganda level, the USSR portrayed its part in the conflict as that of dampening the crisis, helping to end the fratricide in Jordan, and thus forestalling U.S. intervention. Nasser's efforts to obtain a cease-fire were praised, and it seemed clear that the USSR was not anxious to be identified with the Palestinian or Syrian policy of unseating Hussein.

The key to Soviet behavior appears to be that the stakes for Moscow in the crisis were not very great. Thus it did not take much of a combined U.S.-Israeli threat to make the crisis seem unduly risky. There is little doubt that Moscow appreciated that the United States and Israel did perceive major interests as being involved, and thus their threats could not be easily dismissed. Since the USSR had not committed its prestige to the success of the Syrian, let alone the Palestinian, adventure, it suffered no humiliation in adopting a policy of restraint. If the United States or Israel had actually committed forces, or if Nasser had been actively involved in support of the Syrians, then the USSR would have been placed in a more dangerous position and might have reacted more aggressively. But as long as the issue remained localized and involved primarily Jordan and the Palestinians, there was no reason for the USSR to risk confrontation with the United States. It was, then, comparatively easy for the United States to convince the USSR to adopt a restrained position in the crisis. For the USSR it was a case of the wrong crisis at the wrong time over the wrong issue. The USSR had not provoked the crisis, it had not encouraged Syria to send troops into Jordan, and its best friend in the area, President Nasser, was placed in an extremely awkward position by the conflict.[62] All in all, the USSR must have felt the United States was deliberately overreacting by placing a large share of the blame on it.

The Regional Participants

The United States treated the Jordan crisis as a superpower test of wills. But there was a genuine and probably more critical regional dimen-

62. Malcolm H. Kerr, *The Arab Cold War,* 3d ed. (Oxford University Press, 1971), chap. 7.

sion to the crisis in which Jordan, Syria, the Palestinians, Egypt, and Israel were the main actors. The United States had little apparent influence on the behavior of the Palestinians, the Syrians, and the Egyptians. In each case, although U.S. objectives were probably understood well enough the more immediate source of pressure was Jordan or Israel. Those two actors did, however, tailor their behavior in important respects to what they perceived to be U.S. intentions and objectives.

Jordan

The Jordanians, and King Hussein in particular, were confident of their ability to deal with the Palestinian guerrillas and with the Iraqi division stationed in Jordan. When it came to Syria, however, Hussein was anxious to find help wherever it might be available. In an all-out war Syria might very well prevail because of its great advantage in armor and air power. Although Jordan and Israel had developed a discreet relationship based on mutual interests after 1967, it was not sufficiently strong to support, nor was Hussein so foolhardy as to make, a direct appeal to Israel for help against Syria. Thus the United States played a crucial role in coordinating Hussein's requests for aid and Israel's preparations to act.

Hussein's main fear was that the disguised and tentative Syrian intervention would become a blatant invasion aimed at occupying Amman. In the first days, however, the Syrian Air Force had not intervened, nor was Damascus irreversibly committed to the battle. The useful fiction remained that the tanks from Syria were those of the Palestine Liberation Army. Syria could still back down without dishonor. But if Hussein were to commit his own air force, how would the Syrians react? And what would he do if Syrian tanks approached the outskirts of Amman? Before acting on his own, Hussein sought answers from the United States on whether it would intervene, or whether Israel might act, if the Syrians did not back down. Once reassured that U.S.-Israeli aid would be forthcoming *in extremis,* Hussein committed his air force on September 22, and by early morning the next day the Syrians had withdrawn. To some unmeasurable degree Hussein's willingness to take the risk of using his air force rested on the knowledge that the United States and Israel would respond to any successful Syrian counterattack. Insofar as this contributed to Hussein's self-confidence, it played a major role in the resolution of the crisis.[63]

Israel

Israel was also attentive to U.S. preferences in preparing to deal with the Jordanian crisis. Even if Nixon and Kissinger had been indifferent to Hussein's fate Israel might well have tried to deter a full-scale Syrian invasion. The Israelis held several trump cards. First, their air force was without doubt the most effective in the Middle East. It could quickly and surgically go into action, either in Jordan itself or within Syria. Second, Israel had mobilized nearly 400 tanks in the Golan Heights; a diversionary armored strike toward Damascus would have forced the Syrians to consider withdrawal of their forces in Jordan. Third, the Israelis could easily cross the Jordan River and confront Syrian tanks in the area north of Irbid. At the same time they could clean out pockets of guerrillas who used the border area for attacks upon Israel.

If left to their own devices, the Israelis would probably have opted for the combination of air power and intervention into northern Jordan. For King Hussein, however, this was an unattractive alternative, since he would then face the problem either of openly conspiring with the Israelis or of finding himself confronted with their unwelcome and perhaps unyielding presence within his territory once the fighting stopped. Air support was one thing, but any Israeli ground action, in his view, should be confined to Syrian territory.

The important role of the United States was, through consultation with Israel and Jordan, to ensure that Israel would not move at the wrong time or in the wrong manner from Hussein's point of view. At the same time, Nixon and Kissinger were prepared to provide some guarantees to the Israelis that their security would not be gravely endangered if Israel agreed to act in accord with Jordanian and U.S. requests. In particular, direct action against Syria might raise the risk of Soviet reaction or might

63. Some of those who worked closely with Hussein during this period have stressed in interviews with the author that even without U.S. assurances the king, under strong pressure from the army and from his key adviser Wasfi Tal, would have ordered the counterattack. Tal, who was related by marriage to Syrian General Tlas, seemed confident that the Syrian Air Force would not intervene, according to one source.

even bring Egypt into the conflict. Israel's willingness to play a role, but to do so with restraint and concern for King Hussein's wishes, was largely due to this U.S. guarantee, backed by the visible military power of the Sixth Fleet.

Other Arab Actors

Apparently the U.S. threats to intervene and the corresponding military maneuvers were most influential with respect to partners sharing the same goals. Hussein was probably emboldened to take risky actions, and the Israelis were persuaded to adopt a delicate and potentially dangerous position toward Syria. Curiously, the Syrians, Iraqis, Palestinians, and Egyptians showed few signs of having taken the U.S. moves nearly as seriously. In each case, either they had their hands full with more immediate problems and the U.S. threats made little difference, or they were already divided in their objectives and were easily persuaded to end the crisis short of actions that would draw Israel or the United States into the fray.

The Syrian decision to withdraw its tanks from Jordan was no doubt based on several factors. U.S. and Jordanian officials both gave priority to the performance of the Jordanian armed forces, then to the threat of Israeli and U.S. intervention, and finally to Soviet pressure. The only necessary addition to this list is the fact of internal political division between the Jadid and Asad factions in Syria.

Outcomes

The Jordanian crisis was resolved successfully from the U.S. point of view. The primary regional objective was to keep Hussein in power, thus averting a broadening of the Arab-Israeli conflict, and one means to this end was pressure on the USSR to restrain the Syrians. While the substance of Soviet-Syrian contacts remains unknown, the USSR apparently did act to restrain the Syrians at the crucial moment. One suspects that it was not a particularly difficult task, because of the factional divisions in Damascus, nor was it in all likelihood the decisive element in the Syrian decision to withdraw.

U.S.-Israeli Relations

A number of direct consequences can be traced to the outcome of the Jordanian crisis. Most dramatically, U.S. relations with Israel and Jordan were greatly strengthened. Levels of economic and military aid increased substantially to both countries. Israel was increasingly seen by the U.S. government as a useful stabilizing factor in the area, at least until the unanticipated outbreak of war in 1973. As Israel became stronger after 1970, and the Palestinian guerrillas faded from the scene, the status quo seemed to stabilize. Complacency set in. Egypt's President Anwar Sadat apparently decided to go to war in October 1973 to upset this "no war, no peace" situation. That he was able to do so testifies to the degree to which the Israelis had let their guard down in the years following the 1970 Jordanian crisis.

Superpower Relations

Although the demonstration of U.S. firmness probably did make it easier to develop the bases of détente in the next two years, the Jordanian crisis in itself was not vital to the overall U.S.-USSR relationship. Its consequences for the Soviet position in the Middle East are also hard to assess. Within two years of the crisis Sadat had asked them to leave Egypt. A year later, in 1973, they were actively helping Egypt and Syria in a war against Israel. Five years after the crisis Egyptian-Soviet relations had reached a low point. But little of this could be traced directly to the Jordanian crisis.

China was more than a marginal consideration to the United States during the crisis. The decision to develop a new relationship with China had already been made in Washington. It would clearly depend for success on the Chinese belief that the United States was capable of standing up to Soviet pressures. A weak United States would not attract much attention in Peking. Thus one possible benefit of the strong U.S. stance in September 1970 was to convince the Chinese that a relationship with the United States would pay dividends. The Chinese posture during the crisis itself was enigmatic. Their revolutionary support of the Palestinians was tempered by advice against the resort to terrorism and warnings of the dangers of factionalism within the PLO.

The PLO and Syria

The most enduring losses after the Jordanian crisis were suffered by the PLO and the Jadid faction in Syria. The PLO was completely expelled from its remaining bases in Jordan in July 1971, moved underground for a period, then resurfaced in Lebanon and Syria. It remained a political force of consequence in the area but its military potential and its autonomy were greatly reduced. As for the Jadid faction in Syria, it was ousted in November 1970 in a coup d'état led by General Hafiz al-Asad. The new regime has been noticeably more moderate and has succeeded in bringing a degree of political stability to Syria in the years since the Jordanian crisis.

Jordan

King Hussein was able to restore his full authority in Jordan but at the price of becoming the pariah of the Arab world. In the months following the crisis his new prime minister, Wasfi Tal, completed the task of removing the fedayeen from Jordan altogether. In retaliation, the fedayeen assassinated him in November 1971 in Cairo, depriving Jordan of the talents of its most effective prime minister in recent history. Two years later, however, Jordan sent forces to Syria to help the Asad regime during the October war against Israel.

U.S. Policymaking

The only other consequence of note that can be traced to the Jordanian crisis involved the status of Nixon and Kissinger in the foreign policymaking establishment of the United States. The successful outcome of the crisis no doubt redounded to Nixon's advantage and helped to lay the basis for his claims of foreign policy expertise. Following the Jordanian crisis Nixon was able to show progress in relations with both China and the USSR, culminating in his trips to both countries in 1972. Those *coups de theatre* helped to soften the continuing public disenchantment over policy in Southeast Asia. The Jordanian crisis can thus be seen as one of the early steps in establishing the foreign policy record that helped Nixon to win reelection in November 1972.

President Nixon and Kissinger saw the outcome of the Jordanian crisis as a clear victory for the United States. Since Israel had played a key role in the development of the contingency plan for intervention, the U.S.-Israeli relationship was greatly strengthened, not so much from gratitude as from the belief that a strong Israel would be a strategic asset to the United States. As the Soviet position in the Middle East began to unravel in 1971 and 1972, Washington officials were confirmed in their belief that the U.S.-Israeli "alliance" had strategic significance. As in the Israeli case, this contributed to an insensitivity to the dangers of the status quo and an inattentiveness to the signs of war in 1973. The surprise of October 1973 would probably not have occurred but for the mood created in September 1970.

The Jordanian crisis brought Kissinger onto the scene of Middle East politics. After September 1970 the State Department did not recapture control over policy toward the Arab-Israeli conflict until Kissinger became secretary of state in September 1973. Bureaucratically, this was an important development. It helped to ensure the failure of the State Department diplomatic initiative on reopening the Suez Canal in 1971. That failure in turn contributed to the Egyptian-Syrian conviction that the only alternative was the use of force. In brief, 1970 helped lead to 1973 through several different channels.

Evaluation

U.S. policy in the Jordanian crisis can be judged a limited success in terms of its stated objectives. To some degree U.S. power did no doubt contribute to the willingness of the USSR to restrain Syria, insofar as that was an important aspect of the crisis. But it was certainly Jordanian and Israeli power that made the greatest impression on the Syrians, not the U.S. threats or the Soviet pleas for restraint. At best, the U.S. military contribution to the outcome of the crisis was modest.

Insofar as the United States played a key role, it was primarily through its diplomacy, not through its military posturing. Obviously, force and diplomacy do go hand in hand, and the United States was able to deal effectively with King Hussein and with the Israelis because of its overall strength, not just in the Mediterranean, but worldwide. But the real contribution depended on subtlety, not brute power, especially in urging King Hussein to rely on his own forces first and in negotiating with the

Israelis to make their power available in a restrained yet responsive manner. To some degree the two countries would have acted similarly without the United States, but the essential coordination and sense for timing and nuance would have been missing. The United States was an important middleman between Jordan and Israel. A weak United States would have had less credibility in that role.

U.S. behavior during the crisis was consistent with the national interest as broadly understood at the time, and it was certainly in tune with the President's desire to convey a firm image to the Soviet leaders. As such, the policy adopted can be defended, and its consequences were on the whole advantageous to the United States at least in the short run. But the crisis does raise serious questions about the willingness or ability of top decisionmakers to appreciate the local dimensions of a crisis. By concentrating almost exclusively on the U.S.-Soviet relationship, Nixon and Kissinger let themselves be manipulated by the local parties. Israel was able to portray itself as a bulwark against Soviet power; Hussein emerged as a key to stability in the Arab world. The concerns of Egypt, Syria, and especially the Palestinians were lost in the euphoria of having faced down the USSR. This suited Israel and Jordan well enough, but it led the United States to turn a blind eye toward the mounting frustrations of the status quo for the leaders in Damascus and Cairo. Only the October 1973 war was capable of shaking the U.S. and Israeli leaderships out of the complacency and self-congratulation born of September 1970. That was an unnecessarily high price to pay.

In short, the U.S. use of force and diplomacy in the September crisis was probably wise but it rested on somewhat shaky premises at least insofar as the Middle East was concerned. The administration chose to treat the Jordanian crisis as a test of superpower wills, primarily for global reasons. At that level of abstraction, U.S. policy succeeded in making a useful point with the Moscow leadership. But having decided to treat what was essentially a regional crisis as if it were a global one, the administration continued to view the region in terms of U.S.-Soviet relations. Caught in a perceptual trap largely of its own making, it failed to respond to regional trends that ultimately resulted in a war of much greater consequence than that of September 1970.

CHAPTER EIGHT

The Dominican Republic, 1961–66

JEROME N. SLATER

FROM 1961 through 1966, U.S. policy toward the Dominican Republic represented the most massive, sustained intervention in the internal affairs of a Latin American state by the United States since the period of U.S. imperialism in the early twentieth century. Washington used a wide variety of the instruments of power and influence available to it, including multilateral diplomacy and political pressure, economic rewards and sanctions, and, most important, threats of and the actual use of military force, to shape the internal politics of the Dominican Republic. U.S. policy during this period was designed to achieve three major objectives. In the order of their probable priority, they were: (1) to prevent the establishment of a radical, Castroite regime in the Dominican Republic in the aftermath of the Trujillo era; (2) to establish in the Dominican Republic a stable, democratic, moderately progressive, but strongly anti-Communist regime that would serve as the model—the "showcase for democracy"—for the kind of political system the Alliance for Progress was designed to encourage throughout Latin America; and (3) to set the precedent and create the machinery for collective inter-American action against dictatorships in general, but which might later be used specifically against the Castro regime in Cuba.

To understand the context of the events during the period 1961–66, it must be recalled that the Dominican Republic has been closely tied to the United States ever since the U.S. military interventions of 1905 and 1916, in which U.S. Marines had been used to enforce the general U.S. policy of preempting potential European intervention in unstable Caribbean states. After the 1916 intervention the United States occupied the Dominican Republic for eight years, not departing until it had created a centralized Dominican army and placed it under the control of a young army officer, Rafael Trujillo, Sr., thought by his Marine supporters to be a reliable, pro-American leader who would support stable, democratic government. Trujillo, however, used his power to establish one of the most murderously effective feudal dictatorships in recent Latin American history. Despite its initial disappointment the United States maintained close and friendly relations with Trujillo, typifying the general marriage of convenience between the United States and rightist Latin American dictators, who were assured of U.S. support as long as they repressed their local Communists and supported U.S. foreign policies.[1] For nearly thirty years, no one more fervently adhered to U.S. policies than Trujillo. Toward the end of the 1950s, however, U.S. attitudes toward his regime began to shift, partially because of domestic anger at Trujillo's efforts to silence his critics even in the United States (for example, the disappearance of Dominican exile Jesus de Galindez, an instructor at Columbia University), partially as a result of growing Latin American bitterness at Washington's support of repressive regimes. The most fundamental reason for this shift in attitude was that the victory of Fidel Castro over Fulgencio Batista in Cuba seemed to demonstrate that support of the right might no longer be the best way to avoid radicalism in Latin America, but might rather be fostering it.

Moreover, toward the end of 1959, for the first time since he had come to power, Trujillo's grip on the country began to slip. A number of clandestine opposition groups were formed, and the political situation suddenly became fluid. The general environment in the Dominican Republic, in fact, seemed to be uncomfortably similar to that in Cuba in the last days of Batista, and the Eisenhower administration became seriously concerned that a sudden collapse of Trujillo's rule could lead to chaos and the emergence of a second Castro. "Batista is to Castro as Trujillo is to ————," was the implicit assumption, and Washington wanted to ensure that it could help fill in the blank. As a result, the United States began to

1. In 1945–47, however, Assistant Secretary for Latin American Affairs Spruille Braden did attempt to use U.S. diplomatic and economic leverage on behalf of democracy. The failure of the Braden efforts, especially in Argentina, led to the abandonment of such efforts.

cast about for a way to get rid of Trujillo and at the same time to ensure a responsible successor.

Initially, the primary vehicle for U.S. strategy was the collective break in diplomatic relations and the economic sanctions imposed by the Organization of American States (OAS). This occurred in 1960, after Trujillo attempted to arrange the assassination of President Romulo Betancourt of Venezuela, one of the most outspoken anti-Trujillo leaders in Latin America. Going beyond the OAS call for all member states to end shipments of petroleum and trucks to the Dominican Republic, the United States also cut back imports of Dominican sugar, the primary source of export earnings for the Trujillo regime. Moreover, it is now known that the U.S. Central Intelligence Agency (CIA) worked actively with dissident groups in the Dominican Republic plotting against Trujillo's life, and clandestinely shipped small arms to some of these groups.[2]

Ousting the Trujillos, 1961

On May 31, 1961, Trujillo was assassinated, leaving a shattered, leaderless, demoralized society. The primary concern of the U.S. government was to ensure that a new Castro did not emerge from the chaos, and also —but a distinctly secondary goal—to use the opportunity to press for the establishment of democracy in the Dominican Republic. The framework and priority of U.S. objectives was succinctly summarized in John F. Kennedy's oft-quoted remark: "There are three possibilities . . . in descending order of preference: a decent democratic regime, a continuation of the Trujillo regime or a Castro regime. We ought to aim at the first but we really can't renounce the second until we are sure we can avoid the third."[3]

Within a few days of the assassination the Kennedy administration reinforced the Caribbean "ready force" that had remained in the general vicinity of Cuba and/or the Dominican Republic since 1959. Within days the United States placed in the area as a "routine training exercise" a major naval force, including three aircraft carriers (*Intrepid, Shangri-La,* and

2. For details on the CIA plots, see Howard J. Wiarda, *Dictatorship, Development and Disintegration,* vol. 2 (Xerox University Microfilms, 1975), pp. 838–43, and the "Summary of the Report of the Special Senate Committee on Intelligence," *New York Times,* November 21, 1975.

3. Quoted by Arthur M. Schlesinger, Jr., *A Thousand Days: John F. Kennedy in the White House* (Houghton Mifflin, 1965), p. 769.

Randolph), five support ships, and numerous surface combatants, as well as the 4th Marine Expeditionary Brigade of approximately 5,000 men. Already in the area was a Marine battalion landing team aboard the helicopter carrier *Boxer,* and it was accompanied by other amphibious ships.[4] According to *New York Times* reports at the time, the military moves were designed both as a precaution in case American citizens had to be evacuated and as a show of force to back forthcoming U.S. diplomatic efforts to influence the internal Dominican situation. It has also been suggested that these moves might have been part of a contingency plan to intervene militarily in the Dominican Republic to forestall a Castro takeover.[5]

Within hours after the assassination the Trujillo family had moved to crush all internal opposition to their total domination over the country. Joaquin Balaguer, who had been closely tied to the Trujillo family for decades, had been serving as nominal president since August 1960 and he remained in office; Rafael ("Ramfis") Trujillo, Jr., was named to head the armed forces, and his uncles, Hector and José Arismendi Trujillo, remained as key figures behind the scenes, controlling substantial private armies.[6]

Aside from Balaguer and the Trujillo family, the other major actors on the Dominican political scene who were the targets of U.S. military displays and diplomatic maneuvers were:

1. The regular Dominican armed forces, the primary source of political power in the country. Within the military the key figures were Brigadier General Pedro Rodriguez Echevarria, commander of the Santiago military base, and Fernando A. Sanchez, chief of staff of the Air Force.

4. *New York Times,* June 2–4, 1961; Wiarda, *Dictatorship, Development and Disintegration,* p. 854.

5. According to Abraham F. Lowenthal, "Just days after the Bay of Pigs, President Kennedy personally approved a contingency plan for landing troops in the Dominican Republic which stressed as the principal policy guideline that the United States could not afford and would not permit the imposition in the Dominican Republic of a pro-Castro or pro-Communist government. This theme was repeated time and again in presidential instructions to U.S. officials concerned with the Dominican Republic." Abraham Lowenthal, *The Dominican Intervention* (Harvard University Press, 1972), p. 26. See also the memoirs of Chester Bowles, who cryptically refers to the "successful resistance" of the Kennedy administration to "pressures" for a military takeover of the Dominican Republic after Trujillo's assassination, in order to forestall a feared takeover by Castro. Chester Bowles, *Promises to Keep: My Years in Public Life, 1941–1969* (Harper and Row, 1971), p. 342.

6. Wiarda, *Dictatorship, Development and Disintegration,* pp. 846–47; Thomas M. Millington, "U.S. Diplomacy and the Dominican Crisis," *SAIS Review,* vol. 7 (Summer 1963), pp. 25–26.

Their objectives in the aftermath of the assassination are not clear, but it seems reasonable to assume they were primarily concerned to maintain or perhaps expand their own personal power. Rodriguez Echevarria seems to have sided with Balaguer, and as a result he soon emerged—if only briefly—as the dominant figure.

2. The Union Civica Nacional (UCN), a conservative, middle-class, but anti-Trujillo opposition party that came out into the open after the assassination. The UCN was headed by Viriato Fiallo.

3. Juan Bosch, who had been in exile for decades and returned to the Dominican Republic to form the Partido Revolucionario Dominicano (PRD), initially a party of the democratic left, to compete with the UCN after the hoped-for collapse of the Trujillistas.

In the immediate aftermath of the assassination the Kennedy administration had two immediate objectives: to maintain order and to liberalize the Balaguer/Ramfis regime. The ultimate objective was to create a stable, democratic, anti-Communist government. The maintenance of order was considered crucial because, in the short run, the chances of a Communist takeover would increase if chaos and a breakdown of police and army control followed the assassination. In the last year or so of his rule Trujillo had retaliated against the U.S. sanctions by allowing increased Communist activity in the Dominican Republic, and a Castroite group called the Fourteenth of June Movement was active in the working class areas of Santo Domingo. In the long run the U.S. government felt that the minimization of Communist influence depended upon the creation of a democratic regime, capable of meeting the legitimate demands and grievances of a people oppressed for thirty years by a savage totalitarian regime.

The objectives of order and democracy might have been compatible in the long run but there was considerable tension between them in the short run. The requirements of a policy that sought to maximize order would have demanded unstinting U.S. support of Balaguer, the Trujillos, and their supporters in the police and military, for they were probably capable of suppressing Communist (and, of course, all other dissident) activities by brute force. On the other hand, a policy that sought to maximize the chances for democracy would have required immediate and severe U.S. pressures to break the power of the military, force out Balaguer and the Trujillos, and to hold free elections.

Faced with this dilemma, the Kennedy administration split the difference. From the evidence now available it cannot be ascertained whether this was the conscious decision of a united administration aware of the risks of emphasizing one element to the exclusion of the other, or whether it was in fact more in the nature of a nondecision and merely the result of differing opinions within the U.S. government. There were apparently several areas of disagreement.[7] First, there were differences between those who wished to emphasize order and those who stressed establishing a democracy. The former were generally more disposed than the latter to view Balaguer favorably; this was not necessarily the case, however, for a second area of disagreement was whether Balaguer sincerely intended to liberalize the Dominican government as he was promising, or whether his real objective was to preserve the status quo behind a meaningless facade of "reforms." Finally, there was uncertainty over whether Balaguer, whatever his intention, had the leadership capabilities and the power base to control either the extreme left or the extreme right.

In the context of these various disagreements or uncertainties, the Kennedy administration initially chose to back Balaguer, Ramfis, and the armed forces, while at the same time attempting to induce them to liberalize the worst features of the Trujillo era and prepare for democratic elections. As Kennedy put it: "Balaguer . . . [is] our only tool. . . . The anticommunist liberals aren't strong enough. We must use our influence to take Balaguer along the road to democracy."[8]

The primary instruments of U.S. policy were the economic leverage provided by the OAS sanctions and the reduction of U.S. sugar imports, backed by a show of military force. Responding to U.S. recommendations, the OAS agreed to maintain the economic sanctions until there was substantial evidence of progress toward democracy; meanwhile, the U.S. Navy Caribbean "ready squadron," consisting of the U.S. carrier *Boxer,* several amphibious vessels, and a Marine battalion of about 1,200 men, remained in Dominican waters.[9]

The Crisis of November 1961

In the ensuing months the Balaguer regime took some small steps toward liberalization. At the end of the summer it requested the OAS to end the embargo and the United States to resume its sugar purchases. In early

7. The ensuing discussion is based on a series of interviews with government officials in 1962. As these interviews were on a not-for-attribution basis, I cannot identify particular individuals with particular policy positions.
8. Schlesinger, *A Thousand Days,* p. 770.
9. Wiarda, *Dictatorship, Development and Disintegration,* p. 854.

September the OAS sent a committee to the Dominican Republic to re-evaluate the situation. Balaguer and Ramfis promised the OAS group that they would continue the reform process and open negotiations with opposition leaders to form a coalition government. But the UCN and the PRD both urged the OAS and the United States to continue the sanctions, arguing that the reforms had been a sham and that the existing regime was nothing more than a continuation of Trujillism. Apparently convinced by this argument, the OAS decided to maintain the sanctions and the Kennedy administration resolved to continue the sugar embargo and increase diplomatic pressures on Balaguer and Ramfis to reach an agreement with the opposition. A turning point in the hesitant movement toward democracy was apparently reached in mid-November when most of the Trujillo family, although not Ramfis, bowed to the pressures and left the country. In response to this and to other indications of progress, on November 14 the United States proposed in the OAS a partial lifting of the economic sanctions.[10]

On November 16, however, Hector and Arismendi Trujillo—the "wicked uncles"—returned to the Dominican Republic to attempt to block the liberalization process and restore the family dictatorship. If they had succeeded, of course, all the efforts of the U.S. government for the previous two years would have gone for nought. Recognizing this, the Kennedy administration decided to do whatever might be necessary, including ordering an armed intervention, to block the reestablishment of Trujillism. In reaching this decision the administration undoubtedly was influenced not only by a general commitment toward democracy but by concern that a new Trujillo dictatorship might resume the flirtation with Castro and the USSR that Trujillo, Sr., had pursued during his last year in power.[11]

Finally, on November 18, Ramfis Trujillo became convinced that his best course of action was to resign and leave the country. Washington now

10. For details on the May 31–November 14 period, see ibid., pp. 846–52; the *New York Times* daily reports; and Jerome Slater, "The United States, the Organization of American States, and the Dominican Republic, 1961–1963," *International Organization*, vol. 18 (1964), p. 274.

11. For details on this point and on Trujillo's use of the Dominican Communist party leader Maximo Lopez Molina to frighten the United States, see Wiarda, *Dictatorship, Development and Disintegration*, p. 833; and John Bartlow Martin, *Overtaken by Events* (Doubleday, 1966), p. 83. Lopez had been imprisoned by Balaguer on November 14, and U.S. officials might have been concerned that a new Trujillo government would once again release him and allow him to attack the United States verbally, as the Trujillos had done in the past.

also sought to force the wicked uncles to leave and thus to end the Trujillo family's control of the Dominican Republic. The U.S. government was also eager to prevent one of the family's henchmen—General Fernando Sanchez—from seizing power. The Kennedy administration communicated its intention to the Trujillos and Sanchez explicitly through U.S. officials in the country and through a series of diplomatic and military actions. The military threat left the crucial Dominican figures with no doubt that they had little choice but to comply.

On November 16, within hours after it became known that the Trujillos had returned to the Dominican Republic, the United States asked for an urgent meeting of the OAS Council in Washington, and Assistant Secretary of State for Inter-American Affairs Robert Woodward asked that action on the previous U.S. request for a partial lifting of the sanctions be delayed. The next day Secretary of State Dean Rusk held a news conference in which he warned that the United States would not "remain idle" if the Trujillos returned and tried to "reassert dictatorial domination."[12]

Rusk's speech was couched in general terms, but administration sources told reporters from the *New York Times,* the *Wall Street Journal,* and other leading newspapers that the U.S. government had definitely decided it would forcibly intervene if necessary to prevent the restoration of Trujillism.[13] These leaks, prominently featured in leading American newspapers, could hardly have escaped the attention of the Dominicans.

To back up these threats of force a large U.S. naval task force, consisting of the aircraft carrier *Franklin D. Roosevelt,* the helicopter carrier *Valley Forge,* and other amphibious ships with 1,800 Marines on board, the cruiser *Little Rock* (flagship of the U.S. Second Fleet), twelve destroyers, and a number of landing craft appeared off the Dominican coast on November 19. They were just outside the three-mile limit but in plain sight of Santo Domingo. On the same day, jet fighters from the *Roosevelt* streaked along the Dominican coastline in a display calculated to awe and intimidate the Trujillos and the Dominican military.[14]

12. The text of the press release is in *Department of State Bulletin,* vol. 45 (December 4, 1961), p. 931; for Woodward's action, see ibid., p. 932.

13. See the stories by Tad Szulc in *New York Times,* November 17 and 20, 1961, and by Philip Geyelin, *Wall Street Journal,* November 20, 1961.

14. For details on the makeup of the naval force and the objectives of the military display, see U.S. Department of the Navy, Atlantic Fleet, *U.S. Atlantic Fleet, Second Fleet Historical Report, 1961;* Martin, *Overtaken by Events,* pp. 82–83; Wiarda, *Dictatorship, Development and Disintegration,* p. 853; *New York Times,* November 18–20, 1961.

Meanwhile, the head of the U.S. consulate in Santo Domingo, John C. Hill, and a special representative of President Kennedy, Arturo Morales, met with the Trujillos and Sanchez and bluntly told them that U.S. military power would, if necessary, be used to force the formation of a provisional government headed by Balaguer. The previous evening, moreover, the U.S. military liaison, Marine Lieutenant Colonel Edwin Simmons, had met with Rodriguez Echevarria to ascertain that Rodriguez supported the U.S. military actions. Other commanders, who were not so close to U.S. officials, were warned not to support the Trujillos.[15]

All of the Dominican targets received the message. While the exact details of the mixture of threats and promises made by U.S. officials are not known, it is reasonable to assume that all the Dominican targets recognized that their continued political power, status, wealth—perhaps even their lives—depended upon U.S. support or at least the absence of direct U.S. opposition. In any case, the desired action was forthcoming. On the evening of November 19, while the jets continued their fly-bys and Spanish-language broadcasts from the offshore ships warned the Dominicans that the Marines were prepared to come ashore, Balaguer made a speech on the national radio station urging "all Dominicans, military and civilian, to unite behind the legitimate power and avoid the danger that menaces our sovereignty."[16] At about the same time, Dominican planes under the control of Rodriguez Echevarria bombed the San Isidro Air Base outside Santo Domingo, where Ramfis and other Trujillist generals, including Fernando Sanchez, had been massing troops. With the game clearly up, Ramfis, the wicked uncles, and Sanchez fled the country on November 20 and the plot collapsed.

Aftermath of the Crisis

In the next two months the U.S. government stepped up its pressures for further democratization in the Dominican Republic. It backed its diplomatic efforts with the economic sanctions still in force and the continuing presence of the U.S. fleet off the coast. On several occasions administration sources publicly stated that the U.S. Navy would remain in

15. *New York Times,* November 18–21, 1961; Lt. Col. Edwin H. Simmons, "Military-Political Situation in the Dominican Republic," *Office of Naval Information Review* (May 1962); interview of Simmons by Stephen S. Kaplan, February 10, 1975.
16. *New York Times,* November 20, 1971; on the Spanish-language broadcasts, see Wiarda, *Dictatorship, Development and Disintegration,* p. 853.

Dominican waters until the situation was "fully clarified," or as long as there was a danger of "political disintegration."[17] The major focus of administration efforts was to protect Balaguer from potential threats from either the extreme right or left until he was able to broaden his government to include the moderate democratic opposition and prepare for elections. In fact, however, Balaguer himself clearly wanted to hold on to power, and became a major obstacle to meaningful democratization. Finally, faced with pressure from the United States and growing domestic opposition, including a successful general strike supported by Fiallo and Bosch, Balaguer agreed to resign. He was replaced by a seven-man council of state, dominated by the UCN, which pledged to hold elections at the end of 1962.

A final military effort to block this process, this time led by Rodriguez Echevarria and very probably backed by Balaguer, collapsed when the United States moved the *Little Rock* and the Second Caribbean Amphibious Ready Squadron and Landing Force closer in to shore off Santo Domingo, and Hill informed Rodriguez that the U.S. government was prepared to treat him as it had the wicked uncles.[18]

In late January the fleet was withdrawn, the OAS sanctions were lifted, and the United States resumed its sugar purchases, although U.S. representatives in the Dominican Republic continued to use their influence to back the council of state and to ensure that the elections would be fair.[19] Among the instruments of U.S. influence were several U.S. naval ship visitations to Santo Domingo and ostentatious ceremonies and dinners aboard them for council of state leaders. Whether the United States would actually have been willing to use force in the event of a threatened coup

17. *New York Times*, November 21, 25, and 27, 1961.

18. *New York Times*, January 20, 1972; Wiarda, *Dictatorship, Development and Disintegration*, pp. 854–55; *U.S. Atlantic Fleet, Second Fleet Historical Report, 1961*; interview with John C. Hill.

19. The extent of U.S. influence on the internal politics of a supposedly sovereign state is rather vividly illustrated in Martin, *Overtaken by Events*, in which he reports a conversation he had with Bosch and Fiallo shortly before the elections: "We, the United States . . . support free elections. . . . We intend to exert our influence to see that such elections are held. We intend to see that the winner is able to take office. We intend to use our influence to see that his government is not dominated by the military or the police" (p. 227). When Bosch and Fiallo quibbled at some of the details of the electoral process arranged by the United States, the Venezuelan ambassador, who had worked closely with Martin on the matter, reprimanded them: "We diplomats are up to here with the ingenuity of you two" (p. 229).

was another matter. Presidential emissary and later Ambassador to the Dominican Republic John B. Martin writes that he was "privately" convinced that the United States "absolutely would not permit a Castro/ Communist takeover," that he was "almost as certain" force would be used to prevent a new Trujillo coup, but that he "was far less certain" that action would be taken against a rightist coup.[20] However, no coups were attempted, and in December 1962 Bosch defeated Fiallo in the elections, presided over and in effect guaranteed by the U.S. embassy.

The Role of the OAS

During the course of the crisis the OAS had been dominated by the United States and had acted, in effect, as an instrument of U.S. policy. As such it gave U.S. actions at least the color of a collective enterprise, and thus helped reduce possible nationalistic, anti-American reactions in Latin America and in the Dominican Republic itself. Moreover, by making the U.S. economic pressures part of the official peacekeeping functions of an international organization, the OAS gave the Dominican opposition leaders—whose strategy was to bring to bear a maximum of external as well as internal pressures on the Balaguer regime—a degree of maneuver that nationalistic pride might otherwise have denied them. It was one thing for the Dominicans—Bosch, Fiallo, and others—to plead repeatedly with the OAS to maintain sanctions against their own nation and against the wishes of their government, but it might have been quite another if they had been forced to communicate their appeals directly to the United States without the OAS screen.

Outcomes

The activist U.S. policy in 1961–62 and the subsequent course of events in the Dominican Republic illustrate both the benefits and the limitations of the political use of military force as an instrument of U.S. foreign policy. In the short run U.S. policy was remarkably successful. As a direct result of its combined economic leverage and military threats the U.S. government was able to induce all the major Dominican actors to conform to its objectives. Moreover, there were no external costs to the

20. Ibid., p. 196; see also pp. 121–22, 192–97, 255, 271, for details on Council of State visits to U.S. warships and U.S. thinking about potential military coups.

U.S. actions; on the contrary, the Trujillo regime had been in such bad odor around the world that U.S. policies, even including the military threats and deployments, had *enhanced* the image of the Kennedy administration in the Dominican Republic, in the United States, and throughout Latin America. The appearance of the U.S. Navy off the coast led to mass demonstrations of popular approval in the streets of Santo Domingo; Juan Bosch enthusiastically praised the action; and in the United Nations the Dominican foreign minister, responding to a Cuban attempt to have the United States labeled an aggressor, replied: "Blessed be the moment when the American fleet came to Dominican waters."[21] In the United States the actions of the Kennedy administration aroused little widespread or sustained popular attention, but were widely praised on the editorial pages as wisely conceived and brilliantly executed.[22] Throughout Latin America the widespread hatred of Trujillo outweighed the traditional antipathy toward U.S. intervention in the internal affairs of hemispheric states, so most Latin American governments either supported the U.S. actions or tacitly acquiesced in them.

It seems reasonable to suppose that the show of force and the accompanying threats to use it if necessary were crucial to the achievement of U.S. objectives during the November and January crises. The economic pressures undoubtedly helped, but even though the Trujillistas (including Balaguer and Rodriguez) understood full well that those pressures would continue if they attempted to reassert their rule, they were apparently prepared to ignore them ruthlessly, for in each case coups were averted or reversed only after the military displays.

Whatever the undoubted immediate success of U.S. policies, however, subsequent developments in the Dominican Republic cast considerable doubt on their longer term success. Though the Bosch government was democratically elected and began a broad program of social and economic reform, the U.S. government soon became disenchanted with it, and the Kennedy administration did not repeat its earlier threats and military displays to deter the military coup against Bosch of September 1963. It was clear, then, that in the long run the creation of a stable and democratic political system in the Dominican Republic depended on in-

21. *New York Times,* November 25, 1961.
22. For example, see *New York Times* editorials of December 1, 1961, and January 20, 1962.

ternal conditions that were only partially subject to U.S. influence. Still, the destruction of the brutal totalitarianism of Trujillo in 1961–62 was no small accomplishment. During this period the requirements of the national interest and more universalist values had happily coincided. Although the United States had prevented a return to Trujillism not so much from devotion to democracy per se as from fear of communism, the results were a clear gain for the Dominican people and for humanity as well as for U.S. policy.

Evaluation

The ouster of the Trujillos in November 1961 also suggests some more general lessons about the relationship between the use of force and the achievement of objectives by U.S. policymakers. First, the United States was able in this incident to exercise complete strategic control. Aside from certain other Latin dictators, the Trujillos had no external political allies. Even more important, especially with regard to the U.S. decision to use force, the Trujillos could expect to receive no material support from any quarter and the United States could act with complete military confidence.

This was also true, of course, in June immediately after the assassination of Rafael Trujillo. But then the administration did not act explicitly to oust Trujillo's heirs—that is, the administration did not then commit itself to the objective it espoused in November. When it did so commit itself, Washington allowed no doubt as to what would constitute an acceptable outcome. In short, it issued an ultimatum. Moreover, communications with the principal targets in the Dominican Republic were unobstructed.

At the same time, within the Dominican Republic the targets had no ideological commitments. Pragmatic and interested primarily in their personal well being, the Trujillos and their immediate supporters were persuadable. Indeed, Ramfis, who was the most influential in the group, probably lost the stomach to resist the U.S. demands even before force was used.

The Trujillos also had no support within their own country. While there was no popular movement to oust them violently from power, neither was there any die-hard support for them. Aside from the vast apathetic majority, those who were politically active and both the business and social elites were wholly in favor of having the Trujillos leave the country. Furthermore there was no nationalist sentiment against "Yankee intervention."

Finally, the Trujillos did not even control the armed forces. Aside from those officers who straddled the fence, effective military power, small as it may have been, was more in the hands of General Rodriguez Echevarria than anyone else. His support of the U.S. action pulled the rug from under the Trujillos. Thus the earlier cultivation of Rodriguez Echevarria proved of great value.

If the United States had undertaken decisive action against the Trujillos in June 1961 it might have encountered greater difficulty. At that time there was no overt opposition within the Dominican Republic, and the Trujillos held much firmer control over the military, notwithstanding the participation of a number of military men in the assassination plot. The outcomes would probably have been the same but the dangers would have been greater.

Considering Washington's goals, an even greater use of force—such as an actual intervention of the sort that occurred in Lebanon in 1958 and in the Dominican Republic in 1965—would have had no greater value. Both the Trujillos and Rodriguez Echevarria might not have believed that the United States was really committed to its objectives had they not seen a major military force offshore, however. They also might not have believed it had they seen only a few surface combatants. The plain sight of Marines and aircraft carriers, however, was surely something different. In this context the military force, placed clearly in sight, seemed convincingly threatening; coupled with a verbal ultimatum it became anything but a bluff. The Trujillos' only alternative to complying with the U.S. demands was a futile and inconsequential resistance. Being the pragmatists that they were, they folded.

The ability to set in motion the events that occurred between the decision to oust the Trujillos and the inauguration of Juan Bosch did not prove that the United States could effect a radical change of regime no matter how much it might have wished to. In the end, Bosch was completely dependent on the United States. Washington did not take any military action to prevent the coup against him; even more important, the more Washington soured on Bosch, the more *certain* the coup became. Bosch would not have been so dependent had the military been gutted and rebuilt. This could only have been accomplished by force or the direct threat of force from U.S. military power. The Dominican military might have collapsed without violent resistance, but U.S. troops would almost certainly have had to be landed in the Dominican Republic.

The 1965 Crisis

Juan Bosch took office in early 1963, amid high hopes in both the Dominican Republic and the United States that solid progress had been made toward the reestablishment of democracy. There was no doubt that the Kennedy administration initially gave its strong—even enthusiastic— support to the Bosch government; it promised the Dominican Republic substantial economic support under the Alliance for Progress, and gave Bosch the grand treatment in Washington just before he entered office.[23]

The glow faded very quickly, however. The U.S. government, advised by Ambassador Martin, became increasingly disenchanted with Bosch's nationalism; with his determination to engage in substantial social reform measures, which alienated Dominican businessmen, landowners, and the Catholic church; and, most important, with his refusal to crack down on radical groups. In a matter of months the administration had completely soured on Bosch, considering him at best ineffective and, at worst, possibly even a "deep-cover Communist."[24] U.S. economic assistance programs to the Dominican Republic were soon cut back, and these and other indications of U.S. coolness toward Bosch encouraged plotting against him among the rightists and the military. In late September—only seven months after taking office—Bosch was overthrown and sent into exile by a military coup led by Colonel Elias Wessin y Wessin, commander of the key San Isidro Air Base outside Santo Domingo. The rationale for the coup, predictably enough, was that Bosch was delivering the country to the Communists. Martin did not really agree with this assessment, despite his own misgivings about Bosch, and he tried hard to prevent the coup, but his insistence on the Communist threat had helped to legitimize the plots against Bosch and undercut U.S. efforts to persuade the military to stay out of politics.

The coup was greeted in Washington with distaste, but the disillusion with Bosch discouraged any effective action to reverse it. In the last

23. *New York Times*, January 11, 1963; Martin, *Overtaken by Events*, p. 308.
24. Martin, *Overtaken by Events*, p. 347.

frantic hours before the coup, Martin asked to have an aircraft carrier sent to Dominican waters to make the kind of show of force that had earlier proven so effective. The State Department sharply refused, however, and warned Martin not to commit the United States in his moves to save Bosch. Not only would military force not be used or even threatened, but there would be no repeat of the heavy economic pressures of the previous few years. To be sure, diplomatic relations were suspended and economic and military aid were temporarily cut off in an effort to induce the new junta to hold free elections. In the ensuing weeks, however, the State Department progressively softened its pressures, especially when the junta began to warn that U.S. attitudes were encouraging "Castroite revolutionaries." Finally, in mid-December 1963, with a handful of the inevitable "guerrillas" in the hills and a piece of paper from the junta promising "free elections" in a year and a half, the United States capitulated. It reestablished diplomatic relations, restored economic assistance, and replaced Martin with a new ambassador, W. Tapley Bennett, a conservative foreign service officer. Bennett quickly established warm ties with the head of the junta, Donald Reid Cabral, a wealthy businessman. Among Americans Reid was fondly known as "Donny" Reid and considered a safe, sound, pro-American force for stability. Among Dominicans, however, Reid was frequently referred to as "El Americano"; some even considered him an agent of the U.S. Central Intelligence Agency.

By early 1965 the Reid government was in deep trouble. Whatever chance it might have had to gain popular support had been lost because of Reid's authoritarian methods and lack of personal charisma and because of the government's stiff austerity program, which had created high unemployment and widespread discontent. Immediately after the 1963 coup public reaction had seemed apathetic, but a year later there had been a substantial spread in sentiment for a return to constitutional government in general and to Juan Bosch in particular, especially among students, intellectuals, and professionals. In late January 1965 the PRD and its main rival on the moderate left, the PRSC (Social Christians), had met with Bosch at his exile home in Puerto Rico and had formally agreed to work together to reestablish the constitutional government; the agreement became publicly known in the Dominican Republic and was widely approved. Meanwhile, most ominously, the armed forces, the government's last bastion of power, were becoming disgruntled by Reid's efforts to stamp out military corruption and to remove some of the most venal of the remaining Trujillists.

The final straw was Reid's increasingly obvious intention to cancel the elections scheduled for the fall of 1965 or to rig them to maintain himself in power. By early spring it had become evident that a major blowup was imminent; a few weeks before the revolution, Bennett had warned the State Department that "little foxes, some of them red, are chewing at the grapes."[25]

The uprising of April 1965 began not so much as a revolution but as a military coup designed at first simply to bring down the Reid government. In the early morning of Saturday, April 24, two Army barracks, under the leadership of a small group of young colonels and acting in concert with PRD leaders, seized and imprisoned the army chief of staff and declared themselves in revolt against the government. Within a few hours a number of other officers had joined the uprising and taken their units with them, swelling the ranks of the "constitutionalists," as they called themselves, to about 1,000 to 1,500 men.

The original participants in the coup were a rather mixed bag, not all of them simply pro-Boschists or democratic idealists. Many, among them the initiators of the insurrection on April 24, had indeed opposed the 1963 coup, were ashamed of the military's Trujillist heritage, and had established close contacts with Bosch. Others, however, had rather doubtful qualifications as revolutionary heroes. Some were pro-Balaguer Trujillists who had been plotting on their own; they had joined the movement because they assumed its aim was not the direct return of Bosch to the presidency but the holding of new elections, which they believed Balaguer stood a good chance of winning. Many of the leading figures had entirely disreputable records, having been Nazi SS officers, foreign legionnaires, and shock troops from Trujillo's personal commando unit.[26] Colonel Francisco Caamaño, soon to emerge as the leading military figure in the constitutionalist camp, was the son of a Trujillo general known as "The Butcher" because of his enthusiastic services to "El Jefe," and Caamaño himself had served as the head of a hated police riot squad that was anti-Bosch and specialized in breaking up leftist demonstrations. Perhaps such men were simply opportunists and adventurers; perhaps, as seems more

25. Quoted by Rowland Evans and Robert Novak, *Lyndon B. Johnson: The Exercise of Power* (New American Library, 1966), p. 513.

26. On the background of the constitutionalists, see José A. Moreno, *Barrios in Arms* (University of Pittsburgh Press, 1970); and Abraham F. Lowenthal, "The Dominican Republic: The Politics of Chaos," in Arpad von Lazar and Robert R. Kaufman, eds., *Reform and Revolution: Readings in Latin American Politics* (Allyn and Bacon, 1969).

persuasive in the case of Caamaño himself, they were seeking atonement for their past lives.

Whatever the motives of the initial participants, the uprising quickly gained widespread popular support. Two events helped transform the military coup into a populist uprising: first, PRD leaders seized Radio Santo Domingo and urged the populace to take to the streets in support of the movement; second, late Saturday and early Sunday morning, constitutionalist officers passed out arms to thousands of civilians (whether this was planned or spontaneous is not yet known) to broaden the base of the movement and counter any possible reaction from the bulk of the armed forces. Until that point the civilians working with the constitutionalists were mostly middle-class, college-educated students, lawyers, engineers, technicians, and young businessmen, frustrated by a system in which they had no purpose and no meaningful future. The distribution of arms, however, brought large sectors of the urban lower class into the ranks (estimates range from 2,500 to 10,000 armed *combatientes*), giving the movement something of a mass base as well as providing most of the actual armed fighting men.

By Sunday morning it was apparent that the military had ignored Reid's orders to crush the uprising. Reid resigned and went into hiding. Because of Reid's widespread unpopularity, and the still unclear nature and ultimate purpose of the insurrection, the regular military leadership was at first unwilling to take decisive action. By Sunday afternoon, however, the situation had begun to change. The constitutionalists named a close associate of Bosch as provisional president to remain in office only until Bosch could return and reassume the presidency. Meanwhile, jubilant crowds surged through the streets of Santo Domingo all day Sunday, chanting for Bosch's return. Thus there could no longer be much doubt that a victory of the revolution would return Bosch to power and short-circuit the promised elections, in which Balaguer would also participate. The regular military detested Bosch, fearing, undoubtedly correctly, that a triumphant Bosch, backed by the defecting constitutionalist military and what amounted to a well-armed civilian militia, would probably seek to destroy their power and position in the Dominican Republic. As a result, by late Sunday afternoon substantial military opposition to the movement developed, led by (now General) Wessin y Wessin at the San Isidro Air Base.

On Sunday afternoon planes from San Isidro attacked the National

Palace and other constitutionalist positions in Santo Domingo, and armored units from San Isidro and other nearby military bases entered the city. In the next two days it appeared that the revolution was doomed, as the constitutionalists were under heavy attack by apparently superior forces in Santo Domingo, and the revolution had failed to spread to the countryside or any other important city. By Tuesday afternoon, however, the tide had somehow turned. The "loyalist" tanks were bottled up in the narrow streets of the working class sections of Santo Domingo, and were either destroyed or captured intact by the constitutionalists. Outside the city the remainder of Wessin's forces refused to enter the fray, and many began to desert. By the next day the remnants of the regular military forces had been mopped up, and the revolutionaries turned their attention to the police stations inside the city. Post after post fell to the constitutionalists, whose armaments swelled as they captured new armories. By Wednesday night, April 28, the military and police inside Santo Domingo had completely collapsed, and the constitutionalists were about to go on the offensive and attack San Isidro itself, now defended by probably no more than several thousand demoralized troops.

U.S. Behavior

The overriding U.S. concern during the Dominican revolution was, as in the earlier Dominican crisis, to avert at all costs a second Cuba. There were at least four separate reasons behind this policy.

1. A second radically anti-American regime in the Caribbean would be another blow at the historical policy of maintaining a general position of predominance throughout the Central American Caribbean area, a policy first given expression in the Monroe Doctrine and considered an axiomatic objective of U.S. foreign policy ever since.

2. In the more specific circumstances of the cold war, policymakers feared that another Communist or Castroite regime in the Caribbean would undermine U.S. prestige and credibility around the world, present the USSR with another possible site for military bases or even missile launchers close to U.S. borders, and psychologically undercut U.S. efforts in Vietnam. President Lyndon Johnson was reported to have said, "What can we do in Vietnam if we can't clean up the Dominican Republic?"[27]

3. It was widely believed that no administration, and especially not a

27. Quoted in Martin, *Overtaken by Events,* p. 661.

Democratic one, could survive in office if it failed to prevent a new Castro in this hemisphere. Johnson remarked: "When I do what I am about to do, there'll be a lot of people in this hemisphere I can't live with, but if I don't do it, there'll be a lot of people in this country I can't live with."[28]

4. Finally, there were a number of indications that government officials even at lower levels feared for their careers if they could be charged with "losing the Dominican Republic,"[29] just as a whole generation of China specialists was wiped out after Mao's victory, and to a lesser but still substantial degree, Cuban specialists found their careers aborted after Castro's victory in Cuba.

Thus, before the 1965 crisis there was an overwhelming predisposition throughout the U.S. government to err on the "safe" side—to move hard and fast whenever there was even a small possibility of a new Castroite regime in the Caribbean.

No wonder, then, that from the very outset of the revolution the U.S. embassy in Santo Domingo expressed its concern at indications of Communist support of the constitutionalist uprising. As a result, the State Department quickly instructed the embassy to use its influence with still uncommitted Dominican military officials to encourage them to resist. Working through its military attachés, the embassy did urgently press the military chiefs to unite and "do everything possible to prevent a Communist takeover." It may very well be that their efforts proved decisive with those commanders who were still wavering. In Santiago, for example, the Dominican Republic's second largest city, the importunings of the U.S. consul barely averted the defection of an important army base and the passing out of arms to thousands of pro-Bosch civilians; the visit of a U.S. military attaché to the provincial army garrison at La Vega apparently helped persuade the commander to remain loyal to the Reid government.[30] There is no doubt that U.S. officials had advance notice of and approved the decision of Wessin and other military commanders to attack the constitutionalists on Sunday afternoon.

28. Quoted in Charles W. Roberts, *LBJ's Inner Circle* (Delacorte, 1965), p. 205.
29. Much of the research for this study draws on my not-for-attribution interviews with U.S. and Dominican actors and on my access to the cable traffic between the U.S. embassy and the State Department. The sole restriction imposed on use of material gathered from these sources was that I not directly cite individuals or specific cables. I have chosen to handle this restriction by using such phrases as "there are a number of indications," or by quoting directly from individuals or documents without further attribution.
30. Lowenthal, *Dominican Intervention*, p. 201.

At the same time that the U.S. embassy was encouraging the use of force against the constitutionalists, it was rejecting entreaties by PRD leaders and constitutionalist military officials to use its good offices to help negotiate a cease-fire. Since the U.S. government wanted the uprising defeated, and until at least Tuesday night believed that the military would prevail, it saw no reason to intercede. On the contrary, one U.S. official brutally told the constitutionalists, "If I had Wessin's power, I would use it too." Ambassador Bennett later advised PRD leaders that the only thing he would do for them was advise them to surrender.[31]

During the first few days of the revolution the Johnson administration had been reluctant to become directly involved in military assistance to the loyalist forces, let alone to land U.S. forces. On several occasions Bennett had told Wessin and other Dominican military leaders not to expect any armed U.S. assistance; the State Department even denied temporarily a request from Ambassador Bennett that Wessin's forces be provided with fifty walkie-talkie sets. By Tuesday, April 27, the fourth day of the revolution, Washington was becoming worried that the military might not prevail after all, and the 82nd Airborne Division was placed on alert for possible intervention.[32] The next day, in response to increasingly pessimistic reports from the U.S. embassy, Rusk told Bennett that the United States did not want to intervene "unless the outcome is in doubt." Several hours later Bennett sent his famous (or infamous) "critic[al]" cable, saying that the military and police were on the verge of defeat at the hands of "Castro-type elements," and recommending the immediate landing of U.S. troops. All twelve embassy political and military officers concurred in the recommendation, and Thomas Mann later claimed that "all those in our Government who had full access to official information were convinced that the landing of additional troops was necessary."[33] (Aside from the President himself, of course, the key Washington officials apparently were Kennedy M. Crockett, chief of the State Department's Bureau of Caribbean Affairs; Under Secretaries of State George Ball and

31. For details on U.S. actions see ibid., p. 83; and Jerome Slater, *Intervention and Negotiation: The United States and the Dominican Revolution* (Harper and Row, 1970), pp. 24–26.

32. Lowenthal, *Dominican Intervention,* p. 89.

33. "The Dominican Crisis: Correcting Some Misconceptions," Address before the Inter-American Press Association, San Diego, California, October 12, 1965; text appears in *Department of State Bulletin,* vol. 53 (November 8, 1965), pp. 730–38; quotation from p. 736.

Thomas Mann; Secretary of State Dean Rusk; and White House National Security Adviser McGeorge Bundy.)

There is no doubt at all that the U.S. intervention was motivated from the outset by fear of a Communist takeover. The official explanation at the time was that the intervention was undertaken solely to save American lives endangered by the fighting. To a very limited degree this factor might have played some role in the decision, for it was certainly true that the *potential* for serious danger to American and other foreign citizens was considerable. It was also true that Bennett had reported (inaccurately, as it later developed) several attacks on Americans. But the evidence is overwhelming that fear of communism was uppermost in the minds of both the embassy personnel and administration officials in Washington. In any case, of course, U.S. troops were in fact deployed in a manner designed to prevent a constitutionalist victory, and then remained in the Dominican Republic for nearly seventeen months thereafter.

On the other hand, it is not accurate (as Theodore Draper and others have argued) that the United States intervened to prevent a Boschist victory per se. It was certainly true that most U.S. officials had only contempt for Bosch and would not have been happy to see him back in office, but that was not the reason for the intervention. On the contrary, the United States made no move even to interrupt Bosch's communications with PRD leaders from his home in San Juan nor did they attempt to prevent him from returning to take command of the constitutionalist forces. Bosch's decision to remain in San Juan was his own, and he was later severely criticized for it in the Dominican Republic. Washington was concerned about the Communists or Castroites in the revolutionary movement, not the Boschists. The State Department felt that even if Bosch were restored to the presidency, his alleged weakness and incompetence would ensure that the Communists would quickly outmaneuver him and take over the government.

On the evening of April 28, American troops began landing in the Dominican Republic, the first direct military intervention by the United States in a Latin American country in nearly fifty years. The military moves had four immediate objectives: to shore up the remnants of the regular Dominican armed forces and prevent their complete disintegration; to prevent any further military advances by the constitutionalists, especially a projected drive toward San Isidro; to contain the revolution itself in Santo Domingo and prevent it from spreading to the countryside;

and to set the stage for either a direct military attack on the constitution-alists or for an imposed military stalemate before a negotiated political settlement.

For several weeks after the initial troop landings, the U.S. government remained undecided, because of both internal disagreements in Washing-ton and changing circumstances inside and outside the Dominican Repub-lic, as to whether it should crush the constitutionalists militarily—either by the direct use of U.S. troops or by indirect support of the reconstituted and rearmed Dominican military forces—or settle for some kind of po-litical compromise. There was no doubt that in the early days after the intervention the government leaned toward a military solution. On the morning of April 29 Ambassador Bennett was told by the State Depart-ment that the President had not yet authorized the use of U.S. troops in offensive actions against the constitutionalists, but that U.S. officers should be used "to help San Isidro develop operational plans to take the rebel stronghold downtown."[34] While this cable was going out, however, the OAS Council was meeting in emergency session to discuss the crisis. On the afternoon of April 29 it unanimously voted to seek a cease-fire in the Dominican Republic. The United States supported the call for a cease-fire, probably in part because of the political costs of opposing it, but also because the regular Dominican military was in much greater need of a re-spite than the constitutionalists.

As a result of the cease-fire, Bennett received new instructions from the State Department on April 30: discussions with San Isidro about immediate military action against the constitutionalists were to be shelved, and the Dominican military leaders were to be informed that the conflict was now entering a political phase. Despite this initial U.S. support for the cease-fire, there were numerous indications that military action later was far from ruled out. For example, at the same San Isidro meeting at which Bennett informed the Dominican commanders that they had to ac-cept a cease-fire because U.S. troops would not be used in offensive action against the constitutionalists, the generals were also told that the cease-fire would give them a chance to regroup and prepare themselves for possible action later against the constitutionalists; in the meantime U.S. military officers would continue working with the generals to help them plan tactics for an attack. The cease-fire, in short, was apparently viewed at first as a holding action, pending further developments in the Domini-

34. Martin, *Overtaken by Events,* p. 658.

can Republic and a buildup of U.S. forces and the Dominican military. Although the truce was precariously maintained in the next few days, pressures continued to build for a frontal attack on the constitutionalists by U.S. forces. The U.S. military, under the command of General Bruce Palmer, wanted nothing more than to be allowed to "clean up" the constitutionalist zone. General Palmer, like most of the other U.S. military men involved in the intervention, initially took a very hard line on the use of force, chafing at the constraints the Johnson administration placed on him and pressing for a "military solution." Later, however, especially under the guidance of Ellsworth Bunker, his views moderated considerably.

Whatever the personal views of the American military men, they remained under strict political control throughout the intervention and subsequent occupation. At the same time Ambassador Bennett, who had earlier indicated his misgivings about the cease-fire and the prospect of negotiations, repeatedly complained to Washington that the cease-fire was protecting the constitutionalists from the rejuvenated military and was giving them an unwarranted political advantage, allowing them to consolidate their strength and improve their bargaining position. There are indications that Thomas Mann shared these views and urged President Johnson to authorize direct military action. On the morning of April 30, former Ambassador John Bartlow Martin was asked by Johnson to go to Santo Domingo to open a channel of communications with the constitutionalists; at the same time, he received the impression that he had possibly no more than a day or two to prevent "another Hungary," a U.S. slaughter of the constitutionalists.[35]

Gradually, though, the possibility of military action faded into the background. By the end of May a definite decision had been reached to seek a negotiated political settlement and to avoid not only direct military action against the main body of the constitutionalists (in mid-May, the United States had allowed Dominican troops to attack a constitutionalist sector of Santo Domingo), but less oppressive measures as well, including a blockade of food and water or the termination of electrical power to sectors controlled by the constitutionalists. (The decision to seek a negotiated settlement did not preclude the use of force for self-defense, which on occasion may have been rather broadly defined.) A number of factors

35. Ibid., pp. 661–62, 672.

seem to have been involved in this decision. It was clear that Johnson was reluctant to authorize the direct use of U.S. troops unless it was absolutely "necessary,"[36] and there is some evidence that McGeorge Bundy, and later Ellsworth Bunker, steadfastly opposed the use of U.S. troops. There is no doubt that the OAS involvement in the situation was also an important restraining factor.

Whatever the initial reasons for U.S. support for a cease-fire negotiated by the OAS, once in effect it took on a life of its own. Even when it later became clear that the constitutionalists were the primary beneficiaries of the cease-fire, the United States could not blatantly violate it without enormous political costs, particularly in light of the frequent public warnings from the OAS Council (meeting in nearly continuous session in the first weeks of the crisis) and from Latin American political leaders against U.S. support for, or acquiescence in, military action. Moreover, within a few days the United Nations had also become involved, and the presence in the Dominican Republic of a UN mission that was clearly sympathetic to the constitutionalists was an additional constraint. Still another factor was the military estimate that a direct attack on the densely populated, well-defended constitutionalist stronghold would result in extremely extensive damage and in high casualties among noninvolved residents as well as among the U.S. and constitutionalist forces. The consequence of that would inevitably be domestic and international revulsion at what would surely have been widely seen, as Martin predicted, as a Hungarian-type action. Finally, and perhaps most important of all, the successful deployment of U.S. troops across the middle of Santo Domingo had bottled up the rebels in a small part of Santo Domingo and sealed them off from the rest of the country, thus easing U.S. fears that a failure to take harsh action might lead to a new Vietnam. With a Communist takeover now impossible, the United States could afford to seek a political solution, especially since it would obviously have considerable control over the kind of solution that eventually emerged.

The Military Deployment

The first American troops to land on Dominican soil were 500 Marines brought in by helicopter on April 28. They came from U.S. Naval Task

36. Lowenthal, *Dominican Intervention,* pp. 115–20.

Group 44, stationed a few miles off the coast of Santo Domingo. The force included the helicopter carrier *Boxer* and the following other amphibious assault and support ships: *Rankin, Raleigh, Ft. Snelling, Wood County,* and *Ruckankin.*[37] The Marines landed on the grounds of the Hotel Embajador, the major Dominican hotel, which had been designated as the departure point for Americans and other foreigners wishing to be taken out of the country. Soon after this, military transport planes began an around-the-clock airlift, ferrying in two battalions (6,500 men) of the 82nd Airborne Division from Fort Bragg, North Carolina, to the San Isidro Air Base, still controlled by Wessin's troops. In the next forty-eight hours the paratroopers moved out from San Isidro and advanced along the road to Santo Domingo, eleven miles away. They met no resistance and took up positions at the Duarte Bridge, which spans the Ozama River and is the principal route from Santo Domingo to the east. They also took up positions all along the eastern bank of the Ozama River, directly across from the main constitutionalist sector of Santo Domingo. By April 30, 1,700 Marines and 2,500 soldiers were in the Dominican Republic.

Meanwhile the U.S. military buildup in and around the Dominican Republic continued. On May 1 the 4th Marine Expeditionary Brigade (5,500 men) was deployed into San Isidro from Camp Lejeune. By May 2 the offshore naval force had been reinforced by a second helicopter carrier (the USS *Okinawa*) and the cruiser *Newport News,* including additional elements of the 2nd Marine Division. On May 3 a Marine detachment from the *Newport News* landed in Santo Domingo.[38]

By May 2 the initial purposes of the intervention had been accomplished: the collapsing Dominican armed forces had been shored up, a constitutionalist offensive against San Isidro had been prevented, and foreign nationals had been evacuated from the country. Troops and heavy armor continued to pour into San Isidro, their purpose now to prevent the spread of the revolution to the countryside and to surround the constitutionalist forces with vastly superior armed might. On May 3 the paratroopers moved across the Duarte Bridge into Santo Domingo, establishing an armed corridor through the middle of the city and linking up

37. Kenneth O. Gilmore, "The Truth about Santo Domingo," *Reader's Digest* (May 1966).
38. The data on the U.S. military buildup are drawn from the following sources: *U.S. Atlantic Fleet, Second Fleet Historical Report, 1966; U.S. Department of the Navy, Marine Corps Headquarters, Historical Division, A Chronology of the United States Marine Corps,* vol. 4, pp. 2–3; Gilmore, "The Truth about Santo Domingo."

with the Marines at the Embajador, on the western edge of the city. This maneuver was ostensibly a response to an OAS request that a neutral "international security zone" be established in the city to enforce the cease-fire and protect remaining foreigners, but its more important purposes were to divide the constitutionalist zone and to cut off the main body of the rebel fighters from their access to the countryside, bottling them up in a small downtown area with their backs to the sea. The overwhelming power of the U.S. forces ensured that there was little resistance from the constitutionalists. By the time the U.S. buildup was completed on May 9, there were 23,000 U.S. troops in the country (the remaining seven battalions of the 82nd Airborne Division arrived on May 8), with massive amounts of heavy armor. An additional 3,300 Marines and a 35-ship task force were stationed offshore. The task force included two aircraft carriers and numerous surface combatants—a force almost half as large as the one then engaged in a full-scale war in Vietnam.[39] With the Vietnam situation very much in mind, the Johnson administration was taking no chances: the massive show of force was designed to avert new trouble through an awesome demonstration of power or, at worst, to prepare for a nationwide occupation.

While the constitutionalists were being surrounded in Santo Domingo American forces moved into the countryside, though much less ostentatiously. A number of small U.S. teams, in particular Special Forces units in civilian clothes, were stationed throughout the countryside to establish a U.S. presence, survey economic needs, report on local political conditions, and, most important, establish liaison with local police and military units.

With the situation so well in hand, the United States began to reduce its forces in the Dominican Republic by the end of May. By mid-June all of the Marines had been withdrawn, and by mid-November the principal U.S. military unit remaining in the country was a brigade of the 82nd Airborne. The U.S. military presence remained dominant, however, throughout the negotiating period that followed the major fighting and intervention, and during the tenure of the provisional government that was established thereafter.

39. Lowenthal, *Dominican Intervention,* p. 112; U.S. Department of the Army, "Memorandum on Army Contingency Operations" (May 21, 1974; processed) (includes data on 82nd Airborne Division actions in the Dominican Republic in 1965); Gilmore, "The Truth about Santo Domingo."

The Negotiating Phase

With the Dominican military saved, the constitutionalists surrounded, and the rest of the country quiet, the United States shifted its attention to efforts to gain a political solution, though both threats and the actual use of military force were still to play a significant role in support of the Johnson administration's political objectives.

The immediate U.S. objective in the ensuing negotiations was to establish a temporary Dominican government, either a coalition made up of moderate, non-Communist constitutionalists and representatives of more conservative groups supporting the military, or a "Third Force," excluding all participants on either side of the recent fighting. After this projected government was formed and had established its authority throughout the country, new elections for a permanent government would be held. The Johnson administration seemed genuinely committed to free elections, though with some qualifications. First, it was doubtful that the United States would have supported new elections if the government thought there was any chance that the Communists might win; in fact, however, there was no such chance. Second, and *perhaps* more significant, several high-level officials have privately conceded that the U.S. decision to press for genuinely free elections was at least in part influenced by secret CIA-sponsored polls taken shortly before the revolution, which showed that Balaguer, rather than Bosch or an even more radical Dominican political figure, would be likely to win. On the other hand, other U.S. government officials minimize the importance of this consideration, noting that the polls were not considered decisive, that the revolution and the U.S. intervention might well have changed the political context, that it was not certain that Balaguer would actually be willing to run, and that in any case the United States remained firmly committed to free elections even when it appeared that Bosch was more likely to win them. In the longer run, the Johnson administration sought the establishment of a stable democratic political system in the Dominican Republic, progressive but firmly anti-Communist, backed by strong but reformed, professionalized armed forces under firm civilian control.

The Dominican Targets of U.S. Behavior

Before describing the major Dominican actors and their political stakes in the crisis, we should take note of the overall character of Dominican politics. According to all specialists on Dominican politics (especially Howard Wiarda and Abraham Lowenthal), political behavior in the Dominican Republic tends to be non-ideological, non-programmatic, unstructured, and uninstitutionalized, with individuals rather than "parties" dominating, and motivation best understood in terms of individual opportunism and personal ambition rather than genuine differences over public policy. Thus, according to Lowenthal, Dominican politics are marked by a constantly shifting pattern of alliances and cliques, a battle of the "outs versus the ins," disguised, to be sure, as party or ideological conflict but bearing little genuine resemblance to the superficially similar political structures of more politically developed societies.[40] This view tends to exaggerate the purely opportunistic character of Dominican politics and, by implication, also exaggerates the ideological or programmatic character of the politics of the industrialized societies, but there is clearly something to it and the reader should bear it in mind in the ensuing pages.

There were five major actors, or groups of actors, in the 1965 crisis.

1. The regular Dominican armed forces. As noted earlier, for nearly the entire history of the republic the military have been the main source of political power, especially when they were united or, as in the Trujillo era, dominated by a single *caudillo* (leader). After Trujillo's assassination they divided into a number of factions under the almost feudalistic control of individual generals. The main concern of most of the Dominican generals was to maintain their privileged position in Dominican society so they could continue to enjoy the power and plunder that went along with it. A few, to be sure, seemed to stand for something—for example, some of the younger officers who defected to the constitutionalists because of genuine democratic ideals and a desire to cleanse their own profession of its brutality and corruption, and, on the other hand, a few genuinely fanatic anti-Communists, particularly Wessin y Wessin. Most of the others, however, were cautious opportunists whose behavior was a function of their latest estimate of the prevailing political winds.

2. Of this group one of the most unprincipled was Antonio Imbert.

---

40. In Lowenthal's words, "the continuing kaleidoscope of Dominican politics... [is] virtually unchecked by program commitments or mediating institutions." *Dominican Intervention*, p. 38. Moreno, *Barrios in Arms*, also tends to minimize the significance of true ideological conflict in the Dominican Republic, and, Martin, *Overtaken by Events*, refers to the "swirling dance of Dominican politics." The major works embodying this point of view are Lowenthal, "The Dominican Republic: The Politics of Chaos," and Howard Wiarda, *The Dominican Republic: Nation in Transition* (Praeger, 1969).

Imbert had been an important figure in Dominican politics since 1961 for three major reasons: (a) he was one of the two survivors of the original group of sixteen or so who planned the successful assassination of Trujillo (in fact, it was said, Imbert was the man who had actually fired the mortal shots); (b) he had a fairly substantial private army to support him; and (c) far from least, John Bartlow Martin had always been fascinated by him and frequently acted to maximize Imbert's political power. Imbert was a power-seeker pure and simple. He was part of Trujillo's retinue for years, rising to become governor of Puerto Plata in 1948; later, however, there was a family feud with Trujillo, and Imbert's brother died in one of Trujillo's prisons. It was generally agreed that personal revenge rather than principle accounted for Imbert's role in the assassination, and Imbert maneuvered for political power afterward. He was not a career military man but had been appointed a general in the army after the assassination and been assigned troops to protect him against the revenge of the Trujillists. He later became chief of police under the Reid government and augmented his private army to a force of some 2,000 men.

3. Juan Bosch, the symbolic leader of the revolution. Because Bosch remained in San Juan until six months after the crisis, however, it is unclear how much direct influence he actually exercised.

4. The constitutionalists, comprising three different groups: (a) A group of civilian PRD supporters of Bosch, headed by Antonio Guzmán, a wealthy but liberal landowner who was minister of agriculture in Bosch's short-lived government. Guzmán and other PRD leaders were the most politically sophisticated of the constitutionalists and did most of the negotiating with U.S. representatives. (b) The constitutionalist military leaders, headed by Caamaño. They willingly deferred to the PRD leaders once the actual negotiating had begun, and on several occasions emphasized that they would abide by any solution reached between the United States and the PRD. (c) The radical political leaders of the Castroite 14th of June movement and two small Communist parties. Their power rested primarily on their (perhaps shaky) control of many of the tougher street fighters or commandos; but whatever their initial power, it faded in the face of the overwhelming U.S. military superiority and the more moderate positions of the PRD and regular constitutionalist military leaders.

5. A shifting group of "Third Force" Dominican business and political

leaders, to whom the United States turned when negotiations for a provisional government between the rightists and the constitutionalists broke down. The leading figure in this group came to be Héctor García-Godoy, also a wealthy landowner but one who had ties to both Bosch and Balaguer, as foreign minister under the Bosch government and later as a vice-president of Balaguer's Partido Reformista. Basically a moderate progressive, whose political and social philosophy was not very different from that of the general democratic left of Latin America (from which Bosch himself had originally derived his inspiration), he initially had broad support from the Balagueristas, the moderate sectors of the PRD, and the independents.

Somehow a political solution had to be negotiated that would at least be acceptable to the Johnson administration, the Latin American members of the OAS Ad Hoc Committee, the constitutionalists, the Dominican military, and key elites in Dominican society. At a slightly further remove, but still exerting a general influence and setting the outermost boundaries of the ultimate solution, were U.S. domestic opinion, the OAS as a whole, Latin American opinion, and world opinion as expressed through the United Nations.

The ensuing negotiations represent a classic case of what Alexander George and his associates have called "coercive diplomacy," understood to mean the use of both rewards and sanctions to achieve limited political objectives.[41] Coercive diplomacy is distinguished from pure diplomacy in that the use of force may be explicitly threatened if negotiations should break down, or they may be implicit from the structure of the situation; it is distinguished from pure coercion by its use of bargaining, compromise, and rewards. The carrot and stick are employed alternatively and selectively to affect the target's resolve; however, the target's own interests (as Thomas Schelling has pointed out)[42] must be sufficiently accommodated to avoid resolute resistance. All of these elements were clearly present in the Dominican situation.

There is no doubt that the use of coercive diplomacy was a conscious strategy of the U.S. government, employed on behalf of specific objectives. There was also, however, considerable vacillation and internal

41. Alexander L. George, David K. Hall, and William E. Simons, *The Limits of Coercive Diplomacy: Laos, Cuba, Vietnam* (Little, Brown, 1971).
42. Thomas C. Schelling, *Strategy of Conflict* (Oxford University Press, 1960), chap. 7.

division within the government over both the objectives and the degree of force that should be employed on their behalf. The most systematic research on the policymaking process within the U.S. government during the Dominican crisis has been done by Abraham Lowenthal, who concludes that "the evidence now available does not permit confident statements about the perceptions and perspectives of many of the relevant actors; differences among presidential advisers in Washington are particularly hard to define, for instance, and evidence about the president's own views and actions is still fragmentary and uncertain."[43] It is reasonably clear, however, that there were substantial internal differences about the degree to which the United States should employ force simply to impose its will on recalcitrant Dominicans during at least three phases of the crisis: (1) in the first week or so after the landing of U.S. forces, when the U.S. military commander in the Dominican Republic, Ambassador Bennett, and probably Thomas Mann in Washington were urging the destruction of the constitutionalists; (2) during the May–June negotiations over the formation of a government to be headed by Antonio Guzmán, in which the leading American negotiator, McGeorge Bundy, apparently tried but failed to stop U.S. support for a military offensive by Imbert's forces against part of the constitutionalist forces; (3) and during the summer negotiations that finally eventuated in the formation of the García-Godoy provisional government, in which Ellsworth Bunker successfully resisted State Department suggestion for further military pressures on the constitutionalists.

Allowing for these internal differences and/or vacillations, however, within several weeks after the military intervention, an overall U.S. strategy did emerge: to impose a firm military stalemate, to demonstrate to extremists on both sides in the Dominican crisis that they could not achieve their maximum objectives—the destruction of their opponents—and, after the logic of the situation had fully registered, to negotiate a compromise political settlement but one that fully satisfied the primary U.S. objective, the avoidance of a Communist or radical Dominican government. These objectives were communicated quite specifically and explicitly to all the major Dominican actors, and U.S. words were frequently backed by a variety of actions that made the messages both unmistakable and irresistible. During the course of the negotiations the United States did not hesitate to remind the Dominicans, through words

43. Lowenthal, *Dominican Intervention,* p. 150.

and actions, of its ability to impose a military solution if either side became too recalcitrant. Beyond its overwhelming military power the United States had other important sources of leverage.

1. Washington sent a succession of high-level diplomats to the Dominican Republic. Within a few days after the troops had landed Ambassador Bennett and the U.S. embassy were effectively replaced by prestigious and powerful presidential emissaries: first John Bartlow Martin, then McGeorge Bundy (accompanied by Thomas Mann and Cyrus Vance, deputy secretary of defense), and finally Ellsworth Bunker. The Dominicans were well aware that the U.S. negotiators had direct access to President Johnson, and this lent additional weight to their diplomatic efforts.

2. The United States carried out a massive propaganda campaign in the Dominican Republic on behalf of its objectives. The country was flooded with experts on "psychological warfare" from the CIA and Defense Intelligence Agency, the U.S. Information Agency covertly set up and controlled radio stations and newspapers behind an "OAS" or apparently independent "Dominican" facade, U.S. Army communications units jammed constitutionalist radio stations, and leaflets were airdropped throughout the countryside. In sum, a wide variety of both open and covert propaganda efforts were employed to back the U.S. position and to discredit Dominican groups opposed to it.[44]

3. Finally, the U.S. government had considerable economic leverage, particularly over the "loyalist" forces led by Imbert: For several months during the summer of 1965 the salaries of the entire Dominican public sector, including those of the police and armed forces, came either directly from the U.S. government or from the Dominican Central Bank, which was physically under the military control of the United States.

The first step in the U.S. negotiating strategy was to set up a Dominican government that could serve as a provisional source of some Dominican authority pending new elections and could act as a counterbalance—however artificial—to the constitutionalists, enabling the United States to press for a "middle solution." The task of setting up this stopgap government was assigned to John Bartlow Martin, who, to the surprise and dismay of a good many Dominican specialists in the State Department and at the embassy, turned to Antonio Imbert, whose known opportunism,

---

44. For details, see Slater, *Intervention and Negotiation,* especially pp. 113–14, and Lowenthal, *Dominican Intervention,* especially pp. 4, 205–06.

predilection for power, and widespread unpopularity in the Dominican Republic made him a most peculiar choice. Moreover, Martin ignored his instructions to make it clear that the new government would be only provisional and would not receive diplomatic recognition from the United States. Instead, Martin promised Imbert a blank check and recognition within twenty-four hours. Predictably enough, Imbert immediately set out to form a military dictatorship and to destroy the constitutionalists and any other opposition, imprisoning, torturing, and even murdering hundreds of Dominicans. Lyndon Johnson was furious—"I'm not going down in history as the man responsible for putting another Trujillo in power"—and within a few weeks McGeorge Bundy was sent to Santo Domingo to try to undo the damage and restore the situation to one from which a genuine compromise could be reached.[45]

Bundy's negotiating strategy was to attempt to separate the moderate constitutionalists from the more radical groups, and the bulk of the Dominican military from the Trujillists, extreme rightists, and followers of Imbert. The Imbert regime in and of itself was not considered a serious problem, for it had little popular support in the Dominican Republic, only the unenthusiastic support of most of the military leaders; it had a bad press around the world; and it was heavily dependent on U.S. political and economic support. To the constitutionalists Bundy offered the removal of the Imbert regime in favor of a provisional government, headed by PRD leader Antonio Guzmán, that would oust Wessin and other Trujillist military holdovers, end terrorism, and rule by genuinely democratic methods until free elections could be held. To the Dominican military Bundy offered firm U.S. assurances that they would not be destroyed by a Bosch or Boschist government, and that all Communists or Castroites would be exiled or interned in concentration camps. When negotiations bogged down, largely because of Guzmán's principled refusal to exile constitutionalist and Castroite leaders, the United States used more forceful persuasion: U.S. troops allowed Imbert's forces to cross their lines and brutally attack the northern sector of the constitutionalist zone, which had been separated from the main body of the constitutionalists when the United States established its armed corridor through the center of the city. The evidence is mixed on whether the United States participated in

45. The Johnson quotation is from Evans and Novak, *Lyndon B. Johnson*, p. 525. For details on the establishment of the Imbert regime, see Slater, *Intervention and Negotiation*, pp. 57–65.

or provided direct support to the attack. At the time a number of newspaper and television men reported that U.S. troops did join in the fighting.[46] This, however, was angrily denied by U.S. officials, even in unofficial
statements long after the affair. Moreover, at the height of the fighting, the
embassy reassured Washington, in response to an urgent State Department request for a report on the matter, that the newspaper stories were
manifestly false. There were several lower level unauthorized actions and
mistakes, the embassy admitted, but it reiterated that U.S. forces were
still under strict orders not to allow the movement of any armed groups
through their lines. On the other hand, it is also true that earlier in May
U.S. generals were instructed to explain to Dominican military commanders that the projected corridor through the city would help free
loyalist forces to take the offensive; they were further ordered to help their
Dominican counterparts to draw up plans for attacking the constitutionalists, with the rebel forces north of the corridor specifically suggested as
the first target. Thus, whatever the exact degree of U.S. involvement, the
record leaves little doubt that Washington at a minimum acquiesced in the
Imbert attack, in the hope of eliminating the constitutionalist channel to
the countryside, increasing the pressures on the constitutionalists in the
negotiating process, and reopening the important industrial area in the
northern sector of the city. There is evidence that Bundy himself opposed
the attack, or at least the obvious U.S. acquiescence in it, and sought to
have it stopped, but Mann and other hard-liners were apparently more
persuasive to Johnson.

After several days of massive destruction the northern sector was completely under the control of the military. The tactic proved only partially
successful. While it did contribute to softening the resistance of many of
the constitutionalists to any compromise settlement, and demonstrated to
them that their very existence depended on U.S. policy, it did not change
Guzmán's mind about deportation. Even more important, it only stiffened
the resistance of the armed forces to the establishment of a government
they felt would be dominated by Juan Bosch. In fact, with U.S. and other
foreign newspapers angrily attacking the Johnson administration's cold-
blooded support of Imbert's brutality, and with the regular military now
backing Imbert's insistence on a complete "clean-up" of the remaining

46. See especially *New York Times,* May 20 and 21, 1965; Tad Szulc, *Dominican Diary* (Delacorte, 1965); Selden Rodman, "A Close View of Santo Domingo,"
The Reporter (July 15, 1965).

constitutionalist zone, the United States was forced to turn the stick in the other direction. Washington firmly informed Imbert and the military that the United States would allow no further military actions against the constitutionalists; just to make sure, U.S. tanks were placed across the runways at San Isidro, and half the U.S. artillery emplacements surrounding the constitutionalist zone were turned around to face the regular military.[47] As Imbert realized that his own hopes to retain power depended on firm U.S. support, he was forced to give up plans for further military action. Still the negotiations broke down, for reasons that are not entirely clear but apparently centered on growing doubts within the U.S. government that a Guzmán regime—particularly one that adamantly refused to undertake the draconian control of radicals that Washington considered essential—would be sufficiently "reliable." Bundy was replaced by Ellsworth Bunker, under very general instructions to seek a middle-of-the-road provisional government, one not associated with the constitutionalists, the rightists, or the existing Imbert regime.

Though there continued to be internal differences within the U.S. government, especially over matters of tactics in the continuing negotiating deadlock, Bunker quickly established himself as the dominant U.S. figure on the Dominican question. On a number of occasions, differences between Bunker and the U.S. embassy, the State Department, or the U.S. military command in the Dominican Republic had to be taken to the White House, and Bunker's position invariably prevailed. When it became clear to other U.S. officials that Bunker had the personal confidence of and direct access to Johnson, and did not hesitate to make use of it, his predominance was accepted as a fact of life and the internal conflicts diminished.

The two major initial conflicts, primarily between Bunker and the U.S. military, but also to a degree between Bunker and the State Department, were (1) whether the constitutionalists were to be accepted on at least an equal plane with the Dominican military and the Imbert junta, as a contending party whose demands had to be genuinely accommodated in any effective settlement, and (2) the degree to which the threat of force against the constitutionalists was to be kept alive as a means of negotiating leverage against them. On both issues, Bunker took the more liberal posture, and his views prevailed. If anything, the views of the moderate con-

47. Dan Kurzman, *Santo Domingo: Revolt of the Damned* (Putnam, 1965), pp. 264–72.

stitutionalists were taken more seriously than those of the Dominican military and certainly those of the Imbert regime, and Bunker firmly refused to allow any further military displays against the constitutionalists. There was one possible exception to this policy, though it is quite ambiguous. In mid-June, after persistent sniper fire against their lines, U.S. troops advanced into the constitutionalist zone, occupying about another fifty square blocks and killing sixty-seven constitutionalists or bystanders. The evidence generally suggests that this was not a deliberate political tactic, but simply a massive military overreaction by local U.S. commanders to minor constitutionalist provocations. It was not unnoticed in Washington, however, that the constitutionalist negotiating posture softened somewhat after the attack.

The negotiations continued stalemated for some months, with no further U.S. military actions or threats. From time to time the State Department would almost wistfully inquire of Bunker if there was "a possibility of a constitutionalist ceasefire violation to which the U.S. dominated IAPF [Inter-American Peace Force] could react and take additional blocks in the rebel area,"[48] but Bunker stood firm. As a matter of fact, initially Bunker's major effort was simply to convince Imbert and the military that the United States was firmly committed to a negotiated settlement and that it would allow no further military actions against the constitutionalists. This message was communicated repeatedly to the Dominican military, both verbally, through the public statements of U.S. officials and private warnings, and by U.S. actions—the blocking of Dominican airfields and the symbolic reversing of U.S. artillery positions, as well as the seizure of all major oil depots by U.S. forces to deny fuel to Dominican military aircraft and tanks.

By the end of the summer of 1965 Bunker's tactics, described by himself as "patience with persuasion and pressure," had paid off: extremists on both sides had been isolated, the U.S.-created fait accompli was acknowledged, and Héctor García-Godoy—who was acceptable to Bunker, the moderate constitutionalists, and, more reluctantly, the bulk of the military—had emerged as the most likely head of the provisional government. Imbert remained adamant but he was no problem; when all the pieces of the overall settlement had fallen into place, the United States simply announced that there would be no further "OAS" assistance to the Dominican Republic until the García-Godoy government took office.

48. See note 29, above.

This aid paid for nearly the entire budget of the Imbert regime, including the salaries of the police and the military, and other sources of potential revenue, particularly the Dominican Central Bank, had been taken over by IAPF units. Imbert was left with no choice but to resign.

The García-Godoy Government

García-Godoy took office on September 3, 1965, committed to hold genuinely free elections within nine months and to rule by democratic methods until then. The U.S. government fully supported these objectives, and had even modified its initial insistence on harsh measures against the constitutionalists when García-Godoy proved no less adamant than Guzmán had been: not only would there be no deportation or internment of radical groups, but the 14th of June movement would even be allowed to participate in the electoral process. The shift in the U.S. position was a result not only of García-Godoy's insistence on the issue, but also of Washington's confidence that García-Godoy (unlike Guzmán) had both the will and the leadership ability to prevent any outright Communist grab for power. Even more fundamental, by the end of the summer it was clear that the combination of U.S. military power and the relative lack of Dominican popular support of radicalism of any kind made the specter of a "Communist takeover" wholly unrealistic, even to the most conservative of U.S. policymakers.

The real problem for the García-Godoy government during the ensuing months—particularly when it became clear that both he and Bunker were genuinely committed to free elections, which Juan Bosch might win —was not the left but the right. From the inception of the García-Godoy government Bunker very clearly and explicitly committed the United States to its full support, including the use of the IAPF to prevent a coup. But public statements of U.S. intentions and even stronger private warnings to the Dominican military were not sufficient, for, on a number of occasions in the next six months, listed below, force had to be threatened or actually deployed to prevent both rightist coups and threatened massacres of the constitutionalists.

1. One of García-Godoy's first major actions was to fire Wessin and break up his private tank force at the San Isidro Air base. Both García-Godoy and Bunker agreed that Wessin would have to go because of his known proclivities for military coups and the widespread hatred of him

among Dominicans since he had ordered the bombardment and strafing of Santo Domingo during the revolution. In response to García-Godoy's order on September 5 removing him from the head of the San Isidro unit, Wessin mobilized his tanks and began moving toward Santo Domingo. But Bunker ordered the IAPF to block Wessin's advance, and Wessin was then personally escorted to a U.S. military plane by high-ranking U.S. Army officers and flown to Miami to occupy a newly created Dominican "consulate" there.

2. In mid-October García-Godoy learned of a pending plan by the military to send forces into the constitutionalist zone, ostensibly to search for weapons. When the military refused to obey his order to desist, García-Godoy (with Caamaño's private acquiescence) asked Bunker to send IAPF forces into the zone for general peacekeeping purposes. Bunker complied, and at the same time the United States ostentatiously landed sixteen new tanks near Santo Domingo.

3. In mid-November García-Godoy and the U.S. embassy learned of a rightist plot (apparently involving Antonio Imbert) to seize the city of Santiago, proclaim a new government, and attempt to rally Dominican military support behind it. At García-Godoy's request an IAPF unit flew to Santiago to occupy the airport and other key points. At the same time Bunker issued a warning that any attempt to overthrow the government would be in clear defiance of OAS efforts to restore democracy in the Dominican Republic. In the face of this show of force the Santiago police and military units refused to cooperate with the conspirators, and the plot collapsed.

4. In mid-December an IAPF unit was flown into Santiago to rescue Caamaño and about 100 other constitutionalists, who were besieged in a hotel by local police and military units. The IAPF group interposed itself between the two forces, obtained a cease-fire, and transported the constitutionalists back to their base outside Santo Domingo, itself under heavy guard by the IAPF.

5. The most serious challenge to the García-Godoy government came in early January 1966, when García-Godoy announced on nationwide radio that he was sending both Caamaño (and other major constitutionalist leaders) and the three leading regular military commanders out of the country, in the interests of order and reconciliation. The announcement triggered an open rebellion of the military. On January 6 army units seized the government radio and television stations and began a roundup

of "Communists" in all parts of the country. With the García-Godoy government in imminent danger of being overthrown, Bunker ordered the IAPF to protect the National Palace and to force the army units out of the radio and television stations. To avoid an open clash with the IAPF —actually U.S. troops known to be under the direct political control of Bunker—the armed forces backed down. The military chiefs, however, still refused adamantly to give up their offices. In the ensuing weeks a general strike protesting military defiance paralyzed Santo Domingo, and García-Godoy spoke of resigning if he could not bring the military under control. In response, Bunker had the Navy move the Caribbean Ready Squadron (the naval presence had earlier been reduced to this regular area force) closer to shore, and promised García-Godoy that the IAPF would comply with a request to remove the military chiefs from the scene, as Wessin had been removed several months earlier. Faced with Bunker's firmness and visible U.S. military deployments, the Dominican military chiefs ended their defiance and left the country, replaced by men García-Godoy considered amenable to democratic civilian control.

In a more fundamental sense, however, the basic reform of the Dominican military that had been an initial U.S. objective after the intervention was never undertaken. Although there was no doubt that the United States was genuinely interested in helping create an apolitical, professionalized armed force, it gave higher priority to preserving the military as a bastion of anticommunism. To push hard on reform in the aftermath of the revolution, U.S. officials feared, might so disrupt and demoralize the military that they would lose their remaining effectiveness and leave the door open to radicalism. In principle there was no essential inconsistency between fundamental reform and basic preservation, but in practice there was, as the presumed exigencies of one crisis after another led cautious U.S. officials to postpone serious efforts to restructure the armed forces until some future time when the situation would be more propitious. During the summer of 1965 priority had been given to winning military assent for a political settlement, so Bunker was unwilling to take any actions that might antagonize the armed forces. During the García-Godoy government, though the worst of the remaining Trujillist military were weeded out, the continuing civilian-military crisis seemed to preclude more far-reaching measures, so the reforms would have to wait until after the elections. Once Balaguer was in office and U.S. troops were withdrawn, however, the United States lost most of its leverage (and, probably, much of its interest) in the matter. Many of the Trujillist military men were actually brought back into active service by Balaguer. Although there has been little published about the Balaguer government, it seems apparent that there have been few fundamental changes in any aspect of Dominican society, least of all in the armed forces.

The Elections and the U.S. Withdrawal

In June 1966 Joaquin Balaguer defeated Juan Bosch by a surprisingly large margin in what most observers, even many who were initially skeptical, consider to have been genuinely free elections. While there is no doubt that the Johnson administration was very happy with the outcome, there has been no evidence that it covertly interfered in the electoral process. Indeed, only persistent and sustained U.S. pressures, including the threat of military force, ensured that the elections were held at all. Of course it cannot be gainsaid that the Dominican vote for Balaguer might have been substantially influenced by the very fact of the U.S. intervention and the known U.S. distaste for Bosch. A vote for Balaguer under these circumstances might have been seen as a vote for stability, the easing of domestic conflict, and the end of foreign military intervention.

The electoral campaign began in effect when Juan Bosch returned to the country at the end of September 1965. His return was bitterly opposed by the military, but they were overruled by García-Godoy and Bunker. On September 25 Bosch made a triumphal entry into Santo Domingo, his route from the airport heavily guarded by the same U.S. military units (now down to two brigades of the 82nd Airborne Division) that five months earlier had been landed to block an uprising intended to return him to office.

During the ensuing months Bunker and the new U.S. ambassador, John C. Crimmins, a liberal career foreign service officer, went to considerable lengths to convince Bosch, the Dominican military, and even the U.S. civilian and military officers in the country that the Johnson administration was *really* committed to free elections. By April 1966 many of the key conservative State Department and embassy officials who had favored the initial intervention had been replaced by liberals: Crimmins had replaced Bennett, Mann resigned soon after it became clear that he was regularly losing out in policy conflict with Bunker, and Crockett was replaced by C. Allen Stewart, a former ambassador to Venezuela during the Betancourt regime and a strong supporter of the democratic left in Latin America. In early March 1966 very explicit written directions were given to the IAPF and all U.S. embassy, AID, and CIA personnel, reiterating that the United States was neutral, and directing all concerned to avoid any actions or statements contrary to that policy or that might be interpreted as expressing even an unofficial U.S. preference for a Balaguer victory. At the same time, Crimmins and Bunker met repeatedly with Dominican political figures, in particular with Bosch and, on the other side, the military and other Dominican rightists, in an effort to make it "crystal clear" (as a State Department cable to the embassy put it) that the United States would use all its influence to ensure a genuinely free electoral process.

Obviously, even genuinely free elections would have been rendered absurd if Bosch had been elected only to be overthrown by a new military coup shortly thereafter. A good part of the U.S. diplomatic effort, therefore, was also directed toward convincing both Bosch and his enemies that the United States was fully prepared to work with Bosch if he should win, provide his government with substantial economic assistance, and most important of all, keep the IAPF in the country at Bosch's request for a considerable period to deter any attempts to overthrow him. Naturally, such support would not be unconditional; Bosch would have to keep the Communists under control and refrain from trying to destroy the military or even replacing its top commanders with constitutionalist military leaders. There were a number of indications, however, that Bosch intended to follow cautious, nonprovocative policies.

On the eve of the elections, which most State Department and embassy officials expected would be won by Bosch, the State Department told Bunker and Crimmins to reiterate to all major Dominican actors that the United States expected García-Godoy to use force if necessary to uphold the results of the elections if they should be violently challenged from either the left or the right. The IAPF would be employed if the Dominican military joined in any anti-Bosch action.

No action was necessary, however, as Balaguer's victory was quietly accepted by all important Dominican sectors, and the withdrawal of the U.S. and Latin American troops in the IAPF was begun. An agreement between Bunker, Balaguer, and García-Godoy established that the withdrawal would be gradual, taking about three months if all went well. The least important troops would leave first, and the withdrawal could be slowed down if a new major crisis should warrant such action in the eyes of both the Dominican and U.S. governments. The country remained relatively peaceful, and the last U.S. forces departed on schedule in September 1966, thus ending the most sustained *political* use of military force by the United States in the twentieth century.

The Role of the OAS and the UN

As in the 1961 crisis, the United States was able to act in the Dominican Republic through the OAS and thus obtain perhaps a marginal degree of collective legitimization for actions that were, in all essentials, unilateral in fact. The original military intervention, of course, was not authorized by the inter-American organization, but OAS units were involved in the subsequent negotiation process and Latin American contingents were added to U.S. forces later to form the Inter-American Peace Force.

It is difficult to be sure what real difference, if any, the involvement of the OAS made in the course of events in the Dominican Republic. As discussed earlier, it is plausible that the initial OAS call for a cease-fire and the subsequent arrival of an OAS negotiating committee and OAS Secretary-General José Mora in the country played a role in inhibiting U.S. military action against the constitutionalists, though there were other factors also. Later, the negotiations for the García-Godoy government and the use of the IAPF to support his regime were held formally under the auspices of a three-man Ad Hoc Committee of the OAS, consisting of Ellsworth Bunker and representatives from Brazil and El Salvador. There are some observers who believe that the Latin Americans on the committee played a useful complementary role to Bunker in the negotiations and may have had some impact on U.S. policy, but no one doubts that Bunker was by far the dominant figure and that his power stemmed from his unofficial role as a presidential emissary rather than his official one as U.S. representative to the OAS. Finally, the IAPF, though formally commanded by a Brazilian general, was completely dominated by the United States. The force consisted of about 11,000 U.S. troops, 1,100 Brazilians, and token contributions of several hundred soldiers from Costa Rica, Honduras, Nicaragua, and Paraguay. To the extent that there was a significant international component to the IAPF it actually hindered rather than helped a settlement, for the Brazilian commander was a rather primitive rightwinger who openly favored the Dominican military and dragged his heels on several occasions when the Ad Hoc Commitee asked the IAPF to cooperate with the García-Godoy government. However, the *real* commander of the IAPF was General Bruce Palmer, in command of the U.S. forces, and he was left in no doubt that his real orders came from Ellsworth Bunker, who was fully prepared on several occasions to order U.S. troops to act independently in support of U.S. policy if the Brazilian had not finally cooperated.

The overall role of the OAS in the Dominican crisis, then, was at best peripheral to that of the United States. The United States did make several unsuccessful efforts to get some of the more important relatively liberal Latin American states, in particular Venezuela and Mexico, to play a greater role. The marginality of OAS participation reflected the unwillingness of most states in the hemisphere to become involved in the crisis, inhibited as they were by the tradition of nonintervention, by domestic opposition, and by a reluctance to be associated with actions that might turn out to be disastrous. But even somewhat greater participation by other Latin American countries would not have much altered the fact of U.S. domination, for the Johnson administration was clearly not going to accept dilution of its control over the main lines of its policies.

Similarly, the marginal involvement of the United Nations in the crisis probably had at most only a slight effect on the overall outcome. The Dominican situation was brought before the Security Council on May 1 by the USSR. The United States initially sought to exclude any UN role, resorting to its traditional argument that the involvement of the OAS made UN action unnecessary. But when it became clear that there was little sympathy with this ploy, even among a number of Latin American states who in the past had supported it, the United States reluctantly acceded to the appointment of a special representative of the secretary general to report on the situation. Secretary General U Thant appointed as that representative José Mayobre, a former high official in Betancourt's government in Venezuela. By all accounts, Mayobre was forceful, highly intelligent, and sympathetic to the PRD group among the constitutionalists. It is clear that he did not limit his role to reporting, but established close contacts with the constitutionalists and worked vigorously behind the scenes to help bring about a political settlement acceptable to the democratic left. After considerable initial resentment of Mayobre, U.S. officials in the Dominican Republic came to admire him. They even found him useful as a channel of communications with the constitutionalists. Similarly, García-Godoy worked closely with Mayobre because of his access to Bosch and the constitutionalists. Nevertheless, other channels of communication were available, and it is almost certain that the outcome would have been the same without Mayobre.

Conclusions

In 1961 and 1965 the United States used military displays and military deployments on behalf of the overriding political objective of its Latin American policy—to avoid a new Castroite regime in the Caribbean. In assessing such political uses of military force we may ask three critical questions:

1. Was the use of U.S. armed force *necessary* to achieve U.S. objectives, in the sense that nonmilitary instruments were unavailable or had been exhausted?

2. Was the use of armed force *successful?*

3. Was the use of armed force *justified,* in terms of both morality and the relative costs and benefits to overall U.S. foreign policy in the longer run?

I have already sought to answer these questions with regard to the 1961 case, and I need here reiterate only the main conclusions: The military pressures on Dominican political leaders after the assassination of Rafael Trujillo were *necessary* to get rid of the Trujillo family and to induce a new regime to undertake political reform; they were *successful* in the short term, though over the longer run political reform depended far more on internal circumstances in the Dominican Republic than on U.S. actions; and they were both morally and politically *justified.*

The 1965 case is considerably more complicated. We can answer the three questions only by first posing some others. How much does the United States need to worry about a Communist victory in another Latin American or Caribbean country? How much risk was there, in fact, in the Dominican revolution of 1965? Did the United States exhaust all reasonable alternatives before it turned to the use of force?

Let us begin with the last two questions. It is my view that the intervention was a mistake, even within the framework of the established

No Second Cuba policy. Not that the fear of a successful Communist revolution in the Dominican Republic was a figment of the Johnson administration's fevered imagination, for (as I have elsewhere sought to demonstrate[49]) by April 28 there was indeed *some* risk that Communist or Castroite forces might emerge victorious from an uncontrollable revolutionary upheaval. My argument, rather, is that the U.S. government did not exhaust the opportunities for influencing the Dominican upheaval before the military intervention, and that even by April 28, when the opportunities had passed, the risk was still not sufficiently great to justify the predictably enormous political and moral costs that the intervention entailed.

What might the United States have done before April 28 to influence the Dominican situation? Here it must be recalled that the United States probably had greater influence in the Dominican Republic than in any other state in the world, perhaps matched only by its influence in Cuba before the Castro revolution. As a result of a history of intervention in the early twentieth century, the economic sanctions and military displays of the 1960–62 period, and the extraordinary role the United States had been playing in the day-to-day politics of the Dominican Republic in the preceding five years, Dominican political actors were accustomed to giving heavy weight indeed to anticipated U.S. reactions in their political behavior. Thus there is every reason to believe that appropriate U.S. actions and statements between April 24 and 28 could have avoided the necessity for military action. The most crucial pre-intervention error the United States made was failing, or more precisely refusing, to use its considerable influence to aid the moderate, non-Communist PRD leadership within the constitutionalist movement, vis-à-vis both the rightist military and the Castroite forces. Thanks to the general hostility to Bosch throughout the U.S. government and the generally conservative political attitudes of key officials in the U.S. embassy, the embassy deliberately refused a number of opportunities to mediate during the crisis. Had it not chosen to remain aloof, wishfully anticipating a military defeat of the revolution, there was a strong possibility that the United States could have used its influence to ensure that control of the movement was retained by the moderate leadership. In that way it would have averted the Communist threat—whatever its magnitude—and Juan Bosch could have peacefully returned to the presidency with at least the acquiescence of a divided and confused military. If U.S. diplomatic mediation had failed, Washington might simply

49. Slater, *Intervention and Negotiation*, pp. 35–42.

have announced that it would by no means allow a Communist victory in the Dominican Republic and would use its full economic and, if need be, military power to prevent it. Specifically, the government could have threatened to end all economic assistance to the Dominican Republic, suspend its imports of Dominican sugar, and once again deploy powerful naval groups to Dominican waters. In view of the effectiveness of these actions in the 1960–62 period, such a show of U.S. determination would have had great credibility and almost surely considerable effect on the actions of all the Dominican actors, including the radicals.

Thus (still accepting for the moment the underlying premises of U.S. policies), even if the United States had tried and failed to ensure a democratic outcome, it still could have chosen to do nothing more for the moment than reiterate its No Second Cuba policy in strong terms and ostentatiously deploy strong naval forces to Dominican waters, while waiting until the Dominican situation sorted itself out. To be sure, this course of action might itself have posed serious risks, as State Department officials are quick to point out. The longer the delay, the more resistance a later intervention would be likely to meet. Even worse, the longer the delay, the greater the likelihood that the whole crisis would become entwined in the larger cold war conflict. As the State Department saw the matter, the United States *had* delayed in Cuba, taking strong action only after the political orientation of the Castro government was unmistakably clear. By that time it was too late to do anything effective about it. Relatively small-scale military actions like the Bay of Pigs had failed completely, and larger-scale direct U.S. military intervention would have risked a major confrontation with the USSR.

These arguments are by no means implausible or indefensible. Nonetheless, I remain persuaded that on April 28 the balance of costs and risks was still clearly on the side of nonintervention. Consider the costs of the U.S. military actions:

1. The intervention was almost universally opposed around the world. It was in direct defiance of international law, made a mockery of the inter-American system, and, along with the escalating Vietnam War, it seemed to reflect "impetuous and doctrinaire anticommunism; a reckless reliance on military force . . . a penchant for putting action ahead of calculation."[50]

2. The intervention contributed massively to the sharply increased

---

50. Richard P. Stebbins, *The United States in World Affairs, 1965* (Harper and Row for the Council on Foreign Relations, 1966), p. 68.

public alienation from the U.S. government, and even the political system as a whole, within the United States itself. Along with the Vietnam crisis it was seen as both the symbol and the inevitable outcome of a pathologically anti-Communist policy. Of course no one can say what the permanent costs of the Dominican intervention have been to this country's political and social fabric, but surely it played a role in the general domestic crisis of the ensuing decade.

3. Within Latin America the intervention dealt a death blow to the Alliance for Progress and the policy of nonrevolutionary democratic change that underlay it. One of the major premises of the alliance had been that the privileged classes of Latin America and their allies in the military, the church, and the established political parties could be persuaded to support democratic change, or at least to recognize that the forces for democratic change were the only realistic alternative to much more radical and violent change. But the Dominican intervention opened the possibility of another alternative—the United States might, at the moment of truth, bail out the oligarchies rather than let them face the consequences of their own inadequacies and their steadfast addiction to an outmoded and unjust status quo. And indeed (though of course many other factors played substantial roles), in the ensuing years Latin American politics became increasingly polarized between the radical left and the extreme right, and the hopes of the early 1960s that the democratic left would prevail have been bitterly dashed.

On the other hand, what were the risks of deferring military intervention until it should become absolutely "necessary"? The prospect that the USSR would have committed itself to the protection of a radical government in the Dominican Republic, in the face of a firm U.S. threat to take military action to prevent a new Cuba, must be considered as nil. It is of course easier to be confident of such an assessment in retrospect, for the USSR did in fact remain on the sidelines throughout the crisis. Even at the time, however, the previous Soviet caution in the Cuban missile crisis strongly indicated that it would follow a noninterventionist course in any future Caribbean crisis that the United States again defined as critical to its national interests, much as the cautious behavior of the United States in the 1956 Hungarian revolution allowed the USSR correctly to predict similar behavior in the Czechoslovakian crisis of 1968.

Until now, I have been arguing from within the framework of established policies—that is, that a U.S. intervention would have been justifiable if it had been *really* necessary to prevent communism from coming to power in another Latin American or Caribbean country. I have not challenged the No Second Cuba policy itself, but simply its application in the Dominican Republic. This assumption must now be squarely faced. To return to the first of the questions posed earlier: In what way would another Communist government in the Caribbean threaten U.S. security, threaten it so massively as to require military intervention against a genuinely indigenous revolution?

It is my view that the Caribbean is in fact of no great significance to the United States. The only importance of the Caribbean today is psychological—the Caribbean is important because we think it is.[51] Unfortunately, because of the very nature of this self-fulfilling prophecy, a serious argument could be made that in 1965 if the U.S. government had passively accepted an actual—not potential—Communist victory in the Dominican Republic there would have been very severe domestic and international consequences. Domestic considerations did in fact play a crucial role in the U.S. decision to intervene—the fear that the American people would not stand for passivity in the event of a new Castro in this hemisphere. And in the prevailing climate of opinion that fear might very well have been justified. The continued existence of the Castro government is no longer a domestic issue, but one need only recall the hysteria of the early 1960s over the Cuban revolution—"Only ninety miles away," "Cuba is a dagger pointing at the heart of America"—to understand the Johnson administration's concern. With the Cuban missile crisis still a very live memory, reasonable men could and in fact did fear that a successful Communist revolution in the Dominican Republic might well jeopardize the future of the Democratic party, if not of American liberalism in general. Even short of that, a new Communist revolution in the hemisphere could certainly have made politically impossible a more flexible and relaxed policy toward the entire Communist world, and it might have set back for years U.S. willingness to seek a détente in the cold war.

Similarly, a failure to act against an unmistakably Communist revolution in the Caribbean might have produced serious destabilizing consequences in the rest of the world. A new Communist government in the hemisphere would not in fact threaten U.S. security, but the United States had been proclaiming since the Castro revolution that it would. Although

51. Jerome Slater, "The United States and Latin America: Premises for the New Administration," *Yale Review*, vol. 64 (October 1974), pp. 1–10.

a genuinely indigenous revolution was in fact a far cry from international Communist aggression, the United States had been loudly denying such a distinction. An indigenous Communist government in the Caribbean would in fact almost certainly be independent of Moscow, Peking, or Havana, but the United States had been minimizing the significance of pluralism in the Communist world. Thus, caught in the crisis, the government could not suddenly reverse itself and deny the manifest implications of its policies, without inviting dangerous consequences elsewhere in the world. Assuming (as seems plausible) the existence of a militant Kremlin faction favoring pressing on with the cold war, the price of nonaction in the Caribbean might have been more aggressive Soviet behavior elsewhere, say in Berlin or the Middle East. If Washington refused to act in the Caribbean, which the United States itself had insisted was essential to its national security, why would it live up to its commitments in areas outside its immediate sphere of influence?

The United States in 1965 was a prisoner of its own oversimplifications, myths, outmoded policies, and self-fulfilling prophecies. To reiterate the major points of my argument: (1) the overall No Second Cuba policy was an error, based on obsolescent premises, which should have been abandoned before the crisis ever arose; (2) because that had not been done, however, it is arguable that, in the domestic and international environment prevailing in 1965, the United States had trapped itself into the necessity of intervening against an actual Communist revolution; (3) in the Dominican crisis itself the United States had failed to exercise its influence in a constructive manner to avert a potential Communist threat. In any case, its intervention on April 28 was premature, for the evidence of Communist influence in the constitutionalist movement was not nearly sufficient to justify the predictable political and human costs of the intervention. The appropriate course, even within the framework of existing policy, would have been to intervene only if an unmistakably Communist government had actually come to power.

In addition to the intervention itself, the United States made a number of serious errors in the post-intervention period. The landing of U.S. troops should have been directed not only at forestalling whatever danger there was of a Communist takeover, but also at curbing the Dominican military, strengthening the non-Communist democratic elements in the constitutionalist movement, and restoring Juan Bosch to the presidency. As the troops landed the United States might have made the following announcement: "In view of the possible threat of a Communist takeover of a revolutionary movement in the Dominican Republic, as well as the serious dangers to both foreign and Dominican lives, the United States has been forced to intervene militarily. The purpose of this intervention, however, will be not only to prevent a new Castro in the Western Hemisphere but also to end the fighting, restore order, prevent a military takeover, and restore the constitutional president to his office." Once the troops were on the ground, it would not have been difficult to isolate completely the Communist elements within the constitutionalist movement and ensure that they would not be in any position to dominate the government. Had the United States thrown its weight behind Bosch, instituted far-reaching reform of the Dominican military, and in other ways used its power unequivocally on behalf of progressive democracy, the intervention probably would have been welcomed by most Dominicans and it would have been viewed far differently in the United States and Latin America.

In fact, however, the United States used excessive force against the constitutionalists and failed to use enough force to curb the terrorism of the Dominican police and military. Although the Johnson administration had proclaimed as one of the principal reasons for the intervention the need to save lives in a bloody civil war, most of the estimated 3,000 Dominican deaths occurred after the intervention, some of them in clashes between the constitutionalists and U.S. troops and the rest at the hands of a Dominican military that the United States had rescued from probable annihilation in April and thereafter helped protect and rebuild.

The most inexcusable U.S. action during the entire period of the intervention, in my view, was its support of Imbert's military attack in May on the constitutionalist sector in northern Santo Domingo, which ended in the brutal slaughter of hundreds of constitutionalists and innocent civilians. In one sense, this might be looked upon as a successful use of military force for political purposes, for it did indeed generate additional pressures on the constitutionalists in the negotiating process. But the fact was that the constitutionalists were helpless anyway in the face of 23,000 American troops and a rebuilt Dominican police and military, and they knew it. In such circumstances, to have taken lives deliberately in exchange for slight political advantage was morally questionable, to put it as mildly as possible.

On the other hand, once the negotiating process had begun in earnest in the summer of 1965, the continued presence of U.S. troops and their occasional deployment, especially to prevent the attempted coups against the García-Godoy government, was absolutely essential to the realization of U.S. political objectives, which in turn were both politically and morally praiseworthy—namely, putting an end to rightist terrorism against the constitutionalists and establishing a democratic and progressive provisional regime to preside over the holding of free elections. Though U.S. forces remained in the Dominican Republic for eighteen months, after the first weeks their primary function was less to occupy the country than to keep the peace, less to dictate U.S. objectives than to ensure that the majority of Dominicans could give effective expression to their own political will.

Was the intervention ultimately a "success"? Even if we ignore the moral and political costs of the actions of the first few weeks, and the failure to exhaust nonmilitary alternatives, it would be hard to say. There is no Communist government in the Dominican Republic today, but that is not to say there would have been if the United States had not intervened. The United States did weed out the worst of the Trujillists from the Dominican military, but ultimately, despite its initial intentions, it failed to use the opportunity to engage in truly fundamental reform of the military. The United States did seek a democratic solution and presided over free elections, but once its troops were withdrawn it lost most of its leverage over internal Dominican affairs, and few observers think that the Balaguer regime has done much to establish stable, democratic, and progressive government in the Dominican Republic over the longer run.

Moreover, even if the Dominican intervention were not such a flawed "success," it would not be a very useful model or precedent for other such political uses of military force because of the special circumstances of the Dominican case and even because of the great amount of sheer luck. "The Dominican Republic was a comparatively easy place for the United States to intervene and from which to withdraw,"[52] not only because its size and proximity to the United States enabled rapid and massive military intervention, but also because thirty years of Trujillism had so fragmented and demoralized Dominican society that the conditions for a nationalist resistance movement against the U.S. intervention did not exist.[53]

52. Abraham F. Lowenthal, "The Dominican Intervention in Retrospect," *Public Policy*, vol. 18 (Fall 1969), p. 144.
53. The remainder of this chapter was prepared by Stephen S. Kaplan.

As in November 1961, the United States had complete strategic military control of the situation in 1965. Moscow was of no mind to become more than rhetorically involved, and Cuba had no capability to support the constitutionalists once the United States intervened. U.S. forces did not have to face any military opposition that had a strong base of support in the countryside. The opposition, which consisted of the constitutionalists, was located in a narrow geographic area and could be quickly isolated. Nevertheless, an action to root out the constitutionalists violently would have been bloody. Had ideologues of the left actually gained control of the constitutionalist forces compromise would not have been so likely, and there might well have been disastrous political consequences. As it was, neither side had the military capability to stage a successful offensive. The troops on both sides quickly perceived that any such action was out of the question. All they could do was resist—and that only for the sake of a longer term political effect. In short, strategic and local isolation, minimal capabilities, and the absence of long-term political plans and ideological commitment all combined to allow the 23,000 U.S. troops a relatively easy time of it.

Finally, it is interesting to consider what might have been the result of a lesser action, such as was carried out in November 1961. Certainly the political repercussions would not have been so great; but could the situation have been stabilized and similar outcomes been obtained by explicit and direct threats to the principals, coupled with only the offshore appearance of a large naval and amphibious force?

It is very probable that the situation had gone too far—unless the constitutionalists saw U.S. troops in the Dominican Republic, they might not have believed the United States was serious. Threats and a naval presence might not have been enough. The constitutionalists could have done little to prevent the intervention even if they had been fully aware of U.S. intentions beforehand. It also is *possible* that they may have felt an early compromise in the absence of U.S. troops would yield more than could be expected if troops actually did land. In short, the best answer is "who knows?" but it would not have been especially risky to find out. At the least a six- or eight-hour ultimatum could have been issued.

Perhaps a more serious problem than the willingness of the constitutionalist leaders to compromise was the ability of the United States forcefully to communicate an ultimatum to the right people on short notice. During the period of near chaos when the U.S. troops landed, the relations between the embassy and the constitutionalists were complicated both by difficulty in communicating and by mutual distrust.

More significant though was that, unlike the situation in 1961, power was largely in the streets. It is reasonable to hypothesize that without U.S. troops on the ground the constitutionalist leaders could not have enforced a compromise without seriously endangering their own positions. The situation was unstable, and an agreement with one group of leaders might have led only to that group's replacement by another—and more radical—group. The emplacement on Dominican soil, rather than offshore presence, of U.S. troops may also have made it easier for the constitutionalist leaders to compromise, insofar as their followers were more impressed by the actual dominance of U.S. forces on the ground than by the mere threat of it.

Still another factor to consider is what would have been the result of a brief cease-fire in place. Both the loyalists and the constitutionalists had a tremendous fear as well as hatred of each other. This situation would probably have resulted in a series of broken cease-fires, ending only when one of the two sides destroyed the other. It is difficult to imagine that a provisional government of the García-Godoy type would have come to pass and that such free and fair elections as were held in 1966 would have taken place.

In the long run, apart from the holding of elections and the inauguration of a popularly elected government in 1966, can we consider that the U.S. intervention was justified? It is true that Washington has not had to worry about communism in the Dominican Republic, and Balaguer is no Trujillo. On the other hand, a decade later there is very little democracy in the Dominican Republic. The country is not a "showcase" of anything.

In sum, then, one might conclude that by ousting the Trujillos in 1965 the two worst extremes were proscribed. The realities of both, however, were always questionable: Trujillo's heirs probably were not made of the same stuff as El Jefe, and the Communists probably would not have been able to seize power in 1965 or thereafter. In a constructive and longer term sense these interventions had little effect; as a society and as a polity, the Dominican Republic has followed its own rather than any U.S.-directed course.

CHAPTER NINE

The Berlin Crises of 1958–59 and 1961

ROBERT M. SLUSSER

IN THE PERIOD from November 1958 to October 1961 the divided city of Berlin served as the focal point of a continuing international conflict that pitted the USSR and its allies against the Western alliance of the United Kingdom, France, and the United States. Chronologically, the action centering on Berlin falls into two distinct segments: (1) the Berlin crisis of 1958–59, which opened on November 27, 1958, with a Soviet note calling for withdrawal of the Western occupation forces from West Berlin and its conversion into a "free city" under a new agreement to be negotiated by the Western powers with a six-month deadline; this crisis reached its muted and inconclusive end ten months later when Soviet Premier Nikita S. Khrushchev joined President Dwight D. Eisenhower in an agreement to hold negotiations on the Berlin question without the pressure of a Soviet-imposed deadline; and (2) the Berlin crisis of 1961, which began in February of that year with a Soviet note to the Federal Republic of Germany; escalated sharply in June, when the USSR announced another six-month deadline, this time for the conclusion of peace treaties with the East and West German states; reached a climax on August 12 when the USSR and its East German allies established a physical barrier, the Berlin Wall, between the Soviet-occupied sector of East Berlin and the three Western-occupied sectors of the city; and finally receded after a tank confrontation between the United States and the USSR along the sector boundary in the divided city in October.

Between the two Berlin crises there intervened a period during which

343

significant changes took place in the relative strength and internal power relationships of the USSR and the United States and their respective allies. The second Berlin crisis was therefore by no means a mere replay of the first. The 1961 crisis took up the conflict in a new international context, with differing strategies on either side, and with a different conclusion. The two crises, nevertheless, can usefully be regarded as "all a single tapestry,"[1] or, in a longer perspective, as phases in a single extended struggle for world supremacy between the USSR and the United States.

Historical Background

Berlin became the focal point of the Soviet-Western struggle as the result of a series of decisions, agreements, and actions taken during and shortly after the Second World War.[2] The European Advisory Commission decided at a meeting in September 1944 to divide a defeated Germany into three zones of occupation, to be administered by the three principal allies, the United States, the United Kingdom, and the USSR. At the same time the commission agreed that the German capital, Berlin, should be administered jointly by the three powers, each occupying a sector of the city. Despite the fact that Berlin lies some 110 miles east of the border separating the Soviet zone of occupation from those of the Western allies, no provision was made at that time to guarantee Western rights of access to the city.

At the Yalta Conference in February 1945 the three powers agreed to invite France to share in the occupation of postwar Germany and Berlin. When the war in Europe ended, therefore, Germany was divided into four zones of occupation, and Berlin into four occupation sectors. It was agreed that the nation and its capital should be administered as undivided en-

1. Alexander L. George and Richard Smoke, *Deterrence in American Foreign Policy: Theory and Practice* (Columbia University Press, 1974), p. 395.
2. The historical background of the Berlin crises is covered in Jean Edward Smith, *The Defense of Berlin* (Johns Hopkins Press, 1963), pp. 1–130, and, more briefly, in Jack M. Schick, *The Berlin Crisis, 1958–1962* (University of Pennsylvania Press, 1971), pp. ix–xvi. For a useful documentary survey, see Senate Committee on Foreign Relations, *Documents on Germany, 1944–1970*, 92:1 (GPO, 1971). The evidence on the division of Germany is analyzed in two recent books: Tony Sharp, *The Wartime Alliance and the Division of Germany* (Oxford University Press, 1975), and John H. Backer, *The Decision to Divide Germany: American Foreign Policy in Transition* (Duke University Press, 1978).

tities by the four powers acting together. Arrangements for ground and air access to Berlin from the Western zones were agreed on orally by Soviet and Western military authorities at the end of June 1945, and were later spelled out in more precise detail.[3]

The occupation zones and sectors were originally thought of as temporary administrative arrangements having no long-term significance. Increasingly sharp disagreements between the USSR and the three Western powers, however, soon led to the breakdown of four-power administrative machinery in Germany and Berlin. In place of a single united but occupied Germany, there developed in the postwar years two separate German states, the Communist-ruled German Democratic Republic (GDR) in what had been the Soviet zone of occupation, and the Federal Republic of Germany (FRG), created by the merger of the three zones occupied by the Western powers.

In occupied Berlin, four-power administrative machinery also broke down as the result of the unbridgeable gulf between Soviet policies and those of the Western powers, so that Berlin was split into Soviet-controlled East Berlin and the three Allied-occupied sectors that constituted West Berlin. In the period between April 1948 and July 1949 the USSR imposed a blockade on Berlin by blocking Western access via the road, water, and rail routes to West Germany, but refrained from taking the final step of challenging Western access to the city by air, with the result that the Western powers were able to mount an airlift which finally forced the USSR to lift the blockade. The agreements reached by the four occupying powers after the Berlin blockade implicitly confirmed Western rights of access to the city.[4]

In the 1950s the GDR, with Soviet approval, began to stake a claim to East Berlin as its capital and as a legal part of its territory. From time to time East German spokesmen asserted that West Berlin, too, was part of the territory of the GDR and by rights should be incorporated into it. A particularly bold claim of this kind was made just before the onset of the 1958–59 crisis by Walter Ulbricht, first secretary of the Communist-controlled Socialist United Party of Germany (SED), the dominant political force in the GDR.[5] The Western powers steadfastly resisted claims of this

3. *Documents on Germany, 1944–1970*, pp. 21–22, 46–54.
4. Ibid., pp. 154–56.
5. Geoffrey Barraclough, *Survey of International Affairs, 1956–1958* (Oxford University Press, 1962), pp. 582–83, citing *Neues Deutschland*, October 28, 1958.

kind, however, insisting on their rights of occupation. When the USSR, in September 1955, transferred to East German authorities responsibility for control of civilian traffic from West Germany to Berlin, the Western powers declared that the USSR was still bound by the wartime agreements on Berlin and could not assign to the GDR the rights and responsibilities that devolved upon the USSR as a result of those agreements.[6] In particular, they insisted that the USSR must continue to respect their rights of military access to West Berlin via the arterial highways (*autobahns*), railroads, canals, and air corridors. Reluctantly, the USSR accepted these demands.

Shaped by the occupying powers, the two German states took sharply divergent paths in political, economic, military, and cultural policies. East Germany, under the rule of the SED, enacted a series of measures designed to create a socialist society on the Soviet model, while West Germany, with help and encouragement from the United States, adopted the economic system of capitalist free enterprise and a democratic political structure. Partly as a result of these policies, West Germany entered a period of rapid economic expansion, with a sharp rise in the economic well-being of the population, while East Germany encountered grave difficulties in its economic policies and was unable to match the prosperity increasingly characteristic of the FRG.

In the competition of the two politico-economic systems the divided city of Berlin came to play a fateful role. Surrounded by the territory of the East German state but closely linked with West Germany, West Berlin symbolized the economic prosperity and political freedoms of the West in the midst of the state-controlled economy and regimented political system of the East German state. The Western allies, conscious of the symbolic value of West Berlin as an outpost of freedom in Communist-controlled Eastern Europe, lavished funds on its economic growth and deliberately made it a showpiece of capitalist democracy.

From the Soviet and East German standpoint, the material contrast between prosperous West Berlin and the drab Eastern sector of the city was a constant irritant. The situation was really intolerable to the Soviets because West Berlin provided an easy escape route to the West for East Germans dissatisfied by conditions in the GDR and lured by the prospect of steady employment, political rights, and cultural diversity in West Germany. In 1957 and early 1958 the GDR implemented a series of

6. *Documents on Germany, 1944–1970*, pp. 276–77.

measures designed to accelerate the socialization of agriculture and industry, measures that resulted in further curbs on individual rights. The result was a greatly increased flow of population from East to West Germany via West Berlin. By September 1958 the tide was running at the rate of over 10,000 a month, with a cumulative loss to the GDR of over three million inhabitants over a ten-year period. Since young people and professionally trained specialists constituted a high proportion of the migrants, the GDR could not tolerate the loss indefinitely.

The stability and viability of the GDR, in turn, were matters of paramount importance to the USSR, which maintained in East Germany the twenty divisions that constituted its principal military force in Europe, the guarantee of continued dominance over the empire it had carved out for itself in Europe during the Second World War.

The conflict between the two German states inevitably involved the rival alliance systems headed by the USSR and the United States. After the formal division of Germany the GDR became a member of the Soviet-controlled Warsaw Pact organization, while the FRG was incorporated into the North Atlantic Treaty Organization (NATO). To counter the military threat to the Western position posed by Soviet armed power and the clandestine rearmament of East Germany, the Western allies step by step lifted for the FRG the restrictions on German rearmament agreed to by the wartime allies at Potsdam in 1945. In December 1957 the NATO Council resolved to station intermediate-range ballistic missiles in West Germany, as well as nuclear weapons under U.S. control, a move the USSR promptly denounced as a threat to its peace and security.[7]

By 1958 West Berlin had come to represent to the USSR the most acute aspect of a dangerous and threatening situation. The problem of how to remedy the situation was one not easily solved, however, because the United States possessed superior strategic power in nuclear weapons and delivery vehicles and had repeatedly proclaimed its commitment to the defense of Western occupation rights in West Berlin. U.S. strategic superiority, however, was based in large part on manned heavy bombers, whereas the USSR had devoted special attention to the development of heavy rockets capable of serving as intercontinental ballistic missiles (ICBMs). In October 1957 the USSR startled the world by putting into orbit the world's first artificial satellite, Sputnik I, using a heavy rocket-launcher for the purpose. Soviet spokesmen were quick to point out the

7. Schick, *Berlin Crisis,* pp. 7–8.

military implications of the feat. In November 1958, as part of the buildup surrounding the onset of the first Berlin crisis, Soviet Premier Nikita Khrushchev strongly hinted that Soviet armaments factories were producing ICBMs on a regular basis.[8] The implication he wished to convey was obviously that the USSR had succeeded in overcoming U.S. strategic superiority, or was likely to do so in the near future. Like much else in Khrushchev's policies, however, this implication was based on a bluff: having developed the prototype rocket launcher used to put Sputnik I into orbit, Soviet planners had decided to avoid the heavy expenditures needed to achieve large-scale production of the ICBMs, and were in fact producing only a small number of the new weapons.[9]

Khrushchev's bluff was not fully exposed until September 1961, when reliable new information on the deployment of Soviet ICBMs became available to the United States through reconnaissance satellites. Top leaders in the United States had been aware of the hollowness of Khrushchev's claims well before September 1961, however, thanks in large part to photographic evidence obtained by the high-level U-2 flights over Soviet territory inaugurated in 1956. But the United States maintained official secrecy with regard to these flights until they were inadvertently exposed in May 1960, when the USSR finally succeeded in bringing one down. U.S. leaders could not, therefore, counter Khrushchev's claims convincingly, with the result that public opinion in the West tended to take the Soviet leader's boast seriously, a situation Khrushchev exploited to Soviet advantage.

The international context within which the first Berlin crisis developed was therefore a highly complex one, in which real Western strength and illusory Soviet claims competed on apparently equal terms. Khrushchev and his colleagues were undoubtedly well aware of the real strategic balance, but they had compelling reasons to try to effect a change in the status of West Berlin by challenging Western rights in the city. It was this action that precipitated the crisis of 1958–59.

8. Arnold L. Horelick and Myron Rush, *Strategic Power and Soviet Foreign Policy* (University of Chicago Press, 1966), p. 50, citing *Pravda*, November 14, 1958.

9. On the "politics of Soviet missile deception," see Horelick and Rush, *Strategic Power and Soviet Foreign Policy*, pp. 35–70 and 105–16. They argue that Soviet actions in the Berlin crises can best be explained as arising from a Soviet strategy of bluff and deception.

Major Participants in the 1958–59 Crisis and Their Relationships

Before taking up a detailed analysis of the 1958–59 crisis it will be useful to make a few observations about the principal participants in the crisis and their relationships.

The USSR and the German Democratic Republic

On the Soviet side the major actors were the USSR and its client state, the GDR. Vastly unequal in size, resources, and power though they were, the relationship between the two was not simply one of Soviet dominance and GDR subservience. The point is well made by a British historian of the Berlin crises: "It is important not to ignore the part played by the East German government throughout the crisis. It has, within its limited room of maneuver, shown remarkable ingenuity and tenacity in persuading the Soviet Union to accept its own objectives."[10] Well aware of the high stakes the USSR had invested in East Germany, GDR leader Walter Ulbricht was able on occasion to act with great boldness and even seeming recklessness, secure in the knowledge that in the final analysis the USSR could not afford to disavow him.

One reason Ulbricht was able to wield an influence on Soviet policy disproportionate to the size and importance of the GDR was that the Soviet leadership was by no means unified in its objectives. Bold and risky statements or actions by Ulbricht might therefore on occasion find tacit support from individuals or factions in the Soviet leadership that favored a high-risk Soviet foreign policy.

The split in the Soviet leadership was the direct result of recent developments in the evolution of the Communist party of the Soviet Union (CPSU). In June 1957 Khrushchev had won a narrow victory against the so-called anti-party group, a coalition headed by former Chairman of the Council of Ministers Georgi Malenkov and former First Deputy Chairmen Vyacheslav Molotov and Lazar Kaganovich, with support from a

10. Philip Windsor, *City on Leave: A History of Berlin, 1945–1962* (Praeger, 1963), p. 205n.

number of other high-ranking figures in the Presidium.[11] Khrushchev's victory was achieved in part thanks to support from tactical allies who had no real liking for him or his policies, internal as well as foreign, and who presented an increasingly serious challenge to his dominance after June 1957. This situation added an additional element of bluff to Khrushchev's position as Soviet leader in international affairs: not merely was he claiming for the USSR strategic power it did not have but he was claiming for himself a stature that was not justified by the facts. In this instance, however, Khrushchev's bluff was not fully exposed until October 1964, when he was ousted as the result of a clandestine conspiracy mounted by his domestic opponents. Before that date most Western analysts of Soviet politics were convinced that Khrushchev wielded unchallenged power in the formulation of Soviet foreign policy, and Western political leaders in general subscribed to that view.[12]

China

Though not directly involved in the Berlin crises, the People's Republic of China (PRC) played a significant role in shaping Soviet foreign policy in the period 1958–61. Formally, in both the 1958–59 and 1961 crises, the PRC supported Soviet policy, but during this period its leaders grew increasingly critical of what they saw as Khrushchev's tendency to seek an accommodation with the United States. (Needless to say, numerous other issues were involved in Chinese Communist criticism of Soviet policies in the Khrushchev era.)

It was during the 1958–61 period that the split between Moscow and Peking, which had deep historical roots, first became manifest. The Sino-Soviet split had a notable effect on the divisions in the Soviet leadership, polarizing it into pro-Peking and pro-Western factions. Thus another ele-

---

11. For a concise history of the "anti-party group," see Roger Pethybridge, *A Key to Soviet Politics: The Crisis of the Anti-Party Group* (Praeger, 1962).

12. For example, British Prime Minister Harold Macmillan, after his trip to Moscow in February–March 1959, recorded in his diary the opinion that "Mr. Khrushchev is *absolute* ruler of Russia and completely controls the situation." Harold Macmillan, *Riding the Storm, 1956–1959* (Macmillan, 1971), p. 633; italics in the original. Subsequently, however, Macmillan reconsidered, and when he published this diary entry in 1971 he added the comment, "Perhaps the only change I would wish now to make in this appreciation regards the undisputed supremacy of Khrushchev. He had not the strength of Stalin, for he had eschewed, or could not rely on, Stalin's chief weapon—the Terror." Ibid., p. 634.

ment of bluff was added to Soviet foreign policy during this period, since the publicly proclaimed unity between the two principal Communist states masked their increasingly divergent views on a whole range of problems, including foreign policy.[13]

Poland

A minor but not unimportant part in the genesis and development of the Berlin crises was played by Poland. Postwar Poland, which had received sizable accessions of territory at Germany's expense in 1945, felt seriously threatened by West German rearmament, membership in NATO, and possible access to U.S. missiles and nuclear weapons, since a rearmed and resurgent West Germany might one day decide to use its new-found military power to try to recapture its lost eastern territories. To guard against this danger, in October 1957 Polish Foreign Minister Adam Rapacki proposed the establishment of a nuclear-free zone in central Europe, including the two German states (the so-called Rapacki Plan), a suggestion for which Soviet spokesmen promptly voiced support but which the Western powers refused to accept, with the result that the plan was moribund well before the onset of the 1958–59 crisis.[14]

More immediately germane to the subject of the present paper is the fact that it was at a meeting of the Polish-Soviet Friendship Society in Moscow that Khrushchev delivered the speech of November 10, 1958, which marked the opening of the 1958–59 crisis. It has been argued that in demanding a major change in the situation in Berlin on that occasion, Khrushchev was responding in part to Polish fears and pressures.[15]

The Western Alliance

Dominating the Western alliance was the United States, with the United Kingdom as its closest partner, France as a more distant ally, and a number of smaller states as members of NATO. Rapidly gaining in power, prestige, and international stature was the Federal Republic of

13. In the extensive literature on the Sino-Soviet dispute, Donald B. Zagoria's pioneering study, *The Sino-Soviet Conflict, 1956–1961* (Princeton University Press, 1962), is still required reading.

14. On the Rapacki Plan and its fate, see Barraclough, *Survey of International Affairs, 1956–1958*, pp. 562–64.

15. Ibid., p. 587.

Germany, since 1954 a member of NATO and a principal contributor to its military strength, with eight divisions under arms.

Within the Western alliance there were marked differences of opinion over the policy to be pursued in the Berlin crises. The British, led by Prime Minister Harold Macmillan and Foreign Secretary Selwyn Lloyd, consistently favored negotiations, preferably at the level of heads of state, and deprecated the actual or threatened use of force. The French, under President Charles de Gaulle, were far less optimistic about the prospects of negotiations with the USSR, and tended to see merit in the use of limited force to defend Western rights in Berlin.

The West German Republic maintained close links with France and shared its views on Berlin, but its policies in the Berlin crises were marked by a perceptible though never fully acknowledged inconsistency: On the one hand the FRG, under the aging but indomitable Chancellor Konrad Adenauer, was unalterably opposed to any change in the status of West Berlin that might weaken its ties to West Germany; on the other hand, the FRG leadership feared that the use of force by the Western powers in defense of their rights in West Berlin might escalate into a war that would inevitably be fought on German territory and in which countless German lives would be lost.[16] Adenauer therefore advocated an unyielding Western posture in Berlin, but shrank from calling for any substantive actions to back up Western firmness. Less inhibited in his attitude toward the use of limited force by the Western powers was the socialist mayor of West Berlin, Willy Brandt, a vigorous and outspoken man who made a number of significant contributions to the shaping of Western policy in the Berlin crises.

The United States

Within the United States there were diverse and conflicting views among policymakers in the government and armed forces. The first Berlin crisis occurred at a time when a historical phase of U.S. foreign policy, that dominated by Secretary of State John Foster Dulles, was drawing to a close. In part this was because of the rapid advance of the illness that claimed his life in May 1959. In large part, however, it reflected the in-

16. For a perceptive analysis of the ambiguities of West German policy, see Catherine McArdle Kelleher, *Germany and the Politics of Nuclear Weapons* (Columbia University Press, 1975), pp. 86, 334n.

creasing failure of Dulles's policy of opposing to the threat of Soviet aggression the counterthreat of "massive retaliation," that is, an all-out attack on the USSR with U.S. strategic air power employing nuclear weapons. Originally formulated in 1954, the doctrine of massive retaliation had become increasingly suspect. By 1957 even Dulles himself was beginning to cast about for some alternative strategy that would possess greater plausibility and that would lend a greater degree of flexibility to U.S. policy.[17]

Dulles's policies usually enjoyed the support of President Eisenhower, who not only admired Dulles as a statesman but found him eminently compatible as a friend and adviser. Eisenhower was not, however, simply a mouthpiece for Dulles's views, without substantive ideas of his own. Increasingly, as Dulles's illness reduced his capacity to provide leadership in U.S. foreign policy, Eisenhower began to strike out on his own. After Dulles's death Eisenhower took a number of steps of which Dulles would certainly have disapproved, most notably the July 1959 invitation to Khrushchev to visit the United States.

Despite its increasing vulnerability to criticism, the doctrine of massive retaliation continued to enjoy the support of the Eisenhower administration throughout the 1958–59 crisis. An important corollary of the doctrine, to which the Eisenhower administration also subscribed, was avoidance of the use of force on a limited scale for limited objectives. In part, as Morton Halperin and others have pointed out, this attitude was a result of a general American disinclination to engage in limited wars.[18] To a large degree, however, it was based on fiscal considerations: Eisenhower placed a high value on maintaining the fiscal stability of the federal government, feared the unsettling effect an accelerated arms race would have on the budget, and therefore diligently curbed any tendency to use force in ways that might escalate into a larger conflict.

Within the U.S. military establishment the doctrine of massive retaliation was subjected to searching criticism. Defense Secretary Neil McElroy and General Nathan Twining, chairman of the Joint Chiefs of Staff,

17. In his article, "Challenge and Response in U.S. Policy," *Foreign Affairs,* vol. 36 (October 1957), pp. 25–43, Dulles entertained the possibility that tactical nuclear weapons might hold out the prospect of waging limited nuclear war.

18. Morton H. Halperin, *Limited War in the Nuclear Age* (Wiley, 1963), p. 19. A similar point is made in Herman Kahn, *On Escalation: Metaphors and Scenarios* (Praeger, 1965), p. 17. Obviously, on a few occasions, the Eisenhower administration violated this precept, the landing in Lebanon in 1958 being a case in point.

went along with the administration's fiscal limitations on the armed forces budget, but the Army chief of staff, General Maxwell D. Taylor, was openly critical of the doctrine of massive retaliation and its corollary, the avoidance of the use of limited force. Summing up his critique, Taylor formulated a doctrine known as "flexible response"—the development of a broad range of military capabilities, including conventional weapons, which would enable U.S. policymakers to choose the kind and degree of force appropriate to a given situation, instead of being limited, as they increasingly found themselves with the doctrine of massive retaliation, to a choice between threats of all-out war or acquiescence to Soviet demands.[19]

A vocal and outspoken critic of U.S. military and foreign policy in the Eisenhower administration, Taylor became a major influence on the making of policy in the Kennedy administration, which accepted his principle of flexible response as the basis for its program of arms buildup and diversification, and which put into effect some of his recommendations, including the use of limited force to achieve specific ends.

The Effect of Dulles's Illness and Death

The increasingly serious illness of Dulles in the period from December 1958 to April 1959 made it more and more difficult for him to exercise leadership in U.S. foreign policy, and his death in May 1959 left the United States temporarily without a strong figure in foreign policy formulation. Christian Herter, who succeeded Dulles as secretary of state, never achieved the degree of intimacy with Eisenhower that had made Dulles's position so strong, nor did he have the same prestige and influence with U.S. allies.

Sensing an opportunity to display increased British initiative in the Western alliance, Macmillan made a trip to Moscow for bilateral talks with Khrushchev in February and March 1959. These meetings may have helped lessen the danger of overt Soviet-Western conflict by persuading the Soviet leader to agree to holding a conference of foreign ministers preparatory to a summit meeting of heads of state.[20]

19. For Taylor's critique of the doctrine of "massive retaliation," see his *The Uncertain Trumpet* (Harper, 1960), pp. 47–79.

20. For Macmillan's account of his talks with Khrushchev, see his *Riding the Storm*, pp. 592–634.

In the 1961 crisis, by contrast, U.S. leadership of the Western alliance was not seriously challenged by the British. Macmillan, who was still prime minister, found Kennedy a compatible personality, however much he might deplore some American initiatives in foreign policy. In any case, by 1961 the British were forced to recognize that they no longer commanded sufficient power to justify a larger part in the determination of policy for the Western alliance.

The Problem of Soviet Policy Formulation

Throughout this study, hypotheses will be advanced about the struggle for power in the Communist party of the Soviet Union and the effect of that struggle on the formulation and conduct of Soviet foreign policy. In analyzing Soviet policy in the Berlin crises of 1958–59 and 1961 the need to face this problem appears inescapable.

Three explanations for Soviet policy formulation in this period have been advanced by Western analysts. The first, which may be called the traditional view, holds that decisionmaking in the realm of foreign policy was the sole prerogative of Khrushchev, as the result of his being both first secretary of the party and, in the government, chairman of the Council of Ministers or premier. In this view, Khrushchev had the power to take, singlehandedly, foreign policy decisions that were binding on his colleagues in the party Presidium as well as on all subordinate officials and institutions. If Khrushchev was absent from the Kremlin on extended tours (as was frequently the case), his colleagues in Moscow pursued as best they could the policy lines laid down by Khrushchev. If sharp zigzags occurred in Soviet foreign policy (this too was frequently the case), the explanation was to be sought either in the vagaries of Khrushchev's own temperament and shifting priorities, or perhaps (and not all followers of the traditional interpretation were willing to make this concession) in some form of institutionalized pressure on him.[21]

21. The classic formulation of the "traditional" point of view is Merle Fainsod, *How Russia Is Ruled*, rev. ed. (Harvard University Press, 1963). On p. 583 Fainsod writes: "Khrushchev, like Stalin before him, tolerates no derogation of his own authority, permits no opposition to raise its head within the Party, and insists that the Party function as a unit in executing his will." A "traditionalist" view of the Berlin crisis is given in Schick, *Berlin Crisis,* which has served as one of the principal sources for the more recent study by George and Smoke, *Deterrence in American Foreign Policy.*

Challenging the traditionalists is a "collectivist" school, which sees the formulation of policy in the Khrushchev era as a group process with the "collective leadership" in the Presidium playing a major role. Even the collectivists, however, subscribe to the view that foreign policy remained the prerogative of Khrushchev, though they are more willing than the traditionalists to make allowance for group pressures on him.[22]

A third approach to the problem, which can be characterized as a "radical collectivist" view, is set forth in my book, *The Berlin Crisis of 1961,* and in a number of shorter writings based on the same concept.[23] This approach, which serves as the basis for the present study, holds that Khrushchev's position was at all times subject to internal pressures and that a continuing struggle for power took place in the USSR in the Khrushchev period. This power struggle had a direct and at times decisive effect on the formulation of foreign as well as domestic policy.

Ideally, perhaps, a study of this kind should present not just one point of view but all three. Limitations of space rule out this procedure. The "radical collectivist" approach will be used throughout this study, but due attention will be paid to other hypotheses where appropriate.

The Berlin Crisis of 1958–59

The immediate prelude to the crisis of 1958–59 was a speech by Khrushchev at a meeting of the Soviet-Polish Friendship Society in Moscow on November 10, 1958, in which he demanded that the Western

22. The principal "collectivist" studies of the Khrushchev era are Michel Tatu, *Power in the Kremlin from Khrushchev to Kosygin* (Viking Press, 1969); Sidney I. Ploss, *Conflict and Decision-Making in Soviet Russia: A Case Study of Agricultural Policy* (Princeton University Press, 1965); and Carl A. Linden, *Khrushchev and the Soviet Leadership, 1957–1964* (Johns Hopkins Press, 1966). Tatu and Linden treat both foreign and internal policy.

23. The principal publications in which I have presented my views, in order of publication, are "Die Sonderstellung Belorusslands," *Osteuropa,* vol. 14 (November 1964), pp. 851–64; "America, China, and the Hydra-Headed Opposition: The Dynamics of Soviet Foreign Policy," in Peter H. Juviler and Henry W. Morton, eds., *Soviet Policy-Making: Studies of Communism in Transition* (Praeger, 1967), pp. 186–269; *The Berlin Crisis of 1961: Soviet-American Relations and the Struggle for Power in the Kremlin, June–November 1961* (Johns Hopkins University Press, 1973); and "The Presidium Meeting of February 1961: A Reconstruction," in Alexander and Janet Rabinowitch, with Ladis K. D. Kristof, eds., *Revolution and Politics in Russia: Essays in Memory of B. I. Nicolaevsky* (Indiana University Press, 1972), pp. 281–92.

powers give up their occupation rights in West Berlin (which he erroneously attributed to the Potsdam agreement of 1945), "and thereby make
it possible to create a normal situation in the capital of the German Democratic Republic." The USSR, he said, would "hand over to the sovereign
German Democratic Republic the functions in Berlin that are still exercised by Soviet agencies," in other words, responsibility for administration of the city, including control of Western access rights. To back up his
demand Khrushchev voiced a threat of force, warning that the USSR
would regard any attack on the GDR as an attack on the Soviet Union
itself and on its Warsaw Pact allies.[24]

At the very onset of the crisis, therefore, Khrushchev raised the conflict over Berlin to a test of strength between the USSR and the Western
powers, with the threat of force if Soviet demands were not met.

Three days before Khrushchev's speech Secretary Dulles had reaffirmed the determination of the United States to defend its rights in West
Berlin, "if need be by military force."[25] Basic U.S. strategy in Berlin thus
continued to be reliance on the U.S. strategic deterrent. Khrushchev's
speech on November 10 made it necessary for U.S. policymakers to re-
define this strategy and to spell out its implications. With regard to
Khrushchev's speech, Eisenhower claims to have "at once recognized the
dangerous potential of the Russian declaration," but he promptly decided
that no reply was called for. Militarily, in his judgment, "our forces in the
city were token garrisons only. Berlin's actual defense lay only in the
West's publicly expressed intention that to defend it we would, if necessary, resort to war."[26] Underlying Eisenhower's decision was the belief
that increased expenditures on armaments would endanger the economic
stability of the United States. Eisenhower was, in fact, convinced that a
major goal of the USSR in precipitating a crisis over Berlin was to provoke the United States into unnecessary arms outlays.[27] In addition, Eisenhower thought that "too much eagerness to counter Khrushchev's statement would give the impression that our government was edgy. . . . So,
for the moment, we said nothing."[28]

24. *Documents on Germany, 1944–1970*, p. 353.
25. Senate Committee on Foreign Relations, *Documents on Germany, 1944–
1961* (GPO, 1961), p. 339. Dulles's assertion of U.S. rights in Berlin was made in
rebuttal to Walter Ulbricht's claim to the entire city for the GDR.
26. Dwight D. Eisenhower, *The White House Years: Waging Peace, 1956–1961*
(Doubleday, 1965), p. 330.
27. Ibid., p. 336.
28. Ibid., p. 331.

Thus the U.S. decision not to respond promptly to Khrushchev's November 10 challenge, either verbally or with limited force, was a reasoned one based on a consistent long-term evaluation of U.S.-Soviet relations. This is not, of course, to say that the decision was necessarily a wise one; from the standpoint of deterrence strategy, Alexander George and Richard Smoke make the cogent charge that "the administration apparently did not recognize that the *absence* of an American reaction to the November 10 speech was more likely to have a negative effect on the Kremlin's image of the U.S. than the presence of an appropriate and expectable reaction."[29]

Three days before Khrushchev's speech Soviet fighter planes attacked U.S. reconnaissance planes in two separate incidents, one over the Baltic Sea, the other over the Sea of Japan. The U.S. planes, according to a note sent to the USSR on November 13, "withheld fire and did not in any way menace the Soviet aircraft."[30] Although there is no evidence directly linking the November 7 plane incidents to the Berlin crisis, the correspondence generated as a result of the incidents added a note of tension to U.S.-Soviet relations in the period. Furthermore, the plane incidents provided an opportunity for the United States to draw a line beyond which it would not refrain from the use of force in response to future Soviet attacks, and thus to some extent served as a counterweight to the administration's decision to ignore Khrushchev's challenge to the Western position in Berlin.

On November 14 the USSR took its first overt step toward tightening the noose around West Berlin by detaining three U.S. Army trucks on the autobahn just outside Berlin. General Lauris Norstad, the U.S. commander-in-chief in Europe, informed Washington that unless instructed otherwise he intended to send a convoy along the Berlin-Helmstedt autobahn as a test. If the Soviets held up the convoy and if verbal protests did not secure its prompt release, Norstad planned to use the "minimum force necessary" to extricate it.[31]

In the Defense Department, meanwhile, General Maxwell Taylor was at work on a contingency plan for the defense of Berlin by conventional means.[32] U.S. and NATO military planners, however, were overruled by

29. George and Smoke, *Deterrence in American Foreign Policy*, p. 406. Italics in the original.
30. *Department of State Bulletin*, vol. 39 (December 8, 1958), p. 909.
31. Eisenhower, *Waging Peace*, p. 331.
32. *New York Times*, November 13, 1958. For Taylor's defense of his contingency planning for West Berlin, see his *Uncertain Trumpet*, p. 8.

Eisenhower on the grounds that the proposed action ". . . should first be made known to our allies. To give time for consultation an order was sent temporarily suspending all convoys to Berlin."[33]

The November incident, seen as a probing operation by the USSR, fits neatly into Herman Kahn's "escalation ladder," corresponding to his Rung 7, " 'legal harassments'—retortions."[34] If Soviet action was in fact designed to test Western willingness to use force to defend its rights, George and Smoke draw the appropriate deduction: "With hindsight it is difficult to avoid the conclusion that the Soviet leaders, possibly surprised at the lack of an initial Western reaction, were dipping a second toe in the water."[35]

If the USSR was taking an inclusive view of its relations with the United States, however, the firm tone of the U.S. note of November 13 regarding the November 7 plane incidents should have served as an indication of the limits beyond which it would be dangerous to press the United States. From the very outset, therefore, the Berlin crisis of 1958–59 was circumscribed in its possible ramifications, lending force to Kahn's view that the crisis was "more ostensible than real."[36] Conscious of U.S. strategic superiority, and never completely certain that the United States could be relied on not to use its power, Khrushchev and his colleagues moved cautiously, testing each stage before advancing to the next one and leaving themselves plenty of room for maneuver or retreat if the United States and its allies showed any intention of forcibly resisting Soviet demands. It was at the exploratory stage, probably, that the use of limited force by the Western powers had the best prospects of heading off a full-scale international conflict over Berlin. Yet it would be unrealistic to censure too severely the Western policymakers who ruled out the use of limited force at this point. Until the full extent of the Soviet demands was known, Western leaders felt they must move cautiously, avoiding the twin dangers of panicking or overreacting.

Soviet Pressure on West Germany

West German Chancellor Konrad Adenauer, a focal point of Khrushchev's attack, was far less complacent about the Soviet threat than was the Eisenhower administration. Two days after Khrushchev's November

33. Eisenhower, *Waging Peace,* p. 331.
34. Kahn, *On Escalation,* p. 72.
35. George and Smoke, *Deterrence in American Foreign Policy,* p. 406.
36. Kahn, *On Escalation,* p. 54.

10 speech, without awaiting the U.S. response, the West German government warned the USSR against "any unilateral renunciation" of the international agreements on the four-power status of Berlin.[37]

To exert pressure on West Germany the USSR on November 20 sent its ambassador in Bonn, A. A. Smirnov, to inform Adenauer of Soviet plans. Deeply shaken, Adenauer on the next day sent British Prime Minister Harold Macmillan an urgent message stating that Smirnov had "informed him [Adenauer] brutally that his government intended 'to liquidate the occupation statutes concerning Berlin.' " Convinced that "the Soviet Union is resolved to make the Berlin question a test for the policy of the free world," Adenauer asked Macmillan to use British influence in Moscow "with a view to drawing the attention of the Soviet government to the fateful consequences of such a decision." In response, Macmillan sent Khrushchev a message on November 22 warning him that "the British government have every intention of upholding their rights in Berlin which are soundly based."[38]

With surprising inconsistency, however, the West German government chose just this moment to sign a supplementary trade agreement with the GDR, thus ". . . inadvertently confirming [Dulles's] view that one could do business with the East Germans in strictly operational terms without granting them diplomatic recognition."[39]

Thus, in the absence of strong leadership by the United States, other members of the Western alliance were responding to the Soviet challenge in various and uncoordinated ways. The results, coupled with the U.S. action in halting convoys to Berlin, could only encourage the USSR to take the next step up the escalation ladder. What Eisenhower himself characterized as a "low-key" announcement on November 21, to the effect that the United States' "firm intentions in West Berlin remain unchanged,"[40] did nothing to alter this perception.

A final stimulus to Soviet boldness, if any were needed, was provided by Dulles at a news conference on November 26 in which he gave a comprehensive analysis of his perception of Soviet goals in Berlin. These Dulles saw as limited to increased recognition and stature for the GDR.[41]

37. Keesing's Contemporary Archives, *Germany and East Europe since 1945* (Scribners, 1973), p. 154.
38. Macmillan, *Riding the Storm*, pp. 571, 572.
39. Schick, *Berlin Crisis*, p. 33.
40. Eisenhower, *Waging Peace*, pp. 331–32.
41. *Department of State Bulletin*, vol. 39 (December 15, 1958), p. 953. See also Schick, *Berlin Crisis*, p. 33.

Dulles indicated that the United States would be willing to deal with East German authorities as agents of the USSR in supervising Western access to Berlin. As to the possible use of force to defend Western rights, Dulles dismissed the question as "academic," since he saw no indication that the USSR or East Germany intended to impede Western access to Berlin.[42]

The Soviet Notes of November 27

Seventeen days after Khrushchev's November 10 speech the USSR formally opened its campaign on Berlin with notes to the three Western allies calling for a change in the status of West Berlin. In the notes the USSR announced that it regarded as "null and void" the wartime agreements concerning the occupation of Germany and the administration of Greater Berlin; that it intended to transfer its functions under these agreements, including control of Western access rights, to the GDR; that while it preferred to see West Berlin reunited with the eastern sector of the city and established as the capital of the GDR, it was willing to accept a "free city" status for West Berlin, under four-power guarantee and with the possibility of UN support; and that while it would continue to respect Western rights in the city for six months, if the Western powers had failed to accept Soviet demands at the end of that period, it would turn its functions in the city over to the GDR.[43]

Implicit in the notes was the threat of force if the Western powers failed to accept Soviet demands. The onus of initiating the use of force, however, was placed on the Western powers: If they refused to negotiate new access agreements with the GDR or refused to accept the "free city" proposal, it would be they, the Soviet notes asserted, who would thereby reveal their "intention to resort to force and drag the world into a war over Berlin." For its part the USSR asserted that any aggressive action against the GDR, a signatory to the Warsaw Pact, "will be regarded by all its participants as an act of aggression against them all and will immediately cause appropriate retaliation."[44] The USSR thus made shrewd use of the distinction between force and violence, as George and Smoke point out.[45]

42. *Department of State Bulletin,* vol. 39 (December 15, 1958), p. 953.
43. For the full text of the Soviet note to the United States, see *Department of State Bulletin,* vol. 40 (January 19, 1959), pp. 81–89.
44. Ibid., p. 88.
45. George and Smoke, *Deterrence in American Foreign Policy,* p. 439.

By its notes of November 27 the USSR presented a series of non-negotiable demands to the Western powers involving the surrender of their rights in West Berlin, under a six-month deadline and with the implied military power of the USSR and its allies to back up the demands. The notes thus raised the struggle over Berlin to the level of a test of strength between the USSR and the Western alliance. Soviet strategy in the crisis, as George and Smoke point out, was based on the implied allegation—erroneous, as both the Soviet leaders and those of the United States knew—that the USSR enjoyed not merely local military superiority in Berlin but strategic superiority over the United States and its allies.[46] In this situation, a refusal by the Western powers to use limited force to defend their rights in Berlin could be hailed by Soviet spokesmen as proof of their claim to strategic superiority, even though the West's restraint might be, and in fact was, motivated by other considerations entirely. Thus the West was put in a position from which the only way it could effectively challenge exaggerated and unsubstantiated Soviet claims was to demonstrate a willingness to use limited force, even at the risk of escalating the crisis. In their approach to this dilemma the two U.S. administrations involved, that of Eisenhower in 1958–59 and Kennedy in 1961, took diametrically opposed attitudes toward the use of limited force.

The Impact of Fiscal Considerations on U.S. Policy

It is frequently assumed by writers on U.S. foreign policy that the Eisenhower administration's decision not to use limited force in the 1958–59 crisis was dictated by conceptions based ultimately on Dulles's foreign policy strategy.[47] An equally potent influence in shaping U.S. views, however, was Eisenhower's determination to maintain fiscal stability and his belief that a major Soviet goal in precipitating the crisis was to force the United States into additional military expenditures that would unbalance the budget. During the opening phase of the 1958–59 crisis, when the USSR was cautiously feeling its way, Eisenhower was making a determined effort to keep the lid on a different kind of escalation—that of government expenditures, including those for the armed services. Thus, on November 19, Eisenhower instructed all heads of federal departments

46. Ibid., p. 396.
47. This viewpoint, for example, characterizes Schick, *Berlin Crisis*.

and agencies to live within the reduced budgets assigned to them for fiscal 1960, beginning in July 1959.[48]

In pursuit of this policy Eisenhower invited the Joint Chiefs of Staff and the armed forces service secretaries to a stag dinner at the White House on December 3, at which Treasury Secretary Clinton Anderson delivered "a very able statement concerning the importance of a balanced budget and a stable dollar." Army Chief of Staff General Maxwell D. Taylor, while accepting the established monetary ceiling on the defense budget, argued that even within that limitation the country was not getting "the most defense for our money." His effort was unavailing, however: "In the end the 1960 budget followed the same pattern as the former ones."[49] At year's end, Hanson W. Baldwin, the *New York Times*'s military specialist, reported that "cut-back, scale-down and cancellation are the order of the day" in the armed forces.[50]

Thus the decision by the Eisenhower administration not to use limited force in the opening phase of the crisis was shaped primarily by fiscal considerations based on a long-term view of the U.S.-Soviet relationship, in the context of which the tension over Berlin was regarded as a factor of temporary and secondary importance. Instead of U.S. policy in the crisis being dictated primarily by the foreign policy views of Dulles, it would be more accurate to say that Dulles's policies were tailored to fit within the restraints imposed by the fiscal policies of Eisenhower and Anderson, just as the Joint Chiefs of Staff and the defense service chiefs were expected to carry out their functions within the restraints dictated by the budgetary limitations set by Eisenhower and Anderson.[51]

The Impact of Domestic Politics on Soviet Policy

At a time when the policies of the United States were being strongly influenced by domestic considerations, the foreign policy of the USSR was being shaped in part by alterations in the power relationships within the

48. *New York Times,* November 23, 1958.
49. Taylor, *Uncertain Trumpet,* pp. 70–71.
50. *New York Times,* December 30, 1958.
51. The chairman of the Joint Chiefs, General Nathan F. Twining, accepted the budgetary limitations called for by the Eisenhower administration. In his book, *Neither Liberty nor Safety: A Hard Look at U.S. Military Policy and Strategy* (Holt, Rinehart and Winston, 1966), p. 119, Twining asserts that the United States *did* possess military flexibility, even in the era of massive retaliation. Unfortunately, he does not comment directly on the administration's decision to avoid the use of limited force at the outset of the Berlin crisis of 1958–59.

ruling Communist party and the Soviet government. Just as the USSR was making the opening moves in its Berlin campaign of late 1958, a major shift occurred in Khrushchev's position within the ruling Presidium which altered his personal priorities and goals in a way that had a direct bearing on the outcome of the crisis.

In November 1958, when he was just beginning to build tension over Berlin, Khrushchev had still not fully won his struggle against the "anti-party group" which had tried to unseat him in June 1957. At that time only the three ringleaders in the anti-Khrushchev coalition—Molotov, Malenkov, and Kaganovich—had been expelled from the Presidium, leaving a number of others in the Presidium who had supported the "anti-party group" but whose opposition to Khrushchev was not publicly disclosed at that time. One of these still undisclosed opponents of Khrushchev was Nikolai A. Bulganin, who had held the post of Soviet premier from February 1955 until March 1958, when he yielded it to Khrushchev. He retained his seat on the Presidium until September 1958. Even at that late date, however, he still balked at publicly admitting his support for the anti-Khrushchev coalition in 1957. It was not until December 18, 1958, at a plenum of the party Central Committee, that Bulganin finally confessed to his part in the "anti-party conspiracy."[52] The unmasking of Bulganin, a major triumph for Khrushchev, came shortly after a momentous change in the Soviet government. On December 9 control of the secret police (KGB, Committee for State Security) was taken from General Ivan A. Serov, a long-time associate of Khrushchev and a veteran secret police official; two weeks later it was announced that the vacant post had been assigned to Alexander N. Shelepin, a party functionary whose career had been mainly in the Soviet youth organization (Komsomol), in which capacity he had provided valuable support for Khrushchev before and after the June 1957 showdown.[53]

The appointment of Shelepin and the unmasking of Bulganin were accompanied by a third event that bears the unmistakable imprint of Khrushchev's style. On December 17 the Soviet government abruptly and without the usual diplomatic formalities requested a U.S. visa for Deputy Premier Anastas I. Mikoyan, generally regarded as a close associate of Khrushchev.[54] Mikoyan's visit to the United States, which took place

52. *New York Times,* December 19, 1958.
53. For Serov's dismissal, see *New York Times,* December 9, 1958. Shelepin's appointment is reported in *New York Times,* December 26, 1958.
54. *New York Times,* December 19, 1958.

in January 1959, proved to be the opening move in an ultimately successful campaign by Khrushchev to obtain an invitation to visit the United
States himself. His efforts to achieve this goal ran parallel with and at
times intersected the Soviet campaign on Berlin, adding a note of com-
plexity to Soviet policy and in the end decisively affecting Soviet strategy
in the crisis.

Development of the Sino-Soviet Conflict

Khrushchev's sudden decision to angle for an invitation to visit the
United States must be seen in the light of the growing tension between the
Soviet leadership and the Chinese Communists. The conflict between
Moscow and Peking played a major role in shaping Khrushchev's policies
toward the United States, and thus constituted one of the determining fac-
tors in the Berlin crises.

A turning point in the Sino-Soviet conflict was Khrushchev's decision
not to honor a secret Soviet-Chinese agreement of October 1957, under
which the USSR was obligated to provide China with assistance in the development of an atomic bomb. Although the breaching of the 1957 agreement was not publicly disclosed until 1963, it was implied in Khrushchev's
opening speech to the Twenty-first Congress of the CPSU on January 27,
1959, when he called for the establishment of a nuclear-free "zone of
peace" in the Far East.[55]

Another factor in cooling Soviet-Chinese amity was the challenge to
Soviet doctrinal supremacy offered by Chinese development of the so-
called people's communes in the summer of 1958, and the claims made by
the Chinese that they had hit on a short-cut to the building of a socialist
society which had eluded the Soviet Communists. It was in part because of
the need to rebut this challenge that the USSR decided to stage a special
party congress, the Twenty-first, in order to reestablish Soviet claims to
doctrinal supremacy.[56]

The tendency toward an estrangement between Moscow and Peking

---

55. Leo Gruliow and others, eds., *Current Soviet Policies III: The Documentary
Record of the Extraordinary 21st Congress of the Communist Party of the Soviet
Union* (Columbia University Press, 1960), p. 59, citing *Pravda*, January 28, 1959.
William E. Griffith, *The Sino-Soviet Rift* (MIT Press, 1964), p. 12, dates the can-
cellation of the 1957 USSR-PRC agreement on atomic aid in June 1959, but the
Khrushchev speech cited shows that the decision had been taken well before that
time.
56. Linden, *Khrushchev and the Soviet Leadership*, pp. 82–85.

helped exacerbate existing conflicts in the Soviet leadership and thereby introduced an element of ambiguity and uncertainty into the formulation of Soviet policy. Khrushchev, increasingly critical of the Chinese, hesitated between two opposite lines for Soviet policy toward the United States: on the one hand, he felt the need for a resounding symbolic victory over the United States that would validate his handling of Soviet foreign policy, solidify his internal position, and permit him to redirect Soviet investment priorities away from armaments and heavy industry toward agriculture, consumer goods, and the chemical industry; on the other hand, he was attracted by the prospect of a deal with the United States that would reduce tensions and allow the USSR to lower its expenditures for defense.

The leaders of the internal opposition, of whom Frol Kozlov and Mikhail Suslov are the most readily identifiable, maintained unremitting pressure on Khrushchev to adopt a hostile stance toward the United States and its allies and to moderate or end entirely the escalating conflict with Peking.[57] Sharing the views of the internal opposition were several officials who helped shape Soviet policy during the Berlin crises, notably Soviet Foreign Minister Andrei Gromyko and Soviet Ambassador Mikhail Menshikov.[58] Much of the Soviet hard line on Berlin in the period 1958–59 can be attributed directly to Gromyko, who was a far from negligible factor in the formulation of Soviet foreign policy, contrary to the views of Eisenhower and others who regarded him as a mere mouthpiece of Khrushchev's policies.[59]

57. A full-scale study of the role of the internal opposition in shaping Soviet foreign policy in the period 1958–60 has not yet been carried out. My 1967 article, "America, China, and the Hydra-headed Opposition," was designed to provide the basic framework for such an analysis. See n. 23 above.

58. The view that Gromyko and Menshikov were hard-liners on policy toward the United States is based on the analysis of data from their careers, actions, and statements over the period 1956–64.

59. In March 1959 Eisenhower received a cable from Llewellyn Thompson, U.S. ambassador in Moscow, predicting that if Gromyko represented the USSR in the forthcoming Geneva conference of foreign ministers, "We could expect little progress." Eisenhower, *Waging Peace*, p. 359. Eisenhower assumed that this was because "apparently Gromyko did not enjoy the confidence of Khrushchev to the extent that he was empowered by the Kremlin to negotiate seriously on important issues; he was little more than a messenger and one, I often thought, whose every word and action, including his bad manners, were dictated by his Soviet master." Ibid. Even when Gromyko candidly disclosed during the Geneva conference of foreign ministers that a Soviet demand for a one-year termination of Western rights in Berlin had been made on his own initiative, Eisenhower's reaction was one of tolerant amusement. Ibid., p. 400.

Further Soviet Warnings and U.S. Responses

On December 11, 1958, the Soviet news agency Tass issued a statement warning that "any attempt to force a way into Berlin" by military means would be regarded as an attack on the GDR which would bring the Warsaw Pact into action, with the possibility of nuclear war.[60] The Tass statement was no doubt issued in response to a flurry of Western press reports that the United States and NATO planned to send an armed truck convoy over the autobahn to West Berlin in order to test Soviet intentions and emphasize Western determination to remain in the city.[61]

In the face of the top-level U.S. decision early in the crisis *not* to use limited force, however, Western military commanders had not merely to sidetrack their contingency plans but to play down even those actions that might have been interpreted by Soviet leaders as meaningful displays of limited force. Thus, when the U.S. garrison in West Berlin was reinforced by six M-59 armored personnel carriers toward the end of December 1958, army spokesmen denied that the move had any connection with the Soviet demands.[62]

Toward the end of January 1959 Eisenhower convened a meeting of Defense and State Department officials to discuss the Berlin situation. By this time the general outlines of the Soviet position had been clarified, though no essential modifications had been introduced into the position announced in the notes of November 27. Mikoyan, after his visit to the United States, had indicated some flexibility in the six-month deadline for Western acquiescence in the demand for "open city" status for West Berlin,[63] and the details of the Soviet position had been drawn more precisely in a draft peace treaty with the GDR, produced on January 10, together with a note restating the Soviet position.[64] These documents indicated no letup in Soviet pressure to force the Western powers out of Berlin, with or without a six-month deadline.

By late January 1959, therefore, the Eisenhower administration realized that the Soviet challenge was not merely to the precarious Western position in Berlin, but extended to the entire strategic relationship between the USSR and the United States, and that the administration must there-

60. Barraclough, *Survey of International Affairs, 1956–1958*, p. 586.
61. *New York Times*, November 25, 1958; *New York Herald Tribune*, November 21, 1958; *Washington Post*, December 19, 1958; Schick, *Berlin Crisis*, p. 12.
62. *New York Times*, December 30, 1958.
63. *New York Times*, January 25, 1959.
64. Texts in *Documents on Germany, 1944–1970*, pp. 390–411.

fore draw up equally comprehensive plans to meet the Soviet challenge. In Eisenhower's words,

> To show the Soviets that we meant business, the Chiefs of Staff were instructed to send sufficient replacements to Europe to fill out the rosters of all our military units. . . . This routine movement of replacements would be done quietly but quickly; it was certain that the Soviets would detect the movements and would probably interpret them correctly as evidence of our determination.[65]

At this point, however, a serious difference of opinion emerged between Dulles and the military chiefs. Dulles, convinced of the need to marshal the forces of world public opinion in support of Western rights in Berlin, felt it was still too early to sanction the limited use of force. Eisenhower supported Dulles, but on military grounds, considering that "one division was far too weak to fight its way through to Berlin and far more than necessary to be a mere show of force or evidence of determination."[66]

By the time of the meeting in late January, however, Eisenhower was no longer as reluctant to use limited force as he had been earlier, and the meeting thus resulted in a distinct hardening of U.S. policy, reflected in a six-point plan which Eisenhower describes as follows:

> The plan, as I approved it at the meeting, included these steps: (a) A refusal to acquiesce in any substitution of East Germans for Soviet officials in checking the Western occupying powers' movement to and from Berlin. . . . (b) A decision to begin quiet military preparations in West Germany and Berlin prior to May 27, sufficient to be detected by Soviet intelligence but not sufficient to create public alarm; (c) Should there be any substitution of East German officials for Soviets, a small convoy with armed protection would attempt to go through, and if this convoy were stopped, the effect [*sic:* error for effort?] would be discontinued and the probe would fire only if fired upon; (d) Transit would then be suspended and pressure would be brought to bear on the Soviets by publicizing the blockade and taking the matter to the United Nations Security Council and, if necessary, to the General Assembly. In these circumstances our further military preparations would be intensified by observable means such as the evacuation of dependents from West Berlin and possibly from all Germany; (e) In the event that this moral and other pressure was not sufficient, use of additional force would be subject to governmental decision; (f) We would at once attempt to bring about a foreign ministers' meeting with the Soviet Union to be held about the middle of April.[67]

In effect, then, the late January plan outlined a series of graduated steps up the escalation ladder in which the use of limited force would be sanctioned, but carefully circumscribed with safeguards to ensure against

65. Eisenhower, *Waging Peace,* p. 340.
66. Ibid., pp. 340–41.
67. Ibid., p. 341.

too rapid or uncontrolled an escalation, and with due attention to Dulles's insistence on the need to educate world public opinion as to the basic issues in the conflict underlying the apparently superficial technicalities. The hardened U.S. position was almost immediately reflected in a firmer U.S. response to a new Soviet challenge. On February 2 the USSR caused a tie-up on the Berlin-Helmstedt autobahn by demanding, for the first time, the right to inspect the contents of a U.S. military convoy. When the noncommissioned officer in charge of the convoy refused, Soviet troops forcibly detained the convoy. In accordance with the plan drawn up at the late January meeting, the United States thereupon sent the USSR a stiff note characterizing the Soviet action as "a clear violation of the United States' right of access to Berlin," and calling on the Soviet government not only to permit the convoy to proceed unchecked, but "to ensure against a repetition of the incident."[68] To dramatize the incident and emphasize U.S. firmness, Eisenhower called a special press conference, at which he repeated the U.S. charge. Soviet response was quick: "Three and one half hours after the American note was delivered in Moscow the convoy was released."[69]

The convoy incident brought into the open a serious divergence between U.S. and British policies. Faced by a similar Soviet demand for inspection of a military convoy, British authorities promptly complied.[70] That this difference at the local level reflected real differences at the top was made plain when Dulles conferred with Macmillan in London on February 4. Informed by Dulles of the substance of the late January meeting and its decisions, Macmillan interpreted the report to mean that Dulles had *"completely abandoned"* earlier U.S. contingency plans for the use of limited but substantial force in probing operations on the autobahn to Berlin.[71]

Macmillan's Trip to the Soviet Union

Critical of what he regarded as excessive U.S. willingness to contemplate the use of force, and apprehensive lest the unresolved crisis over Berlin suddenly escalate into a more serious conflict, Macmillan made a

68. Text of the U.S. note in *Department of State Bulletin,* vol. 40 (February 23, 1959), pp. 271–72.
69. Smith, *Defense of Berlin,* p. 197.
70. Geoffrey Barraclough, *Survey of International Affairs, 1959–1960* (Oxford University Press, 1964), p. 28n.
71. Macmillan, *Riding the Storm,* pp. 587–88. Italics in the original.

bid in mid-January for his own and British leadership of the Western alliance by proposing that he and British Foreign Secretary Selwyn Lloyd go to Moscow in an effort to steer the crisis away from the danger of military confrontation and toward negotiation.

Macmillan first informed Washington of his intention to visit the USSR on January 20 and received a warm and prompt response, the Americans expressing "complete confidence" in the British leader.[72] The visit was formally announced on February 5, and opened with Macmillan's arrival in Moscow on February 21.

Although approved in advance by the Americans, Macmillan's trip disclosed new differences of opinion within the Western alliance. When Dulles paid a visit to French President Charles de Gaulle after leaving London he found the French leader unenthusiastic about the proposed trip, which he feared would encourage the Soviet leaders to believe the Western powers were eager to open negotiations before expiration of the six-month deadline imposed by the USSR.[73] Remembering the fateful role played in the genesis of World War II by French failure to oppose by force Hitler's reoccupation of the Rhineland in 1936, de Gaulle, in Eisenhower's words, "seemed to be prepared to use force a little more suddenly than we felt advisable."[74]

In his talks with de Gaulle, Dulles admitted there was a possibility that war might come if Khrushchev acted rashly, but he said the United States considered retention of its rights in West Berlin to be vital; efforts to negotiate with the Soviet leader were therefore essential in order to avert disaster. Before he left France, Dulles explained to senior American officials there his plan for a "political offensive" against the Communists in East Germany designed to recapture the initiative for the Western alliance and to make more effective use of the attractive power which West Germany had demonstrated in relation to the population of the GDR. As the ultimate payoff for such an "offensive," Dulles saw the weakening of Communist controls in the GDR and the undermining of Soviet power in Europe.[75] Surprisingly, Dulles seems not to have realized that East Germany and the USSR would not sit idly by while their position was being weakened by a massive population flow from East to West Germany. In a

72. Ibid., pp. 582–83.
73. *New York Times,* February 5, 1959.
74. Eisenhower, *Waging Peace,* p. 343.
75. Roscoe Drummond and Gaston Coblentz, *Duel at the Brink: John Foster Dulles' Command of American Power* (Doubleday, 1960), pp. 214, 215.

sense, Dulles's "political offensive" succeeded all too well: by encouraging East Germans to flee to the West it forced the GDR leaders to demand action by Moscow to protect their own interests and those of the USSR. There is thus a direct connection between Dulles's conception of West Germany as a "magnet" acting on East Germany and the Soviet campaign to force the Western powers out of West Berlin in order to end its availability as an escape route for dissatisfied citizens of the GDR.

Diplomatic Moves Preceding Khrushchev's Visit and the Foreign Ministers' Conference

Unbeknownst to the British, the movement toward high-level, bilateral Soviet-Western contacts was already under way by the time Macmillan formed his plan for visiting Moscow. The first indication that Khrushchev had developed a yearning to see the United States was the abrupt Soviet request for a visa for Mikoyan on December 17, 1958. Evidently, the report Mikoyan gave Khrushchev on his return was encouraging, for on February 5 Khrushchev pointedly raised the subject of his possible visit to the United States, and extended a broadly formulated invitation to Eisenhower to visit the USSR.[76]

Eisenhower lost no time in rebuffing this feeler. On the day after Khrushchev's speech White House press secretary Jim Hagerty announced that Eisenhower had no plans to visit the USSR, especially in view of the rather roundabout way in which the invitation had been extended. The statement nevertheless "left the door open in [the] event future developments would suggest a visit to the USSR in the cause of peace."[77] As to the possibility of Khrushchev visiting the United States, the statement on February 6 ignored it completely, just as Eisenhower did when the subject came up at his February 10 press conference.[78] For the moment, therefore, Khrushchev's wish had been frustrated, but he had planted a seed in the minds of Eisenhower and his advisers that would eventually germinate.

THE TRAWLER INCIDENTS. Rapid and unimpeded cable communications between Washington and the Western capitals—London, Paris, and Bonn—was an essential requirement for maintenance of a working unity

---

76. *Current Soviet Policies III,* p. 203, citing *Pravda,* February 6, 1959.
77. Eisenhower, *Waging Peace,* pp. 343–44. For the text of the statement, see *Department of State Bulletin,* vol. 40 (March 2, 1959), p. 297.
78. Eisenhower, *Waging Peace,* p. 344.

within the alliance. It was therefore a matter of considerable concern when a Soviet trawler, the *Novorossiisk,* was discovered engaged in deep-water grappling operations in an area where a series of breaks in the transatlantic cables had been occurring. On February 26, after several incidents in the period February 21–25, the U.S. Navy put a boarding party onto the *Novorossiisk* to investigate whether its crew had violated the 1884 Convention for the Protection of Submarine Cables, to which the USSR was a party, and two days later the United States sent the USSR a cool but firm aide mémoire reporting the Navy's action.

In its reply of March 4 the Soviet government protested the U.S. action and asserted that information in its possession showed that the *Novorossiisk* had "caused no damage of any kind" to the transatlantic cables. The note then went on to charge that "the detention of the Soviet trawler was undertaken with provocative purposes," including "an attempt to strain Soviet-American relations." The incident was formally closed with a U.S. note of March 23 rejecting the Soviet protest and setting forth the facts in the case as reported by U.S. naval personnel, which it charged added up to "a strong presumption" that the *Novorossiisk* had in fact violated the 1884 Convention. The note concluded with the taciturn warning that the U.S. government "will continue to fulfill its international obligations with regard to the protection of submarine cables."[79]

THE AGREEMENT TO HOLD A CONFERENCE OF FOREIGN MINISTERS. It was a longstanding policy of Eisenhower to refuse to attend a summit meeting until a conference of foreign ministers had made substantial progress toward the settlement of outstanding international problems, including Berlin. An invitation to attend a foreign ministers' conference was presented in a note from the United States to the USSR on February 16, 1959, together with the laconic warning that the Western powers "reserve the right to uphold by all appropriate means their communications with their sectors of Berlin."[80]

The British tended to regard U.S. insistence on successful preparatory work at the foreign ministers' level as an unnecessary complication. Strongly convinced that only Khrushchev could negotiate meaningfully

79. Texts of U.S.-Soviet communications appear in *Department of State Bulletin,* vol. 40 (April 20, 1959), pp. 555–58. Eisenhower calls the Soviet Union action "conceivably an accident," but labels it "suspicious." Eisenhower, *Waging Peace,* p. 356.

80. *Department of State Bulletin,* vol. 40 (March 9, 1959), p. 333; Gillian King, ed., *Documents on International Affairs, 1959* (Oxford University Press, 1963), pp. 9–11.

for the USSR, Macmillan considered the American position a regrettable and time-consuming formality. Unwilling to challenge the American position head-on, however, Macmillan in his talks with Khrushchev in Moscow spoke in favor of a conference of foreign ministers but with the clear implication that he really favored the convocation of a summit meeting. Since there was a meeting of minds with the Soviet leader on this point, it is not surprising that the USSR in a note to the Western powers on March 2 accepted the U.S. proposal for a foreign ministers' conference. Balancing this concession, however, was an insistence that the agenda of the proposed conference conform to the position taken by the USSR in its November 27 deadline note and subsequent statements, including acceptance of the "free city" status for Berlin and the conclusion of a German peace treaty. In an apparent concession, however, the note relaxed the six-month deadline by suggesting that the conference should meet in April and should last "not more than two or three months."[81] Like earlier Soviet communications the March 2 note contained a strong warning against the use of force by the Western powers.

A different approach was reflected in the Soviet-British joint communiqué issued the following day at the conclusion of Macmillan's visit to Moscow. At British request, this document included a reference to the possibility of "some method of limitation of forces and weapons, both conventional and nuclear, in an agreed area of Europe, coupled with an appropriate system of inspection."[82] Like the Rapacki Plan, which it resembled, this aspiration was doomed to remain unfulfilled.

Renewed Debate in the United States over the Limited Use of Force

Despite Eisenhower's efforts to avoid the use of limited force in Berlin, the problem refused to go away. At a press conference on February 25 Eisenhower spoke of undefined "plans" for defending Berlin, implying that the Western powers had some undisclosed alternative to "massive retaliation."[83] On March 5, however, Secretary of Defense McElroy, in rejecting the army's request for an increase of conventional forces, de-

81. Text of the Soviet note in *Department of State Bulletin,* vol. 40 (April 13, 1959), pp. 508–11. See also Schick, *Berlin Crisis,* p. 59; Smith, *Defense of Berlin,* p. 198; Eisenhower, *Waging Peace,* p. 345; Macmillan, *Riding the Storm,* pp. 623–24.
82. King, *Documents on International Affairs, 1959,* p. 12.
83. *New York Times,* February 26, 1959.

clared that it would be impossible to limit a war over Berlin, and raised the specter of a preventive war by the West if the USSR was perceived to be preparing an attack.[84]

In a March 7 *Saturday Evening Post* article, former Secretary of State Dean Acheson urged the administration not only to prepare contingency plans for the defense of Berlin, which he characterized as crucial to the Western position in Europe, but also to mobilize the army and initiate a crash program for the production of ICBM's in order to head off an anticipated Soviet lead.[85]

In an effort to clarify the administration's position on the use of limited force, Eisenhower held several meetings with congressional leaders on March 6, at which he endeavored to convince the doubters that the administration's policy of reducing the armed forces by 30,000 men "in the midst of a critical period" was sound from the long-range point of view. Eisenhower admitted that war might result if the administration was miscalculating, but he assured the congressional representatives that even in that case the United States "had the courage and the means to follow through successfully." He ruled out completely any effort to match Soviet forces in central Europe and said nothing about the use of limited force to defend West Berlin.[86]

Still the critics of the administration refused to be silent, and at a press conference on March 11 Eisenhower made another attempt to explain his position, prompting Morton Halperin to remark that "it was perhaps in Berlin . . . that the policy of trying to defend local areas by strategic retaliatory threats was most in evidence. The Eisenhower administration, in effect, seemed to rule out the possibility of defending Berlin by ground action."[87]

Budgetary considerations still, as earlier in the crisis, underlay Eisenhower's opposition to the use of limited force; the *New York Times* reported his position as being that "even if Congress appropriates increases for conventional forces he would not expend the appropriations."[88]

The subject came up again at a press conference on March 12 when

---

84. Barraclough, *Survey of International Affairs, 1959–1960*, p. 22; Schick, *Berlin Crisis*, p. 52, citing *Christian Science Monitor*, March 9, 1959.

85. Dean Acheson, "Wishing Won't Hold Berlin," *Saturday Evening Post* (March 7, 1959), p. 30–31, 85–86.

86. Eisenhower, *Waging Peace*, pp. 348–49.

87. Halperin, *Limited War in the Nuclear Age*, p. 23.

88. *New York Times*, March 12, 1959.

Eisenhower said, "We are certainly not going to fight a ground war in Europe. What good would it do to send a few more thousand or indeed even a few divisions of troops to Europe?" But when asked directly if the United States was prepared to use nuclear weapons if necessary to defend West Berlin, Eisenhower hedged, finally admitting that "destruction is not a good police force."[89]

Dissatisfaction with the administration's policies was not slow to appear, both in the Pentagon, where General Taylor voiced approval of Acheson's call for the strengthening of conventional forces, and at NATO headquarters, where General Norstad asked for supplemental forces to meet the "deadline crisis."[90]

In an attempt to calm the mounting storm Eisenhower delivered a television address to the American people on March 16, providing a full-scale review of U.S. policy and its long-term goals. Once again he re-affirmed U.S. determination to maintain its links with West Berlin, but he ruled out any move to strengthen U.S. conventional forces, claiming that existing U.S. strategic power gave the nation the capacity "to rapidly apply necessary force to any area of trouble."[91]

Counterbalancing this strong emphasis on U.S. strategic power, Eisenhower stressed the administration's willingness to negotiate with the USSR, both at the foreign ministers' level and at the summit. It was the latter component of the speech, far more than the emphasis on U.S. military power, that caught the public mood of the moment. The Berlin crisis was about to enter a phase of negotiations in which the actual employment or threat of force would seem out of place. Before agreement was reached on negotiations, however, there was a last flare-up of tension.

THE HIGH-ALTITUDE PLANE INCIDENTS. Just as the USSR and the Western powers were slowly moving toward an agreement to hold a conference of foreign ministers on the Berlin question a new source of conflict was injected into Soviet-Western relations. On March 27 the U.S. Air Force, in a test of Soviet reactions, flew several large-capacity transport planes to Berlin above the customary 10,000-foot level. Soviet fighters buzzed the American planes, whereupon the United States asserted that it did not

---

89. *New York Times,* March 13, 1959.
90. *New York Times,* March 15, 1959, and *Washington Post,* March 15, 1959, p. 1. See also the testimony of General Taylor before the Preparedness Investigating Subcommittee of the Senate Committee on Armed Services on March 11, 1959, in *Major Defense Matters,* Hearings before the Senate Armed Services Committee, 86:1 (GPO, 1959), pt. 1.
91. *Department of State Bulletin,* vol. 40 (April 6, 1959), pp. 469–71.

recognize any limitation on its right to fly at any level in the air corridors to Berlin.[92]

The USSR protested the flights on April 1, and two days later Soviet fighter planes again buzzed U.S. planes in the air corridor.[93] On April 4 the USSR sent a further note, suggesting that the United States was attempting to sabotage the forthcoming conference of foreign ministers.[94]

Rejecting the Soviet protest on April 13, the United States repeated its high-altitude flights on April 15, this time from a base in northwest France. Despite renewed Soviet buzzing the operation was carried through successfully.[95] The net effect of the flights was to arm the Western powers with a new technical capability and thereby to strengthen their negotiating position at the conference of foreign ministers.[96] They also confirmed the U.S. position that no technical limitations could be imposed by the USSR on Western flights to Berlin.

PREPARING FOR THE GENEVA CONFERENCE. When the three Western ambassadors in Moscow presented the notes of March 26 proposing a conference of foreign ministers to meet in Geneva on May 11, they added a suggestion that unilateral actions by any of the four powers in the period of preparation for the conference should be avoided.[97] The USSR seized on the suggestion as the basis for a challenge to current Western military preparations. In a note of April 21 Moscow charged that the United States was trying to strengthen the nuclear armament of some of its NATO allies and to speed up plans to station U.S. rocket bases on their territory.[98] As evidence of its charges the Soviet note cited a recently concluded agreement for the stationing of U.S. rockets in Italy and the preparation of similar agreements with Greece, Turkey, and West Germany.[99] The Soviet

92. Schick, *Berlin Crisis*, p. 77.
93. Smith, *Defense of Berlin*, p. 201.
94. *Department of State Bulletin*, vol. 40 (May 4, 1959), p. 633.
95. Schick, *Berlin Crisis*, p. 77. Text of U.S. note of April 13, rejecting the Soviet protest, in *Department of State Bulletin*, vol. 40 (May 14, 1959), pp. 632–33.
96. Barraclough, *Survey of International Affairs, 1959–1960*, p. 28n, considers that "acceptance of the restriction would have made an airlift by high-flying jet supply aircraft impossible."
97. The Western ambassadors' suggestion is referred to in the Soviet note of April 21, 1959, *Department of State Bulletin*, vol. 40 (May 25, 1959), p. 742.
98. Ibid., p. 741.
99. On March 30, 1959, a State Department spokesman announced that final agreement had been reached between the United States and Italy on the delivery of intermediate-range ballistic missiles to the Italian armed forces, in accordance with a decision of the NATO heads of government in December 1957. U.S. Department of State, *American Foreign Policy: Current Documents, 1959* (GPO, 1963), p. 512.

charges were repeated at a meeting of the Warsaw Pact foreign ministers held in Warsaw on April 27–28.[100] In separate notes rebutting the Soviet charges, the NATO Council on May 7 and the U.S. government a day later justified the measures on the grounds of the danger of Soviet aggression.[101]

Stiff Western words were accompanied by stiff actions. By this time the steps to reinforce U.S. units in Germany, which had been decided on at the late January meeting, were no doubt being carried out. In addition, the U.S. Sixth Fleet at this time held a series of exercises designed to put it in a state of combat readiness. On May 9 the Sixth Fleet conducted exercises in the western Atlantic with two aircraft carriers ready for redeployment and the *Intrepid* and the *Franklin Delano Roosevelt* in an advance state of readiness; these were later joined by the *Saratoga* and the *Essex*.[102] Finally, on May 5, the United States and West Germany signed an "agreement on cooperation in the use of atomic energy for mutual defense purposes" at Bonn.[103]

By its statements and actions immediately before the opening of the Geneva conference of foreign ministers the Eisenhower administration thus deliberately brought to Soviet attention evidence of its military and naval power and of its readiness for action. The U.S.-West German agreement on atomic weapons, concluded less than a week before the opening of the conference, was a particularly pointed sign of the administration's lack of concern over Soviet sensibilities, since opposition to West Germany's access to nuclear weapons was widely believed to be a major motive behind the Soviet campaign in Berlin. It seems scarcely open to doubt that the Eisenhower administration took these steps on the eve of the foreign ministers' conference on Berlin with the deliberate intention of stressing U.S. strategic power.

The Geneva Conference of Foreign Ministers

The conference of foreign ministers opened in Geneva on May 11 and continued until August 5, with a recess between June 21 and July 13, for

100. Barraclough, *Survey of International Affairs, 1959–1960*, p. 29.

101. NATO Council note in *Department of State Bulletin*, vol. 40 (May 25, 1959), p. 739; U.S. note, ibid., pp. 740–41.

102. U.S. Department of the Navy, Naval Historical Center, Operational Archives, "Short of War" Documentation, Special List No. 2, and J. C. Donaldson, Jr., "Memorandum to Director of Naval History and Curator for the Navy Department" (August 20, 1969; processed).

103. Text in *American Foreign Policy: Current Documents, 1959*, pp. 644–48.

a total of twenty-five sessions. During the conference both the USSR and the Western powers presented comprehensive proposals on Berlin and Germany. As the conference dragged on, both sides introduced modifications into their original positions. At the end, however, no agreement had been reached, though there had been some narrowing of the gap between the two sides' positions and there were a few points on which their views coincided—for example, that the level of Western occupation forces in West Berlin should not be increased.

In an analysis of the use of force in the Berlin crises it is neither necessary nor desirable to provide a detailed account of the proceedings of the conference.[104] The questions to be asked are, first, whether the use or threat of force by either side played a significant part in producing the agreement to hold the conference, and second, whether the use or threat of force during the conference significantly affected its proceedings.

The answer to the first question would appear to be yes. British fear that if negotiations were not initiated before the May 27 deadline the USSR might resort to the use of force motivated Macmillan's visit to Moscow for bilateral talks with Khrushchev, and it was that visit, more than any other factor, that produced Soviet agreement to participate in a foreign ministers' conference. Here too force may have played a role: realization that the United States was neither intimidated by Soviet threats nor impressed by Soviet claims for strategic superiority may have induced Khrushchev to agree to a conference at the foreign minister level at a time when he had made it clear that he greatly preferred a summit conference of heads of state.

The conference was divided into two phases, from May 11 to June 21 and from July 13 to August 5. During the first phase, neither side made any overt moves of a military nature, and on May 19 the United States even canceled the projected transfer of a Marine battalion to West Berlin.[105]

Threats and counterthreats, however, there were in plenty during this first phase. On May 23 a Soviet note protested U.S. plans to provide

104. A full documentary record of the conference is given in Department of State, *Foreign Ministers Meeting, May–August 1959, Geneva* (1959). For comprehensive summaries of its proceedings, see Schick, *Berlin Crisis*, pp. 77–96; Barraclough, *Survey of International Affairs, 1959–1960*, pp. 30–39; Richard P. Stebbins, *The United States in World Affairs, 1959* (Harper, 1960), pp. 150–57.

105. Department of the Navy, Marine Corps Headquarters, Historical Division, *A Chronology of the United States Marine Corps*, vol. 3 (1971), p. 41.

atomic weapons to West Germany, a step that it warned would have "extremely dangerous consequences for the cause of peace."[106] The United States simply brushed aside this warning, asserting that it was not worth a formal reply. Between May 25 and June 4 Khrushchev headed a Soviet delegation to Albania, where he made a number of bellicose speeches, attacking among other things the U.S. moves to establish NATO rocket bases in Italy and Greece. Shortly after his return to Moscow, in a speech on June 6, Khrushchev proposed the establishment of a nuclear-free zone in the Balkans,[107] with the warning that if the West rejected the proposal the USSR would be "forced to set up missile bases closer to the bases of the aggressors," in Albania and Bulgaria. Five days later, in Riga, he made a similar proposal with regard to the Scandinavian countries and the Baltic.[108]

Khrushchev's verbal belligerence reached a climax on June 23, just at the beginning of the three-week recess in the foreign ministers' conference. In an interview with Averell Harriman, Khrushchev restated the Soviet position on Berlin in the most uncompromising terms and for added emphasis threw a temper tantrum, shouting, "If you send in tanks they will burn, and make no mistake about it. If you want war, you can have it, but remember it will be your war. Our rockets will fly automatically."[109] In his memoirs Eisenhower gives further details:

Khrushchev announced his intention to terminate Western rights in Berlin and boasted of rockets poised in China. He claimed that Soviet fighters could shoot down our air-breathing long-range missiles and made lavish claims regarding the quantity and capabilities of the Soviet ICBMs. He alleged that for an expenditure of 30 billion rubles on ballistic missiles the Soviets could destroy every industrial center in the United States and Europe, but that he, of course, *preferred* not to do so![110]

Apparently timed to coincide with Khrushchev's outburst were new Soviet attempts to transfer to East German authorities jurisdiction over military traffic between West Germany and West Berlin. At about the same time, the East German customs police for the first time attempted to

106. Text in *Department of State Bulletin,* vol. 40 (June 15, 1959), pp. 866–67.
107. For the formal Soviet proposal on establishment of a nuclear-free zone in the Balkans, in a note sent on June 25, see *Department of State Bulletin,* vol. 41 (August 3, 1959), pp. 160–61.
108. *Pravda,* June 12, 1959.
109. Averell Harriman, "My Alarming Interview with Khrushchev," *Life,* vol. 47 (July 13, 1959), p. 33.
110. Eisenhower, *Waging Peace,* p. 404. Italics in the original.

interfere with an American military train.[111] Not all the military muscle-
flexing was on the Soviet side, however; on July 12 columnist Joseph
Alsop reported that Western military convoys were now heavily armed
and NATO aircraft were being deployed out of France into West Germany.[112]

Eisenhower's Invitation to Khrushchev

It was at this moment of apparent deadlock at the Geneva conference,
with Khrushchev uttering increasingly belligerent statements and the
United States stressing its readiness to defend the access routes to Berlin,
that Soviet-U.S. relations suddenly took an entirely unexpected turn, one
that rendered the conference of foreign ministers virtually irrelevant.

At a meeting with a group of U.S. governors in the Kremlin on July 7,
Khrushchev indicated that he would regard favorably an invitation to visit
the United States. Eisenhower, at a press conference the following day,
professed surprise at the suggestion but did not rule it out completely.[113]
A number of State Department officials, including Under Secretary of
State Robert D. Murphy, had been drawing up a recommendation to
Eisenhower for an exchange of visits by him and Khrushchev.[114] Suitably
prepared by this groundwork, Eisenhower made a quick decision: in an
effort to overcome the impasse at Geneva he would invite Khrushchev to
visit the United States, with the explicit condition that substantial progress
toward an agreement on Berlin must first be achieved by the foreign
ministers' conference. In Eisenhower's mind the condition and the invitation were indissolubly linked. Inexplicably, however, in the plans he
drew up for extending the invitation, the link was weakened by the fact
that Murphy was to deliver the invitation itself in writing to Soviet Deputy
Premier Frol Kozlov when he left New York for Moscow on July 11 (at
the conclusion of a ten-day trip to the United States to open a Soviet
exhibit in New York), but Murphy was to deliver *orally* the message
concerning the need for progress at the foreign ministers' meeting.[115] For
reasons that he fails to make clear, Murphy neglected to deliver the oral

111. Ibid., p. 406.
112. *New York Herald Tribune,* July 12, 1959; Schick, *Berlin Crisis,* pp. 89–90.
113. *American Foreign Policy: Current Documents, 1959,* p. 878.
114. Robert D. Murphy, *Diplomat Among Warriors* (Doubleday, 1964), p. 438.
115. Eisenhower, *Waging Peace,* p. 405.

message to Kozlov, with the result that the invitation to Khrushchev was made with no strings attached.[116]

To understand Khrushchev's prompt and favorable response to Eisenhower's invitation and the significant alteration it produced in his foreign policy goals, attention must be directed briefly to developments in Soviet-Chinese relations and the closely related Soviet-Albanian relations.

After the Twenty-first Congress of the CPSU, which closed on February 5, 1959, the Soviet and Chinese Communist parties established a tenuous truce in the covert polemics conducted between them earlier.[117] Tension between the two parties continued to smolder, however, and by May it was threatening to spread to relations between the USSR and the Albanian Communist leadership. Khrushchev's visit to Albania in late May "must be viewed as a final unsuccessful effort to avert [Albanian party leader] Hoxha's alliance with Mao against him."[118]

Soviet refusal to honor the secret 1957 agreement on atomic aid to China followed on June 20, 1959, according to a Chinese statement issued on August 15, 1963.[119] On July 18, in a speech at Poznán, Khrushchev launched an indirect but unmistakable attack on the Chinese Communists for their program of setting up "people's communes," and thereby, in Donald Zagoria's words, "tore the 21st Congress truce to shreds."[120]

Eisenhower's invitation to Khrushchev thus arrived at a critical moment in Khrushchev's complex and risky policy maneuvers toward the Chinese Communists. Evidently the invitation appeared to Khrushchev as an unexpected and providential way out of the impasse into which his policies had led him. The negotiations on Berlin at Geneva were making little progress, and the United States was showing an increased willingness to resist by force Soviet and East German encroachment on Western access to Berlin.

Because his earlier interest in soliciting an invitation to visit the United States had been rebuffed, Khrushchev had patched up his quarrel with Peking, meanwhile accepting Macmillan's proposal for a British visit to Moscow. The Soviet-Western agreement on the convocation of a conference of foreign ministers grew out of that visit. Now the moment of choice

116. Murphy, *Diplomat Among Warriors*, p. 438.
117. Zagoria, *Sino-Soviet Conflict*, pp. 133–34.
118. William E. Griffith, *Albania and the Sino-Soviet Rift* (MIT Press, 1963), p. 34.
119. Griffith, *Sino-Soviet Rift*, p. 351.
120. Zagoria, *Sino-Soviet Conflict*, p. 134.

between Peking and Washington had arrived: relations with the Chinese were going from bad to worse, the Albanians had begun to side openly with Peking, and the foreign ministers' conference was hopelessly bogged down. The Eisenhower invitation offered Khrushchev a new option, that of a deal with the United States. No wonder he snapped it up eagerly. With the U.S. invitation secure, Khrushchev quickly launched his doctrinal attack on the Chinese in his July 18 speech at Poznán.

Under these circumstances the foreign ministers' conference lost its reason for existence. The USSR was no longer interested in it, and even a last-minute compromise offer by the Western powers, with new concessions, failed to evoke a favorable Soviet response.[121]

Why did the USSR fail to consolidate the gains it had achieved at the foreign ministers' conference? Partially, it would seem, the reason was strategic in nature. As Horelick and Rush point out, "acceptance [of Western concessions] would have committed the USSR, at least temporarily, to the status quo in all other respects and therefore might have lessened Soviet freedom to renew pressure at will."[122]

The failure of the Soviet 1958–59 campaign in Berlin, according to George and Smoke, resulted from their inability to convince the West that a significant shift had occurred in the USSR's favor in the strategic balance of power. Less convincing is the same authors' assertion that the Western powers' success in weathering the 1958–59 crisis without substantial impairment of their position in Berlin was due in part to the fact that "the NATO Allies displayed unexpectedly great skill in achieving the necessary degree of unity within the alliance."[123] Although an adequate working level of unity *was* displayed by the Western powers at Geneva, the general tendency of their diplomacy throughout the crisis was to drift slowly but inexorably in the direction of more and more damaging concessions to the Soviet position. The fact that the Soviet leaders saw matters in that light is indicated by Gromyko's statement on August 5, sum-

---

121. Jean Edward Smith writes, "The final days [of the Geneva conference] between the submission of the Western and Soviet plans on July 28 and the adjournment . . . were an extremely critical period for the West. Had Gromyko accepted the final Western proposals, West Berlin's hope of survival would have been destroyed." Smith, *Defense of Berlin*, p. 208. Smith's position is contested by James L. Richardson, *Germany and the Atlantic Alliance: The Interaction of Strategy and Politics* (Harvard University Press, 1966), pp. 270–71.

122. Horelick and Rush, *Strategic Power and Soviet Foreign Policy*, p. 121.

123. George and Smoke, *Deterrence in American Foreign Policy*, p. 402.

ming up the results of the conference from the Soviet viewpoint. "It can hardly be questioned," he said, "that our conference has made progress towards a realistic [read: acceptable to the Soviets] approach to the settlement of questions relating to West Berlin."[124]

We come back, then, to the question raised earlier: why did the USSR fail to consolidate its gains at Geneva as the basis for further encroachment on the Western position in Berlin? I would argue that any attempt to answer this question solely with reference to deterrence strategy, and with the implied assumption of a unitary process of Soviet policy formulation, is bound to produce unsatisfactory results. I believe it is essential to take into account both the internal tensions in the Soviet leadership and the sudden escalation of the Sino-Soviet conflict, which occurred just before the Geneva conference concluded. In my view, it was Khrushchev's perception of a new option in his policy toward the Chinese Communists which produced the abrupt shift in Soviet policy that led the USSR to accept termination of the foreign ministers' conference just as the West was on the point of making damaging concessions. Neither diplomatic skill nor the use of force was involved, though both had been displayed earlier in the crisis in ways that had smoothed the path for this unexpected denouement.

Eisenhower and Khrushchev at Camp David

The final act in the 1958–59 Berlin crisis was played out in the United States, during the visit of Khrushchev from September 15 to 27. To provide a suitable buildup, the USSR staged a spectacular space exploit just before Khrushchev's arrival. On September 12 the USSR launched *Lunik 2*, a moon rocket with a weight of more than 3,300 pounds (1,500 kilograms).[125] The effect on U.S. policymakers was minimal, however, because the United States had itself just achieved an important strategic goal: on September 1 the Atlas ICBM was declared operational.[126]

124. King, *Documents on International Affairs, 1959*, p. 76.
125. The September 1959 moon shot, as Harry Schwartz notes, "gave Nikita S. Khrushchev much to boast about when he toured the United States as President Eisenhower's guest." *New York Times*, December 11, 1972, p. 39. An authoritative British survey calls the moon shot "an astonishing demonstration of Soviet technological skill, a feat of enormous propaganda value, and a reminder that leadership in the 'space race' was one of the main reasons for the Soviet leader's reception in America." Barraclough, *Survey of International Affairs, 1959–1960*, p. 41.
126. *New York Times*, February 9, 1961.

The Eisenhower-Khrushchev talks, held at Camp David in the final days of the Soviet leader's visit, were marked by a direct test of wills in which the President emerged the victor. Eisenhower describes the incident in his memoirs:

As we were obviously at an impasse, he and I, by common consent, moved away from the remaining members of the conference, taking with us again only his interpreter, Oleg Troyanovski. He talked about Germany and Berlin without rancor, but obviously felt he had committed himself so firmly that he saw no way to retreat from his position. However, the Chairman finally said he recognized my determination in this matter and said he would take steps publicly to remove any suggestion of a time limit within which he would sign a Soviet-East German peace treaty, thus making the future of Berlin a proper subject for negotiation, not one for unilateral action. I replied that by this concession he was putting the matter back into the status quo ante, with the result that all of us could honestly seek for a decent solution to the problem of a city divided.[127]

Evaluation: The Use of Force in the 1958–59 Crisis

The West emerged from the Berlin crisis of 1958–59 with its basic positions intact. Not only had the local Soviet challenge in Berlin been successfully faced but the larger Soviet challenge to the Western strategic position had been defeated. In achieving these successes the use of force played a key role, but one that must be seen in the total context of Soviet-Western and Soviet-Chinese relations.

Throughout the crisis the Eisenhower administration drew a consistent distinction between strategic power, which it maintained at a level superior to that of the USSR, and limited conventional power. In the interests of economy the administration consistently played down the use of limited conventional force. The strategic equivalent of this approach was Dulles's doctrine of "massive retaliation" and its corollary of avoiding the use of limited force.

There is abundant evidence to support the views of analysts such as Jack M. Schick or Alexander George and Richard Smoke that the Eisenhower administration's policy with regard to the use of force in the 1958–59 Berlin crisis was not entirely successful. In particular, its failure to use limited force early in the crisis to signify its determination to defend its position in Berlin may well have encouraged the USSR to press ahead with its efforts to force the Western allies out of Berlin.

127. Eisenhower, *Waging Peace*, pp. 446–47.

Once the crisis had been precipitated by the Soviet "deadline note" of November 27, 1958, the use or threat of force by either side became one of several optional moves in a strategic game, a test of wills and of willingness to move up the escalation ladder. Here, in the long run, U.S. strategic power, the confidence of the U.S. leadership in that power, and its recognition by the Soviet leadership proved decisive. Diplomatic skill was displayed on both sides, perhaps more effectively in the Western alliance, where serious differences of opinion over the best tactics to pursue on the Berlin question threatened at times to disrupt the working unity of the alliance.

In the end, however, it was not the West but the Soviet-Chinese alliance, seemingly so strong at the outset of the crisis, that cracked under the enormous strain imposed by the Soviet challenge to Western strategic supremacy. That historic break would have been sufficient in itself to ensure that the next Soviet challenge to the Western position in Berlin would operate with substantially different ground rules than those that obtained in 1958–59. Even more directly pertinent is the fact that in 1961 there was a new administration in Washington, with a radically altered position on the use of force, strategic as well as conventional.

Between Two Crises: September 1959 to February 1961

The meeting between Eisenhower and Khrushchev was followed by a long interval—nearly a year and a half—during which the Soviet-Western conflict over Berlin moved from the stage of acute crisis to that of chronic irritant. The meeting, however, had solved none of the basic problems underlying the conflict, but had merely led to an agreement to negotiate on them without the pressure of a fixed deadline. Deprived of leverage, the USSR for the time being dropped its campaign on Berlin, though without formally withdrawing any of its claims or demands. Soviet leaders had failed to achieve any significant alteration in the status of West Berlin, having neglected to pin down the West on those points it was prepared to concede (for example, a ceiling on Western troop strengths in West Berlin), and had thus thrown away the advantages won by their pressure tactics at Geneva. Consequently, the interval between crises resulted in no significant shifts in either the Soviet or Western positions. Examining the international context in which the 1961 crisis unfolded, however, makes it apparent that fundamental and far-reaching changes had taken place in the interval since the last crisis.

Deepening of the Sino-Soviet Conflict

During the crisis of 1958–59 the conflict between Moscow and Peking, though deep and unresolved, had remained hidden. Neither side had given any public indication of its existence, and until the final months of the crisis it did not directly affect Soviet behavior in its Berlin campaign. By the time of the 1961 crisis, however, the Sino-Soviet conflict had been openly acknowledged by both sides and was a factor the Soviet leadership had to take into account in its strategic calculations. As the 1961 crisis developed, moreover, the split between Moscow and Peking deepened the internal conflicts in the Soviet leadership in ways that had a direct bearing on Soviet goals and tactics.

The U-2 Incident and the Breakdown of the Paris Summit Conference

A strong desire for a summit conference on Berlin and Germany had been a persistent theme in Khrushchev's maneuverings throughout the 1958–59 crisis. Forced to delay his wishes in this regard by Eisenhower's insistence on preliminary progress at the foreign minister level, Khrushchev came back to the summit proposal in the summer of 1960 at a time when the Geneva conference of foreign ministers seemed doomed to failure. By agreeing at Camp David to lift the threat of a deadline on negotiations over Berlin, Khrushchev was finally able to obtain Eisenhower's assent to a summit conference.

Although the four heads of government duly assembled in Paris in May 1960, the Paris summit conference broke up in disorder before any substantive action had been taken. The immediate cause of this fiasco was a sequence of events that began on May 1, when the USSR finally succeeded in forcing down over its territory a high-altitude reconnaissance plane, the U-2, piloted by Lt. Francis Gary Powers.[128] Concealing for several days the fact that they had downed the plane and captured Powers alive, Soviet leaders permitted U.S. authorities to entangle themselves in

128. For a concise account of the U-2 incident and its effect on the Paris summit conference, see Richard P. Stebbins, *The United States in World Affairs, 1960* (Harper, 1961), pp. 28–30.

a succession of cover stories before disclosing the truth. Still hoping to salvage the summit meeting, Khrushchev now called on Eisenhower to disavow responsibility for the U-2 flights and apologize to the Soviet government, but Eisenhower refused.

At this point Khrushchev staged one of his famous temper tantrums, storming out of the meeting place just as the conference was scheduled to begin, despite efforts by Macmillan and de Gaulle to smooth things over. Western fears that Khrushchev might seize this moment to carry through his long-standing threat to sign a peace treaty with East Germany were eased, however, when he made a speech in East Berlin a few days later pledging that the USSR would not reopen the Berlin question until another summit conference could be arranged, in six to eight months—in other words, after the U.S. presidential elections had been held and a new administration was in power in Washington.[129]

The United States did not get off scot-free from the U-2 incident, however. On May 30 Soviet Defense Minister Roman Malinovsky warned that if U.S. planes made overflights of Soviet territory in the future, the USSR would not only shoot down the aircraft but would "deal a crushing blow to the bases from which they take off." Malinovsky said he had issued an order to the commander-in-chief of the Soviet rocket troops "to strike at the take-off base of an aircraft if it violates the space of the Soviet Union and the socialist countries."[130]

The grave implications of the new Soviet stance are underlined by Horelick and Rush: "Thus, for the first time, Soviet leaders threatened to strike allies of the United States, possibly with nuclear weapons, in response to other than a physical attack on the USSR, one of its allies, or a friendly third power."[131]

The Growing Internal Challenge to Khrushchev's Power

The U-2 incident, with its revelation of prior Soviet inability to prevent these flights, and the collapse of the Paris summit conference on which Khrushchev had staked so much of his prestige resulted in a sharp upsurge of internal opposition to his dominance. At a plenum of the party Central Committee on May 4 his position was weakened by a series of

129. *New York Times,* May 21, 1960.
130. Ibid., May 31, 1960.
131. Horelick and Rush, *Strategic Power and Soviet Foreign Policy,* p. 75.

sweeping changes in the leading bodies of the Communist party and the Soviet government, the most important of which was a drastic reduction in the size of the Secretariat from ten members to five, with the removal of a group of loyal followers of Khrushchev. In the new Secretariat, Frol Kozlov, a staunch opponent of Khrushchev's initiatives in internal and foreign policy, joined forces with Mikhail Suslov, another long-time critic of Khrushchev.[132]

Kozlov was the principal beneficiary of the May 4 changes and thereafter presented the most direct challenge to Khrushchev's dominance. Kozlov's triumph was incomplete, however, since Khrushchev had been able to retain control of a key position in the Secretariat, that of secretary for cadres, the occupant of which enjoys the power to make changes in party bodies throughout the USSR in the name of the Central Committee. At the May 4 plenum Leonid Brezhnev, at that time a loyal supporter of Khrushchev, had continued as secretary for cadres. Brezhnev, therefore, became the next target of Kozlov in his drive for power.

The RB-47 Incident and Its Consequences

From the standpoint of the internal opposition the shooting down of the U-2 was a highly successful operation, resulting as it did in serious inroads into Khrushchev's power. It was to be expected, therefore, that an attempt would soon be made to repeat the incident.

On June 30 Khrushchev left Moscow for a state visit to Austria. On the next day, July 1, Soviet fighter planes shot down an unarmed U.S. reconnaissance plane, an RB-47, over the Barents Sea. The repetition of the U-2 incident was under way with the advantage, from the standpoint of the internal opposition, that this time Khrushchev was not in Moscow. There is, in fact, evidence to indicate that he first learned of the action only on July 6, the date on which, visibly upset, he abruptly cut short his visit to Austria.[133]

Just as in the U-2 incident, the USSR for a time kept silent about the shooting down of the RB-47 and even offered to send a cruiser to join in the search for the missing plane. The United States announced the failure of the plane to return to its base but issued no cover story. Washington,

132. Ploss, *Conflict and Decision-Making in Soviet Russia*, p. 184.
133. For an eyewitness account of Khrushchev's reaction, see *Neue Zürcher Zeitung*, July 7, 1960.

in fact, possessed accurate information indicating that the plane had been at least thirty miles from Soviet territory and headed *away* from the USSR when it was overtaken by Soviet fighter planes and shot down.[134] The British, despite their natural skepticism after the U-2 fiasco, fully accepted the U.S. evidence, Macmillan going so far as to characterize the incident as "a fake."[135]

A fake, but staged by whom and for what purpose? The answer to these questions, I believe, can be found in the Soviet internal political struggle. Baffling if one considers it as an action ordered or approved by Khrushchev, the shooting down of the RB-47 makes excellent sense if it is regarded as a step by his internal opponents to force him to sacrifice Brezhnev and hand over to Kozlov the post of secretary for cadres. These actions were in fact taken at the next plenum of the Central Committee, which met from July 13 to 16.[136]

The sacrifice of Brezhnev, however, was not the only price Khrushchev had to pay to extricate himself from his predicament. Two other concessions were forced from him, both having a direct bearing on Soviet foreign policy.

1. On July 9, in the first major speech delivered after his hurried return to Moscow, Khrushchev pledged missile aid to Cuba in case the United States threatened it with invasion.[137] That he made this pledge unwillingly and under pressure is shown by the fact that he later did his best to water it down, stressing that the missiles being offered were merely "symbolic."[138]

2. An even more serious consequence for Khrushchev was a drastic impairment of his status within the "collective leadership." The new arrangements, which were publicly demonstrated for the first time on July 17, "reflected the triumph of collective leadership," in Tatu's view. "The effect had been to upgrade the role of the Presidium to a marked extent and correspondingly to downgrade Khrushchev."[139]

The reduction in Khrushchev's stature was graphically demonstrated when the Soviet press failed to publish the full text of a speech he delivered

134. Eisenhower, *Waging Peace,* p. 568.
135. Harold Macmillan, *Pointing the Way, 1959–1961* (Harper and Row, 1972), p. 237.
136. *Pravda,* July 17, 1960.
137. Ibid., July 10, 1960.
138. *New York Times,* October 29, 1960.
139. Tatu, *Power in the Kremlin,* p. 112.

on July 17, whereas it *did* publish the full text of Suslov's speech at the same meeting. It was ten months later that Khrushchev's speech was published.[140]

Khrushchev's position was weakened at a time when Soviet policy toward the United States was marked by greatly increased militancy. There were sharp conflicts between the two powers in the Congo, in the disarmament negotiations at Geneva, at the United Nations, and in Japan, where Communist riots in June forced the Japanese government to cancel an invitation to President Eisenhower. These developments, coupled with the uncertainties of U.S. foreign policymaking in the period after Dulles's death, helped create a widespread impression that the foreign policy of the Eisenhower administration was being systematically undermined by the USSR and its allies on a global scale. An authoritative British observer sums up the situation as follows:

During the weeks between the collapse of the Geneva [disarmament] talks on 27 June and the re-assembly of the United Nations on 17 September the condition of world politics deteriorated in an alarming way. Basically, it is probably fair to say that this deterioration was the consequence of the failure of American policy to keep pace with the changes in world conditions which had been so distinctive a feature of the past three or four years. . . . In many ways, indeed, this period must be accounted a low-water mark in the conduct of American policy.[141]

The Shift in U.S. Military Thinking

During the summer of 1960, as the presidential campaign got under way, a profound shift took place in the U.S. attitude toward the use of military force as an element in foreign policy, a shift reflected in the views of both major parties. In a campaign platform adopted on July 12 the Democratic party stated that America's first task under a new administration would be to "restore our national strength—military, political, economic, and moral," and "to recast our military capacity in order to provide forces and weapons of a diversity, balance, and mobility sufficient in quantity and quality to deter both limited and general aggression."[142]

In the Republican party, too, there were influential voices calling for

140. A shortened version of the speech was published in *Kommunist*, no. 7 (1961), pp. 3–16.
141. Barraclough, *Survey of International Affairs, 1959–1960*, p. 534.
142. Stebbins, *The United States in World Affairs, 1960*, p. 34.

change. On July 23, shortly before he was nominated for President, Vice President Richard M. Nixon reached an agreement with New York's Governor Nelson Rockefeller which defined the "two imperatives of national security in the 1960s" as:

a. A powerful second-strike capacity—a nuclear retaliatory power capable of surviving surprise attack to inflict devastating punishment on any aggressor, and

b. A modern, flexible and balanced military establishment with forces capable of deterring or meeting any local aggression.

In a direct break with the economy-minded policies of the Eisenhower era, the Nixon-Rockefeller statement continued: "The United States can afford and must provide the increased expenditures to implement fully this necessary program for strengthening our defense posture. There must be no price ceiling on America's security."[143]

Stung by the implied criticism, Eisenhower showed that he felt the need at this time to stress American military power. In a message to Congress on August 8 he disclosed that while "he still had no plans to increase defense spending in any substantial way, despite the recent 'intensification of Communist truculence,' " he had ordered certain practical measures

within the framework of the existing program: deployment of additional aircraft carriers to the Sixth Fleet in the Mediterranean and the Seventh Fleet in the Pacific; steps to increase the operational readiness of the Strategic Air Command and the ground forces; and an expansion of certain long-range programs, particularly those relating to the Polaris missile system.[144]

Helping to brighten the record of the Eisenhower administration was "a series of remarkable current accomplishments in the missile and space field," including the first test firing on July 20 of two Polaris missiles from the nuclear submarine *George Washington,* and the 5,000-mile test-firing of a Titan missile on August 30.[145] It was the cumulative record of the Eisenhower administration, however, that Kennedy attacked during the campaign, most extensively and systematically in a speech before the American Legion convention at Miami Beach on October 18, 1960.[146]

143. Theodore H. White, *The Making of the President 1960* (Atheneum, 1961), pp. 388–89.
144. Stebbins, *The United States in World Affairs, 1960,* p. 35.
145. Ibid., p. 36.
146. For the advance release text of the speech, see *Freedom of Communications, Part 1: The Speeches, Remarks, Press Conferences and Statements of Senator John F. Kennedy,* S. Rept. 994, 87:1 (GPO, 1961), pp. 1154–59.

Kennedy traced the relative decline in U.S. military power to 1953, when the development of the hydrogen bomb had led to the emergence of long-range missiles as the "key to future military power." Whereas the USSR "decided to go all out in missile development," however, "here, in the United States, we cut back on funds for missile development. We slashed our defense budget. We slowed up the modernization of our conventional forces until, today, the Soviet Union is rapidly building up a missile striking force that endangers our power to retaliate—and thus our survival itself."

To remedy this situation, Kennedy offered a four-point program: first, "immediate steps to protect our present nuclear striking force from surprise attack"; second, a crash program for the production of Polaris submarines and Minuteman missiles to "close the missile gap by providing us with an invulnerable retaliatory force"; third, a program of modernizing and giving increased mobility to conventional forces; and fourth, a fundamental reorganization of the Defense Department.

During the campaign Kennedy made it clear that he expected a "most serious crisis over Berlin" to confront the President in the early days of the new administration,[147] and in the third of his television debates with Nixon he pledged to "meet our commitments to maintain the freedom and independence of West Berlin."[148]

Continuing Soviet Claims and Threats

Throughout the inter-crisis period Khrushchev continued to make exaggerated claims for Soviet strategic power. Thus in a speech on October 6, 1959, he declared that the Soviet Union was "ahead of all countries in the production of missiles."[149] A month later he told a group of journalists, "Now we have accumulated such a quantity of missiles, such a quantity of atomic and hydrogen warheads that if they [the Western powers] attack us, we could wipe all our potential enemies off the face of the earth." He went on to describe a visit to a Soviet munitions plant which, he said, "produced on the assembly line 250 missiles with hydrogen war-

147. See his remarks of September 29, October 16, and October 23, 1960, ibid., pp. 405, 613, 710.

148. *Freedom of Communications, Part 3: The Joint Appearance of Senator John F. Kennedy and Vice President Richard M. Nixon,* S. Rept. 994, 87:1 (GPO, 1961), p. 205.

149. *Pravda,* October 8, 1959.

heads."[150] In Budapest on December 1 Khrushchev boasted that the USSR had enough nuclear-tipped rockets to "raze to the ground all our potential enemies."[151] In the same speech he revived the threat to sign a separate peace treaty with East Germany, and directed a particularly sharp attack against West German Chancellor Adenauer.

One purpose of Khrushchev's boasts, it soon became clear, was to cushion the shock of a major military cutback which he announced on January 14, 1960—reduction of the size of the Soviet armed forces by some 1,200,000 men.[152] The speech in which he made this announcement contained the assertion that the USSR was "several years ahead of other countries in the creation and production of ICBMs," as well as an apocalyptic vision of the horrors of a future nuclear war, in which "not a single capital [or] industrial center would escape attack, not merely during the first days but during the first minutes of the war." And once again Khrushchev raised the threat of a separate peace treaty with East Germany, "with all the attendant implications," if the West failed to agree to Soviet demands on Berlin.[153]

Toward the end of February Khrushchev repeated the peace treaty threat, adding that such an action "would mean the immediate cancellation of all allied rights in East Germany, including Berlin."[154] In a speech delivered on a trip to France toward the end of March, Khrushchev ridiculed the military value of the Western garrisons in Berlin and said that if the West put as many as half a million additional troops there, "it would be easier to smash them."[155]

Khrushchev's steady hammering on the issue of a German peace treaty, together with his fraudulent claims and distortions of the historical record, finally goaded U.S. officials into making a formal rebuttal. On April 4, 1960, Secretary of State Herter categorically reaffirmed the U.S. commitment to West Berlin, and on April 20, Under Secretary of State Douglas Dillon warned Khrushchev that the United States was not prepared to

150. Ibid., November 15, 1959.
151. Ibid., December 2, 1959.
152. Ibid., January 15, 1960.
153. Ibid. For analysis, see Horelick and Rush, *Strategic Power and Soviet Foreign Policy,* pp. 58–59, 66–67; and Roman Kolkowicz, "The Impact of Technology on the Soviet Military: A Challenge to Traditional Military Professionalism" (Rand Corp., 1964), pp. 7–9.
154. *New York Times,* March 1, 1960.
155. *New York Herald Tribune* (European edition), March 26–27, 1960.

negotiate on the "distorted picture of the German problem" drawn by Soviet spokesmen.[156]

Under particularly heavy pressure at just this time from the internal opposition, Khrushchev responded with one of his most bellicose utterances, delivered at Baku on April 25.[157] The collapse of the Paris summit conference was soon followed, however, by Khrushchev's pledge not to reopen the Berlin question for another six to eight months. The respite was brief. By the time of his trip to Austria at the end of June, Khrushchev was once again raising the threat of a separate East German peace treaty.

The Flareup of the Berlin Issue, July–December 1960

At a diplomatic reception on June 29, 1960, Khrushchev told the West German ambassador, Hans Kroll, that "the Berlin question could no longer remain unresolved" and that if a solution was not found soon he would be forced to conclude a peace treaty with East Germany "without further delay." Kroll received the impression that Khrushchev "was under strong pressure from the 'Ulbricht group' in the Presidium and could not extend the Berlin pause indefinitely."[158]

One reason for Khrushchev's sense of urgency was revealed in a Soviet note of June 30 protesting West German plans to recruit for the West German army in West Berlin.[159] Another touchy issue was a plan for the West German lower house (Bundestag) to hold an autumn session in West Berlin as it had done for several years. At a press conference on July 8 Khrushchev warned that if the session was held the USSR "would then consider signing an East German peace treaty in the same month."[160]

Undeterred, the West German government not only went ahead with its plans but added several rallies of West German refugee organizations clamoring for the return to Germany of territory lost to Poland and the USSR after the Second World War. Not surprisingly, the East German and

---

156. *Department of State Bulletin*, vol. 42 (April 25, 1960), p. 638, and vol. 42 (May 9, 1960), p. 725.

157. *Pravda*, April 26, 1960. For analysis, see Tatu, *Power in the Kremlin*, pp. 49–50, and Stebbins, *The United States in World Affairs, 1960*, pp. 82–83.

158. Hans Kroll, *Lebenserinnerungen eines Botschafters* (Kiepenheuer und Witsch, 1967), pp. 460–61. Kroll does not explain what he means by the "Ulbricht group," but elsewhere (p. 366) he cites evidence of a link between Kozlov, Ulbricht, and Gromkyo.

159. *Pravda*, July 1, 1960.

160. *The Times* (London), July 9, 1960.

Soviet governments strongly objected to these plans, and the conflict soon reached a stage of acute tension.

The Berlin mini-crisis of 1960, which lasted from early July through the beginning of December, had certain characteristics that set it apart from the two major Berlin crises, those of 1958–59 and 1961. First, the principal actors in 1960 were not the great powers but the two German states. Second, the USSR in 1960 did not stress the issues of strategic rivalry and East-West conflict. Third, the threat to sign a peace treaty with East Germany and thereby to end Western occupation rights in Berlin was not voiced. In searching for an explanation of these aberrations, one notes that throughout most of the period of conflict in 1960 Khrushchev either was not in Moscow or was occupied with other matters, for example, the eighty-one-party conference in November.

Since the 1960 mini-crisis was primarily a tug-of-war between the two German states, it is appropriate that it finally eased when the West German government at the end of November withdrew an earlier threat to cut off interzonal trade unless the East German government lifted its restrictions on travel from West Germany to West Berlin. The mini-crisis served to keep alive the great power tensions over Berlin, however, and reminded both sides that neither the Berlin question itself nor the larger question of the strategic balance between the United States and the USSR had been settled.

Crosscurrents in Soviet Policy, Early 1961

As the time neared for the inauguration of a new administration in Washington, Khrushchev seemed intent on improving relations with the United States. At a New Year's Eve reception in the Kremlin he expressed the hope that "in the new year the United States of America and the Soviet Union will turn a new page, as it were, in their relations."[161]

Prospects for better Soviet relations with West Germany also seemed bright. At the same reception, Khrushchev had a long talk with FRG Ambassador Kroll, in the course of which he expressed pleasure at the signing of a Soviet-FRG trade agreement, and even had some rare words of praise for Adenauer. He warned Kroll, however, that "the German problem must be solved in 1961," to which Mikoyan added: "Khrushchev could not hold out much longer against the pressure being brought to bear

161. *Pravda,* January 2, 1961.

on him for some time by certain circles—he was obviously referring to the Ulbricht lobby in the Presidium."[162]

Unfortunately, Khrushchev's wishes for an improvement in relations between the United States and the USSR seemed incompatible with Soviet actions in Laos, where extensive Soviet military aid to the insurgent Pathet Lao was producing a direct threat to the stability of the Laotian government. Nevertheless, Khrushchev himself delivered the most crushing blow to Soviet-American détente just as the Kennedy administration was making its last-minute preparations to take power. He did this in a major speech on January 6, 1961, given before a select audience of Soviet ideologists and party savants.[163]

Khrushchev's speech had as one of its principal themes the typology of wars from the standpoint of Marxism-Leninism. The USSR, he said, would try to prevent the outbreak of general nuclear wars; it was also opposed to "local wars" that might develop into general nuclear wars. What Khrushchev called "wars of national liberation," however, were "sacred," and he pledged that Communists would support such wars "wholeheartedly and without reservation."

There remained a danger, he continued, that the capitalist nations might attack the USSR, but this threat could be averted by combining peaceful coexistence and disarmament. The ultimate goal of a Communist world, which had been called for in the final statement issued by the eighty-one-party conference, could best be achieved, he asserted, not by force but by the victory of communism in "intensive economic, political, and ideological struggle within the limits of peaceful coexistence." Khrushchev gave particular attention to West Berlin, where, he said,

the positions of the United States of America, Britain, and France have proved to be especially vulnerable. . . . These powers cannot fail to realize that sooner or later the occupation regime in that city must be ended. It is necessary to go ahead with bringing the aggressive-minded imperialists to their senses, and [to compel] them to reckon with the real situation. And should they balk, then we will take resolute measures, we will sign a peace treaty with the German Democratic Republic.

It would be difficult to overstate the impact this speech made on the Kennedy administration and the extent to which it shaped the thinking of

162. Kroll, *Lebenserinnerungen eines Botschafters*, p. 472.
163. The speech, delivered to a joint meeting of the Higher Party School, the Academy of Social Sciences, and the Marx Engels Institute, was published in *Kommunist*, no. 1 (1961), pp. 3–37.

Kennedy and his advisers on the whole subject of U.S. policy toward the USSR. According to Schlesinger, the speech "made a conspicuous impression on the new President, who took it as an authoritative exposition of Soviet intentions, discussed it with his staff, and read excerpts from it aloud to the National Security Council."[164]

It seems probable that one of Khrushchev's major purposes in delivering the speech was to defend his concept of "peaceful coexistence" against his critics in Peking and elsewhere.[165] Seen from this angle, the devastating effect the speech produced in Washington was simply an unfortunate by-product of what was intended for Communist ears. Even if one accepts this analysis, however, the fact remains that the January 6 speech seriously reduced the possibilities of a thaw in Soviet-U.S. relations and contributed mightily to the skepticism with which the new administration viewed Soviet expressions of a desire for an improvement in those relations.

The Crisis of 1961

Analyzing the complex issues involved in the Berlin crisis of 1961 is a difficult task at best. It becomes far more difficult if some of the basic facts in the situation are misstated through ignorance or carelessness. Unfortunately, serious errors have crept into otherwise well-documented accounts of the crisis and have been accepted as established facts in later studies. Two of these errors have a direct bearing on U.S. and Soviet strategies in the opening phase of the 1961 crisis:

1. Several studies assert that Kennedy, shortly after taking office, sent a message to Khrushchev requesting a delay in negotiations on Berlin in order to give the new administration time to prepare its position.[166] No evidence has been found, however, to support this assertion. It may result from confusion with a request the Kennedy administration *did* make, and which the Soviets accepted, for a delay in resumption of the three-power talks at Geneva on a test-ban agreement.[167]

164. Arthur M. Schlesinger, Jr., *A Thousand Days: John F. Kennedy in the White House* (Houghton Mifflin, 1965), pp. 302–03.

165. For the view that the speech was in part "directed at Communist China," see Richard P. Stebbins, *United States in World Affairs, 1961* (Harper, 1962), p. 65, and Zagoria, *Sino-Soviet Conflict*, p. 352.

166. Schick, *Berlin Crisis*, p. 139. See also George and Smoke, *Deterrence in American Foreign Policy*, pp. 414, 422, 424.

167. *Facts on File* (1961), pp. 33, 62.

2. It has been maintained that Khrushchev told U.S. Ambassador Llewellyn Thompson in January 1961 that "his prestige was engaged in Berlin and he had waited long enough to make his move."[168] Available evidence indicates, however, that Khrushchev made this statement to Thompson not at their meeting in Moscow on January 21, 1961, but a month and a half later, when they met again at Novosibirsk on March 9.[169]

Straightening out these errors and misconceptions is not a mere niggling over dates: the evaluation of Soviet and U.S. strategy in the 1961 crisis is directly affected by the question of when and how Khrushchev first broached the matter with an authoritative U.S. representative.

Between Khrushchev's two meetings with Thompson a significant change occurred in the Kennedy administration's perception of the U.S.-Soviet strategic balance. During the 1960 campaign Kennedy had referred frequently to the so-called "missile gap," a period during which the United States was believed to be endangered by a Soviet lead in the production of ICBMs.[170] Shortly after taking office, however, the Kennedy administration discovered that there was in fact no "missile gap," a conclusion that Defense Secretary Robert S. McNamara disclosed to an off-the-record press briefing on February 6.[171] McNamara's statement, though accurate, was considered inexpedient by Kennedy, who told a press conference two days later that studies he had ordered of the U.S. strategic position were not yet completed "and therefore it would be premature to reach a judgment as to whether there is a gap or not a gap."[172]

For the Soviet leadership, however, which had been basing its foreign policy strategy on the inflated claims that had helped give rise to the

168. George and Smoke, *Deterrence in American Foreign Policy*, p. 419.

169. George and Smoke cite Schlesinger, *A Thousand Days*, p. 347. Schlesinger's account of the Khrushchev-Thompson meeting is ambiguous as to the date, however. For a circumstantial and probably accurate account of the March 9 meeting, see *New York Times*, March 18, 1961.

170. For example, in a speech in Chicago on November 4, 1960, Kennedy said, "We are now entering the age of the missile gap, when our nuclear striking power, backed up by larger, more mobile conventional forces, may no longer necessarily convince the Russians of our capacity to survive a surprise attack and also be able to strike back at their willingness to fight." *Freedom of Communications, Part 1*, pp. 895–96. On the "missile gap" as a campaign issue, see Schlesinger, *A Thousand Days*, p. 317.

171. *New York Times*, February 7, 1961.

172. Harold W. Chase and Allen H. Lerman, eds., *Kennedy and the Press, The News Conferences* (Crowell, 1965), p. 20.

"missile gap" theory, the cat was out of the bag with McNamara's disclosure of February 6.[173] Something, it was clear, would have to be done.

The Presidium Meeting of Mid-February 1961

I have presented elsewhere the evidence pointing to a meeting of the Presidium of the Communist party of the Soviet Union in mid-February 1961, and will therefore confine my discussion at this point to a summary of my conclusions.[174] It should be stressed that the following analysis is a hypothesis, but in my view it offers a more satisfactory explanation of the known facts than any alternative interpretation. It is also crucial for an understanding of Soviet policies in the later stages of the 1961 crisis.

The meeting was called, I believe, on the insistence of Khrushchev's critics and opponents in the Presidium, as the result of their realization after McNamara's February 6 press briefing that the U.S. leadership was now aware of the facts about Soviet missile production and consequently about U.S. strategic preponderance. Khrushchev, who at the time was engaged in an extended tour of agricultural centers in the provinces, was forced to hurry back to Moscow to face his critics and, together with them, work out a new foreign policy strategy. It should be remembered that at this time—February 1961—Khrushchev's decisionmaking powers were still subject to the restraints imposed on him at the July 1960 plenum.

The collapse of the myth of Soviet strategic preponderance had especially serious implications for Soviet policy in Germany. In the 1958–59 crisis Khrushchev had used greatly exaggerated claims for Soviet strength as a means to force the Western powers to withdraw from Berlin, a retreat that would have solved the acute problem of population drain from East Germany. As the result of Soviet failure to achieve its goals in the 1958–59 crisis this problem had not been solved, and by early 1961 it was more acute than ever.

At the New Year's reception, Khrushchev had told the West German ambassador that the German question must be "solved" in 1961. Now, with McNamara's disclosure, the foundation on which Khrushchev's Ber-

173. For the effect of McNamara's disclosure on Soviet strategy, see Horelick and Rush, *Strategic Power and Soviet Foreign Policy,* p. 80.
174. "The Presidium Meeting of February, 1961: A Reconstruction."

lin strategy had been based had crumbled. It was urgently necessary to adopt a new policy, one that would end once and for all the debilitating drain on East Germany's vitality caused by the availability of the West Berlin escape route.

The principal decisions which, in my view, the Presidium took at its mid-February meeting were designed to achieve this goal. Khrushchev was given six months to demonstrate that *his* approach to the problem—diplomatic and military pressure on the Western allies to force them out of West Berlin—could produce the desired result. If he failed, the security and viability of the East German state would be assured by physically sealing off West Berlin from the Soviet-occupied eastern sector of the city and from the surrounding territory of the East German state.

I believe that a corollary to this program, with its maximum and minimum goals and its fixed time limit, concerned the testing of nuclear weapons. Since early November 1958 the USSR, like the two principal Western atomic powers, the United Kingdom and the United States, had been observing a de facto ban on testing, despite mounting pressure from military spokesmen on both sides and their political allies to resume testing. There is good reason to believe that Soviet leaders decided at the February 1961 meeting to begin making preparations for a new test series, scheduled to start shortly after the expiration of Khrushchev's six-month time limit for a solution to the East German problem.[175] It seems likely that this decision was an optional one, related to the decision on Berlin: If Khrushchev failed to force the Western allies out of the city, the test series would be launched after expiration of the six-month period as soon as the technical preparations were complete.

Khrushchev Initiates the Soviet Campaign

A cardinal piece of evidence in support of the view that a meeting of the Presidium took place in mid-February 1961 is an aide-mémoire on Germany which the Soviet government sent Adenauer on February 17, 1961.[176] In this document all the familiar Soviet proposals on Germany were restated, but in rather muted form and with a new note of respect for

175. Dr. Hans A. Bethe, an American nuclear physicist, believed that preparations for the Soviet test series, which began on September 1, 1961, must have started at least as early as March 1961. See his article, "Disarmament and Strategy," *Bulletin of the Atomic Scientists,* vol. 18 (September 1962), p. 18.

176. Text in *Documents on Germany, 1944–1961,* pp. 635–41.

and even pleading with the West German chancellor, so often in the past a target for Khrushchev's abuse. Muted, too, were the note's claims for Soviet military power: In place of the old boasts of supremacy appeared the sober statement, "The Soviet Union and its friends have everything they need to uphold their just cause in a fitting manner."[177] The note hinted strongly at a time limit without, however, actually specifying one.

Without waiting for a reply from the West German government (the reply was not, in fact, forthcoming until July 12), the USSR published the text of the note on March 3, thereby serving public notice of the formal reopening of its Berlin campaign. In his meeting with Thompson in Novosibirsk on March 9, Khrushchev cited the note as the basis for Soviet policy in Germany.[178]

At the end of March the Warsaw Pact Political Consultative Committee met in Moscow, with Walter Ulbricht presiding, to consider measures for "further strengthening their defensive capacity and consolidating peace throughout the world." The communiqué issued on March 31 called for signature of "a peace treaty with both German states and, in this connection, rendering harmless the hotbed of danger in West Berlin by converting it into a demilitarized free city."[179] George and Smoke cite a West German journalist's later report that Ulbricht at the meeting "demanded that he be allowed to close the border between East and West Berlin. But the other East European countries opposed such a move on grounds both of embarrassment and of the risk of a violent Western response; and the USSR stated that it would be necessary first to determine how Kennedy's Berlin policies might differ from Eisenhower's."[180]

George and Smoke note that "the reliability of this account may be open to question"; in my view it can be recognized as a fabrication, based on a gross exaggeration of the policymaking capabilities of the Warsaw Pact organization. Ulbricht was far too experienced a Communist functionary not to realize that the place to apply pressure was not a meeting of the Consultative Committee but the Presidium of the Communist party of the Soviet Union. It is far more likely, in my view, that the meeting of the Warsaw Pact committee was convened by the USSR for the purpose of coordinating the satellite nations' foreign policies with that of the USSR

177. Ibid., p. 639.
178. *New York Times*, March 18, 1961.
179. *Pravda*, March 31, 1961.
180. George and Smoke, *Deterrence in American Foreign Policy*, pp. 437–38, citing *Der Spiegel* (August 15, 1966), p. 27.

in the unfolding campaign on Berlin. If my reconstruction of the February 1961 Presidium meeting is close to the truth, Ulbricht already knew by the time of the Warsaw Pact meeting that, one way or another, his problems with West Berlin were going to be solved in the fairly near future.

To ensure maximum publicity for his renewed drive to force the Western allies out of Berlin Khrushchev now resorted to one of his favorite procedures, an interview with a prominent Western journalist. To mark the importance he attached to the event he invited one of the most respected of American news analysts, Walter Lippmann, for a lengthy discussion at Sochi, in the course of which he presented his case for the signing of a German peace treaty that would "fix" the German frontiers and give a legal foundation to the existence of the "three elements of Germany"—the two German states and the free city of West Berlin.[181]

Failing this, Mr. Khrushchev proposed . . . a temporary agreement for three years while the "two Germanies" negotiated some form of unification, perhaps a loose confederation. If no agreement were reached during that period, the legal rights of the occupying powers would lapse. Failing that, he returned to his original threat to conclude a separate peace treaty with the East German state, which would thereby obtain full sovereignty over the access routes to West Berlin. If the west then refused to do business with the East German state and tried to use force to enter Berlin, the Red Army would interpose itself across the access routes and blockade Berlin.[182]

Khrushchev assured Lippmann that he would not precipitate a crisis over Berlin until he had had a chance to talk face to face with Kennedy, and he disclosed confidentially that "there was the possibility of a meeting with the President early in June either in Vienna or Stockholm."[183]

To give added impact to the publication of Lippmann's report, Khrushchev resorted to another well-tried device, a new demonstration of Soviet technical and scientific prowess. On April 12, two days after the Lippmann interview, the USSR achieved a milestone in the exploration of space with the successful launching of the world's first manned space flight. Using a 10,395-pound (4,725-kilogram) space ship, Major Yuri

181. Lippmann's account of the interview was published in *New York Herald Tribune*, April 17, 18, and 19, 1961, and, with an additional note, in his book, *The Coming Tests With Russia* (Little, Brown, 1961).

182. D. C. Watt, *Survey of International Affairs, 1961* (Oxford University Press, 1965), p. 224.

183. Lippmann, *Coming Tests With Russia*, p. 27.

Gagarin made an orbital flight that circled the earth in one hour and 48 minutes and then landed safely.[184] Unfortunately for Khrushchev, the effect of his well-planned journalistic coup was spoiled by a totally unrelated development that captured the headlines of the world press just as Lippmann's report was beginning to appear: the attempted invasion of Cuba by U.S.-trained anti-Castro refugees from Cuba, an attempt which was preceded by an air raid on Havana on April 15 and which ended in ignominious defeat four days later when Castro's forces rounded up the last survivors of the invasion force at the Bay of Pigs. For Khrushchev, the most ominous aspect of the Bay of Pigs invasion was the possibility that the United States might intervene directly on the side of the invaders, thereby forcing the USSR to make good on Khrushchev's pledge to use Soviet missiles in the defense of Cuba against U.S. aggression. Kennedy's decision not to support the invaders with U.S. military power, and the message he sent Khrushchev on April 18 informing him of this decision, lifted the shadow of that danger.[185] Khrushchev could breathe a little easier, reassured by this indication that the new occupant of the White House was a prudent man who wished to avoid a direct confrontation with the USSR.

Before Khrushchev could feel fully confident about the risks involved in precipitating a new Berlin crisis, he felt the need for direct contact with the new U.S. President. It was not until May 4, however, that the USSR indicated an interest in accepting Kennedy's invitation of February 22— if it was still valid.[186] What happened between April 10, when Khrushchev spoke to Lippmann of the meeting with Kennedy as a possibility, and May 4, when he moved to make it a reality? Among other things, there was a distinct improvement in Khrushchev's position in the Presidium as a result of the temporary elimination of his most implacable foe, Frol Kozlov. On April 17, Kozlov, an ardent proponent of Soviet military aid to the Laotian insurgents, attended a state dinner for Prince Souvanna Phouma of Laos that marked Soviet acceptance of the establishment of a neutral Laos. This was Kozlov's last public appearance until early June.

184. For the technical specifications of the Gagarin flight, see F. J. Krieger, "Recent Soviet Advances in Aerospace Technology" (Rand Corp., February 1962), p. 10.
185. Text of Kennedy's message is in *Department of State Bulletin,* vol. 44 (May 8, 1961), pp. 661–62.
186. Hugh Sidey, *John F. Kennedy, President* (Atheneum, 1963), p. 165.

"Diplomatic sources" in Moscow, the *New York Times* reported in late May, explained his absence from public view as the result of a mild heart attack.[187]

The eclipse of Kozlov was promptly followed by a number of signs that Khrushchev's position had been strengthened, including the belated publication of his speech of July 17, 1960. Soviet acceptance of Kennedy's invitation came early in this period of the strengthening of Khrushchev's position, and it seems reasonable to suggest that the earlier delay in responding was due, at least in part, to opposition from Kozlov, who had shown himself a staunch critic of any move toward improving Soviet relations with the United States.

By early May, then, the broad outlines of the new campaign on Berlin were clearly visible, though the USSR had not yet made any specific demands. What had the Kennedy administration been doing meanwhile to prepare for the "most serious crisis over Berlin," which Kennedy himself had predicted the U.S. would face by the spring of 1961?[188]

The Kennedy Administration's Initial Changes in Defense Strategy

In analyzing the Kennedy administration's response to Soviet words and actions in the Berlin crisis of 1961, a clear distinction must be made between the overall policies worked out by the President and his advisers, based on their view of the United States' strategic posture and its ability to meet its commitments on a global scale, and the specific policies and actions they adopted to achieve U.S. goals in Berlin and Germany. Admittedly these two areas were closely related and frequently overlapped, but in principle they remained separate and distinct. Failure to recognize this difference can lead to faulty evaluation of U.S. moves in the crisis and to the confusion of long-term and short-term goals.[189]

Highly critical as he had been of the Eisenhower defense policies, as President-elect Kennedy made it one of his first priorities to obtain a comprehensive review of existing military power in relation to current or anticipated needs. In assigning this task to his new defense secretary,

187. *New York Times,* May 24, 1961.

188. See Kennedy's remarks at Wilmington, Delaware, on October 16, 1960, in *Freedom of Communications, Part 1,* p. 613.

189. George and Smoke, with their focus on deterrence, tend to blur this distinction and to assume that all major defense moves initiated by the Kennedy administration in the first half of 1961 were directly related to the Berlin crisis.

Robert S. McNamara, Kennedy signaled his conscious break from the Eisenhower era by laying down the basic principle that "under no circumstances should we allow a predetermined arbitrary financial limit to establish either strategy or force levels."[190]

McNamara's preliminary survey, as summarized by Sorensen, found that U.S. military policy was characterized by

1. A strategy of massive nuclear retaliation as the answer to all military and political aggression, a strategy believed by few of our friends and none of our enemies and resulting in serious weaknesses in our conventional forces.

2. A financial ceiling on national security, making military strategy the stepchild of a predetermined budget.

3. A strategic nuclear force vulnerable to surprise missile attack, a nonnuclear force weak in combat-ready divisions, in airlift capacity and in tactical air support, a counterinsurgency force for all practical purposes nonexistent, and a weapons inventory completely lacking in certain major elements but far oversupplied in others.

4. Too many automatic decisions made in advance instead of in the light of an actual emergency, and too few Pentagon-wide plans for each kind of contingency.[191]

McNamara's preliminary report was in Kennedy's hands in time to provide the basis for some recommendations in the new President's first major pronouncement on national policy, his State of the Union message sent to Congress on January 30, 1961.[192] In this statement Kennedy set as the national goal the establishment of "a Free World force so powerful as to make any aggression clearly futile," and he disclosed that he had instructed McNamara to reappraise the nation's entire defense strategy, with preliminary conclusions due by the end of February. Meanwhile, as stop-gap measures to remedy what he regarded as the most glaring inadequacies in the nation's existing defense posture, Kennedy called for an increase in the airlift capacity for conventional forces and an acceleration of the Polaris submarine program and of missile output. The rationale underlying these measures, as well as the entire massive arms buildup the Kennedy administration carried through in its first year in office, was defined in the State of the Union message as follows: "If we are to keep the peace, we need an invulnerable missile force powerful enough to deter

190. Theodore C. Sorensen, *Kennedy* (Harper and Row, 1965), p. 603. See also William W. Kaufmann, *The McNamara Strategy* (Harper and Row, 1964), p. 48.

191. Sorensen, *Kennedy*, p. 603.

192. Text in *Public Papers of the Presidents of the United States: John F. Kennedy, 1961* (GPO, 1962), pp. 19–28. Hereafter *Public Papers, 1961*.

any aggressor from even threatening an attack that he would know could not destroy enough of our force to prevent his own destruction."[193]

By the middle of March McNamara had completed his comprehensive review of U.S. defense capabilities. On the basis of his findings Kennedy sent to Congress on March 28 a Special Presidential Message, which included what Sorensen calls "the first full statement of a coherent national defense doctrine for the age of mutual nuclear capabilities."[194] The heart of this section of the message, which was to serve as one of the basic principles of the Kennedy administration's defense policies, was the statement:

Our strategic arms and defenses must be adequate to deter any deliberate nuclear attack on the United States or our allies—by making it clear to any potential aggressor that sufficient retaliatory forces will be able to survive a first strike and penetrate his defenses in order to inflict unacceptable losses upon him.[195]

The goal Kennedy set for the nation, therefore, was neither strategic parity with the USSR nor a modest level of superiority, but a preponderance so decisive that the Soviet leaders would be under no temptation to launch a nuclear-missile attack on the United States. This goal, clearly stated in the March 28 message, in no way constitutes an admission of U.S. strategic inferiority vis-à-vis the USSR.

Included in the March 28 message were recommendations for a rapid buildup of conventional (nonnuclear) forces, requiring an additional $650 million.[196] The purpose of these moves was essentially based on the arguments voiced earlier by such critics of the Eisenhower-Dulles doctrine of "massive retaliation" as General Taylor. As Sorensen points out,

Kennedy inherited in 1961 a 1956 National Security Council directive relying chiefly on nuclear retaliation to any Communist action larger than a brush fire in general and to any serious Soviet military action whatsoever in Western Europe. . . . Because NATO strategy had a similar basis, no serious effort had

193. Ibid., pp. 23–24.
194. Sorensen, *Kennedy*, p. 604.
195. *Public Papers, 1961*, p. 231. For Sorensen's formulation of the doctrine, see his *Kennedy*, p. 610. Essentially the same principle formed part of the Nixon-Rockefeller agreement on national defense of July 23, 1960; see White, *The Making of the President 1960*, p. 389. The broad area of agreement on this issue between Kennedy and the liberal wing of the Republican party helps explain how he was able to get his requests for greatly increased defense spending through Congress.
196. Schlesinger, *A Thousand Days*, p. 318.

been made to bring its force levels up to full strength, and our own Army had been sharply reduced in size.[197]

Development of tactical nuclear weapons, on which Dulles had once pinned his hopes, did not appeal to Kennedy as an answer to the search for greater flexibility, although his administration "increased the development and deployment of those weapons world-wide, and by 60 percent in Western Europe alone." Kennedy's skepticism in this area was the result of his inability to see any real difference between the use of the "small" nuclear weapons and the larger strategic bombs. It was his belief that "once an exchange of these weapons started . . . there was no well-defined dividing line that would keep the big bomb out."[198]

To solve this dilemma, the administration developed "the new Kennedy-McNamara doctrine on conventional forces," which Sorensen summarizes as follows:

The essence of this doctrine was choice: If the President was to have a balanced range of forces from which to select the most appropriate response for each situation—if this country was to be able to confine a limited challenge to the local and nonnuclear level, without permitting a Communist victory— then it was necessary to build our own nonnuclear forces to the point where any aggressor would be confronted with the same poor choice Kennedy wanted to avoid: humiliation or escalation.[199]

The "Kennedy-McNamara doctrine," first articulated in the message of March 28, 1961, was further developed in a "Special Message on Urgent National Needs" which Kennedy presented before Congress on May 25. In this message he requested additional funds to upgrade and strengthen the regular Army, special forces and unconventional warfare units, the reserves, and the Marine Corps. Implementation of these plans, he said, "will allow us to almost double the combat power of the Army in less than two months, compared to the nearly nine months heretofore required."[200]

The doctrine on which this military buildup was based, according to Sorensen, was "the heart and hard core of his [Kennedy's] military response to the 1961 Berlin crisis."[201] That being the case, one is confronted by a seeming paradox: the enormous military buildup carried through by

197. Sorensen, *Kennedy*, p. 625.
198. Ibid., pp. 625, 626.
199. Ibid., p. 626.
200. *Public Papers, 1961*, p. 401.
201. Sorensen, *Kennedy*, p. 627.

the Kennedy administration in its first three months in office, a buildup that raised total defense expenditures by nearly $1 billion (excluding foreign military aid),[202] was undertaken before the Kennedy administration showed any real awareness that a new crisis in Berlin was about to break out. For despite all Kennedy's warnings in the 1961 campaign that a new Berlin crisis was to be expected no later than the spring of 1961, he and his advisers seem largely to have ignored the numerous indicators that pointed to imminent trouble in that area.

The Kennedy Administration's Perception of the Berlin Situation, January–May 1961

The problem of Berlin had preoccupied Kennedy long before he entered the White House. In an interview in December 1959 he had expressed the hope for a "long-range solution" of the problem, through some form of Soviet-Western agreement "which would respect the relative position of both of us in that section of Europe and still permit Berlin to live easier,"[203] and he returned to the theme in a speech of June 14, 1960.[204] The next month, early in the presidential campaign, he accepted an offer by Adlai Stevenson to prepare a report on foreign policy which, when it was delivered in mid-November, included Berlin among the questions requiring the new administration's "immediate attention."[205]

By the time Kennedy took office, however, the most urgent foreign policy problem confronting Washington appeared to be the threatened collapse of the American-sponsored government in Laos in the face of a Soviet-supported insurgent drive, and perhaps for that reason Kennedy and his advisers devoted little attention to Berlin.[206] It was not until early

202. Stebbins, *The United States in World Affairs, 1961*, p. 31. This figure does not reflect additional funds requested in Kennedy's message of May 25, 1961, including $100 million for weapons procurement and $60 million for expansion of the Marine Corps to 190,000 men. *Public Papers, 1961*, p. 401.

203. John F. Kennedy, *The Strategy of Peace*, edited by Allan Nevins (Harper, 1960), p. 214.

204. Schick, *Berlin Crisis*, p. 143.

205. Schlesinger, *A Thousand Days*, pp. 155–56. Schlesinger does not identify any specific proposals on Berlin in the Stevenson report, but elsewhere (p. 346) mentions Stevenson as one of the Democrats who "were prepared to trade legal points for definitive guarantees of Allied presence and access" to Berlin.

206. No reference to Berlin occurs in the inaugural address (January 20), the State of the Union message (January 25), or the two special messages on defense of March 28 and May 25.

March that the administration began seriously to concern itself with the Berlin problem, and then the stimulus was evidently the publication in the Soviet press on March 3 of the Soviet aide-mémoire to West Germany of February 17.[207] There followed a flurry of statements by spokesmen of the administration: a press conference statement by Rusk affirming U.S. intentions to maintain its rights in Berlin; an official denial of reports that the United States was considering reducing its garrison in Berlin; and a statement by newly appointed Ambassador-at-Large Averell Harriman that "all discussion on Berlin must begin from the start,"[208] a statement Schlesinger characterizes as "a move to disengage Kennedy from the concessions the Eisenhower administration had made in 1959 and even more from the ones we had been informed Eisenhower was ready to make at the 1960 summit meeting in Paris."[209]

The ominous report sent by Ambassador Thompson on his March 9 meeting with Khrushchev, however, seems finally to have prodded Kennedy into turning his attention toward Berlin. It was at about this time that Kennedy asked Dean Acheson "to undertake special studies of the problems of NATO and Germany," not because he shared Acheson's hard-line views on Berlin but because he "considered Acheson one of the most intelligent and experienced men around and did not see why he should not avail himself of 'hard' views before making his own judgments."[210] There was still no sense of urgency, however, nor any realization that a new crisis might be brewing; Kennedy's special defense message of March 28 contained no reference to Berlin as a potential trouble spot, and apparently his staff completely missed the clear warning signal in the Warsaw Pact communiqué published on March 31.[211]

When Kennedy played host to British Prime Minister Harold Macmillan in early April the most urgent item on the agenda was the crisis in Laos, but time was found for Acheson to present a preview of his report on Berlin. The report followed closely the lines Acheson had developed

207. "The publication of the Soviet Note forced the U.S. administration to demonstrate publicly its inflexibility on Berlin." Watt, *Survey of International Affairs, 1961*, p. 219.
208. *New York Times,* March 9, 1961.
209. Schlesinger, *A Thousand Days,* p. 348.
210. Ibid., p. 380.
211. Schlesinger, *A Thousand Days,* p. 347, remarks, "As late as the end of March 1961, a Moscow meeting of the Warsaw Pact countries adjourned without mention of Berlin."

in his March 1959 critique of the Eisenhower-Dulles policy on Berlin. As summarized by Schlesinger, Acheson said it looked

as if the Soviet Union planned to force the Berlin issue this year. He did not believe that Berlin could be satisfactorily settled apart from the larger question of Germany; and he saw no prospect of any agreement on either Berlin or Germany compatible with the interests of the west. Therefore, when Khrushchev moved to cut off West Berlin the allies must instantly demonstrate their determination to stand up to the Soviet challenge. Skipping over possibilities of diplomatic or economic response, Acheson crisply offered a formidable catalogue of military countermeasures, concluding tentatively in favor of sending a division down the *Autobahn*. . . . If the Russians repulsed the probe, then at least the west would know where it stood, and it could rally and rearm as it did during the Korean war.[212]

It seemed like a replay of the debate between the Eisenhower administration and the British in the early months of 1959, except that this time Macmillan kept silent, leaving the task of advocating the diplomatic approach to his foreign secretary, Lord Home.[213]

Whether because he found Kennedy a sympathetic personality, considered it futile to combat Acheson's vigorous presentation of his thesis, or recognized that the United States was now boldly reasserting its leadership of the Western alliance, Macmillan seems to have gracefully accepted the role of a supporting rather than a principal actor in the drama that was about to unfold. The communiqué issued at the end of the Kennedy-Macmillan talks mentioned the "critical problem of Laos and Vietnam," and expressed hope for an agreement with the USSR in the test-ban talks at Geneva, but said nothing about Berlin.[214]

Berlin was prominently featured, however, in a joint statement issued on April 13 by Kennedy and Adenauer following the latter's two-day visit to Washington. The statement blandly ignored the Soviet proposals on Berlin and Germany, instead affirming the position of the two heads of government

that only through the application of the principle of self-determination can a just and enduring solution be found for the problem of Germany including Berlin. They renewed their pledge to preserve the freedom of the people of

212. Ibid., p. 380.
213. In his memoirs, Macmillan avoids entirely any discussion of Acheson's presentation. Macmillan, *Pointing the Way*, pp. 348, 352. According to Schlesinger the major British critique of the Acheson report was delivered by Lord Home. Schlesinger, *A Thousand Days*, pp. 380–81.
214. *Public Papers, 1961*, p. 252.

West Berlin pending the reunification of Germany in peace and freedom and the restoration of Berlin as the capital of a reunified country.[215] The final base to be touched in Kennedy's contacts with the leaders of the Western alliance was Paris, where he planned to see de Gaulle at the end of May. Khrushchev's acceptance of the bid for a rendezvous at Vienna, however, had the effect of converting the Kennedy–de Gaulle meeting into a curtain-raiser before the main show. The two statesmen found themselves in agreement on the need for firmness in Berlin in case the USSR applied pressure. De Gaulle was reported to believe that "Khrushchev must be made to recognize that fighting around Berlin would mean a general war . . . the last thing Khrushchev wanted," to which Kennedy replied that "Khrushchev must understand that if necessary, we would go to nuclear war."[216]

The Vienna Meeting

To get set for his meeting with Khrushchev, Kennedy systematically canvassed the views of Americans who knew the Soviet leader at first hand or who had talked with him recently, and boned up on the records of previous summit meetings as well as on a collection of Khrushchev's major speeches. On the eve of his departure for Europe he told Hugh Sidey, the White House correspondent for *Time* magazine, that he had "two main considerations" in his forthcoming talks with Khrushchev: (1) the impasse in the nuclear test-ban talks, with mounting pressure in the United States for a resumption of testing and the growing (and well-founded) suspicion that the USSR was preparing to resume testing, and (2) the need "to warn Khrushchev on Berlin." "The President and all his Soviet experts," Sidey wrote, "felt that Berlin would be the real trouble spot of the year."[217]

Recognizing as he did the high probability that a new international crisis over Berlin was about to break out, why did Kennedy not take some specific action to signal U.S. determination to maintain its rights there? Why, in effect, did he wait for Khrushchev to make the first move? The answer to these questions cannot be found in the difficulties of coordinating policies within the Western alliance, as had been true at an analogous

215. Ibid., pp. 265–66.
216. Schlesinger, *A Thousand Days*, pp. 349–51.
217. Sidey, *John F. Kennedy, President*, pp. 167–69.

stage in the 1958–59 crisis. Then there had been sharp disagreements between the United States and its allies over the risks inherent in the use of limited force as proposed by U.S. and NATO military commanders. Now there seemed general agreement that some form of limited force might have to be used.

Kennedy's restraint, it seems likely, was the result of his realization that U.S. and NATO military forces were completely unprepared for any serious test of strength with the USSR. Pentagon contingency plans for trouble in Berlin, McNamara reported in early May, "assumed almost immediate resort to nuclear war."[218]

It seems probable that Kennedy's realization of the imminence of a new crisis in Berlin, coupled with his discovery of the inadequacy of U.S. forces to cope with a situation calling for the application of limited military force, contributed to his decision to ask Congress on May 25 for additional funds to strengthen the conventional armed forces and increase their mobility.

THE ENCOUNTER AT VIENNA. In the two days Kennedy and Khrushchev spent together at Vienna (June 3 and 4), the American leader found his Soviet counterpart a tough and unyielding adversary. On the Berlin issue especially, the clash between the two men was direct and unmitigated. Despite Kennedy's categorical statement that Berlin was "a matter of the highest concern to the United States" in which "our national security was involved,"[219] Khrushchev asserted that

no force in the world could prevent the USSR from signing a peace treaty by the end of the year. No further delay was possible or necessary. The sovereignty of the German Democratic Republic . . . would have to be observed. Any violation of that sovereignty would be regarded by the USSR as an act of open aggression against a peace-loving country with all the consequences ensuing therefrom. If East German borders—land, air or sea borders—were violated, they would be defended.[220]

The most Khrushchev was willing to concede was that

a face-saving interim agreement might be reached to cover the next six months, but the USSR could no longer delay. Any continued Western presence inside East Germany after a peace treaty had ended the war would be illegal, humiliating, and a violation of East Germany's borders—and those borders would be defended. Force would be met by force. . . . The decision to

218. Schlesinger, *A Thousand Days*, p. 388.
219. Sorensen, *Kennedy*, p. 584.
220. Ibid., p. 585.

sign a peace treaty in December (unless there was an interim six months' agreement) was firm and irrevocable.[221]

To nail down the Soviet position still more firmly, Khrushchev gave Kennedy an aide-mémoire on Germany at the end of their meeting, in which the same position was restated, though with a less categorical insistence on the six-month deadline.[222]

KHRUSHCHEV'S POSITION AND MOTIVES AT VIENNA. The encounter with Khrushchev at Vienna was so "sobering" to Kennedy[223] that a widely accepted evaluation of the meeting has grown up picturing the Soviet leader as "bullying" or "browbeating" the American President, often with the added inference that Khrushchev's overbearing manner was the result of his belief that Kennedy had shown himself weak-willed and irresolute in the Bay of Pigs disaster and could therefore be pushed around on Berlin.[224] Sorensen suggests that this evaluation, which he dismisses as a "legend," may have resulted from "over-management" of the press by Kennedy, who "wanted no one to think that the surface cordiality in Vienna justified any notion of a new 'Spirit of Geneva, 1955,' or 'Spirit of Camp David, 1959.' "[225]

Sorensen is on the right track, I believe, in the explanation he offers for the widespread misconception of Kennedy's role at Vienna, but he fails to explain Khrushchev's behavior. I have postulated that a decision was reached in the CPSU Presidium in mid-February 1961 to "solve" East Germany's security problem either along the lines of Khrushchev's program of a peace treaty with East Germany and the conversion of West Berlin into a "free city" or by physically severing West Berlin from the Soviet-occupied eastern sector. Khrushchev, in this view, was given six months to show he could solve the Berlin problem his way; if he failed, the alternative plan would be implemented.

221. Ibid., pp. 585–86.
222. Sorensen, *Kennedy*, p. 586, notes that the aide-mémoire "confused the question of deadlines."
223. Kennedy repeatedly used this term or one of its variants to describe the Vienna meeting in his radio and television report to the American people on June 6. Text in *Public Papers, 1961*, pp. 441–46.
224. For an early and influential analysis along these lines, see James Reston, "What Was Killed Was Not Only the President but the Promise," *New York Times Magazine,* November 15, 1964, pp. 24–25, 126–27. Reston, a senior *New York Times* correspondent, was the first American journalist to interview Kennedy after his meeting with Khrushchev.
225. Sorensen, *Kennedy*, p. 550.

Knowing as he did that by mid-February 1961 the policy of strategic bluff on which he had based his Berlin campaign in 1958–59 was no longer serviceable, Khrushchev faced a difficult task. Only by putting intense pressure on the United States could he hope to achieve his goal, yet the prospects for success in 1961 were far slimmer than they had been in 1958–59, when at least some prominent Americans accepted Soviet claims for strategic superiority over the United States.

Another difficulty in Khrushchev's task was his ignorance of Kennedy's views and character. If the USSR precipitated a new crisis over Berlin, there was a definite risk that the United States might respond by using its superior nuclear arsenal. Khrushchev's confidential disclosure to Lippmann that he would not unleash a new Berlin crisis until he had had a face-to-face meeting with Kennedy indicates his perception of this danger, as does the concern he manifested over the possibility of U.S. intervention in the Bay of Pigs invasion.

A paradoxical conclusion that emerges from this line of analysis is that Kennedy's best hope of avoiding a new crisis over Berlin lay in playing the part of an irresponsible, trigger-happy hothead, who might easily react to new Soviet pressure in Berlin by unleashing his heavy weapons— in effect, imitating Herman Kahn's description of a teenager playing the game of "chicken" who gives "the appearance of being drunk, blind, and without a steering wheel."[226] Instead, Kennedy stressed the need for both sides to exercise caution and restraint, and went to great lengths to convey to Khrushchev his concern that war between the United States and the USSR might result from miscalculation or misunderstanding on either side.[227]

At Vienna Kennedy completed the process of reassuring Khrushchev as to his sobriety and restraint, which he had begun with his letter to the Soviet leader pledging that the United States would not intervene directly in the Bay of Pigs invasion. The Vienna meeting served Khrushchev as a testing ground with regard to the degree of risk involved in launching a new Berlin crisis, and he was therefore stating the simple truth when he said, in a radio and television report to the Soviet people on June 15, that the Vienna meeting was "more than worth while and, more than that, it had to be held." He went on to say that he had "formed the impression that President Kennedy appreciates the great responsibility that rests with

226. Kahn, *On Escalation*, p. 11.
227. Schlesinger, *A Thousand Days*, pp. 360–61.

the governments of two such mighty states," and he expressed the hope that "the time will come when Soviet-American relations will improve."[228]

During the Vienna talks Khrushchev raised the subject of nuclear testing, saying, in Sorensen's paraphrase, that "Kennedy's defense requests put pressure on him to increase his forces, just as both of them were under pressure from their scientists and military to resume nuclear tests." Sorensen quotes Khrushchev as saying, "But we will wait for you to resume testing and, if you do, we will."[229]

The Formal Opening of the Soviet Campaign

Reassured by his talks with Kennedy as to the American leader's sobriety and healthy fear of nuclear war, Khrushchev now took a series of steps that constituted his opening bid in the new Soviet campaign on Berlin. He had to work fast: On the hypothesis that the "collective leadership" in February had set a six-month deadline for a solution of the Berlin question, Khrushchev had a scant two months remaining. The military buildup already launched by the Kennedy administration constituted a sobering warning that any Soviet attempt to intimidate the United States would make little headway, while the Soviet recognition that the American leaders now knew the facts about Soviet ICBM strength still further lengthened the odds against Khrushchev.

From Khrushchev's standpoint, nevertheless, the effort to win a diplomatic victory over the United States in Berlin was worth making, not only because there was an outside chance it might be successful—a prospect that must have appealed to the gambler in Khrushchev—but for more cogent reasons: first, it would give him a new opportunity to appear before the world as *the* Soviet leader, brandishing his rockets and ordering the West to abandon its outpost in Berlin; second, even if, or rather especially if, it failed, it could serve as a smoke-screen behind which preparations could go forward for implementing the minimum goal adopted at the (hypothetical) mid-February meeting of the Presidium, the physical sealing off of West Berlin. That action, as Khrushchev could not fail to realize, also entailed a certain element of risk, since it would be a direct

228. *Pravda,* June 16, 1961. See also Schlesinger, *A Thousand Days,* p. 378, for Khrushchev's positive evaluation of Kennedy as a result of the Vienna meeting.
229. Sorensen, *Kennedy,* p. 544. See also Schlesinger, *A Thousand Days,* p. 373.

violation of the four-power agreements on the administration of Greater Berlin, which the Western allies had pledged themselves to defend. Sealing off West Berlin, however, while risky, would mean a far less provocative challenge to the Western powers than the threat or actuality of interference with their rights of access to the city. They might even feel a certain sense of relief if Khrushchev and Ulbricht solved their problem in Berlin by means that left the Western position in the city intact. There was only one serious drawback to this line of reasoning, from Khrushchev's standpoint: In order to make a credible opening bid he would have to grant certain concessions to the Soviet military establishment, since their support would be essential to his endeavors.

Against this background, we can summarize Khrushchev's opening moves in the 1961 crisis.

1. On June 15, as already noted, Khrushchev broadcast a report on the Vienna meeting to the Soviet people in which, for the first time in public, he announced the end-of-the-year deadline for the conclusion of a peace treaty with Germany. The speech was far less bellicose than many he had delivered during the 1958–59 crisis, however, and contained not only words of praise for Kennedy but a strong defense of the Khrushchev version of peaceful coexistence.

2. Six days later, at a formal meeting in Moscow to mark the twentieth anniversary of the Nazi attack on the USSR, Khrushchev, wearing the uniform of a lieutenant general (his wartime rank as a political adviser), delivered a ringing call for the elimination of the danger of a new war through signature of a peace treaty with East Germany by the end of the year. Again he stated, as he had to Kennedy at Vienna, that the USSR would resume nuclear testing only if the United States did so.[230] Again, even more than at Vienna, he showed an awareness of the heavy costs of military escalation. Citing the Kennedy administration's $2.5 billion military buildup he said:

The Soviet government is doing everything in its power to end the arms race and to remove from the people's shoulders the heavy burden of military expenditures. Unfortunately, the imperialist powers are answering our call to compete in the production of material and spiritual values with increased military expenditures and expansion of their armed forces. This may confront the Soviet Union with the necessity of increasing allocations for armaments too, in order to strengthen and improve our defenses and, if necessary, also

230. *Pravda*, June 22, 1961.

increasing the numerical strength of our armed forces in order, on the basis of our might, to ensure peace and peaceful coexistence.[231]

An extensive section of Khrushchev's June 21 speech was devoted to extolling the Soviet rocket troops and "their capacity to strike a retaliatory blow . . . which will inevitably punish an aggressor if he nevertheless decides on an act of folly and unleashes a new war."[232] Strikingly absent, however, were the claims for Soviet superiority in ICBM production that had marked so many of Khrushchev's speeches in 1958–59.

A prominent feature of the June 21 meeting was the presence of a solid phalanx of Soviet military leaders, headed by Defense Minister Malinovsky. By their speeches and physical presence the top brass were rendering public testimony to their solidarity with the First Secretary–Premier.

3. The price Khrushchev was required to pay for the military leaders' support was disclosed in a speech he delivered on July 8 to a class of graduating cadets. Citing the recent increases in the U.S. military budget, Khrushchev stated that "the Soviet government had been forced to issue instructions to the Minister of Defense to suspend temporarily, pending a special order, the reduction in the armed forces planned for 1961," and to put through a 3 billion ruble increase in military expenditures for the current year—approximately a 25 percent hike. Khrushchev defended these moves as "temporary," and asserted, not very convincingly, that they would not result in a lowering of Soviet funds for investment in consumer goods, agriculture, and other nonmilitary needs.[233]

While Khrushchev was carrying out these steps the East German political boss, Walter Ulbricht, was manifesting unmistakable signs of incipient euphoria. At a press conference on June 15 Ulbricht almost openly predicted the construction of a wall to seal off West Berlin and dropped broad hints that this action would mean the end of unrestricted Western access to the city by air.[234]

Kennedy Girds for the Crisis

The Vienna meeting brought Kennedy face to face with the crisis he had so long expected. Khrushchev's double-barreled approach—his un-

231. Ibid.
232. Ibid.
233. *Pravda,* July 9, 1961. For an analysis of the economic implications of Khrushchev's speech, see Abraham S. Becker, "Soviet Military Outlays Since 1955" (Rand Corp., July 1964), p. 50.
234. *Documents on Germany, 1944–61,* pp. 652–64, 658–60.

yielding oral presentation of the Soviet position (given, it should be noted, under the watchful eyes of two hard-liners on Berlin, Soviet Foreign Minister Gromyko and Ambassador to the United States Menshikov), followed by the statement of the same demands in the aide-mémoire (obviously prepared in advance of the meeting, and thus carrying the approval of the full Presidium, including the now recovered Kozlov) left no room for doubt that the long-anticipated storm was at hand. One illusion was still left to Kennedy, however, that he had six months in which to prepare before the USSR lowered the boom. A great deal of the acute tension of the next few months was because the Soviets made their key move, the construction of the Berlin Wall, on August 12, at a time when Kennedy thought he still had several months to maneuver and negotiate. It was widely believed in Washington that the USSR might announce its decision to sign a peace treaty with East Germany at the Twenty-second Congress of the Communist party of the Soviet Union, due to take place in the second half of October. Another favored date was late September, following scheduled elections in West Germany.

Not that Kennedy procrastinated; his actions during June and July conveyed a sense of urgency that reflected his "somber" clash with Khrushchev at Vienna. The British too, this time, seemed reconciled to the need to reply to Soviet pressure with limited force. In London, on June 5 and 6, Kennedy told Macmillan that

military planning in Berlin had to be stepped up. They would have to decide what the West should do in a series of contingencies—if the Russians signed the treaty but made no changes in the existing arrangements; or if they interrupted the civilian supply of West Berlin; or if they interfered with military traffic.[235]

This time Macmillan raised no strong objections.

Significantly, Kennedy's catalog of possible Soviet actions concentrated on steps Khrushchev had frequently threatened to take but which the USSR, in fact, never took, and omitted two it *did* take—the building of the Berlin Wall and the resumption of nuclear testing. By placing heavy emphasis on the alleged intention to sign a peace treaty with East Germany by the end of the year, and by assuring Kennedy that the USSR would not resume testing unless the United States did so first, Khrushchev had thrown sand in Kennedy's eyes and had maximized the factor of surprise in preparation for the forthcoming Soviet campaign.

235. Schlesinger, *A Thousand Days,* p. 376.

One positive result of Khrushchev's truculence at Vienna, from Kennedy's standpoint, was that it helped persuade Congress that the military buildup he had been calling for was indeed necessary. On June 21 Congress passed a $12.6 billion procurement bill not only covering the missiles, warships, and aircraft Kennedy had requested but including half a billion dollars for the continued procurement of heavy bombers, which he had not.[236]

During this period of mounting tension Acheson finally produced the report on Berlin which Kennedy had called for in March. Schlesinger describes the report, which has not yet been published, as "a long and powerful paper," and summarizes it as follows:

Acheson's basic thesis . . . was that West Berlin was not a problem but a pretext. Khrushchev's *démarche* had nothing to do with Berlin, Germany or Europe. His object, as Acheson saw it, was not to rectify a local situation but to test the general American will to resist; his hope was that, by making us back down on a sacred commitment, he could shatter our world power and influence. This was a simple conflict of wills, and, until it was resolved, any effort to negotiate the Berlin issue per se would be fatal. Since there was nothing to negotiate, willingness on our part to go to the conference table would be taken in Moscow as evidence of weakness and make the crisis so much the worse.

Khrushchev had only dared precipitate the crisis, Acheson continued, because his fear of nuclear war had declined. Our problem was to convince him that this complacency was misplaced and that we would, in fact, go to nuclear war rather than abandon the status quo. This called for the buildup—prompt, serious and quiet—of both our conventional and nuclear forces. . . . The moment there was an interruption of access itself, we must act: first an airlift—and then, if that could not be sustained against Soviet counter-measures, a ground probe in force too large to be stopped by East German troops alone. . . . There was a substantial chance, Acheson said, that the necessary military preparations would by themselves cause Khrushchev to alter his purpose; but he added frankly that there was a substantial possibility that nuclear war might result.[237]

Although the major thrust of his paper was its emphasis on military power, Acheson also considered the possibility of negotiations, but only after Khrushchev had retreated in the face of the Western arms buildup.

Acheson's paper generated a fierce debate in the administration between the "hard-line" advocates of a military response to the Soviet challenge and those, including some ranking Soviet affairs specialists, who

---

236. Stebbins, *The United States in World Affairs 1961,* p. 41, citing 75 Stat. 94.
237. Schlesinger, *A Thousand Days,* pp. 381–82.

believed Khrushchev's objectives might be limited and open to bargaining.[238] Gradually it became clear that the President himself, who had sat "poker-faced" (Schlesinger's description) through Acheson's preliminary presentation in April, was among the advocates of negotiation. Throughout the 1961 crisis he was to emphasize repeatedly the need to present something more than a military response to the Soviet challenge, the need to have a positive negotiating position as an alternative to the threat of armed conflict. Here, however, Kennedy found himself entangled in the thorny problem of coordinating a position with America's allies, a problem that was to prove one of his most frustrating experiences throughout the crisis. Even to get prompt action from the State Department turned out to be unexpectedly difficult, and Kennedy fumed at what he regarded as the excessive time it took to prepare an official reply to the Soviet aide-mémoire of June 4. When one was finally forthcoming he liked it so little that he asked Sorensen to prepare a shorter, more cogent variant, with the result that there were two U.S. replies, the State Department note issued on July 17 and Sorensen's variant, which appeared two days later.

Meanwhile, on June 28 Kennedy issued a statement designed to leave no doubt in Soviet minds about the unalterable determination of the United States to maintain its position and rights in West Berlin. The statement raised the conflict to the level of a test of fundamental U.S. policy. "This is not just a question of technical legal rights," Kennedy said. "It involves the peace and the security of the people of West Berlin. It involves the direct responsibilities and commitments of the United States, the United Kingdom, and France. It involves the peace and the security of the Western world."[239]

U.S. and Soviet Maneuvering, July–August

Khrushchev's speech to the graduating cadets, in which he announced an increase in Soviet military spending, was immediately accepted in Washington as a formal statement of the Soviet intention to force the issue and to lay down a direct challenge to the United States. At a meeting of the National Security Council on the day after Khrushchev's speech, Kennedy ordered a comprehensive review of U.S. military capa-

238. Ibid., pp. 382–83.
239. *Public Papers, 1961*, pp. 476–77.

bilities.[240] The meeting saw a sharp debate between supporters of Acheson's "hard-line" approach and his critics, who believed a willingness to negotiate was essential if catastrophe was to be avoided. The latter group, which included presidential adviser Arthur M. Schlesinger, Jr., had been encouraged by Kennedy to prepare a summary of their views as an alternative to Acheson's call for all-out military preparations, including the proclamation of a national emergency.[241]

While the debate was raging, Soviet Ambassador to Washington Mikhail Menshikov indiscreetly expressed in public a view that he had no doubt been cabling back to Moscow, namely that "when the chips are down, the American people won't fight."[242] Asked to comment at a news conference on July 19, Kennedy said dryly, "We intend to honor our commitments."[243]

Kennedy's formal response to Khrushchev's opening bid in the conflict over Berlin took the form of a radio and television report to the American people on July 25.[244] In it he summed up everything he had learned in the long struggle over Berlin stretching back to the Second World War. The speech crystallized his thinking on the whole complex of problems centering on Berlin: the historical origins of the problem and the legal basis of Western rights in the city; the reason Berlin had become "the focal point where our solemn commitments . . . and Soviet ambitions now meet in basic confrontation"; the way in which Communist challenges in Berlin and elsewhere had tested and strengthened the Western alliance; the relationship between the current crisis and the administration's long-range buildup program; the willingness of the United States to consider "any arrangement or treaty in Germany consistent with the maintenance of peace and freedom, and with the legitimate security interests of all nations"; and—in a final lapidary summation, the basic issue starkly set forth: ". . . we seek peace—but we shall not surrender." Kennedy closed with a fervent warning of the danger of nuclear war resulting from "any misjudgment on either side about the intentions of the other," and an appeal to the American people for understanding and support.

From the standpoint of the present study the most significant passage

240. *New York Times,* July 11, 1961.
241. Schlesinger, *A Thousand Days,* pp. 387–88.
242. Slusser, *The Berlin Crisis of 1961,* pp. 64–65.
243. *Public Papers, 1961,* p. 520.
244. Text in ibid., pp. 533–40.

in the July 25 speech was the list of additional military measures Kennedy said he would ask Congress to authorize, as follows:

1. An additional $3.247 billion for the armed forces.

2. An increase in the army's total authorized strength from 875,000 to approximately 1 million men.

3. Increases in the active duty strength of the Navy by 29,000 and of the Air Force by 63,000.

4. A doubling and tripling of draft calls in coming months, the extension of terms of duty of some military officers on active service, and the call-up of certain reserve units, including Army National Guard divisions, Air Force Reserve air transport squadrons, and Air National Guard tactical squadrons.

5. Retention or reactivation of ships and planes previously headed for retirement, together with deactivation of B-47 bombers.

6. The procurement of nonnuclear weapons, ammunition, and equipment.

Kennedy also called for an additional $207 million in civil defense appropriations, bringing his total new defense budget requests to $3.454 billion. This brought to more than $6 billion the increases he had requested since January, with a resulting projected deficit of over $5 billion. Appropriately, part of the July 25 speech was concerned with an analysis of the nation's economic health, which Kennedy asserted was strong enough to sustain the effort he called for.

Kennedy's July 25 speech and the measures it set in motion mark the real turning point in the Berlin crisis of 1961. The program it outlined constituted both a reasoned response to the Soviet challenge and a massive counterchallenge, which had behind it the entire weight of the U.S. economy, now well on its way to recovery from the stagnation that had marked the final years of the Eisenhower administration.

Reports of Kennedy's July 25 speech reached Khrushchev two days later at Sochi, where he was vacationing. An American, John McCloy, Kennedy's special representative for Soviet-U.S. disarmament talks, was present and able to observe and report Khrushchev's reaction.[245] Stripped of its emotional rhetoric, it boiled down to an admission that the USSR would not attempt to meet the massive U.S. challenge. Khrushchev gave McCloy no hint of any decision to seal off West Berlin, but he did reveal

245. Slusser, *Berlin Crisis of 1961*, pp. 88–93.

that Soviet technical preparations for the resumption of nuclear testing were well advanced and that they included the detonation of a mammoth 100-megaton bomb. Another fact Khrushchev did not divulge to his American guest was that he was host that day to a delegation from communist North Vietnam and that a decision was taken at about this time to grant that nation Soviet military aid, with which it would be able to expand its program of infiltration and subversion against noncommunist South Vietnam.

I conclude therefore that Khrushchev's response to Kennedy's July 25 speech included the following decisions: (1) to drop out of the military arms race; (2) to initiate steps leading to the physical isolation of West Berlin; (3) to go ahead with preparations for the resumption of nuclear testing; and (4) to grant Soviet military aid to North Vietnam, as an economical means of countering the massive buildup of U.S. military power called for by Kennedy.

The August Climax: The Berlin Wall

There is evidence suggesting that Khrushchev's decision to switch from the maximum to the minimum goal on Berlin was approved by the collective leadership at an unannounced meeting of the Presidium early in August, and communicated to the leaders of the satellite nations at a conference of the Warsaw Pact powers on August 3–5. To help minimize the danger that the Western allies, especially West Germany, would react violently to the construction of the Berlin Wall, Khrushchev delivered a series of inflammatory speeches and public statements threatening the West with dire consequences if it dared challenge Soviet policy in Germany.[246] To maintain the Soviet cover story, however, he still defined that policy in terms of the signing of a peace treaty with East Germany no later than the end of the year.

Among those who recognized the likelihood of an imminent Soviet–East German move to choke off West Berlin were those who had the most to lose, the alert citizens of the GDR. Forewarned by Khrushchev's renewal of the Soviet campaign on Berlin at Vienna, record numbers of East Germans streamed into the West Berlin refugee centers during July and early August. In a series of legislative measures the GDR tried to stem

246. Ibid., pp. 95–96, 100–104, 107–14.

the flow, but the effect was simply to heighten the sense of panic that had begun to grip East Germany.[247]

To provide an additional guarantee against any Western inclination to use force in Berlin, the USSR moved two divisions into positions around the city just before construction of the wall began.[248] Somehow, the increasingly clear indications of a Soviet–East German decision to close the border in Berlin failed to register in Washington, though there were some perspicacious U.S. officials who wondered aloud why East Germany didn't solve its refugee problem by stringent border control measures.[249]

Viewed as a problem in tactics, the border-sealing operation was a model of effectiveness. When the East German border police put up the first obstacles along the East-West sector line on the night of August 12–13 they caught the Western nations totally unprepared, and a period of disarray and confusion followed in Washington.[250] The most urgent question now confronting Kennedy was whether the East German action—a clear violation of the wartime agreements on the four-power administration of Berlin—should be contested by force. He decided that it should not, for reasons Sorensen summarizes:

All agreed . . . that the Wall . . . was illegal, immoral and inhumane, but not a cause for war. It ended West Berlin's role as a showcase and escape route for the East, but it did not interfere with the three basic objectives the West had long stressed: our presence in West Berlin, our access to West Berlin and the freedom of West Berliners to choose their own system. Not one responsible official—in this country, in West Berlin, West Germany or Western Europe—suggested that allied forces should march into East German territory and tear the Wall down.[251]

If force was inapplicable as a response to the wall, there were other ways in which it could be and was employed to express American determination. Even before the wall went up, Congress authorized the call-up of as many as 250,000 reservists.[252] This was followed by the authorization of additional sums for weapons procurement on August 3.[253] On

247. Smith, *Defense of Berlin*, pp. 257–66. See also Schick, *Berlin Crisis*, pp. 157–59.
248. *New York Times*, July 19, 1961, and August 14, 1961.
249. Notably Senator J. William Fulbright, in a speech on July 30. See Schlesinger, *A Thousand Days*, p. 394.
250. Schlesinger, *A Thousand Days*, p. 395.
251. Sorensen, *Kennedy*, pp. 593–94. See also Schick, *Berlin Crisis*, pp. 171–73; Schlesinger, *A Thousand Days*, p. 402.
252. Stebbins, *The United States in World Affairs 1961*, p. 42, citing 75 Stat. 242.
253. Ibid., citing 75 Stat. 243.

August 6 the U.S. Third Army and 40,000 Air Force reserves conducted Operation Swift Strike I, just before the call-up of reserves.[254] After the construction of the wall U.S. military actions came thick and fast. On August 14 the Navy announced it would hold 26,800 officers and men on active duty for six to twelve months beyond normal terms.[255] On August 16, 113 Reserve and National Guard units were alerted and 84,000 enlistments were extended beyond normal release dates.[256] These moves were made in line with the program announced in the President's speech of July 25, though they may have been accelerated by the sense of urgency that resulted from the wall. That action, with its revelation that the Western powers had been, in effect, preparing for the wrong challenge, generated pressure for a military response, especially in West Berlin itself, where the construction of the wall and the apparent inability of the West to take any effective countermeasures were creating a serious morale problem. It was primarily to meet this need that Kennedy on August 17 ordered the dispatch to West Berlin of a battle group of 1,500 men along the autobahn from West Germany.[257] Here at last, it seemed, was the contingency plan for which Acheson, Taylor, and others had been calling, but under very different circumstances from those they had envisaged: instead of being a move to warn the USSR against taking a decisive step in the Berlin situation, it was a move designed to prop up West Berlin's sagging morale *after* a definitive Soviet move. In size and scope, too, the battle group operation differed from earlier contingency plans, which had usually called for the employment of at least a division. By reason of its diminutive size the battle group's deployment was clearly a symbolic gesture: It was too small to represent any real challenge even to the East German "people's police" or any effective reinforcement to the Western garrison in Berlin; it *was* large enough to make plain the continuing U.S. commitment to West Berlin.

The period during which the battle group was en route to Berlin across

254. U.S. Department of the Army, Third Army, *History of the United States Third Army, 1918–1962.*

255. Barbara H. Gilmore, comp., *Chronology of Naval Events, 1960–1974* (Department of the Navy, Naval Historical Center, Operational Archives).

256. Department of the Army, Office of the Chief of Military History, *U.S. Defense Policies from World War II* (Army Historical Series).

257. Kennedy's decision was prompted by an urgent letter from Willy Brandt calling attention to the dangerous threat to West Berliners' morale posed by the wall. Schlesinger, *A Thousand Days,* pp. 395–96.

East German territory provided some of Kennedy's most anxious moments, but the operation was carried out successfully and achieved its aim: the U.S. commitment to West Berlin had been visibly reaffirmed and the morale of its citizens began to recover from the low ebb of the immediate post-wall depression.[258]

One inadvertent by-product of the movement of the battle group to Berlin was the establishment of a precedent that gave the Soviets added leverage over U.S. troop movements along the autobahn. According to Schick, the commander of the battle group, in order to expedite its passage, "accepted a Soviet request at the checkpoint to dismount his troops for a head count," a request U.S. commanders had previously refused. "His action," writes Schick, "stuck as official practice between 1961 and 1963."[259]

An important part of Kennedy's strategy in the 1961 crisis was to persuade America's major allies, Britain and France, to shoulder a larger part of the military burden. In this effort he had only mixed success. The British, though willing to support the United States verbally, were hard put to come up with any actual reinforcements, since they were suffering the adverse effects of a financial crisis coupled with sharp demands on their available troop reserves in Kuwait. The French, too, though sympathetic to U.S. policy in words, made little tangible contribution to the Western buildup. In the immediate aftermath of the construction of the Berlin Wall, however, both nations did order reinforcements for NATO forces in Germany: on August 17 it was reported that the French had announced plans to strengthen their ground and air forces in West Germany and continental France, while the United Kingdom was reported to have ordered limited reinforcement of its tactical units in West Germany and the recall of an armored unit from Kuwait to serve as the nucleus of a new strategic reserve division capable of reinforcing the British Army of the Rhine.[260]

U.S. response to the heightened tension generated by the Berlin Wall included the passage by Congress on August 16 of two key measures: a $46.5 billion defense appropriation covering virtually all the points specified in Kennedy's speech of July 25, as well as funds for extra bomber

---

258. Sorensen, *Kennedy*, p. 594. See also Schlesinger, *A Thousand Days*, pp. 396–97.
259. Schick, *Berlin Crisis*, p. xv.
260. *New York Times*, August 18, 1961.

procurement and a further $180 million for accelerated development of the supersonic B-70 bombers; and a bill providing the extra funds Kennedy had requested to launch the U.S. program to land a man on the moon by 1970.[261]

The Opposition in the Kremlin Takes Charge

Immediately after the construction of the wall, and as soon as it was clear that the Western powers were not going to challenge that act by force, Khrushchev left Moscow for an extended vacation in Sochi. There is evidence to indicate that he returned to the Kremlin briefly on August 16 to take several actions: to dispatch a personal message to Adenauer reassuring the West German leader about Soviet intentions in Berlin, and to order the recall of the Soviet ambassador to Albania.[262] Shortly thereafter Khrushchev resumed his interrupted vacation, and he remained at Sochi until the end of August.

During the period Khrushchev was absent from Moscow, the Soviet and East German governments took a series of steps constituting a more direct challenge to the Western position in Berlin than any previous Communist actions.

1. On August 22 the East German government closed all but one of the border crossing points in Berlin open for "foreigners," including members of the Western occupation forces, and ordered the establishment of a 100-meter no-man's-land on either side of the sector boundary.[263]

2. On the following day, Soviet notes were sent to the three Western allies accusing them of using the air corridors to West Berlin to transport "revanchists, extremists, saboteurs, and spies," and for the first time threatening direct Soviet interference with Western access to the city by air.[264]

The August 23 note for the first time presented a direct challenge to rights Kennedy had explicitly vowed to defend. Washington's response was prompt and clear. A White House statement issued on August 24 called the Soviet charges and allegations "false, as the Soviet government

261. Stebbins, *The United States in World Affairs 1961*, p. 42, citing 75 Stat. 342 and 75 Stat. 365.

262. Slusser, *Berlin Crisis of 1961*, pp. 140–42.

263. Watt, *Survey of International Affairs, 1961*, p. 250.

264. *New York Times*, August 25, 1961. See also Schlesinger, *A Thousand Days*, p. 398.

well knows," and it warned that "any interference by the Soviet Government or its East German regime with free access to West Berlin would be an aggressive act for the consequences of which the Soviet Government would bear full responsibility."[265]

This time the United States and its allies responded with almost equal alacrity, and on August 26 the United Kingdom and France sent protests to the USSR restating the warning contained in the U.S. statement of August 24.[266] Meanwhile, to counter the GDR border control measure ordered on August 22, the U.S. commandant in Berlin on the 24th ordered the deployment of a thousand troops, with tanks, along the East-West sector border.[267]

3. On August 29 the Soviet government announced the "temporary deferment" of reservists from the Soviet Army and Navy, a move explicitly linked with the "immediate conclusion of a German peace treaty . . . by the end of this year."[268]

4. On the following day the Soviet government announced it would resume the testing of nuclear weapons. Professing reluctance to take this step, the note said the USSR had been forced to do so "under the pressure of the international situation being created by the imperialist forces."[269]

While these actions were being taken in Moscow, Khrushchev, in Sochi, was stressing the Soviet desire for negotiations on Germany as a means to head off the threat of war between the USSR and the Western powers. On August 24 he told columnist Drew Pearson of his desire for talks with the Western powers on Berlin and Germany, and two days later he sent an urgent message to C. L. Sulzberger, senior diplomatic correspondent of the *New York Times,* proposing an interview. (The interview with Sulzberger took place after Khrushchev's return to Moscow, on September 5.)[270]

The complex and apparently contradictory pattern of Soviet policy in the period from August 22 to 31 is interpreted in diametrically opposite ways by the "traditionalists" and myself. Schick, for example, sees the bellicose Soviet statements and actions of this period as means to apply

265. *Public Papers, 1961,* pp. 568–69.
266. *Documents on Germany, 1944–1961,* pp. 756–57.
267. *U.S. Defense Policies from World War II.*
268. *Pravda,* August 30, 1961.
269. Ibid., August 31, 1961.
270. Slusser, *Berlin Crisis of 1961,* pp. 145–48, 190–210.

further pressure to the West and as responses to Kennedy's program of military buildup. Soviet resumption of nuclear testing, according to Schick, was intended "to underline the lunacy of war."[271] My explanation for the "dialectical contradictions" of Soviet policy in this period is simple: During Khrushchev's absence from the Kremlin, his internal opponents seized control of Soviet policymaking and put through a series of measures that brought the USSR and the Western powers close to the brink of war.[272]

An advantage of this approach is that it provides an explanation of the no less confusing and apparently contradictory pattern of Soviet foreign policy in the period from early September to the end of October 1961. Following are the principal moves in chronological order:

1. The new Soviet nuclear test series began on September 1 and continued thereafter at short intervals until October 31, when the USSR detonated a super-bomb with a yield estimated at 50 megatons.

2. On September 12, when addressing a congress of the North Korean Communist party in Pyongyang, Kozlov disclosed that the December 31 deadline for the signing of a peace treaty with East Germany had been lifted.

3. The next day Soviet fighter planes buzzed two U.S. commercial airliners en route to Berlin. This was the last direct Soviet threat to Western access to Berlin by air during 1961, however; in the words of a British observer, "A turning point in the crisis seemed to have been reached and passed."[273]

4. On September 20, before Kozlov had returned to Moscow, U.S. and Soviet negotiators reached agreement on a statement of basic principles to govern disarmament talks between the two powers.[274]

5. On September 24 a personal emissary of Khrushchev sought out Pierre Salinger, White House press secretary, and delivered a confidential message to Kennedy from Khrushchev assuring him that "the storm in Berlin is over."[275]

6. Finally, on October 17, in his opening address to the Twenty-second Congress of the Communist party of the Soviet Union, Khru-

271. Schick, *Berlin Crisis,* pp. 175, 178.
272. See Slusser, *Berlin Crisis of 1961,* pp. 147–49, 183, 214–15, 225, 387.
273. Watt, *Survey of International Affairs 1961,* p. 262.
274. Slusser, *Berlin Crisis of 1961,* pp. 226–29.
275. Ibid., quotation on p. 207; see also pp. 239–42.

shchev told the West what it was anxiously waiting to hear: "The question of a time limit for the signing of a German peace treaty will not be so important if the Western powers show a readiness to settle the German problem; we shall not in that case absolutely insist on signing the peace treaty before December 31, 1961."[276]

With this lifting of the deadline one might think the 1961 crisis was finally over. Not so: there was to be one final moment of acute tension, a Soviet-U.S. tank confrontation in Berlin on October 27. Before considering that event, however, I will summarize U.S. military actions in the period from early September through mid-October.

U.S. Military Moves, September–October

Spurred on by the Soviet actions of the last ten days of August, the U.S. armed forces in September and October rapidly embarked on the program of expansion and upgrading called for in Kennedy's speech of July 25. During the second half of 1961 the strength of the armed forces was increased by 300,000 men, with a call-up of some 158,000. U.S. forces in Europe were strengthened by 40,000 men, supported by about three hundred tactical fighter planes, more than 100,000 tons of equipment, and several thousand military vehicles.[277]

The following list of specific actions is not complete but it conveys a vivid impression of the sense of urgency that animated U.S. policymakers at this time:

1. On September 2 four fighter squadrons (seventy-two planes) were sent to Europe to participate in war games.[278]

2. On September 5, after Khrushchev's rejection of a personal plea from Kennedy and Macmillan to halt the Soviet series of atomic tests, Kennedy ordered the resumption of underground testing by the United States. The first U.S. test in the new series, a small-yield improvised shot because of the lack of advance preparations, took place on September 15.[279]

---

276. *Pravda*, October 18, 1961.
277. Sorensen, *Kennedy*, p. 627.
278. Robert W. Coakley and others, comps., *U.S. Army Expansion and Readiness, 1961–1962* (Department of the Army, Office of the Chief of Military History).
279. Slusser, *Berlin Crisis of 1961*, pp. 210–13, 225.

3. Between September 7 and 26, the 101st Airborne Division together with the 1611th Air Transport Wing (C-135s), other units, and forces from Greece, Italy, Turkey, and the United Kingdom took part in NATO Exercise Checkmate I.[280] Ships of the Sixth Fleet in the Mediterranean also participated in the exercise.[281]

4. On September 13, nearly 2,000 naval air reservists were recalled to duty.[282]

5. Between September 15 and 25 the 101st Airborne Division took part in Exercise Checkmate II at Adana, Turkey.[283]

6. On September 19 two Army National Guard divisions and 249 smaller reserve and guard units were ordered to active duty.[284]

7. On September 20, two ships of the Sixth Fleet, the *Newman K. Perry* (DDR-883) and the *Haynsworth* (DD-700) visited Eregli, Turkey, during a cruise of the Black Sea.[285]

8. During the period from August to December 1961 the following Air National Guard units were called to active duty: the 102nd Tactical Fighter Wing, the 152nd Tactical Control Group, and the 7108th, 7117th, 7121st, 7122nd, and 7131st Tactical Wings.

9. During the second half of 1961, U.S. Air Force Europe was augmented by eight TAC fighter squadrons, subsequently supplemented by eleven National Guard tactical fighter and reconnaissance squadrons.

10. On October 14–15, operation Sky Shield II was conducted, the largest air defense maneuvers ever held up to that time.

11. During October the 1611th Air Transport Wing, employing thirteen C-118s, moved Air National Guard units to Europe in Operation Stair Step.[286]

280. Department of the Army, 101st Airborne Division, *History of the 101st Airborne Division, 1942–1964.*

281. Department of the Navy, Sixth Fleet, *History of the Sixth Fleet, Calendar Year 1961.*

282. *Naval and Maritime Chronology. Compiled from Ten Years of Naval Review* (Naval Institute Press, 1973), p. 10.

283. *History of the 101st Airborne Division, 1942–1964.*

284. *U.S. Army Expansion and Readiness, 1961–1962.*

285. *History of the Sixth Fleet, Calendar Year 1961.*

286. U.S. Department of the Air Force, 1611th Air Transport Wing, "History of the 1611th Air Transport Wing, July–December 1961," and Department of the Air Force, U.S. Air Force Europe, Office of History, *Historical Highlights: United States Air Forces in Europe, 1954–1973*, prepared by R. Bruce Harley (USAFE Historical Monograph Series, no. 4, 1974).

The Tank Confrontation of October 27

The Twenty-second Congress of the CPSU opened in Moscow on October 17 with a lengthy report for the Central Committee by Khrushchev, in the course of which he announced the lifting of the December 1961 deadline for the signing of a peace treaty with East Germany. Following this contribution to the relaxation of international tensions, Khrushchev pushed on to what was evidently, in his eyes, the central task of the Congress—discussion and approval of a new party program (the first since 1919), the major feature of which was the forecast that the USSR would enter the era of full communism by 1980.

Contrary to Khrushchev's hopes and expectations, however, the Twenty-second Congress turned out to be a tense and dramatic battleground, marked by sharp clashes between the Communist party of the Soviet Union and those of Albania and China. During the congress Khrushchev reopened old party wounds with a slashing attack on Stalin, culminating in the demand for the removal of his corpse from the mausoleum on Red Square. Finally, the congress witnessed a vigorous battle between Khrushchev and his followers, on the one side, and party functionaries opposed to him on the other, over the question of his powers as first secretary, a battle that ended in Khrushchev's defeat and the elevation of Kozlov to the position of number two man in the Secretariat.[287]

It was while these turbulent developments were taking place in Moscow that the tank confrontation of October 27 occurred. The event presents a sharp challenge to analysts of Soviet policy. Why did the USSR choose this particular moment, ten days after Khrushchev had defused the crisis, to bring tension in Berlin close to the flash point, with the issue of war or peace dependent on the steadiness of nerves of tank crews and their commanders?

"Traditionalist" analysts of the Berlin crisis meet this difficulty in various ways, none of them very satisfactory. Schick simply ignores the tank confrontation.[288] George and Smoke mention it but dismiss it as one of a series of "minor probes around Berlin" by the Soviet forces, though they concede it was "the most spectacular." At a later point in their analysis,

287. Developments at the congress are analyzed in Slusser, *Berlin Crisis of 1961,* chap. 9.

288. Schick's analysis jumps from Khrushchev's announcement of the lifting of the deadline on October 17 (*Berlin Crisis,* p. 184) to a meeting of the NATO Ministerial Council on December 13–15 (ibid., p. 186).

they downgrade it still further, calling it "probably unnecessary," and citing it as one of a series of actions by General Lucius Clay that "caused a number of very sharp Western reactions to local incidents" in Berlin.[289]

The issue at stake, as Clay recognized, was the Soviet and East German challenge to the continuing validity of the wartime four-power agreements on the administration of Berlin, providing for the right of unimpeded access by Western military personnel to all sectors of the city, including that occupied by the USSR. This right was challenged on October 22 by an administrative measure enacted by East German authorities, the demand that Western military personnel in civilian clothes present identity cards to the East German border police when entering East Berlin. This action, which led directly to the tank confrontation, constitutes, in the view of a British observer, a break in the pattern of Soviet policy after Khrushchev's speech of October 17 "which is difficult to properly explain."[290]

The explanation, as I have tried to show in *The Berlin Crisis of 1961,* is a complicated one involving: (1) the drastic deterioration in Soviet-Albanian and Soviet-Chinese relations that occurred at the Twenty-second Congress; (2) Khrushchev's unsuccessful attempt to reestablish his unchallenged authority over the party, using the anti-Stalin issue as his principal weapon; (3) Kozlov's covert defiance of Khrushchev, his siding with the Chinese, and his conniving with Ulbricht to stage a direct provocation to Western rights in Berlin; and (4) Kozlov's ultimate triumph, achieved by means of the pressure exerted on Khrushchev by the tank confrontation, which was called off by the USSR as soon as word was received in East Berlin of the outcome of the struggle for power in Moscow.[291]

Whatever explanation of the tank confrontation one accepts—and it is an event that urgently demands explanation—the only aspect of the incident relevant to the present study is the use of force by the USSR and the United States. The point at which Soviet forces reluctantly moved their tanks up to the sector boundary, facing those previously deployed by the United States, signified the Soviet leadership's acknowledgment

289. George and Smoke, *Deterrence in American Foreign Policy,* pp. 416, 440. General Lucius Clay, a hero in the eyes of West Berliners, had been sent to West Berlin at the end of August as Kennedy's personal representative. Slusser, *Berlin Crisis of 1961,* p. 172.
290. Watt, *Survey of International Affairs 1961,* p. 271.
291. Slusser, *Berlin Crisis of 1961,* pp. 339–461.

that the four-power administrative structure of Berlin still retained its validity and a tacit admission that the USSR could not turn over to East German authorities its responsibilities in the city. The withdrawal of the Soviet tanks on the morning of October 28 amounted to a confession that they had been defeated in the test of wills. Seen in this light, the tank confrontation marked the real climax of the entire U.S.-Soviet tug-of-war that had started with Khrushchev's speech of November 10, 1958.

October 28 can be regarded as the end of the Berlin crisis of 1961. There were to be flareups and tension in early 1962, but when the next major Soviet-U.S. test of will occurred, Cuba, not Berlin, was to be the focus. For some time, the U.S. military and naval buildup continued under the momentum generated by the events of August–October 1961. Over the next two years, however, most of the reserve and National Guard units called to active duty in 1961 were demobilized. On August 1, 1962, for example, the Navy released all reservists.[292] The crisis in Berlin was over, but not the struggle for supremacy between the USSR and the United States.

A Comparative Evaluation, 1958–59 and 1961

It remains to strike a balance and evaluate the effectiveness of military force as a tool for the achievement of national goals in the two Berlin crises. The task can be accomplished most expeditiously by making a point-by-point comparison.

1. *The use of limited force.* During the 1958–59 crisis the United States strove to avoid the use of limited force, fearing that it might lead to an escalation toward the nuclear threshold. Considerations of expense were also involved: acutely conscious of the enormous cost of the nuclear arsenal on which he placed his major reliance for deterrence, Eisenhower was determined to avoid anything that might create a demand for additional military expense.

U.S. reluctance to use limited force in the opening phase of the 1958–59 crisis may well have encouraged the USSR to develop its campaign in Berlin more fully than it would have done had it been faced at the outset by a show of U.S. firmness.

292. J. S. Donaldson, Jr., "Memorandum for Director of Naval History and Curator for the Navy Department," August 20, 1969.

In the opening phase of the 1961 crisis, too, the United States failed to use limited force, even though Kennedy had explicitly broken with the Eisenhower administration's insistence on fiscal restraints on military spending. Nevertheless, the Kennedy administration, though recognizing the high probability of a new Soviet-inspired crisis in Berlin, refrained from taking any action—for example, a token reinforcement of the U.S. garrison in Berlin, which might have conveyed to the USSR a realization of the U.S. determination to maintain its position there.

There were several reasons for this restraint: the failure of U.S. intelligence to pick up the signs of impending crisis probably played a part, but the major reason was no doubt Kennedy's discovery of the unpreparedness of the U.S. military establishment to take effective limited action in Berlin. Whatever the reason, the effect of U.S. inaction in 1961, as in 1958, was to encourage Soviet leaders to push ahead with their plans.

2. *The use of conventional force.* A clear-cut difference between the two administrations was their attitude toward the use of conventional force. Pinning its hopes for deterrence on "massive retaliation" using nuclear weapons and striving to keep a lid on other military expenditures, the Eisenhower administration cut back on army strength and adopted a no-growth policy for the conventional forces. In contrast, Kennedy strongly endorsed a program of building up the conventional forces, and relied on them for his major military moves in the 1961 crisis.

There were four main examples of the use of force by the Kennedy administration during the 1961 crisis, each designed to serve a specific purpose.

a. Kennedy's July 25 speech can be interpreted as a logical step in his long-range plans to strengthen U.S. military power and increase its flexibility. It thus represents the continuation of the policy set forth in his messages to Congress of January 30, March 28, and May 25. Taken as a whole, the 1961 military expansion was the Kennedy administration's response to the Soviet strategic challenge dating back to the launching of Sputnik I in 1957 and to Khrushchev's subsequent exploitation of Soviet space achievements to convey the impression that the strategic balance had shifted decisively in the USSR's favor.

Viewed in the context of the Berlin crisis, the July 25 speech served as a massive response to Khrushchev's deadline challenge at Vienna and his subsequent announcement of an increase in Soviet military spending. The July 25 speech achieved its immediate purpose in forcing Khrushchev to drop out of the bidding at this point, but it entailed certain concealed corollaries that went far to nullify the advantage thus gained for the United States: first, the building of the Berlin Wall; second, the Soviet resumption of nuclear testing; and third—conjecturally—a Soviet decision to extend aid to North Vietnam.

b. Kennedy's order sending a battle group down the autobahn to Berlin on August 17 represented a calculated risk designed to help restore the morale of West Berlin after the jolting impact of the construction of the wall. By keeping the size of the force small enough to rule out any thought on the part of the Soviet leaders that he was offering a direct challenge to them, Kennedy managed to achieve his goal without enlarging the conflict.

c. The program of call-ups, maneuvers, war games, and nuclear test shots in September 1961 constituted the realization of the measures Kennedy had called for in his July 25 speech, and which Congress had approved on August 1, 3, and 16. Seen in relation to the immediate context of the Berlin crisis, these moves might be criticized as a case of locking the barn after the horse is stolen—this on the assumption that the construction of the wall marked the turning point in Soviet strategy in the crisis. In the larger context of the continuing U.S.-Soviet strategic rivalry, however, the September 1961 moves were an essential part of the U.S. effort to establish clear-cut strategic predominance over the USSR and thereby recapture the diplomatic initiative on a world scale that the Eisenhower administration had come close to losing. The September 1961 buildup also served as the indispensable background to the final conflict in the crisis.

d. The tank confrontation in Berlin on October 27, far from being irrelevant or unnecessary, was a direct affirmation by the United States of its determination to retain its rights in Berlin and to force the USSR to observe its obligations under the wartime agreements for four-power administration of the city. To achieve these goals it was necessary for U.S. decisionmakers to have an insight into the issues at stake and a willingness to risk a violent or unpredictable Soviet response rather than yield rights the United States considered vital. Soviet action in the confrontation showed that their decisionmakers understood the issues at stake equally clearly, and that they accepted, though grudgingly, the U.S. demands.

3. *The use of nuclear weapons and ICBMs.* With regard to the use of

nuclear weapons and ICBMs the two administrations differed in degree rather than in kind. A severe critic of the Eisenhower administration's record in this field up to the end of 1961, Kennedy found on taking office that the level of U.S. strategic power was higher and that of the USSR lower than he had believed and asserted during the 1960 presidential campaign. Kennedy's recognition in February 1961 that there was no "missile gap," however, did not induce in him a sense of complacency or a willingness to stabilize the strategic balance at the existing level; rather he accepted the doctrine that the United States, as a nation that would never initiate a nuclear exchange with the USSR, must have a strategic arsenal so powerful and so invulnerable that it could take the full brunt of a surprise nuclear attack by the USSR and still have enough reserve power to destroy the Soviet capacity to wage war.

In the 1958–59 crisis, which broke out just after the beginning of the Soviet-Western de facto test ban agreement, nuclear weapons played a largely symbolic role. It was Khrushchev's exaggerated claims for Soviet superiority in missile production and emplacement that provided the major leverage in Soviet strategy.

During the 1961 crisis Soviet claims to ICBM superiority were drastically toned down, once the Soviet leadership realized that the United States knew the truth about the strategic balance. This enforced moderation, however, may have had a direct bearing on the Soviet decision to begin preparations for the resumption of nuclear testing.

Renewed testing by both the USSR and the United States was one of the most regrettable aspects of the 1961 crisis, and here the U.S. leadership seems fairly clear of responsibility, at least on the existing public record. Especially harmful were the massive Soviet tests in the atmosphere, which produced extensive radioactive fallout. Since the crisis in Berlin was over before the 50-megaton blast of October 31, 1961, and since the United States by that time had given ample evidence of its readiness to meet the USSR at the negotiating table, the Soviet resumption of testing cannot be explained as a means of exerting pressure on the West to consent to negotiations.

4. *Negotiations and the use of force.* In *The Berlin Crisis,* Schick argues that the Kennedy administration, by combining the offer to negotiate with the use of limited force, actually helped prolong the 1961 crisis.[293] The logical conclusion would seem to be that U.S. leaders would

293. Schick, *Berlin Crisis*, p. 237.

have been better advised to eschew the search for a common meeting ground with the USSR in the Berlin conflict and to limit their response to the Soviet challenge to military actions. One detects here an echo of the Acheson thesis.

Granted that the mixture of professed willingness to negotiate and limited force that Kennedy employed may have encouraged some Soviet leaders to believe that the USSR could achieve its goals by intimidation, it is difficult to accept the view that Kennedy's two-track approach was a mistake. In the long-range view, one of the greatest achievements of the Kennedy administration in foreign policy was the nuclear test-ban treaty of August 5, 1963, which for the first time since 1945 brought the USSR and the United States together on a matter of fundamental international importance. It seems highly doubtful that the USSR would have signed the test-ban treaty had Kennedy not held the door open to negotiations all along, even at the moments of greatest U.S.-Soviet tension.

The Eisenhower administration, too, tried to mix force with the willingness to negotiate, but since it never succeeded in convincing the USSR of its determination to hold fast in Berlin, since its threat to use nuclear weapons was regarded with widespread skepticism, and since it eschewed the use of limited force, its negotiating position was weak. Only Soviet failure to cash in on the concessions made by the West at the Geneva conference of foreign ministers in 1959 prevented a serious erosion of the Western position in Berlin. Similarly, the collapse of the Paris summit meeting in May 1961 fortuitously saved the Eisenhower administration from making new concessions on Berlin. It was by luck, then, rather than by good management or skillful planning that the Eisenhower administration managed to weather the 1958–59 crisis in Berlin and its sequel at the Paris summit meeting. The same thing cannot be said, however, of the other foreign policy defeats the Eisenhower administration suffered in the summer and fall of 1960.

The Kennedy record is not without blemishes: His administration made a number of serious blunders in 1961, not only at the Bay of Pigs but elsewhere, including (at least in the opening phase of the crisis) Berlin. Given the nature of the Soviet campaign in Berlin, however; given the impossibility of knowing what the real Soviet goals were and how far they were willing to go to achieve them; given the Soviet capacity to inflict heavy damage on the West in a surprise attack, using either nuclear or conventional weapons or both; given the unpredictability of

Soviet moves and the impossibility of knowing the real power relations within the Soviet leadership—given all these things, I believe Sorensen is justified in his assertion that Kennedy's objectives at Berlin were achieved, and that "his conventional force build-up had helped prevent a confrontation over Berlin that might otherwise have reached the nuclear level."[294]

"One never knows, of course," Schlesinger writes,

what would have happened if Kennedy had ordered full mobilization, or if he had rushed straight to negotiation, but either extreme might well have invited Soviet miscalculation and ended in war. Instead he applied power and diplomacy in a combination and sequence which enabled him to guard the vital interests of the West and hold off the holocaust.[295]

Both Sorensen and Schlesinger, of course, were prominent members of the Kennedy administration and avowed admirers of Kennedy himself, and their evaluation of his record has not won universal acceptance. But no one who has made a thorough study of Soviet policy in the Berlin crises (and the staunchest critics of Kennedy have not done so)[296] can easily deny that he underwent a testing period of extreme danger in 1961 or that he came through it with, on the whole, remarkable success.

294. Sorensen, *Kennedy*, p. 629.
295. Schlesinger, *A Thousand Days*, p. 404.
296. For two characteristic examples of the literature critical of Kennedy, see Louise FitzSimons, *The Kennedy Doctrine* (Random House, 1972), and Richard J. Walton, *Cold War and Counterrevolution: The Foreign Policy of John F. Kennedy* (Viking Press, 1972).

TEN

Yugoslavia, 1951, and Czechoslovakia, 1968

PHILIP WINDSOR

THIS CHAPTER will examine two critical situations in Eastern Europe that led the United States to take demonstrative military action. The use of armed force in a crisis—even where that use is purely demonstrative—reflects a series of difficult decisions. In the case of Eastern Europe the difficulty is the greater since it is clearly an overriding interest of the United States to avoid war with the USSR. The role of military force is therefore bound to be circumscribed. But it is also ambiguous. If the movement of forces is regarded as *purely* demonstrative, and if it is understood that it could never lead to war, then it is unlikely that it would demonstrate anything at all. The purposes of military action must therefore vary. They can range from an indication of resolve, and interest in the outcome of a crisis, to the attempt to reassure allies and convince opponents of an existing commitment; they can include a clear warning to an adversary that a crisis could indeed lead to war. But the very fact that the risk of war might be entailed in a use of force intended primarily to demonstrate support or commitment suggests that the scale and movements of forces are likely to be restricted. From demonstrating commitment to declaring war is a major step. For the most part, the chief concern of the United States was to demonstrate interest or commitment. The use of force could be—and was—significant; but it was generally on a small scale.

Nonetheless, the fact that the United States took little overt military action should not obscure the importance of what it did. First, in purely historical terms, the cases under consideration here demonstrate the restraints upon U.S. action taken in response to Soviet military intervention in Eastern Europe. American reaction here is bound to be qualitatively as well as quantitatively different from that undertaken anywhere else in the world, for it constitutes a challenge to Soviet power in its own sphere. Yet any consideration of wider American interests, in particular the political confidence of the Western European countries, can require that some U.S. action be taken. In this sense, a consideration of American responses is of more than historical importance: the goals and impacts of what would otherwise appear to be pretty trivial military action can be of much greater importance than their scope and scale might suggest.

Even the significance of such restricted movements can be appreciated only within the context of a political analysis of the interests and interactions concerned. I shall suggest the nature of these interactions and shall hope in so doing to indicate the limitations, as well as the effectiveness, implicit in the use of American force. The political context—though vastly different in 1968 from what it had been in 1951—was characterized in both cases by a very complex interplay of considerations, involving Soviet policies in Eastern Europe, the reactions of certain Eastern European countries to those policies, the security of the United States, and the reactions of the Western European countries when confronted with this interaction. I will demonstrate how the use of force—both in its demonstrative capacity and in its wider implications—was informed by the political context.

I will also suggest that the use of force in such circumstances was necessarily directed toward more than one objective. As already observed, force could serve one of several different functions. But in certain cases, including the two under consideration here, it had to serve more than one at a time. The targets of U.S. military action were both the Western European nations *and* the USSR. This, too, dictated the way in which the decisions to take military action came about.

Although such considerations are common to the two cases, there is also an immense difference between them. In the case of Yugoslavia in 1951 the United States was still concerned with establishing a direction for its foreign policy. If that foreign policy was posited on the idea of containment, it was still far from clear where the lines of containment were to be drawn—precisely because Yugoslavia provided an ambiguous and difficult case—or whether Tito would prove a viable instrument in its execution. For these reasons, and because American policymakers were uncertain about both Soviet intentions and Yugoslav objectives, initial U.S. reactions to the case of Yugoslavia were essentially reactive in nature and were characterized by slow and deliberate decisionmaking. I shall argue that the decision to supply military aid was the culmination of a decision process that hardened and formalized the changes that had already come about.

In Czechoslovakia in 1968 the case was very different. The primary consideration of U.S. policy was to prevent an existing situation from degenerating into a new one involving other Eastern European nations and possibly bringing the threat of war. Containment was by then recognized as a mutual process in which both superpowers sought to avoid the threat of war or the uncertainties that could lead to conflict. Yet the attempt to confine the crisis also meant that the real possibility of war had to be invoked.

I shall begin with an analysis of the background to the Yugoslav situation and show how the decision to extend military aid arose from the originally more revolutionary decision to give the country economic assistance.

Yugoslavia, 1951

On June 28, 1948, the Communist Information Bureau (Cominform) passed a resolution expelling the "Tito clique" from the Soviet camp and from any participation in the world Communist movement.[1] This was a particularly important date in Serbian history, Vidov Dan, a day of national mourning commemorating the Serbian defeat by Turkish armies at Kossovo in 1389.[2] For Stalin to proceed to this ultimate action on Vidov Dan was, in terms of the Serbian national consciousness, almost equivalent to the Arabs' attack on Israel on Yom Kippur. Probably Stalin had no idea of its significance; but beyond the ignorance suggested, Stalin also confirmed the rightness and tactical superiority of Tito's moves during the quarrel that had led to the expulsion.

1. The word "camp" had of course acquired a technical meaning, indicative of enduring hostility, since Stalin's declaration of February 1946 that the world was irrevocably divided into two antagonistic camps.
2. The point is made by John C. Campbell, *Tito's Separate Road* (Harper and Row for the Council on Foreign Relations, 1967), p. 12.

For two months the USSR and Yugoslavia had done nothing but exchange polemics. The USSR had withdrawn its military mission in Yugoslavia. A long letter, signed on behalf of the Central Committee of the Communist Party of the Soviet Union (CPSU) by Georgi Molotov and Josef Stalin, accused Tito and his principal comrades—Milovan Djilas, Svetozar Vukmanovic, Boris Kidric, Alexander Rankovic, "and others" —of being "questionable Marxists." During the ensuing exchanges, Tito chose to fight his battle not on ideological grounds but by importing a new principle, that of national independence, into the organization that had been designed to obliterate it—the Cominform. Ultimately, by his action of expelling them on Vidov Dan, Stalin demonstrated that an ideological quarrel had indeed turned into a nationalist principle. At the same time, the very fact that Tito's expulsion occurred on the day observed by the *Serbs* underlined the disparateness of the nations he was trying to weld together. It was of no particular significance to Croats or Slovenes or Montenegrins—let alone, of course, to the Moslems in Bosnia. Like Stalin, Tito had chosen an authoritarian ideology to force his peoples to work together in the construction of socialism.

This situation created a dilemma for the United States. Tito was clearly no Western democrat. Originally supported by the British in the Second World War and later by other Western allies, Tito was encouraged by Stalin at a comparatively late date. Yet immediately after victory, he turned against the Western powers with considerable ferocity. The first threat of a military clash between the Western and Communist allies occurred when Tito's forces threatened to advance into Carinthia and were faced down by Allied forces under General Harold Alexander. There was one other moment at which matters came to the verge of open conflict: at Trieste, which Tito tried to occupy in 1945. Yugoslavia had pushed harder on Trieste than the USSR was willing to contemplate. Tito had even warned "outside powers" in a public speech against treating Yugoslavia's vital interests lightly. (A letter from the Soviet leadership subsequently reproached Tito on this matter and invited him to explain himself to the Cominform.)[3] Yugoslavia had also expressed its territorial ambitions by proposing to the USSR that it bring Bulgaria into the Yugoslav federation as the seventh republic.

The U.S. policy of containment took shape in 1947, partly as a response to the Soviet threat to Greece and Turkey but also as a device to

3. As he emphasized in his speech in Ljubljana, May 27, 1945.

contain Communist influence in general. "Communist influence," though principally equated with Soviet influence, also had other guises. In American and Western eyes, Yugoslavia was in some ways the most ferocious member of the socialist camp.[4] Tito, while seeming to be a Stalinist in his domestic policy, behaved remarkably like a Trotskyite in his foreign policy. His disputes with both the USSR and Bulgaria over the nature and degree of support to be given to the Markos "government" in Greece seemed to cast him as the most expansive and aggressive member of the socialist bloc. Perhaps, indeed, he was.

Given this background, it would not be easy for any U.S. administration suddenly to see Yugoslavia as the arch-challenger of the USSR. After all, it was only with great reluctance that the Yugoslavs agreed to play this role—in which they had been cast by Stalin rather than themselves. One could go further: it was the very energy and drive of Yugoslav national ambition under Tito that had made the country appear to be the most aggressive Communist state. If these same qualities subsequently precipitated the break with the USSR, if Stalin recognized them as a menace, it might nonetheless appear from the U.S. perspective that they merely provided confirming evidence of the expansionism of the socialist camp as a whole. The USSR believed in the socialist camp; Yugoslavia believed in the socialist camp; why should the United States not do so?

Hence the American dilemma. Could the United States believe that this aggressive, neo-Stalinist, anti-Western country had *really* broken with Stalin? In the American public and in Congress skepticism prevailed over hope. Indeed, a widely respected Yugoslav immigrant historian, Alex Dragnich, wrote a book—*Tito: Moscow's Trojan Horse*—which found a wide resonance in the United States at the time. If one accepts the original premise of a Communist monolith, the implications of such a title are not easy to dismiss: different states can be assigned by the center to different functions. If other European Communist parties were controlled from Moscow, was Yugoslavia a real or an apparent exception? If Stalin had been foolish enough to turn down the funds made available to the USSR under the original Marshall Plan proposal, and if such funds were nonetheless needed, why not use one of the Soviet satellites to attract them?

4. Stalin, indeed, appears to have shown some apprehension about Yugoslav policy. See the chapter "Disappointments," in Milovan Djilas, *Conversations with Stalin* (Harcourt, Brace and World, 1962).

However, all the evidence seeming to confirm Yugoslavia's role as an active and aggressive protagonist of Communist expansionism could also be interpreted to indicate that its relations with the USSR were those of inherent conflict. The needs of the multinational state that had emerged from the bitter and bloody divisions of the war did not necessarily coincide with the need for overall solidarity. To stress their expansionist tendencies to the greater glory of the socialist camp might help the Yugoslav authorities to cover up such divisions. But when their very expansionism and aggression brought them into conflict with the rest of the socialist camp they had to choose between ideological purity as defined by Stalin and national unity as defined by Tito. Stalin helped them choose national unity. A percipient observer might be able to see that Yugoslav expansionism could imply a real conflict with Moscow. Such an observer was present in Belgrade in the person of Cavendish W. Cannon, the American ambassador. He recognized shortly before June 28 that Yugoslav-Soviet relations were going seriously wrong.[5] He also suggested that the dissension would provide the United States with a major policy breakthrough.

It is worth remembering that this was the period in which the Berlin blockade was reaching full intensity; in which, only a few months before, the Communist takeover in Czechoslovakia had seemed to confirm that there was no prospect whatever of any country's being able to provide a bridge between East and West—and that, if it tried, its leaders were likely to be defenestrated and its people brought firmly under Eastern control. This period also preceded the North Atlantic Treaty Organization (NATO). There was *no* Western security organization that committed the United States to Western Europe. Such Western European defense agreements as existed were embryonic (and destined to be stillborn). In such circumstances, the idea that the most ferocious member of the socialist camp should strike a stance independent of the two blocs, should reverse the fate of Czechoslovakia, was not easily acceptable. Neither the President nor his national security advisers were disposed at first to take the ambassador's prognostication seriously.

The events of 1949 soon impelled the responsible authorities in Washington to change their minds. These events were of two kinds. First, the Cominform countries in Eastern Europe attempted to isolate Yugoslavia diplomatically and then economically. This process was accompanied by a war of nerves in which the USSR threatened to establish a new, "legiti-

5. Campbell, *Tito's Separate Road*, p. 15, emphasizes Cannon's importance.

mate" Yugoslav Communist party, and in which the Cominform members openly discussed the prospects of guerrilla war against the "Tito clique."[6] The threat of guerrilla war was amplified by a very large number of border incidents, which began almost as soon as Yugoslavia had been expelled from the Cominform. As is usually the case, the precise origin of such incidents is not clear. It appears that their origin lay in the attempt of Yugoslav frontier guards to prevent pro-Soviet refugees from escaping. They very rapidly became part of an established pattern, in which the Soviet satellites—especially Albania and Bulgaria, which flanked the eastern and western borders of Yugoslavia's Macedonian salient—attempted to intimidate the country and wear down the resistance of its defense forces. Indeed, the incidents were so numerous that Yugoslavia claimed 219 frontier clashes and 60 violations of its air space within fourteen months of its expulsion from the Cominform. This pattern of developments in Eastern Europe was shortly accompanied by a Yugoslav counterattack in the United Nations. This was the second event that precipitated a change of mind by U.S. decisionmakers. There were also objective reasons.

Strategically, the Yugoslav defection from the Soviet bloc breached the Adriatic fortress of the Cominform defenses, isolated Albania, and saved both Austria and Greece from encirclement. Economically, it deprived the bloc of raw materials valued at about $100 million a year.[7] Politically, the import of Tito's challenge to Stalin could not be measured: communism was no longer equated with Stalinism. Although these factors would soon be appreciated, the United States had, understandably, acted on the assumption that Stalinism and communism were identical. There was not yet any way to translate the distinctions into policy.

What I would like to suggest is that there was no conceptual scheme of reference, no alternative system into which Yugoslavia could easily be fitted.[8] Moreover, because the polemics between Tito and Stalin had

6. Stephen Clissold, *Yugoslavia and the Soviet Union, 1939–1973: A Documentary Survey* (Oxford University Press for the Royal Institute of International Affairs, 1975), p. 55.

7. Economic Commission for Europe, *Annual Report May 1948 to May 1949*, UN Doc. E/1328-E/ECE/104 (Lake Success, 1949).

8. Unfortunately the relevant volume of the *Foreign Relations of the United States* has not yet appeared. A useful discussion of this subject is found in *The United States in World Affairs, 1951* (Harper and Row for the Council on Foreign Relations, 1952), pp. 256–58.

largely been kept secret, to all but a very few the expulsion from the Cominform came as a surprise. "No hint of the growing tension between Moscow and Belgrade had been given, and there had been no sign of any relaxation in [Yugoslavia's] intransigent anti-Western policies or the pace of her revolutionary domestic changes."[9] But the difficulties went further. Stalin accused Yugoslavia of defecting to the "imperialist camp"—a charge so patently absurd, as Yugoslavia's own continuing record demonstrated, that it was very hard to make sense of the quarrel from either the Yugoslav or the Soviet point of view. Finally, and most important, there was no knowing whether Tito could last—even if the conflict was genuine. Stalin himself did not believe it. "I will shake my little finger," he told his colleagues, "and there will be no more Tito. He will fall."[10] Stalin, after all, was well placed to know. So was Tito. Tito himself was particularly concerned *not* to emphasize the split between himself and Stalin. When the fifth full congress of the Communist party of Yugoslavia (the first full congress since the fourth, illegal, congress of 1928) opened on July 21, Tito appealed to the party's pride in its wartime achievements, its success in "building socialism" in Yugoslavia, and the patriotism of the Yugoslav people in general. Although in so doing he reemphasized the appeal to national independence he had already detailed in his exchange with Stalin, he was very careful not to indicate any hostility between Stalin and himself. On the contrary, he emphasized "our faithfulness and solidarity with the Soviet Union," and stressed the pain it brought him to be called nationalist rather than internationalist.[11] His quarrel was not with the USSR but with the Cominform.

The Change in the U.S. Appraisal

Stalin believed that Tito would fall. Tito believed that he was in danger, and rightly so. In fact the danger was to continue for some years. It was already apparent in the manner in which the USSR sought to infiltrate and subvert the Yugoslav intelligence service, local party organizations in Croatia, Bosnia, Montenegro, and Macedonia, and in the Soviet attempt to set up a Yugoslav government-in-exile in Rumania. This last effort was prevented only by the timely shooting of its intended head as he tried to

9. Clissold, *Yugoslavia and the Soviet Union*, p. 55.
10. According to Khrushchev, "Secret Speech," February 25–26, 1956.
11. Clissold, *Yugoslavia and the Soviet Union*, p. 213.

cross the Yugoslav-Rumanian frontier. It was certainly helpful to Yugoslavia that Rankovic had learned Stalinist methods so well. According to his own account he arrested 8,400 Cominform sympathizers. If this figure is true it means either that Stalin had a very strong base inside Yugoslavia or that the Yugoslav authorities were very worried. In this combination of national and international circumstances, it took a bold man to suggest that Tito's quarrel with Stalin provided the United States with much of a chance.

Only in early 1949 did the State Department conclude that the ambassador in Belgrade was right, and that the break was real.[12] A change in the procedures for export licensing was then made so that U.S. exports to Yugoslavia would be freed of the trammels that impeded deliveries to other Communist countries. But the U.S. government had merely accepted what had already happened; it had not yet begun to frame a deliberate policy to ensure the survival and strength of Yugoslavia. It was, perhaps, the resistance of those hostile to the concept of trading with the country that helped to endow it with a more purposive significance (for example, Defense Secretary Louis Johnson, who held up the export of a steel mill for some months until President Harry Truman finally intervened against him in August).[13] The President's action was taken on overtly political grounds, and by then it was becoming clear that the survival of Yugoslavia's national independence, regardless of its Communist allegiance, was in the political interest of the United States.

The United States was (yet again) helped to this conclusion by Stalin's own actions. After the summer of 1948 commercial relations between Yugoslavia and the USSR, Czechoslovakia, and Albania were first seriously curtailed and finally stopped. A Soviet-Yugoslav trade agreement of December 1948 reduced the volume of trade between the two countries by 88 percent.[14] Czechoslovakia had been particularly reluctant to break off trade relations with Yugoslavia but in 1949 it was finally forced to do so. Until then, Yugoslavia's trade relations with the Western world were

12. This appears to have been a European Affairs Department evaluation, not something with which the secretary of state was immediately concerned. Dean Acheson makes no mention of it in his memoirs. Documentary sources give no indication of how the evaluation was arrived at.

13. An episode discussed by Campbell, *Tito's Separate Road*, p. 16.

14. For this and following figures, see Peter Calvocoressi, *Survey of International Affairs, 1951* (Oxford University Press for the Royal Institute of International Affairs, 1954), p. 222. Hereafter *Survey*.

confined to Italy, Sweden, and the U.S. and UK zones of Germany. From 1949 on it was forced by the facts of the Cominform economic blockade to expand trade where it could. This need was the more pressing since the country had embarked on a wildly ambitious five-year plan in 1947, a plan whose first year had more or less worked successfully but only because it was heavily subsidized by the Soviet Union. With both trade and subsidies withdrawn, not only could the plan no longer succeed but the lopsided economy it had already begun to bequeath could no longer survive.

By summer Yugoslavia had asked the Export-Import Bank of Washington for a loan. In September the bank announced that it had granted a loan of $20 million. In October the United States helped Yugoslavia to secure a loan of $2.7 million from the International Bank and a further loan of $9 million from the International Monetary Fund. These organizations had until that point shown a marked reluctance to extend assistance to Yugoslavia, whose infrastructure was regarded as totally inadequate for the scope and level of its economic planning; they seem to have regarded it (quite rightly) as a country trying to create capital by borrowing abroad rather than investing capital borrowed from abroad. The difference was of course fundamental. If Yugoslavia had been able to persist in its attempts to create an autarchic, balanced economy on the Stalinist model, it would have used up all available resources and been unable to repay loans in any financially acceptable form. It would have been condemned to trading by barter and any money poured into it would have been money down the drain. The U.S. intervention was certainly decisive in securing this aid and, in so doing, involving Yugoslavia in the general pattern of international trade. In December the British government, too, granted Yugoslavia a credit of £8 million ($22.4 million).

Yugoslavia now needed Western, and especially U.S., help to survive. Was this going to make a difference to its foreign policy?

In fact, foreign policy changes were coming about rapidly. First, and most important, Foreign Minister Edward Kardelj had announced in July 1949 the closing of the frontier with Greece, though at first this could have been interpreted as ambiguous. The Yugoslav-backed Markos forces were losing anyway and the American-backed Alexander Papagos had been able to take the offensive since the beginning of 1949. Moreover, a renewal of agitation on the Macedonian issue prompted speculation among the Greek guerrillas that Yugoslavia would cease to support them

—and even that it might turn against them. In May of 1949 Stalin had already suggested, through Andrei Gromyko at the United Nations, that the United States, the USSR, and the United Kingdom might arrange a cease-fire, and the closing of the frontier, in Greece. This proposal had been rejected as an attempt by Stalin to compensate for his military defeats in Greece. When Tito closed the frontier, did this mean that he was acting as Stalin might have wished anyway or that he was striking out on a new line of foreign policy? The situation appears to have been paradoxical. For now it was a staunch Cominformist, N. Zachariedis, who led the last (and disastrous) Communist offensive in the Greek civil war. Yet Djilas has reported that Stalin, before that, had wished the war to be ended. So it was a supporter of Stalin who led the last offensive of the Greek Communists while the hitherto expansionist Tito withdrew support. In a sense, therefore, Tito was now only doing what Stalin had already advocated.

In announcing the closing of the frontier with Greece, Tito went out of his way to denounce the Greek "monarcho-fascists" as much as the erstwhile allies of the socialist camp. Moreover, while he was skillful enough to bring in a reference to his own hopes for economic aid at the time he announced this major reversal of Yugoslav foreign policy, he nonetheless stressed that "we have and shall establish economic relations *without making any political concessions,* and everyone is aware of this."[15] Although, objectively speaking, the closing of the Greek frontier was the most significant policy change Yugoslavia had made since its expulsion from the Cominform, the import of this change for its future relations with the Western powers was by no means clear.

Less ambiguous was a move in the autumn—that is, while the loans already mentioned were being negotiated or announced. At the UN General Assembly Yugoslavia denounced the aggressive actions of the USSR. The import of that action was twofold. First, Yugoslavia now publicly uncoupled its foreign policy from its ideological alignment and from the assumption that its ideology or foreign policy in any sense coincided with that of the USSR. Second, it was now emphasizing that the principles of the UN Charter—stressing as they did the sovereign equality and independence of all member-states—applied to relations among Communist countries as much as to those among other nations. If this sounds like a truism, it is a truism that the USSR has frequently been at pains to ignore,

15. Speech at Pola, July 10, 1949.

and it was certainly not in keeping with the norms of behavior between Eastern European Communist parties.[16]

The question therefore arose: if Yugoslav policy toward the West and in the United Nations now coincided with Yugoslavia's new economic orientation, did the economic assistance granted by the United States also imply the beginnings of a closer relationship with Yugoslavia? Did it, indeed, imply the beginnings of a commitment?

It was at first unclear whether there would be a commitment. Tito was certainly not asking for Western military aid. In fact, even as late as 1951, he still insisted that he would not dream of doing so. But what of the United States? In the first instance, it too was careful not to raise the question of possible defensive assistance to Yugoslavia. It was concerned primarily with the need to make further economic aid available if the country should need it. But it would appear that contingency studies were undertaken in the Pentagon to determine how Yugoslav military resistance could be strengthened.[17] The most significant indication of a new appraisal came in December, when the new U.S. ambassador to Yugoslavia, George V. Allen, said to the press on taking leave of the President:

The President confirmed that the United States is unalterably opposed to aggression whenever it occurs or threatens to occur. Furthermore, the United States supports the principle of the sovereignty of independent nations. As regards Yugoslavia, we are just as opposed to aggression against that country as any other, and just as favorable to the retention of Yugoslavia's sovereignty.[18]

By the end of 1949, therefore, U.S. economic aid, undertaken so hesitantly at the beginning of that year, had already expanded to include an interest in Yugoslavia's security and an implicit warning that the United States would not lightly see it threatened.

The danger of invasion and war appeared to remain serious throughout 1949. Indeed, *Pravda* wrote later (February 13, 1957) that in the middle of that year the decision to invade had been taken, but that it was called off at the last moment. Yet throughout all this Tito was adamant that Yugoslavia would look to its own defenses. He planned for a system of defense in depth, relying essentially on the lessons of partisan warfare drawn from the Second World War, which his Soviet military advisers had earlier treated with a coolness approaching contempt; and he clearly re-

16. These points are well brought out by Campbell, *Tito's Separate Road,* p. 17.
17. Ibid.
18. Ibid.

garded it as essential to the pursuit of such a strategy that the Yugoslav people should be prepared to fight a war of *national* defense. It might even be accurate to suggest that, if he really feared an imminent invasion, there was little prospect that Western help could arrive in time or in sufficient quantity to enable him to use other tactics. Tito was therefore unlikely to ask for any military assistance of a nature that might modify his defense planning.

Equally, it would have proved as difficult for the United States to offer specific military assistance to Yugoslavia as it was for Tito to ask for it. But one development of the greatest importance had already occurred, and it provided the background to the events in the offing. This was the arrival of U.S. troops in Europe. NATO began to change, during the course of 1950, from a declaratory alliance to a full-scale military organization, and the essence of the organization lay in the willingness of the United States to provide a permanent force in Europe. Tito was careful not to refer to this presence, and indeed his references to NATO were, then as ever since, couched in the most hostile terms. But the knowledge that U.S. forces were now continuously prepared to do combat with the USSR cannot have failed to strengthen his resolve, even when he was most apprehensive of attack. And, as he was shortly to demonstrate, he was certainly not averse to accepting moral and military support from the naval forces that the United States had brought into the NATO area.

Meanwhile, also during 1950, two catastrophes brought about a major change in the relations between Yugoslavia and the United States. The nature of Soviet policy, of Yugoslav attitudes, and of U.S. commitments were all focused and transformed by these events. The first was the outbreak of the Korean War; the second was the disastrous drought in Yugoslavia.

The Twin Disasters and the U.S. Commitment

The effect of the Korean War was twofold. On the one hand, it showed that the United States could take swift and powerful action even in circumstances and in a theater in which it was taken by surprise; and it helped to establish the credibility of the U.S. will to fight, even in areas where it had no specific commitment. The war was thus extremely helpful to Yugoslavia, should the country need reassurance or Stalin need a warning.

On the other hand, it seemed also to confirm a different possibility. Both the U.S. and Yugoslav governments agreed in the first instance that the USSR was fighting a war by proxy in Korea. It is perhaps difficult at this distance to understand the impact of such views in 1950. But if one looks back, it is clear that much U.S. diplomatic maneuvering between 1947 and 1950 had been directed at the USSR. (If there was another power whose activities had worried the U.S. government, it was precisely Yugoslavia.) The commitments made between 1947 and 1949 were directed at the overwhelming strength of the USSR in areas where the two powers were likely to compete. Now it appeared that Stalin might be able to pursue his expansionist policies without involving his own country directly at all. Americans would be killed, and North Koreans and Chinese would be killed, but no Soviet citizens would be killed. Moreover, any attempt to call him, to threaten the USSR directly, would only have put the Europeans at risk; to the best of my knowledge, such a course was never even considered. The USSR was sitting pretty. But where did that leave Tito? It left him confronting the very considerable danger that the USSR might attack Yugoslavia *by proxy,* just as it had acted in Korea.

Tito and Truman "agreed" that a satellite attack of the kind that had occurred in Korea could also occur in Europe, and that Yugoslavia was a likely target. The argument was based not only on the general view that the Korean War represented a potential decoy for U.S. forces and might be followed by military action in Europe while the United States was engaged elsewhere, but also on the facts that the Hungarian and Bulgarian armed forces were being greatly strengthened and that the USSR was concentrating its own troops on the borders of Yugoslavia. Any of the numerous border incidents and clashes that occurred continuously throughout this period could have provided the occasion for a major war.

At the same time the effects of the Korean War were being felt in this way, the drought of 1950 made it urgent to consider an increased program of economic aid. The drought, and the imminent threat that the Yugoslav economy might collapse, induced the United States to extend its program of aid. The combined problems of the drought and the Korean War helped to mark the transition from exclusively economic aid to a program that included military assistance as well—in part because Tito was now forced by the position of his country to request aid directly from the United States, a step he had hitherto consistently avoided. Now, however, he had to contemplate an extensive defense expenditure in the most unfavorable of conditions. Not only was the drought cutting heavily into overall production, it was also depriving Yugoslavia of the export potential which alone could provide it with the means of importing necessary industrial or military equipment. There was no alternative to officially requesting aid from the United States.

Hitherto, as has been made clear, U.S. aid had reached Yugoslavia by decision of the executive branch. It had been channeled through trade controls, through the Export-Import Bank, and through as generous an interpretation as possible of existing aid legislation. In part, this pattern continued. In November 1950, for example, the administration made available $15 million, under the Mutual Defense Assistance Act, for food that was nominally for the Yugoslav armed forces. It also made arrangements in the same period to transfer to Yugoslavia $11.5 million worth of flour stored in Germany and Italy under the European Recovery Act. Also, part of a third Export-Import Bank loan of $15 million was diverted to food purchases for Yugoslavia.[19] Although these interpretations testified both to the ingenuity of the administration and to its sense of urgency, there was no aid agreement, which would of course have been a requirement for aid to be authorized under the Marshall Plan. And there was no overall strategy for either the provision or the administration of aid to Yugoslavia.

At the same time, however, there were suggestions that Yugoslavia was now receiving *military* aid. Tito certainly dropped hints to this effect between the summer and autumn of 1950, but he never specified the kind or amounts of aid that he was receiving. His later requests for military equipment and his continuous insistence on Yugoslavia's intention to purchase arms through normal commercial channels suggest that he was not, in fact, receiving any great supplies of equipment or armaments. It is probable that he was referring to the administration's interpretation of existing legislation and in particular to the Mutual Defense Assistance Act. But the situation on both sides began to change when the President recalled Congress in November 1950 for a special session and, among other issues, put the case for emergency aid to Yugoslavia.

In a sense, all that has been said so far provides no more than the background for the U.S. decisions on aid to Yugoslavia in 1951; but it should be clear that this is not *merely* background. Rather than marking a break

19. Ibid., p. 23.

in the conduct of U.S. foreign policy, the decisions grew out of a process that had begun with Cannon's suggestions in the summer of 1948 and that had developed continuously ever since. But the transformation of the international situation in 1949 and the twin emergencies of 1950 helped to accelerate this process and to bring about an important change in the manner and in the scope of providing aid to Yugoslavia. The most significant aspect of this situation is the transformation of a policy: originally designed as a short-term pragmatic measure and dedicated only to the proposition that Tito should be kept afloat, aid was changed by the domestic and foreign pattern of events into a regular and full-scale commitment, international in scope. The United Kingdom and France joined with the United States in establishing a regular program of economic and military aid. It is apparent that by the end of 1950 the United States, France, and the United Kingdom had all decided that Tito's Yugoslavia now represented a major Western interest, and that without any form of alliance commitment they were prepared to subsidize and support the country. Even the limited military aid supplied by executive action on an ad hoc basis in the latter half of 1950 represented a degree of U.S. commitment. The United States was now not only giving help but also signaling support for the country. As more than one voice suggested at the time, if the United States had shown the degree of commitment to Korea that it was now prepared to show Yugoslavia, the Korean War would never have happened.

The basic transformation, therefore, had already occurred by November 1950. Before examining the nature and the impact of the events that followed, it is worth considering in more detail the motives behind the U.S. decisions. These were of two kinds: strategic and political.

The Motives for U.S. Decisions

In strategic terms, the decision to extend ongoing aid to Yugoslavia was taken over a period in which Yugoslavia itself was beginning to change its foreign policy. The general reasons outlined earlier indicate that this was already a significant gain for the Western powers. Yugoslavia lost its virtual protectorate over Albania, it withdrew from the civil war in Greece, and it deprived the USSR of an important strategic asset in the Balkans and on the Adriatic. If Yugoslavia remained an ally of the USSR, Soviet power reached to the borders of Italy and extended along the whole eastern shore of the Adriatic. Neutral Yugoslavia virtually ensured that Italy and the Mediterranean would not be immediately threatened by the USSR; it moved Soviet power—even before the foundation of NATO— back to the middle of the Balkan peninsula; it isolated Albania from Soviet support; and it meant that Soviet and satellite forces would be tied down by the need to confront or contain Tito's own thirty-three divisions. The very fact of subtracting these thirty-three divisions from the combined strength of the Eastern bloc represented a considerable Western gain; but if they were threatened with hostile action from Hungary, or Bulgaria, effectively removing even more of the Soviet potential, the gain was multiplied. Thus, even a neutral Yugoslavia constituted an effective Western ally. There is little doubt that some Western analysts at the time were inclined to exaggerate Tito's military power—much as the United Kingdom had exaggerated Poland's military power in 1939. But it was hard to exaggerate the military *importance* of an independent Yugoslavia.

Moreover, it was possible that if war were coming in Europe anyway, and if it was as likely as not to start in Yugoslavia, then that country would be a positive ally of the West. This possibility had two implications. The first lay in the defense of Italy; the natural geographical frontier of Italy runs down the Ljubljana Gap, and not, like its political frontier, through the middle of the Venetian Plain. Greece too, if Yugoslavia were disposed to cooperate, could be defended much more effectively. These were the essential strategic considerations. They could look like parts of a higher risk policy than in fact they were, for the question was bound to arise whether aid to Yugoslavia would involve the United States in war. But this question need only be asked to be dismissed. Except for Senator Robert A. Taft, very few Americans considered that U.S. aid would drag the United States into another war. On the contrary. By both its practical and its demonstrative effect such aid might help to deter another war. And if war did occur, a friendly Yugoslavia would represent a tremendous asset.

The political considerations were rather different and were longer term in their implications. There is little evidence to suggest that they were important in the transformation and institutionalization of U.S. aid that took place in 1950–51. As rationalizations of the decisions taken then they make a certain limited sense; but it would appear that the rationalizations were after the fact. In any event, the argument, as subsequently expressed, was that Yugoslavia represented the first major defeat for the

Soviet policy of imposing total control in Eastern Europe, that Tito had accomplished this on his own, and that this precedent was of the greatest importance for the future. Not only that, Stalin had realized the importance of Tito's stand, as the trials of the "Titoists" in Eastern Europe were beginning to show. If the Western powers could show that they were willing to help Yugoslavia maintain its independence, but without trying to influence or change its system of government, they would surely encourage other forces in Eastern Europe that might be anxious to reassert the principle of national sovereignty but were inhibited from doing so by fear that this would drive them back into the arms of capitalism.

Whether or not these arguments were seriously considered at the time, the really interesting point about the political and strategic considerations is that they suggested opposite conclusions. Aid given for strategic reasons should be administered in the interests of the United States and the Western powers, should give the United States the right to see that it was spent on objectives that matched U.S. priorities. In other words, it implied supervision. But the argument that Tito's precedent might encourage the other Communist bloc nations was surely an argument for the limitation of aid, for the clear understanding that it would not challenge the Yugoslav model of socialism that was then beginning to emerge. So aid given for the political reasons suggested here would have to be free of checks and restraints. Both these sets of considerations were to find expression in practical politics in the coming months. The program of military aid rose initially from the ad hoc prescriptions of economic aid, but the two were to be sharply distinguished before long.

So far, the argument has been that the decision to implement a program of military aid to Yugoslavia in 1951 cannot be understood without reference to the whole train of developments since 1948. But two events in the last weeks of 1950 stand out. The first, in November, was that President Truman asked the specially reconvened Congress to consider an extended program of aid—and he did so on strategic as well as political and humanitarian grounds. The House on November 12, and the Senate on November 14, voted the Yugoslavia Emergency Relief Act, which authorized the expenditure of $50 million. It secured considerable majorities in both houses: 60 to 21 in the Senate, and 225 to 142 in the House. The $50 million was itself significant, but much more important was the fact that the aid program was now institutionalized; that it no longer depended on ad hoc decisions by the executive branch or on clever interpretations of legislation; and that the Congress, by a very substantial majority, agreed with the executive analysis. Thereafter the way was clear for Yugoslavia to be included in the regular appropriations of the Economic Cooperation Administration, and for the United States to work with the United Kingdom and France on a regular international program.[20]

The second event was related to Korea rather than to Yugoslavia. Following dire warnings from General Douglas MacArthur in Tokyo, the Joint Chiefs of Staff signaled to U.S. commanders the world over that "the situation in Korea has greatly increased the possibility of general war" and ordered them "to increase their readiness."[21] Under this directive the U.S. Mediterranean Fleet was ordered to sea at the end of the first week in December. As I have suggested, both Tito and Truman feared the possibility of war in Yugoslavia. The movements of the U.S. Sixth Fleet were dictated, certainly, by global considerations, but there is little doubt that the question of Yugoslavia was predominant at the time, at least as far as the Mediterranean was concerned. During the spring and summer of 1951 the Sixth Fleet was reinforced on several occasions, and on at least one of these occasions the reinforcements arrived shortly after Tito had made a declaration of his willingness to fight. By the end of 1951 Tito cruised on a U.S. aircraft carrier during a port visit it made to Yugoslavia. Now that economic aid had been transformed into a regular program of assistance, and that significant military support was, at least indirectly, being offered, the question was how to transform this military aid into a direct and overt program. As I have indicated, the commitment already existed—and in the case of Yugoslavia it was the aid that followed the commitment. But how did the decision to expand economic into military assistance come about?

The Decisions of 1951

Two aspects of the U.S. aid to Yugoslavia are worth noting. The first was that the aid was officially military, but largely economic. Yugoslavia did receive a minor amount of specific military supplies, but much of what reached the country was food, nominally destined for the armed forces but intended in practice to relieve the effects of the drought. The second point followed from the first: the aid was formally military because that

20. Ibid., pp. 23–24.
21. See *United States in World Affairs, 1951*, pp. 25–26.

represented the simplest way of getting help to the country. The amendment of the Mutual Defense Assistance Act of 1949, in the form it took in July 1950, required a presidential finding that military aid could be extended to a European country, other than the members of NATO or Greece and Turkey (indeed, it resulted principally from the range of considerations involved in the Greek and Turkish attempts to join NATO), "whose strategic location makes it of direct importance to the defense of the North Atlantic area and whose immediately increased ability to defend itself . . . contributed to the preservation of the peace and security of the North Atlantic area and is vital to the security of the United States."[22] But presidential findings provided no scope for the kind of supervision the United States soon thought desirable or for the provision of aid in the quantity Yugoslavia might want. Any extended program of aid had to meet these two requirements. The transition toward such a program began early in 1951 and it began largely in Yugoslavia.

The changes in Yugoslav foreign policy that began in 1949 gathered momentum in 1950. Already in 1949 the United States had shown its recognition of the new trends at work in Belgrade by supporting Yugoslavia against much Soviet (and, originally, British) opposition for the "Eastern European" seat on the Security Council. In 1950 it began to reap its reward. After the outbreak of the Korean War, Yugoslavia voted for the Uniting for Peace Resolution to override the Soviet veto in the Security Council. But the implications of the Korean War did not stop in the United Nations. In February 1951 Tito declared to the Partisan Guards Division that they must now be prepared to resist aggression *in any part of Europe* if Yugoslav independence was thereby threatened; to drive the message home he remarked that a local war in Europe was now hardly possible.[23] Later, Kardelj uttered an explicit warning against the USSR. "We shall not," he told the Foreign Political Committee of the National Assembly, "allow anyone to stage a new Korea in Yugoslavia; that is to say, to throw this or that satellite or several of them against Yugoslavia while he himself is supposedly protecting peace."[24]

Tito made his declaration in February, Kardelj in July. They are juxtaposed here to emphasize the change in Yugoslav policy during the first

22. Amendment to the Mutual Defense Assistance Act of 1949.
23. It was, to make it as explicit as possible, also reported in *Tanjug Weekly Bulletin*. See *Survey*, p. 211.
24. See *United States in World Affairs, 1951*, pp. 25–26.

six months of 1951. The terms of Kardelj's speech made it unmistakably clear that he was referring to the USSR. Who was Yugoslavia to "allow" or "not allow" a particular course of Soviet action? In effect, surely, he was proclaiming general war in the event of even a satellite attack upon the country. What had happened in the meantime to inspire such confidence?

It might be convenient to summarize the nature of the U.S. involvement up to this point and to indicate actions taken by the U.S. government in the early part of 1951. First, the executive branch had already shown that it was prepared to interpret the Mutual Defense Assistance Act in such a manner that it could be used to extend economic aid to Yugoslavia. Second, Tito was desperate for further economic aid and shortly made it clear that he was prepared to couch his request for assistance in terms that made it possible under the act. Third, a sympathetic intermediary was present in the person of the U.S. ambassador in Belgrade. Fourth, Yugoslavia had approached the British government in the hope of obtaining a long-term loan,[25] but at that stage the British government, while able to help to some degree, could hardly be regarded as more than another intermediary. This was the background to the decisions that now followed, but those decisions indicated an increasing degree of support—military as well as economic—for Yugoslavia.

To consider the economic support first: U.S. and British experts[26] were apparently agreed that Yugoslavia needed a long-term loan of $400 million to $500 million for capital investment, and that otherwise the economy was threatened with collapse. But the current economic crisis was far more immediate, and the government officially informed the United States and the United Kingdom in March that without raw materials to a total value of some $30 million the country's factories would have to close within ninety days. At the end of March it requested a grant of $20 million from the United States and £4 million ($11.2 million) from the United Kingdom for the purchase of raw materials. In its request to the United States the Yugoslav government declared that these materials were needed to maintain the country's military program, and in so doing put the request within the terms of the Mutual Defense Assistance Act. Within a few days (on April 9) the Foreign Office and State Depart-

25. *Survey*, p. 242.
26. Ibid. Quoted without attribution. See pp. 242 ff.

ment began discussions in London. They were to continue until June, and were to be joined by the Quai d'Orsay, but Truman acted before they were anywhere near conclusion. On April 16 he informed Congress that he had authorized the expenditure of $29 million under the act to enable Yugoslavia to obtain raw materials "critically" needed to support its armed forces. In a letter to the chairmen of the House Armed Services Committee and the Senate Foreign Relations Committee he defended his decision with the argument that the Yugoslav shortage of raw materials would jeopardize the country's ability to defend itself, and so weaken the security of the United States. The following day Ambassador Allen was able to implement the decision through an exchange of notes with the Yugoslav deputy foreign minister. The British government, for its part, decided that it could afford to find the £4 million requested by Yugoslavia by the end of May. All three Western governments, which concluded their discussions in mid-June, were agreed that short-term emergency measures were one thing but long-term measures, such as a guarantee of the Yugoslav deficit which would enable Belgrade to obtain a loan from the World Bank, were another, and would require some evidence that the Yugoslav economy was viable. They objected to the enormous emphasis still placed on investment in Yugoslav economic planning; they desired the country to divert more of its resources to exports—not only agriculture, but also commodities like nonferrous metals—and they wished to see some investment diverted from heavy industry, on which, following the proper Stalinist model, it was still concentrated. *Yugoslavia rejected all these arguments,* as an unwarranted interference in its internal affairs and a Western attempt to keep the country in a backward condition of neocolonial dependency.

In itself this act of rejection suggests that Tito was desperate for short-term economic aid, but that he could afford to be obstinate over the longer term questions once that was assured. In that sense it provides support for the argument above. But it also suggests that the differences in criteria for the provision of economic aid on the one hand and military aid on the other now had to be faced. Were the three Western powers going to make economic aid conditional or unconditional? The answer was soon clear. The three powers had reached agreement, and though it was not officially published it was clear that they were prepared to cover the deficit until the middle of 1952 (the United States bearing 65 percent of the cost, Britain 23 percent, and France the remaining 12 percent) and that this help would be unconditional.[27] Moreover, Herbert Morrison, now British foreign secretary, announced to the House of Commons that among the criteria considered was the strengthening of Yugoslavia against the Cominform, which was of "the utmost importance." Tito had won— in economic terms. But it was also announced that the proposed aid would not include arms, which would be "bought in the ordinary way."

But what of the military decisions the United States had been taking at the same time? Here it is important to distinguish between the general and the particular. In general terms, the United States was clearly anxious to preserve Yugoslav independence, and this policy found expression in the general reinforcement of the Sixth Fleet. In the middle of March the Second Battalion of the Sixth Marine Regiment arrived in the Mediterranean. This was a reinforced battalion, with two attack transport ships, one attack cargo ship, one high-speed transport ship, one dock-landing ship, and three other landing ships. In other words it was a force prepared for shore intervention at short notice.[28] Nowhere in the Mediterranean was such an intervention more likely than in Yugoslavia. Not only did the presence of such a force give point to Tito's remarks to the Guards Division in February that war in Europe was unlikely to be confined to any one country; it must have powerfully assisted the transition from that original statement to Kardelj's later, more explicit, warning to the USSR. And later in March a relief force for the Mediterranean Fleet arrived, six weeks early, specifically to cover the "politically critical spring period." This relief force consisted of an aircraft carrier (probably the *Coral Sea*), eleven destroyers, a submarine, and an oiler. At the same time, the force it was relieving remained until its scheduled departure date. The Mediterranean Fleet represented an exceptionally powerful force in the ensuing weeks.[29] Finally, in the fourth week of May, this fleet was augmented by another aircraft carrier, one light cruiser, and another destroyer.[30]

In general terms, therefore, the United States was showing demonstra-

27. Ibid., p. 243.

28. U.S. Department of the Navy, *U.S. Naval Forces, Eastern Atlantic and Mediterranean,* November 1, 1950, to July 1, 1951.

29. *CVAN-70 Aircraft Carrier,* Hearings before the Senate-House Armed Services Joint Subcommittee, 91:2 (GPO, 1970), p. 361.

30. Department of the Navy, *U.S. Naval Forces, Eastern Atlantic and Mediterranean, July 1, 1951, to June 14, 1952.*

tive support for any Mediterranean country that might come under the threat of attack from the USSR or its satellites. Such general support certainly heartened and encouraged Tito, but the prospect of more particular military assistance was bound to raise problems of its own.

If Tito had exploited the possibility of a military threat to Yugoslavia as a means of securing economic aid, he had nonetheless always been careful to preserve his economic independence and the political system that went with it. How much more careful would he be to secure his military independence? It should now be clear that the United States and Yugoslavia were moving, by a parallel process, to opposite conclusions on the subject of military aid. For if the United States were to extend Yugoslavia proper military assistance, and not merely economic aid in a military disguise, would it not demand the controls that went with it? For this reason, Tito had at the beginning of the year emphatically refused military aid. But he was about to lose this battle.

In his speech to the Guards Division in February, Tito defended his decision to seek economic assistance from the West. This, he said, would make the country stronger, both as a socialist country and "in general." But he also said that there was no intention of seeking military aid: it could not be accepted because the Cominform would hold it as proof of the existence of U.S. bases. He even went so far as to spell out the price that was entailed:

We must leave aside training in up-to-date technique, precisely because they wish to depict us as those who are preparing for war. . . . However, the moment we see that attack on us is imminent, matters will be different. Today, we think that the final moment has not yet come.[31]

Was there here a point of agreement between Tito and Senator Taft— that aid would constitute more in provocation than it would be worth in defense? In any event, it is clear that Tito was keeping his options open, but at the same time trying hard to steer clear of military assistance. At the end of the month he suggested in an interview that Yugoslavia could resist attack by the combined forces of its satellite neighbors, but hedged on the question of whether it could also fend off Soviet "volunteers"[32]— the question itself showing how much the model of Korea preoccupied everyone. He was also asked whether Yugoslavia would request Western assistance if the difference between its neighbors and itself became over-

31. *Survey*, p. 245.
32. *New York Times* and *Manchester Guardian*, March 1, 1951.

whelming. He replied that it would do so *if its independence were threatened by an aggressor*. It would appear that he was in fact consistently trying to avoid committing himself to a program of Western military assistance but also hoping that aid would be rushed to him if he had to ask for it.

This was, however, the period in which Tito was also trying to maximize Yugoslavia's potential military danger to obtain economic assistance. The two policies, in fact, appear quite consistent. In each case he was suggesting that there might not be any immediate danger but that there was a long-term need to build up the country's military potential. For this reason, the argument that he had in fact already decided to ask for Western military aid seems unconvincing.[33] What he had decided on, however, was the purchase of Western military equipment—in particular, captured German stocks from the Second World War.

In January Djilas had already visited London, where he had presented a modest list of the items Yugoslavia wished to buy commercially. But a few weeks later he presented a more comprehensive list,[34] which was transmitted by the British government to the United States and France. This was in April, at the same time as the Anglo-American discussions on the scope and scale of economic aid. It would seem, therefore, that from now on the two (and then three) governments were agreed on considering all forms of aid to Yugoslavia together. The question naturally arises at this point of who made the decision. It was probably the United States, in the persons of the ambassador in Belgrade, Assistant Under Secretary of State for Europe George Perkins, who had visited Belgrade in February, and presumably the secretary of state and the President.[35]

The decision to ask for extensive rather than minimal military purchases also represented a change in Yugoslav policy. Whereas minimal purchases could have been managed either from income or from economic aid, extensive purchases represented a real request for assistance. On April 11 *Borba* published an authorized statement from Veljko Vlahavic, the president of the Council for Foreign Affairs, saying that the

33. The otherwise excellent *Survey* appears to me to be mistaken on this point. Tito did not ask for assistance, which would seem at least to imply credit terms. He was concerned only with *buying* arms. By confusing the two, *Survey* has missed the most important point in the transition of Tito's policies.

34. Ibid. No date is specified.

35. "Presumably" because there is no evidence that the question was considered when Perkins returned.

intensified rearmament of the neighboring satellites, the increase of frontier incidents, and general threats had persuaded Yugoslavia to ask for both the means of strengthening its own arms industry (which could be interpreted as economic aid) and facilities for purchasing weapons (which could only be interpreted as military aid). If there had been a change and the change had happened in April, why did it?

In March the four powers had discussed the agenda for a prospective conference. On this occasion, as before, Gromyko had flatly refused to include the rearmament of Hungary, Rumania, and Bulgaria as a subject for discussion. It was not so much that he had refused yet again as it was the general context and tension of the moment. The three Eastern European countries, as Yugoslavia had already been quick to point out, had intensified their rearmament; it was only recently (in January) that the United Nations forces had regained the initiative in Korea after suffering a series of disastrous setbacks and, as the Joint Chiefs of Staff had indicated, "the possibility of general war" had risen sharply; finally there had been a resurgence of border incidents. Later in the year Yugoslavia was to complain to the United Nations that groups were being sent into the country from Bulgaria, Hungary, and Albania to carry out diversion and sabotage, with the assistance of the "state organs" of those governments and the direct blessing of Soviet forces. The interesting aspect of this complaint was that the Soviet Union did not deny the increase in the number of incidents; indeed it went out of its way to emphasize it—while, of course, putting all the blame on Yugoslavia.

On June 8 Kardelj told the Foreign Affairs Committee of the Yugoslav Assembly that the army chief of staff was already in Washington discussing the purchase of military equipment. He pointed to the rearmament of Rumania, Hungary, and Bulgaria as the principal reason for this purchase. In fact, Chief of Staff Colonel-General Koca Popovic had been in Washington since mid-May, as the Department of Defense now announced. A few days after Kardelj's announcement it was reported in the *New York Times*[36] that U.S. "officials" were willing to supply Yugoslavia with substantial quantities of military assistance. Popovic was told that facilities for purchasing the equipment would be made available if Yugoslavia still insisted on purchasing the equipment (as it was still trying to do) but that the volume requested indicated an application for aid under the Mutual Defense Assistance Act. Was it purely the scale of Yugoslav

36. June 12, 1951.

requests which induced the Department of Defense to suggest an application under the act, or was it the desire to exercise some check on the deployment of arms? The subsequent agreement and deployment suggest the latter.

It was apparent that Yugoslavia's determination to catch up with its neighbors was now exercising a pressure contradictory to its determination to purchase arms on a purely commercial basis. On June 18 General Koca Popovic announced that he had discussed whether Yugoslavia would qualify for aid under the Mutual Defense Assistance Act with both General Omar Bradley and Secretary of State Dean Acheson. Since the country had already received aid under the act, the discussions must have dealt more with the conditions than the principle, but nonetheless represented the second major change in Yugoslavia's position. Yugoslavia had now been brought to request formal military assistance, and the request was presented to Dean Acheson by the Yugoslav ambassador to the United States, Vladimir Popovic, at the end of the month. The ambassador declared that there was no immediate crisis, but he also pointed to the continuous pressure from the East and announced that what Yugoslavia wanted was heavy armaments as soon as possible. Finally he remarked that the transactions would be "within the framework" of the Mutual Defense Assistance Act. This was the public transaction. But in private the United States had already anticipated Yugoslavia's actions and the Department of Defense had sent Yugoslavia a quantity of arms in the middle of May. In itself this was no more significant than the limited amounts that had been dispatched after the outbreak of the Korean War. What was important was that the shipment was financed from the department's own funds and that the announcement was held up until the formal negotiations were completed. It was later reported that the value of this shipment was $3 million.[37] The final act in this whole process was the Yugoslav decision to *purchase* arms, diverting to that purpose some of the $29 million of economic aid it had just received.

Thereafter, the real questions would be the scale and level of armaments supplied by the United States and the agreements it was possible to reach on a bilateral basis between the United States and Yugoslavia on the use of this help. In this regard, two U.S. visits to Yugoslavia were of particular interest. The first was by Averell Harriman at the end of August. At this moment in his varied and distinguished career Harriman

37. *Survey*, p. 248.

was Mutual Security administrator. His visit was therefore of some moment. But he emphasized in a press conference at the time that he was there on the initiative of the Yugoslav government and that he had no advice to offer. This was apparently monumental tact, for he had discussed economic and military assistance with Tito, agreed with his analysis of the dangers of war, and promised an increase in both economic and military aid. He also suggested that Yugoslavia's defense industries could do with a bit of help. Later he went to London and Paris, where he apparently discussed the question of Yugoslavia with Clement Attlee and René Pleven.[38]

The second visit occurred in October. It had been preceded by a mission of the chief of operations of the Yugoslav Army (Major-General Sumonja) and its chief of supply (Major-General Kilibarda) to Washington to confer with Secretary of Defense George Marshall. On October 14 the chief of staff of the U.S. Army, General J. Lawton Collins, arrived in Belgrade. In retrospect it is clear that Collins's visit was designed to help Yugoslavia reach a military aid agreement. The same Marshal Tito who had ceaselessly warned about the dangers of overreliance on the West now allowed Collins to inspect Yugoslav military installations in Skopje (headquarters of the military region that guarded the approach from Bulgaria), Macedonia, Bosnia, and Slovenia. He also observed military exercises involving tanks, artillery, and aircraft. Collins made no secret of the fact that he was greatly impressed by the Yugoslav forces, and subsequently became a champion of Yugoslav interests in the Pentagon.[39] On this occasion Tito is reported to have told him that Yugoslavia now had forty-two divisions (it was normally assumed at the time of the break with Stalin that he had had thirty-three), that he particularly wanted tanks, and that he was by now determined to defend Yugoslavia on the frontiers and not through a retreat into the mountains. Collins agreed publicly with him that the Yugoslav forces were far more than mere guerrillas, and thereafter the two men continued to state from their respective positions that what Yugoslavia needed and was building up was a regular army of high caliber.

Collins had arrived on October 14. On October 27 it was announced in the *New York Herald Tribune* (it had by then become an open secret in Washington) that Yugoslavia was ready to sign a military assistance

38. *Daily Telegraph,* August 30, 1951.
39. See Campbell, *Tito's Separate Road,* p. 27.

agreement, including an American Military Assistance Advisory Group (MAAG), as was the normal procedure under other agreements in the Mutual Defense Assistance program. The MAAG was to be led by Brigadier General John W. Harmany. The *Tribune* added that Collins had promised Tito that the MAAG would not spy on Yugoslav defenses or roam around the country.

The final act in this protracted decision process came on the last day of October, when Tito himself announced at a press conference that the agreement would be signed shortly. When asked what the United States would receive in return for its help, he declared that the United States would now have a friendly country by its side if hostilities broke out *anywhere in Europe*. In a letter to the House Armed Services Committee and the Senate Foreign Relations Committee on November 7, President Truman announced that Yugoslavia would receive economic and military assistance under the Mutual Security Act of 1951. (The act was substantially the same, in this regard, as the amended Mutual Defense Assistance Act of 1950, except that it gave the President a somewhat wider latitude by substituting the word "important" for the word "vital" in its reference to the security interests of the United States.) The military aid agreement was signed in Belgrade on November 14 by Marshal Tito and Ambassador Allen. The United States had effectively created a commitment from which it would be impossible to back down without losing its credibility on a global scale. Just as Ambassador Allen had supervised the transition from a general commitment to Yugoslav independence to a more particular commitment to help the country *maintain* its independence, so too the movement of U.S. warships helped to translate the general into the particular.

On December 17, just over a month after the military aid agreement had been signed in Belgrade, the heavy cruiser *Des Moines* visited Rijeka.[40] The attack aircraft carrier *Coral Sea* visited Yugoslavia in the same month. Marshal Tito now laid aside all his eloquent warnings against Western entanglement, and cruised on board.[41] These visits—the cruise in particular—were obviously highly demonstrative. The United States was showing both its commitment to Yugoslav independence and its ability to intervene on its behalf. Tito was showing how far his policies

40. Department of the Navy, Naval Historical Center, Operational Archives, "Short of War" Documentation, Special List Nos. 1 and 2.
41. *CVAN-70 Aircraft Carrier*, Hearings, p. 361.

had changed, and how far he had accepted a new alignment. And for some time thereafter an increased momentum was maintained in the developing relations between the two. Also in December Yugoslav officers and noncommissioned officers were sent to the United States for training. Relations between the MAAG and the Yugoslav military authorities did remain prickly and suspicious, but the ambassador was usually able to restore a degree of harmony and also to ensure that the military cooperation program served U.S. as well as Yugoslav interests. Plans were announced later for direct Yugoslav-Italian military talks and also for U.S.-Yugoslav strategic discussions. What did the United States achieve in the short term by the decisions it took in 1951?

Effect of the Decisions of 1951

It was suggested earlier that the greatest moment of danger for Yugoslavia probably occurred in the summer of 1949. But if it is true that plans for an invasion were first laid and then abandoned by the USSR in these months, this certainly did not mean that the danger had passed. It persisted throughout 1950 and 1951 and probably reached a high point again in the spring of 1951. During that period, between the outbreak of the Korean War and the signing of the military assistance agreement, U.S. officials at almost every level of government had voiced the concern that the Korean episode might merely be the prelude to a Soviet attack in Europe, or the precedent for satellite action in "gray areas." Averell Harriman emphasized after his conversations with Tito that the most likely cause for such an attack would be a miscalculation on Stalin's part of the U.S. will to resist. Aid to Yugoslavia was therefore both a prophylactic measure and a signal to the USSR that the U.S. will was unimpaired. Equally, it allowed the main burden of defense preparations to rest on Yugoslavia, according with both Yugoslav interests and desires and the need of the United States not to become overextended at a time when it was still building up its military strength.

The principal result of the decision, therefore, was to uncouple the question of Yugoslavia from the global situation, making it a separate and serious issue in superpower military relations. It rescued Yugoslavia from the status of a "gray area," dependent for its fate on calculations in Moscow of the U.S. will or capability to resist an attack. Instead it harnessed the U.S. will to the Yugoslav will, U.S. intervention capacity to the Yugoslav ability to fight. In so doing it decisively transformed the situation: from now on, it was clear that any attack on Yugoslavia would carry with it the risks of a European—and therefore a general—war. This mutual reinforcement of will and capacity effectively deterred any further prospect of a Soviet or satellite attack on Yugoslavia.

U.S. aid in 1951 also had another effect. In 1951 Yugoslavia had, after all, changed its position decisively. Not only had it accepted U.S. military assistance, it had also cosponsored, along with the United States, a UN resolution denouncing the USSR's aggressive attitude toward Yugoslavia and calling for a normalization of Soviet-Yugoslav relations. Yugoslavia had circulated among the Western governments a White Book containing details of Soviet harassment, of the military buildup on Yugoslavia's borders, and of the frontier incidents—2,000 in all—that had taken place over the past three years. Speaking before the Ad Hoc Committee of the United Nations in November, Djilas also detailed the course of Soviet-Yugoslav relations.

It was in 1951, in this sense, that Yugoslavia marked its definitive break with the USSR. At first sight this might appear absurd: Yugoslav foreign policy had already begun to change in 1949; Yugoslavia had been anxious about the possibility of a Soviet military attack for a long time. But it is perhaps too easy from today's perspective to take it for granted that Yugoslavia could never have effected a reconciliation with the USSR. The fact that it did not tempts one to overlook too easily the degree to which many Yugoslav leaders—Tito not least of them—long remained anxious to do so. The acts of denunciation in 1951, Yugoslavia's association with the tripartite economic aid agreements, and the acceptance of U.S. military aid all marked the turning point at which Yugoslavia became, in foreign policy, effectively an ally of the West. Even if its function as a sub-rosa military ally was both limited and temporary, this turning marked an immense political and strategic gain for U.S. interests—a gain whose effects are still apparent.

But there was also a significant short-term consequence. At the time of Collins's visit to Belgrade, the Supreme Allied Commander, Europe, General Dwight Eisenhower, had sent him a message that NATO could reasonably expect some quid pro quo for the help it was now sending Yugoslavia.[42] What kind of reward was this? This is where the country's military deployment assumes a new significance. Collins had agreed with

42. From *Declassified Documents Reference System*, microfiche no. (75)168A.

Tito that Yugoslavia needed a frontier defense manned by regular forces, not a guerrilla defense based in the mountains. But *what* frontier defense? Collins, after all, went first to Skopje—indicating the existing Yugoslav interest in defense against an attack from Bulgaria. But the supplies built up after the agreement were directed primarily to the equipment of those Yugoslav divisions stationed in the area of the Ljubljana Gap.[43] In other words, American military aid *was* directed not merely to the overall strengthening of Yugoslavia but also to a reinforcement of the NATO potential, even though the most direct danger to the country lay in the possibility of a satellite attack on its other flank.

These were the principal effects of the decisions of 1951—an immediate military consequence and a longer term foreign policy consequence. But they also raise a question about the longer term consequences of U.S. military aid.

The Longer Term Consequences

During the negotiations that followed the Popovic visit to Washington, culminating in the Collins visit to Belgrade, Tito was of course anxious to show that he was in no sense turning into a Western stooge. Shortly after March 1953 Yugoslavia abandoned any prospect of strategic discussions with the United States, even though in the summer of that year the 317th Troop Carrier Wing carried mobile training equipment to Belgrade.[44] The Yugoslav-Italian military talks came to very little, and throughout 1953 the Yugoslav general staff made preparations for a better balanced defense. This indicated one side of Tito's determination to recover his freedom from the United States as the threat from the USSR receded. But there was also (from the Western standpoint) a more positive aspect.

Although Tito was anxious after 1953 to dissociate himself gradually from the very close dependence on the United States he had built up, his overall foreign policy was not deflected from its course by the news of Stalin's death. Tito was, no doubt, less apprehensive about the effects of association with small states than with big ones. Nonetheless, the small states were Western allies and, after 1952, members of NATO. In Feb-

43. Campbell, *Tito's Separate Road*, p. 27.
44. U.S. Department of the Air Force, 317th Troop Carrier Wing, "Historical Data, 317th Troop Carrier Wing, Medium, July–August, 1953."

ruary 1953 Yugoslavia signed a treaty of friendship and cooperation with Greece and Turkey. By August 1954 this entente had turned into a military pact in which the three countries gave each other mutual guarantees against attack, and Yugoslavia undertook to take into account the NATO obligations of the other two. The Balkan Pact was interesting as an indicator of Tito's views, of the assurance he now felt he had received from the West, and of the fact that—even after the death of Stalin and the fall of Beria—he was still prepared to proceed along his tortuous but carefully chosen path. In the end, then, even by the lowest estimate, Tito's foreign policy had become mobile and flexible, but the mobility and flexibility were now sustained by the United States and its military commitment. The commitment was implicit but it was there when needed—as, for example, when Tito called upon it in 1968, ten years after the supplying of arms under the Mutual Security Act had come to an end.

In sum, the United States succeeded totally in its major objectives, succeeded partially and temporarily in the incidental objective of creating a link between Yugoslav and NATO defense needs, but also succeeded in the longer term transformation of the political and strategic equations in the Balkans. Two final questions are worth mentioning. The first relates to the process of decision; the second to the relevance of the decisions of 1951 to any future actions concerning Yugoslavia.

The Process of Decision

The developments that led to the 1951 agreement were dependent throughout on Yugoslav initiatives. It was Tito who had to bring himself to ask for military aid, just as it was Tito who was capable of changing his foreign policy to suit the economic requirements of his country. It was Tito who sent Popovic to Washington, who hoped at first to purchase arms commercially, who finally changed his mind, and who subsequently invited Averell Harriman to Yugoslavia. U.S. policy was in this sense reactive. Through the original economic program it had become committed to keeping Tito afloat; but the transition to military assistance depended on him, and he was at first very reluctant to become too dependent. Nonetheless, even in a reactive rather than an active role, and even faced with an obdurate supplicant, the United States showed considerable skill and understanding in its response to Tito's move. The credit for the initial perception of the implication of Tito's break with Stalin must go to Ambassador Cannon. Economic aid was thereafter transformed into military aid. The 1950 commitment seems to have grown out of the events preceding it, rather than by conscious decision, and to have been related more to the President's changing view than to any State Department analysis. The State Department, particularly Secretary of State Dean Acheson, took it for granted that Tito was on the Western side and that this was a view shared by the United Kingdom.[45] Finally, the Department of Defense appears to have played the decisive role in extending substantial military aid to the country. Its action in granting $3 million worth of aid from its own funds indicated the seriousness with which it viewed both the potential threat to and the potential worth of Yugoslavia, even while Tito was still hesitating to apply for more extensive (and perhaps more legal) assistance. Thereafter, once the major decisions of principle had been reached, it was perhaps the visits of Averell Harriman, but more particularly of General Collins, that inclined Tito to accept the conditions of aid and to swing Yugoslav defense into a posture that would be of direct use to NATO.

The final question is the relevance of 1951 to any thinking about Yugoslavia today, but that can be understood more clearly after a discussion of the events arising out of the crisis in Czechoslovakia in 1968.

Czechoslovakia, 1968

In examining those aspects of the crisis arising from the Soviet invasion of Czechoslovakia in 1968 that affected U.S. policymaking it will be necessary to indicate the character of the crisis and some of the developments that led to the invasion. In essence the crisis was internal to the Warsaw Pact; the United States had to deal only with its repercussions. Yet these repercussions were in many ways more threatening to international peace than the invasion itself, involving U.S. demonstrative military action and diplomatic action. For once the crisis widened to include a possible threat to Rumania, Yugoslavia was also affected, causing grave concern in the United States.

U.S. military actions following the Soviet invasion of Czechoslovakia were very limited; the diplomatic import of these actions and the kind of signal they conveyed to the USSR mattered most. The task of the United

45. See Dean Acheson, *Present at the Creation* (Norton, 1969), p. 327.

States was not to take extensive or dramatic military measures but to choose the right signals—and in so doing to secure the acquiescence of its NATO allies. Although the invasion of Czechoslovakia did not itself make much difference to the power *balance* in Europe, it did bring about changes in the power *structure*—the disposition of forces, the potential order of battle—and these were naturally of concern to NATO. Most important, the major interest of the United States was predicated on the assumptions that a stable relationship with the USSR had to be preserved and that the risk of a nuclear confrontation in Europe had to be avoided. It was fundamental to this view that each superpower visibly respect the other's sphere of interest. U.S. action, therefore, had to protect broader U.S. interests without appearing thereby to threaten the USSR. All these considerations together created a complex set of requirements, which I shall examine in some detail.

Background

In one sense the USSR could be said to have *resolved* the crisis by the act of invasion. This is the view that might be taken by those who attach importance to the conventions of crisis management.[46] Czechoslovakia represented a threat to the political and ideological cohesion of the socialist bloc, and Soviet action prevented this threat from developing. Even more emphatically, the Soviet invasion prevented the intramural crisis of the Warsaw Pact from becoming a confrontation between the Warsaw Pact and NATO. But such a view, while schematically plausible, not only is morally unattractive but also overlooks some of the distinctive characteristics of the crisis itself. These characteristics, as they developed between Alexander Dubcek's accession to power in January 1968 and the invasion by Warsaw Pact troops on August 21, were roughly as follows.

First, it was very clear that the USSR was reluctant to invade. Pressure within the Central Committee for an invasion had certainly been evident as early as April.[47] Yet it was not until the very last minute—perhaps

46. See Coral Bell, *The Conventions of Crisis: A Study in Diplomatic Management* (Oxford University Press for the Royal Institute of International Affairs, 1971).

47. Philip Windsor and Adam Roberts, *Czechoslovakia, 1968* (Chatto and Windus for the International Institute for Strategic Studies, 1969), p. 39.

shortly after August 10[48]—that the actual decision to invade was taken. Second, Soviet reluctance to invade was accompanied by an equally evident determination to treat the democratization program in Czechoslovakia as a matter affecting the security of the socialist camp, and not merely as a matter of ideological disagreement. Increasingly, between April and August, the Soviet leaders used the Warsaw Pact as the main instrument of their discussions with the Czechoslovaks.

Third, these twin considerations—Soviet reluctance to invade and Soviet determination to use security as an instrument of control—in fact intensified the crisis. Soviet reluctance to invade encouraged some Czechoslovak leaders to believe that they could manage developments slowly and avoid the risk of outright confrontation. Every attempt made by the Soviet and Warsaw Pact leaders to contain and control the developments in Czechoslovakia was interpreted by the Czechoslovak press and people as a threat, and this view encouraged continually more radical demands. In the very attempt to keep some kind of control—which meant both placating the USSR and maintaining popular support—the Czechoslovak government found instead that it was losing control. Concessions to the Soviet leadership were unacceptable at home; concessions to popular demand were unacceptable to the USSR. In this manner, and largely because of the dilatoriness of the Soviet decision, the Czechoslovak government was reduced to helplessness.

What do these considerations together amount to? At one level it is comparatively simple to treat the invasion of Czechoslovakia as a matter of purely intramural concern to the Warsaw Pact, with very little bearing on either détente or security relations in Europe; but on another level it it very difficult to do so. Did the crisis mean that it was now going to be dangerous for Eastern European countries to move toward greater internal liberalization, or was there a fundamental difference between the democratization proposed in Czechoslovakia and the patterns of liberalization that were emerging elsewhere? Did the USSR recognize such a difference? Or was the invasion a prelude to wider intervention in Eastern

48. It was on August 10 that the New Party Statutes were promulgated. The view that it was this event which finally triggered the Soviet decision was widespread in 1968. Signor Manlio Brosio, the quondam Secretary-General of NATO, argued then that all the evidence suggested that the Soviet decision was taken only in these last ten days. Subsequently, Czechoslovak sources, including the draft memoirs of the late Jozef Smrkovsky, have confirmed that this was their reading too.

European affairs? The enunciation of the "Brezhnev doctrine" in the form of an authoritative article in *Pravda* and in statements by Brezhnev himself could be read either way. Indeed, during the complex period of negotiations between the Czechoslovak leaders and the Soviet troops, a period in which the Czechoslovaks appeared at first unexpectedly successful in recapturing much of their autonomy, it is probable that the Soviet leadership itself had not yet decided.

However, one thing was unmistakably clear: détente had led to the crisis. This was only an apparent paradox, for in reality such a crisis had been inherent in the progress of détente. For some years, the USSR had apparently been prepared to accept that détente entailed a relaxation of control in Eastern Europe. This had been a major premise of Gaullist diplomacy. Indeed, this relaxation of Soviet control—the dismantling of the apparatus of economic supervision, the loosening of interparty ties, the formal acceptance of "separate roads to Socialism" at the Twenty-first Congress of the Communist Party of the Soviet Union (CPSU) in 1959—appeared to have gone so far that it was possible for acute observers of Eastern European politics to discuss the "collapse of the Soviet empire."[49] But the seeds of crisis began to grow from such discussions. If ultimate Soviet authority were challenged, or the ideological basis of a fraternal party were threatened, the USSR might feel itself impelled to take corrective action. If the price for détente had initially appeared to be a relaxation of control, that relaxation might now seem to imply more dangerous developments. The difficulty for Western observers lay in determining the likely impact of Soviet action in Eastern Europe.

In fact, further crisis could have had any of three potential results. The first could have been a change in the overall balance of military power in Europe through the heavy reinforcement of Soviet forces there. The second could have been changes in the power structure through the realignment and redeployment of Soviet or other Warsaw Pact forces, necessitating an overhaul of the NATO order of battle. The relocation of Soviet forces in Czechoslovakia did subsequently oblige Western commanders to take account of the greater flexibility that this conferred upon the Warsaw Pact forces. Although not a major factor, it was nonetheless a factor in the restructuring of German and U.S. forces in the central area. Thus, while the invasion made no great difference to the overall

49. See Ghita Ionescu, *The Break-up of the Soviet Empire in Eastern Europe* (Penguin Books, 1965).

power balance, it did change the power structure. The third and most serious consequence could have been a major upheaval in Europe leading to an East-West confrontation and the danger of war, triggered either by emotional and nationalist interests of Western nations, as in the case of a conflict involving East Germany, or else by Soviet intervention in areas of strategic importance, as in the case of Yugoslavia.

This was the background against which the United States had to consider the action it should take following the Soviet occupation of Czechoslovakia. The crisis was not a neat and tidy affair, confined to the Warsaw Pact alone; its implications ranged over very important areas of East-West relations. In framing a possible pattern of response the United States had to take into account its principal opponent, the USSR; its friends, in this case principally the NATO countries of the central area; and finally, others who, while not necessarily directly concerned with the conflict, might find themselves caught up in its implications.

The USSR

The relationship of Soviet and U.S. objectives in the aftermath of the invasion of Czechoslovakia is in one sense clear. The primary concern of the United States was inevitably to demonstrate to the USSR that, although it disapproved of the Soviet action, it would in no sense interfere in the Soviet sphere of influence. Equally, the USSR sought to reassure the United States that its actions against Czechoslovakia in no way represented a threat to the U.S. position in Western Europe.

Indeed, at the moment that the invasion was under way (some three hours after the first Soviet troops landed at Ruzyne Airport in Prague), the Soviet embassies in Washington, London, Paris, and Bonn all sought interviews with the foreign ministries of the governments to which they were accredited. In the case of the United Kingdom, the Soviet emissary apparently delivered a message in two parts.[50] The first part indicated that the Soviet action was directed exclusively against Czechoslovakia, that it would be of short duration, that Soviet troop movements, particularly in East Germany, need be no cause for alarm, and that the USSR

50. I was told of this by Lord Chalfont, at that time minister of state at the Foreign Office, who received his Soviet visitor at 2 A.M. London time. Some confirmation of his report is provided by Harlan Cleveland, at that time American ambassador to NATO, in his article "NATO after the Invasion," *Foreign Affairs,* vol. 47 (January 1969), p. 253.

hoped that its action against counterrevolutionary forces in Czechoslovakia would not impair relations between the British and Soviet governments. The second part was shorter and consisted simply of a warning that any attempt to intervene would mean a world war. Indeed, it ended with a verbal assurance: "If you interfere, we will blow you off the map." Subsequent conversations with members of the Foreign and Commonwealth Office in London have indicated to me that, as far as liaison between Washington and London permitted them to know, the contents of the message delivered in Washington were very similar—although no doubt the second part was expressed somewhat less tersely. In other words, the two superpowers already understood that military action by one against the other's sphere of influence in Europe would leave no alternative but general war. By the same token that U.S. military power was helpless to come to the aid of Czechoslovakia, U.S. military power also remained a viable and completely credible guarantor for Western Europe. But the first level of understanding, although of primary importance in containing the crisis, did nothing to deal with its implications. What was the relationship of the objectives of the two powers at other levels?

The invasion of Czechoslovakia occurred at a moment when the intermittent progress toward East-West détente was about to be transformed into a steadier working relationship. President Johnson was due to visit Moscow very shortly afterward, and it was hoped that his visit would lead to an effective beginning of the strategic arms limitation talks (SALT). Had this been the case the United States would have begun in a very good bargaining position vis-à-vis the USSR, and with some hope that the talks could reach a speedier conclusion than in fact they have. But it was not possible simply to go ahead as planned, although Kosygin publicly pleaded that the President do so. Although the Soviet invasion apparently had much less emotional impact on the U.S. public than its action in Hungary twelve years earlier, American opinion had nonetheless to be considered. The emotional shock in Europe was intense. And in the European perspective it was not merely a matter of emotional shock. First, the invasion did prompt questions about the nature of the new power structure, a point that West German Chancellor Kurt Kiesinger raised with President Johnson. And second, the invasion meant that after a period of relative assurance that Soviet behavior was becoming more or less rational and predictable, Soviet reactions were again as aggressive as ever. The

President of the United States could not appear to condone such behavior if he needed to assure Western Europe of the validity of a continuing American commitment. There was therefore a temporary disjunction between the Soviet objective of gaining a freer hand again in Eastern Europe, while leaving the East-West détente unimpaired, and the U.S. objective of demonstrating that, though world security implied U.S.-Soviet understanding, this did not imply Soviet freedom to invade another state without paying some kind of price. But because the disjunction was temporary the price was small. The United States initially confined its reaction to canceling President Johnson's visit to Moscow and postponing SALT. At this level, again, the nature of the superpower relationship helped confine the crisis in Czechoslovakia to the status of an intramural affair. The uncertain implications of the crisis and the Brezhnev doctrine for further developments in Europe later propelled the U.S. government to new action, which will be examined later, and which seems to have implied a change of mind in the United States. The initial U.S. military response to the crisis in Czechoslovakia was to carry on as usual. The troops were temporarily returned to Europe and some exercises were advanced in date, actions intended to demonstrate U.S. resolve at a time when the Czechoslovakian crisis was threatening to spread. But even then the primary purpose was to reassure the Western Europeans.

The NATO Allies

Although the shock and uncertainty felt in Western Europe after the invasion were profound, the principal Western European governments were unanimous in minimizing the importance of the Soviet action. French Prime Minister Michel Debré declared that traffic accidents could not be helped. Chancellor Kiesinger was obviously concerned about the possible effects of changes in the power structure. Indeed, he proposed strategic discussions in NATO about the effects of Soviet redeployment,[51] but it made no difference to his view of détente; he merely declared that there was no alternative. The British made deploring noises but that was all. European reactions were no doubt due to the nature of their several exchanges with the Soviet government. At no time was *any* form of sanction discussed among Western European leaders.

There was no framework within which Western European governments

51. *New York Times*, September 5, 1968.

could discuss common action except NATO. NATO's primary concern, by definition, was to assure the security of its member states, and its attempts at political coordination, for which the machinery was created after the Suez crisis of 1956, had proven ineffective. In any case there had been astonishingly little prior discussion in NATO of possible reactions to a Soviet coup de main in Czechoslovakia. NATO's concerns, even when considering the likelihood and possibilities of such action, had been limited to an assessment of its security implications for Western Europe. The alliance was devoid of adequate machinery for political consultation and ill-prepared to cope with anything beyond the military implications of the crisis itself. Thus NATO could not serve as any vehicle for European consultation, with or without the United States, about European interests and/or potential action vis-à-vis the USSR in the aftermath of the invasion.

Consequently, the predisposition implied in superpower relations to contain and control the Czechoslovakian crisis as an intramural problem found little opposition among the United States' NATO allies. As Europeans they were ill-prepared to ponder the wider implications of the crisis for pan-European relations. As members of NATO they were concerned primarily with military security. Thus any superpower reaction indicating that the USSR was not mounting a serious threat, and that the United States *was* prepared to deal with any contingencies that might arise, was pretty satisfactory to the European governments. The first of these assurances was conveyed directly to the USSR. The second was served in purpose by a NATO "Yellow Alert." In fact, so far as I have been able to ascertain, this Yellow Alert not only provided a very low level of readiness but was also extremely inefficient. It seems to have been conducted very much more through the press than through any active military preparations. Indeed, there were some units, from at least two different national contingents in Germany, which were not involved at all, and even some senior officers who were practically unaware that it was going on.[52] All the evidence suggests that NATO's contingency measures were adopted at a comparatively low level of decisionmaking, that they were not and were not intended to be comprehensive, and that the major decisionmaking centers in the United States (the National Security

52. As recounted to me by senior (colonel and above) U.S. and British officers at a conference shortly afterward. Neither all German nor all U.S. forces in Germany were involved.

Council, the President, the Joint Chiefs, and the centers of command)
were barely involved. The Yellow Alert was a routine precautionary
measure, and one that was fully within the competence—and indeed the
duties—of the Supreme Allied Command, Europe (SACEUR) and the
group commanders to carry out on their own. Even so, it fulfilled the
U.S. objective: to indicate to its NATO allies a basic degree of commitment and readiness. This was the maximum that the European governments seem to have desired. Furthermore, a low-level, routine precautionary measure of this nature would be consistent with the state of
U.S.-Soviet relations, in the sense that it would reinforce the prevailing
understanding that neither power was prepared to tangle with, or allow
the other to tangle with, the opposing sphere of influence.

The U.S. military and diplomatic response to the Soviet action thus
did not have to meet any requirements of conflicting interests. It could
serve the objectives of U.S. relations with the USSR and with the NATO
allies simultaneously. Such a posture might no longer suffice today to
meet the requirements of both the European and the Soviet relations of
the United States, but that is because the Western European governments
are now capable of articulating a greater, a more distinctive, and a more
comprehensive interest in the process of détente than they were then. It is
also because in 1968 détente was still an experimental notion; by now that
notion has been fleshed out with at least some minimal conditions and
requirements, which have transformed the approach to détente in the
West. Experimental enthusiasm has given place to scrutiny, but such a
transformation also indicates a more articulate interest in détente itself.

The Issue of Rumania

The possibility that the Brezhnev doctrine might be extended to include
Soviet action against other troublemakers in Eastern Europe could not be
excluded in the aftermath of the invasion of Czechoslovakia. There were
two kinds of considerations involved. The first was that a generalized upheaval could follow from such a train of events, and thereby drag in the
Western powers, particularly if it spread to East Germany. But while
such a possibility was and remains the gravest potential consequence of
such action, it was also the most remote. The diplomatic success of the
Soviet Union in involving four other Warsaw Pact nations with the invasion seemed to indicate that the consequences would *not* spread. (Indeed,

one might suggest that one major concern of Soviet policymakers was not merely to legitimate their action in their own eyes and those of others by dressing it up as a Warsaw Pact rescue operation, but also to demonstrate that the crisis would not spread by showing how ready other Eastern European governments were to come in with them.) But the second consequence was of great potential gravity—and it was also very much less remote. One Warsaw Pact member, Rumania, had been excluded from previous meetings designed to intimidate the Czechoslovaks and had not been invited to participate in the invasion. It had moreover been a persistent troublemaker both in the Pact and in COMECON since 1964.

Yet Rumania's military significance in the Soviet bloc scarcely mattered; Czechoslovakia was of the greatest importance, as *Pravda* pointed out on September 4:

Let [him] who is interested in this—including men of letters—outline the Czechoslovak borders sharply on the map of Europe and see what the situation of the Socialist countries would be. This is a wedge dividing the Warsaw Treaty countries. The DDR and Poland remain to the North, Bulgaria and Romania to the South, without any direct communication between them, and soldiers of the Bundeswehr and American soldiers would appear directly on Soviet frontiers.

Because its lines of communication ran both North-South and East-West, Czechoslovakia was a vital factor in Warsaw Pact calculations. As such it was a member of the more important "Northern Tier"; it received relatively up-to-date equipment and was required to take part in significant strategic exercises. None of this applied to Rumania. In breaking the military cohesion of the pact, Rumania had no effect on Soviet security: the Soviet government merely punished it, as it did for its show of independence over the Six Day War, by withholding arms supplies. Even such a punishment, however, emphasized Rumania's insignificance. One might suggest, in fact, that the potential for Soviet threats to Rumania had been severely curtailed by the development of the Warsaw Pact, for the greater emphasis that was placed on Eastern European participation in Soviet defensive strategy necessarily entailed a higher degree of multilateralism within the pact itself. Thus in the late 1960s the organization seems to have undergone a paradoxical development: on the one hand, it was used to contain any tendencies toward Eastern European autonomy (by bringing together under a security rubric considerations ranging from the economic to the ideological); on the other hand, the emergence of the pact as an important instrument of Soviet security planning meant that a degree of free-voice participation was conferred on the satellite members of the organization. In this sense it is probably true that Rumania, far from being threatened, was actually protected by the Warsaw Treaty. In the case of Czechoslovakia, of course, the treaty had proven fatal. But this reflects the difference between the Northern and Southern tiers, and the emphasis the Soviet leadership laid upon each. More than that, it reflects the importance attached to the Czechoslovak ideological challenge. It remains, therefore, to see whether Moscow felt Rumania's political position was sufficiently challenging, in the wake of the invasion of Czechoslovakia, for it to change its repressive tolerance to threat; whether, in fact, the Warsaw Treaty would no longer protect Rumania but rather expose it to danger. This depended not on strategic considerations but on the politics involved, and on the impact of those politics in the counsels of the Kremlin.

Rumania had never challenged the "leading role of the Party";[53] on the contrary, it ceaselessly reaffirmed it. Rumania did not threaten, as Czechoslovakia had threatened, to make nonsense of the principles by which political life in the USSR and the states of Eastern Europe was conducted, by showing that socialism could be achieved without the totalitarian apparatus of state and party control. On the contrary, it ceaselessly reaffirmed the necessity for such control—the original Rumanian quarrel with the USSR dated from the *Soviet* decision to de-Stalinize.[54] But this very apparatus of control, this maintenance of the leading role of the party, had enabled Rumania to adopt a consistently independent policy.

Early in 1968, therefore, the Soviet leadership had faced a challenge on two fronts: on the one hand, the *ideological* challenge offered by Czechoslovakia; on the other, the *political* challenge to Soviet authority offered by Rumania. But the Rumanian challenge was based on an ultramontanism more papist than the Pope. On the assumption that détente *had* implied a relaxation of Soviet control in Eastern Europe, Moscow had appeared able to accept the ultramontane independence of Rumania. But once it had taken the risk of occupying Czechoslovakia, and discov-

53. A consideration which, in the months before the invasion, had been paramount in Soviet and Warsaw Pact reproaches to the Czechoslovak Central Committee. See, for example, the "Warsaw Letter" of July 15, 1968.

54. See R. V. Burks, "The Rumanian National Deviation," in Kurt London, ed., *Eastern Europe in Transition* (Johns Hopkins Press, 1966), pp. 93–113.

ered that Western reaction was restrained, the temptation was strong to deal with the alternative difficulty of political independence too. The question was bound to arise, once the first step had been taken, whether the Brezhnev doctrine did not imply the invasion of Rumania.

Rumania and the Soviet Leadership

It is necessary to distinguish among different tendencies in the Soviet leadership. On the whole, it is true to say that the ruling triumvirate of Leonid Brezhnev, Aleksei Kosygin, and Nikolai Podgorny had been reluctant to contemplate the invasion of Czechoslovakia—or, if they contemplated it, to carry it out. But they were under considerable pressure from other influential members of the Politburo or regional party bosses—for example, Tolstikov of Leningrad or Shelest of the Ukraine (an area that was particularly sensitive to developments in Czechoslovakia, partly because of the local Ruthenians, partly because areas of the Ukraine could receive Slovak television). Both Alexander Shelepin and Yuri Andropov were ambivalent, as was the whole leading apparatus of the KGB, but a number of senior military commanders had been in favor of invasion from the spring onward.[55] The invasion, when it came, did not resolve the dilemma of the Soviet leaders, for they were still confronted by those who were pushing for sterner measures and those who, on the other hand, were concerned that the internal consequences in the USSR itself might prove too repressive. After all, the principal leaders of the CPSU were anxious to clip the wings of a Tolstikov as well as to stem the potential threat from a Dubcek. (Tolstikov was subsequently sent to languish in a representational post in Peking.) Even if they were prepared to go ahead with the invasion they ensured strict discipline among the Soviet troops in Czechoslovakia, and on the whole the behavior of the forces there testified to the effectiveness of this discipline.[56] But if the Soviet leaders were reluctant to proceed to Draconian measures, and if, on the other hand, the population of Czechoslovakia was united behind its government in a prolonged campaign of skillful and

55. *Le Monde* obtained access to a report of the meeting of the Central Committee of the CPSU held on March 29, 1968. See *Le Monde*, April 1, 1968.
56. The deportment of Soviet troops was on the whole remarkably restrained. By far the least disciplined were the Poles.

stubborn resistance, there was some danger that the whole matter would be seen not as a reassertion of Soviet authority, but as a blow to the authority and prestige of the leadership, especially of Brezhnev.

Within this context, the problem of Rumania was particularly pressing. The Rumanian party leader, Nicolas Ceausescu, had received a delirious welcome in Prague when he visited Czechoslovakia shortly before the invasion. So had President Tito of Yugoslavia. Immediately afterward, both these leaders denounced the invasion in the strongest terms—Rumania indeed declared that it was a violation of the Warsaw Treaty, and called for the immediate withdrawal of Soviet forces. In the United Nations and in every available forum Yugoslavia and Rumania did all they could to demonstrate their support for Czechoslovakia. But if they had been able by such means to encourage the Czechoslovak government in its attempts at resistance, the carefully controlled action, which had been directed exclusively at Czechoslovakia, might in fact have proven ineffective within that country and incalculable in its consequences throughout the Warsaw Pact countries and Eastern Europe as a whole.

I have been arguing that the invasion of Czechoslovakia did not merely fail to resolve the dilemmas of authority for the Soviet leadership but that it positively accentuated them, at least temporarily. This was of great importance to any U.S. response. For if the operation had been as successful as it was smooth, if there were no effective resistance inside Czechoslovakia, if Czechoslovakia had not had the moral support of the two other Eastern European countries, if this had not threatened to prolong and extend the crisis—then American reaction would have been comparatively simple. It would have had to meet only two requirements: demonstrating the inviolability of the respective spheres of the two superpowers, and reassuring the friendly and allied nations in Western Europe. Indeed, these purposes were interdependent, and U.S. reaction in the immediate aftermath of the crisis served them both. But if the crisis threatened to go beyond Czechoslovakia it would be much more difficult to serve both purposes at once. Action taken to demonstrate U.S. commitment and concern in Europe could risk a superpower confrontation. Action taken to avoid such a confrontation could risk the impression that the United States was backing down from its commitments in Europe. If that impression had gained ground, it would have been a disservice to both U.S. objectives at once: not only would it have discouraged the Western

European allies of the United States, it would also have encouraged the hawks in Moscow. Such an outcome would have helped to spread the crisis and to ensure that it became more difficult to manage.

I shall argue that the U.S. government showed itself aware of the balance of necessities in framing its reactions and, moreover, that it changed its mind on how to react. In the first days after the invasion President Johnson was adamant that he would not go to Moscow, and he was explicit about the need to demonstrate U.S. displeasure to the Soviet leaders.[57] But at the same time he refused Kiesinger's request for a Western summit to discuss the strategic consequences of the invasion, reportedly because he did not wish to give Moscow the impression that displeasure could turn into active hostility.[58]

Later it became necessary to reconsider the whole approach of the United States. According to some contemporary reports, this reconsideration began because of the adverse effect on European governmental opinion of its early, limited reaction.[59] But there does not appear to be much substance to these speculations. The European leaders knew the score; they had received their several messages from Moscow; they were not so unsophisticated as to believe that a challenge to the principle of the two blocs in Europe would in any way increase their security. Indeed, they were much more likely to be alarmed by any sign of overreaction on the part of the United States. But when the implications of the crisis began to stretch beyond the Warsaw Pact and to involve areas in which the United States had traditionally taken an interest, it was necessary to reassert the validity of U.S. commitments. The key to the change, and to the new position adopted by the United States, lay in the relations between Yugoslavia and Rumania.

Yugoslavia and the Rumanian Question

Yugoslav foreign policy has, to a remarkable extent, reflected the internal balance of forces within the country. Tito has always had three separate kinds of problems to contend with: the relations between the different nationalities and republics that make up Yugoslavia; the relationship among the different tendencies within the League of Communists;

---

57. *New York Times*, August 22, 1968.
58. *New York Times*, September 5, 1968.
59. Ibid. See also Cleveland, "NATO after the Invasion," pp. 259–65.

and the relationship between centralized planning and local autonomy. Tito has had to juggle these factions not only on the basis of internal compromise but also on the basis of his foreign policy. There are many forces in Yugoslavia favoring a rapprochement with the USSR: the Macedonian people and leaders are traditionally Russophile; a number of Yugoslav economists are inclined to argue that the economic future of the country lies in association with the Council for Mutual Economic Assistance (CMEA) rather than with Western Europe; on ideological grounds, some of the leading party figures are apprehensive that their rivals and colleagues have inclined too far toward an "Italian" form of socialism. In such circumstances Tito's foreign policy has been bound to be erratic. But, while erratic, it has always been logical.

It follows that Soviet-Yugoslav relations have served different functions at different times when considered within the whole context of the Soviet system in Eastern Europe. In 1956, for instance, one might suggest that if Tito did not actively abet he did at least help to condone and even make possible the Soviet intervention in Hungary. At that time the pattern of Soviet-Yugoslav reconciliation was based on the notion that de-Stalinization would not get out of hand and that Yugoslavia would not encourage it to do so. Conversely, assured as it was that Yugoslavia would do nothing to upset the cohesion of the bloc during the period of de-Stalinization, Khrushchev's Russia could afford to acknowledge its independence—as well as its fraternity. Both gained something and neither threatened the other. But 1968 was a different case. It was different because Tito had *shared* many Soviet assumptions. The previous year he and Brezhnev, in strikingly similar language, had warned their followers that Western imperialism was on the offensive again and that the forces of counterrevolution were beginning to triumph. There were general grounds for this view, ranging from Indonesia, where the largest Communist party outside the bloc had been physically eliminated, to the Six Day War, in which the one ally of the United States had scored such a spectacular triumph over the clients of the Soviet Union. But Tito also had particular grounds for concern. Yugoslavia had recently embarked on its most pronounced pro-Western course since 1948, but this orientation had been accompanied by internal fears of what today might be called destabilization. There were repeated warnings of the need for vigilance against NATO subversion and denunciations of those inside the country who were trying to undo socialist achievements. The rumors of financial scandal which surrounded the death in an automobile accident of the pro-Western Yugoslav Prime Minister Krajger in that period also complicated the issue. Tito was anxious. He began to steer the country toward a more neutral international position, and checked the pace of internal reform. And in the middle of all this came the Prague Spring.

Tito's primary concern in 1967 and 1968 was that events in Czechoslovakia should not develop too fast—the more so as the students of Belgrade University were hopeful that they should. Although he went in person to quell the students' revolt, Tito was shaken by the events, occurring as they did not in some remote Ljubljana but under his own nose in the capital. Even so, his principal concern was to separate the internal consequences from the external aspects of the developments in Czechoslovakia. In spite of the widespread reports that he warned Dubcek against the course he was taking, there is no evidence that he did anything of the kind. Equally, for internal reasons, he certainly could not condemn Dubcek when the invasion came, he had to condemn *it*. These considerations contributed to the quandary in which he found himself. He had agreed with the Soviet leaders that there was a danger of a general Western offensive in the world. He had watched and shared their alarm at the potential repercussions of the Czechoslovak reform. He had also watched them slowly resolve to put an end to the pace of reform in Prague in the only way they knew. But, *by the same token,* he knew that they would now have to face further pressures. Would the Soviet leaders stop at Czechoslovakia, or would they tidy up dissent elsewhere in the bloc, too, and were they threatening Rumania?

If they did threaten Rumania, Yugoslavia's internal situation would be transformed. There is no suggestion whatsoever that Soviet leaders ever contemplated attacking Yugoslavia, but Soviet divisions would be stationed on two of Yugoslavia's borders: the Rumanian and the Hungarian. Such a situation would vastly complicate the problems of Yugoslav defense. More than that, the country was already in 1968 concerned with the problem of what to do in the event of Tito's death. While there might not have been any immediate possibility of a Soviet attack, the possible contingencies were wide open. But the problem goes further. There has been a persistent tendency in Yugoslavia to seek an accommodation with the USSR, a tendency that was partly the outcome of Tito's own desire to normalize relations.

Tito obviously could not welcome a Soviet threat to Rumania even if he shared a belief in the correctness of the Soviet analysis. Any Soviet action of that nature would have been bound to polarize Yugoslav society between those who were prepared to appease the USSR and those who were prepared to fight it. Tito had consistently avoided such a situation since 1948. Even worse, the polarization, while in some ways cutting across nationality boundaries, could also have reinforced national divisions inside the country. With or without a direct Soviet threat the Yugoslav polity could have fallen apart.

The Nature of Yugoslav Reaction

Tito had no choice. He had to act against the eventuality that Soviet forces might enter Rumania. In fact, largely because he understood Soviet anxieties, he had to be especially cautious to ensure that these anxieties did not threaten his own position and his own state.

If there were any danger of a Soviet move against Rumania, Yugoslavia would do all it could to prevent it. On its own Yugoslavia was powerless; it could only prevent a move against Rumania by widening the implications. These considerations made Yugoslavia a potential target of U.S. interest and action in the aftermath of the Soviet invasion of Czechoslovakia. The principal U.S. interest was, inevitably, to contain the crisis—to prevent it from developing into a threat of war. Much as it might have deplored the Soviet action, in this sense it saw eye to eye with the USSR. The original U.S. interest in and reaction toward Yugoslavia had to be reconsidered. The Yugoslav interest lay in widening the crisis, the U.S. interest in containing it. How, then, was the United States to react in the area of the third target of its behavior?

The question of Rumania provided Tito with the opportunity to maximize his own defense potential. But because the manner in which he did so was by no means clear-cut, it is worth drawing a distinction between the kind of support Yugoslavia might desire and the kind it might not welcome. The Yugoslav concept of general people's defense has always contained internal contradictions. The economic development of the country and the growth of urbanization hinder the application of the doctrine in its pure form as it developed after 1945. Beyond that, while the requirements of a loosely organized, regionally based defense are sometimes compatible with Tito's policies of decentralization, sometimes they are incompatible with his alternative policies of recentralization. Further, the relationship between an organized army and the irregular units of a people's war has never been clearly defined. In other words, Yugoslav defense planning, although by no means worthless, tended at that time to be a mess; and it was bound to remain such as long as it was a variable function of the requirements of domestic policy. Yet in a sense Yugoslavia could afford this mess, and it could afford it precisely because it had no allies.

Since Yugoslavia separates the main body of the NATO allies in Europe from their own southern flank, and to a degree also separates the central area of the Warsaw Pact from its southern part, and since it further separates NATO from the Warsaw Pact in the Adriatic, it would obviously make a tremendous asset for either alliance. By the same token, each alliance has a strong interest in preventing the other from advancing in Yugoslavia. The unwritten security provided by this position helps to assure the Yugoslav leaders of outside help in the event of attack by either outside party. Equally, it gives the Yugoslav government the strongest possible incentive to avoid a permanent commitment to any one alliance. This in turn reinforces the capacity for adjustment in domestic politics. The ideal defense policy for Yugoslavia in the short term, therefore, is to be able to conduct its own defense in every direction, but in the long term to act as a detonator for a wider conflict.[60] Tito appears to have been seeking this position in 1968, and developments in Europe handed it to him.

First, the Yugoslav League of Communists protested massively against the Soviet invasion. A resolution passed by the Central Committee of the League refused

to recognize any agreements—open or tacit—regarding spheres of interest which transform the small nations into the pawns of power politics. . . . Today, as before, we are resolved to use all our forces and means to defend our independence, revolution and our own way of socialist development . . . and also oppose any provocative action geared towards weakening the strength of our resistance and interference from any quarter whatever.

This was on August 23. On August 25 *Pravda* attacked both Yugoslavia and Rumania for "giving active assistance to the Czechoslovak anti-socialist forces . . . it is precisely in Belgrade and Bucharest that the political adventurers from Prague who find themselves outside Czecho-

60. Dennison I. Rousinow quoted an anonymous Yugoslav diplomat in these terms in "The Yugoslav Concept of All-National Defense," *American Universities Field Staff Reports*, 1972.

slovakia during this period are weaving their intrigues." The USSR was at least implying a threat to extend the crisis.

The Fundamental Importance of Rumanian-Yugoslav Relations

Rumania had already evinced considerable alarm at the prospect of Soviet action. A week before the Soviet move into Czechoslovakia, Ceausescu had declared in the restricted-circulation Army journal *Apararea Patriei* that Rumania had taken direct steps to strengthen its armed forces. A week later, on the day of the invasion, the minister of the armed forces, Colonel-General Ion Ionita, issued an order of the day in which he demanded that the Rumanian Army be ready "at a moment's notice" to defend the country's independence and sovereignty. This was also carried in *Apararea Patriei,* and the same issue contained a heartening account of the "excellent fighting ability" of the Rumanian forces.[61] Rumania was clearly preparing to fight if necessary and, more important, signaling its readiness as clearly as possible to the USSR.

In the light of such Rumanian activity and of the Soviet verbal attacks on both Rumania and Yugoslavia, and in the light of the fact that the Central Committee of the League of Communists had declared, two days after the invasion, that the invasion of Czechoslovakia also represented a danger to Yugoslavia itself, it would be surprising if there had been no consultations between Yugoslavia and Rumania. Their "defense agreement" is frequently referred to but its import is still a matter for conjecture. It is not an official treaty, it is not embodied in any communiqué, and indeed I have even heard NATO officials deny its very existence. But it is probable that a close and detailed understanding was reached during the meetings between Tito and Ceausescu, and the USSR certainly showed suspicion of its nature. Indeed, for the next two years or so, the USSR from time to time denounced "Balkan Pactism."[62] All Yugoslav sources confirm the existence of an understanding but they disagree about its nature.

If there were any question of a Soviet invasion of Rumania, would Yugoslav troops enter that country to help it resist? Or would Yugoslavia merely support Rumanian resistance with material and moral backing?

61. *Apararea Patriei,* August 21, 1968.
62. For an account of these denunciations, see *Keesing's Contemporary Archives* (November 13–20, 1971), p. 24934: Rumania.

Or would Yugoslavia open its territory to Rumanian forces, and thus provide a sanctuary for continued resistance, even at the risk of a Soviet attack on Yugoslavia itself? In view of the doubts, contradictions, and general secrecy surrounding the agreement it is impossible to do more than conjecture.

But some considerations are worth bearing in mind. Short of fighting side by side with Rumanian forces in Rumania, Yugoslavia would not be able to do very much in terms of material help. Medical supplies and similar aid might have been offered; but Yugoslav weapons were very different from those standard in Rumania. Questions of training, ammunition, and environmental support for the weapons themselves would have made it very difficult to incorporate significant supplies into the Rumanian forces at short notice. It therefore seems unlikely that the "agreement" would have relied on large-scale material help from Yugoslavia. Of the two remaining alternatives, direct Yugoslav participation seems inherently unlikely. It would have weakened Yugoslavia's own defense while not doing very much to impede a determined and massive Soviet advance. Moreover, the *prime* political purpose of associating Yugoslavia with the defense of Rumania would have been served equally well by using Yugoslav territory as a sanctuary. That would have left Yugoslavia free, had the need arisen, to defend itself with its own combination of regular and irregular war. My own conjecture is therefore that Yugoslavia was prepared to become a passive rather than an active ally of Rumania in the event of Soviet invasion. Equally, this would have served the detonating purpose of Yugoslav defense policy, by creating a general crisis out of an intramural crisis and turning a Warsaw Pact action into a threat to Western interests.

Was there any likelihood that the eventuality would arise at all? On August 21, Soviet and Warsaw Pact forces had invaded Czechoslovakia. Two days later the Central Committee of the League of Communists of Yugoslavia had protested in a resolution that it construed this action as a potential danger to Yugoslavia itself. Two days after that *Pravda* had accused both Rumania and Yugoslavia of harboring and supporting the political adventurers from Prague. Was this accusation to be followed by any Soviet military activity?

Two points need to be considered here. The first is whether the U.S. government would fall in with Tito's conception of Yugoslav interest and defense by construing a threat to Rumania as a threat to Yugoslavia. The second is whether it would allow the USSR time effectively to mount a threat to Yugoslavia. The answer to the first is that it did, and to the second that it didn't.

The U.S. government was soon to show that it was concerned about the pattern of developments in Eastern Europe. NATO, too, soon abandoned its original low profile. Both, in fact, were to take measures that would indicate a determination not to allow the crisis to extend to Yugoslavia. On August 30 President Johnson had in a speech indicated his concern at a new pattern. The next day, Press Secretary George Christian publicly announced that President Johnson had been watching developments in Eastern Europe and receiving messages on the situation at his ranch "all day." It was clear that a new and potentially disturbing set of developments was beginning to exercise both the United States and NATO. These developments were not—and could not have been—related purely to Czechoslovakia.

For a few days toward the end of August the USSR did appear to be strengthening its forces in Bessarabia near the Rumanian border. But this was not a large-scale reinforcement, and there is no suggestion that serious preparations were made to invade Rumania. Moreover, any analyst of Soviet defense planning would have concluded that a swift and effective invasion would not be immediately feasible. After a prolonged buildup, and with massive logistical support, the USSR had launched a large, swift, and precise operation in Czechoslovakia. But in these latter days of August troops were still pouring into Czechoslovakia—they were not yet leaving it. Half a million men were tied down there. Moreover, these included allied forces from the Warsaw Pact, and it would have been unlikely in the extreme that the Soviet leaders, having taken such care to associate their allies with them in the invasion of Czechoslovakia, would now spoil the effect by going it alone in Rumania. Finally, there is some evidence that Soviet leaders had been concerned about the possibility of military resistance in Czechoslovakia;[63] they could be virtually certain of it in Rumania. After all, Ceausescu had just made it clear that if the USSR contemplated an attack on Rumania, Rumania would fight.[64]

63. For example, the USSR had distinctively marked the roofs of all its military vehicles to distinguish them from Czechoslovak vehicles of the same make to ensure that, in the event of resistance, it would not mistakenly strafe its own soldiers.

64. See *Apararea Patriei,* August 14, 1968, for Ceausescu's own statement and the even stronger statement by Ionita.

All factors point to the same conclusion: that the USSR was not *yet* ready to invade.

This did not mean, however, that it might not be ready one day, perhaps before very long. In the aftermath of the invasion of one country, in the context of the anxiety to reassert the control of the leadership inside the CPSU that the invasion itself had demonstrated, and confronted with powerful voices demanding further action, the Soviet government might have been tempted to act. One should not exaggerate the risk; for even if such significant military figures as Marshal Ivan Grechko, the minister of defense, and Marshal Ivan Yakubovsky, the commander-in-chief of the Warsaw Pact, were to show in the following months a strong predisposition to use the pact to tighten Soviet authority in Eastern Europe, they were also the best placed to know that a Soviet invasion of Rumania could not be undertaken in a hurry. In 1969 Yakubovsky proposed a Warsaw Pact "fire brigade" for mobile intervention; this was certainly viewed with alarm by Rumania, but it indicates a desire to remedy deficiencies that were still obvious in the autumn of 1968. So one might suggest that the pressures for immediate action did not arise from the military but from the hard-liners among the politicians, notably Shelest. But Rumania was faced with a threat which, while neither immediate nor tangible, had a potential for growth.

Equally, Western reaction to the "traffic accident" was, at the governmental level at least, remarkably restrained; would the West really raise its voice if somebody else fell victim to the same heavy traffic on Warsaw Pact territory? Finally, the argument that "you can do it once but not twice" barely stands up in such a context. There were, it is true, some repercussions inside the Soviet armed forces after the invasion. Many Soviet troops were astonished and demoralized by their reception. (Indeed some units were thereafter transferred to the Far Eastern Maritime Province—presumably in the hope that they would recover their spirits when faced with the prospect of fighting the Chinese.) On the other hand, the invasion had been a highly successful military operation. The fact that it was run so smoothly must in many cases, and particularly perhaps among junior officers, have greatly strengthened morale. Indeed, only a minority of the Soviet forces was exposed to the arguments, the demonstrations, and the general harassment of Czech and Slovak protesters. Not everyone was stationed in Prague or Bratislava or even Banska Bistrica. Most soldiers were quartered in the countryside, many in newly evacuated Czechoslovak army barracks where they had little contact with the population. One could not really suggest that Soviet forces and Soviet officers were too demoralized to undertake further action.

Therefore, while there is nothing to suggest that the USSR was yet *ready* to invade Rumania, the option was available, and even small-scale troop movements could give some indication that it was being considered seriously. At this point the Yugoslav interest in widening the crisis and the U.S. interest in containing it coincided.

The Evolving Pattern

For Ceausescu, the best and indeed the only available deterrent to a Soviet occupation was the threat to fight. This might or might not have been enough; but for Tito the deterrent would be immeasurably strengthened if the attack on a Warsaw Pact member in the context of an intramural crisis could be transformed into an international crisis by implicating Yugoslavia. It would also give the United States the opportunity to help to deter even an attack within the confines of the Warsaw Pact by showing that it could no longer be so confined. Tito's actions in helping transform the intramural into the international crisis also gave President Johnson the chance to put it back behind walls. The Yugoslav dimension served both Tito and Johnson. For Yugoslavia it helped to involve the United States as an actively interested participant in decision, and thereby to provide the detonator Tito sought. For the United States it provided the occasion to demonstrate an interest that could not have been demonstrated if the crisis had been confined to members of the Warsaw Pact alone. President Johnson was now able to point out to Soviet leaders the potential dangers of further action, and to do so well before their option had hardened into an intention. He did so in the speech on August 30 at San Antonio, Texas. In this speech, only nine days after the occupation of Czechoslovakia and in the middle of the Soviet-Yugoslav polemic, the President referred first to the fact of the occupation. Then he went on to suggest that it "might be repeated elsewhere in the days ahead in Eastern Europe." He followed with the grave warning words: "Let no one unleash the dogs of war."[65]

At one level this might appear to be a vague warning of the "we-will-not-stand-idly-by" variety, since Johnson, now a lame-duck President, undone by the war in Vietnam, was hardly in a position to engage the United States in new and dangerous entanglements. This explanation,

65. Universally reported in the American and British press, September 1, 1968.

though not necessarily invalid, does not indicate either the subtlety or effectiveness of Johnson's warning. It was vague, undoubtedly, but there was merit to this vagueness. Johnson named neither the potential target of Soviet ambitions nor the possible course of U.S. action. The statement's strength lay in these omissions. If the President had referred openly to Rumania he would probably have been told, sharply and explicitly, that the members of the Warsaw Pact were capable of settling their differences among themselves, and it would have been much harder to follow up his ominous but nonetheless implicit warning with any explicit threat or action. By keeping his subject area as ill-defined as he did, he was able to prevent the USSR from imposing boundaries. But there was more to it than that: his *threat* was also vague. He did not commit the United States to any specific course of action, and that was no doubt necessary in terms of domestic politics. Yet it was also vital to his foreign policy considerations. If he had hoped to save Rumania from the threat of invasion by deliberately invoking U.S. military power he could have done so by only one means: the threat of nuclear war. What consequences would such a threat have had? There are only three possibilities: one, that the USSR would have invaded Rumania and the United States would have backed down; two, that the USSR would have backed down; three, that neither would have backed down and that everybody would have had a nuclear war. In such circumstances, to avoid the traditional choice "between annihilation and surrender" was no more than common prudence; but even more, on this occasion the choice would have been loaded against the United States. For *if* the USSR had been openly contemplating the invasion of Rumania, and *if* the President had explicitly mentioned this and threatened war (but especially nuclear war), then the USSR would have been almost *obliged* to invade. To retreat from its traditional sphere within the Warsaw Pact in the face of an overt U.S. threat would obviously have had unforeseeable consequences. Every country in Eastern Europe would have felt free to defy Soviet power; the whole sphere would have crumbled; no Soviet government could have survived. An explicit threat would have created such a challenge to the authority of the Soviet leaders that they would have had to respond. In making the vaguer threat Johnson was thus making the more effective and meaningful threat.

While avoiding the pitfalls of being too explicit about either the target or the threat, he *was* conveying a genuine threat. Quite apart from showing that President Johnson's speech writers had read *Julius Caesar* (actually, a very appropriate text in the case of that particular President), the phrase "to unleash the dogs of war" was both more meaningful and more credible than any bigger threat. It implied that the United States, and perhaps the NATO allies, would do *something*. What they might do was not to be ascertained. One could presume that it might entail only flying supplies to Yugoslavia.[66] It was in any case unlikely that U.S. or NATO troops would be sent to Yugoslavia in the first instance. But even if airborne supplies were followed by seaborne supplies, this might mean an attempt to neutralize Soviet naval forces in the Adriatic or even to prevent them from entering the Adriatic through the Strait of Otranto. The difficulties and the dangers of escalation would be obvious and this would apply whatever the terms of the Yugoslav understanding with Rumania. In other words, President Johnson was threatening that if an unspecified action were taken against an unspecified Eastern European country, the unspecified U.S. response would make it very difficult to keep control. And indeed the "threat to lose control" has been eloquently argued by Thomas Schelling to be a highly effective form of available deterrence.[67] If there were any temptations in the Kremlin to translate their invasion option into a serious intent, the President's strategy worked.

On the same day that Johnson delivered his speech the Soviet ambassador in Yugoslavia, Ivan Benediktov, formally acting on the instructions of the Central Committee of the CPSU, made a public statement that

the Central Committee of the Party and the Soviet government are astonished in the highest degree that the leadership of the League of Communists of Yugoslavia and the Yugoslav government should have taken the same line as those countries which have adopted measures designed to give active support to [the counterrevolutionaries].[68]

This was, in fact, the height of Soviet protest. Thereafter Tito continued to protest vehemently against the doctrine of limited sovereignty, and he called for the withdrawal of the Warsaw Pact forces from Czechoslovakia.

66. Occasionally Yugoslav military commentators do discuss the idea of receiving external assistance, but usually only in vague and guarded terms. See, for example, Colonel Andre Gabelic, "The Universal Substance of General People's Defense," *Vjesnik* (Zagreb), January 11, 1971. Also General Rade Hamovic, *Narodna Armija* (Belgrade), December 23, 1966. Adam Roberts, *Nations in Arms* (Chatto and Windus for the International Institute for Strategic Studies, 1976; Praeger, 1976), takes up in chapter 6 some of the contingencies NATO might have to consider.

67. Thomas C. Schelling, *Arms and Influence* (Yale University Press, 1966), pp. 92–125.

68. Clissold, *Yugoslavia and the Soviet Union*, pp. 297–98.

But the Soviet reactions suggested a basic anxiety to cool matters, and by December *Pravda* was assuring the Yugoslavs that they had no cause for alarm. By then Tito also, seesawing in the opposite direction as usual, was beginning to emphasize the need for good relations with the USSR. The crisis had passed, and passed very quickly. The coincidence of Tito's attempt to extend its implications and the U.S. desire to limit its implications had (though at the price of Czechoslovakia) ensured that a major upheaval did not follow from the original Soviet action.

This cannot all be ascribed to the effects of a single speech. Rather, the speech may be seen as serving three functions. In the first place, obviously it was intended as a warning to the USSR. In the second, it also marked the change of mind in U.S. policymaking that I referred to above. The carefully studied and restrained approach that characterized the first week after the invasion was now abandoned in favor of an equally studied but more minatory series of gestures. These military gestures were low key but they were explicitly intended to convey both a degree of reassurance to Western Europe and an indication to the USSR that the United States was observing the situation with concern. In the third place, the speech provided the framework for more general follow-up action in NATO. The gestures and the follow-up were at least as important as the speech itself. For without them Johnson's warning could have been forgotten, or dismissed as a temporary reaction in the emotional atmosphere following the invasion. It had, after all, been an intelligent bit of preemption, but it is one thing to preempt before the active need has arisen, it is another to continue the threat when it is attended by risk. It is, therefore, worth considering the gestures that followed the speech, and the more extended follow-up action that was taken later.

The Military Gestures

As I have suggested, the gestures were rather insignificant in themselves, but in the context of the moment they had a certain political significance. It is worth recalling that in the immediate aftermath of the invasion the U.S. Army had declared that it would continue with the "rotation" plans, which meant an effective reduction of its forces in West Germany by some 34,000 men. The rotation was about 75 percent complete in August and was meant to be completed toward the end of the year.[69] But early in September, that is, in the days immediately after

69. *New York Times,* August 22, 1968.

President Johnson's speech, Pentagon officials were taking a modified line. They do *not* appear to have amended their intentions to proceed with the overall force reduction, and they still ruled out any dramatic moves. For instance, it was decided not to send an extra battalion of U.S. troops to Berlin (an obviously sensible decision unless the U.S. government wished to extend the crisis to that flashpoint), not to adopt forward emergency positions in Europe (which was presumably why the NATO alert was only yellow and why it was so unremarkable), and not to indulge in any substantial increase in border reconnaissance. As has already been indicated, Kiesinger's proposal for a NATO summit was also rejected. But the Supreme Allied Commander, General Lyman Lemnitzer, was given permission to increase observation along Czechoslovakia's border with West Germany, though only in light formation.[70] And now Pentagon officials began to hint that some of the troops recently withdrawn from Europe would be flown back for military maneuvers.[71]

Such maneuvers were not of course an innovation. Indeed, they were implicit from the beginning in the whole concept of rotation, whereby some U.S. forces were withdrawn from Europe in order to save foreign exchange costs, but kept on a footing of moderate readiness to return and flown back periodically for exercises. (This refers to the formations, not the troops themselves: a formation consisting of Vietnam veterans in Bavaria might consist of raw recruits in Kansas, but would be expected to train for the same functions.) But while there was no suggestion that maneuvers should be increased, they were to be advanced. This was the more striking in view of the fact that the Joint Chiefs had previously recommended that they should be postponed. It was the view of the Joint Chiefs that the cost (about $9 million) would have warranted a postponement until the autumn of 1969, because of the strains to which both the U.S. defense budget and the U.S. balance of payments were subject at that time. Postponement until the following autumn would have allowed the cost of the maneuvers to be covered by funds for the following fiscal year. To advance them now would mean finding an extra $9 million from available funds; this provides an indication of the seriousness the Joint Chiefs attached to demonstrating U.S. commitment.

The important word is commitment. The prime purpose of this particular exercise was to assure the Western European allies. For at the beginning of September the U.S. ambassador to NATO proposed that if

70. Ibid., September 17, 1968.
71. Ibid., September 5, 1968.

other NATO members also took action to strengthen the alliance, the United States would send four squadrons of F-4 fighter-bombers to Germany to take part in maneuvers in November or December. This action was to be followed by the arrival of two brigades of mechanized infantry early in the next year.[72] Because these two brigades were from the 24th Infantry Division and consisted of inexperienced conscripts, one might suggest that to delay their arrival until the early winter of 1969 was to give them time to train. More important, what was being proposed was the advance of the *Reforger* exercise from the autumn through the winter, and most important was the fact that these proposals were conditional on some sort of matching exercise by the other NATO allies. The chief emphasis of U.S. policy at this time was clearly to encourage the Western European countries by demonstrating the U.S. commitment, but even this depended on participation by the other members of NATO. Though there is no direct evidence to support it, I would argue that such participation was important because, in the new context created by Johnson's warning, the United States was determined to secure NATO support for any moves it might make in the defense of Yugoslavia and in withstanding any potential threat to Rumania.

This view will appear more substantial if one examines the third aspect of the significance of the San Antonio speech. Obviously, any gestures of reassurance to the members of NATO constituted a signal to the USSR. Mere commitment where commitments were already explicit, inside the NATO framework, would not necessarily warn the USSR of U.S. interest in areas where the commitment was only implicit, as in the case of Yugoslavia. But if the third aspect, that of a more extended follow-up to President Johnson's warning, could associate NATO with the U.S. interest in Yugoslavia, it would be seen that the initial gestures also served a fundamental purpose. What, then, of the alliance and Yugoslavia?

Yugoslavia and the NATO Follow-up

In the months after the initial crisis the U.S. government sought to achieve some kind of understanding with Yugoslavia as well as support from the NATO allies. It should be emphasized that it did not pursue either of these tasks with any particular urgency. This was no doubt a tribute to the confidence on all sides after the end of August that the

72. Ibid., September 17, 1968.

USSR had no intention of proceeding immediately against Rumania. The most striking evidence for this lack of urgency is that Yugoslavia did not at any point ask for new arms supplies, nor for any resumption of the U.S. military assistance that had ended ten years previously.[73] Early in October Yugoslav officials nonetheless began a concerted series of attempts to enlist Western support. They intensively pursued diplomatic contacts with the Western governments—that is, France, Germany, the United Kingdom, perhaps Italy, and certainly the United States. Probably the highlight of this period occurred when Yugoslav Foreign Minister Marko Nikezic met Secretary of State Dean Rusk at the United Nations.[74]

At the same time the United States made another demonstration of interest in Yugoslavia, though it was little publicized. On October 4 a U.S. destroyer from the Sixth Fleet called at Dubrovnik. This visit had more impact when it was followed, on President Johnson's orders, by a visit from Under Secretary of State Nicholas de B. Katzenbach. Katzenbach had been going to visit Europe anyway, but Johnson instructed him to stop in Belgrade, where he remained from October 17 to 19. Reports of this visit indicate that Tito neither asked for nor received any "guarantees," but that he did receive "assurances" with which he was more than content.[75] Shortly thereafter, at a NATO Council meeting which had been advanced to November from its normal December date, Dean Rusk was reported by *The Times* (London) to have declared forthrightly that Yugoslavia and Austria were part of NATO's area of security interest. It was further reported that he said NATO would consider as very serious any Soviet move against Rumania or Albania.[76]

Apparently there was now a very high degree of American-Yugoslav understanding, which was also being translated into NATO terms. This did not mean NATO had made any commitment to send forces to Yugo-

73. Adam Roberts, *Nations in Arms*, pp. 188–94, quotes responsible American and Yugoslav officials, who all agreed on this point.

74. The Yugoslav prime minister, Mika Spiljak, had already declared in a parliamentary speech on September 23 that Yugoslavia attached great importance to closer ties with the West, and stressed the "great significance" of relations with the United States. During this period Yugoslav diplomatic activity was energetically conducted and attracted public attention. See, for example, *International Herald Tribune*, October 11, 1968: "Yugoslavia reported seeking Western help if invaded."

75. *Daily Telegraph* (London), reporting from Belgrade, October 19, 1968.

76. *The Times* (London), November 16, 1968. It is worth noting that not all accounts name Albania. See, for example, *International Herald Tribune*, November 29, 1968.

slavia in the event of a Soviet attack on Rumania or even of direct Soviet-Yugoslav conflict. Almost certainly, however, it did include an understanding, bolstered by a degree of planning, to reinforce the country with military supplies.[77] Even such measures would carry the implication that the dogs of war might be let slip. In other words, a built-in element of deterrence had now been created, and President Johnson's warning at the end of August had taken the form of NATO action by the end of November.

The widening of the crisis had led to its containment. On November 5 NATO had returned two infantry brigades to West Germany for the exercises that had been moved up to the beginning of 1969. The very prompt reactions on the part of the U.S. government had certainly contributed substantially to the resolution of the crisis.

But the Soviet threat to Rumania was not yet dead. By maneuver, by verbal attack, by withholding supplies, and by other measures, the USSR had frequently appeared to threaten Rumania between 1964 and 1968. Such activities had been fairly intense in the spring of 1967 after Rumania recognized West Germany. Early in 1969 the threat appeared briefly to have gathered momentum again. Ceausescu once again delivered a warning: in a speech to the Great Electoral Meeting in Bucharest he declared that although there was no danger at that moment from *outside reactionary forces,* the Rumanians were *nevertheless* ready to fight:

I want to declare that should anybody try to touch our Socialist achievements, he will come up against the resistance of a 20-million strong, closely united people, determined to fight with all its energies and with all sacrifice, with every means available, in defense of its new life, of the sacred right to liberty and independence.[78]

In fact the Soviet maneuvers of this period had already been preceded by advanced U.S. maneuvers. On January 6 nearly 12,000 U.S. troops and 96 fighter bombers prepared to leave the United States for exercises in the Grafenwöhr area of Germany. Two days later a total of some 17,000 redeployed U.S. troops began their exercise about twenty-five miles from the Czechoslovak border. It is worth recalling that in June the German forces had canceled their summer maneuvers in a similar area in order not to give the USSR any pretext for acting against Czechoslovakia on security grounds. Now that the invasion had occurred the

77. *The Times* (London), November 28, 1968.
78. *Scinteia* (Bucharest), February 19, 1969.

United States was replying demonstratively. On January 9 began the largest helicopter assault exercise ever held in West Germany, involving the forces of the United Kingdom, the Federal Republic, and the United States. The maneuvers ended on February 5—some three weeks before Ceausescu's speech. These maneuvers demonstrated U.S. support and NATO readiness and they helped to remind the USSR that its principal concern must be with the Western powers and not with Rumania.

Vesna 69, a large Warsaw Pact exercise, began in the last days of March. But the participation was exclusively Northern Tier and it took place only in Poland, East Germany, and Czechoslovakia.[79] Similarly, there were naval exercises in the Black Sea, but naval exercises could hardly constitute a threatening prelude to a land invasion of Rumania. Finally, the USSR held small spring maneuvers in Bulgaria; but it had already been reported that Rumania refused to hold them on its territory,[80] and it was apparently on this basis that the government agreed to participate—a concession, but also a victory. The time scales involved and the scope of the exercises indicate that, although Rumania may have been alarmed by the Soviet moves, it was not actually threatened—it was simply that the threat was not yet undeniably dead. By August, however, Rumania was confident enough to invite President Nixon to make a state visit to Bucharest, a sign that, whatever the threat had been, it no longer existed.

One might indeed suggest that Soviet behavior, already cautious, though ultimately ruthless, in the months between the Action Program of the Dubcek government and the moment of invasion, had since that time become even more notably restrained. It did not intervene in Poland in December 1970, when the government of Wladyslaw Gomulka was overthrown by riots. Indeed, it sedulously maintained the position of a friendly but foreign country with no right to interfere in Poland's internal affairs—this although Gomulka begged for Soviet military support. There can be no single explanation for such behavior: internal conditions in the Soviet body politic, the interests of a developing superpower détente, the fact that in any case the "leading role of the party" did not appear threatened in Poland as it had been in Czechoslovakia—all these factors were probably as important as what had happened between August and November 1968. Moreover, Gomulka was hardly a savable figure: his

79. Radio Free Europe, *Situation Report, Poland,* April 2, 1969.
80. See *The Times* (London), February 7, 1969.

power base had been steadily eroding since 1968, and under his leadership the Polish United Workers party (PUWP) had been bitterly divided. Nonetheless, the fact is that the Soviet government acceded to the overthrow of a government by popular demand. It must have obviously considered its own pragmatic interests in so doing, but it cannot have ignored the experience of the Czechoslovak crisis. It had witnessed a quick military takeover, designed to put an end to an intramural crisis, developing into the threat of a much more widespread crisis; it had seen that it was harder to draw the boundaries between what was inside the Warsaw Pact and what was outside than had previously been assumed; and it had heard the President of the United States warn against unleashing war, precisely in order to help contain the original crisis. The U.S. reaction and its translation into NATO policy cannot have been far from the leaders' minds. But the events of 1968 had some paradoxical consequences, and leave questions to be asked.

The Longer Consequences

The chief consequence of the events of 1968 was the development of the *Ostpolitik* of the West German government. Having shown that they were prepared to use force when necessary, having demonstrated that they no longer accepted that the rules of détente required them to relinquish control in Eastern Europe, the Soviet leaders were able to pursue a more radical détente policy. *If* détente had still been dependent on the relaxation of internal control, there would have been no further détente after 1968. The facts that the Western European governments reacted so mildly to the invasion of Czechoslovakia, and that the United States only postponed but did not break off its attempt to create a strategic détente with the USSR demonstrated that the Soviet leaders could now have both détente *and* tight control in the East. In one sense perhaps it was a major tragedy, but in another sense these same considerations allowed the pursuit of a more energetic and radical détente policy, especially by the West German government.

The Federal Republic of Germany had always been the exception, in Soviet eyes, to the slow process of détente that was developing in the mid-1950s. It was not so much that they needed the threat of a resurgent Germany to keep the Warsaw Pact in order (as has sometimes been suggested) as that, if control were gradually being relinquished in the East, then West Germany was simply going to be too powerful. Its economic strength as well as its geographical position, the fact that a gain for West German diplomacy was automatically a defeat for East German diplomacy in that period, all made this inevitable. But in the new situation created by the Soviet use of force, and in the new context created by the Brezhnev doctrine, there were obvious limits to potential German power. At the same time, West Germany had a new government that was anxious to restore a working relationship with its Eastern neighbors, and above all to establish a dialogue with East Germany. The *Ostpolitik* that followed the invasion was therefore able to lead much further than any détente policy pursued by the previous German governments, to lead indeed to resolution of major European conflicts and to recognition of East Germany itself.

It is tempting to consider this another Soviet victory, and in a sense it was. But it marked certain gains for the West—particularly the elimination of Berlin as a potential source of a third world war—and it also led to a situation in which the nature of détente and the behavior of the USSR are now more clearly on probation than before. This is not the place in which to pursue the course of Soviet diplomacy in the Conference on Security and Cooperation in Europe. But it is worth remarking that the Soviet Union was enthusiastic about this after the invasion of Czechoslovakia, that it clearly saw the prospective conference as one more means of keeping Eastern European developments under control, and that as the conference progressed it became increasingly disenchanted. In Western European eyes the conference was largely a failure. Although the nine EEC countries achieved a common position and maintained it during the conference (no mean achievement for the EEC), they were not able to establish the kind of linkages between security considerations, economic considerations, and questions of Soviet behavior that some of them were hoping for. But they were able to make clear how far conditions had changed since 1968; to demonstrate that in the future Soviet behavior in and toward Eastern Europe would be scrutinized, and that the renewal and regularization of cooperation agreements would be dependent on Soviet observance of the promises already made.

The Questions

What happened after the invasion of Czechoslovakia indicates that the United States was successful in containing a crisis, in preventing the spread of its implications to other countries, even inside the Warsaw Pact, and that it was able to do so largely by indirection: by suggesting that a threat to Rumania would be a threat to Yugoslavia. Obviously, however, this could not have happened if Yugoslavia had not been willing to suggest the same thing. The first question that arises therefore is how far the Yugoslav tail wagged the U.S. dog? The answer is probably not at all. Certainly Tito took bold initiatives. But there seems to have been remarkably little coordination between Yugoslavia and the United States until after President Johnson's speech, and it is unlikely that the speech, in turn, was based on any direct or indirect warning from Yugoslavia about possible Soviet action. Reports at the time suggested that the President was motivated by intelligence reports of the minor Soviet troop movements already discussed.[81] The NATO countries had been taken by surprise when the invasion actually began, having discounted the implications of the large-scale buildup that had preceded the invasion of Czechoslovakia and preferring instead to believe the apparent assurances provided by the meetings between the Warsaw Pact leaders at Bratislava and Cierna-nad-Tisou. By the end of August, however, the United States was anxious to contain the crisis, and the President acted immediately upon any suggestion of further Soviet moves. As I have tried to show, these moves were most unlikely to imply an invasion of Rumania, but the speech was intended to preempt such a possibility. It therefore seems clear that he was acting from U.S. perceptions of U.S. interests, and not in any way at the behest of Yugoslavia.

Nonetheless, the degree of contact and consultation achieved between the United States and Yugoslavia in the weeks following the speech shows a very strong coincidence of interests—a coincidence in which Yugoslavia's determination to extend the implications of the crisis and the U.S. determination to contain them met at the right point and allowed the United States to make an effective and independent decision.

The second question is whether the extension of U.S. and NATO interest to Yugoslavia between September and November 1968 made any difference to Yugoslav foreign policy—in the way that, for example, U.S. aid had prompted a reevaluation in 1951. The answer is none at all. Indeed, Tito was already willing by the end of November to deny that he

81. See, for example, *Sunday Telegraph,* September 1, 1968, and *New York Times,* September 5, 1968. It is further worth noting President Johnson's own reference in the speech to "rumors" (a nice euphemism?) of further impending Soviet action.

had asked for or had wanted any kind of help. Of course, one does not, if one is Tito, allow a U.S. warship to call at a domestic port unless one is hoping for some demonstration of assistance. But in fact he went out of his way to warn NATO to mind its own business.[82] Thereafter, and into the present, he has used many opportunities to insult NATO, to accuse it of wishing to meddle in Yugoslavia's internal affairs, even to drop heavy hints that Western intelligence might lie behind, for example, the infiltration of a few returning Ustashi.[83] But ultimately this is only part of the rules of the game. Tito's foreign policy need not change in the context established by the nature of superpower relations in Europe. If it is understood that he and the Western governments have a common interest in keeping Yugoslavia out of *any* alliance, then his balancing acts will not affect NATO's interests in that country, nor will these interests affect his public behavior.

The third question, how far the events of 1968–69 affected Soviet behavior, cannot be answered directly. Such evidence as there is indicates that the Soviet government was not ready to invade Rumania in the autumn of 1968, and the movements that might have been construed as threatening in the early months of 1969 were in fact very minor. It is possible that the USSR never contemplated attacking Rumania, but the option was there; it was not translated into an intention. What is clear is that the Rumanian government, alarmed at first, was nonetheless able to preserve its independence. In spite of intermittent and sometimes acute stress in their relations, the USSR has never gone near that brink again.

Conclusions

The two sections of this study deal with events that occurred at an interval of twenty years. In the period between 1948 and 1951 the United States was still engaged in the attempt to establish a basic structure of international relations. This attempt implied more than a commitment to Western Europe or the maintenance of troops there. It involved a mutual learning process by the two superpowers that was com-

82. Press conference, November 30, 1968, in response to a question by a correspondent of Austrian Television.
83. Mainly right-wing Croatian nationalists, whose hostility to Tito dates from the Second World War.

plex and, as in Korea, bloody. A crucial element in this process was the definition of boundaries—of both superpower influence and superpower behavior. General war over Korea was successfully avoided, though one might argue that the issues at stake in the event of a conflict over Yugoslavia, affecting as they did the security of the Mediterranean and Southern Europe, were even more important. It is hard to judge how valid were the fears of a satellite attack on Yugoslavia, but the evidence is overwhelming—in the form of 2,000 border incidents in this period, and in a Soviet confession in a subsequent *Pravda* article—that the USSR was seriously contemplating an attack. It was obviously Yugoslav willingness to fight that constituted the prime deterrent. But even this resolute attitude could hardly have been a sufficient deterrent. The USSR had maintained a military mission in Yugoslavia after all, and knew the state of the country's defense; it would have contemplated an attack only if it had been confident of victory. The definition of the boundaries of superpower relations within the newly emerging international order demanded U.S. help for Yugoslavia.

The success of the United States lay in securing Yugoslavia a particular, perhaps even unique, place in the international order. It was uncoupled from the global competition between the superpowers, rescued from the status of gray area, and became instead a country whose security was demonstrably of such interest to the United States that it could not be attacked without the risk of general war. As such it is the only state that, with Western help at a crucial moment, has been able to make good its escape from the Soviet system of control in Eastern Europe. Although the truce lines of 1945 have now hardened into a definitive East-West boundary, Yugoslavia has not crossed either line or joined any alliance. Instead, its independent status has made it a perpetual test case of Soviet intentions, providing a focus for the relations between the two powers in an area that is of vital concern to them both. Such a position has of course given Tito the maneuverability his domestic position requires of him. In this sense the domestic politics of Yugoslavia have perpetually confirmed the international status of the country by imposing upon Tito the need to balance between the two power blocs. This in turn means that a succession crisis after his departure could be of the greatest international importance. Yugoslavia would still be a test case, but would it still be able to balance? I have argued that the process of decision was paradoxical. U.S. aid to Yugoslavia was initially economic, disguised for legal reasons as military aid. Later, after the passage of the necessary legislation, it was possible to give the country a full measure of undisguised economic help. Yet this economic help was primarily designed to ensure Yugoslavia's military security. It was therefore possible, as soon as Tito acquiesced, to transform the economic program into a military program, culminating a process that finally demonstrated the U.S. commitment to Yugoslav security. The striking feature of this commitment is the care that was taken by the United States to associate its NATO allies, the United Kingdom and France, with both the economic and the military assistance. The United States has consistently sought to ensure Yugoslav security, but it has never been alone in evincing concern. This is of great importance in assessing potential reactions to a succession crisis.

The Czechoslovak crisis occurred at a moment when the boundary lines of superpower relations in Europe had long been firmly drawn. I have argued that in the early stage of the Czechoslovak crisis the United States was neither able to take any action nor willing to do anything that might seem to intensify the dangers of a new upheaval. But when the U.S. government later had grounds, however uncertain, to believe that the crisis could be extended it did what it could to contain it. The key element in this case was the state of relations between the United States and Yugoslavia. Tito's unique position again made it possible to develop swift contacts and consultations between the two countries and also made it possible for him to move away from overt dependence on the United States as soon as the crisis had passed. Once again Yugoslavia constituted a test case for superpower relations, and this time the situation enabled the United States to extend a degree of indirect protection even to Rumania, a member of the Warsaw Pact. But in this situation, too, although the United States was anxious in the first instance to demonstrate commitment and support for Western Europe, it made it plain that it would expect Western European participation. The return of the air squadrons to Europe and the rescheduling of the troop maneuvers were made conditional on matching activity from the European members of NATO.

A reasonable conclusion is that in the event of a Yugoslav succession crisis the United States would be most unlikely to take action alone. Obviously, a potential, hypothetical crisis cannot be considered in detail; there are too many variables and too many scenarios. The crisis could take the form of an upheaval in the relations between the different Yugoslav republics—notably between Serbia and Croatia, whose mutual hatred has sometimes been so intense as virtually to threaten civil war. It could take the form of a dispute between "liberals" and "conservatives" in the leadership of the League of Communists. It could take the form of a show-down between those who argue that the real future of the country lies in a closer alignment with the socialist bloc and those who desire a freer pattern of association with the West. Or it could combine all these forms. The most adequate summary I have heard of the future patterns of events in Yugoslavia came from a Marxist historian: "If nothing happens, any-thing could happen. If something happens, nothing will happen." This small dialectical masterpiece points to the crucial consideration. If "some-thing happens"—that is, if there is a serious Soviet threat—it would prob-ably be enough to unite the country in withstanding it, and then "nothing would happen." But if "nothing happens"—that is, if there is no overt Soviet threat to Yugoslav security—any or all of the potential conflicts inside the country might erupt, and then "anything could happen."

Unfortunately, perhaps, by far the greater likelihood is that there will be no overt threat when Tito departs. Precisely because Yugoslavia con-stitutes such an important test case of international relations, the USSR would in all probability show a keen awareness of the importance of not interfering. But if the country were to fall into opposing or even fighting factions, would not the USSR be tempted to offer moral and material sup-port to one or another of them? And would not the Western powers be likely to do the same? The prime interest of everybody might lie in pre-venting such a conflict; but its prevention would also depend on the Yugo-slavs themselves, and their future behavior can be neither guaranteed nor foreseen.

In such a case, surely the most important interest of the Western powers, and especially the United States, would lie in *not* allowing another Angola to develop. It might be tempting to support a liberal like Marko Nikezic; and indeed moral and political support would be highly desirable. But it would be essential to draw a firm distinction between political (or even economic) assistance and military assistance. The "threat to lose control" could become all too real in such circumstances, and on either side.

It might seem, therefore, that I am arguing that military measures are of no importance, and that the past instances considered here are of no relevance. But I would argue exactly the opposite. The *only* way to ensure that outside support for any of the competing forces in Yugoslavia remains confined below the military level is to have sufficient force available and to be able to deploy it sufficiently rapidly to deliver an effective warning to the USSR. (Supplies might in some circumstances be equally relevant.) The United States is unlikely to wish to mobilize and deploy all this force on its own. Obviously the most important elements in any display of force—the Sixth Fleet, the aircraft squadrons—would belong to the United States. But for domestic reasons and on grounds of principle, the United States would almost certainly require the material association of the Western European powers. After all, the United States would have no reason to protect European security if the Europeans themselves were not also interested in doing so.

Contingency planning for a succession crisis would therefore require early involvement by the European members of NATO in any attempts to contain it. Fortunately, many Western European governments are now showing serious (if not altogether accurate) apprehension at the strength of the Soviet forces in Europe and at the Soviet intentions that might feed on such a military superiority. In addition, the West German government has shown a degree of active concern over the future of Yugoslavia. Paradoxically, the importance of the Italian Communist party (PCI) in the process of Italian decisionmaking might give more grounds for hope than for concern. Not only is Yugoslavia Italy's neighbor, but the relations between the leadership of the PCI and at least some sections of the Yugoslav League of Communists are very close. Particularly in the context of Yugoslavia, the influence of Admiral Stansfield Turner (now director of the CIA but previously NATO commander in Southern Europe) could be very welcome to Italian Communist party leader Enrico Berlinguer.

With the necessary degree of European support, therefore, the United States should be able to take the requisite military measures to contain any succession crisis in Yugoslavia. These would demand, first, a high level of readiness in NATO: it is clear that a commitment to Yugoslavia is ultimately credible when it is seen as part of a commitment to Western Europe. Second, it would entail the ability to fly supplies or even intervention forces if need be to Yugoslavia, though again it should be emphasized that such an ability would serve primarily as a deterrent to Soviet action. Third, it should imply the ability of the Sixth Fleet, and if necessary other European naval forces, to deny access to the Soviet squadrons, particularly in the Strait of Otranto. In spite of the current confusion in NATO, there is no reason why such measures cannot be discussed intelligently.

The United States has on two occasions and by different means succeeded in averting threats and containing crises. The possibility of war has proved sufficient to deter the USSR from any actions it might otherwise have contemplated. There is no reason why it should not do so again.

PART THREE

Conclusions

CHAPTER ELEVEN

Learning from the Past

ON APPROXIMATELY three dozen occasions since World War II, the ever changing but relatively placid stream of world events has been punctuated by dramatic confrontations—points at which world tensions, which usually rise or fall only in small increments, increased sharply. The trappings of these crises are familiar to all: late-burning lights at the White House, the Department of State, and the Pentagon; hastily called press conferences at which ominous-sounding prepared statements are read by bleary-eyed officials; and inevitably, briefing charts showing the movements of elements of the armed forces. These movements and other changes in the readiness of the armed forces are the idiom of crisis diplomacy. They serve to better prepare the armed forces should they be called upon to protect U.S. interests in whatever situation is at risk; and they are also used to reinforce, and sometimes to substitute for, diplomacy: to warn, to reassure, and generally to signal U.S. policy intent.

In roughly 180 less serious incidents as well, the United States has made use of its armed forces to protect American interests abroad and to secure various foreign policy objectives. What has been the result of this military activity? By and large, are the prospects for success in such ventures good enough that policymakers should consider the armed forces an important option in these situations? Or should they view use of the military with great caution—because this type of activity often fails to meet its objectives and because sometimes it backfires? More to the point, under what circumstances are discrete uses of the armed forces for political objectives more likely to succeed, and when are they more likely to fail?

515

We have used two methods to answer these questions: an aggregate analysis of a representative sample of all 215 incidents (chapters 3 through 5) and detailed case studies of ten separate incidents (chapters 6 through 10). In this final chapter we draw upon both of these analytic approaches to reach broad conclusions about the efficacy of the armed forces when used as a political instrument, stepping back from the two analyses to see if their findings point in common directions. Typically, the aggregate analyses provide the starting points; the conclusions they suggest are then illustrated by the case studies. Before considering these conclusions, however, readers should remember several cautions.

First, we have examined but one way in which the armed forces can be and have been used in the pursuit of foreign policy objectives. There are others, some of which may be more significant. Indeed, in one sense at least, the fact that a discrete political use of the armed forces took place may be indicative of failure in more fundamental political purposes of military forces. It is mainly when something unexpected and adverse happens, when the positive long-term political effects of the acquisition, maintenance, and deployment of the armed forces break down, that decisionmakers turn to discrete military operations in attempts to mend the fabric of foreign relations.

Second, this study does not assume that there is a cause and effect relationship between a single military operation and any specific decision by a policymaker in a foreign nation; it is simply impossible to determine why—specifically—a certain decision was taken. In most cases the decisionmakers themselves probably did not sort out the relative importance of the various stimuli they received. Even if they did, first-hand accounts of most of the incidents that are considered in the study are not available; and if they were they would not necessarily constitute an accurate historical record. Thus, although we can point out the coincidence between, on the one hand, certain types of military operations in certain kinds of situations and, on the other hand, outcomes that are either favorable or unfavorable from the U.S. perspective, we cannot say with certitude that similar outcomes would not have occurred in the absence of any military operations, or in the face of a markedly different sort of military operation.

Third, there are deficiencies in the amount and type of information that is routinely collected about these sorts of military operations. The problem is not one of access; we doubt that most sections of the study would have been significantly more accurate if they had been founded on classified data. It is simply a question of the precision and completeness of the data that were originally recorded. Thus, in some cases, arbitrary judgments had to be made that we would have preferred to avoid. Despite this caveat, we believe that the information upon which the study is based is ample and precise enough for the conclusions to warrant serious attention.

Finally, and perhaps most important, a distinction should be drawn between utility and wisdom. The former is addressed in this study, the latter is not. In evaluating the utility of political uses of the armed forces, the methodology employed accepts the objectives of U.S. decisionmakers as given and assesses only whether or not those objectives were achieved. The question of the wisdom of establishing those objectives is beyond the scope of this study. Nor do we judge the long-term security consequences of political uses of the armed forces beyond those specific ways in which the nation's security may or may not have been affected by the discrete and immediate situation in which the armed forces were employed.

The Special Role of Force

The weight of evidence is consistent with the hypothesis that discrete uses of the armed forces are often an effective way of achieving near-term foreign policy objectives. The aggregate analyses showed clearly that, when the United States engaged in these political-military activities, the outcomes of the situations at which the activity was directed were most often favorable from the perspective of U.S. decisionmakers—at least in the short term.

In a very large proportion of the incidents, however, this "success rate" eroded sharply over time. Thus, it would seem that, to the degree that they did influence events, discrete uses of military forces for political objectives served mainly to *delay* unwanted developments abroad. Though there is some value in "buying time"—that is, keeping a situation open and flexible enough to prevent an adverse fait accompli—it should be recognized that these military operations cannot substitute for more fundamental policies and actions—diplomacy, close economic and cultural relations, an affinity of mutual interests and perceptions—which can form the basis either for sound and successful alliances or for stable adversary relations. What political-military operations perhaps can do is provide a respite, a means of postponing adverse developments long enough to formulate and implement new policies that may be sustainable over the longer term. Or, if that is not possible, the political use of armed forces may serve to lessen the consequences of detrimental events. However, some of the case studies suggest that even these delaying and minimizing accomplishments cannot always be expected.

In some cases the discrete use of force clearly has been ineffectual. For example, David Hall points out in chapter 6 that U.S. support for Pakistan during the 1971 war with India was a relatively empty gesture because the target actors recognized that under virtually no circumstances would the United States become militarily involved in the war. Consequently, the deployment of the *Enterprise* task force to the Indian Ocean had almost no effect on the decisions of either the immediate actors— India and Pakistan; or the actors indirectly involved—China and the Soviet Union.

In other cases, a discrete political application of the armed forces seems to have been associated with the creation of a situation that remained tolerable for a period of months or, in some cases, years. The intervention in Laos in 1962 was such an incident; the landing of U.S. Marines in Thailand was coincident with the negotiation of a settlement that kept the peace in Laos for several years. U.S. actions to oust the Trujillo family from the Dominican Republic following Rafael Trujillo's assassination, and subsequent actions to support the new government, as described by Jerome Slater in chapter 8, were of a similar character. Following these actions a more acceptable political situation was created in the Dominican Republic that persisted for several years, even though it ultimately foundered in 1965.

Was it worthwhile to use armed forces to obtain positive outcomes that could be sustained only temporarily, whether the duration was of several months or several years? We believe the answer is yes, insofar as an opportunity was gained for diplomacy.

When a positive outcome did not endure, it was usually attributable not to an absence of diplomatic effort, but to the fact that the internal situation within a state, or a specific interstate relationship, was strong and durable and not subject to being permeated by either single or periodic U.S. military actions or by the use of other U.S. policy instruments. Realizing that this was the situation with regard to Vietnam in 1964–65,

American policymakers chose war as the solution, as they did not in the late 1940s in China when Communist forces there triumphed and forced the Kuomintang government of Chiang Kai-shek to flee to Taiwan, in the early 1960s over Cuba when Fidel Castro identified his regime with communism and the Soviet Union, or in the late 1960s against North Korea after the *Pueblo* was seized and a U.S. Navy EC-121 aircraft was shot down.

Finally, in some cases with very special circumstances, discrete political uses of the armed forces contributed to the establishment of new international relationships, such that U.S. interests were protected for decades. For example, following the 1946 visit to Turkey by the battleship *Missouri* and further displays of U.S. military support for Ankara, Soviet pressures on Turkey declined; they have not been renewed in a serious way since. Displays of American military support for Italy prior to the 1948 elections seem to have contributed, along with such other instruments of policy as economic aid and covert support for democratic political parties, to the defeat of the Italian Communist party. The dominance of the Christian Democratic party, which resulted from that election, persisted for more than two decades. Political uses of the armed forces during the Berlin crises of 1958–59 and 1961, described in chapter 9, contributed to creating stable conditions in Central Europe that have continued to exist.

What is the mechanism at work here? How do the armed forces play their special role? The process begins when a given framework of relations among several countries, or a domestic political configuration abroad, is disrupted by something unexpected or at least unwelcome: a domestic upheaval, a new departure in a major power's foreign policy, or perhaps an unexpected armed clash between the military units of hostile states. Regardless of cause, this development often creates uncertainties and a distinct psychological unease among interested parties; at other times it leads directly to an unraveling of the fabric of relations that previously had been established and maintained by existing policies. Under such circumstances (and mindful of the fact that even when favorable outcomes do occur they are likely to persist only over the short term), a discrete demonstration of U.S. military capability can have a stabilizing and otherwise beneficial effect, perhaps persuading the target that the course of wisdom is to alter the undesirable policy.

The effect of the military demonstration will depend to a large extent on whether the target finds the threat credible. A prime example was the arrival of U.S. military forces off the coast of the Dominican Republic in November 1961. That event changed the perceptions of the Trujillo family and their lieutenants as to the United States' willingness to act. Coupled as it was with a clear ultimatum, the action seems to have exerted a powerful influence.

Such a military demonstration may be particularly effective when the actor at which it is directed is not yet fully committed to the course from which the United States hopes to dissuade it. We will never know for sure, but U.S. actions in support of Yugoslavia following President Tito's break with Stalin may have lessened Stalin's inclination to take more aggressive measures against Yugoslavia. Moscow may also have been somewhat deterred from taking action against Rumania following the intervention in Czechoslovakia in 1968, as Philip Windsor suggests in chapter 10. We will return to these distinctions later in the chapter. First, however, it is helpful to examine the mechanisms at work more closely.

In some of the cases studied, the insertion (even symbolically) of U.S. military forces may have provided leverage to U.S. decisionmakers where previously there had not been any. Establishment of a U.S. military presence or operation may furnish an incentive to a foreign leader for considering the wishes of U.S. policymakers. Once U.S. Marines landed in Thailand and the threat of a U.S. intervention in Laos became credible, for example, the United States may have gained a decided edge at the negotiating table. In such a case the prime result is to lessen the potential U.S. loss. Foreign decisionmakers may act to avoid those extreme choices that they fear would precipitate a violent U.S. response. Unless the United States is willing to turn its new military presence into a permanent operation, however, any such demonstrative action is likely to be successful, to the degree it is successful at all, only for a limited time.

The intervention in Lebanon in 1958, described by William Quandt in chapter 7, provides a pointed example of this phenomenon. Although President Eisenhower authorized the landing of U.S. Marines and other forces in Lebanon in July 1958, the President—or at least Secretary of State Dulles—recognized that an American-imposed solution in Lebanon would be unacceptable to most of the Lebanese actors and therefore short-lived. Thus the United States adopted a twofold approach. On the one hand, a massive demonstration of American military power was staged, involving the landing of thousands of American troops. On the other hand, Deputy Under Secretary of State Robert Murphy was dispatched to Lebanon, where, recognizing the political realities of the situation, he negotiated a settlement that was probably more favorable to the actors that opposed U.S. policy than to the presumed American client, President Camille Chamoun. In other words, to the degree that it did influence the situation, the U.S. military demonstration seems to have bought sufficient time to reach new political arrangements that more realistically reflected the distribution of power among competing ethnic and political groups in Lebanon. Without the more realistic political solution negotiated by Murphy, the 1958 U.S. intervention in Lebanon would probably have been associated with a much less favorable outcome. At the same time, without the leverage provided by the U.S. military presence in Lebanon, with its implied threat of greater violence, Murphy might well have failed in his attempt to negotiate a political solution.

Military demonstrations also can ease domestic political pressures on the President from groups demanding more forceful action. In less serious incidents, these pressures—which can originate from ethnic groups, the Congress, friends and political associates of the decisionmakers, and executive branch uniformed and civilian officials, among others—are directed at lower-ranking foreign policy managers. Some of the case studies suggest that insofar as they can help to stabilize a situation, thereby postponing forecast adverse consequences of unexpected developments in international politics, discrete uses of the armed forces may diminish calls for more decisive action. The postponement provides the time needed to gather support within the bureaucracy and in the Congress and the public for the fundamental changes in policy required to accommodate developments. In the absence of the time bought by the military demonstration, these fundamental changes in policy may be more difficult to bring about, and the President might fear that his constituencies, both at home and abroad, will see him as bowing to foreign pressures.

This phenomenon was also demonstrated pointedly by the intervention in Lebanon in 1958. During the spring of 1958, President Eisenhower resisted several requests from President Chamoun for American military assistance. An unexpected event—the coup in Iraq in July—made it impossible to avoid the request any longer. The President feared that further inaction, after the seeming wholesale defeat of American clients in the Middle East, would have negative effects both on the perceptions of decisionmakers in foreign nations and on domestic opinion in this nation. American support for the realistic solution to the Lebanese problem negotiated by Murphy might have been difficult to muster without the symbolism of American strength suggested by the military intervention. In the absence of the intervention, President Eisenhower may have feared the effects of such an apparent concession on opinion both at home and abroad.

Similarly, following American intervention in the Dominican Republic in 1965, Ambassador Ellsworth Bunker negotiated an agreement in which it was all but explicit that the president elected the following year would be either Joaquin Balaguer or Juan Bosch. Balaguer was the last president during the Trujillo era, and a person whom the United States had taken pains to keep out of the Dominican Republic in later years; Bosch was strongly disliked by many American officials and suspected of tendencies that might allow an eventual takeover by the extreme left. The emplacement of U.S. forces in the Dominican Republic not only made an election in the Dominican Republic possible, it made its likely outcome acceptable.

None of this is meant to imply that the gains seemingly associated with discrete uses of the armed forces for political objectives have been fraudulent. The amelioration of pressures for extreme actions is an important benefit, as is the provision of time necessary to build a consensus for a new U.S. policy; so too is the provision of leverage to negotiators. We turn next to a discussion of the circumstances under which these desired outcomes are best attained.

Correlates of Success

Four groups of factors have been associated with the relative success or failure of political uses of the armed forces: the type of objective; the context of the incident; involvement by the Soviet Union; and the nature and activity of the U.S. military forces involved. (Unless noted otherwise, these conclusions refer mainly to short-term outcomes.)

U.S. Objectives

The nature of U.S. objectives may be an important determinant of whether a political use of force is successful. Favorable outcomes when the armed forces were used as a political instrument occurred most often when the objective of U.S. policymakers was to maintain the authority of a specific regime abroad. Such was the case, for example, when naval movements and other activities were undertaken in support of King Hussein during the 1970 civil war in Jordan. Indeed, the aggregate analysis suggests that maintenance of regime authority was the one type of objective associated with the persistence of a favorable outcome over the longer term. The armed forces were least often associated with favorable outcomes when the objective concerned the provision of support by actors to third parties—for example, the many incidents in which U.S. military activity was undertaken in order to persuade the Soviet Union to cease supporting hostile political initiatives by its allies or clients. Between these two extremes there were a reasonable number of favorable outcomes when discrete political uses of the armed forces were undertaken to offset the use of force by another actor. Over the longer term, however, no distinction was found to exist between the frequency of favorable outcomes concerning the use of force by another actor and an actor's support of a third party—in both cases these frequencies were low. Illustrative are the futile attempts during the late 1950s and early 1960s to convince the Pathet Lao and Viet Cong to terminate their insurgencies in Laos and South Vietnam.

Perhaps more significant, the mode in which the armed forces are used as a political instrument may also be an important determinant of success. It is evident from the aggregate analyses that discrete uses of the armed forces for political purposes were more often associated with favorable outcomes when the U.S. objective was to reinforce, rather than modify, the behavior of a target state. This stands to reason. It fits not only with the findings of behavioral psychology but with common sense. Chairman Khrushchev, no doubt, found it much easier *not* to follow through on the various threats he made concerning Europe and the Middle East than he did to withdraw Soviet missiles from Cuba; just as deterring the outbreak of violence is usually an easier task than bringing violence to a satisfactory conclusion.

Human behavior is difficult to change. Individuals tend to be more aware of the risks of change than they are of the dangers of continuing their prevailing course. After all, policies being pursued at any one time are known entities; even when their risks are evident, the dangers of change will often appear more threatening. More to the point, no one—least of all the head of a nation—can afford to be told publicly what he should be doing. Thus, national leaders will resist demands for policy modifications most strenuously when such demands are made publicly, which is usually unavoidable when military power is used.

In short, the aggregate analyses showed that whether a discrete application of military power was made in order to coerce a hostile target state to change its behavior or to encourage a friendly target state to change its behavior, the outcomes were similar; most often they were unfavorable from the U.S. perspective. On the other hand, when U.S. policymakers used the armed forces to coerce a hostile target state to continue to do something (for example, stay at peace), or to encourage a friendly state to remain on the same course, military demonstrations were relatively more often associated with favorable outcomes. This is borne out in the case studies, as well.

Consider, for example, the starkly different outcomes of the Berlin crises of 1958–59 and 1961, and the several incidents in Southeast Asia in the late 1950s and early 1960s. In the former the United States sought essentially to assure allies and to deter certain threatened actions by the USSR and East Germany. Both types of objectives required only that the targets not change their behavior, and both were achieved. Not so favorable, especially over the longer term, were the outcomes of the Southeast Asian incidents, in which the United States sought to compel various Communist actors to stop using force and to induce the government of South Vietnam to behave differently (that is, more assertively). Here both types of objectives required a change of behavior on the part of target states, and only rarely were these outcomes achieved.

To some extent this conclusion may reflect Tolstoy's view that the only decisions that are carried out are those corresponding to what would have happened if the decisions had not been made. In many of the incidents, although U.S. decisionmakers may have thought—or feared—that a target state was prepared or intending to change its behavior, and thus used the armed forces to reinforce existing behavior, the target state actually may have had no such intention. A good example is the U.S. military activity that followed the Soviet occupation of Czechoslovakia. One objective of that action was to deter a Soviet invasion of Rumania. No invasion occurred; hence the military demonstration appears to have been effective. The question, however, is whether Soviet leaders ever seriously contemplated such an invasion. The same may be said about the Soviet Union's not taking violent action against President Tito and Yugoslavia

almost two decades earlier. This is not necessarily to discount the importance of the U.S. military activity—as Windsor points out, U.S. policymakers had other important objectives in mind as well. Still, the proportion of favorable "reinforcement" outcomes that are accounted for by
the "unreality" of the feared target state behavior may be high. Unfortunately, that proportion is impossible to determine empirically.

Political uses of the armed forces were often associated with favorable
outcomes when U.S. objectives were at least loosely consistent with prior
U.S. policies. The purpose of discrete political uses of force must fit
within a fundamental framework of expectations held by decisionmakers
both in this country and abroad if the military activity is to be associated
with a favorable outcome. With regard to the incidents in the sample,
although prior diplomacy was closely associated with positive outcomes,
diplomacy during the course of the incidents themselves was not.

When a treaty exists, or when policymakers have taken pains to make
clear that the United States perceives itself to have a commitment, antagonists are less likely to probe, or to probe only within narrower limits than
would have been the case otherwise, and to leave themselves a way open
for retreat. In other words, antagonists may be less likely to try to present the United States with a fait accompli that could be reversed only
through a major use of the armed forces. Prior diplomacy may have reinforced the antagonists' continued performance of desired behavior, and
thus lessened the significance of a breakdown in relations or the severity
of a crisis. Rather than have to cope with hostile actions, policymakers
in these cases might have only had to respond to hostile rhetoric; alternatively, the behavior modification desired of foreign decisionmakers might
have been less.

Hence, although China initiated the 1958 Offshore Islands crisis by
shelling Quemoy and Matsu, and Chairman Khrushchev threatened Berlin on several occasions, both Peking and Moscow carefully controlled
their behavior during these incidents because they perceived a prior U.S.
commitment (or at least feared the strength of announced U.S. commitments). In the absence of prior U.S. commitment, as in Korea in 1950,
we might surmise that not only would China and the USSR have gone
further in their initial actions, but also that sudden U.S. diplomatic action, even if supported by a discrete political use of force, might have had
a lesser effect. Skilled diplomacy during incidents—for example, by
Robert Murphy in Lebanon, Averell Harriman in Laos, and Ellsworth

Bunker in the Dominican Republic—has typically borne fruit only after ambiguous U.S. military commitments have been underscored by the movement of major military units. Not only should the United States not count on skilled diplomacy being effective in controlling crises in the absence of prior commitments and reinforcing uses of the armed forces, it should aim to avoid such difficult tests in the first place by being quite clear as to what its commitments are.

Similarly, the aggregate analyses suggest that prior U.S. military engagement in conflicts in a region was often associated with favorable outcomes when subsequent discrete uses of military force took place. The fact that the United States previously had been willing to engage in violence in the region may have made the threats or assurances implied by the subsequent military activity more credible. Much less often associated with favorable outcomes were previous political uses of force in the region; the willingness to engage in violence seems to have been the key. Previous discrete political uses of force were associated with favorable outcomes more often, however, when the U.S. objective was to assure a target state so that it would continue to do something. Good examples are provided by U.S. naval demonstrations in the Mediterranean. U.S. military forces have not fought in that region since 1945, yet as concerns the assurance of Israel (and less frequently, Jordan), these displays of naval power were often associated with favorable outcomes. U.S. objectives in situations were far less often attained, however, when the political use of force was meant to modify the behavior of Israel's (or Jordan's) enemies.

In short, prior actual or political uses of force did not seem to be sufficient to compensate for the previously noted difficulty of *modifying* a target state's behavior. Indeed, very little seemed to compensate for the difficulty of modifying behavior; more than any other factor this was the basic determinant of when a discrete political use of force would or would not be associated with the attainment of foreign policy objectives. It overshadowed the diplomacy that accompanied the military activity, the nature of the situation, and the timing, size, composition, and activity of the military units themselves.

Soviet Activity

A second group of factors that seemed to be associated with favorable outcomes in the aggregate analyses included the character of U.S.-Soviet relations and the specific role played by the Soviet Union in an incident. One conclusion that runs counter to prevailing views concerns the possible effect of the U.S.-Soviet strategic nuclear balance on the relative fortunes of the superpowers. We did not find that the United States was less often successful as the Soviet Union closed the U.S. lead in strategic nuclear weapons that had been maintained for the first twenty or so years following the Second World War. Whether or not discrete political uses of U.S. armed forces were associated with positive outcomes seems to have been independent of relative U.S.-Soviet aggregate strategic capabilities. Of course, the United States may have engaged less often in these incidents since the late 1960s precisely because it understood that its chances of success were smaller; as the USSR closed the nuclear gap, the United States may have chosen to participate in incidents more selectively, choosing only those cases in which its chances of success were greatest.

Since this study was not designed to test the effects of the strategic balance, the findings in this regard are clearly tentative. Still, both the aggregate analyses and the case studies provide little support for the notion that decisions during crises are strongly influenced by aggregate strategic capabilities. William Quandt's studies of Lebanon and Jordan, for example, indicate that to the extent that evaluations of the military balance played any role, they were more concerned with the local balance of conventional power. More to the point, most local actors in these incidents seem to have had only a rudimentary and impressionistic sense of relative military capabilities in general.

Soviet political and/or military involvement in the incident itself, on the other hand, was clearly associated with the frequency of favorable outcomes, which were less often favorable when the Soviet Union was involved, particularly when the Soviet Union threatened to employ, or actually employed, its own armed forces in the incident. The seemingly pernicious effect of Soviet involvement was tempered at times when broader U.S.-Soviet relations had been improving, and outcomes were more often favorable when overall U.S.-Soviet relations were characterized by greater cooperation. As in the previous finding, this conclusion is stronger when just those incidents in which the Soviet Union participated were considered, and stronger still when just those incidents were considered in which Soviet military forces were involved.

Nature of the Situation

Outcomes were favorable more frequently when discrete political uses of force were directed at intranational, as contrasted to international, situations. We are not confident about this finding, however, because two other factors that are also closely associated with favorable outcomes are highly correlated with intranational situations: lesser amounts of force tend to be used in intranational situations; and the U.S. objective in these situations is more often reinforcement than modification of behavior.

In the international situations, a positive outcome was most likely if the United States was involved from the very onset of a conflict. This finding complements the previous finding concerning the need for the U.S. objective and the specific use of force to be consistent with the prior framework of relations between the United States and the nations involved in the incident. The case studies bear out the view that in those situations in which the United States was involved initially, such as the Berlin crises of 1958–59 and 1961, U.S. statements of aims and objectives were more likely to be considered seriously. Similarly, U.S. threats or promises implied by the use of armed forces were more likely to be perceived as credible. In the other international situations, when the United States was intervening, so to speak, in a situation that did not concern it directly (or at least not initially), there seems to have been some question in the minds of the other actors whether U.S. threats or promises were credible. Consider the perceptions of Hanoi in the late 1950s and early 1960s and those of the Gandhi government in India during the crisis and then war with Pakistan in 1971, for example. The U.S. military demonstrations then were not taken too seriously at first. Why, North Vietnamese and Indian leaders might have asked, would the United States become involved militarily? Such questions were less likely to be raised in those situations in which U.S. interests were directly and obviously threatened.

Boding ill for the future, the aggregate analyses suggest that the proportion of incidents involving hostility between states appears to be increasing, while there is a decline in situations of an intrastate nature. Less and less is the United States being called upon by governments for support against internal dissidents; rather, the trend is toward being asked by one state for support against another. Insofar as such a shift is discernible, the risks of involvement to the United States, especially in a situation of violence, can only increase. The shift from an intrastate to an interstate focus means that the instruments brought to bear by regional actors will often be more powerful, both diplomatically and militarily. Allies usually act more overtly when they are supporting a state rather than a subnational group; hence, the facing-off of states is more likely to occasion the facing-off of alliances, whether formal or otherwise. Most important, the likelihood of superpower confrontation is increased.

States, unlike subnational groups, also have air forces, navies, and heavily armed ground forces. Thus the level of violence which can be threatened in a crisis or manifested in a conflict is much greater. For a threat by U.S. policymakers to be credible in these circumstances, large and technologically sophisticated forces must be available. Should these forces be committed in a conflict, they might have to be used in strength and be prepared to take significant casualties. The danger that U.S. action of this sort might stimulate a Soviet military response is obvious.

Size, Activity, and Type of U.S. Military Forces Involved in the Incident

It is evident from the aggregate analyses that the firmer the commitment implied by the military operation, the more often the outcome of the situation was favorable to the United States. The analyses showed that forces actually emplaced on foreign soil were more frequently associated with positive outcomes than were naval forces, which can be withdrawn almost as easily as they can be moved toward the disturbed area. The movement of land-based forces, on the other hand, involves both real economic costs and a certain psychological commitment that are difficult to reverse, at least in the short term. This is an interesting finding, not so much because of its novelty—after all, it only confirms the common perception—but because its implications run counter to common U.S. practice. The Navy has been the preeminent military force in discrete political operations. Naval forces participated in more than 80 percent of the incidents; and reliance on the Navy was the case regardless of region, time period, type of situation, and whether or not the Soviet Union participated in the incident.

Naval forces can be used more subtly to support foreign policy initiatives—to underscore threats, warnings, promises, or commitments—than can land-based units, and they can do so without inalterably tying the

President's hand. But it is precisely this last fact that probably diminishes the effectiveness of naval forces in a political role. Foreign decision-makers also recognize that warships can be withdrawn as easily as they can enter a region of tension and, hence, that the commitment they imply is not so firm as that implied by land-based units.

Positive outcomes were particularly frequent when land-based combat aircraft were involved in an incident. This would suggest, particularly in view of the much greater mobility of modern land-based tactical air units, that the Air Force might be used more frequently in political-military operations than has been the case in the past.

The Soviet Union has often utilized land-based air force units in limited ways for political objectives. Soviet pilots and aircraft are reported to have taken part in wars in Sudan, Yemen, and Iraq; a full Soviet air defense system, including interceptor aircraft, was established for a time in Egypt; and Soviet tactical aircraft detachments have made goodwill visits to Sweden and France. In view of our findings, the United States might do well to emulate this greater reliance on land-based air units under certain circumstances. Indeed, the United States may be already moving in this direction. In the summer of 1976, along with a naval demonstration in the Sea of Japan, two U.S. Air Force squadrons were flown to Korea as part of a show of strength following the killing of two U.S. officers. It was reported at the time that these units—one of which originated in Idaho—would have been available for combat missions within fifteen hours of their dispatch.

Such a shift in U.S. practice would not be without its costs, because the use of land-based forces is perceived by foreign decisionmakers as greater evidence of commitment. If the U.S. objective is not so certain, if all that is desired is to take an action that signifies interest and concern but leaves room for maneuver—such as U.S. naval deployments during the Cyprus crises of 1964, 1967, and 1974—then the use of land-based forces would not be advisable. Moreover, in situations in which a military move is intended as a bluff or to screen a political defeat—as seems the case in the Indo-Pakistani War in 1971—the use of land-based air forces would not be advisable. In all these types of situations, naval forces would provide greater flexibility to decisionmakers, and thus would be more appropriate even if their probability of succeeding may be less.

There are other ways to enhance armed forces effectiveness. Outcomes were more often favorable when the units involved actually did something, instead of merely emphasizing their potential capability to intervene—for example by reducing the time delay between a decision to intervene and the actual operation by moving toward the scene of the incident or by increasing their state of alert. The involvement of the military unit in a specific operation, such as mine-laying, or mine-clearing, or patrolling—and certainly when the actual exercise of firepower was involved—seems to have indicated a more serious intent on the United States' part. The movement of the force toward the region of concern by itself could be an ambiguous signal; it might not be clear to foreign decisionmakers what the United States had in mind, or the movement might pass unobserved. A more specific action, giving a clearer signal, thus was more often associated with favorable outcomes.

Positive outcomes were also more likely when the forces involved included strategic nuclear forces. Foreign decisionmakers seem to have perceived the use of strategic nuclear forces—whether or not it was accompanied by a specific threat to use nuclear weapons—as an important signal that the United States perceived the situation in a most serious way. Thus, the employment of nuclear-associated forces—such as Strategic Air Command aircraft or Sixth Fleet carriers when they were central to U.S. plans for nuclear war—served the same purpose as the involvement of military units in a specific activity, or the use of ground forces as compared to naval forces: they bolstered U.S. credibility.

The risks of such a policy should be evident. There is no guarantee that any military demonstration will be successful. When nuclear weapons are involved, and the demonstration is not successful, the result could be disastrous—U.S. policymakers being faced with the choice of admitting the emptiness of the nuclear threat, and thus undermining the credibility of fundamental U.S. commitments, or actually employing nuclear weapons.

Moreover, it may be that positive outcomes have more often occurred when nuclear forces were involved simply because these weapons have been used infrequently—in less than 10 percent of the incidents. The more U.S. decisionmakers turn to nuclear forces—even demonstratively—to ensure the credibility of signals in incidents such as we have described, the more quickly the special message now associated with nuclear weapons might be eroded. Eventually the movement of nuclear forces would not receive much more attention and would not convey any more credibility than movements of conventional forces.

A Last Word

The discrete use of the armed forces for political objectives should not be an option that decisionmakers turn to frequently or quickly to secure political objectives abroad; it should be used only in very special circumstances. We have found that over the longer term such uses of the armed forces were not often associated with positive outcomes. Decisionmakers should thus not expect them to serve as substitutes for broader and more fundamental policies tailored to the realities of politics abroad, and incorporating diplomacy and the many other potential instruments available to U.S. foreign policy.

Moreover, there are dangers in using the armed forces as a discrete political instrument. Symbolic low-level uses of force may be disregarded by antagonists or friends in a situation in which U.S. policymakers have not seriously contemplated the need for, or the consequences of, using larger forces in a more manifest way. Foreign decisionmakers may not perceive important U.S. interests to be involved; the initial U.S. military action may be seen as symbolic of U.S. interest but not of a commitment; foreign decisionmakers may calculate that they will be able to successfully cope with the forces that they expect the United States to bring to bear; or, when an actor feels its very existence is at stake, the calculus may not matter at all. In all these situations there is a risk that lesser military actions may lead to pressures for greater U.S. involvement.

The case studies bear this out: The Castro regime did not yield at the Bay of Pigs, Hanoi and the Viet Cong were not swayed in the early 1960s, and India dismembered Pakistan in 1971. In each case, either the United States suffered humiliation or the fear of exposure embarrassed decisionmakers into escalation and war.

Still, in particular circumstances, discrete political uses of the armed forces often were associated—at least in the short term—with the securing of U.S. objectives or the stabilization of adverse situations while more fundamental policies could be formulated. Thus, at times, and although decisionmakers should view this option with some caution, the discrete use of the armed forces for political objectives seems to have been a useful step in shoring up situations enough to avoid dramatic setbacks, to mitigate domestic and international pressures for more forceful and perhaps counterproductive actions, and to gain time for sounder policies to be formulated and implemented.

As pointed out earlier, however, to reach this conclusion about the apparent *effectiveness* of the armed forces as a political instrument is not to reach any judgment about the wisdom of using the armed forces for these purposes. That is a more difficult question, which can only be answered in the context of the specific choices—and the various costs and benefits associated with each choice—facing decisionmakers at that time.

Over the past three decades, Presidents (or their designated foreign policy managers) have decided that a political use of the armed forces was the wise choice on more than 200 occasions. Although, on the average, there have been fewer such occasions in recent years than there were before the United States became involved in the war in Southeast Asia, the number of times each year when the armed forces are required to serve a political purpose abroad is not trivial.

There is little reason to expect a further decline in this frequency; rather, one should expect an increase. Attempting to predict in which specific future incidents the United States might attempt to gain political objectives by altering the disposition of its armed forces would be imprudent. A few broad inferences, however, are worth considering:

Although it seems likely that the frequency will remain relatively low as compared to the peaks in the early 1960s, some increase should be expected. As the Vietnam War fades from the nation's consciousness, and as other recent blows to the nation's confidence—Watergate, the 1974–75 recession—likewise recede, voices urging a more active U.S. role in world affairs are being heard more clearly, particularly as the international system presents a large number of "opportunities." More frequent political uses of the armed forces may be one result.

Among those situations that have provided the source for the majority of past incidents, those near the eastern Mediterranean remain most active. Crises here might arise not only out of the Arab-Israeli conflict but also out of inter-Arab conflicts, the Cyprus situation, and other disputes between Greece and Turkey. If incidents in the eastern Mediterranean do recur, they are likely to require major committals of force insofar as the local participants are well-armed and the Soviet Union is more than likely to become involved. Elsewhere, as well as in this key region, greater emphasis is likely to continue to be placed on the use of the armed forces to improve or cement relations, as opposed to coercive uses of force.

A number of the problems that previously generated U.S. political-military diplomacy, although now quiescent, remain unsettled and could recur. Although the situation in Southeast Asia seems likely to be an exception, potential sources of renewed U.S. involvement include: (a) the situation on the Korean peninsula; (b) the possibility of renewed Cuban support for insurgencies in the Caribbean; and (c) new Soviet pressure on states in Southeastern Europe (for example, in the event of a crisis in Yugoslavia following the death of President Tito).

In deciding on the structure of U.S. forces and on operational and deployment patterns, it makes sense to consider possible future political uses. Although these decisions must be based on many other factors as well, some of which—particularly those requirements which flow from plans for war-fighting—should be accorded higher priority, if U.S. military forces are acquired and operated solely to meet the needs of the "worst case"—the big war—they will be inappropriately configured for the needs of many more likely cases. The armed forces are an important political instrument. This role should receive close attention in force planning and operational decisions.

Finally, for those circumstances in which U.S. armed forces would almost certainly be employed for political objectives, it might be desirable to make that certainty clear to potential antagonists. Ambiguity is a useful policy device when decisionmakers themselves are uncertain as to what they might do in a given set of circumstances; in still other situations, which are so hypothetical that it is difficult to believe they could occur, complete reticence may be in order. Ambiguity or reticence may not be wise, however, when a problem looms closely ahead and decisionmakers know that they would forcefully respond. To the extent they refrain from making this clear, they may risk a greater likelihood that a threat to U.S. interests will manifest itself and that antagonists, acting under false expectations, will leave themselves less room for retreat. U.S. objectives might still be achieved under such circumstances, but only at an unnecessary and higher cost.

Appendixes

Bibliographical Sources for Incidents

A WIDE VARIETY of sources were examined systematically to identify political uses of the armed forces, as defined, by the United States during the period covered by this study. Additional sources were examined to identify potential situations in which armed forces might have been used as a political instrument, with the aim of guiding research to uncover more incidents. It is doubtful that all the political uses of U.S. armed forces during the period examined were discovered. We are reasonably confident, however, that the list of incidents presented in the next section is virtually complete as regards the information available on an unclassified basis.

This last point deserves amplification. No classified materials were examined in the course of this study. Some documents were declassified, however, upon request. And a number of organizations within the government were, at the least, cooperative. These included:

The Department of the Air Force
Air University
Albert F. Simpson Historical
   Research Center
(Maxwell AFB, Ala.)

The Department of the Army
Army War College
Strategic Studies Institute
(Carlisle Barracks, Pa.)

The Department of the Air Force
Office of the Chief of Staff
Office of Air Force History

The Department of the Army
John F. Kennedy School of
   Counterinsurgency
(Fort Bragg, N.C.)

The Department of the Army	The Department of the Navy
Office of the Chief of	Naval Historical Center
Military History	Naval History Division
Historical Services Division	
	The Department of the Navy
	U.S. Marine Corps Headquarters
The Department of Defense	Director of Marine Corps
Joint Chiefs of Staff	History and Museums
Joint Secretariat	
Documents Division	The Department of State
	Bureau of Public Affairs
	Historical Office
The Department of Defense	
Office of the Comptroller	The National Archives
Historical Staff	General Archives Division

Most of the sources that were examined in compiling the list of incidents fall into the following three categories: official records of military organizations, such as air force, fleet, and division histories; chronologies of international events, such as the quarterly chronology in the *Middle East Journal;* secondary sources, including various events data files and compilations of U.S. military activity prepared for other purposes.

These sources have various strengths and weaknesses. No doubt some biases have entered the analysis because the sources themselves are systematically biased to some degree. For example, naval activity may be reported more frequently than other forms of military activity. Warships simply may be more visible than other military units. Moreover, many documents of potential interest are unavailable as a result of their being classified, filed at local headquarters, or misfiled. Also, historical records are often written unsystematically and only occasionally.

The sources examined are given below.

U.S. Government

U.S. Congress. *Congressional Record,* daily edition (May 14, 1963), pp. A3007–09. "There Is No Peace: 18 Years, 57 Wars," by Lou Hiner, Jr., originally published in the *Indianapolis News.*

———. *Congressional Record,* vol. 118, pt. 4, 92:2 (1972), pp. 3878–90.

———. House. Committee on Foreign Affairs. *Background Information on the Use of United States Armed Forces in Foreign Countries.* 91:2. Washington: Government Printing Office, 1970.

———. Senate-House Joint Subcommittee on Armed Services. *CVAN-70 Aircraft Carrier.* Hearing. 91:2. Washington: Government Printing Office, 1970. (Letter from Adm. T. H. Moorer, Chief of Naval Operations, to Sen. Walter F. Mondale, September 6, 1969, pp. 163–65.) Contains "Summary of Wars/Near Wars Since 1946."

———. Senate. Committee on Foreign Relations. *War Powers Legislation.* Hearing. 93:1. Washington: Government Printing Office, 1973.

U.S. Department of Defense. "Berlin Since World War II: A Chronology." DoD Fact Sheet 2-G, January 2, 1959.

———. *The Pentagon Papers: The Defense Department History of United States Decisionmaking on Vietnam* (Gravel edition). 4 vols. Boston: Beacon Press, 1971.

———. Joint Chiefs of Staff. Joint Secretariat. Historical Division. "Military Actions or Campaigns Undertaken by the United States Which Were Not Supported by a Formal Declaration of War by the Congress." July 30, 1959.

———. Office of the Assistant Secretary for Public Affairs. "Press Briefings" (irregular).

U.S. Department of State. Bureau of Public Affairs. Historical Office. "Armed Actions Taken by the United States Without a Declaration of War, 1789–1967." Research Project No. 806A, August 1967.

U.S. Department of the Air Force. "Incidents Reported Between United States and Communist Bloc Nations." [1963.]

———. Air Forces in Europe. "Headquarters U.S. Air Forces in Europe, History." Monthly: February 1944–June 1948.

———. ———. "Historical Data, U.S. Air Forces in Europe, 1 January–30 June, 1950."

———. ———. Office of Information Services. Historical Division. "A Short History of the United States Air Forces in Europe, 1949–1954." Rev. March 20, 1954.

———. Air Materiel Command. "United States Air Force Postwar Chronology, 1 September 1945–15 November 1950."

————. Caribbean Air Command. "History, Caribbean Air Command." Irregular; 1946–55, not inclusive.

————. Fifth Air Force. "History of the Fifth Air Force." Semiannual; inclusive: January 1, 1949–June 24, 1950; July 1, 1953–June 30, 1955.

————. ————. Office of Information Services. Historical Division. "Fifth Air Force in Formosa, 25 January 1955–1 June 1955."

————. Pacific Air Forces. Historical Division. Directorate of Information. "The United States Air Force in the Pacific." February 1969.

————. Seventeenth Air Force. "History, 17th Air Force." Irregular; inclusive: April 25–June 30, 1953; January–December 1954, vol. 1; January–December 1955, vol. 1.

————. Seventh Air Force. "Pacific Air Command (7th Air Force) Annual History." 1947.

————. Strategic Air Command. "History, Strategic Air Command," vol. 1. Irregular; inclusive: January 1, 1948–June 30, 1950.

————. ————. "The Development of the Strategic Air Command 1940–1973." September 19, 1974.

————. Third Air Force. "Historical Data, Headquarters, Third Air Force." Irregular; inclusive: May 1951–December 1954.

————. Thirteenth Air Force. "Semi-Annual History." 1955.

————. ————. "13th Air Force Operational History, 1 July 1955–31 December 1955," vol. 2.

————. Twelfth Air Force. "Twelfth Air Force History." Semiannual; inclusive: 1948–49, 1951–54.

————. U.S. Air Force Europe. Office of History. "Historical Highlights: United States Air Forces in Europe, 1954–1973." Prepared by R. Bruce Harley. USAFE Historical Monograph Series, no. 4, 1974.

————. 317th Troop Carrier Wing. "Historical Data, 317th Troop Carrier Wing, Medium." Irregular; inclusive: July 14, 1952–October 31, 1952, vols. 1–2; July 1, 1953–August 31, 1953, vols. 1–2; July–December 1958.

————. 464th Troop Carrier Wing. "History of the 464th Troop Carrier Wing (M)." Semiannual; inclusive: January–June 1957; January–June 1958.

————. 513th Troop Carrier Group (Special). "Operation Vittles: Historical Analysis of Problems Involved at Group Level."

————. 1602d Air Transport Wing and 322d Air Division. "History of the 1602d Air Transport Wing (M) 31 March 1969, and 322d Air Division (MATS), 1 April–30 June 1964."

————. 1608th Air Transport Wing. "History of the 1608th Air Transport Wing (H)." 1964.

————. 1611th Air Transport Wing. "History of the 1611th Air Transport Wing." Semiannual; inclusive: 1954–57, 1959–64.

U.S. Department of the Army. Air Corps. Fifth Air Force. "Annual History, 5th Air Force." 1946, vol. 1 and annex 24; 1947, annex 20.

————. ————. Twelfth Air Force. "Twelfth Air Force History." Irregular; inclusive: May 17, 1946–December 1947.

————. Army War College. Strategic Studies Institute. "An Analysis of International Crises and Army Involvement (Historical Appraisal, 1945–1974), Final Report." 1975.

————. Eighth Army. "Eighth U.S. Army Chronology." Semiannual; inclusive: July 1, 1970–June 30, 1971; January 1–June 30, 1972.

————. Eighty-second Airborne Division. "Eighty-second Airborne Division, Summary of Activities." Annual: 1963–72.

————. Fifth Infantry Division (Mechanized). "Annual Historical Supplements." 1965–70.

————. First Armored Division. "Annual History." 1963–73, not inclusive.

————. First Cavalry Division. "Annual History." 1963–73, not inclusive.

————. ————. "First Cavalry Unit History, 1952–1954."

————. First Infantry Division. "First Infantry Division (Mechanized) and Fort Riley History, Annual Supplement." Inclusive: 1963–64, 1970–73.

————. Fourth Infantry Division. "Annual History." Inclusive: 1963–64, 1966–67, 1970–71.

————. Ninth Corps. "Ninth Corps Unit History, 1940–1963."

————. Ninth Infantry Division. "Annual History." 1963–73, not inclusive.

————. Office of the Chief of Military History. "U.S. Army Expansion and Readiness, 1961–1962." Prepared by Robert W. Coakley and others.

————. ————. "U.S. Defense Policies from World War II." Army Historical Series.

――――. Second Armored Division. "Annual Historical Summaries." Inclusive: 1965–69, 1971–73.

――――. Second Infantry Division. "Annual History." 1963–73, not inclusive.

――――. Southern Command. "Headquarters, U.S. Army Forces Southern Command, Annual Report of Major Activities." Inclusive: 1967–70, 1972–73.

――――. Third Army. "History of the United States Third Army, 1918–1962." Annual supplements, inclusive: 1963–66.

――――. 18th Airborne Corps. "Annual Historical Supplement." Inclusive: 1963–64, 1966, 1968–72.

――――. 24th Infantry Division. "History." Annual supplements, 1963–73, not inclusive.

――――. 25th Infantry Division. "Tropic Lightning, 1 October 1941–10 October 1966."

――――. 101st Airborne Division. "Annual History." 1963–73, not inclusive.

――――. ――――. "History of the 101st Airborne Division, 1942–1964."

――――. 193d Infantry Brigade. "Annual History." 1963–73, not inclusive.

――――. 350th Infantry Regiment. "350th Infantry in Occupation with the 88th 'Blue Devil' Division in Italy."

U.S. Department of the Navy. Atlantic Command and Fleet. "Fleet History." Irregular; inclusive: April 1, 1949–March 31, 1950.

――――. Atlantic Fleet. "Annual Report, Commander-in-Chief, U.S. Atlantic Fleet, Fiscal Year 1955."

――――. ――――. "CINCLANTFLT, Annual Report, Fiscal Year 1965."

――――. ――――. "COMSOLANT Command History." Annual; inclusive: 1958–64, 1966–73.

――――. ――――. "Report of the Commander-in-Chief, U.S. Atlantic Fleet." Irregular; inclusive: July 1, 1949–June 30, 1951; August 15, 1951–June 30, 1954.

――――. ――――. "U.S. Atlantic Fleet Command History." Annual; inclusive: 1958–59, 1961.

――――. ――――. "U.S. Atlantic Fleet, Second Fleet Historical Report." Annual; inclusive: 1959–61, 1964, 1966–71.

――――. ――――. "U.S. Atlantic Fleet, Second Task Fleet Command Narrative, 1 October 1946–30 September 1947."

————. ————. South Atlantic Force. "U.S. Atlantic Fleet, South Atlantic Force, Command Narrative." 1946.

————. Caribbean Sea Frontier. "Command Historical Report, Caribbean Sea Frontier." Annual; inclusive: 1959–72.

————. Commander, Guantanamo. "Disorder at Port au Prince and Action Taken by This Command, January 15, 1946."

————. Commander, U.S. Naval Forces Mediterranean. "Report to Commander, U.S. Naval Forces in Europe, Visit to Beirut, Lebanon, December 11, 1946."

————. ————. "Task Force 125, Exercises, August 23–27 and September 5, 1946; Report to Commander, U.S. Naval Forces Europe."

————. Eastern Atlantic and Mediterranean. "Command History." Irregular; inclusive: July 1, 1947–July 1, 1953.

————. First Fleet. "Commander, First Fleet, Command Historical Report." Irregular; inclusive: 1946–59, 1964–65.

————. First Task Fleet. "Commander, First Task Fleet, United States Pacific Fleet, Command Narrative, 1 October 1946–30 September 1947."

————. Middle East Force. "Commander, Middle East Force, Command History." Annual; inclusive: 1949–62, 1966, 1969–70.

————. ————. "Commander, Middle East Force; Report of Operations and Conditions of Command, 1 July 1959–18 February 1960."

————. Naval Forces, Eastern Atlantic and Mediterranean. "U.S. Naval Forces, Eastern Atlantic and Mediterranean." Irregular; inclusive: April 1, 1947–July 1, 1953.

————. Naval Historical Center. Operational Archives. "Chronology of Naval Events, 1960–1974." Prepared by Barbara A. Gilmore.

————. ————. ————. "Short of War" Documentation, Special List. Nos. 1 and 2.

————. Seventh Fleet. "Command History." Annual; inclusive: 1946–64.

————. Sixth Fleet. "History of the Sixth Fleet." May 5, 1959, and annual supplements; inclusive: 1959–64, 1967.

————. Southern Command. "Command Historical Report." 1965, 1968.

————. U.S. Marine Corps Headquarters. Historical Division. "A Brief History of the First Marines." 1968.

————. ————. ————. "A Brief History of the 2d Marines." 1962.

———. ———. ———. "A Brief History of the 3d Marines." 1968.

———. ———. ———. "A Brief History of the 4th Marines." 1970.

———. ———. ———. "A Brief History of the 5th Marines." 1968.

———. ———. ———. "A Brief History of the 9th Marines." 1967.

———. ———. ———. "A Brief History of the 11th Marines." 1968.

———. ———. ———. "A Brief History of the 12th Marines." 1972.

———. ———. ———. "A Concise History of the United States Marine Corps 1775–1969." Prepared by Capt. William D. Parker, USMC (Ret.). 1970.

———. ———. ———. "A Chronology of the United States Marine Corps." Vols. 2–4, 1935–69. 1971.

———. ———. ———. "Marines in Lebanon, 1958." 1966.

———. ———. ———. "The United States Marines in North China, 1945–1949." Rev. ed., 1968.

———. ———. Historical Branch. "Operations, Deployments, and Shows of Force by U.S. Marines Outside Continental Limits U.S. in Peacetime, 1800–1958." N.d.

Letters and Memorandums

Chafee, John H. (Secretary of the Navy). Letter to Sen. Clifford P. Case, September 5, 1969. Contains: "Unclassified Summary of Attack Carrier Support of U.S. Foreign Policy Since the Korean War"; and "Classified Summary of Attack Carrier Support of U.S. Foreign Policy Since the Korean War." Available at U.S. Department of the Navy, Naval Historical Center, Operational Archives.

Donaldson, J. C., Jr. "Memorandum to Director of Naval History and Curator for the Navy Department," August 20, 1969. Available at U.S. Department of the Navy, Naval Historical Center, Operational Archives.

Moorer, Adm. T. H. (Chief of Naval Operations). Letter to Sen. Walter F. Mondale, September 6, 1969. Contains: "Summary of Wars/Near Wars Since 1946." Available at U.S. Department of the Navy, Naval Historical Center, Operational Archives.

U.S. Department of the Navy. Commander, Carrier Air Group Twelve. Memorandum to Commander, Air Force, U.S. Pacific Fleet. Contains: "Operational Report of CVG-12 Deployed for the Period of 3 March

1954–15 September 1954." Available at U.S. Department of the Navy, Naval Historical Center, Operational Archives.

————. Commander, Carrier Division Five. Memorandum to Commander, Air Force, U.S. Pacific Fleet. Contains: "Carrier Division Training During Western Pacific Deployment, Comments on." Available at U.S. Department of the Navy, Naval Historical Center, Operational Archives.

————. U.S. Naval Attaché, Ankara, Turkey. "International Relations, Visit of U.S. Naval Vessels, Intelligence Report." December 1, 1946.

U.S. Embassy, Havana, Cuba. "The Frustrated Plot to Invade the Dominican Republic, Summer 1947." Report no. 4434. Prepared by V. Lansing Collins, Jr., October 17, 1947.

Newspaper and Journal Chronologies

Africa Report (monthly). "News in Brief" (title varies).

Africa Research Bulletin (monthly). "Political, Social and Economic" edition; "Political Developments with Nations Overseas."

Asian Recorder (weekly).

Cahiers de l'Orient Contemporain (quarterly). "Le Moyen Orient et en Politique Internationale."

Current History (monthly). "Chronology."

"Current News" (U.S. Department of Defense, daily).

Middle East Journal (quarterly). "Chronology."

New York Times Index (annual). Subheadings (e.g., 1974): Airplanes, American Nations, Armament, Europe, Far East, Indian Ocean Area, International Relations, Mediterranean Area, Middle East, NATO, Ships and Shipping, U.S. Armament and Defense.

U.S. Naval Institute Proceedings (annual Naval Review issue). "Chronology."

Other Sources

Byely, Col. B., and others. *Marxism-Leninism on War and Army (A Soviet View)*. Moscow: Progress Publisher, 1972.

Cable, James. *Gunboat Diplomacy: Political Applications of Limited Naval Force.* New York: Praeger, 1971.

Cady, Richard H. *U.S. Naval Operations in Low Level Warfare.* Detroit: Bendix Corp., Report BSR 2453, December 1968.

Cady, Richard, and William Prince. *Political Conflicts, 1944–1966.* Ann Arbor: Inter-University Consortium for Political Research, 1974.

Chronology of the Sea Service, 1775–1959. Washington: All Hands, n.d.

Cooney, David M. *A Chronology of the U.S. Navy: 1775–1965.* New York: Franklin Watts, 1965.

George, Alexander L., and Richard Smoke. *Deterrence in American Foreign Policy: Theory and Practice.* New York: Columbia University Press, 1974.

Greaves, Lt. Col. Fielding Lewis. " 'Peace' in Our Time," *New York Times Magazine,* April 14, 1963.

Haas, Ernest B., and others. *Conflict Management by International Organizations.* Morristown, N.J.: General Learning Press, 1972.

Naval and Maritime Chronology, Compiled from Ten Years of Naval Review. Annapolis, Md.: Naval Institute Press, 1973.

Polmar, Norman. *Aircraft Carriers: A Graphic History of Carrier Aviation and Its Influence on World Events.* New York: Doubleday, 1969.

Rapport, Leonard, and Arthur Northwood, Jr. *Rendezvous with Destiny: A History of the 101st Airborne Division.* Greenville, Texas: 101st Division Association, 1965.

Richardson, B. P., and others. *An Analysis of Recent Conflicts.* Arlington, Va.: Center for Naval Analyses, 1970.

Xydis, Stephen G. "The Genesis of the Sixth Fleet," *U.S. Naval Institute Proceedings,* vol. 84 (August 1958), pp. 41–50.

The Incidents

THIS STUDY covers the period from January 1, 1946, through December 31, 1975. We found that the United States used its armed forces as a political instrument, as defined, on 215 occasions during this period.[1]

These 215 incidents are listed in this appendix, with a descriptive phrase and the month and year when the use of armed forces was initiated. In many instances the situation occasioned an almost immediate use of armed forces; in other instances a lag of some months occurred.

It is important to note that certain situations—for example, the political crises in Lebanon in 1958, in the Congo in 1960–64, and in the Dominican Republic in 1965–66—are considered two or more incidents rather than just one. This approach allows a more useful analysis of instances in which there occurred either two or more clear modal uses of U.S. armed forces or a significant change in the nature of the situation.

List of Incidents

1. Coup and civil strife in Haiti	January 1946
2. Security of Turkey	March 1946
3. Political conflict in Greece	April 1946

1. More recent research (done after this study was concluded) turned up three additional U.S. naval actions that occurred in early 1975. In January 1975 a carrier task group was deployed near Cyprus in response to demonstrations there. In early February another carrier group visited Mombasa as a demonstration of friendship toward Kenya and the Kenyatta government. Also that month, two U.S. naval vessels took up a position in the Red Sea, apparently because of fighting between Ethiopian government forces and Eritrean rebels.

4. Civil war in China	April	1946
5. Security of Trieste	June	1946
6. Security of Turkey	August	1946
7. Insurgents in Greece	September	1946
8. Inauguration of president in Chile	November	1946
9. U.S. aircraft shot down by Yugoslavia	November	1946
10. Political change in Lebanon	December	1946
11. Inauguration of president in Uruguay	February	1947
12. Civil war in Greece	April	1947
13. Cuba supports anti-Trujillists	May	1947
14. Security of Turkey	May	1947
15. Security of Trieste	August	1947
16. Elections in Italy	November	1947
17. Improved relations with Argentina	January	1948
18. Security of Berlin	January	1948
19. Security of Trieste	January	1948
20. Arab-Israeli war	January	1948
21. Interests in Persian Gulf	January	1948
22. Security of Norway	April	1948
23. Security of Berlin	April	1948
24. Security of Berlin	June	1948
25. Change of government in China	December	1949
26. Political developments in Indochina	March	1950
27. France–Viet Minh war	June	1950
28. Korean War: Formosa Straits	June	1950
29. Korean War: security of Europe	July	1950
30. Political developments in Lebanon	August	1950
31. Security of Yugoslavia	March	1951
32. Inauguration of president in Liberia	January	1952
33. Improved relations with Spain	January	1952
34. Security of Turkey	August	1952
35. Political developments in Lebanon	November	1952
36. China-Taiwan conflict	February	1953
37. Soviet aircraft fire on NATO aircraft	March	1953
38. End of war in Korea	July	1953
39. Security of Japan/South Korea	August	1953
40. France–Viet Minh war: Dienbienphu	March	1954
41. Guatemala accepts Soviet bloc support	May	1954

42.	France–Viet Minh war: Dienbienphu	July 1954
43.	British airliner shot down by China	July 1954
44.	China-Taiwan conflict: Tachen Islands	August 1954
45.	Election in Honduras	September 1954
46.	Accord on Trieste	October 1954
47.	Nicaragua supports insurgents in Costa Rica	January 1955
48.	Austrian State Treaty	August 1955
49.	China-Taiwan conflict	January 1956
50.	Egypt-Israel conflict: Red Sea	February 1956
51.	British General Glubb ousted in Jordan	April 1956
52.	Egypt nationalizes Suez Canal	July 1956
53.	Suez crisis	October 1956
54.	Security of U.S. military personnel and bases in Morocco	October 1956
55.	Egypt-Israel conflict: Red Sea	February 1957
56.	Political-military crisis in Indonesia	February 1957
57.	Political-military crisis in Jordan	April 1957
58.	Civil strife in Taiwan	May 1957
59.	Coup and civil strife in Haiti	June 1957
60.	Civil strife and elections in Lebanon	June 1957
61.	China-Taiwan conflict	July 1957
62.	Political developments in Syria	August 1957
63.	Indonesia-Netherlands crisis	December 1957
64.	Coup and civil strife in Venezuela	January 1958
65.	Political-military crisis in Indonesia	February 1958
66.	Political crisis in Lebanon	May 1958
67.	Security of Vice President Nixon in Venezuela	May 1958
68.	Americans seized by insurgents in Cuba	July 1958
69.	Political crisis in Lebanon	July 1958
70.	Political crisis in Jordan	July 1958
71.	China-Taiwan crisis: Quemoy and Matsu	July 1958
72.	Insurgents in Cuba	October 1958
73.	Castro seizes power in Cuba	January 1959
74.	Cambodia-Thailand crisis	January 1959
75.	Security of Berlin	February 1959
76.	Atlantic cables cut	February 1959
77.	Cuba supports insurgents: Panama	April 1959
78.	Security of Berlin	May 1959

116. Political instability in Guatemala	December 1962
117. Inauguration of president in Dominican Republic	February 1963
118. Insurgents seize Venezuelan merchantman *Anzoatequi*	February 1963
119. Civil war in Yemen	February 1963
120. Dominican Republic–Haiti conflict	April 1963
121. Withdrawal of missiles from Turkey	April 1963
122. Political crisis in Jordan	April 1963
123. Civil war in Laos	April 1963
124. Civil war in Laos	May 1963
125. Buddhist crisis in South Vietnam	June 1963
126. Dominican Republic–Haiti conflict	August 1963
127. Coup in Dominican Republic	September 1963
128. China-Taiwan crisis	September 1963
129. Security of Berlin	October 1963
130. Indonesia-Malaysia conflict	November 1963
131. Cuba supports insurgents: Venezuela	November 1963
132. Improved relations with Israel	November 1963
133. Assassination of Diem in South Vietnam	November 1963
134. Improved relations with Soviet Union	December 1963
135. Cuba supports insurgents: Mexico	January 1964
136. Security of Panama Canal Zone	January 1964
137. Coup and civil strife in Zanzibar	January 1964
138. Cyprus-Greece-Turkey crisis	January 1964
139. Coup in South Vietnam	January 1964
140. Coup in Brazil	March 1964
141. Political developments in Cambodia	March 1964
142. Security of Guantanamo base in Cuba	April 1964
143. Civil war in Laos	April 1964
144. Elections in Panama	May 1964
145. Civil strife in British Guiana	May 1964
146. Cyprus-Greece-Turkey crisis	June 1964
147. Cuba supports insurgents: Dominican Republic	July 1964
148. Civil war in Congo	August 1964
149. Cyprus-Greece-Turkey crisis	August 1964
150. Insurgents in Haiti	August 1964
151. North Vietnam fires on U.S. ships: Tonkin Gulf	August 1964

152. Indonesia-Malaysia crisis	September 1964
153. Cuba supports insurgents in Venezuela	October 1964
154. Civil war in the Congo: hostages in Stanleyville	November 1964
155. Viet Cong attack Bien Hoa barracks in South Vietnam	November 1964
156. Worsened relations with Tanzania	January 1965
157. Viet Cong attack Pleiku air base in South Vietnam	February 1965
158. Viet Cong attack Qui Nhon barracks in South Vietnam	February 1965
159. Civil war in Dominican Republic	April 1965
160. Cuba supports insurgents: British Guiana	April 1965
161. West German parliament meets in Berlin	April 1965
162. Cuba supports insurgents: Venezuela	May 1965
163. War in Vietnam: withdrawal of troops from Europe	July 1965
164. Political developments in Cyprus	July 1965
165. Civil war in Yemen	August 1965
166. Civil war in Dominican Republic	September 1965
167. India-Pakistan war	September 1965
168. Attempted coup in Indonesia	October 1965
169. Improved relations with Egypt	September 1966
170. Israel attacks Jordan: Samu	December 1966
171. Insurgents in Thailand	December 1966
172. Coup in Greece	April 1967
173. Improved relations with France	May 1967
174. Arab-Israeli war	May 1967
175. Insurgents in the Congo	July 1967
176. Political developments in Cyprus	August 1967
177. Egypt sinks Israeli destroyer *Eilat*	October 1967
178. *Pueblo* seized by North Korea	January 1968
179. Invasion of Czechoslovakia	September 1968
180. Israel attacks Lebanon: Beirut airport	December 1968
181. North Korea attacks South Korean fishing boats	December 1968
182. EC-121 shot down by North Korea	April 1969
183. Civil strife in Curaçao	May 1969
184. Political developments in Libya	November 1969
185. Insurgents in Haiti	April 1970
186. Civil strife in Trinidad	April 1970

187. Civil strife in Jordan	June 1970
188. Arab-Israeli cease-fire agreement	August 1970
189. Civil war in Jordan	September 1970
190. Soviet submarine base in Cuba	October 1970
191. Civil war in Cambodia	January 1971
192. Withdrawal of troops from South Korea	February 1971
193. Duvalier dies in Haiti	April 1971
194. Improved relations with Soviet Union	April 1971
195. Stand-down in Sea of Japan	May 1971
196. India-Pakistan (Bangladesh) war	December 1971
197. Seizure of merchantmen by Cuba	February 1972
198. North Vietnam offensive in South Vietnam	May 1972
199. Breakdown in peace talks with North Vietnam	December 1972
200. Civil war in Laos	February 1973
201. Civil war in Cambodia	February 1973
202. Peace agreement with North Vietnam	February 1973
203. Civil strife in Lebanon	May 1973
204. Civil war in Cambodia	August 1973
205. Arab-Israeli war	October 1973
206. Arab oil embargo	October 1973
207. Civil war in Cambodia	January 1974
208. Egypt-Israel Sinai agreement	February 1974
209. Improved relations with Egypt	April 1974
210. Cyprus-Greece-Turkey crisis	July 1974
211. Arab oil policy	November 1974
212. Collapse of regime in South Vietnam	March 1975
213. Collapse of regime in Cambodia	April 1975
214. Improved relations with Soviet Union	May 1975
215. Cambodia seizes U.S. merchantman *Mayaguez*	May 1975

Sample Selection and Characteristics

AFTER WE HAD decided on a 15 percent (33-incident) sample, the question arose whether the sample should be chosen randomly or structured with reference to particular variables. A random sample is likely to reflect more perfectly the "population" from which it is taken; however, if the sample is not very large, the examination of a variable of particular interest may not be possible. In order to insure against this risk the sample was stratified with reference to four variables: the level of armed forces used in the incident by the United States; the degree and nature of involvement by the Soviet Union and China; the overall quality of East-West relations at the time; and the situational context preceding U.S. action. The list below presents the typologies for these four variables that were used in selecting the sample:[1]

Level of U.S. armed forces used:
  Two or more major components
  One major component
  Standard or minor components only
Degree and nature of USSR/PRC involvement:
  Participated, and threatened or actually used force
  Participated, but did not threaten or use force
  Did not participate

1. Major components of the armed forces when used for political objectives are more than a battalion of ground forces, two or more aircraft carriers (or battleships), or at least one combat air wing. Standard components are more than a company but no more than a battalion of ground forces, one aircraft carrier (or battleship), or one or more squadrons but less than a wing of combat aircraft.

554

Periodization of quality of East-West relations:
  1946–47
  1948–52
  1953–56
  1957–62
  1963–68
  1969–75
Context of U.S. involvement:
  Interstate (incident stemmed from relationship between two or more
    states other than the United States)
  Intrastate (incident stemmed from internal situation)
  United States involved directly (incident stemmed from relationship
    between United States and another actor, or hostile act directed
    at United States)

Table C-1 presents a summary analysis of some of these characteristics
and provides a comparison of the sample with the total 215-incident data
file.

The categorizations of the level of U.S. armed forces used and the
degree of USSR/PRC involvement are rank ordered or scaled. The periodization of the overall East-West relationship may be converted into
a rank ordering by rearranging the various sets of years. It was con-
ceivable that two or more of these three variables might be correlated
with one another and thus perhaps reflect only one or two factors. Not to
entertain this possibility was to risk wasted effort as well as a misleading
analysis. In fact, though, these variables are not correlated with each
other or with any ordering of the situational context typology.

Obviously it was impossible to obtain a perfectly stratified sample,
given the numbers of categories and the actual cell distribution. Nevertheless, this approach was useful insofar as it did provide a sample which
allowed a more valid examination of variables of particular concern.

One hundred and sixty-two cells were obtained by multiplying together the numbers of categories of each variable—as $3 \times 3 \times 6 \times 3$
= 162. Of these, 46 were "dead" cells (i.e., they contained no incidents)
and 83 contained three incidents or fewer. In selecting cases for the
sample we grouped the latter in sets containing one, two, and three incidents, and cases were selected randomly from each set. The remaining

Table C-1. *Comparison of All Incidents and Sample*
Percent

Characteristic	All incidents	Sample
Regional		
Central America/Caribbean	23.3	24.2
East Asia	9.3	9.1
Europe	20.0	9.1
Middle East	17.7	27.3
Southeast Asia	19.1	24.2
Other	10.7	6.1
Time period		
1946–50	14.0	6.1
1951–55	8.4	3.0
1956–60	20.9	27.3
1961–65	34.9	30.3
1966–70	10.7	18.2
1971–75	11.2	15.2
Situational context (A)		
Interstate[a]	29.8	30.3
Intrastate	43.3	45.5
U.S. directly involved	26.0	24.2
Other	0.9	0.0
Situational context (B)		
Violent/hostile act directed at U.S.	68.8	72.7
Nonviolent relations with U.S.		
(friendly or unfriendly)	30.3	27.3
Other	0.9	0.0
Actor		
National government	76.8	76.1
Insurgents/civilian party or group	14.7	16.2
Military faction	3.0	2.6
International or regional		
organization	5.4	5.1

a. Between states other than the United States.

33 cells, containing four or more incidents each, were considered large enough for a random choice to be made from within each cell. The number of cases selected from each cell, or set, was proportional to its relative size. The objective was to approximate, as closely as possible, 15 percent of the incidents in the cell or set.

Bibliography for Utility Analysis

Abidi, Aqil H. H. *Jordan: A Political Study, 1948–1957*. New York: Asia Publishing House, 1965.

Acheson, Dean. *Present at the Creation*. New York: Norton, 1969.

Adams, Nina S., and Alfred W. McCoy, eds. *Laos: War and Revolution*. New York: Harper and Row, 1970.

Adams, Thomas W., and Alvin J. Cottrell. *Cyprus Between East and West*. Baltimore: Johns Hopkins Press, 1968.

Allison, John M. *Ambassador from the Prairie, or Allison Wonderland*. Boston: Houghton Mifflin, 1973.

Aruri, Naseer H. *Jordan: A Study in Political Development (1921–1965)*. The Hague: Martinus Nijhoff, 1972.

Badeau, John S. *The American Approach to the Arab World*. New York: Harper and Row, 1968.

Barber, Willard F., and C. Neale Ronning. *Internal Security and Military Power: Counterinsurgency and Civic Action in Latin America*. Columbus: Ohio State University Press, 1966.

Bohlen, Charles E. *Witness to History, 1929–1969*. New York: Norton, 1973.

Bolt, Beranek, and Newman, Inc. *The Control of Local Conflict: Latin American Case Studies*. Vols. 2 and 3. Waltham, Mass.: 1969. Prepared for U.S. Arms Control and Disarmament Agency.

Bonsal, Philip W. *Cuba, Castro and the United States*. Pittsburgh: University of Pittsburgh Press, 1971.

Bosch, Juan. *The Unfinished Experiment: Democracy in the Dominican Republic*. New York: Praeger, 1965.

Bowie, Robert. *Suez 1956: International Crisis and the Role of Law*. New York: Oxford University Press, 1974.

Bowles, Chester. *Promises to Keep: My Years in Public Life, 1941–1969*. New York: Harper and Row, 1971.

Brandon, Henry. *The Retreat of American Power*. Garden City, N.Y.: Doubleday, 1973.

557

Brecher, Michael. *Decisions in Israel's Foreign Policy.* New Haven: Yale University Press, 1975.

Burchett, Wilfred G. *The Furtive War: The United States in Vietnam and Laos.* New York: International Publishers, 1963.

Butterworth, Robert Lyle, with Margaret E. Scranton. *Managing Interstate Conflict.* Pittsburgh: University of Pittsburgh Press, 1976.

Byrnes, James F. *All in One Lifetime.* New York: Harper, 1958.

——. *Speaking Frankly.* New York: Harper, 1947.

Cable, James. *Gunboat Diplomacy: Political Applications of Limited Naval Force.* New York: Praeger, 1971.

Campbell, John C. *Defense of the Middle East: Problems of American Policy.* New York: Harper, 1958.

Centre de Récherche et d'Information Socio-Politiques (CRISP). *Congo 1959.* 2d ed., rev. Brussels, 1960.

Chen, King C. "Hanoi's Three Decisions and the Escalation of the Vietnam War," *Political Science Quarterly,* vol. 90 (September 1975), pp. 239–59.

Churchill, Winston S. *The Second World War: Triumph and Tragedy.* Boston: Houghton Mifflin, 1953.

Clark, Mark W. *From the Danube to the Yalu.* New York: Harper, 1954.

Copeland, Miles. *The Game of Nations: The Amorality of Power Politics.* New York: Simon and Schuster, 1970.

Crassweller, Robert D. *Trujillo: The Life and Times of a Caribbean Dictator.* New York: Macmillan, 1966.

Djilas, Milovan. *Conversations with Stalin.* New York: Harcourt, Brace and World, 1962.

Dobney, Frederick J., ed. *Selected Papers of Will Clayton.* Baltimore: Johns Hopkins Press, 1971.

Dommen, Arthur J. *Conflict in Laos: The Politics of Neutralization.* Rev. ed. New York: Praeger, 1971.

Draper, Theodore. *Castro's Revolution: Myths and Realities.* New York: Praeger, 1962.

Eden, Anthony. *Full Circle.* Boston: Houghton Mifflin, 1960.

Eisenhower, Dwight D. *The White House Years: Mandate for Change, 1953–1956.* Garden City, N.Y.: Doubleday, 1963.

——. *The White House Years: Waging Peace, 1956–1961.* Garden City, N.Y.: Doubleday, 1965.

Espaillat, Arturo R. *Trujillo: The Last Caesar.* Chicago: Henry Regnery, 1963.

Fagen, Richard R., and Wayne A. Cornelius, Jr., eds. *Political Power in Latin America: Seven Confrontations.* Englewood Cliffs, N.J.: Prentice-Hall, 1970.

Feis, Herbert. *From Trust to Terror: The Onset of the Cold War, 1945–1950.* New York: Norton, 1970.

Ferrell, Robert H. *The American Secretaries of State.* Vol. 15: *George C. Marshall.* New York: Cooper Square, 1966.

Finer, Herman. *Dulles Over Suez: The Theory and Practice of His Diplomacy.* Chicago: Quadrangle, 1964.

Gaddis, John L. *The United States and the Origins of the Cold War, 1941–1947.* New York: Columbia University Press, 1972.

Gardner, Lloyd C. *Architects of Illusion: Men and Ideas in American Foreign Policy, 1941–1949.* Chicago: Quadrangle, 1970.

Gavin, James M. *War and Peace in the Space Age.* New York: Harper, 1958.

George, Alexander L., and Richard Smoke. *Deterrence in American Foreign Policy: Theory and Practice.* New York: Columbia University Press, 1974.

George, Alexander L., David K. Hall, and William E. Simons. *The Limits of Coercive Diplomacy: Laos, Cuba, Vietnam.* Boston: Little, Brown, 1971.

Gerard-Libois, J., and Benoit Verhaegen. *Congo 1960.* 2 vols. Brussels: Centre de Récherche et d'Information Socio-Politiques, 1960.

Glubb, John Bagot. *A Soldier With the Arabs.* London: Hodder and Stoughton, 1957.

Goldenberg, Boris. *The Cuban Revolution and Latin America.* New York: Praeger, 1965.

Goold-Adams, Richard. *John Foster Dulles: A Reappraisal.* New York: Appleton-Century-Crofts, 1962.

Gott, Richard. "The Kuwait Incident," in D. C. Watt, ed. *Survey of International Affairs, 1961.* London: Oxford University Press, 1965.

Haddad, George M. *Revolutions and Military Rule in the Middle East: The Arab States.* Part 1: *Iraq, Syria, Lebanon and Jordan.* New York: Robert Speller and Sons, 1971.

Halberstam, David. *The Best and the Brightest.* New York: Random House, 1969.

Hall, Luella J. *The United States and Morocco, 1776–1956.* Metuchen, N.J.: Scarecrow Press, 1971.

Heikal, Mohamed. *The Cairo Documents.* Garden City, N.Y.: Doubleday, 1973.

Hilsman, Roger. *To Move a Nation: The Politics of Foreign Policy in the Administration of John F. Kennedy.* Garden City, N.Y.: Doubleday, 1967.

Hoopes, Townsend. *The Devil and John Foster Dulles.* Boston: Little, Brown, 1973.

———. *The Limits of Intervention.* New York: David McKay, 1969.

Hoskyns, Catherine. *The Congo Since Independence: January 1960–December 1961.* New York: Oxford University Press, 1961.

Hughes, Emmett John. *The Ordeal of Power: A Political Memoir of the Eisenhower Years.* New York: Atheneum, 1963.

Hussein, King of Jordan. *Uneasy Lies the Head.* New York: Bernard Geis, 1962.

Institute for Strategic Studies. *Strategic Survey 1970, The Middle East.* London: Institute for Strategic Studies, 1971.

Jackson, D. Bruce. *Castro, The Kremlin and Communism in Latin America.* Washington: Johns Hopkins School of Advanced International Studies, 1969.

Johnson, Lyndon B. *The Vantage Point: Perspectives of the Presidency, 1963–1969.* New York: Holt, Rinehart and Winston, 1971.

Kalb, Marvin, and Bernard Kalb. *Kissinger.* Boston: Little, Brown, 1974.

Langer, Paul F., and Joseph J. Zasloff. *North Vietnam and the Pathet Lao: Partners in the Struggle for Laos.* Cambridge: Harvard University Press, 1970.

Laqueur, Walter Z. "Communism in Jordan," *The World Today,* vol. 12 (March 1956), pp. 109–19.

Lederer, William J. *A Nation of Sheep.* New York: Norton, 1961.

Levine, Daniel H. *Conflict and Political Change in Venezuela.* Princeton: Princeton University Press, 1973.

Lieuwen, Edwin. *U.S. Policy in Latin America.* New York: Praeger, 1965.

Lodge, Henry Cabot. *The Storm Has Many Eyes: A Personal Narrative.* New York: Norton, 1973.

Lott, Leo B. *Venezuela and Paraguay: Political Modernity and Tradition in Conflict.* New York: Holt, Rinehart and Winston, 1972.

Love, Kennett. *Suez: The Twice Fought War.* New York: McGraw-Hill, 1969.

Lowenthal, Abraham F. *The Dominican Intervention.* Cambridge: Harvard University Press, 1972.

————. *The Dominican Republic: The Politics of Chaos.* Washington: The Brookings Institution, 1969. Reprint 158.

————. "Foreign Aid as a Political Instrument: The Case of the Dominican Republic," *Public Policy,* vol. 14 (1965).

Lumumba, Patrice. *Le Congo: Terre d'Avenir: Est-Il Menacé?* Brussels: Office de Publicité, 1961.

Macmillan, Harold. *Pointing the Way, 1959–1961.* New York: Harper and Row, 1972.

————. *Riding the Storm, 1956–1959.* London: Macmillan, 1971.

————. *Tides of Fortune, 1945–1955.* New York: Harper and Row, 1969.

Martin, John B. *Overtaken by Events: The Dominican Crisis From the Fall of Trujillo to the Civil War.* Garden City, N.Y.: Doubleday, 1966.

Maullin, Richard. *Soldiers, Guerrillas, and Politics in Colombia.* Lexington, Mass.: Lexington Press, 1973.

Mecham, John L. *The United States and Inter-American Security, 1889–1960.* Austin: University of Texas Press, 1961.

Mercier Vega, Luis. *Guerrillas in Latin America: The Technique of the Counter-State.* New York: Praeger, 1969.

Michel, Serge. *Uhuru Lumumba.* Paris: René Luillard, 1962.

Miller, Merle. *Plain Speaking: An Oral Biography of Harry S. Truman.* New York: Berkeley, 1973.

Millis, Walter, ed. *The Forrestal Diaries.* New York: Viking, 1951.

Mirsky, Jonathan, and Stephen E. Stonefield. "The Nam Tha Crisis: Kennedy and the New Frontier on the Brink," in Nina S. Adams and Alfred W. McCoy, *Laos: War and Revolution.* New York: Harper and Row, 1970.

Morrison, Delesseps S. *Latin American Mission: An Adventure in Hemisphere Diplomacy.* New York: Simon and Schuster, 1965.

Murphy, Robert. *Diplomat Among Warriors.* Garden City, N.Y.: Doubleday, 1964.

Nixon, Richard M. *Six Crises.* Garden City, N.Y.: Doubleday, 1962.

Nutting, Anthony. *Nasser.* London: Constable and Co., 1972.

──────. *No End of a Lesson: The Story of Suez.* New York: Clarkson N. Potter, 1967.

O'Ballance, Edgar. *Arab Guerrilla Power, 1967–1972.* London: Faber and Faber, 1974.

──────. *The Greek Civil War, 1944–1949.* London: Faber and Faber, 1966.

Packard, George R. III. *Protest in Tokyo: The Security Treaty Crisis of 1960.* Princeton: Princeton University Press, 1966.

Payne, James L. *Patterns of Conflict in Colombia.* New Haven: Yale University Press, 1968.

The Pentagon Papers: The Defense Department History of United States Decisionmaking on Vietnam. 4 vols., Gravel ed. Boston: Beacon Press, 1971.

Plank, John, ed. *Cuba and the United States: Long-Range Perspectives.* Washington: The Brookings Institution, 1967.

Quandt, William B., and others. *The Politics of Palestinian Nationalism.* Los Angeles: University of California Press, 1973.

Ridgway, Matthew B. *Soldier: The Memoirs of Matthew B. Ridgway.* New York: Harper, 1956.

Rubinstein, Alvin Z. *The Foreign Policy of the Soviet Union.* 3d ed. New York: Random House, 1972.

Sanchez, Jose Manuel. "U.S. Intervention in the Caribbean 1954–1965: Decisionmaking and the Information Input." Ph.D. dissertation, Columbia University, 1972.

Schlesinger, Arthur M., Jr. *A Thousand Days: John F. Kennedy in the White House.* Boston: Houghton Mifflin, 1965.

Seale, Patrick. *The Struggle for Syria: A Study of Post-War Arab Politics, 1945–1958.* New York: Oxford University Press, 1965.

Selden, Mark, ed. *Remaking Asia: Essays on the American Uses of Power.* New York: Random House, 1971.

Shaplen, Robert. *The Lost Revolution: The U.S. in Vietnam, 1946–1966.* Rev. ed. New York: Harper and Row, 1966.

Shulman, Marshall D. *Stalin's Foreign Policy Reappraised.* Cambridge: Harvard University Press, 1963.

Shwadran, Benjamin. *Jordan: A State of Tension.* New York: Council for Middle Eastern Affairs, 1959.

──────. "The Kuwait Incident," parts 1 and 2, *Middle Eastern Affairs,* vol. 13 (January and February 1962).

Slater, Jerome. *Intervention and Negotiation: The United States and the Dominican Revolution.* New York: Harper and Row, 1970.

Smith, Robert F. *What Happened in Cuba?* New York: Twayne Publishers, 1963.

Sorensen, Theodore C. *Kennedy.* New York: Harper and Row, 1965.

Stephens, Robert H. *Nasser: A Political Biography.* New York: Simon and Schuster, 1972.

Stevenson, Charles A. *The End of Nowhere.* Boston: Beacon Press, 1972.

Talbott, Strobe, ed. and trans. *Khrushchev Remembers,* vol. 1. Boston: Little, Brown, 1970.

Taylor, Maxwell D. *Swords and Plowshares.* New York: Norton, 1972.

————. *The Uncertain Trumpet.* New York: Harper, 1960.

Thomas, Hugh. *Suez.* New York: Harper and Row, 1966.

Tiet, Tran Minh. *Congo: Ex-Belge Entre l'Est et l'Ouest.* Paris: Nouvelles Editions Latines, 1962.

Torrey, Gordon H. *Syrian Politics and the Military, 1945–1958.* Columbus: Ohio State University Press, 1964.

Toye, Hugh. *Laos: Buffer State or Battleground.* London: Oxford University Press, 1968.

Trevelyan, Humphrey. *The Middle East in Revolution.* Boston: Gambit, 1970.

Truman, Harry S. *Memoirs,* vol. 1. Garden City, N.Y.: Doubleday, 1955.

————. *Memoirs,* vol. 2. Garden City, N.Y.: Doubleday, 1956.

Truman, Margaret. *Harry S. Truman.* New York: Morrow, 1973.

Twining, Nathan F. *Neither Liberty Nor Safety: A Hard Look at U.S. Military Policy and Strategy.* New York: Holt, Rinehart and Winston, 1966.

Ulam, Adam B. *Expansion and Coexistence: Soviet Foreign Policy, 1917–73.* 2d ed. New York: Praeger, 1974.

U.S. Congress. House. Committee on Foreign Affairs. Subcommittee on Inter-American Affairs. *Soviet Naval Activities in Cuba.* Hearings. 91:2. Washington: Government Printing Office, 1970.

U.S. Congress. Senate. Select Committee to Study Governmental Operations with Respect to Intelligence Activities. *Alleged Assassination Plots Involving Foreign Leaders.* 94:1. Washington: Government Printing Office, 1975.

U.S. Department of State. *Foreign Relations of the United States, 1946.* Vol. 3: *The Near East and Africa.* Washington: Government Printing Office, 1969.

————. *Foreign Relations of the United States, 1947.* Vol. 3: *The British Commonwealth and Europe.* Washington: Government Printing Office, 1972.

————. *Foreign Relations of the United States, 1948.* Vol. 3: *Western Europe.* Washington: Government Printing Office, 1974.

————. *Report of the Allied Mission to Observe the Greek Elections.* DOS Publication 2522. Washington: Government Printing Office, 1946.

Urquhart, Brian. *Hammarskjöld.* New York: Knopf, 1972.

Weinstein, Martin E. *Japan's Postwar Defense Policy, 1947–1968.* New York: Columbia University Press, 1971.

Weissman, Stephen R. *American Foreign Policy in the Congo, 1960–1964.* Ithaca, N.Y.: Cornell University Press, 1974.

Wiarda, Howard J. *The Dominican Republic: Nation in Transition.* New York: Praeger, 1969.

Wolfe, Thomas W. *Soviet Power and Europe, 1945–1970.* Baltimore: Johns Hopkins Press, 1970.

Woolf, S. J., ed. *The Rebirth of Italy, 1943–1950.* New York: Humanities Press, 1972.

Xydis, Stephen. *Greece and the Great Powers, 1944–1947.* Thessaloniki, Greece: Institute for Balkan Studies, 1963.

Yarmolinsky, Adam. *United States Military Power and Foreign Policy.* Chicago: University of Chicago Press, 1967.

Zasloff, Joseph J. *The Pathet Lao: Leadership and Organization.* Lexington, Mass.: Lexington Press, 1973.

Data on events were also obtained from *Keesing's Contemporary Archives* *The New York Times;* and *U.S. Department of State Bulletin.*

Index

.